lonely planet

Bhutan

Thimphu
p50

Central Bhutan
p126

Eastern Bhutan
p155

Western Bhutan
p78

Bradley Mayhew, Joe Bindloss, Lindsay Brown

PLAN YOUR TRIP

ON THE ROAD

THIMPHU TSECHU FESTIVAL
P24

SNOWMAN TREK P198

TAKTSHANG GOEMBA P95

Contents

Welcome to Bhutan

Bhutan is no ordinary place. It is the last great Himalayan kingdom, shrouded in mystery and magic, where a traditional Buddhist culture carefully embraces global developments.

Low-Volume, High-Value Tourism

The Bhutanese pride themselves on a sustainable approach to tourism in line with the philosophy of Gross National Happiness. Foreign visitors famously pay a minimum tariff of US$250 per day, making it seem one of the world's more expensive destinations. However, this fee is all-inclusive – accommodation, food, transport and an official guide are all provided, so it's not a bad deal. You don't have to travel in a large group and you can arrange your own itinerary. What you won't find is budget independent travel.

Surprising Bhutan

Bhutan is like nowhere else. This is a country where the rice is red and chillies aren't just a seasoning but the main ingredient. It's also a deeply Buddhist land, where monks check their smartphones after performing a divination, and where giant protective penises are painted at the entrance to many houses. Yet while it proudly prioritises its Buddhist traditions, Bhutan is not a land frozen in time. You will find the Bhutanese well educated, fun loving and very well informed about the world around them. It's this blending of the ancient and modern that makes Bhutan endlessly fascinating.

The Last Shangri-La?

So why spend your hard-earned money to come here? Firstly, there is the pristine eastern Himalayan landscape, where snow-capped peaks rise above primeval forests and beautiful traditional villages. To this picture-book landscape add majestic fortress-like dzongs and monasteries, many of which act as a stage for spectacular tsechus (dance festivals) attended by an almost medieval-looking audience. Then there are the textiles and handicrafts, outrageous archery competitions, high-altitude trekking trails, and stunning flora and fauna. If it's not 'Shangri-La', it's as close as it gets.

An Environmental Model

Environmental protection goes hand in hand with cultural preservation in Bhutan. By law, at least 60% of the country must remain forested for all future generations; it currently stands above 70%. Not only is Bhutan carbon neutral, but it actually absorbs more carbon than it emits! For the visitor, this translates into lovely forest hikes and superb birding. Whether you are spotting takins or blue poppies, trekking beneath 7000m peaks or strolling across hillsides ablaze with spring rhododendron blooms, Bhutan offers one of the last pristine pockets in the entire Himalaya.

Why I Love Bhutan

By Bradley Mayhew, Writer

There is much to love about Bhutan, but it's the sacred side of the country I enjoy the most. I love joining pilgrims as they look for saints' footprints in a rock face, or explain monastery history in terms of flying tigers and unruly demons. On one hike alone, a reincarnated lama blessed me with a *thangka* made from the nose blood of a saint and then hit me on the back with the stone footprints of a divine skywalker. From Gross National Happiness to crazy wisdom, a journey to Bhutan is a journey into a different reality.

For more about our writers, see p320

Above: Black Hat Dance (p258)

Bhutan

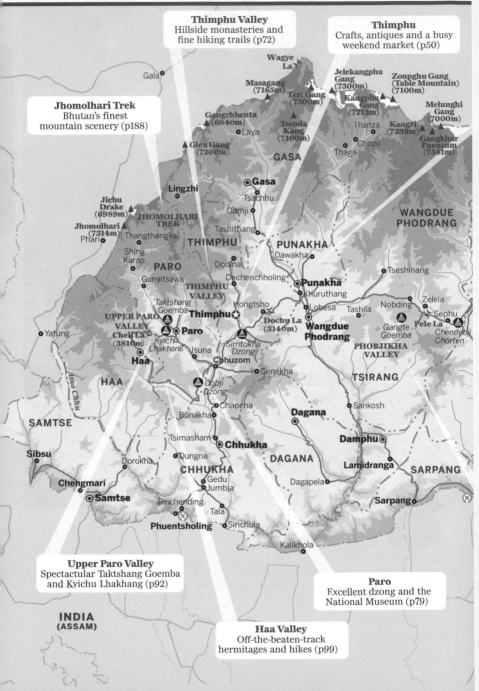

Thimphu Valley
Hillside monasteries and
fine hiking trails (p72)

Thimphu
Crafts, antiques and a busy
weekend market (p50)

Jhomolhari Trek
Bhutan's finest
mountain scenery (p188)

Wagye
La

Gala

Masagang
(7165m)

Teri Gang
(7300m)

Jelekangphu
Gang
(7300m)

Zonpghu Gang
(Table Mountain)
(7100m)

Kangphu
Gang
(7212m)

Melunghi
Gang
(7000m)

Gangchhenta
(6840m)

Laya

Tsenda
Kang
(7100m)

Thanza

Kangri
(7239m)

Gangkhar
Puensum
(7541m)

Gien Gang
(7200m)

Chozo

Thaga

GASA

Jichu
Drake
(6989m)

Lingzhi

Gasa

Tsachhu

WANGDUE
PHODRANG

JHOMOLHARI
TREK

Damji

Jhomolhari
(7314m)

Thangthangka

Tashithang

THIMPHU

PUNAKHA

Phari

Dawakha

Tseshinang

Shing
Karap

Dodina

Dechenchholing

Punakha

PARO

Gunyitsawa

THIMPHU
VALLEY

Khuruthang

Zelela

Hongtsho

Lobesa

Tashila

Nobding

Sephu

Taktshang
Goemba

Thimphu

Dochu La
(3140m)

Wangdue
Phodrang

Gangte
Goemba

Pele La

Chendebji
Chorten

UPPER PARO
VALLEY

Paro

Yatung

Cheli La
(3810m)

Kyichu
Lhakhang

Isuna

Simtokha
Dzong

PHOBJIKHA
VALLEY

Haa

Chhuzom

Genekha

TSIRANG

HAA

Dobji
Dzong

SAMTSE

Chapcha

Dagana

Sankosh

Sibsu

Bunakha

Damphu

Tsimasham

Chhukha

DAGANA

Lamidranga

SARPANG

Chengmari

Dorokha

Dungna

CHHUKHA

Dagapela

Samtse

Gedu
Jumbja

Sarpang

Rinchending

Tala

Phuentsholing

Sinchula

Kalikhola

INDIA
(ASSAM)

Upper Paro Valley
Spectactular Taktshang Goemba
and Kyichu Lhakhang (p92)

Paro
Excellent dzong and the
National Museum (p79)

Haa Valley
Off-the-beaten-track
hermitages and hikes (p99)

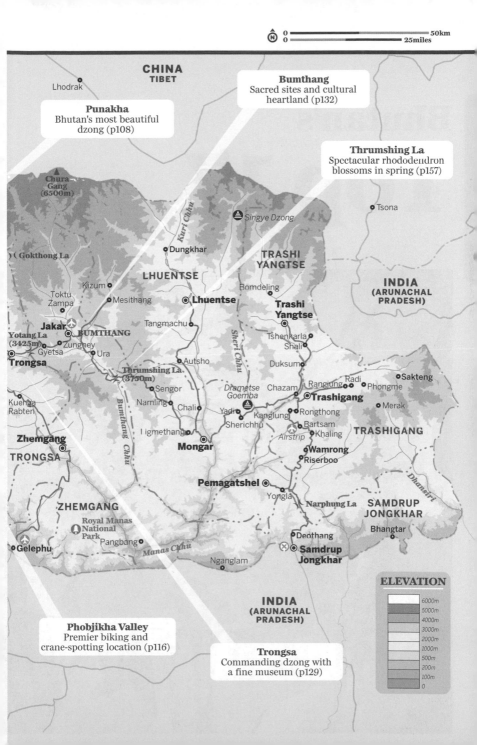

0 ——— 50km
⊛N 0 ——— 25miles

CHINA
TIBET

Lhodrak

Bumthang
Sacred sites and cultural
heartland (p132)

Punakha
Bhutan's most beautiful
dzong (p108)

Thrumshing La
Spectacular rhododendron
blossoms in spring (p157)

○ Tsona

Chura
Gang
(6500m)

⛰ Singye Dzong

) (Gokthong La

○ Dungkhar

**TRASHI
YANGTSE**

Kizum ○

LHUENTSE

Bomdeling ○

**INDIA
(ARUNACHAL
PRADESH)**

Toktu
Zampa   ○ Mesithang   ◎ **Lhuentse**

**Trashi
Yangtse**

Tangmachu ○

Jakar
BUMTHANG

Tshenkarla ○
Shali ○

Yotang La
(3425m) ○   ○ Zungney   ○ Ura
Trongsa   Gyetsa

Autsho ○

Duksum ○

Radi   ○ Sakteng
Chazam Rangjung ○○ ○ Phongme

Thrumshing La
(3750m) ○

*Drametse
Goemba*
⛰

Kuenga
Rabten

○ Sengor
Namling ○ Chali ○

Yadi ○
Kanglung   ○ **Trashigang**   ○ Merak
Rongthong

Zhemgang
TRONGSA

I igmethang ○ ○
Mongar

Sherichhu ○
Bartsam
Airstrip ○ Khaling

TRASHIGANG

Pemagatshel ◎

○ Wamrong
○ Riserboo

ZHEMGANG

Yongla ○

Narphung La

**SAMDRUP
JONGKHAR**

Royal Manas
National
Park   Pangbang ○

Bhangtar
○

○ Gelephu

Manas Chhu

⊗○ Deothang
⊗◎ **Samdrup
Jongkhar**

 Nganglam ○

Dhansiri

ELEVATION

	6000m
	5000m
	4000m
	3000m
	2000m
	1000m
	500m
	200m
	100m
	0

**INDIA
(ARUNACHAL
PRADESH)**

Phobjikha Valley
Premier biking and
crane-spotting location (p116)

Trongsa
Commanding dzong with
a fine museum (p129)

Bhutan's
Top 17

Taktshang Goemba

1 Bhutan's most famous monastery, Taktshang Goemba (p95) is one of its most venerated religious sites. Legend says that Guru Rinpoche flew to this site on the back of a tigress to subdue a local demon; afterwards he meditated here for three months. This beautiful temple clings to the sheer cliffs soaring above a whispering pine forest. The steep walk to the monastery is well worthwhile, providing the most photogenic views of the monastery and the Paro valley, and you can combine a visit with the Bumdrak trek.

Terrific Tsechus

2 Most of Bhutan's dzongs and goembas (monasteries) have annual festivals featuring sacred dance dramas. The largest of these festivals is the tsechu (p33) – with dances in honour of Guru Rinpoche. The dances are performed by monks and laypeople dressed in colourful costumes and painted masks, and the dancers take on aspects of wrathful and compassionate deities, heroes, demons and animals. During the dances, *atsara* (masked clowns) mimic the dancers and perform comic routines, and even harass the audience for money in exchange for a blessing with the wooden phallus they carry! Below: Haa tsechu (p101)

PETER ADAMS / GETTY IMAGES ©

DANITA DELIMONT / SHUTTERSTOCK ©

2

DUCOIN DAVID / GETTY IMAGES ©

3

ANGELO CAVALLI / GETTY IMAGES ©

4

ANDREW STRANOVSKY PHOTOGRAPHY / GETTY IMAGES ©

5

Himalayan Treks

3 Bhutan's treks are physically demanding but hugely rewarding. They are the only way to get close to Bhutan's high mountains and to visit such fabled valleys as Laya and Lingzhi. The Jhomolhari trek (pictured; p188) and Snowman trek in particular rank as two of the world's classic walks. On all treks you will be expertly guided and looked after and your pack will be carried by ponies. Meeting traditionally dressed locals tending their animals according to century-old traditions will be a highlight of your trip.

Archery

4 Bhutan's national sport of archery *(datse)* is exhilarating to watch, with competitions held across the country throughout the year. There are two classes of competition: one for the traditional bamboo bows, and another for the space age carbon-fibre bows that propel arrows at astonishing speeds. The targets seem impossibly tiny and the distance immense, yet the target is hit quite regularly. Narrow misses, bawdy banter and singing and dancing accompany the whoosh of arrows and hoots of delight as the competition heats up. Look for weekend practice sessions at Paro's Archery Ground (p84).

Haa Valley

5 Just a few hours' drive from Paro, over Bhutan's highest motorable road, this little-visited valley (p103) is home to magical cliffside hermitages, ancient temples and charming villages. Accommodation is focused around boutique farmhouses and homestays rather than big group resorts, giving it a more intimate feel. The valley rim is a great place to do some hiking or trekking, either along the Cheli La ridge or up to the Saga La, with its fine views of snow-capped Jhomolhari. Budget a couple of days to beat the crowds.

Punakha Dzong

6 Superbly situated where two rivers converge, Punakha Dzong (p109) is the most dramatic and beautiful example of Bhutanese architecture in the country. Visit in spring to see the famous jacaranda trees splash lilac flowers down the whitewashed walls and red-robed monks wandering on a sea of purple petals. The fortress-thick walls are intimidating and are silent one moment, then warmed with the echoes of giggles in another as a horde of young monks head off for a meal. The dzong's spring festivals rank as the country's most colourful.

Traditional Textiles

7 Hand-woven and embroidered textiles are generally recognised as Bhutan's premier handicraft. Centuries of tradition have honed the techniques of textile dyeing, weaving and stitching. Most of the weavers are women and it is a rare home in Bhutan that does not 'clunk' to the sound of a loom. In addition to the National Textile Museum (p53) in Thimphu, there are small shops throughout the country – particularly in Bumthang and in the far east – selling vibrant fabrics that make beautiful souvenirs.

6

LINEGOLD / SHUTTERSTOCK ©

WHITWORTH IMAGES / GETTY IMAGES ©

ANGELA MEIER / SHUTTERSTOCK ©

Gross National Happiness

8 Gross National Happiness (p209) has become Bhutan's philosophical tagline and an offering to a world grappling with unsustainable 'growth economics'. Based on core Buddhist values, this measurable index is a counterpoint to the economist's Gross National Product. It is also a revolutionary philosophy that places real value on things such as cultural heritage, health, education, good governance, ecological diversity and individual wellbeing. Importantly, it sees economic growth not as an end but rather as a means of achieving quality of life and it's fascinating to see the philosophy in action.

EDDIE GERALD / ALAMY STOCK PHOTO ©

COOPERMOISSE / GETTY IMAGES ©

Bumthang

9 The valleys comprising Bumthang (p132) make up the cultural heartland of Bhutan. The region's ancient goembas, dzongs and temples figured prominently in Bhutan's early development as well as in the foundation of the unique aspects of Bhutanese Buddhism. See the rock imprint of Guru Rinpoche, hoist Pema Lingpa's 25kg chain mail (pictured), and stare into the churning waters of Membartsho, where Pema Lingpa uncovered hidden Buddhist treasures. Bumthang is also one of the best places for day hikes up to some superbly sited monasteries and meditation retreats.

Paro Dzong & National Museum

10 Paro's Rinpung Dzong is a hulking example of the fortress-like dzong architecture that dots Bhutan's major settlements and valleys. The colourful Paro tsechu is held here in spring; the festival culminates with the unfurling of a *thondrol* (huge religious image) depicting the tantric saint Guru Rinpoche. Above the dzong is an old watchtower, the Ta Dzong, now converted into the excellent National Museum (pictured; p83). It's the perfect introduction to Bhutan's cultural heritage.

Arts & Crafts

11 Bhutan's pride in its handicrafts is on show at the schools of Zorig Chusum (pictured; p53) and Bhutan's many handicraft shops. Many items have a utilitarian or religious use, such as bamboo baskets, brass butter lamps or the exquisite wooden bowls hand-turned from intricately patterned burlwood. Silk, cotton, wool and even yak hair is spun, dyed, woven and stitched into cloth and traditional garments. Bhutan's rich painting tradition lives on in the form of intricate *thangkas* (religious pictures), while Bhutanese stamps are must-haves for collectors.

Trongsa Dzong & Tower of Trongsa Museum

12 Sprawling down a ridge towards an ominous gorge, Trongsa Dzong (pictured; p129) sits centrally in Bhutan's geography and in its recent history. Both the first and second kings ruled the country from this strategic position. Inside is a labyrinth of stairways, narrow corridors and courtyards. Overlooking the dzong is the Tower of Trongsa Royal Heritage Museum. Dedicated to the history of the royal Wangchuck dynasty, it has exhibits ranging from royals' personal effects to Buddhist statues.

Thimphu Weekend Market

13 Thimphu's bustling weekend Weekend Market (p53) is the biggest and brightest in the country. The food section is an olfactory overload with dried fish competing with soft cheese and dried chilli to assault your nostrils. Curly fern fronds *(nakey)*, red rice and ground herbal incense are just some of the exotic offerings. Cross the fast-flowing Wang Chhu on the traditional cantilever footbridge to get to the handicraft and textile stalls where you can barter for 'antiques', rolls of prayer flags or even a human thigh-bone trumpet.

Wonderful Wildlife

14 Bhutan has the largest proportion of land designated as protected areas in the world, with 65% of its territory covered in forest and mountains, protecting richly varied habitats and an amazing diversity of plants and creatures, including snow leopards and Bengal tigers. Birdwatchers flock to the monsoon-soaked forests of southern Bhutan, where hundreds of species can be spotted. The endangered black-necked crane winters in central and eastern Bhutan and the reliably returning cranes of the Phobjikha valley (p116) are justifiably renowned. Bottom: Golden takin (p270)

Kyichu Lhakhang

15 Kyichu Lhakhang (p92) is one of Bhutan's oldest, most venerated and most beautiful temples and it sits just a short distance from the gateway town of Paro. The oldest temple in this twin-temple complex is believed to have been built in AD 659 by King Songtsen Gampo of Tibet. The outside grounds hum with prayers and spinning prayer wheels (pictured above left), while inside a treasured 7th-century statue of Jowo Sakyamuni sits in the inner sanctuary. Easy day walks begin in the vicinity of this serene lhakhang.

Thimphu Valley

16 Thimphu (pictured) abounds with museums and cultural attractions, including the Trashi Chho Dzong (p51), which celebrates one of the country's most popular tsechus in autumn. The capital also boasts the country's only real dining and nightlife scene. There are several great hikes around the valley walls, taking in a handful of perfectly positioned monasteries offering excellent views over the city and valley. And just west of Thimphu's centre, Motithang Takin Preserve is your best bet for spotting Bhutan's extraordinary national animal.

Forests & Blooms

17 Although the ethe-real high-altitude blue poppy is the national flower and the cypress the national tree, no plant is more emblematic of Bhutan than the rhododendron. In spring, splashes of red, pink and white rival the multicoloured prayer flags at many high passes, but especially around the Dochu La (p104) en route to Punakha. With some of the Himalaya's most pristine forests, Bhutan beckons amateur botanists with its sheer variety of flora and shades of green. Long drives are inevitable, so remember to stop the car and smell the flowers.

Need to Know

For more information, see Survival Guide (p281)

Currency

Bhutanese ngultrum
(Nu)

Language

Dzongkha

Visas

With the exception of
South Asian Association
for Regional Coopera-
tion (SAARC) tourists,
visitors to Bhutan must
arrange a visa through a
tour agency as part of a
prepaid all-inclusive tour.

Money

Tours are prepaid so
you'll only need money
for drinks, laundry, sou-
venirs and tips; for this,
bring cash as ATMs are
not always reliable.

Mobile Phones

Buy a B-Mobile or Tashi
Cell SIM card for both
local and international
calls, and top up your
credit at phone shops
across Bhutan.

Time

Bhutan Time (GMT/
UTC plus six hours; 30
minutes later than India,
15 minutes later than
Nepal)

When to Go

Jhomolhari Base Camp
GO May–Oct

Punakha
GO Feb–Apr, Oct–Dec

Paro/Thimphu
GO Feb–May, Sep–Dec

Trashi Yangtse
GO Oct–Apr

Phuentsholing
GO Nov–Feb

Alpine: cold/frozen winters, mild summers
Valley: cold winters, warm summers
Lowlands: cool winters, hot summers

High Season
(Mar–May, Sep–
Nov)

➡ The weather is
ideal in spring and
autumn. Book flights
well in advance;
accommodation
options can fill up.

➡ Himalayan views
are best in October,
while rhododendron
blooms peak in
March and April.

Shoulder
(Dec–Feb)

➡ Bhutan has
seasonal tariff
discounts so you'll
save money and see
fewer tourists by
travelling outside the
high season.

➡ The weather
is still pleasant,
though it can be cold
in December and
January.

Low Season
(Jun–Aug)

➡ Monsoon rains
and leeches put an
end to most treks,
although high-
altitude flowers are
at their peak.

Useful Websites

Official Tourism Website
(www.bhutan.travel) Tourist
FAQs, country information and
upcoming festivals.

My Bhutan (www.mybhutan.
com) Travel articles and tourist
information.

Tourism Council of Bhutan
(www.tourism.gov.bt) Approved
tour operators and travel
regulations.

Lonely Planet (www.lonely
planet.com/bhutan) Destination
information, articles, traveller
forum and more.

Kuensel (www.kuenselonline.
com) News from the kingdom.

National Portal of Bhutan
(www.bhutan.gov.bt) Official
government site.

Important Numbers

Bhutan's country code	☑975
International access code	☑00
Ambulance	☑112
Fire	☑110
Police	☑113

Exchange Rates

Australia	A$1	Nu 48
Canada	C$1	Nu 51
Europe	€1	Nu 77
India	Rs100	Nu 100
Japan	¥100	Nu 63
UK	£1	Nu 88
USA	US$1	Nu 69

For current exchange rates, see
www.xe.com.

Daily Costs

Fixed Daily Rate: US$250

➡ All tourists must pay
US$250 per person per day
(US$200 a day from December
to February and June to
August), with a US$40/30
surcharge per person for
those in a group of one/two.
This covers accommodation,
transport in Bhutan, a guide,
food and entry fees, and
includes a US$65 royalty that
goes to the government.

➡ Possible extra charges
include hot-stone baths,
cultural shows, horse riding,
rafting, mountain biking
and tips.

➡ Children under 12 years
are exempt from the royalty
component (US$65).

Budget: Less than US$150

➡ Only Indian tourists and
foreign residents are able to
set their own travel budgets.

➡ Budget hotel: US$20–40

➡ Restaurant meal in
Thimphu: US$7–15

Top end: US$500–1750

➡ Luxury hotel: US$250–1500
above the daily US$250 tariff

Opening Hours

Banks 9am to 5pm (4pm
winter) Monday to Friday, 9am
to 11am or 1pm Saturday

Bars Close at 11pm on weekdays
and midnight on Friday and
Saturday. Closed Tuesday.

Clubs Generally close at
midnight most weekdays, and at
around 2am or 3am on Wednesday, Friday and Saturday

Government Offices 9am to
1pm and 2pm to 5pm summer,
until 4pm winter, Monday to
Friday

Shops 8am to 8pm or 9pm

Arriving in Bhutan

Paro Airport Your guide and
driver will meet you at Paro
Airport to transport you to the
first stop on your itinerary. For
travellers exempt from the daily
fee, taxis are available outside
the airport.

**Phuentsholing, Gelephu &
Samdrup Jongkhar** Your guide
and driver will also meet you if
you arrive at one of Bhutan's
land borders to help with arrival
formalities and transport you on
to the first destination on your
itinerary.

Getting Around

The only way to explore Bhutan
is on foot or by road, or via the
rather limited domestic air
service. If you are travelling on
a tourist visa, the cost of all
transport is included in the price
of your trip and you'll have a
vehicle available for both short-
and long-distance travel.

Air At the time of research,
internal flights connected Paro
to Bumthang, Gelephu and
Yongphula.

Car, Jeep & Minivan Unless you
are on a trek or take an internal
flight, you will be moved around
by minibus, 4WD jeep or car. For
trips to central and eastern Bhutan during winter (December to
February) or the monsoon (June
to September), a 4WD vehicle is
a distinct advantage.

For much more on
getting around,
see p296

If You Like...

Fitting in Like a Local

Get a gho (or a kira) Locals love it when a *chilip* (foreigner) wears Bhutanese national dress, especially during a holiday or festival. (p237)

Watch an archery tournament There's nothing more Bhutanese than the good-humoured banter of a *datse* (archery) or *khuru* (lawn darts) game. (p84)

Hang some prayer flags Earn some good karma by hanging prayer flags at a mountain pass such as Dochu La. (p104)

Overnight in a rural farm-house The digs are simple but the welcome warm – overnight with a local family in Ngang Lhakhang or Khoma. (p146)

Sample some local snacks Try jellied cow skin, dried yak cheese and fresh betel nut at the Paro Weekend Market. (p84)

Walk with pilgrims Join locals on a *kora* (circumambulation) past sacred rocks, meditation caves and shrines at Drak Kharpo. (p97)

Himalayan Treks

The best way to experience rural Bhutan is on foot, especially if you can combine a trek with a festival and the highlights of Paro and Thimphu. Come in October and November for mountain views and March for rhododendron blooms.

Druk Path Trek Bhutan's most popular trek between Paro and Thimphu takes in high-altitude lakes and remote hermitages. (p181)

Jhomolhari Trek A popular trek that combines close-up high-mountain views, remote villages, high passes and yak pastures. (p188)

Laya Trek Perhaps the best combination of scenery and culture, with a visit to the unique people of remote Laya. (p195)

Bumdrak Trek A short and luxurious overnighter, visiting remote chapels and the Tiger's Nest at Taktshang Goemba. (p185)

Snowman Trek One of the world's toughest, most expensive and ultimate treks across the roof of the Bhutan Himalaya. (p198)

Pampering Yourself

Bhutan's top-end travel is anything but tough. Uber-luxury resorts guarantee six-star treatment, with muscle-melting spas and hot-stone massage.

Hot-Stone Bath Stone, wood, hot water and artemisia herbs provide the quintessential Bhutanese experience, available at most tourist hotels. (p283)

Termalinca Resort & Spa Not quite the Promised Land, but the milk-and-honey body wrap comes close; nonguests are welcome at the spa. (p77)

Uma Paro Massage, complimentary yoga and Ayurvedic oil treatments, all featuring Como bath products. (p88)

Zhiwa Ling The Menlha (Medicine Buddha) spa at this luxury hotel offers a red rice or lemongrass body polish. (p89)

Taj Tashi Choose your mood – invigorating masala spice rub or relaxing coconut skin softener? (p61)

Bhutan Spirit Sanctuary All-inclusive spa resort that combines Bhutanese traditional medicine with relaxing spa treatments. (p99)

Tshetob Yingyum Spa Five-star massage without the resort price tag at this downtown Paro spa. (p84)

Wildlife & Wildflowers

Bhutan is a paradise for botanists and birders. Mountain goats and lan-gur are easily spotted; red

PASCAL BOEGLI / GETTY IMAGES ©

WAITANDSHOOT PRODUCTION / SHUTTERSTOCK ©

Top: Trekkers en route to Maurothang, Snowman Trek (p202)

Bottom: Red panda (p271)

pandas are more commonly seen on beer labels than in trees.

Phobjikha valley Winter (end of October to mid-February) offers guaranteed sightings of one of over 400 black-necked cranes. (p116)

Dochu La One of the best places to wander through a magical forest of rhododendron blooms (March and April). (p105)

Motithang Takin Preserve Get up close to Bhutan's odd-looking and endearing national animal. (p56)

Royal Manas National Park The wildlife- and bird-spotting in this subtropical forest ranks as some of Asia's best. (p153)

Day Walks

Sometimes it's just nice to get out of the car and hike to a hillside monastery or temple. Lose the crowds and meet monks, villagers and fellow pilgrims on an equal footing.

Tango & Cheri Goembas Excellent excursion from Thimphu to two of Bhutan's most historic monasteries. (p73)

Taktshang Goemba A two-hour hike up to the dramatic Tiger's Nest Monastery, with more temples above. (p95)

Bumthang valley The best single destination for day hikes to silent meditation retreats and valley viewpoints. (p149)

Ura & Shingkhar Hike between these charming villages, up to a nearby retreat or into Thrumshing La National Park. (p151)

Dochu La Choose between short walks through rhododendron forests and longer hikes connecting nearby monasteries. (p105)

Cheli La Walk downhill to Kila Nunnery, uphill to a sky burial site or combine the two. (p99)

Phobjikha valley Spot black-necked cranes on the lovely, easy Gangte Nature Trail in this charming hidden valley. (p120)

Sacred Sites

Protector deities, spirits and saints lurk behind every pass, river junction and lake in Bhutan. These pilgrim spots are imbued with sacred significance and hold a key to understanding how Bhutanese see their world.

Taktshang Goemba Bhutan's most famous and revered site, tied to the cliff face by little more than the hairs of angels. (p95)

Gom Kora Pilgrims flock to this remote chorten for its collection of rock footprints, relics and bizarre sin tests. (p170)

Changangkha Lhakhang Always bustling with mothers and their babies seeking a blessing from the red-faced protector, Tamdrin. (p52)

Membartsho The serene and sacred 'burning lake', where Pema Lingpa found underwater treasures and performed miracles. (p148)

Chumphu Ney A three-hour walk past waterfalls and medialation caves to a hidden *ney* (sacred place). (p96)

Avoiding the Crowds

Bhutan's big shows are its dzongs and festivals, but don't overlook the charm of the country's smaller, less-visited monasteries and temples.

Juneydrak Hermitage The Haa valley is a great place to get off the beaten track; this timeless hermitage is its highlight. (p102)

Kila Nunnery Perched below the Cheli La, Kila is an hour's walk and about two centuries off the main highway. (p99)

Dumtse Lhakhang Pilgrim paths wind upwards at this snail-shell-shaped chapel past some of the country's best medieval murals. (p83)

Tago Lhakhang A charming and easily missed 15th-century chapel inside a chorten, just south of Paro. (p97)

Dechen Phodrang Sacred stones and towering cypress trees mark this pilgrimage site, seemingly lost in time. (p56)

Gasa Dzong Spectacularly sited fort, reachable by day trip from Punakha, and best combined with the annual tsechu (dance festival). (p115)

Festivals

Many people time their entire trip around one of Bhutan's colourful tsechus (dance festivals). Expect swirling mask dances, playful clowns, spectacular costumes and superb photo opportunities.

Paro Tsechu Popular with groups – and with good reason – but perhaps too popular for some people's taste. (p84)

Ura Yakchoe A quiet rural festival, though the dates are notoriously changeable. Camping is a good idea. (p151)

Punakha Drumchoe One of Bhutan's most unusual festivals re-enacts an ancient battle; held February or March. (p112)

Kurjey Tsechu Brave the monsoon rain and avoid the tourists, plus hit the nearby Nimalung tsechu at the same time. (p143)

Royal Highlander Festival Mountain festival featuring yak beauty competitions, wrestling and horse races. (p195)

Arts & Crafts

Bhutan's arts and crafts vary from sacred murals to bamboo bows. For high religious art visit the dzongs and monasteries, but for handicrafts, try these fascinating places.

National Institute for Zorig Chusum Watch students perfect the Thirteen Arts. (p53)

Jungshi Handmade Paper Factory View the whole paper-making process. (p58)

National Textile Museum Thimphu's impressive complex showcases Bhutan's most impressive art form. (p53)

Nado Poizokhang Incense Factory Breathe in the fragrance of juniper, sandalwood and high-altitude herbs at this factory in Thimphu. (p58)

Khoma Village, Lhuentse Every household has a loom in this remote centre of 'brocade-style' weaving excellence. (p163)

Yathra Workshops, Zungney Shop for hand-woven woollen blankets at these roadside looms on the drive to Bumthang. (p133)

Month by Month

TOP EVENTS

Thimphu Tsechu, September/October

Paro Tsechu, March/April

Punakha Drumchoe, February/March

Ura Yakchoe, April/May

Jampey Lhakhang Drup, October/November

February

The mercury stays low in Phobjikha and Bumthang, but things are warmer in the lower elevations of Punakha and the east, and there are loads of festivals, with few crowds.

✨ Losar

Bhutanese mark their New Year by painting their houses, visiting the local monastery, and holding epic archery and darts tournaments. The event follows the lunar Bhutanese calendar and there are lots of regional variations, so it can happen anytime between mid-January and mid-March.

✨ Nomad's Festival

Highlanders from as far away as Laya and Sakteng attend this tourism fair in upper Bumthang, selling such exotica as conical hats from Laya and fermented cheese from Sakteng. Traditional games and masked dances make it an interesting (if slightly contrived) addition to the festival scene. (p146)

✨ Trashi Yangtse Tsechu

If you want to skip tour group crowds, this three-day tsechu is held at remote Trashi Yangtse's new dzong and features masked dances and the unveiling of a Guru Tsengye *thondrol* (building-sized *thangka*) on the third day. (p171)

March

Spring, from March to May, is an excellent time to visit Bhutan, for both touring and trekking. Mountain views can be cloudy, but the magnificent rhododendrons are in bloom and birdlife is abundant.

✨ Punakha Dromchoe (Drubchen)

The balmy Punakha valley hosts this unique three-day event, the highlight of which is a dramatic recreation of a 17th-century battle, featuring hundreds of costumed warriors. A three-day tsechu then follows. The festival follows the lunar calendar, so it can fall in February. (p112)

✨ Gom Kora

Hundreds of people travel to this pilgrimage site in the east of the country for a night of celebrations and ritual circumambulations of the sacred black rock. It takes place between the 8th and 10th days of the second lunar month, so it can fall in April. (p170)

✨ Gasa Tsechu

A wonderful three-day festival featuring masked dances, the unveiling of a *thondrol* and the performance of a 300-year-old folk song called *goenzhey*. Tsechus are held at the same time at Talo Goemba and Zhemgang Dzong. (p115)

April

April is the second most popular month to visit Bhutan, partly because temperatures are comfortably warm. The Paro tsechu is a big draw and trekking is good.

✸ Paro Tsechu

This popular festival features four days of *cham* (religious dances) followed by the predawn unfurling of a giant *thangka* (religious icon) depicting the eight manifestations of Guru Rinpoche. First-day ceremonies are in Paro Dzong, before the action moves outside. It can also fall in March. (p84)

✸ Chorten Kora

Thousands of pilgrims from eastern Bhutan and Arunachal Pradesh circumambulate this stupa during two fair-like festivals, set two weeks apart. The main festival is from the 13th to 15th of the first lunar month, so it can fall in March.

🏃 Trekking

Warm weather and continued rhododendron blooms at higher elevations make this a fine time to trek, but there's less chance of blue skies at the top of the mountain. Bring some rain gear just in case.

May

Spring's end brings warm and dusty weather, with rain increasing towards the end of the month. Lighter crowds and good weather still make it a good month to visit, though it's hot at lower elevations.

✸ Ura Yakchoe

A small-town vibe marks this three-day festival featuring religious processions, dances and local moonshine. The only problem is that dates are notoriously unreliable. The festival can happen in April, but is only fixed a few weeks in advance. (p151)

June

Monsoon clouds can obscure views and cancel flights at Paro airport during June and July. As the rains intensify, roads can wash away. The wildflowers in the high valleys at this time are spectacular.

✸ Nimalung Tsechu

Bumthang is the place to visit in the fifth lunar month. Nimalung Goemba has a three-day festival starting on the eighth day, with the final day coinciding with the nearby Kurjey tsechu. Can be held in July. (p135)

✸ Kurjey Tsechu

Monks from Trongsa Dzong perform religious dances for this one-day festival in Bumthang. The date also marks the birthday of Guru Rinpoche, which is celebrated by prayer ceremonies across Bhutan. The three-day tsechu at Nimalung Goemba starts two days before Kurjey tscchu. (p143)

📅 Monsoon Madness

The summer monsoon (June to September) dominates Bhutan, which receives more rainfall than any other Himalayan region. The rains peak during July, making road travel to the east precarious, but the lush foliage and fresh mushrooms, mangoes and avocados go some way to compensate.

September

The first half of the month is still rainy, but by the end of it the monsoon has washed the Himalayan skies clear and several big festivals coincide with the beginning of the main tourist season.

✸ Thimphu Tsechu

Crowds can be thick during the four days of spectacular monk dancing in Trashi Chho Dzong – over 3000 tourists attend each year. The event can also fall in October. The preceding three-day *dromchoe* festivities are generally open to Bhutanese only. (p51)

✸ Haa Tsechu

Sleepy Haa only truly wakes during this festival. Monk dances are held on the eighth and ninth days of the eighth lunar month in the courtyard of the Lhakhang Kharpo, before the final day's action moves to Haa Dzong, where a *thondrol* is unfurled. (p101)

✸ Tamshing Phala Choepa

The Bumthang valley offers a double shot of festivals in the eighth lunar month. From the ninth to 11th you can enjoy dances at Tamshing Goemba, before relocating three days later to nearby Thangbi Goemba for three days of festivities. Both festivals can fall in October. (p145)

Top: Paro tsechu (p84)

Bottom: Ura Yakchoe (p151)

October

October is the single most popular month to visit Bhutan. Temperatures are warm, mountain views are clear and tour groups are everywhere. Make your hotel and flight bookings well in advance.

✪⚑ Jampey Lhakhang Drup

Cham dances and bonfires commemorate the founding of this 7th-century temple. The first evening features a midnight 'naked fire dance'. Festivities last from the 15th to the 18th of the ninth lunar month, so it can occur in November. The four-day Jakar tsechu occurs a week before. (p142)

✪⚑ Prakhar Tsechu

This three-day festival at Prakhar Goemba, in the Chumey valley, shares the same dates as the Jampey Lhakhang Drup, so you can easily double up.

🏃 Trekking Heaven

Trekking is superb everywhere in Bhutan in October and this is when most tour companies operate their treks. Nights can be cold at high elevations, but the views of snowy peaks such as 7314m Jhomolhari are superb.

🏃 Royal Highlander Festival

Activities at this new mountain festival in remote Laya include wrestling, horse races and yak competitions, with lots of Layaps in attendance. It takes place in the fourth week of October and may change location. Getting here involves a day's trek from Gasa. (p195)

November

A good month weatherwise, though pack a jumper for the evenings. Several smaller festivals offer a good alternative to the over-visited Paro and Thimphu tsechus. Blacknecked cranes start to arrive in Phobjikha.

✪⚑ Mongar Tsechu

Mongar offers a smaller, more intimate festival experience than most others in Bhutan, with more opportunities for photography and cultural interaction. The little-visited Trashigang tsechu occurs on the same three days, which can fall in December.

✪⚑ Ngang Bi Rabney

This three-day festival at Ngang Lhakhang in upper Bumthang features some unusual dances by noblemen from two local clans, as well as masked dances. The festival can fall in November or December. (p145)

✪⚑ Trashigang Tsechu

A little-visited, three-day festival in the far east that includes the unveiling of a large *thangka* and the displaying of a statue of Guru Rinpoche in the main courtyard on the last day. It shares the same dates as tsechus in Mongar and Pemagatshel. (p166)

December

December marks the beginning of winter, with possible snow at higher elevations, though it's not a bad time for touring western Bhutan. The high passes to Haa and the east may be temporarily snowbound.

✪⚑ Trongsa Tsechu

This is one of the oldest and least-visited festivals in the country. Three days of dancing run from the 9th to the 11th days of the 11th lunar month, so it can be held in January. The final day features the hanging of a giant *thondrol*.

✪⚑ Druk Wangyel Tsechu

This new festival on 13 December features masked dances performed by the Bhutan Army atop the Dochu La, set against a rather splendid backdrop of Himalayan peaks. (p104)

✪⚑ Lhuentse Tsechu

Very few tourists make it to this remote monastic festival, way out in the extreme northeast of the country. Festivities also take place simultaneously in nearby Dungkhar. The festival can be held in January. (p162)

Itineraries

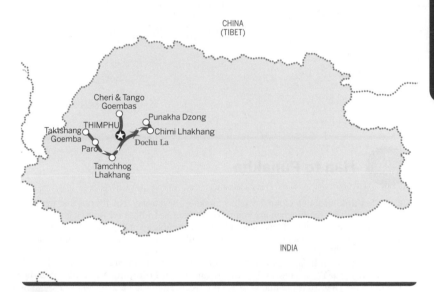

CHINA
(TIBET)

Cheri & Tango
Goembas

Punakha Dzong

THIMPHU

Taktshang
Goemba

Chimi Lhakhang

Paro

Dochu La

Tamchhog
Lhakhang

INDIA

4 DAYS A Long Weekend in Paro & Thimphu

If you have limited time or money, you can get a good impression of Bhutan in just four days by concentrating on Thimphu and Paro.

Count on two full days in picturesque **Paro**, visiting Paro Dzong and the National Museum. On the second day, hike up to the dramatic Tiger's Nest, **Taktshang Goemba**, and visit lovely Kyichu Lhakhang. Get away from the tour buses on the walk from Paro Dzong to Zuri Dzong. After lunch, make the three-hour drive to Thimphu, stopping at the charming **Tamchhog Lhakhang** en route.

On day three you could squeeze in a long day trip over the Dochu La to **Punakha Dzong**, the most beautiful dzong in the country. On the way back to Thimphu, pop into the nearby **Chimi Lhakhang**, the temple of the 'Divine Madman'.

Day four is in **Thimphu**. Go to the weekend market and visit **Cheri Goemba** or **Tango Goemba** in the upper Thimphu valley. If handicrafts are your thing, hit the National Textile Museum and National Institute for Zorig Chusum. Late in the afternoon, drive back to Paro; most flights depart early in the morning.

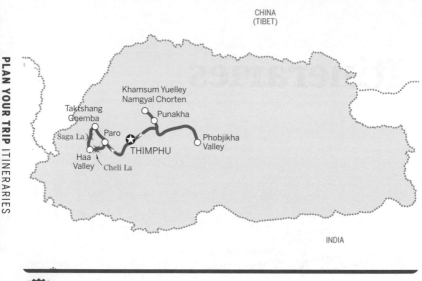

CHINA
(TIBET)

Khamsum Yuelley
Namgyal Chorten

Taktshang
Goemba   Paro   Punakha

Saga La

THIMPHU   Phobjikha
Valley

Haa
Valley   Cheli La

INDIA

7 DAYS · Haa to Punakha

If you're thinking about a four-day trip, consider a seven-day trip. It's not that much more money and, really, when are you next going to be in Bhutan? A week gives you more time to get a feel for Bhutanese culture and enables you to get off the beaten track in either the Haa or Phobjikha valleys, while still seeing the major dzongs and monasteries of western Bhutan.

Figure on two full days in **Paro**, including visits to **Taktshang Goemba** and Kyichu Lhakhang in the Paro valley, and a full day (or two) in **Thimphu**. A few tips: try to be in Thimphu on a Saturday or Sunday to see the weekend market and avoid Paro on Monday, when the National Museum is closed. If you're lucky, you may be able to catch a weekend archery tournament in Thimphu or Paro.

To get off the beaten track, add on an overnight trip to the **Haa valley**. The road goes over the highest drivable pass in Bhutan, the Cheli La, and it's worth a short detour to visit Kila Nunnery or Dzongdrakha Goemba. Arrive in Haa at lunchtime, and spend an afternoon, and maybe the next morning, exploring the Juneydrak Hermitage and Shelkar Drak. If you fancy a taste of trekking, hike the overnight Saga La trek over the mountains to the Paro valley, before continuing on to Thimphu.

With the extra days you can definitely add an overnight trip over the mountains to **Punakha**. This way you'll have time to make the 1½-hour return hike to the nearby **Khamsum Yuelley Namgyal Chorten**, as well as visit Chimi Lhakhang, and maybe even do a short rafting trip.

If you don't visit Haa, you might be able to add on a day trip to the **Phobjikha valley**, especially worthwhile in winter (November to February) when the valley's black-necked cranes are roosting. Bring some warm clothes and a torch (flashlight).

At some point during your trip, ask your guide to arrange a Bhutanese hot-stone bath, available in most tourist hotels (for a charge). Throw in a festival and you have the perfect introductory visit to Bhutan.

PEMA GYAMTSHO / SHUTTERSTOCK ©

CHR. OFFENBERG / SHUTTERSTOCK ©

Top: National Memorial Chorten (p53), Thimphu

Bottom: Punakha Dzong (p109)

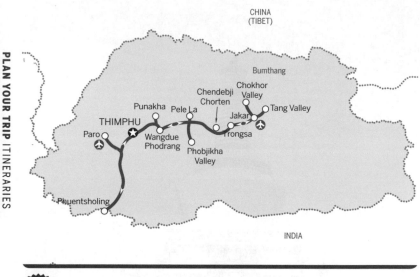

Thimphu to Bumthang

A 10-day itinerary should just about allow you two or three days in Bumthang, with overnight stops in Paro, Thimphu and **Punakha** and a quick stop in Trongsa. But a full two weeks will let you see the same places in more depth, at a more relaxed pace, with time for a couple of day hikes.

Follow the four-day itinerary for your first days. From **Thimphu**, a night in the **Phobjikha valley** will give you a chance to see Gangte Goemba and also view the rare and endangered black-necked cranes (November to February). Phobjikha is a great place to explore on foot.

From Phobjikha, it's a day's drive over the **Pele La** to the superb dzong and museum at **Trongsa** and on to **Jakar** in Bumthang. Leave early, as there's lots to see en route, including the Nepali-style **Chendebji Chorten**, which is a perfect place for a picnic.

If you have two full days in Bumthang, spend one day doing a loop in the **Chokhor valley**, taking in the Jampey Lhakhang, Kurjey Lhakhang and walking to Tamshing Goemba. Your second day here should be spent exploring the **Tang valley**, visiting Membartsho (Burning Lake) and the interesting Ogyen Chholing Museum near Mesithang. If you have an extra day, overnight in the Ogyen Chholing Heritage House and hike down to the road via the remote rural chapels of Choejam Lhakhang and Narut (Pelphug) Lhakhang.

The Bumthang valley is a great place for some hiking, so budget half a day to stretch your legs after a week's driving. From Jakar, it's a two-day drive back to **Paro**, so spend a night near **Wangdue Phodrang**. Better still, fly from Bumthang to Paro and enjoy an extra day there.

If you intend to visit India in conjunction with Bhutan, consider driving from Thimphu or Paro to **Phuentsholing** instead of flying out of Paro; this will add a day to the itinerary. From here you are only a few hours from Darjeeling, Kalimpong and Sikkim, as well as the airport at Bagdogra, which has frequent flights to Delhi and Kolkata (Calcutta).

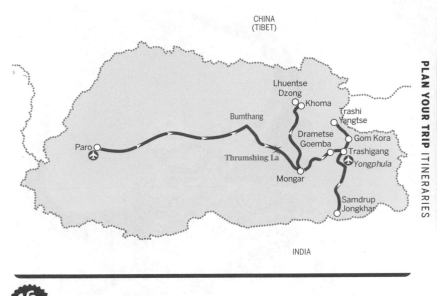

16 DAYS · Eastern Explorations

It takes at least two weeks to make a trip out to the little-visited far east and we'd suggest throwing in a couple of extra days to allow for some rest and recuperation.

There's a lot of driving involved (up to five hours a day in eastern Bhutan) but it is now possible to fly back to Paro from **Yongphula** (near Trashigang). You could also avoid the long drive back to Paro by exiting Bhutan at Samdrup Jongkhar, as long as you have arranged an Indian visa in advance. This is a particularly good trip if you're interested in traditional weaving.

Follow the earlier itineraries from **Paro** as far as Bumthang (or fly there if this is your second trip to Bhutan), from where you can see the highlights of the east in five or six days. From Bumthang, day one takes you on a dramatic drive over the Thrumshing La and Bhutan's wildest road to **Mongar**. Stay here for two nights and make a scenic day trip up to remote **Lhuentse Dzong** and the nearby traditional weaving village of **Khoma**. To cut down on the driving, consider instead a day's hiking off the beaten track around Mongar.

Continue on to funky **Trashigang**, with an optional two- or three-hour detour along the way to **Drametse Goemba**, Bhutan's most important Nyingma monastery. Accommodation standards in the east are not as good as western Bhutan, so bring a sense of humour and some bug spray.

Figure on two nights at Trashigang, with another great day excursion to **Trashi Yangtse**, with stops en route at the pilgrimage site of **Gom Kora**, the old Trashi Yangtse dzong and the Nepali-style Chorten Kora. March and April bring two important pilgrimage festivals to this region. Spend a second day here if you want to go crane-spotting in Bomdeling Wildlife Sanctuary or to hike via the Dechen Phodrang pilgrimage site.

From Trashigang, it's a full day's winding drive down to the plains at steamy **Samdrup Jongkhar**. From there, take a three-hour taxi ride to Guwahati (check in advance for planned strikes) then fly to Kolkata, Delhi or Bangkok, or take the overnight train to West Bengal for Darjeeling and the Nepal border.

Masked participant at Paro tsechu (p84)

Plan Your Trip

Festivals

The exotic, arcane and other-worldly side of Bhutanese culture is on glorious display in its religious festivals. With their masked costumes, dances, music and processions, Bhutan's tsechus are a highlight of the social calendar for most Bhutanese and tourists, so be sure to build at least one into your itinerary.

Need to Know

What to Bring

Dances are long and you don't want to lose your hard-fought-for position, so bring a sun hat, water, snacks, camera and spare batteries, and a collapsible seat or cushion.

Dress Up

Pack a smart set of clothes or even better get a *gho* (robe) or *kira* (skirt) made up – locals will love it and you'll be accepted with open arms.

Offbeat Festivals

Try to visit an off-the-beaten-track festival at a smaller temple, lesser-visited dzong or a festival out in the east.

Two-for-One

Some auspicious dates are celebrated in multiple locations, meaning you can combine festivals, such as the simultaneous tsechus at Gasa and Talo Goemba, near Punakha.

Book Ahead

Hotel rooms and flights into Bhutan fill up quickly during the Thimphu and Paro tsechus, and some top-end hotels introduce a tsechu supplement or minimum stay.

The Tsechu

Bhutan's most dramatic festivals are its tsechus, a series of ritual religious dances *(cham)* performed by spectacularly masked and elaborately robed dancers. The dates and duration of the tsechus vary from one district to another, but often take place on or around the 10th day of the Bhutanese calendar, which is dedicated to Guru Rinpoche.

Usually the tsechus are performed in dzong or monastery courtyards, which can become incredibly crowded as onlookers vie for a position. The tsechu is a grand social event, drawing people far and wide from the surrounding districts. They are not solemn occasions, but are marked by a holiday atmosphere as people put on their finest clothing and jewellery, share their picnics and exchange local news, often engaging in a bit of shopping or gambling in the stalls set up just outside the festival grounds.

Above all the festival is an opportunity to catch up with far-flung friends and relatives, and to be immersed in Buddhist teachings. The Bhutanese believe that they attain merit simply by attending the tsechus and watching the performances of the highly symbolic dances.

The highlight of many tsechus is the unfurling of a giant *thangka* (painted or embroidered religious picture) from a building overlooking the dance arena before sunrise. Such large *thangkas* are called *thondrols* and are usually embroidered rather than painted. The word means 'liberation on sight', and it is believed that one's sins are washed away upon viewing one of these impressive relics.

Tsechu Participation

You'll get the most out of a tsechu if you come prepared to take part and be part of the crowd, instead of an observer taking photos from the sidelines.

During the tsechu dances *atsara* (masked clowns) mimic the dances and perform comic routines wearing masks with long red noses. While entertaining the onlookers, they also help to keep order and have developed the habit of harassing tourists for money. Take it as a good-natured game. If you contribute, you may even receive a blessing from the wooden phallus they carry.

Wherever there is dancing, you should be willing to take part. Traditionally, everybody, including visitors, enthusiastically takes part in the final dance (Tashi Lebey), which concludes all festivities or dance performances. Don't feel shy, just follow the person in front of you and smile for the cameras!

Which Festival?

The Thimphu and Paro tsechus are by far the most popular festivals with tourist groups, and increasing numbers of visitors are discovering the theatrical *drubchoe* in beautiful Punakha. These three are the grandest festivals, on the biggest scale and are true spectacles, but the tourist crowds can be thick at times.

Some old Bhutan hands prefer the smaller festivals or tsechus held in lesser-known regional dzongs and lhakhangs. They may be lighter on spectacle but they provide a more intimate and traditional experience, and you might just be the only foreigners there.

Smaller, lesser-known rural festivals to consider include:

➡ Trashi Yangtse tsechu (p23) in February, and the Chorten Kora (p24) festival in April, both in remote far eastern Bhutan

➡ Buli Mani in February at Buli Lhakhang (p133)

➡ Jakar tsechu in October (p26) or November

➡ Trashigang and Mongar tsechus in November (p26)

➡ Trongsa, Lhuentse and Dungkhar tsechus in December (p26)

➡ Gasa Tsechu (p23) in March/April

In addition to religious festivals there are other cultural celebrations throughout the Bhutanese year, notably Bumthang's Nomad's Festival (p23) in February and Laya's Royal Highlander Festival (p26) in October.

Festival Dates & the Bhutanese Calendar

Festival dates are determined by the Bhutanese lunar calendar, which in turn is based on the Tibetan calendar, but differs from the latter by one or more days. There are online Bhutanese calendars to convert dates – there's even a Bhutanese calendar app! By far the easiest way to determine the main festival dates is on the Tourism Council of Bhutan website (www.tourism.gov.bt), where over 30 festivals are listed with their upcoming dates.

LAKKANA SAVAKSURIYAWONG / SHUTTERSTOCK ©

Monk dancing in the tsechu at Mongar (p159)

PHOTOGRAPHY ETIQUETTE

During festivals you can photograph from the dzong courtyard where the dances take place. Remember, however, that this is a religious observance and you should behave accordingly. Consider the following etiquette:

➡ Use a telephoto lens without a flash.

➡ Don't let your desire for a close-up get in the way of the dancers or block the view of other spectators.

➡ Don't intrude on the dance ground or on the space occupied by local people seated at the edge of the dance area, and if you do end up in the front row, remain seated.

➡ Don't photograph a member of the royal family, if you happen to be at a festival or gathering where they are present.

Plan Your Trip

Booking Your Trip

Despite its image as an exclusive, remote destination, Bhutan is not a difficult place to visit. You can easily organise a journey as a group of friends, a couple or even as a solo traveller, and there is no quota on the number of tourists who can enter the country.

When to Book

Bhutanese tour operators generally prefer a minimum of one month to arrange the logistics, including bank transfers, visa and booking Druk Air tickets. Pinning down your itinerary and tour price may take several weeks of emailing beforehand. If you're timing your trip to coincide with a popular festival, you will need to start several months prior to book Druk Air flights and secure accommodation. For a simple trip in off-season you might be able to get it all arranged in as little as a week.

The Daily Tariff

Bhutan's tourism mantra is 'high value, low impact'. Although there is no restriction on visitor numbers, there is a minimum daily tariff fixed by the government, which is the same whether you stay in hotels or camp on a trek. From this daily tariff, US$65 goes to the government as a 'royalty' and is spent on education, healthcare and the like.

The costs seem steep at first, but when you factor in what that gets you – three-star accommodation, food, private transport (not flights), guides, entry fees, permits, a fully organised trek etc – it's

Need to Know

Fixed Daily Rates

The daily tariff for tourists is US$250 per person per night's stay in the high and shoulder seasons. The rate drops to US$200 per person per day in the shoulder/low seasons (December to February/June to August).

Groups of one/two people pay an additional surcharge of US$40/30 per person.

Tariff Discounts

Children up to five years old travel free, while those aged six to 12 years pay only 50% of the daily tariff.

Full-time students aged under 25, with valid identity cards, get a 25% discount if booking directly with a Bhutanese tour operator.

Discounts are offered on the royalty (not the daily tariff) for longer-stay visitors – 50% (ie US$32.50) from the ninth night and 100% after the 14th night.

Tourists are allowed a royalty-free night (ie US$65 discount) if overnighting in the border towns of Phuentsholing, Samdrup Jongkhar or Gelephu.

not a bad deal. The personal service can be remarkable. A solo trek might include a staff of six and a team of horses. On the other side of the coin, the standards of accommodation and food in the remote east or in homestays in general don't reach 'value for money' status.

Solo travellers and couples can easily travel in Bhutan, though they will pay a surcharge. In fact, the most common group size visiting Bhutan is two people.

Because of the daily tariff, there's little difference in price between agencies. A few travel agencies will offer some discount to people who book with them directly, effectively passing on to you the commission they pay to international companies. Another advantage to booking directly with a local agent is that with no commission to pay, the agent has more funds to allocate to better accommodation. If you book through an Indian or Nepali agent, you may find the Bhutanese agent has less funds to book you into a better hotel, since a commission is going to the agent abroad.

The daily tariff doesn't include luxury accommodation (generally four-star options or above), for which you will have to pay a surcharge, which amounts to paying the bulk of the normal hotel rate. Some agents include visa fees (US$40), drinks and perhaps a cultural show in the daily tariff, while most charge separately for this. Activities such as rafting and mountain biking entail additional fees.

There is talk of doing away with the daily tariff and instead raising the royalty to US$100 and then letting agents charge what they want for a tour. Even if this does happen, it is unlikely to dramatically reduce the daily costs of travelling in Bhutan.

Special Categories

Group Leaders A discount of 50% is given to one person in a group of 11 to 15 people. A free trip is allowed for one member per group exceeding 16 people.

Travel Agents Established tour companies intending to put Bhutan into their programs may apply for a discounted familiarisation tour, but you'll need to provide backup documentation.

Payment Procedure

Tours must be fully paid for in advance in order to get visa authorisation. If you have arranged your trip directly with a travel agent in Bhutan, you must make a wire transfer into a Bhutan National Bank (BNB) account, which is held in Standard Chartered Bank (New York, Tokyo, London, Frankfurt branches). Your agent will advise on all the banking details for transferring the funds and also ask you to send them a copy of the transfer so that it can be matched with BNB's records. The ultimate beneficiary is your travel agent in Bhutan, so you will need their account details (and possibly their IBAN number), but the funds are supposed to be held by the Tourism Council of Bhutan (TCB) until your travel is completed; therefore you have more protection against default on the part of the tour company.

Delays & Cancellation

There is no daily tariff for days of delay in your arrival or departure due to weather conditions, Druk Air problems or roadblocks. In cases of delayed departure, tour operators will simply charge the actual expenses for accommodation, food, transport and any other services required.

Each agency has its own cancellation policy, so check the fine print with your agency. There is no refund if you have to cut a trip short once in Bhutan. Travel insurance is a very worthwhile investment, given that you must make full payment upfront.

Booking a Tour

Unlike most countries, government regulations require foreign visitors to travel with a prepaid itinerary organised through a registered Bhutanese tour company. You can join a prepackaged group tour from abroad or arrange a custom-made program with a Bhutanese operator. Generally there is a great deal of freedom as to where you can go and what you can do. The one thing you can't do is travel without a guide.

By dealing with an overseas agent you will avoid complicated payment procedures and also have a home-based contact in case of queries or special needs, but you'll generally pay more for your trip. If you deal directly with a Bhutanese tour operator, you will have lots of scope to individualise your itinerary, but you'll have to spend time exchanging emails and organising an international bank transfer.

Just because you are paying a high tariff, don't imagine you'll have Bhutan to yourself. During the high season, tourist hotels, the major dzongs and festivals hum with tour groups, especially in Paro. For a more exclusive experience you'll have to head to the lesser-visited monasteries in Haa and central Bhutan, choose the shoulder season, or venture out to eastern Bhutan.

If you're not used to travelling on an organised tour, we suggest you break up your itinerary with the occasional hike, bike ride or visit to a remote monastery to give you that independent travel vibe. Independent travellers will have to get used to not ordering their own food or choosing their meal times; other things, like having your luggage carried to your room, are easier to cope with!

Which Tour Company?

There are more than 200 licensed tour companies in Bhutan, ranging from one-person operations to large organisations with fleets of vehicles and their own hotels.

Large companies, such as Norbu Bhutan Travel, Etho Metho Tours & Treks, Bhutan Tourism Corporation Limited, Yangphel Adventure Travel, International Treks & Tours, Rainbow Bhutan and Gangri Tours & Travels, have more clout to obtain reservations in hotels (some of which they own) and on Druk Air, but they are focused on groups and so may have less time to answer individual enquiries.

One Bhutanese hotelier suggested that the following companies would be large

enough to handle overseas queries, but still small enough that the owner would pay personal attention to your program: Bhutan Travel Bureau, Bhutan Mountain Holiday, Bhutan Mandala Tours & Treks, Sakten Tours & Treks, Thunder Dragon Treks, Windhorse Tours and Yu-Druk Tours & Treks.

A few Bhutanese agencies, such as Blue Poppy Tours & Treks (p38), have offices abroad, which can be useful.

All operators in Bhutan are subject to government regulations that specify services, standards and rates, and tour funds are held by the Bhutanese government and only released to the operator at the end of the tour, so you have safeguards no matter which company you choose. In the event of a problem with your Bhutanese tour company, the Tourism Council of Bhutan (p285) can provide advice and assistance.

Bhutanese Tour Operators

The following list includes a selection of the largest companies. For a complete list, see the websites of the Tourism Council of Bhutan (p285) and the Association of Bhutanese Tour Operators (www.abto.org.bt).

Above Horizon Tour & Treks (☏17612487; Thimphu)

All Bhutan Connection (☏02-327012; www.abc.com.bt; Thimphu)

Bhutan Journeys (☏02-333890; www.bhutanjourneys.com; Thimphu)

Bhutan Mandala Tours & Treks (☏02-323676; www.bhutanmandala.com; Thimphu)

Bhutan Men-Lha Adventures (Adventure Trekking Club; ☏02-321559; www.trekkingbhutan.com; Thimphu)

Bhutan Mountain Holiday (☏02-320115; www.bhutanmountainholiday.com; Thimphu)

Bhutan Tourism Corporation Limited (BTCL; ☏02-324045; www.btcl.bt; Thimphu)

Bhutan Travel Bureau (☏02-321749; www.bhutantravelbureau.com; Thimphu)

Bhutan Travel Club (☏02-336941; www.bhutantravelclub.com; Thimphu)

Bhutan Travelers (☏02-328868; www.bhutantravelers.com; Thimphu)

Bhutan Your Way (☏17164757; www.bhutanyourway.com; Paro)

Bridge to Bhutan (02-331766; www.bridgeto bhutan.com; Thimphu)

Dragon Trekkers & Tours (02-323599; www. dragontrekkers.com; Thimphu)

Etho Metho Tours & Treks (02-323162; www. bhutanethometho.com; Thimphu)

Gangri Tours & Travels (02-321229; www. gangritours.com; Thimphu)

International Treks & Tours (77190149; www. bhutanintrek.com; Paro)

Jojo's Adventure Tours (02-333940; www. jojos.com.bt; Thimphu)

Keys to Bhutan (02-327232; www.keysto bhutan.com; Thimphu)

Lhomen Tours & Trekking (02-324148; www. lhomen.com.bt; Thimphu)

Lingkor Tours & Treks (02-323417, 17171766; www.facebook.com/LingkorToursAndTreks; Thimphu)

Norbu Bhutan Travel (02-340151; www. norbubhutan.com; Thimphu)

Rainbow Bhutan (02-323270; www.rainbow bhutan.com; Thimphu)

Raven Tours & Treks (02-326062; www.raven bhutan.com; Thimphu)

Rural Heritage Bhutan/Xplore Bhutan (02-335672; www.ruralheritagebhutan.com; Thimphu)

Sakten Tours & Treks (02-325567; www. bhutanhimalayas.com; Thimphu)

Thoesam Tours & Trekking (02-365101; www. bhutanthoesamtoursandtreks.com; Thimphu)

Thunder Dragon Treks (02-321999; www. thunderdragontreks.com; Thimphu)

Trophel Tours & Treks (77280901; www. bhutanholiday.bt; Thimphu)

Windhorse Tours (02-326026; www.wind horsetours.com/bhutan; Thimphu)

Yana Expeditions (02-332329; www. yanatravel.com; Thimphu)

Yangphel Adventure Travel (02-323293; www. yangphel.com; Thimphu)

Yu-Druk Tours & Treks (02-323461; www. yudruk.com; Thimphu)

Tours from Abroad

Many overseas travel agencies and adventure travel companies offer trips to Bhutan, though few are real specialists. In addition to removing the hassle of transferring money, they will arrange your flights with Druk Air. Most group tours to Bhutan fly to Paro together.

Australia & Asia

Amala Destinations (www.amaladestinations.com)

Bhutan & Beyond (www.bhutan.com.au)

Druk Asia (www.drukasia.com)

Intrepid Travel (www.intrepidtravel.com)

Tour Bhutan (www.tourbhutan.com.au)

World Expeditions (www.worldexpeditions.com.au)

Continental Europe

Explorator (www.explo.com)

Hauser Exkursionen (www.hauser-exkursionen.de)

Snow Leopard Adventures (www.snowleopard.nl)

UK

Audley Travel (www.audleytravel.com)

Blue Poppy Tours & Treks (www.bluepoppy bhutan.com)

Exodus (www.exodus.co.uk)

KE Adventure Travel (www.keadventure.com)

Mountain Kingdoms (www.mountainkingdoms. com)

USA

Above the Clouds (www.aboveclouds.com)

Asian Pacific Adventures (www.asianpacific adventures.com)

Bhutan Travel (www.bhutantravel.com)

Far Fung Places (www.farfungplaces.com)

Geographic Expeditions (www.geoex.com)

Journeys International (www.journeys international.com)

Mountain Travel Sobek (www.mtsobek.com)

Wilderness Travel (www.wildernesstravel.com)

Plan Your Trip
Planning Your Trek

Where Bhutan's roads and tour buses peter out beckons an untouched wilderness of Himalayan valleys, high peaks and picturesque villages that require visitors to strap on some sturdy boots and start hiking. If you're considering trekking in Bhutan, there are a few unique characteristics to consider when choosing a trek.

When to Go

The first thing to consider while planning your trek is the weather. The second half of October provides the best window for trekking in Bhutan; mid-April comes a close second. However, both these periods fall within high tourist seasons, when flights are booked out and hotel rooms are at a premium, so book well in advance. The popular trekking routes also see a steep rise in human traffic during these periods. No matter when you trek, you are likely to have sporadic, and sometimes heavy, rain, so come prepared.

Best Times

October–November The best overall season, with frequent blue skies and dazzling views. The bright sun makes for pleasant daytime temperatures upward of 20°C, falling to around 5°C at night. Mornings are crisp and clear. Clouds and wind tend to build up after 1pm, but typically disappear at night to reveal spectacular starry skies.

March–May Affords warmer weather and suits those who fancy rhododendrons and other exotic Himalayan flora. However, there is a higher chance of rain, and high passes can be snowed under, especially through March.

December–February Winter is the time to tackle the lowland treks such as the Nabji or Salt treks.

Best Experiences

Best Trek for Bragging Rights
Gruelling, expensive (minimum US$5000) and treacherous, the Snowman trek (p198) is Bhutan's ultimate adventure and a brutal way to earn your trekking stripes.

Best Trek for Himalayan Peaks
The Jhomolhari trek (p188) takes you within arm's reach of Jhomolhari and Jichu Drakye, two of Bhutan's most beautiful summits.

Best Trek for Mountains & People
Experience the unusual culture and fantastic hats of the Layap people in a village at 3700m on the Laya trek (p195).

Best General Trek
Atmospheric monasteries and lovely alpine scenery converge on the Druk Path trek (p181) between Paro and Thimphu.

Best Short Trek
The overnight Bumdrak trek (p185) offers luxury camping, mountain views and a visit to the Tiger's Nest Monastery from above.

TOPOGRAPHIC MAPS

Good-quality maps of Bhutan are difficult to obtain. The entire country has been mapped by the Survey of India at 1:50,000, but these are restricted documents, as are a related series of topographic maps produced by the Survey of Bhutan. Another series is the 1:200,000 Russian Military Topographic set, which takes 10 sheets to cover Bhutan, but its text is in Russian Cyrillic.

In cooperation with an Austrian project, the Tourism Council of Bhutan (TCB) produced large-scale contour maps of the Jhomolhari and Dagala Thousand Lakes treks based on the Survey of Bhutan series. These are the best (although not entirely accurate) trekking references available, but they are extremely hard to find these days.

The weather is warm but not oppressively hot. The second half of February is a possible time to tackle a shorter trek such as Bumdrak or the Saga La.

Avoid

June–August This is when the monsoons descend on Bhutan in all their fury, and it can sometimes rain for days on end. Mudslides are common, trails get dangerously wet and slippery, and there's an army of bloodthirsty leeches waiting to jump on you along the way.

September Alpine wildflowers are in bloom, but the mud remains deep and soggy due to rain. Mountain views are generally blocked out by passing clouds, barring the odd sunny morning.

Schedule Changes

Despite all the planning and advance arrangements involved, itineraries can often be disrupted by several unforeseen factors. Snow can block out tracks, horses can fail to appear on schedule, or horse drivers may consider the trail too dangerous for their animals. These events happen more frequently than you might imagine. Be prepared to take any disappointment in your stride.

Booking Your Trek

Government rules dictate that all treks in Bhutan must be arranged as fully fledged camping trips booked through a tour operator. This is essential, since most routes pass through uninhabited and undeveloped forest areas, and parties must therefore be self-sufficient in terms of provisions, personnel and equipment.

It's also mandatory for trekkers to be escorted by a licensed guide registered with the Tourism Council of Bhutan (TCB). Guides in Bhutan come with varied levels of work experience, and a seasoned trek leader is often hard to find. If you're trekking in the high season, ask your tour operator to arrange for a knowledgeable guide well in advance.

Trekking in Bhutan also involves obtaining a slew of permits for entering national parks, walking through protected areas and engaging in activities such as fishing. Brief your tour operator about your exact plans, so that these permits can be duly obtained.

Although many Bhutanese agents can arrange treks on the most popular routes, you should go with a specialised agent if you're headed off the beaten track. The biggest trek operators are Yangphel Adventure Travel (p284), International Treks & Tours (p38), Yu-Druk Tours & Treks (p38) and Lhomen Tours & Trekking (p38).

Foreign trekking companies that specialise in Bhutan include the following:

Himalayan Expeditions (www.himalayan expeditions.com)

KE Adventure Travel (www.keadventure.com)

Mountain Company (www.themountaincompany. co.uk)

Mountain Kingdoms (www.mountainkingdoms. com)

World Expeditions (www.worldexpeditions.com. au)

What to Pack

Trekking gear is not widely available in Bhutan, so bring all personal equipment with you, preferably in a lockable duffel bag. While packing for the trek, limit your baggage to 15kg and bring a bag that is suitable to be packed on a horse or yak. Each pack animal carries 30kg, and it's expected that one animal will carry the luggage of two trekkers.

Your trek operator will provide two-person tents with thin foam mattresses, eating utensils, kitchen equipment, a kitchen tent and a toilet tent. Sleeping bags are often not provided, and when they are, they aren't of the highest quality, so bring your own. Regulations specify that the operator should provide a first-aid kit and a pressure bag (portable altitude chamber) for high-altitude treks.

What to Expect on a Trek

Trail Conditions

Treks in Bhutan are quite physically demanding due to their lengths, altitude and drastic changes in elevation, but a lot of this depends on the trek. The average daily gain is about 500m spread over 8km to 12km, with the odd 1000m ascent thrown in when campsites are few and far between. There's a lot of side-hill climbing on steep slopes, which means more up-and-down climbing around vertical cliffs, avalanche tracks and side canyons. Camp-sites are sometimes spaced out over long distances, requiring you to walk seven to nine hours in a day. Other days, however, may involve just three or four hours of brisk walking.

Many treks follow ancient trade routes that fell into disuse once roads were built. Some of these trails, especially in eastern Bhutan, have seen scant maintenance for several decades, and route conditions are thus often difficult to predict. The terrain is often very rocky, so tough Vibram soles are a good investment. Thanks to mule, horse and yak traffic, trails are often extremely muddy, especially in spring and early summer, and diversions are quite common. Snow can fall anywhere at any time in the Bhutan Himalaya, but especially on high passes.

You may well find that the end of your trek has been affected by the ever-growing network of farm roads that have exploded across Bhutan in the last 10 years. This can mean the last few hours of your trek are on a scrappy, half-built mud road, which is a very anticlimactic end to a walk.

Jhomolhari trek (p188)

ROMULO REJON / GETTY IMAGES ©

Planning Your Trek

JHOMOLHARI

Difficulty Medium–hard
Duration 7 days
Season April to June, September to November
Good For Mountain views
Summary Bhutan's premier trek offers spectacular views of the 7314m Jhomolhari from a high camp at Jangothang. (p188)

LAYA

Difficulty Medium–hard
Duration 10 days
Season April to June, September to November
Good For Remote mountains and communities
Summary This trek is an extension of the Jhomolhari trek. It offers diverse flora and fauna, as well as a good opportunity to spot blue sheep. (p195)

JHOMOLHARI LOOP (SOI YAKSA)

Difficulty Medium
Duration 6 days
Season April to June, September to November
Good For Mountain views with less time
Summary The shorter version of the main Jhomolhari trek goes to the Jhomolhari base camp at Jangothang, returning via several high lakes and three passes. (p193)

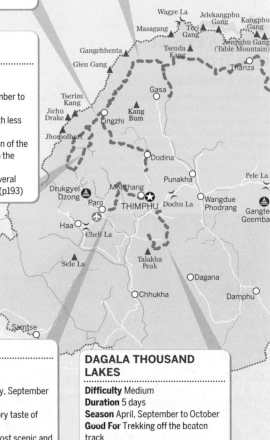

DRUK PATH

Difficulty Medium
Duration 6 days
Season February to May, September to December
Good For An introductory taste of trekking in Bhutan
Summary One of the most scenic and popular treks in Bhutan, following a wilderness trail past several remote lakes. Although it is a short trek, it goes to a high altitude. (p181)

DAGALA THOUSAND LAKES

Difficulty Medium
Duration 5 days
Season April, September to October
Good For Trekking off the beaten track
Summary A short trek, near Thimphu, to a large number of lovely high-altitude lakes; far fewer, however, than the name suggests. (p183)

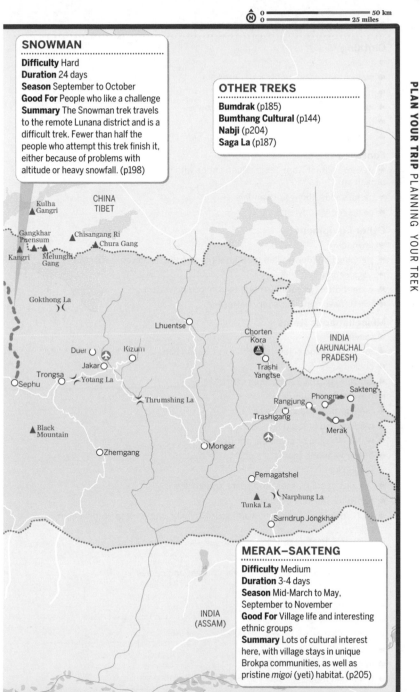

0 ————— 50 km
0 ————— 25 miles

SNOWMAN

Difficulty Hard
Duration 24 days
Season September to October
Good For People who like a challenge
Summary The Snowman trek travels to the remote Lunana district and is a difficult trek. Fewer than half the people who attempt this trek finish it, either because of problems with altitude or heavy snowfall. (p198)

OTHER TREKS

Bumdrak (p185)
Bumthang Cultural (p144)
Nabji (p204)
Saga La (p187)

CHINA
TIBET

▲ Kulha Gangri

Gangkhar Puensum ▲
▲ Chisangang Ri
Kangri ▲ Melunghi Gang ▲ Chura Gang

Gokthong La)(

Lhuentse ○

Chorten Kora

INDIA (ARUNACHAL PRADESH)

Duer ○ Kizum ○
Jakar ○
Trongsa ○ Yotang La
Sephu ○ Thrumshing La

Trashi Yangtse ○

Phongme ○ Sakteng ○
Rangjung ○
Trashigang ○ Merak ○

▲ Black Mountain

○ Zhemgang ○ Mongar

Pemagatshel ○

▲ Tunka La) Narphung La

Samdrup Jongkhar

INDIA (ASSAM)

MERAK–SAKTENG

Difficulty Medium
Duration 3-4 days
Season Mid-March to May, September to November
Good For Village life and interesting ethnic groups
Summary Lots of cultural interest here, with village stays in unique Brokpa communities, as well as pristine *migoi* (yeti) habitat. (p205)

PERSONAL EQUIPMENT CHECKLIST

Clothing
➡ fleece
➡ waterproof jacket, poncho or umbrella
➡ hiking pants or skirt
➡ wicking or quick-drying T-shirts or blouses
➡ long-sleeved shirt
➡ sun hat that covers your ears

Footwear
➡ water-resistant Gore-Tex trekking shoes with hard Vibram soles (properly broken in)
➡ camp shoes, thongs or sandals
➡ socks (polypropylene)

Other Equipment
➡ daypack
➡ sleeping bag (down-filled for high-altitude treks, preferably 800-fill)
➡ silk sleeping bag liner
➡ water bottle (preferably metal to cool boiling water)
➡ torch (flashlight) and spare batteries

Miscellaneous Items
➡ toiletries
➡ toilet paper and cigarette lighter in a Ziploc bag
➡ pocket-knife
➡ sunscreen (SPF 30+) and lip balm
➡ travel towel
➡ biodegradable laundry soap
➡ medical and first-aid kit
➡ water filtration or chemical purification
➡ blister gear and tape
➡ sewing kit
➡ goggles or sunglasses, and spare spectacles
➡ books for the long evenings
➡ stuff sacks for organisation and sturdy plastic bag to keep your sleeping bag dry
➡ second duffel bag or suitcase to leave your city clothes in
➡ trekking poles
➡ mobile phone, battery pack, solar charger and cables

For Treks Above 4000m
➡ down- or fibre-filled jacket
➡ long underwear
➡ woollen hat or balaclava
➡ gloves
➡ gaiters
➡ mountain trekking boots (properly broken in)

For the low-down on Bhutan's mountain trails as well as a sea of information on the flora, fauna, environment and geology of the region, pick up Bart Jordans' comprehensive *Bhutan: A Trekker's Guide*.

Kevin Grange's travelogue *Beneath Blossom Rain: Discovering Bhutan on the Toughest Trek in the World* isn't our favourite mountain title, but it does give a flavour of group trekking in Bhutan.

Yak on Track, by Heather McNeice, is a recent account of a trek through Lunana while raising funds for the Australian Himalayan Foundation.

The Dragon Run: Two Canadians, Ten Bhutanese, One Stray Dog describes a Canadian teacher's 578km run across Bhutan; published by University of Alberta Press in 2017.

Runners will also want to catch *The Snowman Trek* documentary, which follows a group of ultra runners as they tackle the Snowman trek. See www.bluefox entertainment.com.

For general inspiration look at www.greathimalayatrail.com.

Guides & Camp Staff

For a small group, a trekking party typically contains a guide, a cook, a helper and a horseman with his animals. Porters are generally not used in Bhutan, unlike neighbouring Nepal. The guide makes important decisions, and often teams up with the cook to handle the logistics. Larger groups are accompanied by a 'trek organiser' who oversees sundry campsite activities, packers to manage and streamline porterage, and a couple of 'waiters' who serve food and handle kitchen duties. This is not light and fast trekking. On our solo trek along the Druk Path we had six staff and seven ponies!

Accommodation

You will sleep in a tent, with foam pads placed on the floor as a mattress. All your gear goes into the tent with you at night. Staff will often bring you a bowl of warm water each morning to wash with, as well as a piping-hot cup of tea. In some places, there is a stone building that the staff can use for cooking and shelter, which may be available for trekkers to use as a dining room or emergency shelter.

In campgrounds, your tour company will dig a hole and erect a toilet tent, and likely provide a basin of water for washing hands. At night you'll likely get a hot-water bottle to snuggle with. Bring your own water purification, though you can get plenty of boiling water in the evenings at your campsite.

Along some treks such as the Merak–Sakteng and Nabji treks you have the opportunity to stay in village homestays. At other villages you might stay in community-run campgrounds, where profits go into a community fund.

Food & Drink

The food that your camp staff conjur up each day is generally of such quality and quantity that Bhutan is one place where you might actually gain weight while on a trek. Most cooks are adept at tossing together a variety of Western and Asian dishes and you can rely entirely on camp meals. Your cook can even look after any special dietary requirements if given enough notice. All rations are carried from the start of the trek, and food is cooked over stoves fuelled by bottled gas.

Breakfast at camp generally starts with tea in bed and moves on to cereal or porridge, jam and toast, and sometimes eggs, served in a dining tent with unlimited instant coffee or tea. You'll sometimes even be served French fries for breakfast, more proof (if you need it) that Bhutan really is Shangri-La. Midday meals are hot, usually prepared at breakfast time and packed beforehand in a thermos-style metal container with a flask of hot tea. Afternoon brings more tea, and sometimes even snacks of popcorn or nuts. For dinner, you're likely to be served red or white rice, chapatis, lentil soup and vegetables. Fresh meat may be served on the first two nights, and canned fruit cocktails are often thrown in for dessert. All you need to bring is a few muesli bars and a slab of chocolate for moral support.

Pack Animals

In the absence of porters, pack horses (and at higher elevations, yaks) form the lifeline of treks in Bhutan. They carry all personal and common trekking gear, freeing you up to trek with nothing but a daypack. Contractors arrange for animals at the starting point, and their owners accompany them on the trek to arrange their loads and ensure their overall well-being. The ancient *dolam* system in Bhutan allocates specific grazing grounds to each village. For this reason, pack animals often don't cross *dzongkhag* (administrative district) boundaries. Messages are sent ahead so that replacement animals are (with any luck) waiting at the boundary.

Responsible Trekking

Fires

➡ Campfires are technically prohibited and you should decline the offer if your staff suggest one. Bring enough warm clothing and you won't need to stand around one. It's a real dilemma, though, if the horsemen build a fire, or if one is struck as part of a 'cultural show' in a village.

➡ Since 1996, cooking meals over a fire has been prohibited by law, and staff are required to carry a supply of fuel. However, it's a hard rule to enforce, and animal herders sometimes violate the code and cook their own meals over wood.

➡ Burning garbage is offensive to deities, especially within sight of a sacred mountain such as Jhomolhari.

Rubbish

➡ Encourage your guide and staff to pack out all your group's waste. Don't overlook easily forgotten items such as silver paper, cigarette butts and plastic wrappers, including those left behind by others. They weigh little and can be stored in a dedicated rubbish bag.

➡ Sanitary napkins, tampons and condoms cause serious damage to the environment if they are not carried out from a trek.

Human Waste Disposal

➡ Contamination of water sources by human faeces can lead to the transmission of hepatitis, typhoid and intestinal parasites, and poses severe health risks to trekkers as well as local residents and wildlife. A toilet tent will be set up at each camp, so use it.

➡ Ensure that your crew fully fills in the toilet trench afterwards. Some campsites are pockmarked with an unsavoury minefield of half-buried toilet holes.

➡ Where there is no toilet tent, bury your waste. Dig a hole 15cm deep and at least 100m from any watercourse. Consider carrying a trowel for this purpose. Cover the waste with soil and a rock. Use toilet paper sparingly, and burn it or bury it with the waste. In snow, dig down to the soil or your waste will be exposed when the snow melts.

Washing

➡ Detergents and toothpaste, even biodegradable ones, pollute watercourses. For personal washing, use biodegradable soap and a basin at least 50m away from any watercourse. Widely dispersing the waste water allows the soil to filter it fully before it makes it back to the watercourse.

Erosion

➡ Hillsides and mountain slopes are prone to erosion. Sticking to existing tracks and avoiding shortcuts helps to prevent it.

➡ Sometimes a track passes right through a mud patch. Walking through the mud preserves the trail while walking around the edge will increase the size of the patch.

➡ Avoid removing or disturbing plants that keep the topsoil in place.

Cultural Conservation

➡ Thoughtful travellers respect the culture and traditions of local villagers, camp staff and horse drivers.

➡ Giving sweets, money, medicines or gifts to local people, particularly children, encourages begging. If you want to bring something, a range of cheap reading glasses are often much appreciated.

➡ Buying religious artefacts from villagers can deprive them of family heirlooms or precious relics.

Regions at a Glance

Which region of Bhutan you decide to visit will most likely depend on how much time you can afford to spend here. The vast majority of visitors quite naturally focus on the west and Thimphu. With its excellent tourist infrastructure, fantastic sights and spectacular festivals, it allows you to see the most of Bhutan in the shortest amount of time.

Central Bhutan, on the other hand, sees fewer tourists and is a quieter, dreamier collection of alpine valleys and historical monasteries. The winding roads east are for adventurers, weaving researchers and *migoi* (yeti) hunters. It offers warmer, wetter and wilder climes, tougher travel and, some would say, the 'real' Bhutan, untouched by group tourism or even much of the modern age.

Thimphu

Shopping
Museums
Modern Bhutan

Traditional Handicrafts

Thimphu not only has the best handicraft shops in the country, it's also the best place to actually see the products being made, from traditional paper and incense factories to local silversmiths and weaving workshops.

Bhutanese Culture

The best general museums are not in Thimphu (try Paro and Trongsa instead), but for specialised interests such as Bhutanese medicine, traditional country life and the country's rich textile tradition, this is the place.

Cultural Collisions

Thimphu is the beachhead for globalisation in Bhutan. It's the place for contemporary Bhutanese art and culture, as well as espresso coffee and pizza. And there's nowhere better to witness cultural collisions that sum up Bhutan's inherent quirkiness – monks with mobiles and lamas with laptops are a daily sight.

p50

Western Bhutan

Architecture
Trekking
Scenic Views

Religious Monuments

If you only visit two towns in Bhutan, make them Paro and Punakha. The west is blessed with the country's loveliest dzong (Punakha), one of its oldest lhakhangs (Kyichu Lhakhang) and its most dramatic monastery (Taktshang Goemba). These are the big sights that you simply can't miss.

Mountain Exploration

From awesome Jhomolhari to the remote land of Laya, and the well-worn trails of the Druk Path, the west offers you lots of opportunities to combine cultural sights with a walk in the mountains.

Himalayan Majesty

In October or November, a trip to the Dochu La, with its view of Himalayan peaks framed by chortens and prayer flags, is a literal highpoint, rivalled only perhaps by views of Jhomolhari from the upper Paro valley.

p78

Central Bhutan

Architecture
Hiking
Buddhism

Bhutanese Heartland

The heartland of central Bhutan is Bumthang, a delightful collection of Swiss-style valleys sprinkled with golden-roofed chapels, remote red-walled goembas and sacred temples, including the fabulous 1500-year-old Jampey Lhakhang.

Valley Trails

Bumthang offers great day hikes through bamboo forest and yak meadows, past chortens to remote monasteries. The delightful Bumthang Cultural trek goes through moss-covered forests, while the villages of Ura and Shingkhar are great for strolls.

Sacred Landscape

The line separating geography and religion can be fuzzy in Bhutan. Stand where Guru Rinpoche wrestled a snow lion, run your hand over meditation caves etched with the body prints of saints and peer into a lake full of treasure visible only to the virtuous.

p126

Eastern Bhutan

Off the Beaten Track
Dramatic Drives
Handicrafts

Remote Adventures

Bhutan's wild east is for the hardy. Long, winding drives ending in simple accommodation are the norm here. Temples and villages are more traditional and you are likely to have them to yourself. Just don't come during the monsoon.

Changing Landscapes

Roads in the east often inch along sheer cliff faces on a ledge not quite wide enough for two vehicles. Expect a thrilling drive. The variety of landscapes is equally impressive, from the heights of Thrumshing La down to the subtropical plains of India.

Village Looms

Eastern Bhutan is the heartland of the country's rich weaving traditions. Enthusiasts can wander the village looms of Khoma and find out which natural dye comes from insect secretions at Khaling.

p155

On the
Road

Thimphu
p50

Central Bhutan
p126

Eastern Bhutan
p155

Western Bhutan
p78

Thimphu

📞 02 / POP 114,550 / ELEV 2320M

Best Places to Eat

➡ Cloud 9 (p68)

➡ Hayate Ramen (p67)

➡ San MaRu (p68)

➡ Clove Bistro (p67)

➡ Brusnika Russian Cafe (p66)

➡ 7th Restaurant (p68)

Best Places to Stay

➡ Hotel Druk (p61)

➡ Hotel Jumolhari (p59)

➡ Taj Tashi (p59)

➡ Kisa Villa (p64)

➡ Namgay Heritage Hotel (p58)

Why Go?

Strung out along the Wang Chhu, Thimphu is Bhutan's own mini-metropolis, an expanding bubble of shopping complexes, monasteries and chalet-like apartment buildings that reverts quickly to blue-pine forest at the city limits.

Travellers expecting a medieval mood may be disappointed – Thimphu's traditional houses are fast being replaced by multistorey towers – but linger a while and the capital's Bhutanese soul will shine through. Climb up to Changangkha Lhakhang early in the morning, or wander around the Weekend Market in the late afternoon, and you'll see the Bhutan you were expecting: devotees in traditional garb, crimson-robed monks and farmers from the hills coming into town to trade.

For the visitor, Thimphu offers an opportunity to break away from a rigid tour itinerary and enjoy Bhutan's best dining, shopping and nightlife. In place of the traditional, Thimphu offers the realisation of the Bhutanese dream: contented people embracing the modern world, but doing so on their own terms.

When to Go

➡ Post-monsoon, the clear skies and colourful Thimphu *dromchoe* and tsechu festivities make September to November the peak season, but flight and accommodation bookings can be tight.

➡ In spring, rhododendrons in the surrounding hills erupt into flower, while peach trees bloom down in the valley and the Je Khenpo leads the annual procession of monks from Punakha to their summer residence in Thimphu.

➡ Saturday is a good day to be in the city throughout the year, with archery tournaments, expanded opening hours at the dzong, the Weekend Market and the liveliest nightlife, though some sights and all government offices are closed.

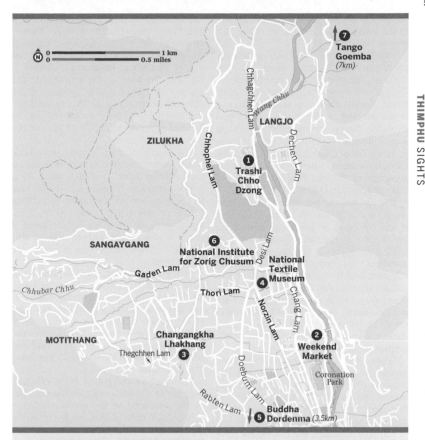

⊙ Thimphu Highlights

❶ Trashi Chho Dzong
(p51) Marvelling at the scale of this grand and serene fortress.

❷ Weekend Market (p53)
Plunging into Thimphu's pungent Weekend Market for incense, local foodstuffs and artefacts.

❸ Changangkha Lhakhang (p52) Joining the morning pilgrims

circumambulating around Thimphu's liveliest temple.

❹ National Textile Museum (p53) Uncovering the intricacies of Bhutanese weaving and embroidery at Thimphu's best museum.

❺ Buddha Dordenma (p55) Looking up in awe at the mighty 51m-tall statue that rises over the city.

❻ National Institute

for Zorig Chusum (p53)
Appreciating the skill of Bhutanese artistry at this school for the 13 traditional arts.

❼ Tango Goemba
(p73) Hiking between the whispering pines to the serene solitude of this Buddhist college, easily combined with a side trip to Cheri Goemba.

⊙ Sights

★**Trashi Chho Dzong**   BUDDHIST MONASTERY
(Map p54; Chhagchhen Lam; SAARC national Nu 300; ⊘5.30-6.30pm Mon-Fri, 9am-5pm Sat & Sun Mar-Oct, 4.30-5.30pm Mon-Fri, 9am-4pm Sat & Sun Nov-Feb) This splendid dzong, north

of the city on the west bank of the Wang Chhu, dominates the valley, looking out over a cascade of terraced fields. It's Thimphu's grandest building by far, and served as the official seat of the Druk Desi, the head of the secular government that shared power with the religious authorities, from the 18th to the 19th centuries. The dzong was the site of the lavish formal coronation of the fifth king in 2008.

The building you see today is actually not the original Thimphu dzong. The first fortress – the Dho-Ngen Dzong (Blue Stone Dzong) – was erected in 1216 on the hillside where Dechen Phodrang now stands, and it was adopted as the seat of Lama Phajo Drukgom Shigpo, who brought the Drukpa Kagyu lineage to Bhutan. The fort was renamed Trashi Chho Dzong (Fortress of the Glorious Religion) when it passed from the descendants of Lama Phajo to Zhabdrung Ngawang Namgyal in 1641.

The Zhabdrung planned to house both monks and civil officials in the dzong, but it was too small, so he built a new dzong lower down in the valley for the civil officials, and this soon become the focus of attention. The upper dzong was eventually destroyed by fire in 1771 and the lower dzong was expanded before also suffering a devastating fire in 1866. Such setbacks are not unusual in the history of a dzong, and the lower dzong was rebuilt, before suffering damage in two further fires and the deadly earthquake of 1897.

When King Jigme Dorji Wangchuck moved his capital to Thimphu in 1962, he began a five-year project to renovate and enlarge the dzong. The royal architect left the *utse* (central tower) untouched, along with the imposing chapel and assembly hall in the courtyard, but the rest of the compound was rebuilt in traditional fashion, without nails or architectural plans. The dzong once housed the National Assembly and now houses the secretariat, the throne room, and offices of the king and the ministries of home affairs and finance. The courtyard to the north of the assembly hall hosts Thimphu's biggest annual bash, the colourful tsechu festivities.

The dzong's whitewashed perimeter walls are guarded by three-storey towers at the four corners, capped by red-and-gold, triple-tiered roofs. The only way to enter the fort is via one of two gateways on the eastern side of the structure. The southern entrance leads to the administrative section (off-limits to visitors), while the northern entrance leads to the monastic quarter, the summer residence of the *dratshang* (central monk body).

Entering the dzong via the northern entrance after a thorough security check, visitors are greeted by depictions of the four guardian kings, while the steps are flanked by images of Drukpa Kunley, Thangtong Gyelpo and Togden Pajo (the founder of nearby Phajoding Monastery). Beyond is the vast, flagstone *dochey* (courtyard) and the *utse*. It's hard not to be humbled by the dramatic proportions of the architecture, and the enclosed silence broken only by the flight of pigeons, the shuffle of feet and the whir of prayer wheels.

The northern part of the compound, which visitors are free to explore, contains the towering **utse**, accessed via a steep wooden stairway. If you're allowed in, look for the 3rd-floor funeral chorten of the 69th Je Khenpo, where pilgrims receive the blessing of betel nut from his nut container. If this intrigues you, head next door to visit the toilet of the Zhabdrung in his former living room.

Nearby in the courtyard is the **Lhakhang Sarp**, a small chapel with handsome mythical beasts supporting its beams. The original *dukhang* (assembly hall) on the edge of the square enshrines a huge statue of Sakyamuni (the historical Buddha) and the thrones of the current king, past king and Je Khenpo. Look to the ceiling for fine mandala paintings.

Northeast of the dzong is an excellent example of a traditional cantilever bridge. To the southeast is the unassuming residence of the current king, while across the river you can see the impressive, step-roofed **National Assembly** (Map p54; Dechen Lam). The small **Neykhang Lhakhang**, west of the dzong, houses the local protective deities Gyenyen Jagpa Melen and Dorji Daktshen, and is off-limits to visitors.

The large open-air courtyard on the north side of the dzong hosts the dances of the annual tsechu festival in September. The dzong's huge Sangay Tsokhorsum Thondrol (painted/embroidered religious picture) is unfurled here at the climax of the tsechu.

★ **Changangkha Lhakhang** BUDDHIST TEMPLE
(Map p54; Thegchhen Lam; ☉ daylight hours) This traditional Bhutanese temple perched like a fortress on a ridge above central Thimphu hums with pilgrim activity. It was established in the 12th century on a site chosen by Lama Phajo Drukgom Shigpo, originally from Ralung in Tibet. Parents come here to get auspicious names for their newborns or blessings for their young children from the protector deity Tamdrin (to the left in the

grilled inner sanctum). Children are blessed by a *phurba* (ritual dagger) and given a sacred thread.

The interior murals are particularly fine. Give the resident astrologer your birth date and he will consult divination charts to decide what kind of protective prayer flags will benefit you. Don't leave without checking out the shrine to the *tshomen* (mermaid) in the central courtyard and then taking in the excellent view from the *kora* (circumambulation) path around the compound. Come early in the morning, before groups arrive, to enjoy Changangkha at its most peaceful.

★**National Textile Museum** MUSEUM
(Map p54; ☑02-336460; www.rtabhutan.org; Norzin Lam; SAARC/non-SAARC national Nu 100/250; ☺9am-4pm Mon-Sat) Thimphu's best museum is part of the Royal Textile Academy. It features a stunning display of ancient and modern textiles, and explores the rich traditions of Bhutan's national arts of *thagzo* (weaving) and *tshemzo* (embroidery). The ground floor focuses on royal *ghos*, including the wedding clothes worn by the fourth king and his four wives. The upper floor introduces the major weaving techniques, styles of local dress and types of textiles made by women and men. No photography is allowed.

The museum shop offers some interesting books and fine textiles. Across the courtyard is the Royal Textile Academy conservation centre, where you can watch a small group of weavers working their looms.

★**National Memorial
Chorten** BUDDHIST MONUMENT
(Map p54; Chorten Lam; SAARC national Nu 300; ☺9am-5pm Mar-Oct, to 4pm Nov-Feb) This large chorten is one of the most visible landmarks in Thimphu, and for many Bhutanese it is the focus of daily worship. The Tibetan-style stupa was built in 1974 as a memorial to the third king, Jigme Dorji Wangchuck (1928–72). Early morning is a great time to visit, as elderly people shuffle meditatively around the chorten, families light butter lamps, and kids dressed in their smartest *ghos* and *kiras* (traditional dress for men and women) rush out a quick *kora* on their way to school.

The whitewashed chorten, with its sun-catching golden finial, has richly painted annexes facing the cardinal directions, and features elaborate mandalas, statues and a shrine dedicated to the popular king. The action continues from dawn till long after dark, but tourists are discouraged from visiting at night to give devotees some respite. Clock the dedicated group of old timers hauling away at room-size giant prayer wheels beside the main entrance.

★**Weekend Market** MARKET
(Centenary Farmers' Market; Map p62; Chhogyel Lam; ☺7am-8pm Sat & Sun) Thimphu's Weekend Market fills a maze-like pavilion on the west bank of the Wang Chhu, just north of Changlimithang Stadium. Vendors from throughout the region start arriving on Thursday and remain until Sunday night, filling the market halls and surrounding streets with produce. The incense area is one of the most interesting, full of deliciously aromatic raw ingredients and pink cubes of camphor and saffron that are used to flavour the holy water given to pilgrims in lhakhangs.

Wander around the stalls and you'll find a pungent collection of dried fish, strips of fatty pork and discs of *datse* (soft cheese), as well as dried chillies, local pickles and condiments and bottles of wild honey from southern Bhutan. During the winter you can even pick up a leg of yak (with the hoof still attached). Depending on the season, look out for banana pods, jackfruit and the curly fern fronds known as *nakey*. The cereals section has red rice and *kapche*, the ground roasted barley beloved by highland Bhutanese and Tibetans (known as *tsampa* across the Himalaya). The action spills over into the surrounding streets, which are a buzz of activity at market time.

Nearby, across a traditional cantilevered bridge, is the weekends-only Handicrafts Market (p69).

★**National Institute
for Zorig Chusum** ARTS CENTRE
(Map p54; ☑02-322302; www.nizc.gov.bt; Pedzoe Lam; adult Nu 100; ☺10am-noon & 2-5pm Mon-Fri, to 4pm in winter, 10am-noon Sat) This institute, commonly known as 'the painting school', operates four- to six-year courses that provide instruction in Bhutan's 13 traditional arts. Students specialise in painting (of both furniture and *thangkas* – painted religious pictures, usually on canvas), woodcarving (masks, statues, bowls), embroidery (hangings, boots, clothes) or statue-making (clay). Students are well used to having visitors while they work and it's fine to take photos.

Greater Thimphu

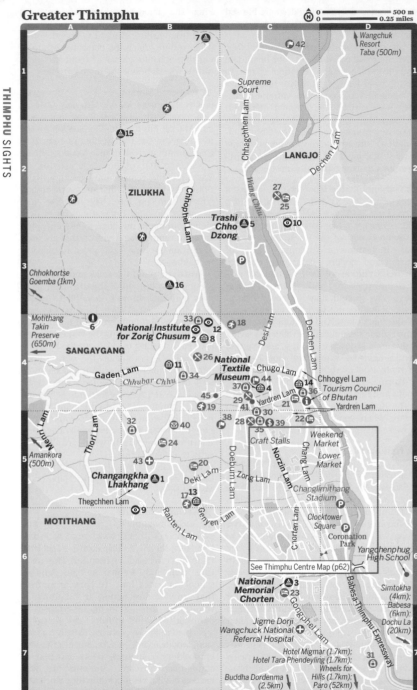

Greater Thimphu

◎ Top Sights
1 Changangkha Lhakhang B5
2 National Institute for Zorig
   Chusum B4
3 National Memorial Chorten C6
4 National Textile Museum C4
5 Trashi Chho Dzong C3

◎ Sights
6 BBS Tower A4
7 Dechen Phodrang B1
8 Folk Heritage Museum B4
9 Nado Poizokhang Incense Factory B6
10 National Assembly C3
11 National Institute of Traditional
   Medicine B4
12 National Library B4
13 Simply Bhutan B5
14 Voluntary Artists Studio Thimphu C4
15 Wangditse Goemba B2
16 Zilukha Nunnery B3

◎ Activities, Courses & Tours
17 Deer Park Thimphu B5
18 Royal Thimphu Golf Club C4
19 Yu-Druk Bike Shop B4

◎ Sleeping
20 Bhutan Suites B5
21 Dorji Elements C4
22 Hotel Golden Roots C5
23 Hotel Tashi Yoedling C6
24 Khang Residency B5
25 Kisa Villa C2

◎ Eating
26 Big Bakery B4
27 Brusnika Russian Cafe C2
   Folk Heritage Museum
   Restaurant .... (see 8)
28 Fu Lu Shou C5
29 San MaRu C4

◎ Shopping
   Choki Handicrafts .... (see 8)
30 Craft Gallery C5
31 Gagyel Lhundrup Weaving Centre D7
32 Nado Poizokhang Incense
   Showroom B5
33 Sangay Arts & Crafts B4
34 Survey of Bhutan B4
35 Tarayana Rural Products C5
36 Tarayana Rural Products C4
37 Traditional Boot House C4

◎ Information
38 Bangladesh Embassy C5
   Bank of Bhutan .... (see 21)
39 Bhutan National Bank C5
40 DHL B5
41 Immigration Office C4
42 Indian Embassy C1
43 Menjong Diagnostic Centre B5
44 Thai Honorary Consulate-General C4

◎ Transport
45 Druk Air B4

It's hard not to be impressed by the skill and discipline of the young students, and their work is sold at fair prices in the school showroom.

Changlimithang Archery Ground
STADIUM

(Map p62; Chhogyel Lam; ☉daylight hours) FREE Most days of the week you'll find arrows flying at the city's most important archery ground, just down from Changlimithang Stadium. Teams compete to hit targets over a distance of 145m, while their competitors pass comment on misses, and sing and dance to celebrate shots on target. Traditional bamboo or high-tech carbon-fibre compound bows are used, and a tournament is quite a spectacle, with lots of good-natured ribbing and camaraderie.

It's a miracle that more archers don't get injured considering how close they stand to the targets. An on-site shop (p69) sells traditional bamboo bows.

Buddha Dordenma
BUDDHIST MONUMENT

(Kuensel Phodrang; ☉9am-5pm, to 4pm in winter) FREE The huge 51m-tall steel statue of Buddha Dordenma commands the entry to the Thimphu valley. The massive three-storey base houses a large chapel full of thousands of donated Buddha statuettes, while the body itself is filled with 125,000 smaller statues of Buddha. The chapel roof has some particularly fine mandalas. The Buddha looks amazing when illuminated at night. The area is called Changri Kuensel Phodrang after the former palace of the 13th Druk Desi that once stood here.

The statue was made in China, cut into pieces and then shipped and trucked in from Phuentsholing – we would've loved to have seen the faces of the local farmers as the super-sized features of the Buddha drove by! The paved road to the site, also known as 'Buddha Point', passes a new Hindu temple and is a popular biking route. A 3.5km mountain-bike trail branches off from just below the Buddha site to Depsi, near

Babesa; in the other direction, you can continue as far as Pangri Zampa.

Dechen Phodrang
BUDDHIST MONASTERY

(Map p54; Gaden Lam) Beyond Trashi Chho Dzong at the north end of town, Dechen Phodrang stands on the site of Thimphu's original 12th-century dzong. Since 1971 it has housed the state *lobra* (monastic school), providing an education for more than 280 novice monks. If you visit during breaks between classes, expect lots of questions from the students!

Simply Bhutan
MUSEUM

(Map p54; ☎ 02-337961; www.simplybhutan.bt; Genyen Lam; SAARC national Nu 300; ⓧ 9.30am-5pm, to 4.30pm in winter) Simply Bhutan is an interactive 'living' museum that gives a quick introduction to various aspects of traditional life in Bhutan. Visitors are greeted with a shot of local *arra* (rice spirit), before being guided through mocked-up village scenes. Along the way, you can dress up in traditional clothes, try out archery and hear songs sung by Bhutanese women as they build houses out of rammed earth. It's touristy, but a good family experience.

There are also souvenir stalls, and a restaurant serving Bhutanese set meals for Nu 500.

Zilukha Nunnery
BUDDHIST MONASTERY

(Thangthong Dewachen Dupthop; Map p54; Gadem Lam) Just off Gadem Lam, on the hillside above Trashi Chho Dzong, this small, friendly nunnery has links to Thangtong Gyelpo, builder of chain bridges across Bhutan and Tibet, and there's an interesting enclosed chorten in the main courtyard. The best way to visit is at the end of the walk from the BBS Tower to Wangditse Goemba.

Motithang Takin Preserve
ZOO

(Sangaygang; adult Nu 300; ⓧ 9am-5pm Tue-Sun, to 4pm in winter) Off the road leading to the BBS Tower, this preserve for Bhutan's curious national animal (p270) was originally established as a zoo, but the fourth king decided this was not in keeping with Bhutan's environmental and religious convictions, and the takin were released into the wild. Unfortunately the animals were so tame they took to wandering the streets of Thimphu looking for food, so this enclosed area was set aside to keep them safe.

Although the entry fee is high, the setting is peaceful and it's worth taking the time to see these oddball mammals. The best time to view the takin up close is early morning, when they gather near the fence to feed.

Folk Heritage Museum
MUSEUM

(Phelchey Toenkhim; Map p54; ☎ 02-327133; www.folkheritagemuseum.org.bt; Pedzoe Lam; SAARC/non-SAARC national Nu 50/200; ⓧ 9am-5pm Mon-Fri, 10am-5pm Sat, to 4pm in winter) Set in a small orchard, this restored rammed-earth and timber building is furnished as it would have been about a century ago, providing a glimpse into rural Bhutanese life. Details that jump out include the antique noodle press, leopardskin bags and Brokpa yak-hair 'spider' hats (available for sale for Nu 1200). There's a short-range archery ground for visitors and the **restaurant** (set lunch/dinner from Nu 350/680; ⓧ 9am-9pm Mon-Sat) here serves good Bhutanese meals.

Voluntary Artists Studio Thimphu
GALLERY

(VAST; Map p54; ☎ 17265449; www.vastbhutan.org.bt; Tarayana Centre, Chhogyel Lam, Chubachhu; ⓧ 9am-6pm Tue-Sun) FREE This studio and art gallery exists to promote local artists, to provide vocational training for young artists and to act as an artists' creative meeting venue. It's a great place to plug into the Thimphu art scene, check out the latest modern and traditional art in the exhibition hall and chat with artists. Some artwork is displayed in the public park outside.

Bhutan Postal Museum
MUSEUM

(Map p62; GPO, Chang Lam; Nu 150; ⓧ 9am-5pm Mon-Fri, 9am-1pm Sat) Below the post office, this small museum is dedicated to the history of the Bhutan postal service, from its earliest days (when messages were delivered from dzong to dzong by the king's bodyguards) to the arrival of modern postage stamps and delivery methods. There are also displays of coins and religious artefacts.

National Library
LIBRARY

(Map p54; ☎ 02-324314; www.library.gov.bt; Pedzoe Lam; ⓧ 9.30am-5pm Mon-Fri Mar-Oct, to 4pm Nov-Feb) FREE The National Library was established in 1967 to preserve ancient Dzongkha and Tibetan texts. For tourists it's of interest mainly for its dzong-like traditional architecture, but the shelves inside are full of important scriptures, made of unbound pages stacked between wooden plates and wrapped in cloth. Dotted here and there are historical photos and on the top floor is a copy of a letter sent from the Druk Desi (secular ruler) to British army officer and surveyor Samuel Turner in 1783.

Historical manuscripts are kept on the top floor and include texts from the famous Tibetan printing presses of Derge and Narthang. Scriptures from all religious schools are represented, including the Bön tradition. Also on display are carved wooden blocks used for printing, and a copy of the world's largest published book – a 2m-tall coffee-table tome called *Bhutan: A Visual Odyssey Across the Last Himalayan Kingdom*. Shoes must be left outside.

National Institute of Traditional Medicine
MUSEUM

(Map p54; ☎02-332949; www.dtms.gov.bt; Serzhong Lam; SAARC/non-SAARC national Nu 100/200; ☺9am-5pm Mon-Fri, 9am-1pm Sat) Established in 1978, this institute collects medicinal plants from remote corners of the Bhutanese Himalaya, and distributes pills, ointments and medicinal teas to regional health-care units around the country. As well as a fully functioning herbal medicine hospital, there's a small museum here covering some of the 300 herbs, minerals and animal parts that Bhutanese doctors (p239) have to choose from.

Of particular interest is *yartsa goenbub* (cordyceps) – actually the bodies of caterpillars and other bugs that have been infested by a parasitic fungus – which is consumed as a form of 'Himalayan Viagra'. The curious 'worm-root' sells for up to US$25,000 per kilogram in China. Also pause to examine the intricate 'Celestial City of Medicine' sculpture in the lobby.

If you're feeling under the weather, the on-site clinic will tell you if your wind, bile and phlegm are in balance and prescribe appropriate medicines or treatments, all free of charge. Lasgang root and gentiana are said to do wonders for a sore throat, while *chozen nagsel* helps in curing all diseases apparently caused by evil spirits.

Zangto Pelri Lhakhang
BUDDHIST TEMPLE

(Map p62; Dungkhar Lam) Close to the Weekend Market, this modern chapel was built in the 1990s as a representation of Guru Rinpoche's celestial abode by Dasho Aku Tongmi, the musician who composed Bhutan's national anthem. The older Mani Dungkhar Lhakhang beside it contains some enormous prayer wheels, and between the two is an elephant skull in a box – reputedly unearthed while digging the foundations.

🏃 Activities

Thimphu is a small town at heart, and it's never hard to escape the commotion. Set off on foot (p76) into the surrounding hills and you can walk all day and hardly see a soul. Most of the walking trails double as mountain-biking tracks, and several local agencies rent out bikes. For information on rock climbing in the area, visit the website of **Vertical Bhutan** (www.verticalbhutan.com).

Yu-Druk Bike Shop
MOUNTAIN BIKING

(Map p54; ☎02-323461; www.yudruk.com; Thori Lam; ☺10am-6pm Mon-Fri, 10am-2pm Sat) Yu-Druk organises mountain-biking tours and guides, and rents out quality bikes for Nu 2000 per day. It can arrange to have you and the bike transported to the start of several rides. It also sells bikes, accessories and Bhutanese-designed cycling gear.

Wheels for Hills
MOUNTAIN BIKING

(☎02-340185; www.bhutanmountainbike.com; near Shearee Sq Mall, Olakha; ☺9am-6.30pm) This mountain-bike shop in south Thimphu rents quality imported mountain bikes for Nu 1800 to 2500 per day. It runs its own tours and can arrange guides, and the shop sells parts and does repairs.

Royal Thimphu Golf Club
GOLF

(Map p54; ☎02-335521; www.golfbhutan.com; Chhophel Lam; green fees SAARC/non-SAARC national Nu 2500/US$60, club hire per day US$30; ☺8am-5pm) This delightful nine-hole course sprawls over the hillside above Trashi Chho Dzong. Brigadier General TV Jaganathan got permission from King Jigme Dorji Wangchuck to construct a few holes in the late 1960s, and the course was formally inaugurated in 1971. It's not cheap, but how often do you get to tee off in sight of a Bhutanese dzong and have to dodge chorten hazards?

Schoolboy caddies are available for around US$10. You don't need to make an appointment to play, but you may have to wait to tee off on weekends. The new clubhouse canteen has decent food and fine views of the greens.

Deer Park Thimphu
MEDITATION

(Map p54; www.deerparkthimphu.org; Nazhoen Pelri Youth Development Centre, Genyen Lam) This small meditation centre opposite Simply Bhutan (p56) offers Tuesday evening meditation classes, short weekend retreats and Buddhist discussions for adults and children, as well as a Friday movie night. See its website for the schedule.

WORTH A TRIP

CRAFT WORKSHOPS IN THIMPHU

Ask your guide to arrange a visit to the following workshops and traditional factories in Thimphu.

Jungshi Handmade Paper Factory (Map p62; 02-323431; Khuju Lam; SAARC national Nu 50; 9am-5pm Mon-Sat) This small factory produces traditional Bhutanese paper by hand using pulp made from the bark of the daphne bush. You can see the whole process, from the initial soaking and boiling of the bark to sorting, crushing, pulping, layering, pressing and drying. Products for sale include lovely decorated paper (Nu 250 to 800 per sheet), plus cards, notebooks, lampshades and calendars. It has a stand among the craft stalls on Norzin Lam.

Nado Poizokhang Incense Factory (Map p54; 02-323107; www.nadopoizokhang.com; Changangkha; 9am-5pm Mon-Sat) FREE Easily Thimphu's sweetest-smelling excursion, this busy workshop churns out about 10,000 sticks of handmade incense monthly, with each stick hand-rolled between wooden blocks and then stacked for air drying. You can watch the whole production process (grinding, extruding, rolling and drying) at the main workshop above Changangkha Lhakhang, or simply browse for the final product at the nearby **showroom** (Map p54; Thori Lam; 9am-7pm Mon-Sat).

Goldsmiths Workshop (Map p62; Dechen Lam; 9am-1pm & 2-5pm Mon-Fri) FREE This government workshop, behind the long-distance bus station, hosts dozens of goldsmiths and silversmiths, making mainly repoussé work, with designs hammered by hand into sheets of metal set into blocks of resin. Many of the metalworkers work on large pieces such as *toranas* (arches found over monastery statues), but they also make small jewellery pieces that are offered for sale to visitors.

Festivals & Events

Thimphu comes alive during the annual *dromchoe* and tsechu festivities, held consecutively over eight to 10 days in September/October, corresponding with the eighth lunar month in the Bhutanese calendar. Normal business grinds to a halt and hotels charge a supplement on their room rates during this period. Given the level of demand, you need to book well ahead to stand a chance of getting a room at this time.

On public holidays such as the Birthday of the Fifth King (21 to 23 February), Birthday of the Fourth King (11 November) and National Day (17 December), there are cultural shows at Changlimithang Stadium and youth-focused music performances in the city's Clocktower Square.

Sleeping

Standard tourist-class hotels are concentrated around Clocktower Square and along Chang Lam, while budget hotels targeting Indian travellers are strung out along Norzin Lam.

Many of Thimphu's best hotels are on the outskirts, but guests may feel a little isolated being so far from the centre. If you intend to explore Thimphu's dining and nightlife scene, stay downtown, but expect some noise from traffic and barking dogs.

Thimphu Centre

Hotel Chophel Norkyi LOCAL HOTEL $
(Map p62; 02-337007; nyendak28@gmail.com; Norzin Lam; d/tr Nu 1800/2500;) At this Indian-style hotel, marble stairs and stone-clad corridors lead to wood-lined rooms with small TVs and little Bhutanese details. It's not lavish, but it is very clean and good value.

Hotel Shantideva LOCAL HOTEL $
(Map p62; 02-336066; hotelshantideva@gmail.com; MKTS Bldg, Clocktower Sq; s/d/tr Nu 2000/2500/2800;) This modern hotel is one of the best Thimphu inns aimed at Indian guests, with chintzy but spotless tiled rooms with heated floors and tasty Indian vegetarian food served in the dining room. Enter at the back of the building.

★**Namgay Heritage Hotel** HOTEL $$
(Map p62; 02-337113; www.namgayheritage hotel.com; Jangchhub Lam; r from Nu 4800, ste Nu 18,000;) A top-end tourist class hotel, Namgay Heritage is a riot of hand-carved timbers. The rooms are less traditional than the five-storey atrium, but are warm and comfortable, with murals on the walls. Perks include the quiet location away from the hubbub, a decent restaurant, a free sauna, gym and indoor pool,

and a great bar across the courtyard serving draught beers, coffee and cakes.

Visiting lamas should splash out on the suite, which comes with its own meditation throne.

★ Hotel Jumolhari
HOTEL **$$**

(Map p62; ☑02-322747; www.hoteljumolhari.com; Wogzin Lam; s/d Nu 4200/4800, deluxe r Nu 5400, ste Nu 6000; ☏) This centrally located hotel swaps the usual Bhutanese interior design for a smart art deco feel and lots of brown and gold tones. The rooms are snug but tastefully decorated and well appointed, and the above-average restaurant serves good Indian dishes, and buffets for groups. For our money, this is the best-value option close to Clocktower Square.

★ Wangchuk Hotel
HOTEL **$$**

(Map p62; ☑02-323532; www.wangchukhotel.com; Chang Lam; r standard/deluxe Nu 4800/5400; ☏) This well-cared-for hotel overlooks Changlimithang Stadium and is a favourite with expats. The wood-panelled, carpeted rooms are spacious, light and conducive to relaxation, and the service is excellent. The outdoor terrace seating is great for a Red Panda beer or espresso at the end of a busy day of sightseeing.

Hotel Tashi Yoedling
HOTEL **$$**

(Map p54; ☑02-338134; www.tashiyoedling.com; Doebum Lam; r Nu 4200-4600; ☏) There's a certain design flair at this bright, modern hotel just south of the centre, but it's the views right over the National Memorial Chorten that steal the show. Even rooms without the view are light and airy, with stylish modern furniture.

Walk Inn
LOCAL HOTEL **$$**

(Map p62; ☑02-330927; walkinn218@gmail.com; Norzin Lam; tw/d Nu 3510/4500; ☏) A spick-and-span new arrival on Norzin Lam, nudging into the Bhutan-tourist-hotel category. There's a spotless restaurant overlooking the town square serving good Indian vegetarian food, and upstairs, marble corridors lead to clean, calm rooms with gleaming white sheets, dragon carpets and wood-effect tile floors. Enter at the back of the building.

Thimphu Tower
HOTEL **$$**

(Map p62; ☑02-335367; www.thimphutowers.com; Clocktower Sq; r from Nu 5400, premium r from Nu 6600; ☏) A business-like business-class hotel facing onto Clocktower Square, with good service and nice little touches, such as free earplugs in the rooms to keep out the noise from downtown. Inside, it's modern rather than traditional and the upper-floor premium rooms boast good views over Changlimithang Stadium. You might need to pay a small supplement to stay here.

Ambient Café Serviced Apartments
LOCAL HOTEL **$$**

(Map p62; ☑17116661; ambientcafethimphu@gmail.com; Norzin Lam; apt per week/month Nu 17,500/38,000; ☏) Upstairs from Ambient Café and run by the same friendly folk, these tasteful one-bedroom apartments have wooden floors, neat marble bathrooms, a small kitchen and lounge and upbeat, modern decor. Access to the rooms is past the cafe's coffee grinder.

Gyelsa Boutique
HOTEL **$$**

(Map p62; ☑02-339191; www.gyelsaboutique.com; Jangchhub Lam; s/d from Nu 3960/5400; ☏) The rooms aren't quite as plush as the stylish black-timbered exterior at this small hotel off the main drag, but the food is excellent and scents of lemongrass waft around the lobby. Rooms have dark wood furnishings and Venetian blinds, and the location is quieter than average for downtown. It's popular with Asian travellers.

Hotel Kisa
HOTEL **$$**

(Map p62; ☑02-336495; www.hhlbhutan.com; Chang Lam; r from Nu 4560; ☏) The expansive rooms at the Kisa are looking a little tired, but the welcome is warm and the location central. Rooms on the higher floors have good views over Changlimithang Stadium. The lobby is a cosy place to hang out with a book, and there's a restaurant and spa.

Hotel Pedling
HOTEL **$$**

(Map p62; ☑02-325714; www.hotelpedling.com; Doendrup Lam; s/d from Nu 4560/5520; ☏) There's a vaguely Nordic feel to the wood-lined rooms at Pedling, which have subtle Bhutanese motifs painted on the walls and lots of light pine furniture. The pleasant staff are a great asset and there's a restaurant and spa. The hotel is owned by Gangte Monastery and often gets visiting Buddhist groups.

★ Taj Tashi
LUXURY HOTEL **$$$**

(Map p62; ☑02-336699; www.tajhotels.com; Samten Lam; r/ste from US$540/804; ☏☒) The striking dzong-like architecture of the five-star Taj Tashi fits effortlessly into the valley, and the elegant interior is full of Bhutanese motifs (note the *dungchen* trumpets as door

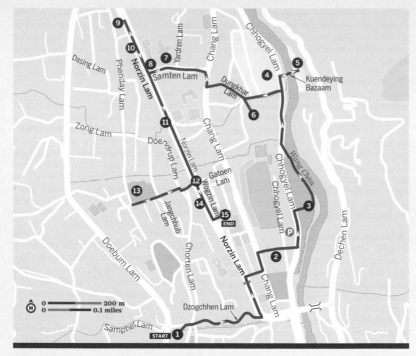

🏃 City Walk
Downtown Thimphu

START NATIONAL MEMORIAL CHORTEN
END CLOCKTOWER SQUARE
LENGTH 4KM; TWO TO THREE HOURS

Start at Thimphu's handsome **①National Memorial Chorten** (p53) and join locals for a ritual circumambulation, then follow winding Dzogchhen Lam downhill to the end of Norzin Lam. Stroll north and turn right after the ornate city gateway to reach Chang Lam and the **②Changlimithang Archery Ground** (p55). If there's an archery tournament in progress, cross carefully to Chhogyel Lam, and walk through the car park to calm **③Coronation Park** (Map p62).

Continue north along the riverbank to Thimphu's animated **④Weekend Market** (p53), then cross the Kuendeying Bazaam bridge to reach the **⑤Handicrafts Market** (p69) on the east bank. Next, follow Dunghkar Lam west, passing the tiered tower of the **⑥Zangto Pelri Lhakhang** (p57). Duck into the compound to see the elephant skull and spin the giant prayer wheels of the adjacent Mani Dungkhar Lhakhang.

Continue along Dunghkar Lam and go north to pick up Samten Lam, passing the imposing hotel **⑦Taj Tashi** (p59). Turn north along Norzin Lam past a string of **⑧handicraft stalls** (p69) and a scattering of traditional earth and timber homes amid the modern towers. Continue north to admire the amazing embroidery and weaving on display in the **⑨National Textile Museum** (p53).

Retrace your steps along Norzin Lam, ducking into **⑩Chula** (p67) for a refreshing cup of masala chai, before following the bazaar south past shops such as **⑪Sephub Gyeltsen Tsongkhang** (p70), piled high with ghos and kiras. You'll soon reach the main **⑫traffic circle** (p61).

Follow the pedestrian path from the traffic circle to the **⑬Bhutan Thailand Friendship Park** (Map p62; Jangchhub Lam; ⊙daylight hours), where the old-fashioned Droma Lhakhang enshrines another giant prayer wheel. Return to Norzin Lam for another refreshment stop at **⑭Ambient Café** (p66) before you drop down to finish up in **⑮Clocktower Square**, the centre of downtown.

handles). The understated rooms are full of dark timber and most have excellent views, particularly the corner suites and the four deluxe rooms with private balconies, where you can relax on a day bed.

The Chig-Ja-Gye restaurant serves superior Bhutanese meals in a lavish dining room full of dark wood and gold trim, and the bar and outdoor terrace are sophisticated places for a quiet drink away from the crowds. There's also a top-end gym, an indoor pool, and one of Thimphu's best spas.

★**Hotel Druk**   HOTEL $$$
(Map p62; 02-322966; www.drukhotels.com; Wogzin Lam; s/d Nu 10,560/12,600, ste from Nu 18,720;) This understated but stylish place is the closest Thimphu has to a grande dame hotel, with an old-world charm that sets it above some of the pricier five-star hotels in town. It's right in the centre on Clocktower Square, and the grand rooms have free-standing bathtubs in open-plan bathrooms and subtle Bhutanese details that complement rather than clash with the *belle époque* styling.

★**Norkhil Boutique Hotel & Spa**   BOUTIQUE HOTEL $$$
(Map p62; 02-330356; www.norkhil.com; Doebum Lam; s/d from Nu 11,520/14,400;) One of a new breed of boutique hotels in Bhutan blending designer decor with a modern, international outlook. It's all tastefully done, and the spacious rooms offer great views over the town or hills. There's a good restaurant, a spa, and a bar with open-air terrace for sipping drinks while looking out over the city.

DusitD2 Yarkay Thimphu   LUXURY HOTEL $$$
(Map p62; 02-339988; www.dusit.com; Chorten Lam; r from US$346;) This new Bhutanese-Thai venture is on the road to the National Memorial Chorten. Each floor has an animal theme, inspired by the Buddhist legend of the Four Harmonious Friends, which extend to the decor in each room and the cuddly toy on each bed (which you can buy to fund local charities).

The top-class facilities include a lobby bar, a nightclub, the elegant Soi 8 restaurant, and a gym, spa and pool. Come for sleek lines and gourmet dining.

Hotel Norbuling   HOTEL $$$
(Map p62; 02-335754; www.hotelnorbuling.com; Chang Lam; r from Nu 7800;) At the upper end of the tourist-hotel category, Hotel Norbuling adds such extras as a minibar and floor-to-ceiling windows, making the most of

the views over the Changlimithang Archery Ground. There's a slightly 1980s feel to the decor, but facilities are good and there's a lobby coffee shop warmed by a *bukhari* heater.

Osel Hotel   BUSINESS HOTEL $$$
(Map p62; 02-344444; www.oselbhutan.com; Phenday Lam; s/d Nu 7320/8040, ste from Nu 18,720;) The four-star Osel has an understated modern style and a full range of in-house facilities, including an atmospheric coffee shop, a spa, restaurant and bar. The suites have fine corner bathrooms where you can take in city views while soaking in the free-standing bathtub. There's a pleasant outdoor terrace and guests have free use of the steam and sauna rooms.

City Hotel   HOTEL $$$
(Map p62; 02-338813; www.cityhotelthimphu. com; Dungkhar Lam; s/d from Nu 5400/6360, apt from Nu 9000;) An upper-end tourist-class hotel, this calm, corporate hotel is light and bright, with large, modern rooms and small terraces in the superior ones. The serviced apartments have a separate lounge and kitchenette, and room to host a party. Expect to pay a surcharge to stay here.

Le Meridien Thimphu   BUSINESS HOTEL $$$
(Map p62; 02-337788; www.lemeridien.com/thimphu; Chorten Lam; r from US$304;) In a prime central location, the five-star Le Meridien Thimpu offers modern designer flourishes in place of traditional Bhutanese trim. Wood-panelled rooms are lavishly appointed, with stylish designer rugs and good city views. Other perks include

DON'T MISS

THIMPHU'S TRAFFIC POLICE

Thimphu is said to be one of only two capital cities in the world without traffic lights (alongside Ngerulmud in Palau). A set was installed a few years back, but residents complained that it was too impersonal, and Thimphu's beloved white-gloved police returned to direct the traffic with the balletic grace of a backing dancer doing a 1980s robot dance. As well as being a classic Bhutanese anachronism, this may well be the city's most photographed spectacle. Moonwalk up to the **roundabout** (Map p62) known as 'traffic circle' on Norzin Lam and enjoy the show.

THIMPHU

Thimphu Centre

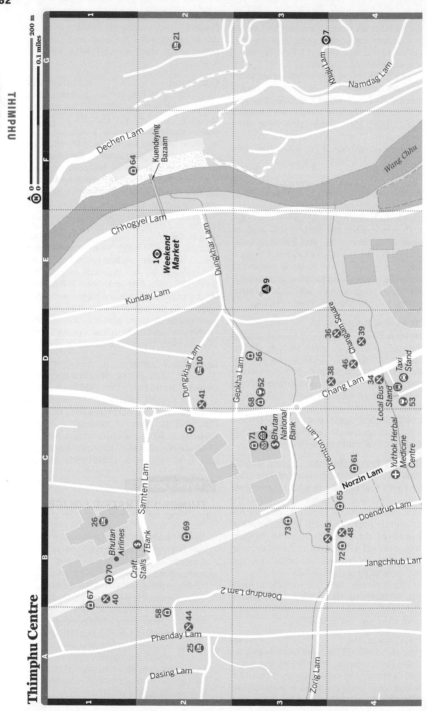

200 m
0.1 miles

G
21
7
Khilu Lam
Namdag Lam

F
Dechen Lam
64
Kuendeying Bazaam
Wang Chhu

E
Chhogyel Lam
Dungkhar Lam
1 Weekend Market
9

D
Kunday Lam
Dungkhar Lam
10
Gepkha Lam
56
68
52
36
Changlam Square
39
38
46
Chang Lam
34
Taxi Stand
Local Bus Stand
53

C
Samten Lam
71
2
Bhutan National Bank
Drentoen Lam
Norzin Lam
61
Yutthok Herbal Medicine Centre

B
26
Bhutan Airlines
70
TBank
Craft Stalls
69
65
Doendrup Lam
73
45
48
72
Jangchhub Lam

A
67
40
Doendrup Lam 2
58
44
Phenday Lam
25
Dasing Lam
Zorig Lam

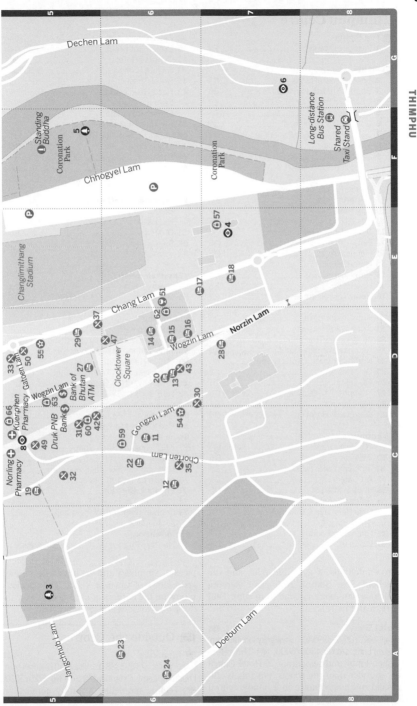

Dechen Lam

Standing Buddha 1

Coronation Park

5 🏛

Chhogyel Lam

Coronation Park

⊙6

Long-distance Bus Station

Shared Taxi Stand

Changlimithang Stadium

⊙57
⊙4

🏛18

🏛17

Chang Lam

✕37

62 🏛51

🏛14 🏛15
🏛16

Wogzin Lam

Norzin Lam

✕33
50 🏛
55 ★

29 🏛

✕47

Clocktower Square

2B 🏛

Wogzin Lam Gatoen Lam

Kuenphen Pharmacy

Bank of Bhutan 27 🏛 ATM

20 🏛

13 🏛
43

🏛66
Norling Pharmacy
8⊙
✕49

Druk PNB Bank $

31🏛
60 🏛
42✕

Gongzin Lam

11 🏛
54 ★

✕30

✕32

22 🏛

35✕
Chorten Lam

59 🏛

12 🏛

19 🏛

🏛3

23 🏛

24 🏛

Jangchub Lam

Doebum Lam

Thimphu Centre

a top-notch spa, a gym and pool, and the excellent Sese Shamu restaurant, serving delicious pan-Asian cuisine (dim sum, Thai curries and more).

Hotel Gakyil HOTEL $$$
(Map p62; ☑02-339640; www.gakyilbhutan.com; Wogzin Lam; s/d Nu 4800/6000; 🛜) The refurbished lobby and restaurant at Hotel Gakyil are grander than the rooms, but this is still a solid midrange choice in a handy, central location. The tidy, wood-lined rooms have a

pleasing simplicity and the higher floors offer good views of town or valley. The spacious rooms on the corners of each floor have windows on two sides and get more light.

🛏 Outside the Centre

★ Kisa Villa HOTEL $$
(Map p54; ☑02-338811; kisavilla01@gmail.com; Lhudrong Lam; r standard/deluxe Nu 3720/5220; 🛜) Feeling more like a family home than

a hotel, this cosy stone property looks out across the river towards Trashi Chho Dzong. Two houses with snug, wood-lined rooms are set in a pretty garden. The best rooms have windows on two sides and views of the dzong from your bed.

Hotel Golden Roots
HOTEL $$

(Map p54; ☑02-330043; www.goldenhotels.in; Chang Lam, Chubachhu; r from Nu 5400; 🛜) Quieter than the hotels right in the centre of Thimphu, this is a solid choice, with neat, wood-floored rooms that get plenty of light, and spotless tiled bathrooms.

Dorji Elements
HOTEL $$

(Map p54; ☑02-333075; www.hoteldorji elements. com; Yardren Lam, Chubachhu; r/ste from Nu 3360/5760; 🛜) This low-key but comfortable three-star hotel has a quiet location a little out of the town centre, close to the National Textile Museum. There's a terrace cafe, the rooms are clean and those on the upper floors have good views. The lobby is decorated with artwork from the nearby Voluntary Artists Studio Thimphu (VAST).

Bhutan Suites
APARTMENT $$

(Map p54; ☑02-333377; www.bhutansuites.com; Deki Lam, Changangkha; ste from Nu 5760; 🛜) Business travellers, NGO workers and passing tourists all appreciate the set-up here. Bright and comfortable suite rooms have underfloor heating, a separate lounge and dining area and mini-kitchens, plus sweeping balcony views over Thimphu. It's away from the centre but close to the Changangkha Lhakhang, and you can order room service from the good vegetarian restaurant or snack in the ground-floor cafe.

Jambayang Resort
HOTEL $$

(Map p62; ☑02-322349; www.jambayangresort. com; Dechen Lam, Taba; s/d from Nu 4025/5175, ste Nu 6900; 🛜) On the east bank of the Wang Chhu, Jambayang Resort sprawls over a series of buildings linked by pathways on the hillside above town. Rooms are comfortable rather than luxurious but the restaurant and terraces overlooking the valley are a big asset. The location is quiet and the welcome friendly.

Amankora
LUXURY HOTEL $$$

(☑02-331333; www.amanresorts.com; r incl full board from US$1895; 🛜) A 'less is more' philosophy presides at this exclusive five-star resort, Thimphu's finest, edging into the forest by a tinkling brook northwest of town.

The graceful cluster of whitewashed buildings resembles a mini dzong, and stone-paved passageways lead past open fireplaces to elegant, wood-lined rooms with *bukhari* heaters, free-standing bathtubs and a touch of futuristic minimalism – Bhutanese-Nordic might be the best description.

Khang Residency
HOTEL $$$

(Map p54; ☑02-339111; www.khangresidency.com; Lower Motithang; r/ste from Nu 6600/10,200; 🛜) This modern block close to the Changangkha Lhakhang eschews the ubiquitous pine cladding found in many hotels for a sleek international feel. The rooms have underfloor heating and space to spread out in, there's a gym, spa and restaurant, and you can rent mountain bikes for Nu 500 per hour.

Premium rooms are good for small groups, as three rooms share a communal TV room and kitchen.

🍴 Eating

Thimphu is the one place in Bhutan where you can break away from the same-same hotel buffets and track down some authentic local and international flavours. Ask your guide to arrange a non-hotel meal in Thimphu to get a taste of the local dining scene.

As well as the town restaurants, don't overlook the charming Babesa Village Restaurant (p77), south of town on the road to Paro.

Thimphu is well stocked with supermarkets, including the expansive **8-Eleven** (Map p62; Gongzin Lam; ⊗8am-9pm) – a good place to pick up local specialities ready packed to travel – and Chuniding Food (p66), great for everything wholesome and organic.

For fresh produce, visit the busy Weekend Market (p53) and the street stalls in **Hong Kong Market** (Map p62; ⊗8am-8pm).

🍴 Clocktower Square & Around

Norzin Lam is lined with cheap local hotels offering simple and inexpensive vegetarian Indian food at lunch and dinner; try the **Hotel New Grand** (Map p62; mains Nu 60-220; ⊗9-11am, noon-3.30pm & 6.30-9pm; 🍴) or **Hotel Ghasel** (Map p62; mains Nu 70-220; ⊗7.30am-9pm; 🍴) for their good South Indian vegetarian dishes, or sample Nepali at the simple, cosy **Cypress Hotel** (Map p62; ☑02-334453; 2nd fl, FCB Bldg; set meals Nu 300, mains Nu 60-250; ⊗9.30am-9.30pm Mon-Sat), which serves good *thalis* (plate meals) on Fridays.

Zombala 2 BHUTANESE $

(Map p62; Norzin Lam; mains Nu 70-140; ☺9am-9pm Wed-Mon) This branch of Thimphu's famous *momo* restaurant serves delicious food in a roomy dining room overlooking Thimphu's main junction. It's deservedly popular with both visitors and locals and serves such tasty local dishes as *momo*s and beef *paa* with chillies and spinach.

Zombala BHUTANESE $

(Map p62; Doendrup Lam; momos per plate Nu 70-95; ☺8.30am-9pm Mon-Sat) Any local will tell you the best *momo*s (deep-fried or steamed dumplings) in town are served at Zombala, a cheap and cheerful local dive near Hong Kong Market. Choose between beef or cheese, and expect to fight for a seat.

★Ambient Café CAFE $$

(Map p62; Norzin Lam; mains Nu 110-350; ☺8am-8pm Fri-Wed; ☎🖉) A warm, friendly bolthole above Norzin Lam, used by many expats as a de facto office. Drinks include good espresso coffee, juices and smoothies, and the food menu runs to vegan breakfasts, buckwheat waffles, sandwiches and pitta pockets, and homemade cakes and ice cream. The owner is a good source of information on local mountain-biking routes.

★Zone INTERNATIONAL $$

(Map p62; 🖉02-331441; Chang Lam; mains Nu 275-550; ☺10.30am-10.30pm Wed-Mon) This expat favourite feels a bit like a small-town American diner, with a Bhutanese twist. The menu runs to burgers and fries, ice cream, ribs (including yak), pizza, *momo*s, hot dogs, and fish and chips. The pub-style tables out front are great for having an evening Red Panda beer.

Bhutan Orchid BHUTANESE $$

(Map p62; 🖉02-336660; Chang Lam; set menus from Nu 400; ☺11.30am-2.30pm & 7.30-9pm) A well-organised restaurant serving Bhutanese set meals, with the chilli toned down for non-Bhutanese palates. You'll get to sample eight local dishes, and the list often runs to less familiar regional specialities such as *hoentey* (stuffed buckwheat *momo*s) and *puta* (buckwheat noodles). *Bukhari* heaters and log tables and chairs add a homey feel.

Bhutan Kitchen BHUTANESE $$

(Map p62; 🖉02-331919; Gatoen Lam; set lunch/dinner Nu 450/490; ☺12.30-2pm & 6.30-9pm) A warm interior and traditional seating make for cosy meals at this Bhutanese place,

serving local cuisine in traditional wooden bowls. Set meals include such local treats as melted hard cheese, red rice, and dried brinjals (eggplants) with chilli. Spice levels are not off the scale, so you can dive into the *ema datse* (chillies with cheese) without calling for the fire brigade.

Art Café CAFE $$

(Map p62; Doendrup Lam; cakes & soups Nu 100-300; ☺9.30am-6.30pm Mon-Sat; ☎) A welcoming taste of the old Thimphu, this small, *bukhari*-warmed coffee shop serves decent filter coffee and delicious cakes, hearty soups, salads and burgers, with daily specials on the whiteboard. It's at the back of a car park near Hotel Pedling.

✖ Rest of Thimphu

Chuniding Food SUPERMARKET $

(Map p62; Changlam Sq; ☺9am-8pm) Chuniding has shelves piled high with organic and local produce, much of it neatly packaged and ready for travel. You'll find everything here from *ema kam* (dried red chillies) and buckwheat cookies to cordyceps and mistletoe tea, and preserved fruit, vegetables and mushrooms.

Cafe Himalaya & Bakery CAFE $

(Map p62; Karsang Bldg, Choeten Lam; cakes & snacks from Nu 150; ☺9am-9pm Tue-Sun; ☎) Fine Lavazza coffee, excellent homemade cakes and snacks such as pizzas and burgers make this modern coffee house a great place to warm up on a cold afternoon.

Sonam Tshoey Ice Cream ICE CREAM $

(Map p62; Changlam Plaza; ice cream Nu 90; ☺9am-8pm Mon-Fri) This watch shop (look for the Tissot sign) doubles as an unlikely purveyor of delicious homemade ice cream. The all-natural vanilla, coconut and chocolate ice creams are scrumptious, plus there are seasonal fresh-fruit sorbets.

Big Bakery BAKERY $

(Map p54; Kawajangsa; bread & cakes Nu 50-150; ☺9am-5.30pm Mon-Fri, 9am-1pm Sat) 🍴 This project trains young Bhutanese with learning disabilities as bakers. Drop in for a cup of coffee and a croissant to help support their work.

★Brusnika Russian Cafe CAFE $$

(Map p54; 🖉02-320888; www.facebook.com/brusnikarussianbakery; Lhudrong Lam; mains Nu 150-650; ☺9am-8pm Tue-Sun) One of

THIMPHU IN...

One Day

Pop out before breakfast to see morning pilgrims paying their respects at **Changangkha Lhakhang** (p52), and after breakfast, stroll along Norzin Lam to the **National Textile Museum** (p53) for a fine introduction to this traditional art form. If it's a weekend, stroll downhill to the **Weekend Market** (p53) for a bit of browsing. On a weekday, visit the **Changlimithang Archery Ground** (p55) to see archers at play, or drop into the National Institute for **Zorig Chusum** (p53) to watch artisans learning their craft. Take advantage of the global food on offer in Thimphu for lunch – **Cloud 9** (p68), **Hayate Ramen** (below) and **San MaRu** (p68) are standout options – then head up to the **Motithang Takin Preserve** (p56) and **Buddha Dordenma** (p55) statue before joining the crowds at **Trashi Chho Dzong** (p51). After dark, sample local brews and local tunes at **Mojo Park** (p69).

Two Days

With a second day in Thimphu, find inner peace on the lovely walk from the **BBS Tower** (p76) to **Wangditse Goemba** (p76) and **Dechen Phodrang** (p56), or make a day trip to **Tango Goemba** (p73) or **Cheri Goemba** (p75), stopping by at **Pangri Zampa** (p72). Take some time for souvenir shopping at **Tarayana Rural Products** (p69) and other craft stores on Norzin Lam, and finish off with a chilli-infused Bhutanese feast at **Babesa Village Restaurant** (p77).

Thimphu's most welcoming cafes, Brusnika is run by a charming Russian-Bhutanese family and looks out over a small park towards Trashi Chho Dzong. It's a fine place to hole up with a book, and the menu runs to tasty pelmeni and blinis, wild thyme tea and delicious home-baked crusty bread.

★**Clove Bistro**   INTERNATIONAL $$
(Map p62; ☑ 77737623; Chang Lam; mains Nu 250-320; ☺ 11am-8.30pm, to 10.30pm Wed, Fri & Sat) There's a pan-Asian flavour at this upmarket bistro serving dishes that draw influence from China, Japan, India and Southeast Asia. It's a calm, grown-up space for lunch or dinner, and the set meals with rice and side dishes are excellent value.

★**Hayate Ramen**   JAPANESE $$
(Map p62; ☑ 02-330240; Dungkhar Lam; mains Nu 155-350; ☺ 11am-9pm Wed-Mon) It's ramen noodles all the way at this inviting, calm Japanese restaurant. Bowls come topped with everything from roast pork to *ebi* (battered prawns), and you can finish off the dish with a suite of condiments, from roasted sesame seeds to *thingye* (Bhutanese pepper). Order an artisanal ale on the side.

Coffee Culture   CAFE $$
(Map p62; Changlam Sq; mains Nu 120-350; ☺ 11am-8pm) A bright, buzzy coffee shop, with a big chalkboard menu of pizza, sandwiches, salads, burgers and wraps, plus

doorstop-thick walnut brownies and full-flavoured cups of joe. The covered terrace is a popular after-work hang-out.

Lemongrass Thai   THAI $$
(Map p62; ☑ 02-339528; 4th fl, Karsang Bldg, Chorten Lam; mains Nu 300-550; ☺ 10am-10pm Tue-Sun; 🐾) Thimphu's best and most stylish Thai restaurant looks out over downtown from the top of a shopping centre, with views towards the National Memorial Chorten and Buddha Dordenma. The menu throws in some interesting Isaan dishes among the familiar strip fries and curries, and groups of four or more can pre-order impressive set menus and Thai hotpots.

Chula   INDIAN $$
(Map p62; ☑ 02-336275; KMT Bldg, Norzin Lam; mains Nu 140-300; ☺ 9am-9pm) Upstairs above the hubbub of Norzin Lam, Chula serves some of the best Indian food in town. You'll find a wide range of tasty Indian staples (including good tandoori, biryani and paneer dishes), served at highly varnished black-wood tables. The set lunch *thalis* (veg/nonveg Nu 250/300) are great value.

Thijha Cafe   CAFE $$
(Map p62; Clocktower Sq; mains Nu 95-450; ☺ 9.20am-10pm) A modern, international-style coffee shop serving Illy coffee, salads, grills, pastas and decent attempts at Indian, continental and full English breakfasts. It's

open later than most places in the evening but not everyone will appreciate the loud music.

Karma's Coffee
CAFE $$

(Map p62; Tashi Rabten Bldg, Phenday Lam; mains Nu 120-230, coffee Nu 90-120; ⏰10am-7pm Mon-Sat; 🛜) Karma's was an early arrival on Thimphu's coffee scene and is still going strong despite lots of competition. The interior is a little dated but it's warm and cosy: bring a paperback and settle in with a cappuccino. There's a smoking room out the back.

Seasons Restaurant
ITALIAN $$

(Map p62; ☑02-327413; Doendrup Lam; pizzas Nu 270-600; ⏰10am-3pm & 4-9pm Wed-Mon) This deservedly popular restaurant specialises in thin-crust pizzas with authentic toppings, but the kitchen also rustles up some excellent salads. It's as big a hit with locals as it is with visitors, and the alfresco patio overlooking Hong Kong Market is the perfect place to enjoy a beer.

★7th Restaurant
INDIAN, INTERNATIONAL $$$

(Map p62; ☑02-322966; Hotel Druk, Wogzin Lam; mains Nu 220-580, buffet dinner Nu 840-1200; ⏰noon-3pm & 7-10pm) The elegant restaurant at the Hotel Druk (p61) elevates the hotel buffet to high art. The spread of dishes roams from Europe to Bhutan and China, but it's the finely crafted Indian dishes that stand out above the pack. The Friday buffet is simply the best Indian meal in Bhutan. There's also an à la carte menu.

★Cloud 9
INTERNATIONAL, BURGERS $$$

(Map p62; ☑02-331417; Chang Lam; mains Nu 240-790; ⏰noon-11pm; 🛜) If you're tired of bland hotel buffets, this stylish restaurant serves the best international menu in town. Come for sourdough pizzas with authentic Italian toppings, fat gourmet burgers with all the trimmings, deli sandwiches and delicious real gelato. You can't miss the ultra-modern silver-grey dining room, in a prime Chang Lam location, with a terrace overlooking Changlimithang Stadium (you can also enter from Clocktower Square).

★San MaRu
KOREAN $$$

(Map p54; ☑02-334496; Norzin Lam; mains Nu 550-1200; ⏰11.30am-3pm & 5.30-9pm) A little slice of Seoul, transported to the centre of Thimphu, this wood-lined Korean restaurant serves excellent soups, stews and, for groups of two or more, delicious beef

bulgogi, barbecued at the table, with all the expected *banchan* (side dishes).

Fu Lu Shou
CHINESE $$$

(Map p54; ☑77385308; Phenday Lam; mains Nu 320-700; ⏰10am-10pm) The most authentic Chinese restaurant in Thimphu, with a huge dining room heated by open fireplaces and a long menu of real Chinese dishes – clay pot pig trotters, double-boiled soup, beef with bitter gourd and the like. Meals come with a side order of snacks and nibbles.

🍷 Drinking & Nightlife

Thimphu has a growing collection of coffee shops; recommended places include Ambient Café, Cafe Himalaya & Bakery and Thijha Cafe.

For a real night out, the city has a handful of proper bars with loud music, draught beer and imported spirits, served till late on Wednesday, Friday and Saturday. No alcohol is served on Tuesday, the national dry day.

★Hi Jinks
BAR

(Map p62; Hotel Druk, Wogzin Lam; ⏰1-10pm Wed-Mon) The sophisticated leather-and-wood bar at the Hotel Druk is the perfect spot for a grown-up pre- or post-dinner drink, especially if you can score one of the bar-side armchairs.

Benez Bar
BAR

(Map p62; 5th fl, Karsang Bldg, Chorten Lam; ⏰10.30am-11pm Wed, Fri & Sat, to 10pm Sun-Tue & Thu) Gazing out over the city from the top floor of a modern block, Benez is popular with a grown-up crowd, who come for the views, the globe-trotting food menu (Nu 150 to 450) and the drinks lined up behind the curving wooden bar. *Bukhari* heaters keep things cosy and there's a separate smoking room.

Space 34
CLUB

(Map p62; ☑17554945; Wangdi Plaza, Chang Lam; ⏰9pm-1am Wed, to 5am Fri & Sat) A lively basement club (entry Nu 300 to 350), with live music and thumping electro beats courtesy of local DJs. It's downstairs in the same building as Lungta Handicraft.

Om Pub
BAR

(Map p62; ☑02-326344; Jojo's Shopping Complex, Chang Lam; ⏰6pm-late Wed-Mon) A relaxing place for young Thimphu movers and shakers, on the 2nd floor of the faded Jojo's building; the entrance is on the north side of the block.

Viva City
CLUB

(Map p62; ☑17601015; www.facebook.com/
clubvivacity; ⊙9pm-2am Wed, Fri & Sun) Live
bands and deafening DJs get the crowds
moving at this youth hang-out behind the
local bus stand.

☆ Entertainment

Thimphu is fairly quiet after hours, but there's
normally some action on Wednesday, Friday
and Saturday. There are a couple of cinemas,
showing Bhutanese films in Dzongkha, and a
handful of music venues with live bands and
singer-songwriters performing.

You could try asking your guide to take you
to a local *drayang* bar. Members of the audience request songs for a fee of around Nu 100,
which are then sung in traditional style by the
performers on stage. However, some *drayang*
venues can feel a bit sleazy, with women dancing for an exclusively male clientele.

★ Mojo Park
LIVE MUSIC

(Map p62; ☑17110975; www.facebook.com/
themojopark; Chang Lam; ⊙5pm-late Wed-Mon)
Thimphu's friendly premier live-music venue
and bar is strong on blues, rock and reggae.
Beers on tap include Amber Ale and Dragon
Stout from the Ser Bhum brewery, and Red
Rice lager and wheat beer from the Namgyal
Artisanal Brewery. Check the Facebook page
for upcoming gigs: most start about 9pm.

Jimmy's Pub
LIVE MUSIC

(Map p62; ☑17113656; www.facebook.com/pg/
Jimmys.pub.thimphu; Gongzin Lam; ⊙8-11pm
Wed,Thu, Sun & Mon, to midnight Fri & Sat) Loud
bands and cold beers set the scene at Jim-
my's, a classic basement bar tucked in
behind the DusitD2 hotel. Bands start
around 9pm on Friday and Saturday.

🔒 Shopping

Many of the souvenirs for sale in Thimphu
are actually made in India or Nepal, and
are marked up in price in Bhutan. However,
there are plenty of interesting Bhutanese
products on sale, including bamboo bows
and arrows, *khuru* (Bhutanese darts) sets,
textiles, baskets, jewellery, incense, books,
Buddhist dance masks and religious items.

In Thimphu's Weekend Market, look out
for local honey, pickles and preserves, or visit
the capital's food stores for beauty products
made from local herbs, Tsheringma herbal
teas and cordyceps preparations (made from
insects infected with a parasitic fungus).

ONE OF A KIND SOUVENIR

The **Philatelic Bureau** (Map p62; GPO,
Chang Lam; ⊙9am-5pm Mon-Sat, 9am-
1pm Sat) at Thimphu's main post office
is the place to come for one of Bhutan's
most unique gifts. Bring a favourite
digital photo in on a USB stick, and staff
will print you a sheet of personalised
stamps with your photo on them. The
stamps are fully functional so you can
use them to send your postcards home.
The process costs Nu 500 for 12 stamps
and takes just a couple of minutes.

★ Tarayana Rural Products
ARTS & CRAFTS

(Map p54; ☑02-329333; www.tarayana foundation.
org; Norzin Lam; ⊙10am-6pm Mon-Sat) ✔ Bhutan's Queen Mother Dorje Wangmo (the
fourth king's wife) established this NGO to
support rural communities across Bhutan
through the marketing and selling of traditional crafts. These include paper products
from Samtse, handwoven scarves, bags and
nettle place mats, and the quality is generally
high. There's a second **shop** (Map p54; ☑02-
330143; ⊙10am-6pm Mon-Sat) in the Tarayana
Centre on Yardren Lam, Chubachhu.

★ Norzin Lam Craft Stalls
ARTS & CRAFTS

(Map p62; Norzin Lam; ⊙9am-6pm) Dozens of
craft stalls line the middle of Norzin Lam
opposite the Taj Tashi hotel. It's the single
best place in Thimphu to shop for crafts,
with stalls selling everything from embroidered boots to handmade paper.

★ Bhutan Traditional
Archery Shop
SPORTS & OUTDOORS

(Map p62; Changlimithang Archery Ground,
Chhogyel Lam; ⊙9am-6.30pm Mon-Sat) This
traditional bow and arrow maker at the
Changlimithang Archery Ground sells bamboo bows, lacquered and strung to order.
Expect to pay Nu 1800 for a bow, Nu 800 for
a hand-spliced string, and Nu 800 for a pair
of arrows with tips.

Handicrafts Market
MARKET

(Map p62; ⊙7am-8pm Sat & Sun) Across the
Kundeyling Baazam cantilevered footbridge
from the Weekend Market, this market on
the east bank sells everything from wooden
bowls and mala beads to printing blocks,
amulets and yak tails. Bargaining is accept-
able, and often needed to bring prices down

to affordable levels. Note that many items sold here are actually imports from Nepal.

Sephub Gyeltsen Tsongkhang CLOTHING

(Map p62; Norzin Lam; ⊗8am-9pm) This is one of Thimphu's best cloth and clothing stores, with ready-made *ghos* costing from Nu 2000 and *kira*s costing from Nu 850, and all the needed accessories. It's also a great place to buy regional woven fabrics from across Bhutan.

DSB Books BOOKS

(Map p62; www.dsbbooksbhutan.bt; Chang Lam; ⊗9am-8pm) Thimphu's best selection of magazines and newspapers, as well as coffee-table and other books on Buddhism, Bhutan and the region. It's on the ground floor of the Jojo Building; enter from the lane behind Chang Lam.

Craft Gallery ARTS & CRAFTS

(Map p54; www.gyalyum.com; Norzin Lam; ⊗10am-6.30pm) Run by the Gyalyum Charitable Trust, a personal project of the Queen Mother promoting traditional arts and crafts, this smart showroom sells high-quality textiles, daphne paper, natural beauty products and other attractively presented craft items. Proceeds fund schools in rural areas.

Dolkar Handicrafts ARTS & CRAFTS

(Map p62; Chorten Lam; ⊗9am-8pm) Opening hours are erratic and the prices are high at this eccentric crafts store, often staffed by a *doma*-nut-chewing grandma, but there are some genuine antiques on sale among the fading bric-a-brac.

Traditional Boot House SHOES

(Map p54; Desi Lam; ⊗10am-7pm Mon-Sat) No prizes for guessing what's on sale at this small shop in a traditional house near the National Textile Museum. Colourfully embroidered *tshoglham* boots cost from Nu 5000 per pair.

Junction Bookstore BOOKS

(Map p62; www.facebook.com/junctionbook store; Wogzin Lam; ⊗10am-8pm Tue-Sun) A bookshop with a community feel (and a weekly reading club), Junction has a small but well-chosen selection of books about Bhutan, and there's a little cafe upstairs.

Above Himalaya Trekking Store SPORTS & OUTDOORS

(Map p62; ☑17162455; Gepkha Lam; ⊗9am-7pm) The best trekking-gear store in town sells and rents sleeping bags, tents, wet-weather gear, solar battery chargers and even bottled oxygen. It also sells traditional basketware backpacks.

Druk Adventure Gear SPORTS & OUTDOORS

(Map p62; Etho Metho Plaza, Norzin Lam; ⊗9.30am-8.30pm) Has a decent stock of outdoor gear, including jackets, boots and bags.

Lungta Handicraft ARTS & CRAFTS

(Map p62; Chang Lam; ⊗8.30am-8.30pm) This place has two floors of souvenirs from across Bhutan and further afield. The best buys here are larger items such as bamboo boxes, burl-wood *dhapa* (bowls), carpets, metal ewers, horse saddles and monastic trumpets. The antiques all have stamped seals from the National Commission of Cultural

---

LOCAL KNOWLEDGE

BUYING A GHO OR KIRA

A *gho* or *kira* (traditional dress for men and women, respectively) makes a great, inexpensive souvenir, and locals will be thrilled if you wear one to a festival in Bhutan. Many tourist shops sell off-the-rack versions, but specialist robe stores on Norzin Lam offer more choices of styles and colours.

Depending on the fabric, a *gho* can cost from Nu 1800 to over Nu 10,000. To get the best fit, allow a couple of days to have an item tailor-made. Don't forget you'll also need to invest in a *kera* (narrow woven belt; Nu 500) and a white *lhagey* (inner liner; Nu 150 to 500). Expect to pay Nu 1000 and upwards for a *kira*, and Nu 750 to 1500 for the accompanying *wonju* (blouse).

Once you have your *gho* or *kira*, you'll probably need help learning how to wear it. You'll also need some instruction on storing the *gho*, which involves folding the pleats origami-style. Video your guide demonstrating it or you'll never remember how!

Recommended clothing stores include Sephub Gyeltsen Tsongkhang (above), and **Dorji Gyeltshen Tshongkhang** (Map p62; Norzin Lam; ⊗9am-9pm), run by the same family and closer to the main square.

RELIGIOUS SHOPPING

As the national capital, Thimphu is crammed with shops selling essential religious objects for the monastery and home. Alongside tourist souvenir shops, you'll find stores specialising in monks' robes, *dhar* (prayer flags), traditional Buddhist books, moulds for making *tsa tsa* (clay stupa offerings), ceremonial *nga* drums and Buddhist statues.

KMT Yangkhil Book Shop (Map p62; Norzin Lam; ⊙8.30am-8pm Mon-Sat, 10.30am-8pm Sun) is particularly well stocked with religious items, while **Gedun Tshongkhang** (Map p62; Wogzin Lam; ⊙9am-7.30pm) specialises in monks' robes and **Dhar Tshongkhang** (Map p62; Phenday Lam; ⊙10am-6.30pm Mon-Sat) is piled high with prayer flags. For traditional woodcarving, look no further than **Samphel Traditional Furniture** (Map p62; Doendrup Lam; ⊙9am-6pm Mon-Sat).

Also look out for ritual *kangling* horns, made from human thigh bones, and *kapala* bowls made from human skulls (just don't ask where the bones came from). Needless to say, overseas customs officers would not look kindly on imported human remains!

Affairs (NCCA), which means they are safe to take through customs.

National Handicrafts Emporium
ARTS & CRAFTS

(Map p62; Norzin Lam; ⊙9am-1pm & 2-6pm, to 5pm in winter) This government-run souvenir emporium has fixed prices and there's a good range of masks, paintings, textiles, and carved wooden items such as traditional food bowls and *arra* pots.

Gagyel Lhundrup Weaving Centre
CLOTHING

(Map p54; ☑02-327534; Changzamtog; ⊙9am-6pm Mon-Sat) This private weaving centre at the south end of Thimphu produces expensive but high-quality hand-woven textiles and has a selection of ready-made garments for sale (scarves, belts, jackets, shawls and *kira*). You can watch weavers at work and photos are allowed.

Choki Handicrafts
ARTS & CRAFTS

(Map p54; www.chokischool.com; Bhutan Handicraft Centre, Thori Lam; ⊙9am-5pm Mon-Sat) Set in a block of craft shops, Choki sells masks, *thangka* paintings, local clothing and other souvenirs. Many of the items are produced by the affiliated Choki Traditional Art School.

Sangay Arts & Crafts
ARTS & CRAFTS

(Map p54; ☑02-339608; Pedzoe Lam; ⊙9am-6pm) You can purchase works by graduates of the National Institute for Zorig Chusum (p53) at this nearby shop, run by a former student.

ℹ Information

MEDICAL SERVICES

There are several pharmacies around the centre supplying medicines, including over-the-counter antibiotics, including **Kuenphen Pharmacy**

(Map p62; Norzin Lam; ⊙9am-9pm), **Norling Pharmacy** (Map p62; Norling Centre, Norzin Lam; ⊙8.45am-8.30pm) and **Namsey Pharmacy** (Map p62; Norzin Lam; ⊙8.30am-9pm).

Consider also the clinic at the National Institute of Traditional Medicine (p57) or the downtown clinic at **Yuthok Herbal Medicine Centre** (Map p62; ☑77642255; Karma Khangzang Bldg, Norzin Lam; ⊙9am-7pm).

For serious medical issues visit the following:

Jigme Dorji Wangchuck National Referral Hospital (Map p54; ☑02-322496; www.jdwnrh.gov.bt; Gongphel Lam) Bhutan's best hospital.

Menjong Diagnostic Centre (Map p54; ☑02-334616; Thegchen Lam) A well-run private hospital.

MONEY

ATMs in Thimphu read the magnetic strip rather than digital chips, so check that your bank approves cash withdrawals via this system. Bhutan's government also blocks international ATM withdrawals from time to time as part of the fight against money laundering, so carry cash as a backup.

Several clothes shops near the main traffic circle offer foreign exchange at better rates than hotels; your guide can show you where to go.

Bank of Bhutan (Map p54; City Mall, Yardren Lam, Chubachhu; ⊙9am-5pm Mon-Fri, to 4pm winter, 9am-1pm Sat) Main branch (with ATM and foreign exchange). This ATM is one of a number dotted around the town centre.

Bhutan National Bank (Map p54; Norzin Lam; ⊙9am-4pm Mon-Fri, to 3pm in winter, 9-11am Sat) Main branch with an ATM and foreign exchange. There's a more central **branch** (Map p62; GPO, Chang Lam; ⊙9am-4pm Mon-Fri, 9-11am Sat) in the same building as the post office.

Druk PNB Bank (Map p62; Norzin Lam; ⊙9am-1pm & 2-4pm Mon-Fri, 9am-noon Sat) Has an ATM that accepts MasterCard, Maestro and Cirrus cards, and changes cash (no travellers cheques).

TBank (Map p62; Tashi Mall, Norzin Lam; ⊘ 9am-5pm Mon-Fri, 9am-1pm Sat) Opposite the Taj Tashi hotel; changes cash.

POST

Many hotels and shops sell stamps and you can drop cards and letters into any post box.

DHL (Map p54; ☑ 02-324730; 19-13 Thori Lam; ⊘ 9am-5pm Mon-Fri, 9am-1pm Sat) Can arrange (costly) international courier services.

Post Office (GPO; Map p62; Chang Lam; ⊘ 9am-4pm Mon-Fri, to 3pm in winter, 9am-1pm Sat) Well organised, with a separate philatelic shop and a small museum.

ℹ Getting There & Away

Thimphu's **long-distance bus station** (Map p62; Lungten Zampa) is on the east bank of the Wang Chhu, below the east end of the bridge (*zampa*) at the southern end of town. (Even the bus depot has a prayer wheel in the courtyard and names its bus companies after the eight auspicious symbols!)

There are over two dozen daily buses (so-called 'vomit comets') to Phuentsholing (Nu 220, five hours), plus several daily services to Paro (Nu 55, 90 minutes) and Haa (Nu 120, five hours) and morning buses to Phobjikha (Nu 150, six hours), Trongsa (Nu 290, seven hours), Bumthang (Nu 385, eight hours) and Gelephu (Nu 370, nine hours). Multiday trips to Mongar, Lhuentse and Trashigang leave less frequently. Most buses to points east of Thimphu pass through Wangdue Phodrang.

Shared taxis depart from an informal **stand** (Map p62; Lungten Zampa) at the south end of the bus station's bus parking area for Phuentsholing (per seat Nu 750), Paro (Nu 250), Wangdue Phodrang (Nu 350) and Punakha (Nu 350). Chartering a whole taxi costs Nu 1000 to Paro, Nu 1400 to Punakha or Wangdue Phodrang, and Nu 3000 to Phuentsholing.

ℹ Getting Around

Most places of interest downtown are within easy walking distance of Thimphu's major hotels, and if you are on a standard tourist package, you will have a vehicle and driver on hand for trips to the outskirts.

Although roads are well signposted, few locals, including taxi drivers, use street names; landmarks and building names will serve you better when asking for or giving directions.

TO/FROM PARO AIRPORT

Most visitors will be met by their driver on arrival. For travellers not on a daily package, the official rate for a taxi from Paro Airport to Thimphu is Nu 972 (90 minutes) but drivers routinely overcharge. Expect to pay Nu 1500 in either direction, or save money by jumping into a shared taxi.

If you have an early-morning flight from Paro (and most are), it's best to spend the night in Paro.

TAXI

For short hops, head to the **taxi stand** (Map p62; Chang Lam) by the local bus stand. Taxi drivers will approach you as soon as you arrive to offer their services, usually for an elevated fare. Meters are rarely used so some bargaining is required. Expect to pay Nu 100 for a short trip in the centre, or you can charter a taxi for the day for local sightseeing for Nu 2000.

AROUND THIMPHU

North of Thimphu

As you travel up the east side of the Wang Chhu, there are good views of Trashi Chho Dzong and the National Assembly. On the opposite side of the river you may catch a glimpse of Samtenling Palace, the cottage that is the king's residence.

Six kilometres north of Thimphu centre is the suburb of Taba, where you can stay at the atmospheric, antique-filled **Wangchuk Resort Taba** (☑ 02-365262; www.wangchukhotel.com; Taba, off Dechen Lam; s/d from Nu 4200/4800), run by the same owners as Thimphu's Wangchuk Hotel and set in a peaceful pine forest near a small goemba built atop the ruins of a former palace.

As you cross back over to the west bank of the Wang Chhu, you'll pass the tree-filled compound of the **Dechencholing Palace**. The handsome building was constructed in 1952 and is used by the Royal Grandmother, so it's off-limits to visitors. North of the palace is the headquarters of the Royal Body Guard (RBG).

Pangri Zampa BUDDHIST MONASTERY
Founded in the early 16th century, this riverside monastery complex houses Bhutan's most important college for traditional astrology. Zhabdrung Ngawang Namgyal stayed here after he arrived in Bhutan in 1616 because the temple appeared in the vision that directed him from Tibet. It's a photogenic stop even if none of the chapels are open, and the whitewashed buildings have colourful curtains on their eaves that

ripple like the dress of a flamenco dancer in the breeze.

The complex gets its name from the cantilevered bridge beside the complex, and the two huge cypress trees in front of the temple are said to be the biggest in the country. The well-respected head astrologer here was entrusted to divine the auspicious date for the king's coronation in 2008. The next-door **Drolma Zhingkham Lhakhang** was built recently by the Royal Grandmother and is dedicated to 21 images of Tara. Above Pangri Zampa, the tall **Dechenphu Lhakhang** is home to Gyenyen, the valley's protective deity, and is off-limits to tourists.

Choki Traditional Art School ARTS CENTRE
(☑ 02-361077; www.chokischool.com; Kabisa; ⊙ open by arrangement) This charitable school trains disadvantaged children in the traditional arts of painting, sculpture and carving. It's in the village of Kabisa, 2km up the east valley road from Pangri Zampa, 10km north of Thimphu. Ask your guide to call ahead to arrange a visit.

Tango Goemba & Cheri Goemba

A trip to the northern end of the valley to visit Tango and Cheri Goembas makes for an excellent day trip from the capital. There's nowhere to eat nearby so bring a water bottle and a packed lunch (if you're on a daily package, your guide can arrange this at your hotel).

After crossing back over to the west bank of the Wang Chhu near Pangri Zampa, the road passes a huge and very photogenic painted **rock painting** of Guru Rinpoche and a line of water-powered prayer wheels, before returning to the east side of the river at Begana. Just before the bridge is the small **Guru Lhakhang**, with some fine murals of protector deities, and on the hillside above is a gleaming white **chorten** styled after the great stupa at Bodhnath in Nepal.

Beyond the bridge, you'll pass some 'self-arisen' rock images of a fish and mongoose and a collection of chortens as the white buildings of Cheri Goemba come into view on the sugarloaf-shaped hill at the end of the valley. About 12km from Thimphu, just past the campus of the **Tago Dorden Tashi Thang Buddhist University**, a side road branches right and climbs to the car park for Tango Goemba and **Dhrolung (Drolay) Goemba** (currently off-limits for a monastic retreat).

If you stay on the main road, it's a short drive to the cluster of village houses and small lhakhang at **Dodina** (2600m), where drivers park for the walk to Cheri Goemba (p75). A handsome covered bridge crosses to a group of Bhutanese-style chortens and carved boulders at the confluence of two streams, marking the start of the trail.

From Dodina, a dirt track continues north into the forested foothills of **Jigme Dorji National Park**, an important habitat for takin, tigers, snow leopards and Himalayan black bears. Guides can arrange short treks in the reserve, or you'll pass through if you walk the Laya trek (p195) or the Jhomolhari trek (p188).

⊙ Sights

★ **Tango Goemba** BUDDHIST MONASTERY
Tango is the residence of Gyalse Rinpoche, recognised as the seventh reincarnation of Gyalse Tenzin Rabgye, founder of Taktshang Goemba. The original monastery was founded in the 12th century but it was the 'divine madman', Lama Drukpa Kunley, who built the present building in the 15th century. Notable for its striking curved frontage, Tango is part of an important university of Buddhist studies – the main campus is down in the valley and monks trek back and forth between the two throughout the day.

In 1616 Zhabdrung Ngawang Namgyal visited Tango and meditated in a nearby cave, and the head lama made a gift of the entire complex. In gratitude, the Zhabdrung carved a sandalwood statue of Chenresig, which he installed in the monastery. Because of its connections to the Zhabdrung, Tango is a popular place to visit during the memorial of his death in April or May, known as the Zhabdrung Kuchoe.

Once you reach the main three-storey goemba there are several chapels to visit, including the 3rd-floor *zimchung* (living quarters) of the fourth Druk Desi, where you can receive a blessing from his walking stick. The timbers of the surrounding compound are adorned with fine carvings of the Buddhist eight auspicious signs. Restoration work is ongoing at the goemba, using materials hauled up from the bottom of the valley on an old-fashioned cableway.

The trail from the car park climbs 280m and takes about 40 minutes if you follow the steeper direct trail, or about an hour if you take the longer, more gradual trail. En

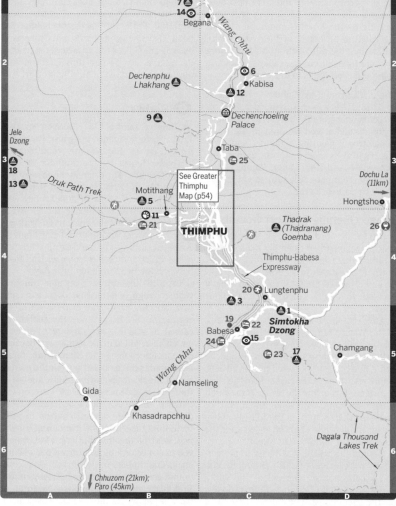

route you'll pass Buddhist quotes to inspire you on the spiritual path.

As you climb to the monastery take the left branch to first visit the meditation cave of the Zhabdrung (Tandin Ney) on a rock outcrop looking out over the valley. Tango gets its name (it translates to 'horse head') from the natural shape of this rocky protrusion. A small chapel enshrines a large crystal that was carried from Tibet and is used in visualisation meditations.

Around Thimphu

Cheri Goemba   BUDDHIST MONASTERY
(Cheri Dorji Dhen) From the river confluence at Dodina, a steep trail climbs for 45 minutes through a forest adorned with prayer flags to Cheri Goemba, established by Zhabdrung Ngawang Namgyal in 1620 as the home for Bhutan's first monk body. A richly decorated silver chorten inside the upper goemba enshrines the ashes of the Zhabdrung's father, whose body was smuggled here from Tibet. Cheri is an important place for meditation retreats, so try not to disturb anyone.

Cheri's *goenkhang* (protector chapel) features the two patron protector deities of Cheri and Tango. From the goemba, it's a steep climb (pilgrims aim to do it without pausing) to the Demon-Subjugating Monastery, built into the cliff where the Zhabdrung overcame the local demons. Look for tame brown goral (mountain goats) grazing the monastery grounds.

Monastic cells are scattered up the steep slopes behind the goemba, which is undergoing major reconstruction work. Traditional building materials are hauled here using a steep cableway running down to the bottom of the valley.

South of Thimphu

There are some interesting things to see south of the capital, including the first dzong built by Zhabdrung Ngawang Namgyal at Simtokha, perched above the road that branches east towards Wangdue Phodrang.

Heading west from Thimphu towards Paro, you'll reach **Babesa**, where a road leads uphill to the **Royal Botanical Garden** (SAARC/non-SAARC national Nu 30/50; ☺9am-5pm, to 4pm in winter) at Serbithang, a popular weekend retreat for Thimphu residents. It's pleasant rather than spectacular, but from the garden's far viewpoint you can see across the valley to the **Gangchen Nyezergang Lhakhang**, an ancient lhakhang that was rebuilt and reconsecrated in 2001.

◎ Sights

★**Simtokha Dzong**   BUDDHIST MONASTERY
(Simtokha) About 5km south of Thimphu on the old road to Paro and Phuentsholing, the handsomely proportioned Simtokha Dzong was built in 1629 by Zhabdrung Ngawang Namgyal. The site is said to mark the spot where a demon vanished into a rocky outcrop, hence the name Simtokha, from *simmo* (demoness) and *do* (stone). The site was also a vitally strategic location from which to protect the Thimphu valley and the passage east to the Dochu La and eastern Bhutan.

Officially known as Sangak Zabdhon Phodrang (Palace of the Profound Meaning of Secret Mantras), Simtokha is often said to be the first dzong built in Bhutan. In fact, there were dzongs in Bhutan as early as 1153, but this was the first dzong built by the Zhabdrung, and was the first structure to incorporate both monastic and administrative facilities. It is also the oldest dzong to have survived as a complete structure. Just above

DAY HIKES AROUND THIMPHU

In addition to the half-day hikes to Tango Goemba (p73) and Cheri Goemba (p75) at the north end of the valley, there are numerous day walks to monasteries and lookout points closer to Thimphu. For more ideas, download a PDF copy of Piet van der Poel and Rogier Gruys' booklet *Mild and Mad Day Hikes Around Thimphu* from www.bhutan-trails.org.

Note that some monasteries close periodically for long-term meditation retreats. Dhrolung (Drolay) Goemba, reached via a two- to three-hour trek from the car park below Tango Goemba, is off-limits to visitors until 2021.

Wangditse Goemba

Starting from the **BBS Tower** (Map p54; ⊘24hr) at Sangaygang, a quiet, and spotlessly clean track runs for 1.7km to the reconstructed chapel of **Wangditse Goemba** (Map p54; above Zilukha), offering stunning views of Trashi Chho Dzong along the way. Wangditse was founded in 1750 but the monastery is in the process of being rebuilt using traditional mud and stone construction techniques, and carving and murals by graduates from the National Institute for Zorig Chusum. Preserved from the original monastery, the inner chapel houses a two-storey statue of Sakyamuni Buddha. Nearby is a local *khuru* (darts) ground.

From this saddle, there are sweeping views across the northern part of Thimphu and the yellow-roofed Supreme Court of Bhutan at the bottom of the spur. If you follow the winding trail steeply downhill in front of Wangditse, you'll reach Dechen Phodrang (p56). On this litter-free trail, you'll have only the scent of blue pines and birdsong for company while you soak up the vista. Allow a couple of hours for the walk and stops at the two monasteries. Alternatively, a smaller trail runs southeast through scrubby forest to the hamlet of Zilukha, home to the interesting Zilukha Nunnery (p56).

Chhokhortse Goemba

Heading west from the BBS Tower, a steep trail climbs directly up the ridge, offering stunning views over the valley, framed by ribbons of prayer flags. Photography is best in the afternoon, but be careful not to photograph the telecommunications installation itself. After 1½ hours of hiking you'll get to a flat saddle, with a tidy new chapel and the time-scarred original **monastery** (Sangaygang), founded in the 14th century and studded with ancient statues of the main deities of the valley. The trail continues uphill for several more hours to reach Phajoding Goemba.

Thadrak (Thadranang) Goemba

A strenuous two-hour uphill hike from the Yangchenphug High School, above the bus stand on Yangchen Lam, will take you through lovely stands of blue pines to the 17th-century Thadrak (Thadranang) Goemba (3270m). The views en route are marvellous and there are several old chapels and monastic cells looking out over the valley.

Phajoding Goemba

It's a steep four-hour walk uphill from upper Motithang to Phajoding Goemba (3950m), a large monastic complex with 10 lhakhangs and more than a dozen monastic residences. Togden Pajo, a yogi from Tibet, founded the site in the 13th century, but most of the buildings were constructed in 1748 through the efforts of Shakya Rinchen, the ninth Je Khenpo.

Getting to Phajoding and back takes most of a day, but to extend the walk, you can ascend another 300m to Thujidrak Goemba. This is the last day of the Druk Path trek (p181) in reverse. On the way back down you can change your route slightly to descend via Chhokhortse Goemba and get picked up at the BBS tower at Sangaygang.

the dzong is Bhutan's Institute for Language and Culture Studies.

During its construction Simtokha Dzong was attacked by an alliance of Tibetans and five Bhutanese lamas from rival Buddhist schools who were opposed to the Zhabdrung's rule. The attack was repelled and the leader of the coalition, Palden Lama, was killed. In 1630 the Tibetans attacked again and took the dzong, but the Zhabdrung regained control when the main building caught fire and the roof collapsed, killing the invaders. Descriptions of the original buildings at Simtokha Dzong were provided by two Portuguese Jesuit priests who visited in 1629 on their way to Tibet.

The fortress was restored and expanded by the third *desi* (secular ruler), Mingyur Tenpa, in the 1670s, and it has been enlarged and modified many times since. The fine murals inside have been restored by experts from Japan. The squat, whitewashed dzong looks more fortress-like than most, and the only gate is on the south side (though the original gate was on the west wall). As you enter, note the murals of the four guardian kings – Vaishravana (north), Dhritarashtra (east), Virudhaka (south) and Virupaksha (west) – protecting the four cardinal directions, and the jewel-vomiting mongoose in the hand of the yellow King of the North.

The **utse** is three storeys high, and prayer wheels around the courtyard are backed by more than 300 slate carvings depicting saints and philosophers. The large central figure in the central lhakhang is of Sakyamuni, flanked by the eight bodhisattvas, and the ceiling is hung with an incredible array of *dhvaja* (victory banners) in brightly coloured silk. The dark murals inside this lhakhang are some of the oldest and most beautiful in Bhutan and the walls are adorned with embroidered *thangkas*.

In the **western chapel** are statues of Chenresig, green and white Taras, and an early painting of Zhabdrung Ngawang Namgyal. Check out the tigers' tails and guns hanging from the pillars in the eastern *goenkhang,* a protector chapel dedicated to the guardians of Bhutan, Yeshe Goenpo (Mahakala) and Pelden Lhamo.

🛏 Sleeping

★ Heritage Home
Babesa HERITAGE HOTEL **$$**
(📱17617027, 02-350880; tenziya7027@gmail.com; Babesa; r standard/deluxe Nu 3000/4800) A gorgeous restoration of a traditional rammed-earth farmhouse, this place feels more like a homestay than a hotel. The home, which is more than 120 years old, is full of trinkets and original features. Some rooms share a bathroom but all are full of dragon rugs and Bhutanese fabrics. It's located just off the road to Paro.

There's a restaurant on the ground floor and a courtyard coffee shop, plus a spa with hot stone baths.

★ Six Senses
LUXURY HOTEL **$$$**
(📱02-341337; www.sixsenses.com; r from US$1212; 🛜) 🍃 Set in carefully tended grounds high above Simtokha, the immaculate new Six Senses is effortlessly refined. There are no TVs in the graceful, timber-filled rooms, but with the sweeping valley views (including from the bathtub) and *bukhari* heaters, you won't mind. Everything is about peace and contemplation: an infinity pond reflects the sky, and a meditation room looks out over the valley.

Termalinca Resort & Spa
LUXURY HOTEL **$$$**
(📱02-351490; www.termalinca.com; Babesa; r/ste Nu 24,120/32,160; 🛜) Perched beside a peaceful stretch of the Wang Chhu, about 7km south of Thimphu, Termalinca packs a lot of comfort into its stone and timber buildings. Scattered around stone courtyards and beautifully tended gardens are multiple restaurants, a gym, spa rooms with a hot stone bath, and enormous wood-panelled rooms decorated in a modern-Bhutan-meets-dynastic-China style.

The long, curved bar looking out over the river is one nice touch; the intricately carved traditional dining room at the end of the grounds is another. Cooking classes, archery lessons and guided hikes are available for a fee. The resort is part-owned by the eldest wife of the fourth king. Discounts are often available.

🍴 Eating

★ Babesa Village Restaurant
BHUTANESE **$$$**
(📱02-351229; Babesa; set menu Nu 600-700; ⏰10.30am-10pm Tue-Sun) About 6km south of Thimphu's centre, this charming restaurant offers traditional Bhutanese cuisine in a rammed-earth village home, one of four still standing incongruously next to the Thimphu–Babesa Expressway. The interior is decorated with antiques and the authentically spicy set menus include such local dishes as ribs with chilli, *lom* (dried turnip leaf) and *mengay,* optimistically described as 'Bhutanese pizza'.

Western Bhutan

Best Places to Eat

➡ Bukhari Restaurant (p90)

➡ Sonam Trophel Restaurant (p90)

➡ Brioche Cafe (p89)

Best Places to Stay

➡ Gangtey Palace (p87)

➡ Lechuna Heritage Lodge (p102)

➡ Uma Punakha (p111)

➡ Dhensa (p111)

Why Go?

Whether you arrive by air at the dramatic, mountain-bound Paro valley or by road at steamy Phuentsholing, it soon becomes clear that you have arrived at an otherworldly destination. Prayer flags flutter from nearly every rooftop, men and women dress in traditional garb, chortens and stupas decorate river and road junctions, and fortress-like monasteries command mountaintops.

The west is the region of Bhutan that most tourists see, and for good reason. It's the heartland of the Drukpa people and is home to the major airport, the capital, the most popular festivals and the most spectacular dzongs (fort monasteries) in the kingdom. Throw in the trekking, the scope to get off the beaten track and the minimal driving times, and the appeal is obvious. Whether it's the beginning of your trip or the only part of Bhutan that you will explore, the west is a spectacular introduction to this magical country.

When to Go

➡ September to November are the ideal (but busiest) months to visit western Bhutan. You'll get great weather, clear mountain views from Dochu La, and dramatic festivals at Thimphu and Wangdue Phodrang.

➡ March and April are also popular, with the Paro tsechu a major draw, as lovely spring rhododendron blooms decorate the high passes.

➡ Black-necked cranes arrive in the Phobjikha valley in late October and early November and stay until February, though you'll want to bring warm clothes if visiting during those months.

➡ Punakha has a milder climate than Thimphu, so has pleasant temperatures even in February.

PARO DZONGKHAG

The Paro valley is without doubt one of the loveliest in Bhutan. Willow trees and apple orchards line many of the roads, whitewashed farmhouses and temples complement the green terraced fields, and forested hills rise on either side to create a beautiful, organic and peaceful whole.

The fertile land, clement climate and network of trade routes from Tibet have provided the people of Paro with a historical importance that survives to this day. For most of the 19th century, Paro held the seat of government and was the commercial, cultural and political centre of the country.

Several treks begin in or near Paro. The Druk Path trek climbs east over a 4200m pass before descending to Thimphu. The Jhomolhari, Laya and Snowman treks all lead west from near Drukgyel Dzong on to Jhomolhari base camp and the spectacular alpine regions of Gasa and Laya.

Paro

✏ 08 / POP 11,500 / ELEV 2280M

The charming town of Paro lies on the banks of the Paro (or Pa) Chhu, just a short distance northwest of the imposing Paro Dzong. The main street, only built in 1985, is lined with colourfully painted wooden shopfronts and restaurants, though these appear under threat as the town grows and multistorey concrete buildings continue to pop up. For now Paro remains one of the best Bhutanese towns to explore on foot and is worth an hour or two's stroll at the end of a day of sightseeing.

◎ Sights

★ **Paro Dzong**   BUDDHIST MONASTERY

(Rinpung Dzong; Map p86; SAARC nationals adult/child Nu 300/150; ⊙9am-1pm & 2-5pm, to 4pm Nov-Feb) Paro Dzong ranks as a high point of Bhutanese architecture. The massive buttressed walls that tower over the town are visible throughout the valley, especially when floodlit at night. It was formerly the meeting hall for the National Assembly and now, like most dzongs, houses both the monastic body and district government offices, including the local courts. Most of the chapels are closed to tourists but it's worth a visit for its stunning architecture and views.

The dzong courtyard is open daily, but on weekends the offices are deserted. Foreign visitors should wear long sleeves and long trousers and remove their hats when entering. Citizens from South Asian Association for Regional Cooperation (SAARC) countries are charged an entry fee but foreign tourists are not, since they pay a daily minimum tariff that includes most entry fees.

The dzong's formal name, Rinchen Pung Dzong (usually shortened to Rinpung Dzong), means 'Fortress on a Heap of Jewels'. In 1644 Zhabdrung Ngawang Namgyal ordered the construction of the dzong on the foundation of a monastery built by Guru Rinpoche. The fort was used on numerous occasions to defend the Paro valley from invasions by Tibet. The British political officer John Claude White reported that in 1905 there were old catapults for throwing great stones stored in the rafters of the dzong's veranda. The dzong survived a 1897 earthquake but was severely damaged by fire in 1907.

The dzong is built on a steep hillside, and the front courtyard of the administrative section is 6m higher than the courtyard of the monastic portion. The road to the National Museum branches down to the dzong's northeastern entrance, which leads into the *dochey* (courtyard). The *utse* (central tower) inside the *dochey* is five storeys tall and was built in the time of the first *penlop* (governor) of Paro in 1649. The richly carved wood, painted in gold, black and ochres, and the towering whitewashed walls reinforce the sense of established power and wealth.

A stairway leads down to the monastic quarter, which houses about 200 monks. The **kunrey**, which functions as the monks' classroom, is on the southern side (to the left) and centred around an image of Buddha aged 16. Look left of the exterior vestibule for the mural of the 'mystic spiral', a uniquely Bhutanese variation on the mandala. Other murals here depict Mt Meru, the legendary centre of the universe, surrounded by seven mountain ranges and four continents.

The large **dukhang** (prayer hall) opposite has lovely exterior murals depicting the life of Tibet's poet-saint Milarepa. The first day of the spring Paro tsechu is held in this courtyard, which fills to bursting point. The views from the courtyard's far windows are superb.

Outside the dzong, to the northeast of the entrance, is a stone-paved **festival ground** (Map p86) where masked dancers perform the main dances of the tsechu. A *thondrol* – a huge *thangka* (painted or embroidered religious picture) of Guru Rinpoche of more than 18 sq metres, is unfurled shortly after dawn on the final day of the tsechu – you can see the

Western Bhutan Highlights

❶ Punakha Dzong
(p109) Exploring Bhutan's most picturesque fortress, the capital of Bhutan from the 17th to the 19th centuries.

❷ Taktshang Goemba (p95) Hiking to Bhutan's most famous sight, the Tiger's Nest Monastery, hanging miraculously from the cliff face.

❸ Paro Dzong (p79) Visiting the courtyards of this hulking dzong, home to the valley's main tsechu festival.

❹ National Museum (p83) Taking a crash course in Bhutanese culture and history at Bhutan's best museum, recently reopened in Paro.

❺ Phobjikha Valley (p116) Spotting black-necked cranes or hitting the biking and hiking trails in this remote valley.

❻ Kyichu Lhakhang (p92) Making the pilgrimage to one of Bhutan's oldest and most beautiful temples.

❼ Haa Valley (p99) Hunting for rare Himalayan flowers and visiting remote monasteries in this little-visited gem.

❽ Chimi Lhakhang (p107) Being blessed with a 25cm penis, if only for a day, at the monastery of the Divine Madman.

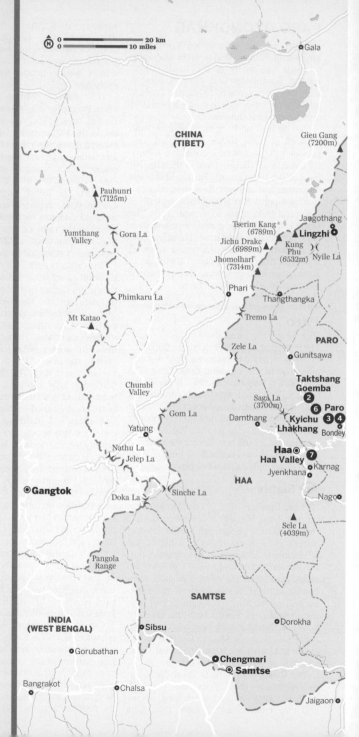

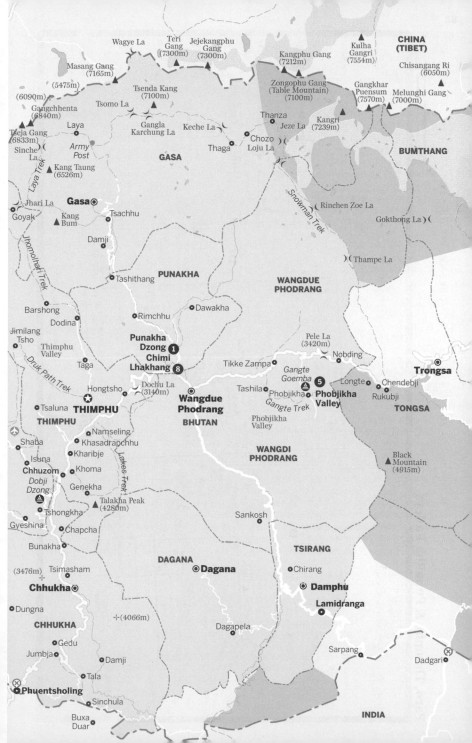

Paro, Thimphu & Punakha Valleys

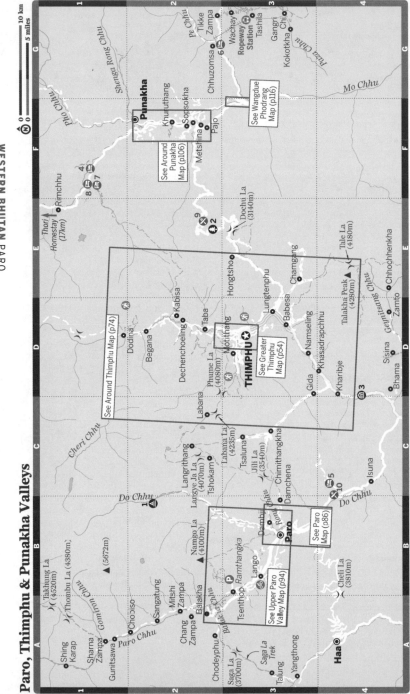

Paro, Thimphu & Punakha Valleys

huge rail upon which it is hung. It was commissioned in the 18th century by the eighth *desi* (secular ruler of Bhutan), also known as Druk Desi, Chhogyel Sherab Wangchuck.

Below the dzong, a traditional wooden covered bridge called **Nyamai Zam** (Map p86) spans the Paro Chhu. This is a reconstruction of the original bridge, which was washed away in a flood in 1969. Earlier versions of this bridge were removed in times of war to protect the dzong. The most picturesque photos of Paro Dzong are taken from the west bank of the river, just downstream from the bridge.

An interesting side note: scenes from Bernardo Bertolucci's 1993 film *Little Buddha* were filmed here.

★ National Museum   MUSEUM
(Gyelyong Damtenkhang; Map p86; ☑08-271257; www.nationalmuseum.gov.bt; SAARC/non-SAARC national Nu 25/200, monks, nuns & children under 10yr free; ☉9am-5pm, to 4pm Dec-Feb, closed national holidays) Perched above Paro Dzong is its *ta dzong* (watchtower), built in 1649 to protect the undefended dzong and renovated in 1968 to house the National Museum. The unusual round building is said to be in the shape of a conch shell, with 2.5m-thick walls. The *ta dzong* suffered damage in the 2011 earthquake but reopened in 2019 as the nation's premier museum.

The 4th-floor entrance kicks off with a description of early history that perfectly illustrates how magic and science are inseparable in Bhutan. Information on Stone Age tools sits next to descriptions of battles between gods and demons. The *thangka* gallery has displays on the four schools of Tibetan Buddhism (Sakya, Nyingma, Gelug and Drukpa). Next is the Namse Phodrang with its collection of bronze statues, notably of the god of wealth Kubera, and it's then down to a collection of relics discovered by Bhutan's treasure finders, featuring 15 links from Thangtong Gyalpo's original iron bridge at Tamchog.

Go down again to the displays on Bhutanese dress and Bhutan's ties with Tibet. The 3rd floor has a royal gallery before it's down once again to the museum's most revered treasures, including a stone egg laid by a mule and a ritual dagger belonging to the protector Dorje Lekpa. An underground tunnel is said to lead from the watchtower to the water supply below.

Cameras are not allowed inside the museum, but you can photograph the *ta dzong* and surrounding grounds. More exhibits (festival masks, natural history and temporary exhibits) are on display in an adjacent annex. The museum plans to raise entry fees to Nu 200/500 for Indians/foreigners.

Driving to the museum involves a 4km loop into the Dop Shari valley. After visiting, you can walk down a path from the museum to the dzong and back to the town, enjoying good views of the valley and of the Ugyen Pelri Palace. Alternatively, you can start the excellent hike to Zuri Dzong (p85) from just above the museum.

★ Dumtse Lhakhang   BUDDHIST TEMPLE
(Map p86; ☉dawn-dusk) Just north of town, by the road leading to the National Museum, is Dumtse Lhakhang, an unusual chorten-like temple that was built in 1433 (some sources say 1421) by the iron-bridge builder Thangtong Gyalpo to subdue a demoness. Look for a mural of Thangtong to the right by the entrance. As you climb clockwise up through the atmospheric three-storeyed mandala-shaped temple core you'll pass some of the finest murals in Bhutan. It's essential to bring a good torch.

The middle floor is devoted to wrathful protectors and the animal-headed deities that the deceased face on their journey through the bardo, the transition between death and rebirth.

Pena Lhakhang   BUDDHIST TEMPLE
(Map p86; ☑caretaker 77227412) Lovely Pena (or Puna) Lhakhang is ignored by most visitors to Paro, but is said to have been founded by

Tibetan King Songtsen Gampo in the 7th century, making it one of the oldest temples in Bhutan. It's easily missed, just past Dumtse Lhakhang, on the east side of the road.

The main inner sanctum certainly has an ancient feel, dominated by a statue of Jowo Nampar Namse that apparently has the power to fulfil wishes. The red-faced protector Pehar lurks in the corner, while to the left of the chapel is the stone footprint of a former Zhabdrung. You may have to call the caretaker to open the building.

Tashi Gongphel
Bhutanese Paper WORKSHOP
(Map p94; ☑17614995; Jiba village; ⊙8.30am-1pm & 2-5.30pm Mon-Sat) **FREE** This small workshop in the Dop Shari valley northeast of Paro town is worth a visit to see how traditional paper is made from local daphne and edgeworthia bushes. You'll see the steps of soaking, boiling, sorting, pounding and laying out the paper on a bamboo screen and then compressing and drying the sheets, a process that takes three days.

The factory is 2km from the turn-off on the road to the National Museum down a rough road; turn left at the chorten. On the hillside behind the factory is the intriguing Singye Drak temple dedicated to the protector Sengdongma.

Paro Weekend Market MARKET
(Map p86; ⊙6am-4pm) Paro's weekend market isn't very large but it has a traditional feel and is a fine introduction to some of Bhutan's unique local products, from organic Tsirang honey to the squares of dried jellied cow skin known as *khoo* (a local snack). The market is busiest on Sunday mornings but the vegetable stalls remain open throughout the week.

As you wander the stalls, look for strings of *chugo* (dried yak cheese), either white (boiled in milk and dried in the sun) or brown (smoked). The fruit that looks like an orange egg is actually fresh husky betel nut, imported from India. The jars of pink paste contain lime, which is ingested with the betel nut. There is also plenty of powdered juniper incense and patties of *datse,* the cheese used in almost every Bhutanese dish.

After visiting the market check out the action in the **archery ground** (Map p86) to the southeast, especially on weekends.

Druk Choeding BUDDHIST TEMPLE
(Map p86; ⊙hours vary) Also known as Tshongdoe Naktshang, the quiet and peaceful Druk Choeding is the town temple and an important historical site. It was built in 1525 by Ngawang Chhogyel (1465–1540), one of the prince-abbots of Ralung in Tibet and an ancestor of the Zhabdrung Ngawang Namgyal.

Chhoeten Lhakhang BUDDHIST TEMPLE
(Map p86; ⊙hours vary) The tower-like Chhoeten Lhakhang is southeast of Paro's town square. The caretaker may allow you to visit the upstairs chapel, which features a central Jowo Sakyamuni, with Guru Rinpoche and Chenresig to the side.

🏃 Activities

Tshetob Yingyum Spa MASSAGE
(Map p86; ☑17630490; www.parospa.com; massage per hr Nu 1700-3000; ⊙9am-9pm) Spa owner Tshewang was a masseuse at Amankora for nine years so you can count on a top-notch massage at this relaxing, locally run spa. Choose between a 60- or a 90-minute Thai full body, head and shoulder, foot or signature hot stone massage (the last option costs Nu 3000/4000 for 60/90 minutes). They also offer a steam bath (Nu 500).

The spa is in Paro town, on the 1st floor behind the Khamsum Hotel. Book a time slot in advance.

Dragon Riders
Mountain Bike Club MOUNTAIN BIKING
(Map p86; ☑17563795; www.facebook.com/DragonRidersBikeClubBhutan) Paro's local mountain-bike club can arrange exciting downhill rides on the valley fringes, and rents and repairs bikes for local rides. Figure on Nu 1800 per day to rent a Trek bike, with an extra Nu 1500 for a guide, or Nu 3500 per day trip with guide, bike and transportation. They can even arrange heli-biking up at Cheli La.

The office/workshop is below the Ama Buffet Restaurant in Paro centre.

✨ Festivals & Events

The four-day **Paro tsechu** is the main religious event of the year, heralding the arrival of spring in March or April. The first day takes place inside the dzong before moving to the *deyankha* paved area just above the dzong entrance. A *thondrol* is unfurled here at dawn on the 15th day of the second month.

🛏 Sleeping

Paro's better accommodation options are in resort-style hotels scattered around the valley, not in the town itself, which caters mostly to local and Indian tourists. The closest options to town are on the hillside west

HIKING & BIKING THE PARO VALLEY

There are several day-hiking options in the Paro valley that allow you to get off the tourist route and have some valley views to yourself.

A great way to end a visit to the National Museum (p83) is with an hour-long hike along the forested hillside to **Zuri Dzong** (Map p86) and then down to the main gate of the Uma Paro hotel, where your vehicle can pick you up. En route you'll pass **Gönsaka Lhakhang** (Map p86; ☉ hours vary), a charming place that predates Paro Dzong. Don't miss the meditation cave here of Pha Drun Drung, the founder of Paro Dzong. The views down over the valley and dzong along this route are unmatched. Zuri Dzong was built in 1352 as a fort and the main building is well protected by double walls and a bridge. There are some particularly fine murals in the upper chapels, one of which is dedicated to the protector Zaa (Rahulla). Once you reach the fence of the Uma Paro hotel, nonguests will have to walk 15 minutes around the perimeter fence to the front gate.

Southeast of Kyichu Lhakhang in the direction of Paro are two hilltop temples that offer a short hike off the beaten track. From the road that leads to the Nak-Sel resort a dirt road branches uphill to the atmospheric but run-down **Tengchen Goemba** (Map p94). From here it's an easy 40-minute stroll (get the monks at Tengchen to show you the confusing initial stretch) past a potential picnic site by a prayer-flag-strewn hill to curve around the ridge to **Dranjo Goemba** (Map p94). This monastic school looks deceptively new, but there are some fine darkened murals inside. Of note here is the mask-like statue of Tsering Ngodup, the Goddess of Wealth, riding a snow lion, with a *drangyen* (lute) hanging to the side. Also here is the funeral stupa of the founder Kichu Barawa and statues of local protectors Shingkhab and Gyenyen. From Dranjo Goemba you can take the shortcut trail down to Pelri Cottages to meet your car and head back to Paro town. It's also possible to hike to both temples from the Dewachen Resort.

A pleasant 40-minute downhill hike leads from the **Kuenga Choeling Goemba** (Map p94) below Sangchen Choekor Shedra on the north side of the Paro vallley down to the interesting **Tsendo Girkha Lhakhang** (Map p94; Tsendona village; ☉ hours vary), where your vehicle can pick you up. Take the lower trail as it curves round into the side valley, then through an orchard to meet the dirt road just before the monastery.

Most ambitious is the tough cardio day hike up from the hospital to Gorena Lhakhang, high on the ridge behind the Hotel Olathang. It's also possible to mountain bike here on an 8km-long dirt road from the Paro–Cheli La road.

Biking routes include cycling up the Paro valley along the quiet northeast bank road, then crossing the footbridge to Kyichu Lhakhang. From here you could take the southwestern dirt road back to Paro via the Dewachen Resort. The cycle up to Drukyel Dzong is another popular ride. To get off the beaten track, try exploring the Dop Shari valley north of Paro.

For single track ask at Dragon Riders Mountain Bike Club (p84) about the trails from the Cheli La to Gorena Lhakhang.

of Paro, in a suburb known as Geptey, which offers great views over the valley.

Hotels increase their rates significantly during the spring Paro tsechu, when every hotel and even local farmhouses are full to bursting point.

🛏 Near Paro Town

Hotel Jigmeling   LOCAL HOTEL $
(Map p86; ☎08-271444; www.bhutanecolodges. com; s/d Nu 2400/2640, deluxe s/d Nu 2520/3000; 🛜) Of the nearly identical local hotels in Paro town that are popular with Indian tourists, the Jigmeling is probably the best, with cosy rooms decorated in earth tones, a porch and balcony seating for the deluxe rooms, and a decent restaurant-bar. It's off the main road so it's quieter than most hotels in town.

Sonam Trophel Hotel   LOCAL HOTEL $
(Map p86; ☎08-274444; hotelsonamtrophel@gmail. com; r Nu 1500-2500, ste Nu 3500; 🛜) If you want to be based in town, this simple but comfortable lodge straddles the local and Indian tourist markets. It doesn't have the sense of space of the valley resorts, but it does allow you to grab a beer in town, if you can put up with a little extra street noise (and the basement club). Spacious deluxe rooms are best.

Paro

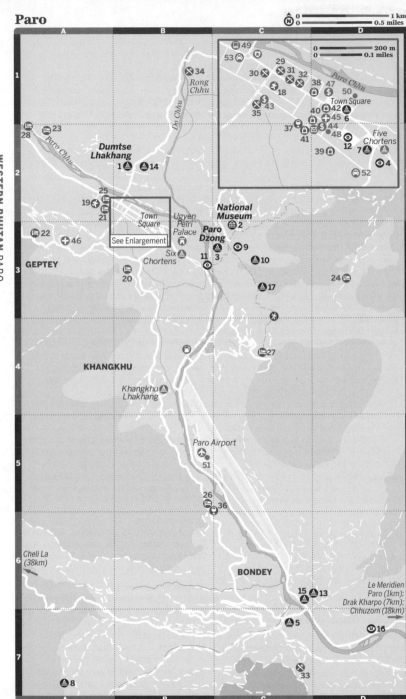

Paro

★ **Gangtey Palace** HISTORIC HOTEL $$
(Map p86; ☑ 08-271301; www.gangteypalace.net; s/d incl breakfast Nu 4180/5185, deluxe s/d Nu 5100/6240; ☎) This 19th-century Bhutanese manor was once the residence of the *penlop* of Paro and it oozes historical charm. The spacious deluxe rooms in the creaking main *utse* offer the most charm, but the standard rooms are also pleasant and the restaurant below has fine valley views. This is one place where you'll want to arrive early in order to savour the atmosphere.

Ask staff to show you the 150-year-old murals in the main tower's altar room.

★ **Tashi Namgay Resort** HOTEL $$
(Map p86; ☑ 17170299, 08-272319; www.tashi namgayresort.com; Damsebu; deluxe r Nu 4680, cottages Nu 5400, ste from Nu 15,000; ☎) This well-run three-star place, on the west bank of the Paro Chhu across from the airport, features great views of the Paro Dzong. Deluxe rooms are well sized and decorated with Tibetan carpets, while cottages are spacious, with their own sitting areas. Try for a riverside room. Beer lovers will appreciate the four draught microbrews from the next-door craft brewery. Service is excellent.

Under construction are more rooms and a pool, which should propel the resort to four stars.

Hotel Olathang HOTEL $$
(Map p86; ☑ 08-271304; www.bhutanhotels.com. bt; Geptey; s/d Nu 3600/4200, cottage s/d Nu 4200/4800, deluxe cottage s/d Nu 4800/5400, ste

s/d from Nu 5100/5640; 🕾) This hotel was built in 1974 for guests invited to the coronation of the fourth king, and with its spacious grounds it still maintains a distinct whiff of grandeur. The main building's rooms are set around a charming courtyard, the peaceful standard cottages share a lounge (great for families), and the private deluxe cottages among the whispering pines are perfect for couples.

Janka Resort   HOTEL $$
(Map p94; ✆08-272352; www.jankaresort.com; Nemjo; s/d Nu 2640/3360, deluxe s/d Nu 4200/4800) There's a rural feel at this well-run resort, yet it's just 2.5km from Paro town. The 19 standard rooms frame the courtyard, with five stylish deluxe rooms in the main farmhouse-style building. Staff can arrange for guests to visit the chapel in the owner's attached farmhouse. The turn-off by the main road is next to an archery ground.

Rema Resort   HOTEL $$
(Map p86; ✆08-271082; www.pororemaresort.com; s/d Nu 4440/4620; 🕾) This well-located resort of 28 rooms offers panoramic views and blends in nicely with the surrounding farmhouses on the quiet north side of the valley, 1.5km from Paro. The new-block rooms are large and fresh (upper-floor rooms with a balcony are best), while the older stand-alone cottages come with a sitting room.

★ Uma Paro   LUXURY HOTEL $$$
(Map p86; ✆08-271597; www.comohotels.com/uma/bhutan; forest/valley view r incl breakfast & dinner US$792/960, ste from US$1224; 🕾🏊) Kudos goes to the Uma for combining traditional architecture with top-of-the-line facilities to create the best hotel in town. Highlights are the excellent restaurant and spa, with a gym, heated indoor pool and herbal hot stone bath. Bathrooms in the standard rooms are surprisingly simple; the valley-view rooms with a balcony are a better choice.

Activities include complimentary yoga classes and the chance to try Bhutanese-style archery (US$25).

★ Nemjo Heritage Lodge   HERITAGE HOTEL $$$
(Map p94; ✆08-271983; www.bhutanlodges.com; Nemjo village; s/d incl breakfast US$150/180, ste US$210; 🕾) For something rural and exclusive, this lovely 70-year-old farmhouse is a tasteful blend of the traditional and stylish, offering just five comfortable rooms. The lower-floor rooms are overpriced but the two top-floor suites are good value for two couples or a family. Book ahead for the

restaurant speciality, a Tibetan-style hotpot known as *gyakok*.

The walled lawn garden with wicker seats gives some outdoor space and the hot stone and herbal *(menchu)* baths are a worthy luxury. Small groups could consider booking the entire lodge. The owners also run the similar Lechuna Heritage Lodge (p102) in Haa.

🛏 Around the Paro Valley

Metta Resort & Spa   RESORT $$
(Map p94; ✆08-272855; www.mettaresort.com; Shomu; s/d Nu 5400/6000; 🕾) This friendly Malaysian-Bhutanese-run place is 6km from Paro in the middle of the valley and is a good place to be based for a couple of days. The duplex deluxe rooms are spacious and stylish, with extras like traditional-style bathrobes and heaters in the bathroom, and the staff are attentive, offering thoughtful touches such as a refreshing welcome drink on arrival.

Other pluses include Asian-influenced food. Avoid the lower-standard rooms below the car park.

Kichu Resort   HOTEL $$
(Map p94; ✆08-271649; www.kichuresorts.com; Lango; r Nu 5400, deluxe r Nu 6600, ste Nu 9600; 🕾) Set in a large complex 5km from Paro, just past the Kyichu Lhakhang, this resort has a sense of space that's missing in many of Paro's newer resorts. The rooms are in octagonal cottages, each with eight rooms; riverside standard rooms are quieter than roadside deluxe options. A cafe, spa and hot stone baths are bonuses.

Dewachen Resort   HOTEL $$
(Map p94; ✆08-271699; www.dewachenresort.com; Nemjo; s/d from Nu 4750/5330; 🕾) The views over the terraced Paro valley from the dining room, warmed by a *bukhari* (wood stove), are what sold us on this hillside collection of ochre-coloured buildings, as did the proximity to local hiking trails and the on-site spa. The private balconies are a nice touch on sunny mornings but room lighting can be frustratingly dim.

Tiger's Nest Resort   HOTEL $$
(Map p94; ✆08-271310; www.tigernestresort.com; s/d Nu 4140/4740, deluxe s/d Nu 4560/5160, ste Nu 6600; 🕾) Just beyond the turn-off to Taktshang in the Paro upper valley, this rural resort, 9km from Paro, offers rare views of Taktshang Goemba. Rooms are comfortable, if a little old-fashioned, while the duplex cottages scattered behind the main building

share a living room, making them great for families or couples travelling together. Hot stone baths are available.

Base Camp Hotel
HOTEL $$

(Map p94; ☏08-270291; www.basecamphotel.com.bt; Balakha; s/d Nu 3000/3600, deluxe r Nu 4200; ☏) This hotel at the far end of the Paro valley is a friendly place, with 15 cosy rooms and outstanding views of the rebuilt Drukgyel Dzong from the garden picnic tables. Mountain bikers will want to plot adventures with the manager Sangay Phuntshok, one of Bhutan's leading bike guides. It's a convenient option if you are trekking to/from Jhomolhari or the Saga La.

If you have a spare day in your itinerary, staff can advise on visits to nearby Jana Goemba and the day hike to the high-altitude lake of Drakey Pang Tsho behind.

★Village Lodge
BOUTIQUE HOTEL $$$

(Map p86; ☏08-272340; www.hhlbhutan.com/the-village-lodge-paro; Tshendona village; s/d Nu 8400/9600; ☏) This charming converted farmhouse, set in rice paddies 9km north of Paro, achieves that rare balance of style, tradition and comfort. Wooden windows and tamped walls are set off by understated modern touches like walk-in showers, and the hallways are decorated with antique leather bags, lending a rustic chic. It's owned by the Norbu Bhutan agency.

★Zhiwa Ling
LUXURY HOTEL $$$

(Map p94; ☏08-271277; www.zhiwalingheritage.com; Satsam Chorten; s/d incl breakfast from US$380/410; ☀☏) This impressive complex, 8km from Paro, boasts an imposing central lodge and lobby, surrounded by a collection of stone towers. Antiques, plush sofas and a spa counteract the austerity (an indoor pool is under construction), and there's even a temple on the 2nd floor, built with 400-year-old pillars from Gangte Goemba.

Most rooms have a balcony, and the royal suite comes with its own altar room. Pottery is handmade and painted on the premises, and the hotel also makes its own fishing flies. Discounts of 40% are available in low season.

Resort at Raven's Nest
RESORT $$$

(Map p94; ☏08-270244; www.bhutanravens.com; Satsam; s/d from Nu 5040/5760; ☏) Scraping the top end of the tourist class is this stylish resort. The modern rooms come with a balcony or terrace and dinner's organic herbs and vegetables come from the attached nursery. If your agent will include it in your

tariff, snap it up. Ask to borrow the *khuru* (darts) for a game.

Nak-Sel
LUXURY HOTEL $$$

(Map p94; ☏08-272992; www.naksel.com; Ngoba; superior/deluxe r US$240/360, ste from US$504; ☏) Luxury at tourist-class prices is what this opulent resort promises and indeed it compares well to properties charging twice as much. The stylish deluxe rooms are worth the extra expense, with underfloor heating and balconies offering views towards Jhomolhari and Taktshang Goemba, while activities centre around the large spa and good local hiking trails. It's 3km up a secluded side valley.

Amankora
LUXURY HOTEL $$$

(Map p94; ☏08-272333; www.amanresorts.com; Balakha; full-board s/d US$1740/1860; ☏) 'Designer dzong' is the theme here, with the half-dozen sleek, rammed-earth buildings secreted among the blue pines. The rooms benefit from the serene setting and muted home-spun fabrics, romantic open-plan bathrooms and traditional *bukhari*s. It's certainly sleek and stylish, but it's hard to justify the price tag. Most guests are on a packaged Amankora multiday journey.

The spa has a wide range of muscle-melting treatments, and there's an intimate restaurant and reading room. The resort is near Balakha village, about 14km from Paro, not far from Drukgyel Dzong.

Six Senses Paro
RESORT $$$

(Map p86; ☏Thimphu 02-350772; www.sixsenses.com; s/d incl breakfast & dinner US$1840/2000; ☏☷) Perched high on the ridge above Paro, next to the ruined Chubja Dzong that once protected the valley's water supply, this new uberluxury resort and spa is quite a drive from town, though the views are breathtaking. The 20 spacious, open-plan luxury rooms and villas are centred around the pool and massage/yoga rooms. Rooms come with the resort's house-made drink infusions.

Ask staff about the 30-minute hike to the Gyemjalo hermitage perched dramatically on the cliffs below the resort.

✖ Eating

★Brioche Cafe
BAKERY $

(Map p86; cakes Nu 150-240; ⊙9am-8.30pm) The espresso is good at this little cafe but the real draw is the wonderful range of pastries, from the signature apple pie to blueberry cake and seasonal fruit tarts. Add a scoop of house-made masala chai ice cream. The owner is a pastry chef at the five-star Aman-kora, so knows exactly what she is doing.

★ Sonam Trophel Restaurant BHUTANESE $$

(Map p86; ☑17641100, 08-271287; mains Nu 180-300, set meals Nu 600; ⊙9.30am-8.30pm Wed-Mon) Sonam is popular with small groups and has excellent home-style Bhutanese cooking adapted to foreign tastes. The best bet is the set lunch (order in advance; minimum six people), which consists of seven dishes, brought to the table (not buffet-style). The *momos* (dumplings), boneless chicken, ginger potatoes and *hentshey datse* (spinach and cheese) are all excellent.

My Kind of Place ASIAN $$

(Map p86; ☑77411784; mains Nu 200, set meals Nu 490; ⊙10am-9pm; 🛜) Stylish, clean and well run, this spacious 1st-floor restaurant has tasty Bhutanese dishes such as *hoentey* (buckwheat dumplings) and *ema datse* (chillies with cheese) with *bhaley* (Tibetan-style bread), but has some interesting Asian dishes too, including Indonesian-style chicken rendang or a curry set with bok choy and garlic potatoes. The personal touch of the owner elevates the place.

Authentic Pizza PIZZA $$

(Map p86; ☑17296305; pizza Nu 260-450; ⊙9am-8.30pm; 🛜) If you need a break from burning *ema datse* or bland hotel buffets, this upstairs joint bakes decent pizzas: eat in the pleasant restaurant area or takeaway to your hotel room (order 20 minutes in advance). For a local twist try the Bhutanese dried beef pizza with caramelised onions.

Lhayabling Restaurant MULTICUISINE $$

(Map p86; ☑17718057; set meals Nu 480-540; ⊙noon-3pm & 6-8pm) This tourist restaurant is unlikely to surprise you, but it's a popular choice with travel agencies and the food is fresh, light and strong on vegetables.

Yue-Ling Restaurant MULTICUISINE $$

(Map p86; ☑77111847; set meals Nu 540-600; ⊙lunch & dinner; 🗷) A good, reliable place frequented by tour groups, Yue-Ling serves fine curries, vegetable dishes, naan and fried *batura* bread. If you want to try some fiery local dishes, ask your guide to bring a taster plate of the food provided to the drivers and guides.

★ Bukhari Restaurant FUSION $$$

(Map p86; ☑08-272813; Uma Paro hotel; set lunch/dinner US$66/102; ⊙11.30am-3pm & 6.30-10.30pm; 🛜) The sophisticated circular restaurant at the Uma Paro hotel is the best in the valley. The set dinner menu changes frequently and focuses on fresh, healthy and locally sourced food. Lunch is simpler and includes the popular Wagyu burger with Bumthang 'Gouda' cheese. There are also set Bhutanese or Indian meals, or you can choose anything from the all-day dining menu.

Bukhari is a small, intimate restaurant, so reserve ahead of time. For that special occasion ask about the expensive but magical private candlelit dinner in the lower courtyard.

Tou Zaiga Restaurant FUSION $$$

(Map p86; ☑77420979; www.bihtbhutan.org; Bondey; set menu Nu 800; ⊙lunch & dinner by appointment) Trainee five-star chefs and timid waitstaff test their skills on lucky tourists at this restaurant run by the Bongde Institute of Hospitality and Tourism. The dishes fuse Western tastes with local seasonal organic produce. Ring the day before to tailor a three-course Bhutanese menu (ask if the shiitake mushrooms are available), otherwise you'll get the less-inspired Western set meal.

The Institute also runs the 13-room Bongde Goma Resort here. It's 1km southwest of Bondey (Bongde) village.

🍷 Drinking & Nightlife

★ Namgyal

Artisanal Brewery MICROBREWERY

(Map p86; ☑08-272977; www.bhutanesebeer.com; ⊙9am-11pm Mon & Wed-Fri, to midnight Sat & Sun; 🛜) Beer drinkers should make a beeline for Bhutan's premier microbrewery (beers Nu 120) to try its flagship Red Rice lager and hoppy IPA (our favourite, only available on tap). The huge taproom and restaurant is a professional set-up, with live music on Friday and Saturday nights, and if you like what you taste, you can can buy bottled beer to go.

A TASTE OF TRADITIONAL BHUTAN

Most tour companies can arrange a hot stone bath and/or Bhutanese meal at a traditional farmhouse. One popular place in Paro is the rustic **Tshering Farm House** (Map p86; ☑17687642; set meals Nu 450; ⊙lunch & dinner by appointment) in the Dop Shari valley, which serves great traditional food and adds artemisia herbs to its traditional-style wooden baths (Nu 1200 to 1500 per person).

If you get peckish, try a scoop of local *sikam* (dried spicy pork) or masala peanuts. For something heavier, the full restaurant (mains Nu 350) offers everything from burgers and steaks to wild tea leaf salad and grilled river prawns, with a suitably beery stout ice cream float on offer for dessert.

Champaca Cafe
CAFE

(Map p86; ☑ 77212057; ⊙ 8.30am-9pm Thu-Tue; ☎) The bright, spacious upstairs of this coffeehouse (coffee Nu 90 to 150) is the best place in town to recover from sightseeing over a reviving espresso hit and free wi-fi. The South Indian coffee is roasted in Thimphu and packs a punch, while the kitchen serves hard-to-find breakfast dishes (granola, waffles etc) plus cakes and light lunches (mains Nu 200 to 300).

Park 76
BAR

(Map p86; ☑ 17630388; ⊙ 11am-10.30pm Wed-Mon; ☎) The only real pub in Paro, this modern place has a sports-bar vibe, with suitably dim lighting, weekend live music and three beers on draught from the local Namgyal Artisanal Brewery (beers Nu 200 to 250). It also offers Bhutanese and Indian bar food, plus full meals like chicken tikka masala with rice.

Book Cafe
CAFE

(Map p86; ⊙ 9am-9.30pm) This modern place serves good Lavazza espresso alongside traditional Bhutanese snacks such as *khule* (breakfast pancakes), *puta* (buckwheat noodles) and the owner's family *bathup* stew recipe. Coffee costs Nu 100 to 150, mains are Nu 150 to 400. There's no wi-fi, as visitors are encouraged to put away their phones; instead there's a wall of books that guests are welcome to read.

🛍 Shopping

Most of Paro's main street now consists of handicraft shops, offering the country's most convenient selection of souvenirs, from prayer flags to fridge magnets. It's worth budgeting an hour or two to pick up some last-minute souvenirs before flying out of Paro Airport.

Lama Tshering Dorji General Shop
RELIGIOUS SUPPLIES

(Map p86; ⊙ 9am-7pm) This monk supply shop is one of several in Paro aimed squarely at locals and monks rather than tourists, but it's a fascinating browse. Items for sale include amulets, divination dice, prayer flags, incense, statuary and butter lamps – everything in fact for your own personal altar. There are also some nonreligious items such as *khuru* darts and bamboo arrows.

Chencho Handicrafts
ARTS & CRAFTS

(Map p86; ⊙ 9am-noon & 1-6pm) Chencho has an interesting selection of local handicrafts, and is particularly strong on weavings, antique *kira*s (women's traditional dresses) and embroidery, as well as woollen carpets. It's a good place to see weavers working on-site. Credit cards are accepted. Nonshoppers can grab a coffee at the next-door Book Cafe, run by the owner's daughter.

Tashi Gongphel Bhutanese Paper
ARTS & CRAFTS

(Map p86; ⊙ 9am-6pm Mon-Sat) This showroom has products ranging from notebooks and cards to sheets of wrapping paper, all created from Bhutanese paper, traditionally made from either daphne (white-coloured paper) or edgeworthia (cream-coloured) bushes. To see the fascinating production process, arrange a visit to the factory (p84) in the Dop Shari valley.

TT Extra
FOOD & DRINKS

(Map p86; ⊙ 9am-7pm) This innocuous local grocery store has a section dedicated to local and organic Bhutanese products, making it a great place to pick up everything from bags of organic red rice and local turmeric to locally produced incense and sesame-like *zhimtse*, all at reasonable prices.

Paro Canteen
FOOD & DRINKS

(Map p86; ⊙ 9am-8pm) A local general store that sells hard-to-find bottles of Red Panda beer for Nu 120, as well as TashiCell SIM cards (bring a photocopy of your passport).

Yuesel Handicrafts
ARTS & CRAFTS

(Map p86; ☑ 08-271942; www.yuesel.com; ⊙ 9am-6pm) This superior souvenir shop has the normal incense, tea, masks, cane boxes, traditional locks and books, but also dried mushrooms, ceramics, and the worm-like cordyceps roots often called 'Himalayan Viagra' (around Nu 500 per piece). Head upstairs for antiques, most of which come with export-ready seals.

Collection of Rare Stamps & Souvenir Shop
GIFTS & SOUVENIRS

(Map p86; ⊙ 9am-6pm) First covers and rare items, like hologram stamps and stamps you can play on a record player, are available here, as well as handmade balms and hand creams from the excellent Bhutanese Mudra brand.

WESTERN BHUTAN PARO

ℹ Information

EMERGENCY

Police Station (Map p86) Northwest of the town square, near the bridge over the Paro Chhu.

MEDICAL SERVICES

Kuenphuen Pharmacy (Map p86; ☏17627060; ⊙9.30am-1pm & 2-9pm) Basic medical supplies; opposite the Made in Bhutan store.

Paro District Hospital (Map p86; ☏08-271571) On a hill to the west of town; it accepts foreigners in an emergency.

MONEY

Bank of Bhutan (Map p86; ☏08-271230; www.bob.bt; ⊙9am-1pm & 2-4pm Mon-Fri, 9am-noon Sat) Your best bet: efficient, friendly and with an ATM.

Bhutan National Bank (Map p86; www.bnb.bt; ⊙9am-4pm Mon-Fri, 9-11am Sat)

Tashi Money Exchange (Map p86; ☏08-271303; ⊙8am-9pm) Exchanges small amounts of cash (US dollars and euros) if you need to change outside of bank hours.

ℹ Getting There & Away

Paro Airport (Map p86; ☏08-271423) is 7km south of Paro town and 53km from Thimphu. There are offices of both **Druk Air** (Map p86; ☏1300, 08-272044; www.drukair.com.bt; ⊙9am-1pm & 2-4pm Mon-Fri, 10am-noon Sat) and **Bhutan Airlines** (Map p86; ☏08-270227; ⊙9am-1pm & 2-5pm Mon-Fri, 9am-1pm Sat, 10am-1pm Sun) in Paro.

Shared taxis run from a **stand** (Map p86) next to the petrol station and also from a **stand** (Map p86) west of the archery ground. The trip to Thimphu costs Nu 250 per seat or Nu 1000 per minivan; to Phuentsholing costs Nu 750 per seat.

Daily Coaster buses to Thimphu (Nu 55, 9am and 2pm) and Phuentsholing (Nu 210, 8.30am) leave from the offices of **Dhug Transport** (Map p86) and other bus companies at the northwest end of town.

For a day's sightseeing by taxi in the Paro valley figure on around Nu 2500.

Upper Paro Valley

The Paro valley extends west all the way to the peaks on the Tibetan border, though the road only goes as far as Sharna Zampa, near Drukgyel Dzong, about 20km beyond Paro. En route it passes half a dozen resorts, lovely rural scenery and some of Bhutan's most famous sights. Beyond the dzong, a side valley leads to the Tremo La, the 5000m pass

that was once an important trade route to Tibet and also the route of several Tibetan invasions.

Kyichu Lhakhang

A short drive from Paro is Kyichu Lhakhang, a highlight of the Paro valley. The temple is popularly believed to have been built in 659 by King Songtsen Gampo of Tibet, to pin down the left foot of a giant ogress who was thwarting the establishment of Buddhism in Tibet. Inside the lhakhang look for a framed image of the reclining demoness (p95) for whom the temple was allegedly built.

◉ Sights

★**Kyichu Lhakhang**   BUDDHIST TEMPLE
(Map p94; SAARC national students/adult Nu 150/300; ⊙9am-noon & 1-5pm Mar-Oct, to 4pm Nov-Feb) Kyichu Lhakhang is one of Bhutan's oldest and most beautiful temples. The main chapel has roots as far back as the 7th century, with additional buildings and a golden roof added in 1839 by the *penlop* of Paro and the 25th Je Khenpo. Elderly pilgrims constantly shuffle around the temple spinning its many prayer wheels, making this one of the most charming spots in the Paro valley. Entry is free to foreign tourists since they are paying their daily tariff.

As you enter the intimate inner courtyard of this historic chapel, you'll see to the right of the doorway a mural of King Gesar of Ling, the popular Tibetan warrior-king, whose epic poem is said to be the world's longest.

The third king's wife, Ashi Kesang Wangchuck, sponsored the construction of the **Guru Lhakhang** in 1968. It contains a 5m-high statue of Guru Rinpoche and another of Kurukulla (Red Tara), holding a bow and arrow made of flowers. To the right of Guru Rinpoche is a chorten containing the ashes of Dilgo Khyentse Rinpoche, the revered Nyingma Buddhist master and spiritual teacher of the Queen Mother, who passed away and was cremated nearby in 1991. There is a statue of him to the left, as well as some old photos of the fourth king's grandmother and the first king of Bhutan. The ornately carved wooden pillars are superb, as are the snow lions that support the flower pots.

The inner hall of the fantastically atmospheric main **Jowo Lhakhang** conceals the valley's greatest treasure, an original 7th-century statue of Jowo Sakyamuni, said to have been cast at the same time as the famous statue in Lhasa. In front of the statue you can see the grooves that generations of prostrators have worn into the wooden floor. King Songtsen Gampo himself lurks up in the upper left niche of the outer room. The main door is superbly gilded with images of curling dragons.

The former quarters *(zimchung)* of Dilgo Khyentse are in a room to the left and still hold his bed and throne.

Dilgo Khyentse Rinpoche's Residence Memorial House
MUSEUM

(Map p94; ☑17531177; Nu 50; ⊙10am-4pm Tue-Sun) Just outside the Kyichu Lhakhang complex is this museum dedicated to Dilgo Khyentse (1910–91), the Tibetan Buddhist rinpoche (reincarnated Buddhist lama) who lived here for some time. The museum is full of the rinpoche's photos and personal effects, including his palanquin and sinus medication, and his Mercedes car and teaching throne are on the grounds. Call in advance as opening hours are somewhat unreliable.

Taktshang

Tucked into a narrow cleft in the wall of the Paro valley, iconic Taktshang Goemba (the 'Tiger's Nest Monastery') is Bhutan's most famous sight and it features on most visitors' itineraries. Reachable only on foot via a relentlessly uphill path, this precariously balanced *ney* (holy place) is the most famous of Bhutan's monasteries and also its most photogenic, hanging onto what looks from afar like a sheer vertical cliff. Tradition says that the building is anchored to the cliff face by the hairs of *khandroma* (*dakini;* female celestial beings), who transported the building materials up onto the cliff on their backs. There is a distinct air of magic to the site.

It is said that Guru Rinpoche flew to the site of the monastery on the back of a tigress (a manifestation of his Bhutanese consort Tashi Kheudren) to subdue the local demon, Singye Samdrup. He then meditated in a cave here for three months.

Milarepa is said to have meditated at Taktshang, Thangtong Gyalpo revealed a *terma* (treasure text) here and Zhabdrung Ngawang Namgyal visited in 1646. Pilgrims from all over Bhutan come to the site. The *penlop* of Paro, Gyalse Tenzin Rabgye, built the primary lhakhang in 1692 around the Drubkhang (also called the Pelphu), the holy cave in which Guru Rinpoche meditated.

On 19 April 1998 a fire (which was rumoured to be arson, to disguise a theft) destroyed the main structure of Taktshang and all its contents. It had already suffered a previous fire and had been repaired in 1951. Reconstruction started in April 2000 at a cost of 130 million ngultrum and the rebuilt site was reconsecrated in the presence of the king in 2005.

⊙ Sights

The paved road to the Taktshang car park branches right, 8km north of Paro, and climbs 3km past a white chorten and the small but charming **Ramthangka Lhakhang** (Map p94) to the trailhead at 2600m.

Getting to the goemba involves a fairly stiff uphill hike of a couple of hours so bring comfortable walking shoes and water. Many Indian tourists ride a horse halfway up to the temple; you can avoid their dust by taking smaller side paths.

If you require a horse, be sure to mention this to your guide in advance so they can book one. Check whether the cost (around Nu 700 per horse) is to be paid by you (likely) or your agency.

Citizens of SAARC countries need to buy an entry ticket at a **ticket office** (Map p94; ⊙7.30am-1pm) by the car park. Non-SAARC tourists don't need a ticket.

THE HIKE TO TAKTSHANG

The only way up to the Tiger's Nest is to walk, ride a horse or fly up here on the back of a magic tiger (the last option is generally reserved for tantric magicians). The 1¾-hour hike is a central part of any tourist itinerary and is unmissable for the spectacular views. It's also a good warm-up hike if you are going trekking. Most people make the walk in the morning to avoid strong direct sun, but photographers should take advantage of the much better afternoon light. Wear a hat and bring water.

The trail climbs through blue pines to three water-powered prayer wheels, then switchbacks steeply up the ridge. If you have just flown into Paro, walk slowly because you are likely to feel the altitude.

Once you reach the ridge there are excellent views across the valley and southwest towards Drukgyel Dzong. After a climb of about one hour and a gain of 300m you will reach a small chorten and some prayer flags on the ridge, which is as far as horses can

Upper Paro Valley

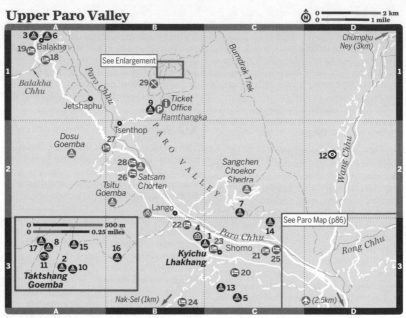

Upper Paro Valley

◎ Top Sights
1 Kyichu Lhakhang	C3
2 Taktshang Goemba	A3

◎ Sights
3 Choedu Goemba	A1
4 Dilgo Khyentse Rinpoche's Residence Memorial House	B3
5 Dranjo Goemba	C3
6 Drukgyel Dzong	A1
7 Kuenga Choeling Goemba	C2
8 Machig-phu Lhakhang	A3
9 Ramthangka Lhakhang	B1
10 Shama Lhakhang	A3
11 Taktshang Viewpoint	A3
12 Tashi Gongphel Bhutanese Paper	D2
13 Tengchen Goemba	C3
14 Tsendo Girkha Lhakhang	C3
15 Ugyen Tshemo Lhakhang	A3
16 Yoselgang	B3
17 Zangto Pelri Lhakhang	A3

⊜ Sleeping
18 Amankora	A1
19 Base Camp Hotel	A1
20 Dewachen Resort	C3
21 Janka Resort	C3
22 Kichu Resort	B3
23 Metta Resort & Spa	C3
24 Nak-Sel	B3
25 Nemjo Heritage Lodge	C3
26 Resort at Raven's Nest	B2
27 Tiger's Nest Resort	B2
28 Zhiwa Ling	B2

⊗ Eating
29 Taktsang Cafeteria	B1

go. It's then a short walk to the **cafeteria** (Map p94; ☑17601682; tea & biscuits Nu 145, buffet lunch Nu 470; ⊙7am-4pm; ✐), at 2940m, where you can savour the impressive view of the monastery over a well-deserved cup of tea. The cafeteria also serves a vegetarian buffet lunch but it's not up to much; you are better off with a packed lunch.

The trail continues up for another 30 minutes to a spring and the basic monastery guesthouse. A cave and plaque marks the birthplace of a previous Je Khenpo; his former residence is just up the hill. A short walk further along the main trail brings you to a spectacular stupa **viewpoint** (Map p94) at 3140m that puts you eyeball to eyeball with the monastery, which looks like it is growing out of the rocks.

From this vantage point Taktshang seems almost close enough to touch, but it's on the

SUBDUING THE DEMONESS

When the Tibetan king Songtsen Gampo married the Chinese princess Wencheng in 641, her dowry included the Jowo Sakyamuni, a priceless Indian statue of the Buddha as a small boy. As the statue was transported through Lhasa, it became stuck in the mud and no one could move it. The princess, known as Ashe Jaza (the Chinese Princess) in Bhutan, divined that the obstruction was being caused by a huge supine demoness, lying on her back with her navel over a lake where Lhasa's main temple, Jokhang, now stands.

In 659 the king decided to build 108 temples in a single day to pin the ogress to the earth forever and, as a by-product, convert the Tibetan people to Buddhism. Temples were constructed at her shoulders and hips, which corresponded to the four districts of central Tibet, and her knees and elbows, which were in the provinces. The hands and feet lay in the borderlands of Tibet, and several temples were built in Bhutan to pin down the troublesome left leg.

The best known of these temples are Kyichu Lhakhang in Paro, which holds the left foot, and Jampey Lhakhang in Bumthang, which pins the left knee. Other lesser-known temples have been destroyed, but it is believed that, among others, Konchogsum Lhakhang in Bumthang, Khaine Lhakhang south of Lhuentse, and Lhakhang Kharpo and Lhakhang Nagpo in Haa may have been part of this ambitious project.

far side of a deep valley about 150m away. The trail descends to a waterfall by the Singye Pelphu Lhakhang (Snow Lion Cave), a meditation retreat associated with Guru Rinpoche's consort Yeshe Tshogyel that's wedged dramatically into a rock crevice. The path then climbs back up to the monastery entrance.

★ **Taktshang Goemba** BUDDHIST MONASTERY (Taktshang Palphug; Map p94; SAARC nationals child/adult Nu 250/500; ⊘ 9am-4pm Oct-Mar, to 5pm Apr-Sep) The 'Tiger's Nest Monastery' is one of the Himalaya's most incredible sights, miraculously perched on the side of a sheer cliff 900m above the floor of the Paro valley. Visiting is the goal of most visitors to Bhutan and while getting there involves a bit of uphill legwork, it's well worth the effort. The monastery is a sacred site, so act with respect, removing your shoes and hat before entering any chapels.

Bags, phones and cameras have to be deposited at the entrance, where your guide will register with the army.

As you enter the complex you pass underneath images of the Rigsum Goempo (Jampelyang, Chenresig and Chana Dorje). Turn to the right and look for the relic stone; Bhutanese stand on the starting line, close their eyes and try to put their thumb into a small hole in the rock as a form of karmic test.

Most groups then visit the **Drubkhang** (Pelphu Lhakhang), the cave where Guru Rinpoche meditated for three months. Outside the cave is a statue of Dorje Drolo,

the manifestation the Guru assumed to fly to Taktshang on a tigress. The inner cave is sealed off behind a spectacularly gilded door and is said to hold the *phurba* (ritual dagger) of the Guru. Murals of the Guru Tsengye, or eight manifestations of Guru Rinpoche, decorate the walls. Behind you, sitting above the inside of the main entrance, is a mural of Thangtong Gyalpo (p100) holding his iron chains.

From here ascend to the **Guru Sungjonma Lhakhang**, which has a central image of Pema Jungme, another of the eight manifestations of Guru Rinpoche. This statue incorporates the ashes of a famous 'talking' image that was lost in the 1998 fire. Various demonic animal-headed deities and manifestations of the deity Phurba decorate the walls alongside the 25 disciples of Guru Rinpoche, while outside is an image of the long-life protector Tseringma riding a snow lion.

Passing a small prayer hall, the **Langchen Pelgye Sengye Lhakhang** on the left has connections to Dorje Phagmo, with a rock image of the goddess's crown hidden in a hole in the floor. The inner chorten belongs to Langchen Pelgye Sengye, a 9th-century disciple of Guru Rinpoche, who meditated in the cave. Behind the chorten is a holy spring.

Further on inside the complex to the left is the **Dorje Drolo Lhakhang**, where the monks sometimes sell blessed lockets, while to the right is the **Guru Tsengye Lhakhang**, which features an image of the

OFF THE BEATEN TRACK

THE PILGRIMAGE TO CHUMPHU NEY

For a fabulous trip into the dreamlike miracle world of Bhutan's sacred geography, budget a day for a hike up to one of Bhutan's most famous *ney* (sacred sites), **Chumphu Ney** (Map p82; Dop Shari valley; ☉dawn-dusk). The focal point of the walk is a venerated 'floating' statue of tantric goddess Dorje Phagmo (Vajravarahi), who is said to have flown here from Tibet and turned into a statue, but it's the pilgrim trails winding up to the complex that are the real attraction to most visitors.

The three- to four-hour walk to the temple follows a beautiful river and passes dozens of *neydo* or sacred natural rock carvings connected to the activities of Guru Rinpoche and his consorts. Unfortunately, a swath of forest was recently cleared to extend electricity to the monks. After two hours or so, a side valley enters from the left and you can spy the lhakhang above you. Shortly afterwards a *kora* (circumambulation) path branches left up the side valley towards a waterfall, before ascending past sin tests, ladders, ledges, meditation caves and natural stone pools to reach the temple.

The main shrine is guarded by police and home to Dorje Phagmo (Vajravarahi), recognisable by the sow's snout behind her right ear. An attendant monk will open a little door under the statue and pass a 10-ngultrum note under her foot to prove that the statue floats unsupported by the ground.

A further 10-minute walk behind the monastery leads to a small prayer-flag-draped waterfall and pool connected to Guru Rinpoche. It's then a two-hour walk back to the car park, which is an hour-long drive from Paro up the Dop Shari valley. You'll need three-quarters of a day for the excursion, but it's well worth it.

monastery's 17th-century founder, Gyalse Tenzin Rabgye. Look down through the glass into the bowels of a sacred cave.

Further up is a butter-lamp chapel (light one for a donation). You can climb down into the original Tiger's Nest cave just above the chapel, but take care as it's a dusty path down a hairy series of wooden ladders to descend into a giant slice of the cliff face.

After visiting the Tiger's Nest and reascending to the previous viewpoint, it is possible to take a signed side trail uphill for 15 minutes to the charming **Machig-phu Lhakhang** (Map p94), where Bhutanese pilgrims come to pray for children. Head to the cave behind the chapel and select the image of the Tibetan saint Machig Labdron on the right (for a baby girl), or the penis print on the cave wall to the left (for a boy). The main statues inside the chapel are of Machig and her husband Padampa Sangye.

❶ Getting There & Away

Taktshang Goemba is located on the eastern side of the Paro valley, about 10km northwest of Paro town, but the only way to reach the monastery is to walk from the end of the access road. All foreign tourists will have their own vehicle as part of a tour; otherwise, negotiate a fare for a taxi in Paro town.

Drukgyel Dzong

Near the end of the paved road, 14km from Paro, stand the ruins of Drukgyel Dzong, built in the 17th century to cement Bhutanese control over what was then the main route to Tibet. Once the Tibetan invasions ceased, this became a major trade route, with Bhutanese rice being transported to the Tibetan town of Phari Dzong as barter for salt and bricks of tea. These days trekking groups headed to Jomolhari base camp have replaced the trade caravans.

◉ Sights

Drukgyel Dzong　　　BUDDHIST MONASTERY
(Map p94; ☉closed) Drukgyel Dzong, now an imposing ruin, was built in 1649 by Zhabdrung Ngawang Namgyal to control the trade and military route to Tibet. The building was used as an administrative centre until 1951, when a fire caused by a butter lamp destroyed it. Major renovations started in 2016 and will continue until at least 2022, meaning the dzong's interior is currently off-limits.

Choedu Goemba　　　BUDDHIST MONASTERY
(Map p94) After a visit to Drukgyel Dzong, you can take a five-minute stroll from the parking area up to the small Choedu Goemba, which houses a statue of the blue-faced local

protector, Gyeb Dole. It's just above the village archery ground.

Paro to Bondey

6KM / 10 MINUTES

Two roads lead south from Paro to the village of Bondey, straddling the Paro Chhu to the southeast of the airport. The winding road on the west bank passes above the airport, Khangkhu village and the Namgyal Artisanal Brewery; a couple of turnouts offer great views of planes taking off and landing. A faster main road runs past the airport on the east bank of the river.

Beyond the turn-off to the Cheli La is 400-year-old **Bondey Lhakhang** (Map p86; ⊙ hours vary), on the west bank of the river. On the east side of the Paro Chhu, beside the main road near the Bondey bridge, is the charming and unusually chorten-shaped **Tago Lhakhang** (Map p86; ☑ caretaker 17616405; Bondey), founded by Thangtong Gyalpo. A circular chapel occupies the upper floor; ask for the key at the next-door Tharpala General Shop if the caretaker is not around (he normally isn't).

A 15-minute uphill hike (or short drive) above Tago is the small **Pelri Goemba** (Map p86; ⊙ hours vary), a rare Nyingmapa-school chapel that was reduced in size after an unwise dispute with the dominant Kagyu school.

Bondey to Thimphu

53KM / 2 HOURS

Figure on about two hours driving from Paro to Thimphu via Bondey, longer if you stop en route. There are some worthwhile off-the-beaten-track detours along the road, so you could easily make this a full day's drive.

Bondey to Chhuzom

18KM / 30 MINUTES

En route to Thimphu, it's worth stopping briefly at **Bondey** to admire its lovely traditional houses and chapels. Just 1km from Bondey is the family-run **Tshenden Incense Factory** (Map p86; ☑ 08-271352; www.tshendenschool.bt; ⊙ 8.30am-1pm & 2-5pm Mon-Sat), where you can see the boiling, dyeing, extruding and drying processes. Get your guide to arrange a visit in advance.

Two kilometres further on at Shaba are two cliff-face religious sites. A short but steep hiking trail near the army commando training centre, just past Le Meridien Hotel, leads for 40 minutes up to **Gom Jalo** hermitage, clinging to the hillside and tended by a handful of nuns. The views are excellent but the chapels themselves are often closed.

A little further on, just past the bridge in Shaba, a rough road heads up for 20 minutes past Eutok (Yutok) Goemba to the higher **Drak Kharpo** (White Cliff), a cliffside monastery where the Buddhist magician-saint Guru Rinpoche meditated for several months before flying off to Dzongdrakha across the valley. The site is well worth the detour for its delightful 20-minute *kora* walking path, numerous sacred stones and small cave complex, where you can join fellow pilgrims as they squeeze their way through a claustrophobic series of sin-absolving tunnels (bring a torch/flashlight). The large split stone at the top of the path is where Guru Rinpoche subdued the local demon Draksen and pilgrims rub their backs and joints on the healing stone before squeezing through the crack. The main lhakhang is built around the meditation cave of Guru Rinpoche and you can see his fingerprints in the rock that he magically displaced when making the cave. Figure on a 2½-hour return detour to visit the complex from the main road.

Near the turn-off for Drak Kharpo is Bhutan Spirit Sanctuary (p99), a top-end spa resort. Also nearby is the **Neyphu Heritage Café** (Your Café; Map p82; ☑ 08-276441; mains Nu 330-550; ⊙ 10am-10pm; ☎ ☑) ✎ , a good lunch spot that was set up by the rinpoche of nearby Neyphu Goemba to generate income for monastery renovations.

Just past Shaba you'll pass the new **Chorten Drimed Namnyi**, a large whitewashed stupa built in 2017 by the fourth king.

At Isuna, 12km from Bondey and 8km from Chhuzom, the road crosses a bridge to the south bank of the Paro Chhu.

About 5km before Chhuzom, the road passes **Tamchhog Lhakhang**, a private temple on the far side of the river that is owned by the descendants of the famous Tibetan bridge-builder Thangtong Gyalpo. The traditional iron bridge here was reconstructed in 2005 using some of Thangtong's original chain links from Duksum in eastern Bhutan. A small cave above the bridge supposedly marks Thangtong's iron mine, as well as the mouth of the snake-shaped hillside that the chapel is built on. It's a 10-minute uphill walk to the lhakhang.

You can almost feel the clocks slowing down as you step into the 600-year-old temple. A *kora* path circles the inner sanctum whose murals include images of dark-skinned Thangtong Gyalpo and his son Dewa Tsangpo. The doorway of the upper-floor *goenkhang* (protector chapel) is framed by rows of skulls and a hornbill beak and is dedicated to the local protector Maza Damsum (it's often off limits though).

Chhuzom, better known as 'the Confluence', is at the juncture of the Paro Chhu and the Wang Chhu (*chhu* means 'river', *zom* means 'to join'). Because Bhutanese tradition regards such a joining of rivers as inauspicious, there are three **chortens** here to ward away the evil spells of the area. Each chorten is in a different style – Bhutanese, Tibetan and Nepali.

Chhuzom is also a major road junction, with roads leading southwest to Haa (79km), south to the border town of Phuentsholing (121km) and northeast to Thimphu (31km). Roadside stalls here offer a good selection of local products, from apples and chillies to dried cheese and jars of *ezey* (chilli, Sichuan pepper, garlic and ginger).

Chhuzom to Thimphu

31KM / 1 HOUR

As the road ascends the Wang Chhu valley, the hillsides become surprisingly barren. Three kilometres past Chhuzom a rough side road leads to Geynikha (Geynizampa) and the start of the Dagala Thousand Lakes trek.

About 6km from Chhuzom is the **Sisichhum Heritage Home** (Map p82; ☑17902417; www.sisichhumheritage.com; Nu 150), a charming centuries-old farmhouse set up to receive visitors. You can see the wooden grain storage bins, old leather bags and a fine altar room, or ask your guide to book a lunch here. The 19th Druk Desi was born here in 1788 and the family has lived here for 11 generations.

After turn-offs to Kharibje and the former hydro plant at Khasadrapchhu, the valley widens at the small village of **Namseling**. Above the road are numerous apple orchards. Much of the fruit is exported, particularly to Bangladesh. In the autumn people sell apples and mushrooms from makeshift stalls at the side of the road.

OFF THE BEATEN TRACK

HIKING BEYOND TAKTSHANG

Instead of returning from Taktshang Goemba to the car park the way you came, you can make an adventurous two- to three-hour hike to higher chapels before descending steeply to the car park on a different path. Budget three-quarters of a day to visit these chapels and Taktshang. You can also see all these chapels as you descend from the Bumdrak trek (p185).

Just to the side of the Machig-phu Lhakhang (p96) a trail climbs a couple of steep metal ladders and then branches right for 15 minutes to the Ugyen Tshemo Lhakhang, or left up to the **Zangto Pelri Lhakhang** (Map p94), named after Guru Rinpoche's heavenly paradise and perched on a crag with great views from the back down to the Tiger's Nest. Roll the dice inside the chapel to improve your chances of conceiving a child.

The **Ugyen Tshemo Lhakhang** (Map p94) has an unusual set of four exterior protectors (one is just above the door entrance) and an interior 3D mandala that you can climb via a series of stairways. Just inside the main entrance are statues of the local protectors Singye Samdrup and red-faced Doley. The only sounds here are the murmurs of wind and water and the creaking of the prayer wheels. If you're keen, you can continue up for 15 minutes to the **Yoselgang** (Yosel Choekorling; Map p94) before returning.

From the back of the Ugyen Tshemo Lhakhang, just beside a hot stone bath used by local monks, descend steeply down the valley for 15 minutes to a right turn-off, past a chorten to the cliff-face **Shama Lhakhang** (Map p94), just next to Taktshang, but inaccessible from there. Look out for *jaru* (mountain goats) here.

Back at the junction where you turned right to the Shama Lhakhang, trails drop steeply for 45 minutes down to the three water prayer wheels just before the car park. Figure on six hours for the entire hike up to Taktshang and down via this alternative route. The descent is best not attempted in wet weather.

The Thimphu expressway drops towards the valley floor and enters **Thimphu** from the south. A second, older road travels via Babesa and Simtokha, enabling you to visit the Simtokha Dzong or bypass Thimphu completely on the way to Punakha.

🛏 Sleeping

Bhutan Spirit Sanctuary   SPA HOTEL $$$
(Map p82;   ☑08-272224;   www.bhutanspirit sanctuary.com; Neyphu Valley; r from US$1584; 🛜🎅) From the moment you select your bath products at check-in, it's clear that this five-star rural resort is all about the spa experience. Rates include a consultation with a Bhutanese traditional doctor and unlimited Bhutanese herbal treatments, featuring *numtsug* hot-oil compressions and *kunye* oil massages. The 24 luxury rooms, with either a balcony or a terrace, all offer bucolic views.

It's a very relaxing place, though you need to devote enough time in the spa to make the price tag worthwhile. Staff can also arrange yoga classes, guided meditations and hikes to nearby Neyphu Monastery, and there's even a spring-fed heated pool and ceramics studio. The resort is between Paro and Chhuzom in a side valley near the turn-off at Shaba. Rates include food, spa treatments and activities. Introductory discounts of at least 40% are on offer.

HAA DZONGKHAG

The isolated Haa valley lies southwest of the Paro valley, hidden behind the high ridge of the Cheli La. Despite easy access to Tibet, the remote valley has always been off the major trade routes and continues to be on the fringes of tourism. The valley is the ancestral home of the Dorji family, to which the Queen Grandmother, Ashi Kesang Wangchuck, belongs. It is the only one of Bhutan's main north–south valleys that is too high for growing rice.

Less than 10% of visitors to Bhutan make it to Haa, but it's a picturesque valley that's ideal for mountain biking and hiking, and there is real scope here for getting off the beaten track. There are at least a dozen monasteries in the valley. Perhaps the best way to visit is to spend a day cycling to the nearby sights.

There are two roads into Haa. One climbs from Paro, crossing the 3810m Cheli La,

DAY TRIP TO THE CHELI LA

If you don't have time to visit the Haa valley, the 35km drive up to the 3810m Cheli La makes an interesting day excursion from Paro and is an excellent jumping-off point for day walks, including to Kila Nunnery or the ridgeline north of the pass. On a clear day there are views of Jhomolhari from the pass, as well as down to the Haa valley.

Bhutan's highest motorable road. The other diverges from the Thimphu–Phuentsholing road at Chhuzom and travels south, high above the Wang Chhu, before swinging into the Haa valley.

You'll need your own transport to explore the Haa valley, though there are taxis in Haa town. Minibuses connect Haa town with Thimphu and Paro.

It's also possible to hike from the Haa to Paro valleys on the overnight Saga La trek (p187).

Paro to Haa Via Cheli La

68KM / 2½ HOURS

From the turn-off at Bondey, south of Paro, it's 2½ hours to Haa over the Cheli La on the highest drivable road in Bhutan. As you start to climb, 5km from Bondey, a side road branches left for 2km to Dzongdrakha Goemba (p100), where a string of chapels perches dramatically on a cliff ledge. The site is one of several where Guru Rinpoche suppressed local demons and is worth the detour.

As you drive up to the pass, past the turn-off to Gorina Goenba, look for the roadside *drub chhu* (holy spring) with rock paintings of Guru Rinpoche and his two consorts. About 20km from the turn-off to Dzongdrakha Goemba is an easily missed turnout (and possible picnic spot) where a dirt road leads to the remote **Kila Nunnery** (off Paro-Haa Hwy), a 9th-century meditation site that is reputedly the oldest nunnery in Bhutan. Around 50 nuns pursue higher Buddhist studies in a series of cliffside buildings. The best way to reach the historic site is via the scenic hour-long downhill hike from the Cheli La.

When you finally crest the Cheli La, join the Bhutanese in a hearty cry of *'lha-gey lu!'* ('May the gods be victorious!'). A sign says

THANGTONG GYALPO: THE IRON-BRIDGE BUILDER

Thangtong Gyalpo (1385–1464) was a wonder-working Tibetan saint and engineer who is believed to have been the first to use heavy iron chains in the construction of suspension bridges. He built 108 bridges throughout Tibet and Bhutan, earning himself the nickname Lama Chakzampa (Iron Bridge Lama).

He first came to Bhutan in 1433 in search of iron ore, and built eight bridges in places as far removed as Paro and Trashigang. You can see some of the original iron links at Paro's National Museum. Sadly, the only surviving Thangtong Gyalpo bridge, at Duksum on the road to Trashi Yangtse in eastern Bhutan, was washed away in 2004.

This Himalayan Renaissance man didn't rest on his engineering laurels. Among his other achievements was the composition of many folk songs, still sung today by people as they thresh wheat or pound mud for house construction, and the invention of Tibetan *lhamo* opera. He was also an important *terton* (discoverer of *terma*) of the Nyingma lineage, attaining the title Drubthob (Great Magician), and in Paro he built the marvellous chorten-shaped Dumtse Lhakhang. His descendants still maintain the nearby Tamchhog Lhakhang.

Statues of Thangtong Gyalpo depict him as a stocky shirtless figure with a beard, curly hair and topknot, holding a link of chains.

the elevation of the pass is 3998m; it's really more like 3810m, but this still makes it the highest paved road in Bhutan. If it's raining in Paro, it's likely to be snowing here, even as late as the end of April.

During the clear skies of October and November you can take hiking trails up the mountain ridge for 1½ hours to spectacular mountain views towards Jhomolhari. Trekking routes continue along the ridgeline for two days to the Saga La.

As you make the steep switchbacking 26km descent from the pass to Haa, you'll soon see the golden roof of the Haa Dzong.

Sights

Dzongdrakha Goemba　　BUDDHIST TEMPLE
(Map p86) The visually splendid but little-visited cliffside retreat of Dzongdrakha Goemba is one of several local sites where Guru Rinpoche did battle with local demons and it's well worth a short detour off the Paro–Cheli La road. A string of four chapels and a large chorten perch on the cliff face. Budget an hour to visit the site.

The first building you come to is the private manor house of **Jongsarbu Lhakhang**, founded in the 18th century by the meditation master Gyanpo Dorje, and fronted by a lovely *suntala* (mandarin) tree. The main statue is of Sakyamuni in his princely Jowo form, flanked by the local protector Tsethsho Chen and a *tshomen* (mermaid spirit).

The **Tsheringma Lhakhang** is dedicated to the goddess of longevity, one of five sisters, depicted riding a snow lion. Climb the

narrow log ladder behind the chapel to the cave-like Droley Lhakhang, which houses local protectors Doley and Shari Tsen alongside a couple of papier-mâché heads that were once used during local festivals. Local parents who have just given birth to a son are supposed to come to this chapel to receive an auspicious name for their child.

Nearby is the **Guru Lhakhang**, where the caretaker will tell you stories about local spirits, flying saints and magical spells, and point out sacred dagger marks in a nearby stone. Behind the main statue is a hidden relic chorten that allegedly has to be enclosed to prevent it flying away; the caretaker can open a little door at the back to reveal part of the chorten. The final building is the small Lhamey Lhakhang.

Haa

08 / POP 2600 / ELEV 2700M

The town of Haa sprawls along the Haa Chhu and forms two distinct areas. Much of the southern town is occupied by the Indian Military Training Team (IMTRAT) camp (complete with a golf course) and a Bhutanese army training camp. Near here is the small dzong and Lhakhang Kharpo monastery. The central bazaar, a couple of kilometres to the north, has the main shops and local restaurants.

The three hills to the south of town are named after the Rigsum Goempo, the trinity of Chenresig, Chana Dorje and Jampelyang;

they also represent the valley's three protector deities.

The scenic road to the north continues past the Talung valley and Chhundu Lhakhang, and ends at Damthang, 15km from Haa town. It would be prudent to turn around before you reach the gates of the large Bhutanese army installation.

⊙ Sights

Lhakhang Kharpo   BUDDHIST MONASTERY

(☑caretaker 77265955; ⊙9am-noon & 1-5pm) Haa's 100-strong monk body is housed not in Haa's dzong (fort monastery) but in the recently renovated Lhakhang Kharpo (White Chapel) complex, just south of the dzong. The atmospheric central chapel has statues of the Tse-la-nam Sum trinity (central Tsepame, Namgyelma and Drolma) and of local protector App Chhundu, and there are also a couple of bamboo-framed mannequins once used during *cham* (ritual dances).

Lhakhang Nagpo   BUDDHIST TEMPLE

A 10-minute walk or short drive behind the Lhakhang Kharpo is the grey-walled Lhakhang Nagpo (Black Chapel), one of the oldest temples in the Haa valley. It is said that when searching out auspicious locations for two new temples the Tibetan king Songtsen Gampo released one black pigeon and one white pigeon; the black pigeon landed here, the white one at Lhakhang Kharpo.

The inner shrine has an ancient statue of Jowo Sakyamuni wearing a lovely crown and jewels. The outer chapel houses a shrine to red-faced protector Drakdu Tsen beside a trapdoor that leads to the underground pool of a *tshomen*. In the grounds outside look for the clay representations of the valley's three sacred mountains.

Shelkar Drak   BUDDHIST TEMPLE

(⊙dawn-dusk) A short excursion up the valley behind the Lhakhang Kharpo is Shelkar Drak (Crystal Cliff), a tiny, charming retreat centre perched on the limestone cliff face. Take the unpaved side road past the Lhakhang Nagpo, by Domcho village, and continue up the hillside towards the recently renovated ridgetop Takchu Goemba (8km). From the small private lhakhang and white chorten of Lungsukha village, a 15-minute walk along a new road leads to the small chapel attended by one lama and one monk.

Inside the main lhakhang look for statues of local protector Dorji Zebar and the site's founder, Choling Jigme Tenzin. Those with a spiritual bent can follow the monks on a 10-minute scramble to the meditation cave of the 11th-century female tantric practitioner Machig Labdrom. It's possible to hike downhill from the lhakhang via the prayer-flag-draped Chimey Dingkha pool to rejoin the main dirt road further down.

Haa Dzong   BUDDHIST MONASTERY

(⊙9am-5pm) Haa's small dzong, known formally as Wangchuck Lo Dzong, is one of Bhutan's newest, built in 1915 to replace a smaller structure. It is inside the Indian army compound (an impressive two-legged *khonying* chorten marks the camp entrance) and so houses several Indian army offices and a rations shop. There's not a great deal to see.

⚡ Activities

Haa Valley View Trail   HIKING

This easy 30-minute walk offers fine views over the Haa valley. The route starts from a bend on the road to the Cheli La and follows the hillside north to a picnic spot, before ending in charming Wangtsa village above Risum Resort, where you can meet your car.

To extend the walk you can continue hiking north for 45 minutes on logging trails over a small pass and down through forest to meet the Juneydrak Hermitage trail.

Meri Phuensum Nature Trail   HIKING

Hardcore hikers up for a long day hike should budget time for this trail, which links Haa's three sacred hills from south to north, starting in Baysa village and finishing in Haa town. You'll need a full day, so bring water and a packed lunch.

Haa Golf Course   GOLF

(green fees weekday/weekend Nu 500/1000; ⊙9am-5pm Thu-Tue) Fans of golfing exotica might want to play nine holes on this course run by the Indian army. The clubhouse/pro shop in front of Haa Dzong offers caddies (Nu 150) and club rental (Nu 250).

🎊 Festivals & Events

The annual **Haa tsechu** is held in the lower courtyard of the Lhakhang Kharpo on the eighth and ninth days of the eighth lunar month (September/October), before a large *thangka* is displayed on the 10th day in the nearby Haa Dzong. The festival takes place at the same time as the Thimphu tsechu, so it's easy to combine both.

WESTERN BHUTAN HAA

The first week of July brings the tourist-oriented **Haa Summer Festival** to the central festival ground in the main town. Events include traditional song and dance, archery displays and plenty of Haa-style dumplings.

🛏 Sleeping

There is one good tourist lodge just outside Haa town, a modern hotel in the town centre, and a couple of farmhouse-style designer lodges in the upper valley.

Over a dozen homestays dot the Haa valley, all in traditional Bhutanese farmhouses and most signposted from the road. For details visit www.communitytourism.bt/haa.

Risum Resort   HOTEL $
(☑08-375350;   risumresort@yahoo.com; Wangtsa; s/d Nu 2400/2640, ste s/d Nu 3600/4200; 🛜) Haa's most popular accommodation is available here in 14 huge, cosy pine-clad duplex suites. The rooms are well heated (important in Haa) but the bathrooms aren't, and can be freezing outside summer. The older block is simpler but also comfortable. The hotel is east of the road linking the northern and southern sections of Haa town.

Ugyen Homestay   HOMESTAY $
(☑17111116;   www.haavalleyhomestay.com; s/d from Nu 935/1100) Owners Ugyen and Bedar warmly welcome guests into their traditional home in Domcho village, just 100m south of the Lhakhang Kharpo; it's a good option if you want a look at family and village life. The mattresses are thick, the toilets are Western, and a hot-stone bath is available (Nu 750 to 1000 per person).

⭐Lechuna
Heritage Lodge   BOUTIQUE HOTEL $$
(☑17347984;   www.lechunaheritagelodge.com; Hatey/Lechu; s/d Nu 4550/5950; 🛜) This beautiful lodge occupies a wonderfully restored farmhouse of just seven rooms sharing five showers and four separate toilets. It's much more comfortable than it sounds because the renovation has been so careful to blend modern comforts with traditional style.

There's a cosy bar downstairs, filter coffee and tea in the common room, a garden courtyard and a communal dining table attached to the separate kitchen. The lodge is 10km north of Haa town in the picturesque village of Lechu, down a 500m pathway, and is a great base for local walks.

Soednam Zingkha
Heritage Farmhouse   HERITAGE HOTEL $$
(☑17170507; www.szingkha.com; Hatey; s/d Nu 4200/4800; 🛜) In the lovely village of Hatey, this 150-year-old manor house has 17 simple but comfortable guest rooms, a small garden, a traditional altar room and a restaurant. Chunky wooden floorboards and traditional wall murals add some charm. Pop across the stream to see the working traditional watermill.

To get here take a right just after the Yak Chhu Zam bridge.

🍴 Eating

Most visitors will eat dinner in their lodge but there is at least one good restaurant in town for lunch. Be sure to try the local *hoentey* dumplings.

Pelden Restaurant   MULTICUISINE $
(☑17687230; mains Nu 130-200, set meals Nu 440; ⊙lunch & dinner) This clean and bright option is the best place to eat in Haa and the only restaurant to regularly receive tourist groups. The *bukhari* is a nice touch in cold weather.

Around the Haa Valley

There are several interesting Buddhist sites and traditional villages scattered around the Haa valley and some fine hiking and trekking on the valley rims, so it's worth budgeting a full day here, especially if you like getting off the beaten track.

⊙ Sights

Juneydrak Hermitage   BUDDHIST SITE
About 1km north of Haa, just before the main bridge, a paved road branches east 1km to Katsho village, from where you can take a lovely 40-minute hike to Juneydrak hermitage (also known as Juneydrag). The cliffside retreat contains a footprint of Machig Labdrom (1055–1132), the female Tibetan tantric practitioner who perfected the chöd ritual, whereby one visualises one's own dismemberment in an act of 'ego annihilation'.

From Katsho village a trail follows the stream past the **Chorten Dangrim** *mani* (prayer) wall for 15 minutes to a two-legged archway chorten (known as a *khonying*). Cross the stream and ascend the trail through a charming rhododendron forest. At a red sign in Dzongkha script, take the trail to the left and climb up to a chorten that marks the entry to the hermitage. You'll need to find the caretaker in his nearby residence in order to gain access to the lhakhang. You climb up steep steps with the aid of a rope before squeezing between a stone entryway guarded by the faded rock painting of a green-faced demon.

From just below the hermitage, a rough trail scrambles up the hillside and curves round the exposed bluff. Don't attempt this if you are afraid of heights or if it's raining; simply return from Juneydrak the way you came. The trail curves around to **Katsho Goemba**, which has fine views down over Katsho village, where your vehicle can meet you. It's worth popping into the temple to see the fine antique *thangkas*. Bring a thermos of tea to drink in the monks' treehouse just outside the goemba.

It's also possible to hike to Juneydrak from Wangtsa village, joining the main trail near the Chorten Dangrim. Figure on 2½ hours from Wangtsa to Katsho village.

Yangthong Goemba   BUDDHIST MONASTERY
(Yangtho Goemba) This monastery in the upper Haa valley is worth visiting, especially if you are heading on the Saga La trek. The charming upper chapels feature murals depicting Zangto Pelri (the paradise of Guru Rinpoche), while *tshomen* are said to inhabit the pool just outside the monastery.

About 5km from Haa, a side road branches right over the river past Yangthong village into the Talung valley. Just before you enter the valley you pass the App Chhundu Pang **ceremonial ground**, which until recently was used for annual yak sacrifices to the local deity App Chhundu.

At the Makha Zampa bridge a side road branches right 1.5km to Yangthong Goemba, up on the ridge. The bridge is one starting point for the two-day Saga La trek (p187), which continues up the Talung valley, crossing the Saga La to reach Drukgyel Dzong the next day.

To get off the beaten track from Yangthong, head across the Makha Zampa bridge for 2km to Talung village and **Tsenkha Goemba** (signposted Changkha), or take the branch road left just before Talung village to curve around for 2km to **Jamtey Goemba**, a historic *lobra* (monastic school).

Chhundu Lhakhang   BUDDHIST TEMPLE
(Gechuka Lhakhang; ☎caretaker 77222258) Eleven kilometres north of Haa is this recently rebuilt local temple, one of several shrines dedicated to the valley's protective deity. Blue-faced App Chhundu and his red-faced cousin Jowya glower from either side of the main altar.

Troublesome Chhundu was banished to Haa by the Zhabdrung after an altercation with Gyenyen, Thimphu's protector. He also had a quarrel with Jichu Drakye of Paro, resulting in Paro's guardian stealing all of Haa's water – and that's why there is no rice grown in Haa. Ceremonies dedicated to Chhundu are still carried out in nearby Yangthang, highlighting how deep Bhutan's roots are with its pre-Buddhist animist past.

The chapel is a five-minute walk down a concrete path below Chenpa (Lechuna) village, 3km north of Yangthang, just past the Yakchu Zam bridge. Call the caretaker if the temple is closed.

Haa to Chhuzom

79KM / 3 HOURS

The road from Haa to Chhuzom allows an alternative to returning to Paro over the Cheli La, and offers a shortcut if you're heading directly from Haa to Thimphu or Phuentsholing. There are several little-visited sights to explore en route.

From Haa town it's 6km to Karnag (also called Kana), 2km further to Jyenkana and then 19km to Nago, with its picturesque water-powered prayer wheels. A few kilometres further is **Bietakha**, its small dzong in precarious ruin after the 2009 and 2011 earthquakes. At Km 40, shortly before the village of Gyeshina, look for the photogenic **Gurugang Goemba** just below the road.

Now high above the river, the road swings into a huge side valley, passing below the village of Susana en route to Mendegang. Around 3km before Susana a new bypass branches right to descend in wide loops to Chapcha on the Thimphu–Phuentsholing road, offering a new shortcut route if you're headed down to India. The road has been built but the bridge across the Wang Chhu remains unfinished, so check with your agency to see if the route is open.

After the basic restaurants of Tshongkha the road descends in and out of side valleys, passing above **Dobji Dzong**, which served as Bhutan's central prison from 1976 and is now a small religious school for 22 monks (the old prison cells are now classrooms!). Milarepa is said to have spent the night here and a paved path leads for five minutes to his holy spring.

The road continues its descent into the Wang Chhu valley to join the main road at Chhuzom. Just before Chhuzom is the new site of Bhutan's main petrol storage facility. From Chhuzom it's 24km (45 minutes) to Paro or 31km (one hour) to Thimphu.

PUNAKHA DZONGKHAG

The Punakha district covers a wide range of terrain, from the heights of the Dochu La to the subtropical riverside monastery of Punakha itself. Some groups visit Punakha on a long day trip from Thimphu but you are much better spending at least one night here.

There's plenty of scope to get off the tour bus in Punakha. The river rafting and mountain biking here are some of Bhutan's best, and several treks begin or end at nearby Gasa Dzong.

It's noticeably warmer in Punakha than in Thimphu or Paro, making it a good early-season destination.

Thimphu to Punakha

76KM / 2¾ HOURS

The drive from Thimphu to Punakha, along the National Hwy and over the Dochu La, leads from the cool heights of Thimphu to the balmy, lush landscapes of the Punakha valley.

Thimphu to Dochu La

23KM / 45 MINUTES

From Thimphu, the route to the east leaves the road to Paro and loops back over itself to become the east–west National Hwy. About a kilometre past the turn-off there is a good view of Simtokha Dzong. The route climbs through apple orchards and forests of blue pine to the village of **Hongtsho** (2890m), where an immigration checkpoint controls all access to eastern Bhutan. Your guide will present your restricted-area travel permit, giving you the chance to use the public toilets or haggle for walnuts, apples and dried cheese with the roadside vendors.

Just south of here, at the end of a bumpy track, is the **Ser Bhum Brewery** (Map p74; ☑ 17116991; www.serbhumbrewery.com; brewery tour Nu 350 per person; ◷ 9am-5pm Mon-Sat), where visitors can tour the tiny craft brewery and enjoy a Bhutan Glory amber ale or Dragon Stout in the small taproom or on the sunny deck.

The road climbs to the **Dochu La** (3140m), marked by an impressive collection of 108 chortens. On a clear day (only really likely between October and February), the pass offers a panoramic view of the Bhutan Himalaya – some groups make special predawn trips up here to catch the views. The collection of chortens was built in 2005 as atonement for the loss of life caused by the flushing out of Assamese militants in southern Bhutan.

Most groups stop for a hot drink at the **Druk Wangyal Cafe** (☑ 17533317; breakfast/lunch Nu 450/590; ◷ 7am-7pm), which offers espresso coffee and a warming *bukhari*. With prior arrangement staff can organise a breakfast buffet for a dawn visit to see the peaks. A panorama painting nearby labels the peaks on the horizon (with different spellings and elevations from those we have used). Gangkhar Puensum (7570m, according to Chinese surveys) is the highest peak that is completely inside Bhutan and is generally considered the world's highest unclimbed peak.

The adjacent **Druk Wangyal Lhakhang** (adult Nu 100; ◷ 7am-6pm) is well worth a visit to view its unique cartoon-style modern murals on the upper floor. Images include the fourth king battling Indian rebels in the jungle, a Druk Air plane and monks using a laptop or reading the *Kuensel* newspaper, alongside a modern history of the kingdom. It's a quintessentially Bhutanese fusion of the 21st and 15th centuries. The giant central butter lamp was offered by the Queen Mother on the occasion of the fourth king's 60th birthday and features images of the first three kings. On 13 December the royal-supported **Dochu La Wangyal Festival** holds *cham* dances against the dramatic background of peaks.

The area near the pass is believed to be inhabited by numerous spirits, including a cannibal demoness. Lama Drukpa Kunley, the 'Divine Madman', built Chimi Lhakhang in the Punakha valley to subdue these spirits and demons.

The hill above the chortens is covered in a lovely rhododendron forest, part of the 47-sq-km **Royal Botanical Park** (Map p82; foreigner Nu 100; ◷ 9am-5pm). There are wonderful blooms between April and June, when you can view 38 of Bhutan's 46 species of rhododendron or spot some of the 220 species of birds. A series of modern bunker-style grottoes are dotted about the

HIKES AROUND THE DOCHU LA

There are several good hiking trails around the Dochu La. Come in spring and you'll be surrounded by lovely rhododendron blooms.

If you just want to escape the car for an hour or two, a couple of downhill trails lead east from the pass. The **Dochu La Nature Trail** (1.3km, 45 minutes) starts near the chortens and ends on the road at the Public Works Department. The **Lumitsawa Ancient Trail** (4km, two hours) continues downhill from here to again meet the road at Lumitsawa. Both trails are sections of the original route between Thimphu and Punakha.

It's possible to walk the entire ancient trail by continuing from Lumitsawa to Thalogang (3km, 90 minutes), then to Thinleygang (4km, two hours), and on to Chimi Lhakhang (6.2km, 2½ hours) via Chandana Lhakhang.

Lungchutse Goemba

Perhaps the best walk in the area is the 7km, three-hour round trip from Dochu La to the hilltop Lungchutse Goemba, which offers excellent views of the Bhutan Himalaya. From a signed trailhead just below the 108 chortens of the Dochu La the trail climbs gradually through rhododendron forest, with some steep sections, for 80 minutes, before branching left to the goemba (right to Trashigang). The 18th-century goemba was founded by the treasure hunter Drakda Doji and is dedicated to local protector Tashi Barwa. Combine the hike with dawn views from Dochu La for a great half-day excursion.

Trashigang Goemba

Trashigang Goemba (3200m) is easily combined with Lungchutse Goemba for a fine half-day walk. It's an easy 60-minute downhill stroll from Lungchutse; follow the electricity pylons on a trail that passes a meditation spot. Built in 1782 by the 12th Je Khenpo, Trashigang is an important meditation centre for around 60 monks and a few anims (Buddhist nuns). In the main chapel ask to see the small chorten that encases a tiny statue made from a tooth of the 22nd Je Khenpo. The various chapels hold statues of 10 or more Je Khenpos who have meditated here over the years. The inner sanctum of the ground-floor *goenkhang* (chapel dedicated to protective deities) is said to conceal the preserved flesh of the goddess Palden Lhamo.

Watch out for the very aggressive dogs here; carry a stick and make sure they are tied up before approaching. From Trashigang it's a steep one-hour direct descent to Hongtsho on the Thimphu–Punakha road, where your vehicle can pick you up. Avoid the far longer dirt road. For the perfect end to a hike finish with a cold amber ale from the nearby Ser Bhum Brewery (p104).

lower forest, with murals depicting varies Buddhist deities.

On the hill just below the pass is the **Dochula Eco Resort** (☑17671418; dochularetreat@gmail.com; s/d from Nu 2160/2760), where some groups overnight in October and November, when views are clearest. The binocular telescope here was a gift from the Kyoto University Alpine Club after members made the first ascent of Masang Gang (7165m) in 1985. Using the telescope, it's also possible to see Gasa Dzong, a small white speck almost 50km to the north.

Dochu La to Metshina

42KM / 1½ HOURS

The vegetation changes dramatically at the pass from oak, maple and blue pine to a moist mountain forest of rhododendron, alder, cypress, hemlock and fir. There is also a large growth of daphne, a bush whose bark is harvested for making traditional paper. The large white chorten a few kilometres below the pass was built because of the high incidence of accidents on this stretch of road.

About 11km below the pass at Lamperi is the entrance to the Royal Botanical Park, and just below the park is **Menchuna Restaurant** (Map p82; ☑17124506; set lunch Nu 480; ☺6am-7.30pm), a popular lunch stop. The proprietor has a business producing embroidered *thangkas,* including some *thondrols* for tsechus, and there's a large gift shop here.

It's a long, winding descent past Lumitsawa to **Thinleygang**, during which the air gets warmer and the vegetation becomes increasingly tropical with the appearance of

Around Punakha

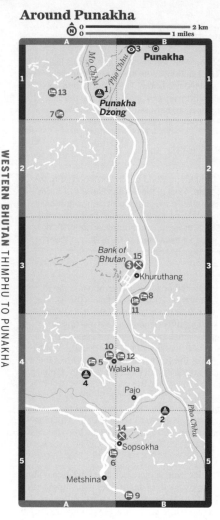

N
0 — 2 km
0 — 1 miles

WESTERN BHUTAN THIMPHU TO PUNAKHA

Around Punakha

◎ **Top Sights**
  1 Punakha Dzong A1

◎ **Sights**
  2 Chimi Lhakhang B5
  3 Nyi Ma Zam Suspension Bridge..........B1
  4 Sangchen Dorji Lhendrub
     Choling Nunnery A4

⌂ **Sleeping**
  5 Dhensa...A4
  6 Drubchhu Resort.............................A5
  7 Dumra Farm Resort..........................A1
  8 Four Boutique Hotel..........................B3
  9 Hotel Lobesa....................................B5
  10 Hotel Zangto Pelri A4
  11 Khuru Resort B3
  12 Meri Puensum Resort......................B4
  13 Zhingkharn Resort A1

✗ **Eating**
  14 Chimi Lhakhang Cafe B5
  15 Phuenzhi Diner B3
     Rinchenling Cafe ....(see 14)

next-door farmhouse, whose family have cared for the shrine for 15 generations.

From Thinleygang monasteries soon start to appear on the surrounding hills; notably Drolay Goemba. The winding road passes a chorten that flows with *drub chhu* (holy water), said to have its source in a lake far above.

The road continues its descent, looping in and out of a side valley, to the road junction and petrol station at **Metshina**, where the road to Punakha branches left off the National Hwy. If you are continuing the 8km to Wangdue Phodrang, stay on the main road.

Metshina to Punakha

11KM / 30 MINUTES

The road to Punakha makes a switchback down past a collection of restaurants, houses and resorts at **Sopsokha**, from where you can visit the Chimi Lhakhang. The stone chorten right in the middle of the road just outside the Drubchhu Resort is proof, if you needed it, that spiritual matters take priority over road safety in Bhutan.

Beyond Sopsokha, the road crosses the small Teop Rong Chhu and swings round a ridge into the valley of the Punak Tsang Chhu. The quiet tarmac road on the far side of the valley offers several mountain-biking options.

cacti, oranges and bamboo. Every November (on the first day of the 10th month), the Je Khenpo and *dratshang* (central monk body) overnight in the lhakhang below the road on their two-day journey from their summer residence in Thimphu to their winter residence in Punakha.

In the valley below Thinleygang is the charming **Chandana Lhakhang** (meaning 'Where the Arrow Landed'): it is believed that when Drukpa Kunley fired an arrow from Tibet to determine his future path, it landed here, causing the saint to detour to Bhutan. The log-cut wooden ladder that the arrow struck is still preserved in the

After another 2km or so, by the village of Wolakha, a road peels off to the left and climbs to the Meri Phuensom and Zangto Pelri hotels and several interesting monasteries. Just above the hotels is the **Sangchen Dorji Lhendrub Choling Nunnery** (foreigner Nu 100; ⏰6am-5pm), which was financed by the fourth king's father-in-law to serve as a Buddhist college for 120 resident anims. The attached ridgetop Nepali-style chorten is visible from as far away as the Dochu La–Metshina road. The nuns generate some income by selling attractive woven bracelets (Nu 50 to 100).

High up on the hillside, the main side road continues relentlessly uphill for 15km to **Talo Goemba**. The main chapel is worth seeing, as are the views, but the monastery really comes alive in March during its tsechu, held at the same time as the Gasa tsechu.

Aorund 5km before Talo, a 1km side road branches left to **Drolay (Dalay) Goemba**, a *shedra* that is home to 150 monks, including a young *trulku* (reincarnated lama). The monastery was founded by the ninth Je Khenpo and is commonly known as Nalanda, after the famous Indian Buddhist university in Patna. Local protectors here include Pelzom Gyelmo, the female consort of Drukpa Kunley.

Back down at the junction just above the nunnery, it's worth branching right to reach the lovely village of Nobgang, or **Norbugang** (Jewel Hill), with its stunning Himalayan panoramas. The **Laptshaka Lhakhang** here is a charming monastery school. This region is home to the families of the fourth king's four wives, who maintain a residence in the upper village.

Back on the main Metshina–Punakha road, just under 2km from the junction and 6.5km from Metshina, is the dusty new town of Khuruthang. All of Punakha's shops were relocated to this charmless concrete grid in 1999. There are several restaurants, local hotels and a Saturday vegetable market.

To the side of the road is the new **Khuruthang Goemba**, built by the Royal Grandmother and consecrated in 2005. The main Zangto Pelri Lhakhang here has excellent ceiling mandalas. The murals on the far wall depict the Zhabdrung and the various dzongs he established. The large Nepali-style chorten here was built by the Indian guru Nagi Rinchen and is said to enshrine a speaking image of Guru Rinpoche known as Guru Sungzheme.

It's a further 3km to a middle school and small park with an excellent **viewpoint** over the Punakha Dzong. A kilometre further on is a parking area and the footbridge leading across the Mo Chhu to the gorgeous dzong.

Chimi Lhakhang

On a hillock in the centre of the valley below Metshina is the yellow-roofed Chimi Lhakhang, built in 1499 by the cousin of Lama Drukpa Kunley in his honour after the lama subdued the demoness of the nearby Dochu La with his 'magic thunderbolt of wisdom'.

Most visitors take the 20-minute trail across fields from the road at Sopsokha to the temple (take a hat and be prepared for wind, dust or mud). The trail leads downhill across rice fields to Yoaka (which means 'in the drain') and on to the tiny settlement of Pangna (meaning 'field'). The path then crosses an orchard before making a short climb to the Chimi Lhakhang. Otherwise it's a 10-minute walk from the car park.

Budget some time for shopping after your visit. The collection of shops by the car park are mostly run by graduates of Thimphu's National Institute for Zorig Chusum, and they sell a good range of woodcarvings, *thangkas* and weavings. Perhaps inevitably there is also an eyebrow-raising choice of souvenir wooden phalluses, from discreet purse-sized options to ostentatious tiger-striped varieties.

The well-run **Chimi Lhakhang Cafeteria** (☑17679501; set meals Nu 480; ⏰lunch & dinner) in Sopsokha is a great place for lunch or tea, with tables lined up against the window overlooking Yoaka and Pangna villages. Close by, the modern **Rinchenling Cafe** (☑17611433; mains Nu 120-200, set meals Nu 480; ⏰9am-5pm; 🐾) is another good option for lunch.

◉ Sights

Chimi Lhakhang   BUDDHIST TEMPLE
(Pangna village; ⏰8am-5pm) The famous Chimi Lhakhang is dedicated to Lama Drukpa Kunley, the 15th-century Tibetan magician, saint and exponent of 'crazy wisdom'. It is for him that every house and shop in the nearby village is decorated with protective phallus symbols. The temple is one of Bhutan's most popular sights, for both foreign tourists and Bhutanese pilgrims.

THE DIVINE MADMAN

Lama Drukpa Kunley (1455–1529) is one of Bhutan's favourite saints and a fine example of the Tibetan tradition of 'crazy wisdom'. He was born in Tibet, trained at Ralung Monastery, and was a contemporary and disciple of Pema Lingpa. He travelled throughout Bhutan and Tibet as a *neljorpa* (yogi) using songs, humour and outrageous behaviour to dramatise his teachings to the common people, earning him the nickname 'Divine Madman'. He felt that the stiffness of the clergy and social conventions were keeping people from learning the true teachings of Buddha.

His outrageous, often obscene, actions and sexual antics were a deliberate method of provoking people to discard their preconceptions and conventions. Tango Goemba is apparently the proud owner of a *thangka* that Kunley urinated on! He is also credited with having created Bhutan's strange animal, the takin, by sticking the head of a goat onto the body of a cow.

His sexual exploits are legendary, and the flying phalluses that you see painted on houses and hanging from rooftops symbolise the lama. Kunley's numerous sexual conquests often included even the wives of his hosts and sponsors and he fathered several children. On one occasion when he received a blessing thread to hang around his neck, he wound it around his penis instead, saying he hoped it would bring him luck with the ladies.

The eyebrow-raising penises you see painted around the villages work on many levels – to protect fertility, as a symbol of Drukpa Kunley's unorthodox crazy wisdom or, as one noticeboard says, to 'symbolise the discomfort that society expresses when facing the truth'.

For a biography and collection of songs, poems and bar-room anecdotes concerning Drukpa Kunley, try Keith Dowman's book *The Divine Madman: The Sublime Life and Songs of Drukpa Kunley*.

Inside the lhakhang you'll see the central statue of the lama and his dog Sachi, as well as statues of the Zhabdrung, Sakyamuni and a 1001-armed Chenresig. To the right is a statue of Kunley's cousin, the founder of the temple. Make a small offering and you'll be rewarded with a blessing from the lama's wooden and bone phalluses and his iron archery set. Childless women come to receive a *wang* (blessing or empowerment) from the saint, while mothers-to-be select their future baby's name from a collection of bamboo slips, leaving with either Chimi or Kunley as one of their child's two names. Other women carry a large wooden phallus around the building perimeter in order to boost their chances of conception.

Murals to the right of the chapel depict events from Kunley's colourful life; the section above the window portray the three demons of the Dochu La. Local protectors depicted in the chapel include Dochula Dom, the demon who Drukpa Kunley subdued at a spot just outside the lhakhang, marked by a black, white and red chorten. The nearby bodhi tree is believed to have been brought from Bodhgaya in India (where Buddha achieved enlightenment under a bodhi tree).

Punakha & Khuruthang

📍 02 / POP 6300 / ELEV 1250M

Punakha sits in a sultry, fertile and beautiful valley at the junction of the Mo Chhu (Mother River) and Pho Chhu (Father River). Commanding the river junction is the gorgeous Punakha Dzong, perhaps Bhutan's most impressive building.

The low altitude of the Punakha valley allows two rice crops a year, and oranges and bananas are in abundance. Birders should keep their eyes peeled for the critically endangered white-bellied heron, which can be spotted in Punakha. Of the global population of only 200, around 34 are in Bhutan.

Most people spend one night in Punakha, before heading on to Phobjikha, but you'll need two nights here if visiting remote Gasa.

All of Punakha's shops and facilities are in the unappealing new town of Khuruthang, 4km to the south.

Punakha served as Bhutan's capital for over 300 years. Here, the first king was crowned in 1907 and the third king convened the Bhutan National Assembly for the first time in 1952. In 2008 the fifth and current king underwent a secret ceremony in the Punakha Dzong, receiving the royal raven crown, before proceeding to a formal coronation in Thimphu.

◉ Sights

Budget a couple of hours to visit Punakha Dzong and then if you have time make the short drive to the Upper Punakha valley or the sights above Wolakha.

★**Punakha Dzong**   BUDDHIST MONASTERY
(student/adult Nu 150/300; ⊘ 9am-5pm Jun–mid-Nov, 11am-1pm & 3-5pm mid-Nov–May) Punakha Dzong is arguably the most beautiful dzong in the country, especially in spring when the lilac-coloured jacaranda trees bring a lush sensuality to the dzong's characteristically towering whitewashed walls. This dzong was the second to be built in Bhutan and it served as the capital and seat of government until the mid-1950s. All of Bhutan's kings have been crowned here. The dzong is still the winter residence of the *dratshang*.

Guru Rinpoche foretold the construction of Punakha Dzong, predicting that a person named Namgyal would arrive at a hill that looked like an elephant. When the Zhabdrung visited Punakha he chose the tip of the trunk of the sleeping elephant at the confluence of the Mo Chhu and Pho Chhu as the place to build a dzong.

A smaller building called Dzong Chung (Small Dzong) housed a statue of the Buddha here as early as 1326. Construction on the current dzong began in 1637 and was completed the following year, when the building was christened Pungthang Dechen Phodrang (Palace of Great Happiness). Later embellishments included the construction of a chapel to commemorate the victory over the Tibetans in 1639. The arms captured during the battle are preserved in the dzong. The Zhabdrung established a monk body here with 600 monks from Cheri Goemba.

Punakha Dzong is 180m long and 72m wide and the *utse* is six storeys high. The gold dome on the *utse* was built in 1676 by local ruler Gyaltsen Tenzin Rabgye. Many of the dzong's features were added between 1744 and 1763 during the reign of the 13th *desi*, Sherab Wangchuk. One item he donated was the *chenmo* (great) *thondrol,* that depicts the Zhabdrung and is exhibited to the public once a year during the tsechu festival. A brass roof for the dzong was a gift of the seventh Dalai Lama, Kelzang Gyatso.

Frequent fires (the latest in 1986) have damaged the dzong, as did the severe 1897 earthquake. In 1994 a glacial lake burst on the Pho Chhu, causing damage to the dzong that has since been repaired.

Access to the dzong is across the Bazam bridge, which was rebuilt in 2008 after the original 17th-century bridge was washed away in floods in 1958. The room above the bridge entrance has displays on the renovations and on Bhutanese cantilevered bridge architecture.

In addition to its strategic position at the river confluence, the dzong has several other features to protect it against invasion. The steep wooden entry stairs are designed to be pulled up, and there is a heavy wooden door that is still closed at night.

The dzong is unusual in that it has three docheys instead of the usual two. The first (northern) courtyard is for administrative functions and houses a huge white Victory Chorten and bodhi tree. In the far left corner is a collection of stones and a shrine to the Tsochen, queen of the *naga* (snake spirits), whose image is to the side.

The second courtyard houses the monastic quarters and is separated from the first by the *utse*. In this courtyard there are two halls, one of which was used when Ugyen Wangchuck, later the first king, was presented with the Order of Knight Commander of the Indian empire by John Claude White in 1905.

In the southernmost courtyard is the temple where the remains of the *terton,* Pema Lingpa, and Zhabdrung Ngawang Namgyal are preserved. The Zhabdrung died in Punakha Dzong, and his body is still preserved in the **Machey Lhakhang** (*machey* means 'sacred embalmed body'), which was rebuilt in 1995. The casket is sealed and may not be opened. Other than two guardian lamas, only the king and Je Khenpo may enter this room. Both come to take blessings before they take up their offices.

At the south end is the *kunrey,* or **'hundred-pillar' assembly hall** (which actually has only 54 pillars). The exceptional murals, which were commissioned by the second Druk Desi, depict the life of Buddha. The massive gold statues of the Buddha, Guru Rinpoche and the Zhabdrung date back to the mid-18th century, and there are some fine gold panels on the pillars. The elaborately painted gold, red and black carved woods here add to the artistic lightness of touch, despite the massive scale of the dzong. This is the only chapel that is reliably open to visitors.

Bhutan's most treasured possession is the **Rangjung ('Self-Created') Kharsapani**, an image of Chenresig that is kept in the Tse Lhakhang in the *utse* of the Punakha Dzong. It was brought to Bhutan from Tibet by the Zhabdrung and features heavily in Punakha's famous *dromchoe* festival. It is closed to the public.

After you exit the dzong from the north you can visit the *dzong chung* and get a blessing from a wish-fulfilling statue of Sakyamuni. The building marks the site of the original dzong. North of the dzong is a cremation ground, marked by a large chorten, and to the east is a royal palace.

Punakha Suspension Bridge
BRIDGE

At 160m long, this bridge northeast of Punakha Dzong is one of Bhutan's longest suspension bridges and it's fun to cross the swaying, prayer-flag-draped walkway over the Po Chhu. The drive here from the dzong takes you past a royal palace and a cremation ground.

🏃 Activities

Mountain Biking

Punakha's **mountain-bike trails** offer some of the best chances to break out the fat tyres, though you'll have to bring your own bike as there's nowhere to rent locally.

A 27km-loop valley ride from Khuruthang crosses the bridge there and heads up the east side of the valley along a feeder road to Samdingkha (14km), crosses the suspension bridge and then returns along a trail to Punakha Dzong (7.5km), finally coasting back to Khuruthang along the paved road.

A longer 40km loop starts from the new town of Bajo, just north of Wangdue Phodrang, and heads up the east side of the valley to Jangsabu (14km), before climbing a technical trail (some carrying required) to Olodama and Tschochagsa (9.5km). From here you can detour to Limgbukha or coast down 10km to the Aumthekha junction, across the river from Chimi Lhakhang, and then pedal back to Bajo and Wangdi. You'll need a guide for this.

Rafting

Punakha is the site of Bhutan's most popular rafting trips. Rafting on the **Pho Chhu** starts with a hike up the side of the river through forest and farmland to the put-in at Samdingkha. The rafting includes a couple of Class III rapids and ends in a bang with the 'Wrathful Buddha' rapid next to Punakha Dzong.

The Khamsum Yuelley Namgyal Chorten bridge, about 6km above Punakha Dzong, is the put-in spot for relaxing rafting and kayaking float trips down the Mo Chhu. This is a very easy scenic float, suitable for all abilities and a good introduction for novices. Agents charge small groups around US$75 per person for the two-hour trip. As the river meanders through the wide valley, you float past one of the queen's winter residences, the king's weekend retreat and some beautiful farmland before taking out just above Punakha Dzong.

Most trips are operated by Druk Rafting Services (p284), through which your agency will make a booking.

🛏 Sleeping

Many people visit Punakha as a day trip from Thimphu but there are several excellent hotels throughout the valley. Most are located in Wolakha, a 10-minute drive from Punakha, or in Sopsokha or Lobesa, 20 to 25 minutes' drive from Punakha. There are several more hotels near Wangdue Phodrang that can be useful as a launch pad for travel further east.

★ Meri Puensum Resort
HOTEL $$

(☑02-584237; www.mpr.bt; Wolakha; r Nu 2640, deluxe r Nu 2880-3240; 🖭) This very popular hotel is 6km south of Punakha, 1.2km up the side road to Talo Goemba. Comfortable, cosy rooms are in cottages that hug the terraced hillside. The garden gazebo (the only place with wi-fi) is a great place to have breakfast or sip on a relaxing beer after a long day's touring.

Some of the back-facing standard cottage rooms can be a bit poky; deluxe rooms are better and have a balcony. None have a wi-fi connection.

Zhingkham Resort
RESORT $$

(☑02-584722; www.bhutanhotels.com.bt; Punakha village; s/d Nu 4800/5400; 🖭) The Bhutan Tourism Corporation Limited (BTCL) opened this large resort in 2016, located above Punakha, with unbeatable views overlooking Punakha Dzong (between us, cottage one has the best views). The 40 rooms have balconies that maximise the picture-perfect vistas. The upper-floor bar and terrace is a tempting place for an afternoon beer or espresso and the restaurant is excellent. *Zhingkham* means 'paradise'.

Four Boutique Hotel HOTEL **$$**
(☏17122217; www.fourboutique.com.bt; s/d Nu 4500/4800; ✴🛜) With its glitzy decor and tiny velvet-clad karaoke bar, the oddly named Four Boutique would feel more at home in downtown Thimphu than on the rural riverbank opposite Khuruthang town. Twelve of the 20 rooms have valley views and the airy restaurant terrace overlooks the river, but there's still a tangible lack of space. Look up at the ceiling mandala as you check in.

Khuru Resort HOTEL **$$**
(☏02-584429; khurupunakha@gmail.com; r Nu 4800; ✴🛜) One of a couple of new three-star hotels across the river from Khuruthang town, this sprawling property caters mostly to large Asian groups. Plus points include the spacious rooms with private balconies overlooking the river, the pleasant modern restaurant and the cheery staff.

Hotel Zangto Pelri HOTEL **$$**
(☏02-584125; zpelri@gmail.com; Wolakha; r Nu 3000-3480; 🛜) Named after the paradise of Guru Rinpoche, this hotel has 45 rooms in a central building and surrounding cottages. Most rooms have fine balcony views, but don't worry if yours falls short as the pleasant grounds and sunny terraces offer plenty of space. The spacious deluxe rooms offer the best value but the smaller cottages have more privacy.

★Dumra Farm Resort BOUTIQUE HOTEL **$$$**
(☏17117488; www.dhumrafarm.com; Logodama; r/ste Nu 6000/7800; 🛜) With just six rooms, this rural retreat has an exclusive, relaxed vibe that offers the prefect antidote to a day's sightseeing. The main farmhouse has been converted into a wonderful top-floor suite and there are five other spacious rooms and a restaurant-lounge building, all set in lovely, peaceful gardens. Ask to have your breakfast served on the terrace overlooking Punakha Dzong.

The owners grow their own herbs and vegetables in the surrounding 3-hectare farm and the gardens are dotted with lemon, guava and avocado trees. Snap it up if your agency will include it in your tariff. The resort is 2km uphill from Punakha and the last section is up a rough road.

★Dhensa LUXURY HOTEL **$$$**
(☏02-584434; www.dhensa.com; Wolakha; d with breakfast US$462; ✴🛜) Dhensa is an excellent top-end choice, mixing clean, modern style with elements of traditional Bhutanese architecture. The calming rooms come with a balcony and all the facilities you could ask for, including a peaceful library and a yoga room. Indulge yourself in the cosy fire-heated wooden hot tub (US$20 per person) or opt for a sensual four-handed spa massage.

🛏 Upper Punakha

The Upper Punakha valley is home to Punakha's most exclusive luxury resorts. In addition to the three existing ones, the Taj group is building a new resort on the east bank of the Mo Chhu.

Amankora LUXURY HOTEL **$$$**
(Map p82; ☏02-584222; www.amanresorts.com; full-board s/d US$1740/1860; ✴🛜) This place is the most intimate of Aman's uberluxury resorts, with only eight rooms in three buildings. The main farmhouse (now the restaurant and reading room) was the former residence of the Queen Mother and features a traditional altar room. The spa reception is in the old farmhouse kitchen, and the outdoor dining area is surrounded by rice fields and orchards.

★Uma Punakha LUXURY HOTEL **$$$**
(Map p82; ☏02-584688; www.comohotels.com/en/umapunakha; d incl breakfast & dinner US$744-1920; 🛜) Upstream along the Mo Chhu valley, 11km (20 minutes) from Punakha, in a lush rural location just north of the Khamsum Yuelley Namgyal Chorten, the Uma is an intimate boutique retreat of just 10 luxury rooms and one- and two-room villas. There are sublime views from the floor-to-ceiling windows over rice fields towards the river and chorten and the service is top-notch.

Ask staff about the hour-long walk from the hotel to the Chorten Nyingpo Dratshang.

Six Senses Punakha LUXURY HOTEL **$$$**
(Map p82; ☏Thimphu 02-350773; www.sixsenses.com; s/d incl breakfast & dinner US$1840/2000; ✴🛜🏊) Six Senses Punakha opened in 2019 on a hillside near the Uma Punakha. There are some striking design elements, including the lounge cantilevered over a pool in an imitation of a traditional Bhutanese bridge. The 16 suites (in four buildings) come with private wrap-around balconies, *bukhari*s, excellent mattresses and luxurious bathtubs, plus James Bond–style pop-up TVs.

Most exclusive are the private villas, housing up to three couples and featuring a private plunge pool. The spa complex has a heated pool and yoga classes, with a 'Guest

PUNAKHA DROMCHOE & TSECHU

The **Punakha Dromchoe** (or *drubchen*) festival in February/March is a dramatic celebration of a 17th-century battle scene. In 1639 a Tibetan army invaded Bhutan to seize its most precious relic, the Rangjung Kharsapani, a self-created image of Chenresig. The Zhabdrung concocted an elaborate ceremony in which he pretended to throw the relic into the Mo Chhu, after which the disappointed Tibetans withdrew.

On the final day of the festival (the ninth day of the first Bhutanese lunar month), a group of 136 people dressed as *pazaps* (warriors) perform a dance in the main courtyard, then shout and whistle as they descend the front stairs of the Punakha Dzong. Next, a procession of monks led by the Je Khenpo proceeds to the river to the accompaniment of cymbals, drums and trumpets. At the river the Je Khenpo throws a handful of oranges symbolising the Rangjung Kharsapani into the river. This is both a recreation of the Zhabdrung's trick and also an offering to the *naga* (lu in Dzongkha), the spirits in the river. The singing and cheering warriors carry their generals back into the dzong as firecrackers explode around them, then mask dances celebrate the Zhabdrung's construction of the dzong.

The three-day **Punakha tsechu**, with *cham* dances in honour of Guru Rinpoche, follows the next day, and on its final day a *thondrol*, which features an image of the Zhabdrung, is displayed. It's one of Bhutan's most spectacular festivals.

Experience Maker' on hand to help with local excursions. The resort is 12km north of Punakha.

🛏 Lobesa

The collection of resorts at the road junction of Lobesa/Metshina are a 30-minute drive from Punakha Dzong but are useful for visiting Chimi Lhakhang or for getting an early start to Phobjikha or Thimphu.

★ Hotel Lobesa   HOTEL $
(☑17612672; p_druk@hotmail.com; Lobesa; r Nu 2160; 🛜) Excellent value for money and super-attentive staff make Hotel Lobesa a popular choice, with 14 spacious rooms and a bright and airy restaurant decorated in stone and wood. Spacious new block rooms have wrap-around balconies offering great views over the spiky spring blooms of a red cotton *(Bombax ceiba)* tree.

Drubchhu Resort   RESORT $$
(☑02-376237; www.drubchhu.com; Sopsokha; s/d from Nu 4320/4800; 🛜) This comfortable three-star resort is built on the site of a former granary, next to a holy spring *(drub chhu)* and with bucolic views over the surrounding rice fields. There are 27 spacious rooms, two of which are wheelchair accessible, and the restaurant grows its own organic greens, bakes its own bread and boasts a lovely terrace.

The resort's roadside cafe should soon double as a bar, stocking beers from Bhutan's burgeoning craft-beer scene.

✗ Eating

★ Phuenzhi Diner   BHUTANESE $$
(☑02-584145; Dungkhar Lam, Khuruthang; set lunch Nu 450; ⊙lunch & dinner) The 'Four Friends' is easily the best eating place in Khuruthang and is well known to guides. The food is delicious and reliable (as is the welcoming air-con) and the decor is cosy. If you don't eat here, your guide will probably book lunch at Sopsokha or at one of the tourist hotels.

ℹ Information

Bank of Bhutan (Khuruthang; ⊙9am-1pm & 2-4pm Mon-Fri, 9am-noon Sat) Changes cash and has an ATM.

Upper Punakha Valley

The road up the west side of the Mo Chhu valley passes several country manors owned by Bhutan's nobility, including the Phuntsho Pelri palace, a royal summer residence. The fourth king's father-in-law built many of the lhakhangs in the valley and owns several hotels, including the Damchen Resort.

On the left side of the road, 4.5km from Punakha, look out for the **Dho Jhaga Lama Lhakhang**, whose pretty gardens surround a huge boulder split miraculously in two. It is said that the Indian guru-magician Nagi Rinchen sent lightning and hail to split the rock to liberate his mother, who was trapped inside. The chapel houses a statue of the guru (to the far right), who is recognisable by the scriptures in his topknot. Rinchen meditated in a cave across the river (behind Sona Gasa, the former palace of the third king), and so is depicted here as a long-haired *drubthob* (hermit-magician). To the far left is a statue of the local female protector, Chobdra, riding a snow lion.

In Yambesa, 7km north of Punakha, is the huge **Khamsum Yuelley Namgyal Chorten**, perched high on a hill on the opposite bank of the river. The 30m-tall chorten (also known as the Nyzergang Lhakhang) took eight years to build and was consecrated in 1999. The chorten is dedicated to the fifth king and serves to protect the country, so it is stuffed with a veritable 'who's who' of Bhutanese demonography; some with raven or elephant heads, others riding snow lions, and most covered in flames. Look in the ground-floor stairwell for one protector riding a brown, hairy *migoi* (yeti). Go to the roof for fine views of the valley.

A bridge provides access to a sweaty 45-minute hike uphill to the chorten. Head off in the morning to avoid the subtropical heat. Ask your guide to point out the wonderfully fragrant *tingye* (flower pepper) plants that grow along the trail beside fields of chillies and beans.

Beyond the chorten, the road leads up past Kabesa village and the Uma Punakha resort to Tashithang and then continues all the way to the Gasa Dzong and the ending point of the Laya trek (p195).

WANGDUE PHODRANG DZONGKHAG

The scenic *dzongkhag* (administrative district) of Wangdue Phodrang is centred on the once magnificent dzong of that name and stretches all the way to the Pele La and Phobjikha valley. South of Wangdi, as it is known locally, towards the southern region of Tsirang, is the giant Indian-financed Punatsangchhu hydroelectric project.

Punakha to Wangdue Phodrang

21KM / 30 MINUTES

It's a half-hour drive from Punakha to Wangdue Phodrang. Follow the road back to Metshina and drive 1.5km to Lobesa, following the Punak Tsang Chhu. Soon the ruins of Wangdue Phodrang Dzong come into view,

along the end of a ridge above the river, just as you pass a series of eight chortens.

The modern bridge over the Punak Tsang Chhu below Wangdue Phodrang replaced the original 17th-century wooden cantilevered structure that was washed away by floods in 1968.

Wangdue Phodrang

🎵 02 / POP 9000 / ELEV 1240M

Legend says that the Zhabdrung Ngawang Namgyal met a small boy named Wangdi playing in the sand on the banks of the Punak Tsang Chhu and was moved to name his new dzong Wangdi – later Wangdue – Phodrang (Wangdi's Palace). The town is still known colloquially as Wangdi.

The ramshackle old town that once lined the road to the dzong has been relocated 3km north to the concrete grid of Bajo new town.

⊙ Sights

Wangdue Phodrang Dzong BUDDHIST MONASTERY

(⊘ closed) The Wangdue Phodrang Dzong (Wangdi) was founded by the Zhabdrung in 1638 atop a high ridge between the Punak Tsang Chhu and the Dang Chhu, clearly chosen for its commanding view of the valleys below. Wangdi is important in the history of Bhutan because in the early days it was the site of the country's second capital. Sadly, the dzong caught fire on 24 June 2012 and was virtually destroyed save for the lower walls. The mammoth task of rebuilding it is expected to continue until 2021.

Legend relates that as people searched for a site for the dzong, four ravens were seen flying away in four directions. This was considered an auspicious sign, representing the spreading of religion to the four points of the compass. After Trongsa Dzong was established in 1644, the *penlop* of Wangdue Phodrang became the third-most powerful ruler, after Paro and Trongsa. The dzong's strategic position gave the *penlop* control of the routes to Trongsa, Punakha, Dagana and Thimphu.

Radak Neykhang BUDDHIST TEMPLE

By the tall cypress trees of the Wangdue district court is this timeless 17th-century temple dedicated to an ancient warrior king. The anteroom has a collection of helmets, knives and shields. Inside are five versions of the local protector deity Radrap, one of whom (Terdak Chenpo) protects the local police, army and royal bodyguards. To the far right is a statue of a local *tshomen*. Roll the chapel dice and the resident monk will read your future.

✷✷ Festivals & Events

The highlight of September/October's **Wangdue Tsechu** is its third and final day when the Guru Tshengye Thondrol, depicting the eight manifestations of Guru Rinpoche, is unfurled in the dzong at dawn. Until the dzong is rebuilt the tsechu will be held in the nearby Tencholing Army Training Centre.

🛏 Sleeping

There's not a great deal of demand for hotel rooms in Wangdi, especially while the dzong is closed for rebuilding. A few people use hotels here as a base to visit Punakha (30 minutes' drive away) or break the drive to Gangte, Trongsa or Bumthang. At tsechu time in autumn, however, the town is packed and rooms are at a premium.

★**Wangdue Ecolodge**　　　LODGE **$$**
(☑17111783, 17353004; www.bhutanecolodge. com; Damina village; s/d Nu 3000/4200; 🕾) 🗲 Sustainable initiatives lie at the heart of this stylish rural retreat of four cottages, from the biogas used for cooking dinner to the organic food in the farmhouse-style restaurant. The eight spacious rooms have wrap-around balconies or a terrace, and are decorated with the owner's fine photographs. The quiet, rural location is a 3km winding drive from Wangdue, above Ngashigaykha in the Rubesa district.

The food is excellent, making it a potential stop for lunch (Nu 600) if you have time to make the detour here.

Kichu Resort　　　HOTEL **$$**
(Map p82; ☑17122659; www.kichuresorts.com; s/d Nu 3360/3720; 🕾) In Chhuzomsa, 9km east of Wangdue Phodrang (Wangdi), this tranquil and relaxing resort of 24 tiled rooms enjoys a lovely landscaped garden overlooking the rushing Dang Chhu. Ask for a riverside balcony room and pack insect repellent for the sand flies (from April to June). After a day's touring you can relax with a cold beer in the riverside bar.

The nephew of the owners is a rinpoche (the title given to a revered lama), so the restaurant serves only vegetarian food.

Punatsangchhu Cottages　　　HOTEL **$$**
(☑02-481942; www.punacottages.bt; s/d Nu 2500/3300, deluxe s/d Nu 3000/3500; 🕾) Also

known as Puna Cottages, this is a good choice, located below the road and next to the Punak Tsang Chhu, 5km from Wangdue Phodrang (Wangdi). Modern rooms vary in size, with some in the main block and others in cottages, while the better deluxe rooms have balconies overlooking the river.

The restaurant is good and the lawn is perfect for a cold beer on a warm afternoon. Deluxe rooms are worth the extra cost. Couples should ask for one of the two riverside cottages.

🍴 Eating

Kinten Hotel　　　DHUTANESE **$**
(☑02-481121; hotelkinten@gmail.com; Bajo; mains Nu 90-150; ⊘lunch & dinner) This local restaurant in Bajo new town serves tasty Bhutanese dishes given some advance warning, making it the best option in the Wangdue Phodrang area. Indian tourists sometimes make use of the 10 rooms here (Nu 1500 to 2500).

❶ Information

Bank of Bhutan (Gase Lam, Bajo; ⊘10.15am-1pm & 2-4.30pm Mon-Fri, 10.15am-noon Sat) Changes cash and has an ATM.
Bhutan National Bank (Gase Lam, Bajo; ⊘9am-3pm Mon-Fri, 9-11am Sat Nov-Apr, 9am-1pm & 2-4pm Mon-Fri, 9-11am Sat May-Oct) Changes cash; next door to the Bank of Bhutan.

Wangdue Phodrang to Pele La

61KM / 1¾ HOURS
The beautiful drive from Wangdue Phodrang east towards the Pele La offers access to central Bhutan and the Phobjikha valley, known for its winter population of black-necked cranes. The pass itself takes you over the rugged Black Mountains, the physical boundary between western and central Bhutan.

Leaving Wangdue Phodrang (Wangdi), the road traverses bare hillsides high above the Dang Chhu. The large riverside building below the road is a jail for prisoners serving life imprisonment.

At the point where the road reaches the new bridge at **Chhuzomsa**, at the confluence of the Pe Chhu and the Dang Chhu, 9km from Wangdi, it is level with the river (Chhuzomsa means 'meeting of two rivers'). Below the small village is the idyllic riverside Kichu Resort.

At **Tikke Zampa** (Wachey Zam), 4km past Chhuzomsa, the road crosses to the

GASA DZONG

The road up the Mo Chhu valley leads north out of Punakha and enters **Gasa Dzong-khag** and **Jigme Dorji National Park**. Until recent times you had to trek this route, but a dirt road now means you can visit Gasa comfortably as a long (148km) day trip from Punakha. The rewards are magical views, wonderful birdwatching and Gasa Dzong. Several treks end at nearby Koina, including the popular Laya trek (p195).

Just 19km from Khamsum Chorten is the village of **Tashithang**. Here the road hugs the Mo Chhu and is wrapped in verdant forests that sing with birdlife. Just stop the car and wander quietly along the roadside to spot shimmering sunbirds, pure blue flycatchers and crested laughing thrushes.

It's another rough 47km drive through forests, terraces and villages, ascending the hillside to the west on switchbacks, before reaching Gasa's **Trashi Thongmoen Dzong**, a remote 17th-century fortress built to protect against Tibetan invasions and surrounded by a dramatic mountain setting. The dzong's *utse* (central tower) sits atop the meditation cave of Drubthob Terkhungpa, the 13th-century Tibetan master who subdued the local protector Gomo and banished him to the pond just behind the dzong.

The dzong's eclectic treasures remain on display: the skeleton of the sheep that followed the Zhabdrung on his journey from Tibet's Ralung Monastery is in the Chanzoe Lhakhang, and the remarkably preserved saddles of the Zhabdrung and his companions are in the *kunrey* (assembly hall).

The wonderful three-day tsechu in March includes the performance of a 300-year-old folk song called *goenzhey*, believed to have been composed by Zhabdrung Ngawang Namgyal when he first came to Bhutan via Laya in 1616.

The famous **Gasa tsachhu** (hot springs) are far below the dzong on the riverbank and reachable by road. The communal baths are primarily a destination for sick or elderly locals who shoehorn themselves into the pools seeking relief from joint pain and other ailments.

A couple of homestays around Gasa offer simple accommodation if you need to overnight.

One good place to stay en route between Punakha and Gasa is the **Thori Homestay** (☏17411991; www.bhutanthoritours.com; per person Nu 1000, meals Nu 200-300) in Damji village, which offers mattresses on the floor and a shared indoor bathroom. If you are lucky you might get served traditional *jengey* – pounded rice, flavoured with *zhimtse* (amaranth seeds). Ask to see the sacred shoes of the Zhabdrung, on display in the altar room.

south bank of the Dang Chhu and begins a gradual climb to the Pele La, passing the newly renovated Wachey Lhakhang. A further 10km on you'll see a superbly located private lhakhang atop a hillock to the left. The road gets steeper as it climbs the valley. In many places the road has been blasted out of the cliff and hangs high above the deep forests of the valley below.

The road detours frequently into side valleys, passing the village of **Kalekha**, the end of the Shasi La hike from the Phobjikha valley. From here it's 12km to the village of Nobding (2640m), where the tourist-friendly **Hotel Kuenphen** (☏17630091; Nobding; set lunch Nu 440; ☺lunch & dinner by appointment; ☎) offers a useful lunch stop just above the village.

A further 7km on is Dungdung Nyelsa, where the old (disused) road to the Pele La branches off. The **Khandu Hotel** (☏17650480; mains Nu 170-190; ☺lunch) here is

a decent back-up food option, and even has a VIP room rather optimistically reserved for visiting ministers and the royal family.

The main road climbs steeply up the hillside for 5km, to the turn-off to Gangte in the Phobjikha valley. In spring the upper hillsides here are covered with red, white and pink rhododendron blossoms.

From the Gangte turn-off, it's a final 3km through forests to the top of the **Pele La** (3420m), which is marked by a new chorten and an array of prayer flags but no real mountain views. On a clear day (admittedly rare in these parts) there is a view of Jhomolhari (7314m), Jichu Drakye (6989m) and Kang Bum (6526m) from a viewpoint 500m down the old road from the pass.

The Pele La marks the western border of the Jigme Singye Wangchuck (formerly the Black Mountains) National Park and is the gateway to central Bhutan.

Wangdue Phodrang

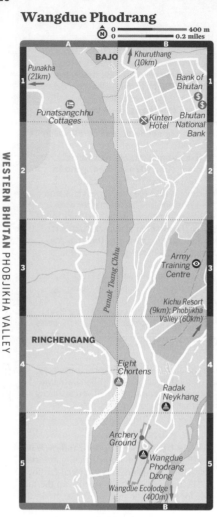

Phobjikha Valley

⏺ 02 / ELEV 2900M

Phobjikha is a bowl-shaped glacial valley on the western slopes of the Black Mountains, bordering the Jigme Singye Wangchuck National Park. Because of the large flock of black-necked cranes that winters here, it is one of the most important wildlife preserves in the country. In addition to the cranes there are muntjacs (barking deer), wild boars, sambars, serows, Himalayan black bears, leopards and red foxes in the surrounding hills. Some people refer to

this entire region as Gangte (or Gangtey), after the goemba that sits on a ridge above the valley.

The valley is snowbound during the height of winter and many of the valley's 4700 inhabitants, including the monks, shift to winter residences in Wangdue Phodrang during December and January, just as the cranes move in to take their place. Even outside winter, temperatures can plummet in the afternoon, so be sure to pack some warm clothes.

The road to Phobjikha diverges from the main road 3km before the Pele La. It's then a 1.5km drive through forests to the new Janchab Chorten marking the Lowa La (3360m), where you may encounter a few stray yaks. After the pass the trees disappear and the scenery switches dramatically to low-lying dwarf bamboo as the road descends past stalls selling yak tails and local weavings to Gangte village and its goemba.

From the goemba junction, the road switchbacks down past the turn-off to the Amankora resort to the valley floor, past extensive russet-coloured fields of potatoes. Gangte potatoes are the region's primary cash crop and one of Bhutan's important exports to India. The local residents are known as Gangteps and speak a dialect called Henke.

◉ Sights

★ **Gangte Goemba**   BUDDHIST MONASTERY
Gangte Goemba enjoys prime real estate, on a forested hill overlooking the green expanse of the entire Phobjikha valley. The extensive complex consists of the central goemba, monks' quarters, a small guesthouse and outlying meditation centres. Much of the interior and exterior woodwork of the 450-year-old goemba was replaced between 2001 and 2008 due to a beetle-larvae infestation.

During a visit to the Phobjikha valley, the 15th-century treasure-finder Pema Lingpa prophesied that a goemba named *gang-teng* (hilltop) would be built on this site and that his teachings would spread from here. Pema Thinley, the grandson and reincarnation of Pema Lingpa, built a Nyingma temple here in 1613, and the larger goemba was built by the second reincarnation, Tenzing Legpey Dhendup. The current Gangte *trulku*, Kunzang Pema Namgyal, is the ninth reincarnation of the 'body' of Pema Lingpa.

The *tshokhang* (prayer hall) is built in the Tibetan style with 18 great pillars around an unusual three-storey inner atrium, and is one of the largest in Bhutan. The inner sanctum houses the funeral chorten of founder Tenzing Legpey Dhendup. The monastery's three-day tsechu (September/October) ends with the hanging of a large *thondrol* on the final day; at other times the huge *thangka* is stored in a steel box in the inner sanctum.

Upstairs is the Machey Lhakhang, holding the central funeral chorten of the sixth Gangte *trulku*. Monks will tell you that when the lama died, his body shrank down to the size of a baby and then the size of a peanut.

★ **Black-Necked Crane Information Centre** WILDLIFE RESERVE
(☑ 17767330; www.facebook.com/cranecentre. bhutan; SAARC adult/student Nu 100/50, non-SAARC national Nu 120; ☺ 9am-5pm) Your first stop in Phobjikha should be the information centre of the Royal Society for Protection of Nature (RSPN), which has informative displays about the black-necked cranes and the valley environment. You can use the centre's powerful spotting scopes and check what you see against its pamphlet *Field Guide to Crane Behaviour*. If the weather's iffy, you can browse the library and watch a 15-minute video.

Star of the centre is Karma, an injured black-necked crane who was discovered as an eight-month-old with a broken wing and now lives in a neighbouring enclosure. It's a rare chance to see these magnificent cranes up close. Donations are accepted for a project to build a bigger enclosure.

Nyelung Drachaling BUDDHIST TEMPLE
(Nyelung Draghaling) Travellers with a sense of the magical will want to visit this unassuming chapel, one of eight residences *(ling)* built by the 14th-century Nyingma Dzogchen master and treasure-finder Longchen Rabjam (Longchenpa). Don't be put off by the plain interior: the resident monk can show you some remarkable relics and tell tales of saints and miracles worthy of Chaucer.

Ask politely and the caretaker may bless you with an old *thangka* whose back bears the handprints of Longchenpa printed in his own nose blood; a golden statue made in Longchenpa's own image; a fossilised horse's tooth; and an iron skillet made by Pema Lingpa, with his thumbprints in it. Your guide will be thrilled.

The next-door protector chapel is dedicated to Dzogchen protector Dza (Rahula), whose nine-headed body is covered in eyes and has a snake's lower half. The bowl of sacred water here comes from a nearby spring and is claimed to have the power to cure epilepsy and paralysis.

The caretaker can point you towards a 10-minute walk to the huge centuries-old cypress tree said to have sprouted from Longchenpa's upside-down walking stick. On the way back you can stop at two sacred springs at the base of the hill, where pilgrims fill up bottles of *drub chhu*. The lhakhang is accessed from a side road just above the Amankora resort.

Longchenpa founded other 'lings' at Tharpaling in Bumthang, Ogyen Chholing Palace in Tang, and Dechen Chholing Goemba in Shingkhar.

WESTERN BHUTAN PHOBJIKHA VALLEY

WATCHING THE CRANES

The marshy centre of the Phobjikha valley means it's best avoided on foot, but it's a perfect winter residence for the flock of around 450 (up from 212 about a decade ago) rare and endangered black-necked cranes (p272) that migrate from the Qinghai-Tibet Plateau to Bhutan in late autumn, typically in the last week of October. The Bhutanese have great respect for these 'heavenly birds' (known locally as *thrung thrung kam*), and songs about the cranes are popular among locals. Between mid-February and mid-March the cranes circle Gangte Goemba and fly back across the Himalaya to their summer breeding grounds in Tibet. One of the most popular folk songs of the people of Phobjikha laments the time when the cranes leave the valley.

The best times to spot cranes are between late October and late February, with the optimum chance between November and January. The ideal times for viewing are at dawn or dusk, when all the birds in the valley congregate for the night. You can watch the birds from the Black-Necked Crane Information Centre's viewing area, from a hide on the Gangte Nature Trail, or even just from the side of the road. Wear dull-coloured clothes, keep your distance and refrain from flash photography.

Phobjikha Valley

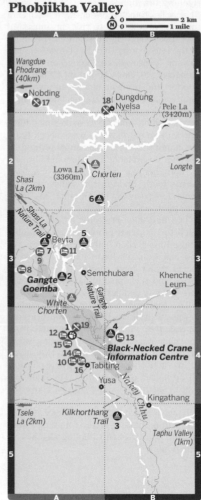

Phobjikha Valley

◉ Top Sights
1 Black-Necked Crane
Information Centre A4
2 Gangte Goemba A3

◎ Sights
3 Damcho Lhakhang B5
4 Khewang Lhakhang B4
5 Kuenzang Chholing Shedra A3
6 Kumbhu Lhakhang A2
7 Nyelung Drachaling A3

⊟ Sleeping
8 ABC Resort A3
9 Amankora Gangtey A3
10 Dewachen Hotel A4
11 Gangtey Lodge A3
12 Hotel Gakiling A4
13 Phuentsho Yangkhil Lodge B4
14 Phuntshocholing Farm House A4
15 Six Senses Phobjikha A4
16 Yue-Loki Guest House A4

⊗ Eating
17 Hotel Kuenphen A1
18 Khandu Hotel B1
19 Wangchuk Lodge A4

Kuenzang Chholing Shedra
BUDDHIST MONASTERY

(☏17674524; gangteng.shedra@gmail.com) This Nyingma-school *shedra* of 300 student monks has a unique fledgling tourist outreach program. Contact the office at least a day before to arrange either a late-afternoon meditation class (not Sundays), to attend an early-morning prayer meeting or just to chat and learn more about the life of the monks. It's a rare chance to gain a deeper understanding of this essential part of Bhutanese life.

Khewang Lhakhang
BUDDHIST TEMPLE

On the east side of the Phobjikha valley, opposite Tabiting, is the 15th-century Khewang Lhakhang, one of the oldest in the valley. It features three impressive two-storey statues of the past, present and future Buddhas *(dusum sangay)*. The lhakhang has a tsechu on the third day of the ninth month, when local men (not monks) do the dancing, celebrating an ancient victory over local demons.

Kumbhu Lhakhang
BUDDHIST TEMPLE

A dirt road leads from the Kuenzang Chholing Shedra up to the Kumbhu Lhakhang (Kumbhu means '100,000 statues'), a protector chapel and meditation-retreat centre dedicated to the ancient Bon deity Sipcy Gyalmo and featuring a statue of the Medicine Buddha on the ground floor. After rain, the road is often impassable and you'll have to make the trip without transport on a 45-minute walk.

Damcho Lhakhang
BUDDHIST TEMPLE

South of Tabiting, the unpaved road down the west side of Phobjikha valley winds past Yusa village to this small but charming chapel, said to be the oldest in the valley, dating to the 14th century.

✨ Festivals & Events

A three-day **tsechu** is held at Gangte Goemba from the eighth to 10th days of the eighth lunar month (September/October), with *cham* and the hanging of a *thondrol* on the final day.

The Royal Society for Protection of Nature (RSPN) initiated and sponsors an annual **Black-Necked Crane Festival** on 12 November. It's primarily an effort to instil conservation values into the people of Phobjikha, but tourists are welcome to watch the festivities, most of which are folk dances staged by schoolchildren.

🛏 Sleeping

Several new hotels are under construction in the valley, so expect more options to open. Note that much of the electricity infrastructure here is underground, which maintains the valley's picturesque, crane-friendly scenery, but the supply isn't all that reliable. Wi-fi is available in most hotels but it's slow.

At least 20 simple homestays are dotted around the valley (half-board costs around Nu 1500 per person). If interested, ask your tour agent in advance or browse www.communitytourism.bt.

Phuntshocholing Farm House   GUESTHOUSE $
(☑17669676; s/d old r Nu 1440/2160, s/d new block Nu 2640/3600) This traditional farmhouse belonging to the sister of the Gangte *trulku* was converted to a hotel in 1994. The simple rooms in the creaking main building are authentic but share bathrooms, so most tourists opt for the back block of six modern rooms, with private bathrooms and heaters. Both share the charming dining room.

Hotel Gakiling   HOTEL $$
(☑17651577; gakiling17@gmail.com; s/d Nu 3480/3840) This locally owned hotel is just behind the Black-Necked Crane Information Centre. The block of 16 wood-panelled rooms offers a comfortable and warm rest, and there are fine valley views from the shared balcony and the *bukhari*-warmed dining room.

Phuentsho Yangkhil Lodge   LODGE $$
(☑17129381; phuenyanglodge2017@gmail.com; s/d Nu 2880/3360) This new lodge on the east side of the Phobjikha valley has cosy pine-clad rooms and is friendly and well meaning, but the lack of wi-fi and usable electrical outlets is frustrating. The main-block rooms are brighter and more spacious than others.

ABC Resort   LODGE $$
(☑02-325012; abclodgegangtey@gmail.com; r Nu 3240; ☎) This new collection of stone-and-wood two-storey cottages is an undiscovered gem. Rooms are comfortable and stylish and the bathrooms are very spacious, with walk-in showers and a changing room, and the cosy restaurant features an open kitchen. The location is also great, surrounded by traditional farmhouses in a quiet part of the Phobjikha valley well away from other resorts.

The resort is in the northwest of the valley, near the Shashi La trailhead, at the end of the Beyta village road.

Yue-Loki Guest House   GUESTHOUSE $$
(☑17772101; s/d Nu 3360/3840) The dining room and the pine-clad rooms in this small, family-run guesthouse are heated by *bukhari*, adding to the cosy ambience. The new rooms are smaller but warmer, with big windows and nicer bathrooms.

★Dewachen Hotel   HOTEL $$$
(☑17162204; www.dewachenhotel.com; Tabiting; s/d Nu 4800/6000; ☎) This impressive stone-and-wood building is a top choice for most travellers. The rooms are large and stylish (corner rooms are best), and the good restaurant has a warming *bukhari* and floor-to-ceiling bay windows that offer great valley views. The name refers to the 'Pure Land' paradise of the Buddha Amitabha.

The hot stone bath and sauna are great for keeping the Phobjikha cold away. If that doesn't work, try a 'dragon warmer', the house cocktail of warm rum, apple juice and Bumthang honey.

★Gangtey Lodge   LUXURY HOTEL $$$
(☑02-340943; www.gangteylodge.com; s/d incl breakfast & dinner US$1044/1104; ❄☎) This 12-suite hotel combines pampered but understated luxury and charming Bhutanese decor, with chunky farmhouse-style wooden beams and an earthy palette of dark browns and creams. All rooms share excellent views over the valley, even from the in-room bathtubs! It's a fabulous mix of style, design and traditional elements, and the Bhutanese food is some of the best in the country.

For activities, the lodge offers guests mountain bikes, guided hikes and free archery, or you can simply take it easy with an in-room massage and soak up the phenomenal terrace views. There's a 50%

HIKING & BIKING THE PHOBJIKHA VALLEY

The beautiful glacial lower valley is peppered with villages, hiking trails and lhakhangs. It's great for exploring by foot or on mountain bike, so make sure you allow an extra half-day here to do this. The rapid spread of farm roads throughout the valley has limited the amount of hiking trails, but this means there's now also great scope for mountain biking.

The best and most popular short walk is the **Gangte Nature Trail** (1½ hours), which leads downhill from the *mani* (prayer) stone wall just north of Gangte Goemba to the Khewang Lhakhang. The trail descends to Semchubara village and drops down right at the chorten into the edge of the forest, before descending to a valley viewpoint, a crane-watching hide and finally the lhakhang.

The tougher three- to four-hour **Shashi La Nature Trail** leads up the valley from the track behind the Amankora Gangtey resort. This was the traditional route taken by the Gangte *trulku* (reincarnated lama) and local farmers when they left the valley for the winter. The path branches off the dirt road by an electrical transformer and climbs gently to a *mani* wall, then swings into a side valley of yak pastures to ascend gently to the white chorten and prayer flags at Shashi La. The stone throne here was once used by the Gangte *trulku* when resting at the pass. From here it's a long, steep descent through old-growth forest to Kalekha on the main Wangdue Phodrang road, where you can meet your car (by the T Wangmo Village Restaurant). This descent is great for birders, who can expect to spot pheasants along the trail, including the beautiful western tragopan.

One excellent mountain-bike route is from Gangte Goemba, along the upper dirt road above the Gangte Nature Trail and into the valley behind Khewang Lhakhang, visiting the village of Gophu before descending to the main valley at Khewang Lhakhang. It's all on dirt roads.

Another good hike or off-road bike route is the **Kilkhorthang Trail**, from the large modern nunnery at Kilkhorthang Lhakhang across the valley to the Damcho Lhakhang, south of Tabiting. A couple of wooden bridges cross the river, one below the lhakhang, another just north of the nearby village of Kingathang.

Alternatively, drive further south from Kingathang into the lovely Taphu side valley and explore on bike from there, climbing up one side of the valley and descending down the other.

---

discount in the low season (which are luckily prime crane-spotting months).

Amankora Gangtey   LUXURY HOTEL $$$
(☏02-442235; www.amanresorts.com; full-board s/d US$1740/1860; ☏) A side road branches off 1km from just below Gangte Goemba to this top-of-the-line lodge. The eight rooms are sleek and stylish and the dramatic picture windows, spa massage and excellent service won't disappoint. It's the smallest and most intimate of the Aman properties in Bhutan.

Six Senses Phobjikha   LUXURY HOTEL $$$
(☏Thimphu 02-341316; www.sixsenses.com; s/d incl breakfast & dinner US$1840/2000; ☏) This luxury eight-room and one-villa hotel opened in 2019 and has much in common with Six Senses properties in Paro, Thimphu and Bumthang, including a good spa and traditional cantilevered-bridge design. It shares an access road with the Hotel Gakiling.

✖ Eating

Wangchuk Lodge   BHUTANESE $$$
(☏77333495; www.wangchukhotel.com; lunch Nu 630, coffee Nu 90-120; ◷8am-8pm; ☏) This eight-bedroom lodge operated by Thimphu's Wangchuk Hotel has a fine dining room offering great views and espresso coffee. The disappointing rooms fail to take advantage of the views, making it a better place for lunch or coffee than for sleeping.

CHHUKHA DZONGKHAG

Unless making an overland crossing to or from India, most Western travellers tend to give Chhukha Dzongkhag a wide berth.

For those who insist on taking the land route, the district effectively consists of the winding road that drops from the mountains through the lush tropical foothills of southern Bhutan to Phuentsholing, a boom town on the international border; Jaigaon, its twin Indian settlement, is on the other side. It's a dramatic road trip and it gives you a sense of geographical continuity that flying into Paro doesn't. En route, you'll pass gigantic ferns that spill onto the road and dozens of silver-threaded waterfalls cascading off high cliffs into the mist, as you descend from the cool Himalayan heights to the sultry Indian plains.

Road improvements have made this an easier (and faster) ride in recent years but blockages can still occur in the monsoon months of May to September.

Thimphu to Phuentsholing

152KM / 4¼ HOURS

The downhill journey from Thimphu to Phuentsholing follows the first highway in Bhutan, built in 1962 by Dantak, the Indian border-roads organisation. This journey took up to 10 days before the highway.

It's still the most important road in the country, and is constantly being widened and improved, most recently in 2017 when a new bypass around Chapcha shaved an hour off the journey. A new road connection from this bypass to Haa will offer a direct route into that valley when it opens.

The first stage of the trip follows the road from Thimphu to Chhuzom (p98; 31km, 40 minutes), part of the overland route between Thimphu and Paro Airport.

Chhuzom to Chhukha

37KM / 1 HOUR

A wide two-lane expressway connects Thimphu to Watsa, 13km from Chapcha. It follows the Wang Chhu valley southward; you can see the road to Haa climbing on the opposite side of the valley. Passing beneath **Dobji Dzong**, which sits atop a promontory high above the river, the road crosses the settlement of Hebji Damchu (2020m).

The Chapcha bypass starts near here, taking a new, more direct route down the Wang Chhu valley, passing the new Tanalung Chhu and Jangtulam Chhu bridges, a couple of local restaurants and a waterfall by the side of the road. The road is susceptible to damage during the summer monsoon rains.

The new road joins the old Chapcha road at the Thegchen Zam (Strong High Bridge) across the Wang Chhu, where your guide will have to register your tour at a checkpoint.

Chhukha to Gedu

38KM / 1 HOUR

The road climbs to a lookout over the 1020MW **Tala hydroelectric project**, where water is diverted through a 22km-long tunnel. From the lookout you can see the transformers and the transmission station, and beside the distribution station is the yellow-roofed Zangto Pelri Lhakhang and the site of the old Chhukha Dzong. The project meets the entire power demand of western Bhutan, with enough surplus to export to India.

Several restaurants at Wangkha offer a good place to break for lunch. The **D2K Hotel** (☑77209043; mains Nu 170, set meals Nu 350; ☺lunch & dinner) is a friendly place with good food, while the nearby **Dam View Restaurant** (☑17643976; mains Nu 200; ☺9am-9pm) has some Indian dishes and a VIP Room with great views into the valley.

The rest of the climb is over the ridge that separates the Wang Chhu valley from the Torsa Chhu drainage. Look out for the spectacular high waterfall visible to the east across the valley. Up ahead is a short bridge over what's left of Toktokachhu Cascade (Takti Chhu), much diminished after a flood brought down a collection of huge boulders.

Atop the Lachugang ridge, at 2020m, is a **Dantak canteen** (mains Nu 55-180; ☺8am-6.30pm), selling cheap Indian fare such as *masala dosa* and sweet milky tea. It also has public toilets (the ones to the right are for 'officers only'). Then comes Asinabari (Field of Hailstones) and the small settlement of Chasilakha (*la kha* means 'grazing field'). The **Chasilakha Lhakhang** here is a new Nyingma-school temple and monastic school featuring the throne of the Gangtey *trulku* who supervises the lhakhang. Look for statues of the local deities Tsanglhep and Am Khangchima.

Another climb leads to Gedu, a highway town with a large business college, several small restaurants and a line of eight chortens in the centre. The Laptshakha Lhakhang at the south end of town has some new murals.

Beyond Gedu, a side road leads downhill to Mirching and the Tala power station, and rejoins the Phuentsholing road just north of Rinchending. It's open to traffic but is a long detour, so is only used if landslides or road-works block the main highway.

Gedu to Rinchending

41KM / 1¼ HOURS

A short distance from Gedu is **Jumja** village, at 2050m. Around a sharp bend is the huge Jumja slide that often wipes away the road during the monsoon, holding up traffic for days on end. Passing the yellow-roofed **Kuenga Chholing Lhakhang** in the village of Kamji, the road turns a corner and begins to drop like a stone all the way down to the plains.

At **Sorchen**, a road-construction camp houses workers who continually repair damage from landslides. From here, it's 7km further to the newly built **Mila Seykhar Guthog**, a replica of a famous seven-storey tower built in southern Tibet by the 11th-century Tibetan sage Milarepa; it's 500m off the road. For more on the tower see www.sml-foundation.org.

It's a further 5km to the immigration checkpoint and petrol station at Rinchending bridge, where Indian travellers will pick up an entry or exit stamp. Just above the checkpoint is the Peling Resort, a quiet alternative to staying down in dusty Phuentsholing.

Rinchending to Phuentsholing

5KM / 15 MINUTES

If you are heading into Bhutan, the roadside stalls above Rinchending are the last place to stock up on cheap subtropical fruit. As you proceed, the prices rise almost as quickly as the altitude.

Just below Rinchending is the small **Kharbandi Goemba**, built in 1967 by the late Royal Grandmother Ashi Phuentso Choedron, who had a winter residence here. The modern temple houses large statues of Sakyamuni, the Zhabdrung and Guru Rinpoche. In the lush grounds there are examples of eight different styles of Tibetan chortens.

Below Kharbandi, the road switchbacks down to Phuentsholing, offering spectacular views over the Torsa Chhu valley as it spills onto the plains.

Phuentsholing

📞 05 / POP 27,700 / ELEV 300M

The small, sweltering border town of Phuentsholing sits opposite the much larger Indian bazaar town of Jaigaon, separated by a flimsy fence and the much-photographed Bhutan Gate. Coming from elsewhere in Bhutan it feels like a congested, noisy settlement bustling with hordes of traders, security personnel and migrant workers. If you're coming from India, however, you will notice an instantaneous improvement in municipal cleanliness and organisation.

Unless it's absolutely necessary to halt for the night, you'll find little reason to linger in Phuentsholing apart from clearing immigration. The thick subcontinental air gets uncomfortably hot and humid in summer. That said, there are a couple of sights to occupy an hour or two, the backstreet bazaars are full of interest and the mix of cultures is fascinating.

Sights

Zangto Pelri Lhakhang BUDDHIST TEMPLE
(☉dawn-dusk) The modern Zangto Pelri Lhakhang, in the centre of the town's main plaza, is a replica of Guru Rinpoche's celestial abode (though we're guessing the original paradise isn't made of concrete!). There's not much to see here, but the surrounding garden is pleasant and the pilgrims spinning prayer wheels offer some fine people-watching on a balmy evening.

Palden Tashi Chholing Shedra BUDDHIST TEMPLE
(☉dawn-dusk) Consecrated in 2014, this Buddhist college in the west of town offers education to around 70 students aged between six and 25 and has some fine murals in its central *tsuglhakhang* (assembly hall). It's worth a quick visit if you aren't goemba-ed out.

Crocodile Breeding Centre ZOO
(SAARC/non-SAARC national Nu 50/100; ☉9am-5pm) Got an hour to kill in Phuentsholing? Perhaps go and snooze with the sleepy marsh muggers and gharials at the Crocodile Breeding Centre, a 10-minute walk north of the bus station. The crocs are fed every other day at around noon.

Sleeping

Centennial Hotel 2008 LOCAL HOTEL **$**
(📞05-251663; www.centennialhotel.bt; Lower Market, Phuensum Lam; r standard/deluxe Nu 1700/1925, ste Nu 2475; 🖳🛜) The Centennial fits somewhere between a local hotel and a tourist hotel and is used mainly by Indian tourists. Rooms are simple but spacious, tiled and clean, and the multicuisine

Phuentsholing

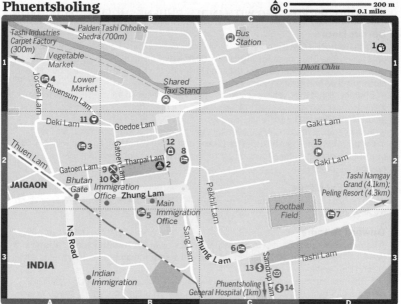

Phuentsholing

restaurant/bar is cool and welcoming. It's one of the better budget options.

★ Hotel Druk Phuentsholing   HOTEL $$
(☏ 05-252426; www.drukhotels.com; Zhung Lam; s/d Nu 4020/4620, ste Nu 10,200; ❄🛜) The salmon-pink Druk is the best tourist hotel in town, boasting comfortable, tastefully furnished rooms (but small bathrooms) spread out around a spacious, manicured lawn. It's in a secluded spot set back from the busy road, behind the customs and immigration office. The multicuisine restaurant serves delicious Indian food.

Park Hotel   BOUTIQUE HOTEL $$
(☏ 05-252986; www.parkhotelbhutan.com; Tharpai Lam; r Nu 3000-6000; ❄🛜) This well-run small hotel in the centre of town has a stylish lobby, a good restaurant and patio seating. Rooms are spacious, modern and clean, if a bit dark; aim to get a quieter back room to minimise the squeal of truck brakes.

Tashi Namgay Grand   HOTEL $$
(☏ 17161067; www.tashinamgaygrand.com; Rinchending; r Nu 4000-5500; ❄🛜❄) This large, new concrete place, 5km outside Phuentsholing, has an odd location, surrounded

❶ BORDER CROSSING WITH INDIA: PHUENTSHOLING TO JAIGAON

Border Hours

The main **Bhutan Gate** is open to vehicles from 6am to 9pm but pedestrians can cross until 10pm. The Bhutanese **Immigration Office** (⊙7am-9pm) for foreigners has fixed opening hours but officers say tourists can knock on the building any time around the clock to get an immigration stamp.

Bhutanese and their vehicles can cross the border freely so you can arrange for your guide to meet you at your hotel in Jaigaon if overnighting there. Otherwise look for your guide at the Bhutan Gate.

When entering Bhutan, Indian travellers need to get their entry permit from the separate **Main Immigration Office** (Zhung Lam; ⊙9am-5pm Mon-Fri) and will need to present a passport, Voter ID card or border card, a passport photo and photocopy of the passport ID pages.

Foreign Exchange

It can be hard to change Bhutanese ngultrum into Indian rupees at Bhutanese banks, so try at moneychangers or the Bhutan border immigration office instead.

Onward to India

When you cross into or out of India remember to stop at the **Indian Immigration post** (MG Rd; ⊙7am-6pm) to get an Indian entry or exit stamp. Indian time is 30 minutes earlier than Bhutan time.

Early-morning minibuses from Phuentsholing bus station to the West Bengal transport hub of Siliguri (Nu 120, four hours) aren't really set up for foreigners, as you would have to persuade them to stop at Indian Immigration en route.

Bhutanese taxis to Siliguri (Nu 3000 to 5000) are available outside the Phuentsholing bus station, or you can find a much cheaper Indian taxi (₹2500) or bus (₹170, four hours) on the other side of the border after you've gone to Indian Immigration to get an entry stamp.

Bhutanese vehicles are free to travel in India so you could arrange for your Bhutanese tour company to drop you in Siliguri for a fee.

by the buildings of Norbu College. The facilities are impressive, with a good outdoor pool, gym and sauna, and the grand deluxe rooms have a balcony, but the design is fairly charmless, with chintzy chandeliers and cheap furniture in the rooms.

Peling Resort   HOTEL $$

(☏77100865; www.pelingresort.com; Rinchending; d/tr Nu 3000/3600, ste Nu 4800; ❋🛜) This modern place on a leafy hill overlooking Kharbandi offers a quiet alternative to staying in dusty Phuentsholing, 5km below. Some of the spacious rooms come with a balcony, and the patio has views down to the plains of India. Avoid an east-facing room on Wednesdays, Fridays and Saturdays when the disco thumps away until 1am. New rooms are under construction.

Orchid Hotel   HOTEL $$

(☏05-254290; www.theorchid.bt; Zhung Lam; r s/d Nu 3500/4000, ste s/d Nu 4500/5000; ❋🛜) The 28 rooms in this modern three-star option are generally very spacious and

some come with pleasant French-window balconies overlooking the football field. The suites are poor value in comparison.

Lhaki Hotel   HOTEL $$

(☏05-257111, India ☏+91 9859217012; lhakihotel@druknet.bt; Pelkhil Lam; s/d from Nu 2645/3450; 🛜) A popular modern hotel with clean and spacious rooms built around a bright and airy lobby. The entrance is off a lane in the upper quarters of town, but the back rooms overlook the noisy main road. Be sure to request a nonsmoking room. Booking is advised as many travel agents lodge their groups here.

Bhutan Ga Me Ga   BUSINESS HOTEL $$$

(☏05-253065; www.bhutangamega.com; behind Mig Cinema Hall; s/d from Nu 4200/5400; ❋🛜❋) This modern option in the centre of the bazaar boasts more style than most. From the espresso in the lobby cafe to the roof terrace and small indoor pool, the facilities are modern, even if the the airless rooms are a tad claustrophobic. Deluxe rooms offer a bit more space for an extra Nu 1000.

✗ Eating

Zen Family Restaurant   CHINESE $$
(☑ 05-251194; Gatoem Lam; mains Nu 250-500; ⊗ 10am-9.30pm; ❋) The Chinese dishes here are tasty and fairly authentic, with some Bhutanese and Thai flavours thrown in, and portions are sized to share, though service is languid. The snappy modern decor is surprisingly sophisticated and the ambience is quiet. You might even find seafood and lobster here if you fancy a last-night blowout.

Kizom Cafe   CAFE $$
(Gatoen Lam; pizza Nu 360-440, coffee Nu 120; ⊗ 9am-9.30pm; ❋ 🛜) For espresso coffee in delicious air-con, this modern and central cafe hits the spot. It also serves smoothies and iced coffee alongside good cakes, desserts and passable pizza, with comfy upstairs sofas. With fresh morning croissants, it's a good place for a breakfast alternative to your hotel.

☗ Drinking & Nightlife

For a bottle of cold beer, stargaze on the roof terrace of the **Hotel Sinchula** (☑ 17110452; hotelsinchulabhutan@gmail.com; Phuensum Lam; ⊗ 5-10pm Wed-Mon) or get a drink from the bar at the Hotel Druk Phuentsholing (p123) and enjoy it in the garden.

🛍 Shopping

Phuentsholing has the cheapest consumer goods in Bhutan and many Bhutanese and Indians come here especially on shopping trips. It's also one of the cheapest places to have a *gho* or *kira* (traditional dress for men and women) made.

Bhimraj Stores   TEXTILES
(⊗ 9am-8.30pm) Located in the central bazaar next to Hotel Namgay, here you can buy a range of cloth from Nu 350 to 950 per metre; you'll need about 4m for a *gho* or *kira*. Figure on tailoring fees of Nu 750 to 1200. A ready-made *gho* retails for between Nu 1700 and Nu 4000.

Tashi Industries
Carpet Factory   HOMEWARES
(☑ 77191046; Jorden Lam; ⊗ 9am-12.30pm & 2-6.30pm Mon-Sat) Anyone interested in carpets is welcome to make a visit to this handmade-carpet factory hidden in the north of town. At 49 knots per square inch, woven from Indian wool and coloured with synthetic dyes, the carpets are not top-notch, but the prices are right, with a 1m-by-2m carpet selling for Nu 9000.

The factory specialises in bulk orders for many of Bhutan's monasteries and also weaves *mathra,* the cloth used for a *gho,* for Nu 250 per sq metre.

ℹ Information

IMMIGRATION

If headed to India you will need to have an Indian visa in your passport as the Indian consulate in town doesn't process visas for foreigners. India e-visas are not valid for this land crossing.

See box on previous page for information on border crossings.

Indian Consulate (p286) Indian travellers headed further into Bhutan who are travelling with a PAN card, driver's licence or Aadhaar card (ie without a passport) will need to come to this office to get an identification slip. This slip needs to be presented to the Main Immigration Office in town in order to get an entry permit and proceed further into Bhutan.

MEDICAL SERVICES

Phuentsholing General Hospital (☑ 05-254825; Samdrup Lam) A 50-bed hospital equipped with a modern lab, operating theatres and a casualty department.

MONEY

Small denomination Indian rupees (₹100 bills and under) can be used freely in Bhutan.

Bank of Bhutan (www.bob.bt; Samdrup Lam; ⊗ 9am-1pm & 2-4pm Mon-Fri, 9am-noon Sat) Your best bet for changing foreign currency into ngultrum; has an ATM accepting Visa, MasterCard and Cirrus cards.

Bhutan National Bank (www.bnb.bt; Samdrup Lam; ⊗ 9am-1pm & 2-4pm Mon-Fri, 9-11am Sat) Changes foreign currency.

POST

Post Office (Samdrup Lam; ⊗ 9am-5pm Mon-Fri, 9am-1pm Sat) Next to the Bank of Bhutan.

ℹ Getting There & Away

Transport companies such as Dhug, Metho, Pelyab and Sernya run frequent Coaster minibuses from the bus station to Thimphu (Nu 220, five hours), with morning services to Paro (Nu 210, five hours), and daily or every-other-day services to Haa (Nu 210, nine hours), Wangdue Phodrang and Punakha (both Nu 300, 10 hours).

Shared taxis depart from outside the bus station and also from a stand on the ground floor of a car park near the river. A seat to Thimphu costs around Nu 550 in a Bolero jeep or Nu 750 in a four-seater car. A seat to Paro costs around Nu 750. A taxi to Thimphu costs Nu 4800.

Central Bhutan

Best Places to Eat

➡ Cafe Perk (p140)

➡ Jakar Village Lodge (p137)

➡ Panda Beer Garden Cafe (p141)

➡ Sunny Restaurant (p141)

Best Places to Stay

➡ Jakar Village Lodge (p137)

➡ Swiss Guest House (p138)

➡ Ogyen Chholing Heritage House (p149)

➡ Marang Forest Lodge (p154)

➡ Mountain Resort (p137)

➡ Yangkhil Resort (p131)

Why Go?

Central Bhutan's fertile and neatly cultivated valleys fringed by evergreen mountains paint a picture of rural near-perfection. This postcard landscape is also Bhutan's cultural heartland, accented by several of the country's oldest and most significant temples and monasteries. In these venerable places of worship ancient and spectacular festivals celebrate Buddhist tradition.

Across the 3420m-high Pele La and the Black Mountains is the magnificent Trongsa Dzong, the western gateway to Central Bhutan. From Trongsa, a short drive over the Yotong La (3425m) leads to the four valleys of Bumthang, a magical region rich with relics, hermitages and sacred sites from the visits of Guru Rinpoche and Pema Lingpa.

Central Bhutan sees fewer tourists than western Bhutan, and nature lovers will relish the opportunities for day hikes along uncrowded trails. To really get off the beaten track, head south to the wildlife-filled jungles of Royal Manas National Park.

When to Go

➡ Central Bhutan, particularly the sunny valleys of Bumthang, makes for a year-round destination: pleasant in summer, and ideal in spring (especially for the rhododendron displays on the mountain passes) as well as autumn

➡ Winters can be cold, especially in Bumthang, but days are usually sunny and there are few tourists – just bring some warm clothes and don't be surprised if the mountain passes are temporarily closed by snow for a day or two.

➡ The southern regions, including Gelephu and Royal Manas National Park, are extremely hot in summer.

➡ Ideally you should time your visit to include at least one of the region's colourful and fascinating festivals, such as those at Ura, Trongsa Dzong, Jampey Lhakhang or Kurjey Lhakhang.

Central Bhutan Highlights

1 **Trongsa** (p129) Exploring the dramatic dzong and Royal Heritage Museum.

2 **Bumthang valleys** (p149) Taking on one of the many excellent hikes.

3 **Royal Manas National Park** (p153) Rafting to see river otters, water birds and hornbills.

4 **Kurjey Lhakhang** (p143) Wandering the temples dedicated to Guru Rinpoche.

5 **Jampey Lhakhang** (p142) Entering one of Bhutan's most significant temples.

6 **Tamshing Goemba** (p146) Circumambulating in a cloak of chain mail made by Pema Lingpa.

7 **Chendebji Chorten** (p128) Picnicking at the stupa patterned after Swayambhunath in Kathmandu.

8 **Ogyen Chholing Palace** (p148) Taking in the superb palace museum.

History

Central Bhutan is believed to be the first part of Bhutan to have been inhabited, with evidence of prehistoric settlements in the Ura valley of Bumthang and the southern region of Khyeng (around Zhemgang). These and many other valleys were separate principalities ruled by independent kings. One of the most important of these kings was the 8th-century Indian Sindhu Raja of Bumthang, who was eventually converted to Buddhism by Guru Rinpoche. Bumthang continued to be a separate kingdom, ruled from Jakar, until the time of Zhabdrung Ngawang Namgyal in the 17th century.

During the rule of the first *desi* (secular ruler), Tenzin Drugyey, all of eastern Bhutan came under the control of the Drukpa government in Punakha. Chhogyel Mingyur Tenpa unified central and eastern Bhutan into eight provinces known as Shachho Khorlo Tsegay. He was then promoted to Trongsa *penlop* (governor).

Because of Trongsa Dzong's strategic position, the *penlop* exerted great influence over the entire country. It was from Trongsa that Jigme Namgyal, father of the first king, rose to power.

Bumthang retained its political importance during the rule of the first and second kings, both of whom had their principal residence at Wangdichholing Palace in Jakar. Several impressive royal residences and country estates remain in the region, including at Kuenga Rabten, Eundu Chholing and Ogyen Chholing.

TRONGSA DZONGKHAG

Trongsa Dzongkhag covers an area of 1810 sq km surrounding the strategic and historically important Trongsa Dzong, with its links to the royal Wangchuck dynasty. The steep and heavily forested countryside, ranging from below 1000m to over 5000m, encompasses the diverse **Jigme Singye Wangchuck National Park**.

Most visitors limit themselves to a stop in Trongsa en route to Bumthang, but a few people branch south here towards Zhemgang and Royal Manas National Park.

Pele La to Trongsa

68KM / 2¼ HOURS

The route between the windswept town of Wangdi (Wangdue Phodrang's colloquial name), in western Bhutan, and Trongsa crosses the Black Mountains over the Pele La (3420m) before entering the broad, heavily cultivated Mangde Chhu valley. The area near Pele La is one place you might see grazing yaks from the road. Recent road widening has made the route an easier and slightly faster journey.

Pele La to Chendebji

27KM / 1 HOUR

From Pele La the road drops through hillsides carpeted with a strange dwarf bamboo called *cham*. This bamboo never gets large enough to harvest for any useful purpose, but when it's small it is a favourite food of yaks and horses.

The road drops into the evergreen forests of the Longte valley, passing below the high village of **Longte**. An easy 30-minute walking path follows the old trail from the pass downhill to Longte. An interesting longer hiking trail climbs from behind Longte through forest and over a pass to drop into the Phobjikha valley near Khumbhu Lhakhang (four hours).

About 9km from the pass, the cosy **Tushita Cafe** (☑17671642; Kemepokto; set lunch Nu 390; ☺8am-5pm) offers fine valley views and makes a good lunch stop.

Lower down into the valley the vegetation changes to bamboo and multihued broadleaved species. The road passes opposite **Rukubji** village, with its cluster of houses, a large school and a goemba at the end of a huge alluvial fan believed to be the body of a giant snake. Surrounding the village are extensive fields of mustard, potato, barley and wheat.

After 1km the road enters a side valley and drops to **Sephu** (2610m), also known as Chazam, next to the new bridge that spans the Nikka Chhu. Upper Sephu is the end point of the epic 24-day Snowman trek through the remote Lunana district.

The lodge-style **Norbu Yangphel Hotel** (☑17858647; hotelnorbuyangphel2007@gmail.com; set lunch Nu 576; ☺7am-11pm), just before the junction, offers a good lunch stop and a chance to sample local *juru jaju* (river moss soup); fresh in August and September, and dried the rest of the year (order in advance).

The road follows the Nikka Chhu to two chortens that mark the river's confluence with the Nyala Chhu. It is then a gentle, winding descent through rhododendrons, blue pines, spruces, oaks and dwarf bamboo to the village of **Chendebji**, recognisable by its cluster of traditional houses and the yellow roof of its lhakhang on the far bank. This was a night stop for mule caravans travelling from Trongsa during the reign of the second king.

Two kilometres beyond Chendebji village is **Chendebji Chorten**, at a lovely spot by a river confluence and a great place for a picnic. The large white chorten is patterned after Swayambhunath in Kathmandu and was built in the 19th century by Lama Shida, from Tibet, to cover the remains of an evil spirit that was killed here. The proper name of this structure is Chorten Charo Kasho; it is the westernmost monument in a 'chorten path' that was the route of early Buddhist missionaries. The nearby Bhutanese-style chorten was constructed in 1982.

Just 500m past the chorten is the riverside **Chendebji Resort** (☑ 77635633; s/d Nu 1500/3000, set-meal lunch/dinner Nu 480/540), a popular lunch spot with excellent food and a well-stocked gift shop.

Chendebji to Trongsa

41KM / 1¼ HOURS

From Chendebji Chorten the road passes a few farms, crosses a side stream and climbs again to a ridge, passing above the village of Tangsibi. The valley widens and the road turns a corner into the broad Mangde Chhu valley. The shrubs along this part of the road are edgeworthia, which is used to make paper. The brown monkeys you will probably see are Assamese macaques.

At Tashiling village you'll see **Tashichholing Lhakhang**, home to the Gayrab Arts and Crafts Training Institute. Inside is an impressive 9m-tall statue of Chaktong Chentong, a 1001-armed version of Chenresig (Avalokiteshvara, the Bodhisattva of Compassion). The particularly fine murals were painted by the 40 monks who study here as part of a six-year course in traditional monastic arts.

Further along the road you can see the pretty nearby village of **Tsangkha**, whose large *shedra* (Buddhist college) just above the road specialises in astrology.

Keep your eyes peeled to the right and you'll catch glimpses of the new 720MW Mangdechhu hydroelectric dam and power station. The Indian-funded project started generating in 2019 and features a 100m-tall dam and a 13.5km-long water tunnel.

After the road weaves in and out of side valleys you finally get a view of Trongsa and the imposing whitewashed dzong that seems to hang in the air at the head of the valley. A

viewpoint next to a small chorten in the centre of the road offers a good place for a photo stop and cup of tea if the **Viewpoint Restaurant** (☑ 17644349; ⊙ hours vary) is open. The dzong looks almost close enough to touch but it is still a 14km drive away.

From here you can walk to the dzong on the **Mangdue Foot Trail**, a tough two-hour track that drops steeply down to a traditional *baa zam* (cantilevered bridge) over the Mangde Chhu before ascending equally steeply to the western gate of the dzong. Your driver will need to drive ahead to the dzong so that the western gate will be unlocked for your arrival.

To reach Trongsa, you make a tedious detour into the upper reaches of the Mangde Chhu valley, cross the raging river at the Bjee Zam vehicle check-post, and then climb again above the north bank of the river, past a waterfall and the Yangkhil Resort, before pulling into town.

Trongsa

☑ 03 / POP 3100 / ELEV 2180M

Trongsa is smack in the middle of the country, set at the strategic junction of roads to Punakha, Bumthang and Gelephu but separated from both east and west by high mountain ranges. The dzong and surrounding town are perched above a gorge, with fine views of the Black Mountains to the southwest. It's a sleepy and pleasant town, lined with traditional whitewashed shops decorated with pot plants. The town received a large influx of Tibetan immigrants in the late 1950s and early 1960s, and Bhutanese of Tibetan descent run most of the shops here.

⊙ Sights

The main road from the west traverses above the dzong and passes the small weekend **vegetable market** (⊙ 7am-4pm Sat & Sun) and tiny **Thruepang Palace** (closed to visitors), where the third king, Jigme Dorji Wangchuck, was born in 1928. A traffic circle by the centre of town marks the junction of the road south to Gelephu. A short walk along this road offers excellent views of the dzong.

Views over Trongsa have been tarnished somewhat by the completion of a 100m-high dam just below the town, part of the Mangdechhu hydroelectric plant.

★**Trongsa Dzong**   BUDDHIST MONASTERY
(☑ 03-521220; ⊙ 9am-5pm, to 4pm Dec-Feb) This commanding dzong, high above the roaring

Trongsa

Trongsa

Mangde Chhu, is perhaps the most spectacularly sited dzong in Bhutan, with a sheer drop to the south that often just disappears into cloud and mist. The rambling assemblage of buildings that comprises the dzong trails down the ridge and is connected by a succession of alley-like corridors, wide stone stairs and beautiful paved courtyards. The southernmost part of the dzong, Chorten Lhakhang, is the location of the first hermitage, built in 1543.

The first construction on the site was carried out by Ngagi Wangchuck (1517–54),

the great-grandfather of Zhabdrung Ngawang Namgyal. He came to Trongsa in 1541 and built a *tshamkhang* (small meditation room) after discovering self-manifested hoof prints belonging to the horse of the protector deity Pelden Lhamo. Trongsa ('New Village' in the local dialect) gets its name from the retreats, temples and hermit residences that soon grew up around the chapel. The dzong was built in its present form in 1644 by Chhogyel Mingyur Tenpa, the official who was sent by the Zhabdrung to bring eastern Bhutan under central control. It was then enlarged at the end of the 17th century by the *desi*, Tenzin Rabgye. Its official name is Chhoekhor Raptentse Dzong, and it is also known by its short name of Choetse Dzong. The dzong was severely damaged in the 1897 earthquake, and repairs were carried out by the *penlop* of Trongsa, Jigme Namgyal, father of Bhutan's first king.

Trongsa Dzong is closely connected to the royal family. The first two hereditary kings ruled from this dzong, and tradition still dictates that the crown prince serve as Trongsa *penlop* before acceding to the throne.

The dzong's strategic location gave it great power over this part of the country. The only trail between eastern and western Bhutan still leads straight through Trongsa and used to run directly through the dzong itself. This gave the Trongsa *penlop* enviable control over east–west trade and the considerable tax revenue to be derived from it. Today most visitors enter through the main eastern gate, but energetic types can make the steep cardio hike on the Mangdue Foot Trail from the viewpoint and enter the dzong via the western gate, in traditional fashion.

The Trongsa *rabdey* (district monk body) migrates between winter (Trongsa) and summer (Bumthang) residences, just as the main *dratshang* (central monk body) does between Thimphu and Punakha.

There are 23 separate lhakhangs in the dzong, though what you get to see depends on which keys are available. Most of the existing fine decoration was designed during the rule of the first king, Ugyen Wangchuck. To the side of the dzong is the archery ground and pavilion where the current king (then crown prince) was crowned *penlop* in 2004.

Rooms to visit include the atmospheric northern *kunrey* (assembly hall) and the impressive next-door Jampa Lhakhang, with a two-storey Maitreya (Jampa) statue. The southern Mithrub Lhakhang houses the funerary chorten of Ngagi Wangchuck. Feel for the footprints worn into the wooden floor by one overly enthusiastic prostrator.

The five-day Trongsa tsechu is held in the northern courtyard in December or January and culminates in the unveiling of a *thondrol* (a giant *thangka* – a painted or embroidered religious picture).

★ Tower of Trongsa
Royal Heritage Museum   MUSEUM
(☑ 03-521220; www.toweroftrongsa.gov.bt; SAARC/ non-SAARC national Nu 100/200; ⊙ 9am-5pm Mon-Sat Apr-Oct, 9am-4pm Mon-Fri Nov-Mar) This watchtower *(ta dzong)* overlooking the dzong now houses an excellent museum. The five floors of displays tell the history of the monarchy through such varied treasures as the 500-year-old jacket of Ngagi Wangchuk, the second king's saddle and a copy of the famous raven crown. You can drive here and then walk back to town down a staircase past several chapels.

As you ascend the floors look for the radio given by American Burt Todd, a friend of the third king who visited Bhutan in the 1950s (the first American to do so) and set up Bhutan's postal system. Other treasures include a fine photo of the kings of Bhutan and Sikkim in Kolkata (Calcutta) in 1905, and a beautiful 1926 document declaring an oath of allegiance to the monarchy.

The most sacred religious item is a copy of the Padma Kathang, a copy of Guru Rinpoche's biography discovered by Pema Lingpa underneath the Jokhang Temple in Lhasa. There are two lhakhangs inside the *ta dzong;* the top-floor Gesar Lhakhang is dedicated to the 19th-century *penlop* of Trongsa, Jigme Namgyal. Two British soldiers are said to have been kept in the dzong's dungeon for several months during the Duar War.

There are sweeping views from the roof, plus a souvenir shop and a ground-floor cafe providing refreshments (and lunch by prior arrangement).

Photos are not allowed in the museum, so leave your camera and phone in your vehicle. There are lockers at the entrance but you'll need to return all the way back there to pick them up.

🛏 Sleeping & Eating

Norling Hotel   LOCAL HOTEL $
(☑ 03-521171; s/d Nu 2160/2700) This concrete local inn in the bazaar has a back restaurant that's a decent place for lunch. The nine upstairs wooden-floored rooms are fairly comfortable and come with private bathrooms, catering to a mix of locals and visiting NGO staff, but are poor value for foreign tourists.

★ Yangkhil Resort   HOTEL $$
(☑ 03-521417; www.yangkhil.bt; Tashipang; s/d Nu 3670/3970, deluxe s/d Nu 4740/5210; ❊ 🛜) This resort, 1.5km west of Trongsa, is an excellent choice, with 21 rooms constructed in five blocks on a terraced hill facing the dzong. All rooms are clean and cosy with ample heating, a balcony and comfortable beds (no TVs). The gardens, with their lovely spring pear blossom, are an ideal place to relax, so arrange your itinerary for an early arrival.

It's worth noting that good Illy espresso coffee (Nu 180) is available at the well-stocked bar. An in-house bakery and outdoor restaurant were under construction at the time of research.

Tashi Ninjay Hotel   HOTEL $$
(☑ 03-521536; tashininjey@gmail.com; s/d Nu 2640/3000; 🛜) The views of the Trongsa Dzong are superb at this inn – make sure you get one of the upper-floor rooms with a balcony. Rooms are comfortable, meals are hearty and the staff are super-friendly, but bring earplugs for the barking dogs. It's the only tourist-grade hotel in the town itself. Wi-fi is currently in the reception only.

Tendrel Resort   HOTEL $$
(☑ 03-521531; tendrelresort@gmail.com; s/d Nu 3300/3510; 🛜) This new place run by the former manager of the Tashi Ninjay Hotel doesn't have great views but it's a solid place, with a pleasant dining room and bar. The upper eight rooms have slightly larger balconies.

Puenzhi Guest House   HOTEL $$
(☑ 03-521197, 17627156; www.puenzhi.bt; s/d Nu 3080/4180, deluxe s/d Nu 4180/4950; 🛜) A 4km drive high above the town leads to this place, run by the former governor of Trongsa. The deluxe rooms are the best – airy and spacious with eagle-eye views down to the *ta dzong,* Trongsa Dzong and the Black Mountains. The older rooms are smaller and more old-fashioned but still cosy and with the same great balcony views.

The restaurant balcony is the perfect place for a sunset beer, while more active types can follow the footpath below the hotel directly down to the *ta dzong.*

Oyster House   BHUTANESE $
(☑ 03-521413; mains Nu 150-180; ⊙ 8am-10pm) This popular restaurant boasts cosy sofa

A HALF-DAY EXCURSION FROM TRONGSA
••

If you have a spare half day in Trongsa or really want to get off the beaten track, consider driving and then hiking up to the **Taphey Goemba** (Taphak Goemba) meditation retreat high on the hillside north of Trongsa. It was built by the first king of Bhutan around the meditation site of 18th-century practitioner Ngawang Tsamphel. Eight monks live at the *drubdey* (meditation retreat), whose main chapel houses a two-storey statue of 1001-armed Chenresig.

From Trongsa take the farm road north to Yuling village to visit its surprisingly ornate **lhakhang**, then backtrack to take the new dirt road up to the car park, 30 minutes' hike below Taphey Goemba.

A further hour's hike uphill from the goemba can take you to Singye Tang on the ridge-line above, for fine Himalayan views north all the way to Gangkhar Puensum (7570m). The path is not easy to find so try to take a local guide.

seating and a sunny terrace with pub tables overlooking the main strip, along with a menu of Tibetan and Bhutanese dishes: *thukpa* (noodles), *momos* (dumplings), and ribs with rice.

❶ Information

Bank of Bhutan (⊘9am-3pm Mon-Fri, 9-11am Sat) Has an ATM.

Bhutan National Bank (⊘9am-3pm Mon-Fri, 9-11am Sat) Also has an ATM.

Hospital On the hillside northwest of town.

Post Office (⊘8.30am-5pm Mon-Fri, 8.30am-1pm Sat)

Around Trongsa

The road that branches off south from Trongsa towards Zhemgang and Gelephu provides access to a couple of interesting sights, including former palaces of the first and second kings of Bhutan.

Kuenga Rabten

The winter palace of the second king, Jigme Wangchuck, is 23km (one hour) south of Trongsa. It's an interesting drive, passing below Takse Goemba (after 17km), several huge waterfalls, and the fertile rice terraces of the lower Mangde Chhu valley. It's a good half-day or three-quarter-day trip from Trongsa and could even make for a fine bike trip if you can arrange to be picked up at Kuenga Rabten. Traffic is light and it's all downhill from Trongsa!

There are about 40 young monks up to the age of 15 studying here. The first storey of the U-shaped building was used to store food; the second was the residence of royal attendants and the army; and the third housed the royal quarters and the king's private chapel. Part of this floor has been converted into a library, and books from the National Library are stored here. Sandwiched between the king's and queen's quarters is the Sangye Lhakhang, with statues of Sakyamuni, the Zhabdrung and Guru Rinpoche. The smoky chapels reek of antiquity.

A 15-minute hike or drive uphill from the building is the **Karma Drubdey Nunnery**, which is being expanded by its hard-working anim (Buddhist nuns).

A further 25km down the valley is **Yundrung (Eundu) Chholing**, the winter palace of the first king, Ugyen Wangchuck. From Kuenga Rabten the road drops down in loops, past Refey village to the river and road camp at Yourmu, and then 2km later branches up a dirt road to the palace. The building belongs to a local Dasho (nobleman) but is looked after by the monastic body, and tourists can normally visit. The 32 young monks are mostly from Tamshing Goemba in Bumthang.

The 2nd-floor *goenkhang* (chapel devoted to protective deities; men only) has a highly venerated chorten of Pema Lingpa, as well as a fabulous collection of arms and a lovely *drangyen* (lute). The entry chapel has some of the finest murals you'll see, depicting the mythical kingdoms of Zangto Pelri and Sukhavati.

BUMTHANG DZONGKHAG

The Bumthang region encompasses four major valleys: Chokhor, Tang, Ura and Chhume. Because the dzongs and the most important temples are in the large Chokhor valley, it is commonly referred to as the Bumthang valley.

There are two versions of the origin of the name Bumthang. The valley is supposed to be shaped like a *bumpa,* the vessel of holy water that is usually found on the altar of a lhakhang. *Thang* means 'field' or 'flat place'. The less respectful translation relates to the particularly beautiful women who live here – *bum* means 'girl'.

Trongsa to Jakar

68KM / 2½ HOURS

The run between Trongsa and Jakar, the main town in Bumthang, is one of the easier and more interesting drives in Bhutan, because it passes numerous villages and goembas as it winds through the Chhume valley. With stops you could easily fill an entire day on this lovely drive.

Trongsa to the Yotong La

28KM / 1 HOUR

The road zigzags up the ridge above Trongsa, climbing steeply past the Puenzhi Guest House and the cremation ground at Dorji Goemba to reach the head of the valley. Eventually the road traverses the top of the valley to a Tibetan chorten and an array of prayer flags atop the **Yotong La** (3425m). The old trade route to eastern Bhutan parallels the modern road as it crosses the pass.

Yotong La to Zungney

24KM / 1 HOUR

The descent from the pass is through firs, then blue pines and bamboo. The road enters the upper part of the Chhume valley, marked by the small roadside Chuchi Lhakhang at Gaytsa (Gyatsa). On a hill a few hundred metres to the north of Gaytsa is the Nyingma school **Buli Lhakhang** built by Tukse Chhoying, the son of Dorji Lingpa (1346–1405) and more recently renovated with assistance from the American Himalayan Foundation. There are about 40 young monks studying here. On the ground floor is the Jowo Lhakhang, with a lovely seated Jampa (Maitreya) and some impressive 12-sided pillars *(kachen).* On the upper floor is the Sangye (Sangay) Lhakhang, named for the statues of the past, present and future Buddhas. These three are flanked by statues of Guru Rinpoche and Dorji Lingpa. A mural by the window also depicts Dorji Lingpa. As you climb the stairwell to this upper storey look for a slate carving of the local protective deity, Yoebar Drakpo. The three-day Buli tsechu in February kicks off with an evening *mewang* (fire blessing) that dates back to pre-Buddhist times. Several black-necked cranes winter in the fields to the northeast of the village.

The red and yellow roofs of **Tharpaling Goemba** are visible above the trees on a cliff to the northeast. The Tibetan Nyingma (Dzogchen) philosopher and saint Longchen Rabjampa (1308–63) founded Tharpaling as part of eight *lings* (outlying temples) and lived here for many years, fathering two children. The goemba has several temples and houses more than 100 monks who study in the attached *shedra.* It's possible to visit here by driving 10km up a sealed road through bucolic countryside or by trekking over the hill from Jakar. The downhill journey makes for a good mountain-bike ride, or you could walk down to the main road via Samtenling Goemba.

Above Tharpaling, at about 3800m, is the white hermitage of **Choedrak**, which consists of two ancient chapels separated by a chorten and a sacred spring. The Thukje Lhakhang to the right has a central 1000-armed statue of Chenresig, the Lorepa Lhakhang, named after the chapel's 12th-century Tibetan founder, contains a stone footprint of Guru Rinpoche and the stone skull of a *dakini (khandroma;* female celestial being). Further uphill is the **Zhambhala Lhakhang**, named after the popular God of Wealth. Pilgrims ask for boons here at a set of circular grooves in the rock behind the lhakhang, which contains the surprisingly grand funeral chorten of Nyoshul Khen Rinpoche, an important Tibetan lama who died in 1999. Pema Lingpa revealed several *terma* (sacred texts and artefacts) hidden by Guru Rinpoche near these monasteries.

Back on the main road, just past the Tharpaling turn-off, a bridge crosses the Gaytsa Chhu and a signposted gravel road leads off 1km to the **Chumey Nature Resort** (☑17114836; www.chumeynatureresort. com; Gaytsa; r/ste Nu 3600/4800; 🔊), a relaxing rural retreat surrounded by fields and forests with several walking trails, including to Domkhar Tashichholing Dzong (30 minutes). The resort even has its own lhakhang and can cater for visitors wishing to learn about Buddhism. Mountain bikes can be hired for valley rides.

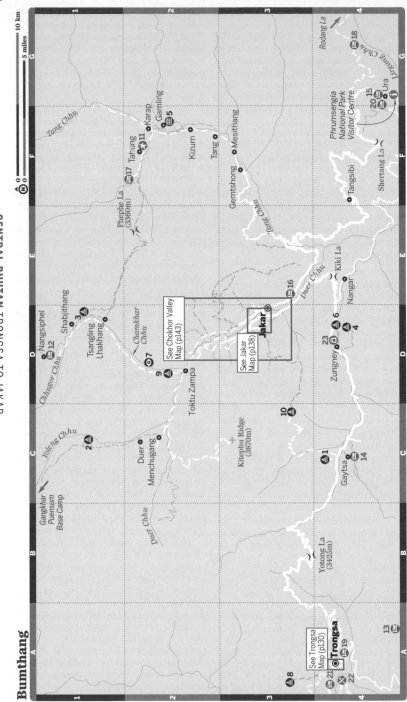

Bumthang

Bumthang

CENTRAL BHUTAN TRONGSA TO JAKAR

The main road continues down the Gaytsa Chhu valley for 2km to Domkhar. A dirt road branches south for 1km to **Domkhar Tashichholing Dzong**, the summer palace of the second king. It was completed in 1937 and is a replica of Kuenga Rabten. It served for years as the residence of the second king's wife, and is now a royal guesthouse (the interior is closed to visitors, although you can visit the courtyard). The monastic school to the south was built in 1968 by the previous reincarnation of the Karmapa, the head of the Karmapa lineage.

Beyond Domkhar village, past Hurjee, is the settlement of **Chhume**, with two large schools alongside more than 500m of straight road, perhaps one of the longest stretches of its kind in the hills of Bhutan. Just before Zungney, at Yamthrak, a paved road branches off 3.5km to **Nimalung Goemba**, an important Nyingma monastery and *shedra* that was founded in 1935 by Dorling Trulku. The ground-floor inner chapel contains a venerated statue of Drolma ('Tara) inside an amulet that was brought from Tibet. Walk behind the altar to see the collection of black hats used during the tsechu on the 10th day of the fifth month (around July). In front of the altar is a large metal box, which holds a *thondrol* depicting the Guru Tshengye, or eight manifestations of Guru Rinpoche. The upper floor is a *goenkhang*. Outside you might catch the monks playing *khuru*, a game that is part darts, part archery. If you want to stretch your legs, a 15-minute trail leads downhill through whispering pines from a line of eight stupas below the main chapel to Prakhar Goemba. Another two

minutes' walk from the goemba, across a small suspension bridge, brings you to the highway, and hopefully your waiting car.

Back on the main road, a short 500m walk from the Yamthrak junction leads to the **Chorten Nyingpo Lhakhang**, a 16th-century chapel whose main relic is a statue of the Zhabdrung's father, Tenpa Nyima (1567–1619). In the grounds look for the white throne from which Tenpa is said to have preached for three years. Further along the main road, just before Zungney, you pass the pool of the 1.7MW Chhume mini-hydro plant, which has been upgraded as a backup supply to Trongsa and Bumthang.

Five minutes further, stop at the two craft shops at Zungney village to watch weavers and dyers in action. Adjacent to the **Thokmed Yeshe Handicraft & Yathra Production Centre** (☏03-641124; Zungney; ☉6am-8pm) is the tiny **Zungney Lhakhang**, said by locals to have been built by Tibetan king Songtsen Gampo as one of his demoness-pinning temples.

Zungney to Jakar

16KM / 30 MINUTES

East of Zungney, **Prakhar Lhakhang** (Zha Lhakhang) is visible on a promontory on the opposite side of the river. It's a delightful two-minute walk to the three-storey lhakhang, which was built as a residence by Dawa Gyaltshen, a son of the famous Pema Lingpa. On the ground floor is a statue of Sakyamuni, crafted by artists from Nepal. On the middle floor are statues of Guru Tshengye, the eight manifestations of Guru Rinpoche. The top floor contains nine small

YATHRA

Hand-spun, hand-woven wool strips with patterns specific to the Bumthang region are called *yathra*. They mostly have geometric designs, sometimes with a border. Three strips may be joined to produce a blanket-like rain cover called a *charkep*.

In earlier days a *yathra* was often used as a shawl or raincoat to protect against the winter cold of Bumthang. They were once made from wool from Tibet; nowadays some of the wool is imported from New Zealand, while most is sourced from nearby Australian-supported sheep-breeding projects.

Since Bhutan does not have the carpet-weaving tradition of Tibet, *yathra* pieces have often served the same function as Tibetan rugs. Today a *yathra* is fashioned into a *toego*, the short jackets that women often wear over the *kira* (women's traditional dress) in cold weather.

chortens and murals that are as old as the lhakhang. The Prakhar Duchoed festival is held here in the middle of the ninth month (October or November) at the same time as the Jampey Lhakhang Drup. Prakhar means 'White Monkey'.

The road follows the valley down past the apple orchards of Nangar and into blue-pine forests. A new bypass branches off the main road here directly to Ura. It's a short climb to the Kiki La, a crest at 2860m marked by a chorten and many prayer flags. Once over the side ridge, the road descends into the Chokhor valley.

Jakar

📋 03 / POP 6243 / ELEV 2580M

Jakar (Chamkhar) is the major trading centre and town of the Bumthang region. Well serviced with resorts and hotels, this will most likely be your base for several days as you visit the surrounding valleys.

Jakar is a bustling two-street town near the foot of the Chokhor valley, and well worth a wander. Most of the shopfronts are relatively new, having been rebuilt after fires destroyed much of the town in 2010. As with several other towns in Bhutan, Jakar has plans to eventually shift location, to the new town of Dekyiling, just north of the Sey Lhakhang. The town roads are complete, but there's been no progress for years and no date has been given for the big move.

There is a strong up-valley wind from the south every afternoon, which makes Jakar nippy in the evenings.

👁 Sights

A traffic circle and the 14th-century **Jakar Lhakhang** mark the centre of the town.

The main street leads east from the town centre to a bridge over the Chamkhar

Chhu. Just before you cross the bridge to leave town, a small **chorten** marks the spot where a Tibetan general's head was buried after the defeat of a 17th-century Tibetan invasion force.

★ Jakar Dzong   BUDDHIST MONASTERY

Jakar Dzong is in a picturesque location overlooking the Chokhor valley; the current structure was built in 1667. Its official name is Yuelay Namgyal Dzong, in honour of the victory over Tibetan ruler Phuntsho Namgyal's troops. An unusual feature here is that the *utse* (central tower) is situated on an outside wall, so there is no way to circumambulate it.

According to legend, when the lamas assembled in about 1549 to select a site for a monastery, a big white bird rose suddenly in the air and settled on a spur of a hill. This was interpreted as an important omen, and the hill was chosen as the monastery's site and for Jakar Dzong, which roughly translates as 'castle of the white bird'. The Zhabdrung's great-grandfather, Ngagi Wangchuck, founded the monastery.

The approach to the impressive dzong, which has a circumference of more than 1500m, is made on foot along a stone-paved path. The entrance leads into a narrow courtyard surrounded by administrative offices. The *utse* is on the east side of the courtyard, and beyond that is the monks' quarters. At the west end of the dzong is a slightly larger courtyard, also surrounded by administrative offices. Behind here is a half-round *ta dzong*. A walled passage leads from the dzong down the hill to a nearby spring – a feature that ensured water could be obtained in the event of a long siege.

Even if the chapels are closed, it's a worthwhile climb for the views of the Chokhor valley from the front courtyard.

Wangdichholing Palace   PALACE

The palace of Wangdichholing was built in 1857 on the battle-camp site of the *penlop* of Trongsa, Jigme Namgyal. It was the first palace in Bhutan that wasn't designed primarily as a fortress. The grand but rather neglected building was used as a *lobra* (monastic school); however, the Bhutan Foundation (www.bhutanfound.org) has started to restore it and convert it into a museum.

Namgyal's son, King Ugyen Wangchuck, the first king of Bhutan, was born in Wangdichholing and chose it as his principal residence. The entire court moved from here to Kuenga Rabten each winter in a procession that took three days. Wangdichholing was also for a time the home of the third king, before he moved the royal court to Punakha in 1952.

There are five giant water-powered prayer wheels inside square chortens just to the north. The sleek modern building next door is the upmarket resort Amankora (p139).

Lhodrak Kharchu Goemba   BUDDHIST MONASTERY

On the hill to the east of Jakar is this large Nyingma monastery, founded in the 1970s by Namkhai Nyingpo Rinpoche, with about 400 monks currently in residence. The *tshokhang* has massive statues of Guru Rinpoche, Chenresig and Sakyamuni.

If you're here between 4.30pm and 6pm from April to November, check out the mass debating in the courtyard of the *shedra*, behind the main monastery, where monks reinforce their theological arguments with a stamp of the foot and a victorious slap. Don't disturb the debates with any photography.

Bumthang Brewery   BREWERY

(☑ 77754900; Bathpalathang; Nu 350 or US$5; ☺ by appointment only Mon-Sat) At this state-of-the-art microbrewery you will learn about the brewing of the Swiss-style unfiltered weiss beer, before sampling the end product in the adjacent Panda Beer Garden Cafe (p141). The brewery tour price includes one bottle of Red Panda beer.

✵ Festivals & Events

Bumthang has several important festivals, of which the most important is the **Jampey Lhakhang Drup**. The celebrations go from the 15th to the 18th days of the ninth lunar month, so it can fall in October or November.

The popular **Kurjey tsechu** is held in June at Kurjey Lhakhang (p143) and includes

a masked dance that dramatises Guru Rinpoche's defeat of Shelging Kharpo.

The three-day **Jakar tsechu** takes place in October or November and features mask dancing in the dzong.

The Nimalung Goemba holds a three-day **Nimalung tsechu**, also in June (it can also fall in July).

In September (or October) in the eighth lunar month, there are dances at Tamshing Goemba for the three-day **Tamshing Phala Choepa** before they relocate to nearby **Thangbi Goemba** for another three days.

The three-day **Ngang Bi Rabney** at the Ngang Lhakhang, high up in the valley, features masked dances and can fall in November or December.

🛏 Sleeping

Most of Bumthang's hotels and guesthouses follow a similar design, with pine-clad rooms and separate dining rooms, and are family-run. More recently, impressive large hotels have been built, providing luxury but lacking cosy guesthouse atmosphere. Many guesthouses and hotels have a *bukhari* (wood stove), though modern heaters are gradually replacing them.

Jakar is Bumthang's main hub and boasts numerous hotels for all budgets. Elsewhere the choice is much more limited, but worth seeking out for genuine cultural immersion.

🛏 Jakar

★ Jakar Village Lodge   HOTEL $$

(☑ 03-631242; www.bhutanlodge.com; s/d Nu 3600/4200, deluxe s/d Nu 4200/4800; ☎) This hotel, situated down a quiet village lane below the dzong, is run by a former *dzongdag* (district administrator) who will regale you with stories as you sample his assortment of teas and freshly ground coffee. Guest rooms are spotless and beds are sumptuous, while the sunny terrace enjoys great views over the valley and up to the dzong.

Boasting some of the best food in Bumthang, the kitchen staff take great care to vary the menu, which includes tasty buckwheat pancakes for breakfast. Bicycle hire is also available.

★ Mountain Resort   HOTEL $$

(☑ 17670668; www.bhutanmountainresort.com; s/d Nu 3420/3540; ☎) This hotel has undergone a stylish makeover, with modern interpretations of traditional stone and wood in its new reception and dining areas and

Jakar

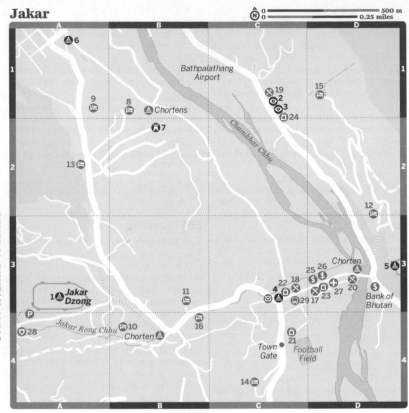

Bathpalathang Airport

Chortens

Chamkhar Chhu

Chorten

Bank of Bhutan

Jakar Dzong

Jakar Rong Chhu

Chorten

Town Gate

Football Field

contemporary-accommodation wing. The rooms are mini suites featuring fabulous valley-view picture windows, electric heaters (though *bukharis* are gradually being installed in all rooms), and separate shower and bath.

A spa, sauna and hot-stone bath are also available.

★ Swiss Guest House   HOTEL $$

(📞03 631145, 17164119; www.swissguesthouse. bt; Bathpalathang; s/d Nu 3240/3360; 🛜) It doesn't get more bucolic than this wooden farmhouse surrounded by apple and pear orchards on a hill overlooking the valley. In 1983 this was the first guesthouse in Bumthang, but there have been plenty of upgrades since then. Rooms in the new wing are spacious and warmed by *bukharis,* with comfy beds and clean bathrooms.

The dining room has the best desserts and is the cosiest in town. There's espresso coffee, and you can get Red Panda beer on draught,

guaranteed fresh since it's brewed just down the road!

Yu-Gharling Resort   HOTEL $$

(📞03-631602; www.yugharlingresort.com; standard/deluxe r Nu 4620/5640, ste from Nu 7080; 🛜) This bold, traditional-style hotel overlooking the valley is almost as luxurious as it is enormous. Rooms are massive and the views are spectacular, particularly from the highly recommended 'cottages' with balconies. Most rooms don't have TVs, but hotel facilities include a spacious bar with a billiard table, espresso coffee, a spa with massage, a sauna and a hot-stone bath.

Kaila Guest House   HOTEL $$

(📞17815583; kailaguesthouse94@gmail.com; s/d Nu 3000/3180; 🛜) This friendly, genuinely welcoming option features a sunny courtyard and a new wing of rooms boasting sumptuous Tibetan carpets, and bathrooms with rain showers. The owner was the cook at the Swiss Guest House for many years, so

Jakar

the food is very good at this unpretentious establishment.

It is a favourite of NGO workers, who get a 20% discount, and the bar, with Red Panda beer on draught, is a great place to plug into what's happening in Bumthang.

Hotel Ugyen Ling   HOTEL **$$**
(☑ 03-631369; www.bhutanhotels.com.bt; s/d/ste Nu 3000/3360/4800; ☎) Owned by one of Bhutan's biggest travel agencies, this walled compound is close to Wangdichholing Palace and offers above-average accommodation, a multicuisine restaurant and a comfortable bar. Standard rooms are almost suites with their separate sitting areas heated with a *bukhari* and a private balcony. The same level of luxury, however, doesn't carry through to the small bathrooms.

River Lodge   HOTEL **$$**
(☑ 03-631287; www.bumthangriverlodge.com; r standard/deluxe/ste Nu 3240/4200/8340; ☎) This popular place has a variety of comfortable rooms overlooking the valley south of town. The lodge has a gregarious and knowledgeable owner, a small spa that offers massage and hot-stone baths, and a bright dining room that has great valley views, good food and a warming *bukhari*. Try the homemade wild strawberry or organic plum jam.

Tashi Yoezerling Guest House   HOTEL **$$**
(☑ 17493493; r Nu 2640-3480; ☎) So new we could still smell the varnish when we visited,

this 12-room hotel is on the hill overlooking town and has views up the valley towards Kurjey Lhakhang. Downstairs is a cosy wood-lined dining room with a wood-fired heater. Only two rooms have king-sized beds, but all rooms are spacious and twin beds can be put together.

Mipham Guest House   GUESTHOUSE **$$**
(☑ 03-631738; r standard/deluxe Nu 4200/4800; ☎) This hidden guesthouse nestles just below the Lhodrak Kharchu Goemba, making it perfect for Buddhist practitioners headed for dawn prayers. The old, *bukhari*-heated rooms are cosy, while the newer rooms are more spacious, have electric heaters and great dzong and town views.

Amankora   LUXURY HOTEL **$$$**
(☑ 02 331333; www.amanresorts.com; full board s/d US$1740/1860; ☎) The last word in luxury in Bumthang, the sleek dzong-like Amankora sits beside Wangdichholing Palace in apple and pear orchards. Rooms are spacious, with king-size beds, soaring ceilings and central, sumptuous bathtubs. Rates include all meals and several activities.

🏠 Chokhor Valley

Gongkhar Guest House   HOTEL **$$**
(☑ 17932073, 03-631288; gongkharhotel@gmail.com; s/d Nu 2706/3000, deluxe s/d Nu 4266/4554; ☎) This excellent hotel, 1.5km southeast of Jakar, has spacious, cosy and comfortable

rooms with *bukharis* and renovated bathrooms. There's a good view of the dzong, garden seating among amazing roses, excellent service, and the food is among the best and most varied in the valley. The deluxe rooms are exceptionally comfortable, though all rooms boast electric heaters and *bukharis*.

Wangdicholing Resort
HOTEL **$$**

(☑ 03-631452, 17670399; wangdicholingresort@gmail.com; Chamkhar; s/d Nu 3120/3240, deluxe s/d Nu 3960/4080, ste Nu 6600; ☎) This well-run resort with a reputable kitchen producing tasty food is on a bluff overlooking the valley to the south of town. The highlight is the relaxing balcony terrace, seasonally festooned with climbing flowers, from where you can savour the view. Rooms are a bit old-fashioned but very comfortable; the spacious corner suites boasting king beds are best.

Rinchenling Lodge
HOTEL **$$**

(☑ 03-631147; rinchenlinglodge@gmail.com; Tashigatsel; r Nu 3420, deluxe r Nu 4200, ste Nu 6600; ☎) This hotel is run by amiable Dasho Jampel Ngedup and family. It has spacious rooms with quality mattresses and an excellent restaurant. Standard rooms line up among the apple trees (avoid the back rooms), and the deluxe rooms come with modern bathrooms and sunny balconies. The hot-stone bath is worth experiencing for its ingenious communication system.

Hotel Jakar View
HOTEL **$$**

(☑ 17637241, 03-631779; hoteljakarview@gmail.com; Jalikhar; s/d Nu 4800/5400; ☎) On the outskirts of town and with great valley views, this brightly painted hotel has just 15 spacious, traditionally decorated, wood-panelled deluxe rooms with modern bathrooms. There's a cosy bar, a *bukhari*-warmed dining room and a large terrace with a firepit.

Yozerling Lodge
HOTEL **$$**

(☑ 17648412; www.yozerling.com.bt; 2736/2880, deluxe s/d Nu 3600/4032; ☎) This friendly, family-run place 2.5km from town certainly could do with a bit of tidying up and gardening, but the comfortable pine-clad deluxe rooms enjoy valley views and are warmed with a *bukhari* and an electric heater. The comfy sofas in the large dining hall make for cosy pre- and post-dinner drinks.

Hotel Peling
HOTEL **$$**

(☑ 03-631222; www.hotelpeling.com.bt; Tamzhing; s/d Nu 3000/3360, ste Nu 4320; ☎) This lavish-looking hotel has huge rooms with wide balconies and great views. Rooms are heated with a traditional *bukhari*, TVs are provided on request and a hot-stone bath is available. Wi-fi is patchy outside of the reception.

✖ Eating

The hotels in Bumthang do a great job feeding their guests hearty local and continental food, and there's even some healthy competition among hotels in the culinary stakes. Because of the altitude, buckwheat is the crop of choice in Bumthang and buckwheat noodles *(puta)* and pancakes *(khule)* are local specialities. The Chamkhar Chhu is famous for its trout, and despite Buddhist prohibitions on the taking of life, fish does mysteriously appear on hotel dinner plates.

★ Cafe Perk
INTERNATIONAL **$**

(☑ 17739217; meals Nu 70-200, cakes Nu 65, espresso Nu 90-150; ◷ 9am-9pm) If you are searching for espresso, this is the place to head for. In addition to coffee, there are cakes, milkshakes, cold coffees and masala chai. The blackboard menu includes banana and buckwheat pancakes, pasta, grilled

---

BEER, BEES & CHEESE: THE SWISS CONNECTION

Bumthang's famous **Swiss Farm** is a mature development project that was established by Fritz Maurer, one of the first Swiss to work in Bhutan. The project introduced cheesemaking, brewing, European honey bees, farming machinery and fuel-efficient wood stoves to the valley, as well as its first tourist guesthouse.

One legacy from the project is Bhutan's celebrated beer, Red Panda, which is brewed at the **Bumthang Brewery** (p137).

Swiss expertise also set up Bhutan's only commercial **cheese factory** (☑ 17928017, 17607239; Bathpalathang; Nu 350 or US$5; ◷ by appointment only 2-4pm Mon-Sat), which is also open to visitors (a tour includes free tasting). If you just want to invest in some cheese and beer for a top-notch Bumthang picnic, head straight to the next-door Yoser Lhamo Shop (p141), which is the main stockist for both enterprises.

sandwiches with fries and other familiar favourites. Picnic lunches can be arranged.

Bumthang Pizza
PIZZA $

(☑17885830; pizza small/medium/large Nu 260/300/350; ☺9am-9pm) Find this pizza joint, the best in Jakar, downstairs, where there are veg and nonveg pizzas made in three sizes, plus a bar. Bhutanese varieties include beef and mushroom, and if you ask for chilli you'll get it in spades.

Sunny Restaurant
BHUTANESE $

(☑17254212; mains Nu 55-150; ☺8am-9pm) There are plenty of small bars and local restaurants along Jakar's main street, though the brightest and cleanest is Sunny Restaurant, with Bhutanese and Chinese dishes offered by a former chef from the Amankora. Popular dishes include cheese/beef *momos* (Nu 55/65) and chilli chicken with rice (Nu 150). Wash it down with a Red Panda beer (Nu 130).

Panda Beer Garden Cafe
INTERNATIONAL $$

(☑77754848; Bathpalathang; pizza Nu 260-280, set lunch/dinner Nu 400/450; ☺9am-5pm Mon-Fri, 9am-noon Sat) Adjacent to and associated with the Bumthang Brewery (p137), this cosy cafe serves meat and veg pizzas, Swiss-style cheesy fondue and raclette dishes, cakes and espresso coffee (from Nu 100). Set buffets for lunch and dinner can be arranged with prior notice. Or if it's just beer and snacks that you want, this is also the place to come.

🛍 Shopping

As in most Bhutanese towns, the shops in Jakar contain a delicious hodgepodge of goods. There are a couple of dedicated handicraft shops on the main street where it's OK to gently haggle for a better price. One item in good supply in Jakar is *chugo* (dried yak cheese). Unless you want to break your teeth, let a piece soften in your mouth for a while before biting into it.

Dragon Handicrafts
ARTS & CRAFTS

(☑17120032; ☺7am-9pm) The most prominent souvenir shop in town has a decent range of books, masks and the like. It accepts credit cards, and you can also rent mountain bikes here. Also of note is a display of a *gho* (traditional dress for men) worn by the first king of Bhutan.

Yoser Lhamo Shop
FOOD

(Bumthang Swiss Cheese & Wine Shop; ☑17607239, 03-631929; Bathpalathang; ☺6am-7pm) Yoser Lhamo is the main outlet for the Swiss Farm enterprises, where soft Gouda or hard Emmental cheese sells for Nu 650 per kilogram. This cheese is made for eating off the block, unlike the soft Bhutanese *datse,* which is used only in sauces.

Gongkhar Handicrafts
ARTS & CRAFTS

(☺8am-9pm) Stocks a small selection of glossy books, DVDs and textiles. This is the place to buy a miniature yak for the pool room...

Bumthang Handicraft Shop
ARTS & CRAFTS

(☺9am-6pm) This shop south of the main bazaar is strong on textiles from eastern Bhutan.

ℹ Information

Bank of Bhutan (☺9am-1pm & 2-4pm Mon-Fri, 9am-noon Sat) Also has ATMs opposite and behind Gongkhar Handicrafts.

Bhutan National Bank (☺9am-4pm Mon-Fri, 9-11am Sat) Also has an ATM opposite Gongkhar Handicrafts.

Pema Yangzom Pharmacy (Bumthang Medical Store; ☑17670906; ☺7am-1pm & 2-7.30pm) For medical supplies.

Police Station (☑03-361113, emergency 113) At the base of Jakar Dzong.

Post Office (☺9am-5pm Mon-Fri, 9am-1pm Sat)

ℹ Getting There & Away

Jakar's Bathpalathang Airport is on the east bank of the Chamkhar Chhu, and operates six Druk Air flights a week to Paro, though timetables change seasonally depending on demand.

Druk Air (☑17110150, 77888887; www.drukair. com.bt) has a ticketing office in Jakar.

Metho Transport (☑17605131) has minibuses from Jakar to Thimphu (Nu 385, nine hours) at 7am.

Taxis congregate next to Jakar Lhakhang.

The **Dragon Ride** (☑17120032; per day Nu 2500; ☺7am-7pm) counter at Dragon Handicrafts rents out mountain bikes, which is a great way to get around the valley's main sights.

Chokhor Valley

To most people the Chokhor valley is Bumthang, and the Chokhor valley is often called the Bumthang valley or just simply Bumthang. If the weather is conducive and you feel like a walk, it's possible to visit Jampey and Kurjey Lhakhangs in the morning, cross the river and have a packed lunch

CENTRAL BHUTAN CHOKHOR VALLEY

at Do Zam, and then visit Tamshing and Konchogsum Lhakhangs in the afternoon. There is also a new road bridge at Do Zam, allowing you to fit in even more sightseeing by car. If you want to see a good selection of valley sights and fit in a hike, you really need three or four days here.

Western Side of the Valley

The road that leads up the western side of the valley connects a string of interesting temples, which are connected in one way or another to the visit of Guru Rinpoche to Bumthang in 746. Mountain biking is a great way to link up the monasteries and continue over to the east bank. You can walk/drive/ride from Jampey Lhakhang over Do Zam's road or suspension bridge.

⦿ Sights

Sey Lhakhang BUDDHIST TEMPLE
Beyond the hospital north of Jakar is the Sey Lhakhang ('*sey*' means 'golden'). Properly known as Lhodrak Seykhar Dratshang, this is a monastic school that was established in 1963. The central figure in the lhakhang is Marpa Lotsawa, a great teacher and translator of the Kagyu lineage.

Jampey Lhakhang BUDDHIST TEMPLE
Up a short side road about 1.5km past Sey Lhakhang, this fabulous temple is believed to have been built in 659 by the Tibetan king Songtsen Gampo, on the same day as Kyichu Lhakhang in Paro, in order to subdue a Tibetan demoness (the temple is said to pin her left knee). The temple was visited by Guru Rinpoche and was renovated by the Sindhu Raja after the Guru restored his life force. It's the one place in the valley that feels truly ancient.

Inside the main Jampey (Jampa) Lhakhang are three stone steps representing three ages. The first signifies the past, the age of the historical Buddha, Sakyamuni. This step has descended into the ground and is covered with a wooden plank. The next age is the present, and its step is level with the floor. The top step represents a new age. It is believed that when the step representing the present age sinks to ground level, the gods will become like humans and the world as it is now will end.

The central figure in the ancient inner sanctum is Jampa, the Buddha of the future, with his feet on an elephant. This is the oldest part of the oldest chapel in Bhutan. The entry to the chapel is protected by an iron chain mail that was made by Pema Lingpa. Look up into the alcove above the entry to see a statue of Guru Rinpoche. He sat in this alcove and meditated, leaving behind a footprint. It is said that under the lhakhang there is a lake with several *terma*.

The inner *kora* (circumambulation) path around the chapel is lined with ancient murals depicting 1000 Buddhas. There are more lovely murals in the atrium. On the right side of the wooden wall divider is an image of Kim-lha, the Goddess of the Home.

On the northern side of the courtyard is the Kalachakra Temple (Dukhor Lhakhang), added by Ugyen Wangchuck when he was *penlop*. The animal-headed deities on the walls are the demons that confront the dead during the 49 days of bardo (the state between death and rebirth). Chimi Dorji, the administrator of Jakar Dzong, added the Guru Lhakhang on the south side of the *dochey* (courtyard), which features statues of Guru Rinpoche, Tsepame and Chenresig. Generations of prostrators have worn the wooden boards smooth on either side of the courtyard entryway.

Behind the main temple are two large stone chortens; one is in memory of the second king's younger brother, the other in memory of Lama Pentsen Khenpo, spiritual adviser to the first and second Bhutanese kings. The four corners of the complex are anchored by four more chortens, coloured yellow, red, white and blue.

The pile of *mani* stones (carved with the Buddhist mantra *om mani peme hum*) in the car park in front of the goemba is called a *thos* and represents the Guardians of the Four Directions.

Each October one of the most spectacular festivals in Bhutan, the Jampey Lhakhang Drup, is staged here. The festival ground and VIP viewing platform is to the left (south) of the chapel. On one evening, after the lama dances, the monastery hosts a *mewang*, when pilgrims jump through a burning archway. Another late-night rite is the naked *tercham* (treasure dance), normally performed at midnight.

Chakhar Lhakhang BUDDHIST TEMPLE
(Iron Castle Temple) Beside the main road, a short distance beyond Jampey Lhakhang, is Chakhar Lhakhang. It's the site of the palace of the Indian king Sendha Gyab, better known as the Sindhu Raja, who first invited Guru Rinpoche to Bumthang. The original

palace was made of iron, hence the name Chakhar; it was said to have been nine storeys high, holding within it all the treasures of the world. The current building was built in the 14th century by the saint Dorji Lingpa.

Although it is easy to mistake it for just a house, this is an interesting temple and worth a short visit. The main statue is of Guru Rinpoche, and there are dozens of masks and black hats that are used during the Jampey Lhakhang Drup festival. Guru Rinpoche took Sindhu Raja's daughter Tashi Khewdoen as his consort – you can see her statue to the left of the altar (flanked by baby elephant tusks), as well as a photo of her stone footprint, one of the lhakhang's most prized relics.

On the ground floor the entrepreneurial caretaker has opened a small museum (Nu 150 entrance fee) that contains farm, household and religious artefacts.

Kurjey Lhakhang
BUDDHIST TEMPLE

This large, active and important temple complex is named after the body *(kur)* print *(jey)* of Guru Rinpoche, which is preserved in a cave inside the oldest of the three buildings that make up the complex. It is at the end of a paved road, 2.5km from Chakhar Lhakhang.

The first of the three temples, the **Guru Lhakhang**, is the oldest and was built in 1652 by Mingyur Tenpa when he was *penlop* of Trongsa. Tucked just below the eaves is a figure of a snow lion with a *jachung* (also called *garuda*) above it, which represents the famous struggle between Guru Rinpoche (appearing as the *garuda*) and the local demon, Shelging Kharpo (as the snow lion). The statue of Shelging Kharpo inside is usually hidden from view.

At the entrance to the lower-floor **Sangay Lhakhang** is a small crawl-through rock passage; Bhutanese believe that in crawling through a narrow tunnel like this you will leave your sins behind. Behind the statues of the three Buddhas is a secret passageway that is said to have once led to Tharpaling.

The upper-floor sanctuary is the holiest in the complex. There are 1000 small statues of Guru Rinpoche neatly lined up along the left wall, plus statues of Guru Rinpoche, Pema Lingpa and Drolma (Tara). The main statue in this sanctuary is again of Guru Rinpoche, flanked by his eight manifestations and eight chortens. Hidden behind this image is the **meditation cave**, where he left his body imprint. The far wall has images of Guru Rinpoche, his manifestations, his 25

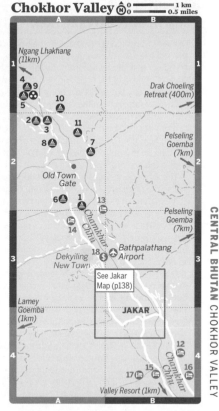

Chokhor Valley

WORTH A TRIP

BUMTHANG CULTURAL TREK

The walk from Ngang Lhakhang in the upper Chokhor valley to the Tang valley is often referred to as the Bumthang Cultural Trek, but most people now do the trek in a single day, staying at simple accommodation in Ngang Lhakhang and more luxurious digs at Ogyen Chholing at the start and end of the walk, respectively. The six-hour walk is easily doable in a day but packs in a tiring 750m climb to the Phephe La.

The walk starts from the Ngang Lhakhang (p145) with a short climb to a meadow at the base of **Draphe Dzong**, which is worth the short detour to explore the ruins of this formerly strategic fort. From here the trail drops to the **Sambitang** campsite (a possible overnight stop). The trail continues across meadows, with a lot of dwarf bamboo, before climbing up to a cold, shadowy forest of birch, sycamore and tall bamboo. Spanish moss drapes the ancient trees, giving an eerie feel to the steep climb.

The climb continues through a rhododendron forest in a dry gully to a rock cairn and a little stone shrine. Tattered prayer flags stretch across the path atop **Phephe La** (3360m), on a forested ridge with big birch and fir trees.

The trail leads down to a stream at 3200m, then into a side valley, passing a small *mani* wall (carved with Buddhist inscriptions) and a *khonying* (two-legged archway chorten). Breaking out into broad yak pastures, the route continues down through fields into a wide valley, where the most prominent of several trails leads downhill to a wooden bridge at 2790m near the village of Tandingang (also known as **Tahung**).

From here a rough farm road leads down to **Tang** village and the main Tang valley. Your vehicle can pick you up here and take you to Ogyen Chholing or you can continue on foot to **Gamling**, a large, wealthy village noted for its *yathra* weaving, about 45 minutes downstream, where a footpath climbs up to a ridge, reaching four chortens and several large houses at 2760m. Ogyen Chholing (p149) is atop the hill to the right. Comfortable rooms and great meals are available at the renovated guesthouse (p149).

If horse riding sounds inviting, you can explore the area around Tandingang or Ogyen Chholing on sturdy Bhutanese ponies by contacting **Pema Wangdi** (✆77373227; Tandingang; per day US$50). For an authentic village overnight in the region try the **farmhouse homestay** (✆77351570; Tandingang; r Nu 1500, breakfast Nu 350, lunch & dinner Nu 400) of Sangay Dawa, who offers lunch to hikers if prearranged.

disciples and various other figures connected with the Guru. The big cypress tree behind the lhakhang is said to have sprouted from the Guru's walking stick.

Ugyen Wangchuck, the first king of Bhutan, built the second temple, the **Sampa Lhundrup Lhakhang**, in 1900, when he was still *penlop* of Trongsa. On the entrance porch are paintings of the Guardians of the Four Directions and of various local deities who were converted to Buddhism by Guru Rinpoche. The white ghostlike figure on the white horse above the doorway to the right is Shelging Kharpo; also here are local protectors Yakdu Nagpo (on a black yak) and Kyebu Lungten (on a red horse). Inside the temple is a towering statue of Guru Rinpoche, this one 10m high, flanked again by his eight manifestations. A smaller image of the Guru sits facing towards Tibet with a defiant stare.

The third building in the complex was built by Ashi Kesang Wangchuck, queen to the third king, in 1984 under the guidance of Dilgo Khyentse Rinpoche. She also had the courtyard in front of the three temples paved with stones and built a wall with 108 chortens around the whole complex. On the porch in front of the temple is a large wheel of life. At the bottom you can see a man being judged, with black and white stones representing his good and bad deeds. There's a mystic spiral mandala on the side of the entrance. Interior murals illustrate various monastic rules and regulations, including the strict dress codes.

The elaborately decorated **Zangto Pelri Lhakhang**, a short distance south of the Kurjey Lhakhang compound, features a kitschy 3D depiction of the paradise of Guru Rinpoche and a wall mural of Ashi Wangchuk enjoying life in the western paradise known as Dewachen. The ground floor has a particularly lovely portable chorten shrine known as a *tashi gomang*.

A five-minute walk up the hillside near the entrance is the Kurjey Drupchhu, a sacred spring where monks come to wash their socks.

The popular **Kurjey tsechu** is held in June and includes a masked dance that dramatises Guru Rinpoche's defeat of Shelging Kharpo. A large *thangka,* called Guru Tshengye Thondrol, depicting the eight manifestations of Guru Rinpoche, is unfurled in the early morning before the dances, which are performed by the monks from Trongsa.

Deothang Goemba BUDDHIST MONASTERY
(Dawathang Goemba) The little-visited but charming Deothang Goemba, known as the Field of the Moon, is just north of Kurjey Lhakhang and dates from 1949. The surprisingly grand main hall has a large image of Guru Rinpoche, with 12 other interesting metal statues to the side. A small, grey image of Thangtong Gyalpo stands above the cabinet to the left.

Luege Rowe BUDDHIST TEMPLE
This lovely and little-visited lhakhang at the far northern end of the valley offers a fine half-day hike. The chapel is named 'Sheeps' Horns' after the sacred horn prints and hoof prints on the cave roof. Pilgrims walk under the roof's nine mandalas and make a wish. The building is locked when the caretaker is away, but it's still a lovely location.

From Kurjey Lhakhang drive beside the Duer Chhu past Taktu Zampa and the village of Menchugang to Jusbi village. From here a path climbs up the forested hillside, sometimes on wooden planks across marshy bamboo groves. After two hours branch left at a junction and 30 minutes later you'll reach a chorten gateway, from where you can see the lhakhang nestled in a fold in the hills.

Back at the junction continue straight for 40 minutes to yak pastures, where a path branches left for the more ambitious hike across the ridge to Shugdrak. After a total of four hours' walking a collection of prayer flags marks a great viewpoint over the Bumthang valley. From here it's less than an hour downhill to Thangbi.

Thangbi Goemba BUDDHIST MONASTERY
(Thankabi Goemba) Thangbi Goemba was founded in 1470 by Shamar Rinpoche and, after a dispute, was taken over by Pema Lingpa. The main chapel of the Dusum Sangay (past, present and future Buddhas) is entered under another of Pema Lingpa's famous chain mails.

Around 20 *gomchen* (lay or married monks) attend here, celebrating a *mani*

(festival) and fire ceremony in the middle of the eighth lunar month (October).

The goemba is a 3.5km drive north of Kurjey Lhakhang on an unpaved road, branching across the river at Toktu Zampa. Along the main road you'll see what looks like mailboxes; these are actually 'milk boxes', where local herders leave their fresh milk for daily delivery down to Jakar.

Hikes start from here to Ngang Lhakhang and to Luege Rowe. For Ngang Lhakhang walk along the road to a small *khonying* (traditional stupa-style gateway), visit the nearby rock painting and traditional water mill and then cross the bridge over the Chamkhar Chhu at Kharsa village.

Shugdrak CAVE
To get well off the beaten track make the short 10-minute hike up to this sacred Guru Rinpoche cave, 2km past Thangbi. A series of ladders leads pilgrims past a lovely butter-lamp shrine to a rock-face chapel, where a monk can point out the stone footprint, handprint and boot print of the Guru.

Pilgrims have stuffed dozens of ngultrum notes into the cracks of the rock wall.

To get here take the dirt side road to the left, just past Goling and Kharsa villages, then drive for 1km to the car park and walk 10 minutes up to the cave.

Ngang Lhakhang BUDDHIST TEMPLE
(Swan Temple) A bumpy 10km drive up the Chokhor valley from Thangbi Goemba is the small region known as Ngang-yul (Swan Land). The site was visited by Guru Rinpoche, but the present Ngang Lhakhang was built in the 15th century by Lama Namkha Samdrup, a contemporary of Pema Lingpa.

Despite the recently renovated exterior, the interior contains some lovely statues and paintings. The primary statue is of Guru Rinpoche, flanked by early Buddhist missionary Shantarakshita and Tibetan king Trisong Detsen. There is a mural of the Zhabdrung on the side wall opposite the altar and an image of Guru Rinpoche on a lotus surrounded by two duck-like swans.

The upper chapel is a *goenkhang,* with statues of the 'Tsela Nam Sum' trinity of Tsepame, Namse and Drolma, with Chenresig standing to the left. The statue of Guru Rinpoche to the right was fashioned by Pema Lingpa himself. Protector deities lurk in the shadows. Hanging from the rafters are masks used in the three-day Ngang Bi Rabney, a festival organised in the middle of the

NANGSIPHEL

This attractive village high in the valley is starting to lure visitors. Also known as Chhok-hortoe, it's a prosperous village that has become wealthy thanks to the centuries-old caravan trade with Tibet and the more recent boom in the *yarsa gomba* (cordyceps) trade.

The annual two-day **Nomad's Festival** is held here on the third weekend in February and features a series of traditional sports, such as shot-put, wrestling, archery, tug of war and even pillow fighting on a pole, along with mask dances. Locals set up stalls selling everything from buckwheat products to fermented cheese.

The village hopes to be a starting point for new treks into the Wangchuck Centennial Park, which is constructing a visitor centre here. The five-hour Orochhoto (Raven's Beak) Trail winds through blue pine and hemlock forest and cliffs above the village, offering fine day-hike potential.

Homestays are available in both Nangsiphel and the surrounding villages of Shabjithang and Dorjung through the community-run **Alpine Organic Homestays** (☑17670870, 17292177; s/d Nu 1430/1650, meals Nu 330). The homestays are simple but offer an inside toilet and a hot-stone bath.

Nangsiphel is around 4km north of the turn-off to Ngang Lhakhang, passing the charming Shabjithang Lhakhang after 2km. Figure on an hour's drive from Jakar.

10th month by the two main clans of the village in honour of the temple's founder.

It's possible to stay overnight at the rural **Balakha Farmhouse** (☑17292062; s/d Nu 1300/1500, meals Nu 350-500), homestay accommodation right beside the lhakhang. Accommodation is simple, but you'll get a comfortable mattress on the floor, a shared organic meal with the family and a clean Western toilet. The friendly owners have looked after the lhakhang for generations.

A bridge over the Chamkhar Chhu means it's possible to drive up to the lhakhang, but it's a much nicer walk (of two hours) from Thangbi Goemba along the true left bank of the river. En route you can detour to explore the 17th-century ruins of Draphe (Drapham, or Damphel) Dzong, a 30-minute gentle uphill walk from Ngang Lhakhang.

The long day hike over the Phephe La (signed 'Febila') to Ogyen Chholing Palace in the Tang valley also begins here, on what is called the Bumthang Cultural Trail (p144).

Eastern Side of the Valley

The best way to visit the eastern side of the Chokhor valley is to walk a couple of hundred metres north from Kurjey Lhakhang, then follow a path east to cross a prayer-flag-strewn footbridge. Note, however, that a new road bridge opened in 2018 and road widening on both sides of the valley is having an impact on this walk. From the bridge you can see a natural formation named **Do Zam**, said to be the remains of a stone bridge that

was built by a goddess trying to meet Guru Rinpoche, but destroyed by a demon.

From here you can follow the east-bank trail south for 30 minutes to Tamshing Goemba. A more interesting 45-minute detour is to take a left after the bridge for 10 minutes to a **manor house**, built by relatives of the second king. From here branch left for two minutes to an impressive **rock painting** of Guru Rinpoche in the form of Dorji Drolo, astride a tiger. Warning: the last 20m of the trail is a narrow goat track on a very steep slope.

Back at the manor house, head uphill to the **Dorji Bi Lhakhang**, with its large white chorten. From here a dirt road descends to Tamshing Lhakhang via the turn-off to Pema Sambhava Lhakhang. You can meet your vehicle at Dorji Bi or Tamshing Lhakhang.

The major influence in the temples on this side of the valley was Pema Lingpa, the great *terton* (discoverer of *terma*) of the 16th century.

◎ Sights

Tamshing Goemba   BUDDHIST MONASTERY
This goemba, formally the Tamshing Lhendup Chholing (Temple of the Good Message), is 5km from Jakar. It was established in 1501 by Pema Lingpa and is the most important Nyingma goemba in the kingdom. Pema Lingpa built the unusual structure himself, with the help of *khandromas,* who, it is claimed, made many of the statues.

On the inner walls are what are believed to be original unrestored images that were painted by Pema Lingpa, though there are even older paintings underneath.

The entrance to the lhakhang is via a courtyard lined with monks' quarters. Upon entering the inner courtyard, directly in front is the small **Mani Dungkhor Lhakhang**, built in 1914 to hold a huge prayer wheel.

The main lhakhang, to your right, has an unusual design, with the key chapel screened off in the centre of the assembly hall, almost like a separate building. In the chapel are three thrones for the three incarnations (body, mind and speech) of Pema Lingpa. During important ceremonies the reincarnations sit here, although a photograph is substituted if one of the incarnations is not present.

The primary statue in the inner sanctuary is of Guru Rinpoche flanked by Jampa (Maitreya, the Buddha of the future) and Sakyamuni. This statue is particularly important because it was sculpted by the *khandromas*. The statue's eyes are looking slightly upward, following the angels in their flight; another unique aspect of the statue is that the Guru is not wearing shoes. Above the altar are two *maksaras* (mythological crocodiles) and a *garuda*. On the walls are the eight manifestations of Guru Rinpoche, four on each side. A small statue of Pema Lingpa occupies a glass case in front of the chapel.

The upper floor forms a balcony around the assembly hall. Pema Lingpa was a short man and it is said that he built the low ceiling of the balcony to his exact height. Around the outside are 100,000 old paintings of Sakyamuni. In the upper chapel is a statue of Tsepame, the Buddha of Long Life, and a large collection of masks that are used for dances. Also here, but off-limits to visitors, is a statue of Pema Lingpa fashioned by the man himself.

There are good views from Tamshing back across the river to Kurjey Lhakhang.

Konchogsum Lhakhang   BUDDHIST TEMPLE

Just 400m below Tamshing, this towering, recently constructed and brightly painted building completely envelops the restored remains of the original temple. That much smaller temple, most of which dates from the 15th century, when Pema Lingpa restored it, was almost destroyed by a butter-lamp fire in 2010. Parts of the original building probably date back to a Tibetan design from the 6th or 7th century.

The old lhakhang retains its central statue of Nampal Namse (Vairocana, one of the five Dhyani Buddhas). On Vairocana's right are Chenresig and Longchem Rabjampa

---

PEMA LINGPA'S CHAIN MAIL

At the side of the dimly lit inner *kora* (circumambulation) path within Tamshing Goemba is a cloak of chain mail made by Pema Lingpa. It weighs about 25kg, and if you can hoist it on to your shoulders it is an auspicious act to carry it around the *kora* three times, including getting down to prostrate before the chapel (three times!) and getting back on your feet.

(founder of Tharpaling Goemba). On Vairocana's left are statues of Guru Rinpoche and Pema Lingpa (said to be a reincarnation himself of Longchem Rabjampa). There is a pedestal in the courtyard in front of the old lhakhang that used to be outside, but has now been internalised within the soaring walls of the new lhakhang. Upon this pedestal sat a large and ancient bell. It is said that when this bell was rung it could be heard all the way to Lhasa, Tibet. The story goes that a 17th-century Tibetan army tried to steal the bell, but it was too heavy and they dropped it, cracking the bell. The fractured bell resides in the new Kudung Chorten Lhakhang in the upper level of the new building.

The modern structure is truly magnificent. Massive, brightly painted columns soar to the mandala-painted ceiling. A perimeter mezzanine features seated statues of various (mind, body and spirit) reincarnations of Pema Lingpa, and virtually every surface has been decorated with intricate murals and designs. Either side of the lhakhang are monks' quarters, signifying that this place is developing, phoenix-like, into a vibrant centre of Buddhist learning.

Pema Sambhava Lhakhang   BUDDHIST TEMPLE

Along the dirt road north of Tamshing, a short steep climb above the valley floor leads to the small Pema Sambhava Lhakhang. The original lhakhang was built in 1490 by Pema Lingpa around the cave where Guru Rinpoche meditated and assumed his manifestation of Padmasambhava. The lhakhang was expanded by Jigme Namgyal, the father of the first king, and restored in the early 1970s.

There are several rock paintings here, as well as a representation of the local protector Terda Norbu Zangpo, who lurks in a corner behind the door beside a leather whip, and the cave itself is painted in rainbow colours. Ask to see the main relic, a conch shell that is said to have flown here from Do Zam. The footpath at the back of the lhakhang leads steeply uphill for 90 minutes to the white cliff of the Drak Choeling retreat centre.

Tang Valley

Tang is the most remote of Bumthang's valleys. It is higher than Chokhor so there's not as much agriculture here, although in places where the soil is fertile and deep the Arcadian scenes are picture-perfect.

From Jakar it's 11km to the road that branches north up the Tang valley. This road climbs past the trail to **Membartsho** (1.3km from the turn-off) and the **Pema Tekchok Choeling Shedra**, a large nunnery, to reach the turn-off to the jumping-off point for the hike to Kunzangdrak. The road then climbs high above the river. After a short descent to the river it's 3km to **Mesithang** and 1km further to the **Ta Rimochen Lhakhang**.

The road becomes gravel after Mesithang and passes a picnic spot before the bridge at **Kizum** (Ki Zam), 22km from the road junction. Across the bridge, a steep gravel road winds up to the mansion and village of Ogyen Chholing.

Membartsho

A five-minute walk from a parking spot at a bend in the road leads to a picturesque pool in a shadowy ravine of the Tang Chhu that is known as Membartsho (Burning Lake). The 27-year-old Pema Lingpa found several of Guru Rinpoche's *terma* here. It's a lovely, if slightly unsettling, spot, where nature, religion and mythology blur into one.

A wooden bridge crosses the prayer-flag-strewn gorge and offers a good vantage point over the 'lake'. Only the enlightened will spot the temple that lurks in the inky depths. The sanctity of the site is made evident by the numerous small clay offerings called *tsha-tsha* piled up in various rock niches.

Under a rock shrine with a carving of Guru Rinpoche flanked by Sakyamuni and Pema Lingpa is a cave that virtuous people can crawl through, no matter how big they are. Beware: it's quite small, and very dusty. Also, don't venture too close to the edges of the ravine for that elusive photo angle. Vegetation hides where the rock ends and a treacherous drop into the river begins. Sadly, there have been several drownings in the swift waters here.

Kunzangdrak Goemba

A stiff 45-minute hike up the hillside above Drangchel village leads to one of the most important sites related to Pema Lingpa. He began construction of the goemba in 1488, and many of his most important sacred relics are kept here.

The first chapel, Wangkhang Lhakhang, has a *kora* path around it, suspended in mid-air, with Chenresig, Guru Nangsi Zilnon (Guru Rinpoche) and his disciple Namkhai Nyingpo inside. Walk around the back of the building to the gravity-defying **Khandroma Lhakhang**, the meditation cave of Yeshe Tshogyel, spectacularly situated against a vertical rock face that seeps holy water. Ask to see the woodblocks and stone anvil bearing the footprint of Pema Lingpa. Finally, cross over the small bridge, past a fire-blackened cleft in the cliff, to the *goenkhang*.

Figure on 2½ hours for the return trip. There is a very rough road to the goemba but this doesn't detract from the hike (the more comfortable option).

Ta Rimochen Lhakhang

Ta Rimochen Lhakhang was built by Pema Lingpa in the 14th century to mark a sacred place where Guru Rinpoche meditated. The original name 'Tag (Tak) Rimochen' (meaning 'an impression of tiger's stripes') is derived from the vertical yellow stripes that stain the dark rock cliff behind the building.

There are handprints and footprints of the Guru and his consort Yeshe Tsogyal on the cliff face, as well as several wish-fulfilling stones, sacred symbols and even an invisible doorway. There are more footprints at the top of the steps leading to the temple. Inside the main chapel, look for a depiction of local protector Lhamo Remaley.

The two huge rocks below the lhakhang represent male and female *jachung (garudas)*. By the road you can see the roadside bathing tub of the Guru and even the buttock marks of Yeshe Tsogyal, worn into the rock during an epic bout of tantric lovemaking.

Ogyen Chholing Palace

From Kizum bridge it's a 3km uphill drive to this hilltop 16th-century *naktshang* (temple dedicated to a warlord or protective deity), originally built by Deb Tsokye Dorji, the one-time *penlop* of Trongsa and a descendant of the *terton* Dorji Lingpa. The present

WALKING THE BUMTHANG VALLEYS

There are plenty of opportunities for day hikes in the Bumthang region, most of which offer a wonderful combination of remote sacred sights, wide valley views and sublime picnic spots.

A good short walk is between Kurjey Lhakhang and Tamshing Goemba via Do Zam and the nearby rock painting of Dorji Drolo, though the new road bridge has increased traffic. You can extend the walk by 15 minutes by walking to Kurjey from Jampey Lhakhang.

Following are the main day hikes:

Pelseling Goemba The half-day hike from the Swiss Guest House in Jakar to the large 'Lotus Grove' Monastery is all uphill (2½ hours), gaining 800m, but is nice and varied, through a mix of forest, meadows and villages, and you are rewarded with great views. A switchbacking 11km dirt road now winds up to the monastery, so you can get picked up at the monastery. Alternatively, descend a different route to Tamshing Goemba for a total of about four hours' walking.

Kunzangdrak Goemba For a remoter hike, drive to Pelseling and then hike over the ridge and around a side valley to this retreat in the Tang valley. Get your vehicle to pick you up there before visiting other sights in the valley.

Tharpaling Goemba A favourite one-way walk is from Lamey Goemba over the ridge to Tharpaling in the Chhume valley, to meet your vehicle there. The trail branches off a logging road 1km past the goemba, which was built in the 1800s as a residence for King Ugyen Wangchuck and now houses a government office. The first two hours are a hard uphill slog through rhododendrons and bamboo, before you finally crest a pass and descend across the bare hillsides of the Chhume valley to the Zhambhala Lhakhang, Choedrak Hermitage and, finally, Tharpaling. The hike offers less in the way of views but has the feel of a pilgrimage, taking in several sacred sites. Check for ticks along this route.

Thangbi Goemba to Ngang Lhakhang A pleasant, largely flat, two- to three-hour hike that avoids the bumpy drive to Ngang Lhakhang by taking the south-bank trail of the Chamkhar Chhu, passing the ruins of Draphe Dzong en route.

Drak Choeling Retreat A 90-minute uphill hike from Pema Sambhava Lhakhang takes you up through forest to the white cliffs of this silent retreat centre (don't disturb the hermits), with sweeping views over the Bumthang valley from a prayer-flag lookout.

Luege Rowe A charming half-day hike to a remote, little-visited lhakhang that feels untouched by time. Continue the route to Thangbi Goemba or make the more ambitious day hike across the ridge to Shugdrak.

structures, including the *tshuglhakhang* (main temple), *utse, chamkhang* (dance house), *shagkor* (residential quarters) and *nubgothang* (guesthouse), are more recent, having been rebuilt after their collapse in an 1897 earthquake.

The family that owns Ogyen (Ugyen) Chholing has turned part of the complex into a **museum** (☑ 17641464; www.oling.bt; Nu 200; ⊙ by appointment) to preserve its legacy. The fascinating and well-captioned exhibits offer real insights into the lifestyle of a Bhutanese noble family. Highlights include a book of divination, a *dakini* dance costume made of bone and the revelation that petrified yak dung was one of the ingredients for Bhutanese gunpowder. Particularly interesting is the section on the once-thriving trade with Tibet, describing how Bhutanese traders

would take tobacco, English cloth, rice, paper and indigo to trade fairs over the border in Lhodrak, to return laden with bricks of Chinese tea, gold dust, salt and borax (an ingredient in butter tea). Bring a torch. An excellent museum booklet (Nu 100) is for sale.

The family living quarters of the palace, in the **Ogyen Chholing Heritage House** (☑ 03-631221; www.oling.bt; r standard/deluxe Nu 3600/4800, set meals Nu 550-800), have undergone renovation and there are 14 traditional yet very comfortable guest rooms combining authenticity with some creature comforts. Proceeds go to the trust managing the palace, museum and its grounds. Your agency can probably also arrange an overnight in a nearby farmhouse.

Instead of leaving by road the way you came, consider making the one-hour walk back down to Kizum bridge via the charming **Choejam Lhakhang**, with its *kora* path and room full of festival masks, and the **Narut (Pelphug) Lhakhang**, built around a sacred cave enclosing a Guru Rinpoche footprint and a shrine to the local protector Garap Wangchu.

Thowadrak Hermitage

The remote hermitage of Thowadrak (Thowa Drak) clings to the highest rocks above the north end of the Tang valley. It is said to have been founded by Mandarava, the Indian consort of Guru Rinpoche, and the Guru himself is believed to have meditated here. The goemba was built by Dorji Lingpa. There are numerous small meditation retreats on the hillside above (don't disturb the hermits) and dramatic views over the valley. Texts relate that the upper valley conceals a sealed gateway to one of Bhutan's *bey-yul* (hidden lands). The only sounds here are of rushing water and the rustle of bamboo.

The six-hour return hike is best done as a day trip from the Ogyen Chholing Heritage House.

Jakar to the Ura Valley

48KM / 1½ HOURS

The road to the village of Ura crosses the bridge to the east of Jakar, then travels south along the east bank of the Chamkhar Chhu, winding around a ridge past the turn-off to the Tang valley. As the road climbs, look back at excellent views up the Chokhor and Chhume valleys.

The road climbs to a chorten, then finally crosses the Shertang La (3590m), also known as the Ura La. Just before the pass you'll get a view of Gangkhar Puensum (7570m) to the northwest and the yellow-roofed lhakhang of Shingkhar village below.

It's then a long descent into the Ura valley. The direct way down on foot from the pass makes for a nice hour-long walk into Ura village. You can also ride this trail on a mountain bike. A couple of kilometres before the turn-off to the village of Ura, which lies below the road, is the turn-off to Shingkhar.

Shingkhar

POP 250 / ELEV 3400M

The village of Shingkhar, made up of only 35 traditional households, is 9km up a good gravel side road and over the ridge from Ura.

There are several good hiking options in the valley. The easiest option is the two-hour return hike to the cliff-hanging **Shamsul Lhakhang**, which offers fine views down the valley. The trail starts from the dirt road 3km above Shingkhar. A longer hike leads up to the Singmi La, along the former trade route to Lhuentse, and multiday treks continue further through Phrumsengla National Park to Songme in the Lhuentse valley.

On the way back to Ura stop at the charming **Somtrang Lhakhang**, with its courtyard megaliths and a meditation retreat in the cliffs above the village. A footpath offers a pleasant walk from here directly down to Ura village. A three-day *kangsoe* festival brings the place to life at the end of the ninth month (November).

THE BURNING LAKE

Two of Pema Lingpa's most celebrated discoveries took place at Membartsho.

The first occurred when a dream told him to go to a point where the river forms a large pool that looks like a lake. After a while, standing on a large rock, he saw a temple with many doors, only one of which was open. He plunged naked into the lake and entered a large cave where there was a throne, upon which sat a life-size statue of Lord Buddha and many large boxes. An old woman with one eye handed him one of the chests and he suddenly found himself standing on the rock at the side of the lake holding the treasure.

Pema Lingpa's second find was the most famous. His previous *terma* had instructed him to return to the lake, but when he did, many people gathered to watch the event and the sceptical *ponlop* (governor) of the district accused him of trickery. Under pressure to prove himself, Pema Lingpa took a lighted lamp and proclaimed: 'If I am a genuine revealer of your treasures, then may I return with it now, with my lamp still burning; if I am some devil, then may I perish in the water'. He jumped into the lake, and was gone long enough that the sceptics thought they'd been proven right. He then suddenly emerged back on the rock with the lamp still burning and holding a statue and a treasure chest. The lake became known as Membartsho (Burning Lake).

⊙ Sights

The **Rinchen Jugney Lhakhang**, on a hill just above the village, was founded by the Dzogchen master Longchen Rabjampa (1308–63).

The village's central **Dechen Chholing Goemba** is headed by Shingkhar Lama, whose predecessor featured prominently in the Bhutanese novel *The Hero with the Thousand Eyes* by Karma Ura. The central lhakhang has its floorboards exposed to show the stone teaching throne of Long-chen. The protector deities are appropriately fierce, except for Rahulla, who looks embarrassed wearing a gorilla mask.

🛏 Sleeping

Shingkhar Retreat GUESTHOUSE **$**
(☑ 17603971, 03-323206; masagang@druknet.bt; s/d Nu 2160/2760) Shingkhar Retreat is a great base from which to explore the village. The rooms are pretty basic, with mud walls and solar electricity, but cosy. Meals are available.

Ura

☑ 03 / ELEV 3100M

Ura is one of the most interesting villages in Bhutan. There are about 40 closely packed houses along cobblestone streets, and the main **Ura Lhakhang** dominates the town, giving it a medieval atmosphere. In colder weather Ura women can still be seen wearing a sheepskin shawl that serves as both a blanket and a cushion.

A few hundred metres beyond Hotel Araya Zamlha (towards Mongar) is the start of the **Ura–Geyzamchu Walking Trail**, a 9km-long, five-hour hike crossing the Wangthang La pass and rejoining the main road at Geyzam Chhu. It's a demanding but rewarding walk through rhododendron, pine forests and alpine meadows along an old trade route. For information and a local guide visit the **Phrumsengla National Park Visitor Centre** (☑ 77192125; admtnp@yahoo.com; ⊙ 9am-5pm Mon-Fri), or ask at Hotel Araya Zamlha.

✴ Festivals & Events

The annual **Ura yakchoe** has gained notoriety as a festival that changes date at the last minute, leaving behind disappointed tour groups on tight schedules. If you do decide to visit for the festival, usually held in May, it's wise to allow a couple of days' leeway in your itinerary.

The three days of masked dances usually start on the 12th day of the third month with a procession carrying an image of Chana Dorji (Vajrapani) from the nearby Gaden Lhakhang down to the main lhakhang. The eve of the festival sees the frantic brewing of *sinchhang* (a spirit distilled from millet, wheat or rice) and late-night exorcisms. Even if it's not festival time, it's a pleasant 15-minute walk from Gaden Lhakhang down to Ura village.

Ura is the centre of Bhutan's matsutake mushroom production, a fact celebrated with recipes, local stalls and other fungi-related fun in August's **Matsutake Festival**.

🛏 Sleeping

Most travellers will pass through the Ura valley, but if you are here for an overnight stay, the **Ura Bangpa Farmhouse** (☑ 77639828; s/d Nu 1600/1900, breakfast Nu 280, lunch & dinner Nu 550) and the **Hotel Araya Zamlha** (☑ 17732699; azherbal05@yahoo.com; r Nu 3600) require booking in advance. During the Ura festival even camping spots are scarce and some groups commute from Jakar, 90 minutes' drive away. At other times further homestay options are generally possible.

SOUTHERN DZONGKHAGS

The two *dzongkhags* (administrative districts) of Zhemgang and Sarpang lie on the southern border of central Bhutan. This region is open to tourism and Gelephu town is connected to Paro by regular flights, yet it remains little visited. Gelephu also offers a remote alternative entry or exit route between Bhutan and Assam in India. The region around Zhemgang was once a collection of tiny principalities, collectively known as Khyeng, absorbed into Bhutan in the 17th century.

For tourists the highlights include superb birdwatching, spotting golden langurs right beside the road, and Royal Manas National Park, which offers wildlife enthusiasts an amazing opportunity to explore an area of unsurpassed biodiversity.

Trongsa to Zhemgang

106KM / 4 HOURS

South of Eundu Chholing the road continues past the villages of Lungtel and Taksila (with its lhakhang above the road), before descending to the bridge at Tongtongphey, which marks the start/end point of the Nabji trek (p204). Past Koshela and Pangzum villages the road swings round the unstable Riotala cliffs slide area, opening up views of Nabji and Korphu villages in the side valley across the river.

After briefly detouring up a side valley the road reaches the Wangduegang turn-off, 86km from Trongsa, where the Zhemgang bypass continues ahead to offer a direct route to Gelephu (114km). The access road to the southern end of the Nabji trek also branches off here. Turn left to take the road to Zhemgang (20km), which zigzags steeply up a side valley, past a *mithun* cattle-breeding centre before finally rolling into Zhemgang.

The sleepy *dzongkhag* centre of Zhemgang is a natural place to break the trip. The surprisingly impressive dzong dates back to the 12th century and is home to about 70 monks and several statues of the valley protector Dorji Rabten. An annual tsechu here in March culminates in the unfurling of a large Guru Rinpoche *thondrol*. The picturesque old town, still bearing the original name of **Trong**, is worth a look. Wander through its cluster of stone houses along a narrow paved central street to visit its charming lhakhang.

In Zhemgang town, the contemporary, concrete **Hotel Valley View** (☑ 17938181, 77938181; s Nu 500, d Nu 1000-1200, meals Nu 250-350) is the best place to stay, but is nothing fancy. Hot water is available in the poorly planned bathrooms. There's a Bank of Bhutan ATM attached.

Zhemgang to Gelephu

131KM / 5 HOURS

After leaving Zhemgang the highway quickly swings into a side valley, passing the **Dueduel Namgyel Chorten** to the turn-off at Dakpa, which leads to the remote but historically important lhakhangs of Buli and Dali. Look for golden langurs along this stretch.

The Zhemgang bypass joins the main highway at the bridge across the Mangde Chhu. Over the bridge and 1km past the new town of **Tingtibi** (some maps still call the location Mangde Chhu) is the turn-off to Gomphu and access to the northern part of Royal Manas National Park. Tingtibi offers a potential lunch spot and even an overnight stop at the **T-Wang Hotel** (☑ 17761427, 03-790004; r Nu 1800, set meals Nu 300-500), whose simple rooms are often used by birding groups as a base to explore Royal Manas National Park.

A huge hydroelectric project nearby will continue to boost Tingtibi for several years. From here it is 98km to Gelephu.

The road south now starts a long climb, swinging around a Nepali-style chorten below **Tama** village. Just above the village is the small but atmospheric Lhamo Lhakhang. The older and more significant Tama Lhakhang, founded by Pema Lingpa, is a further 10 minutes' drive up towards the pass, a short walk from the road.

The road crests the **Tama La**, where vehicles make a *kora* around the white chorten. As you descend the hillside on the far side close your car windows and look for wild beehives on the cliffs above Chapcha. The nearby pagoda at Lungsilgang offers a viewpoint and picnic potential. The road bottoms out at Samkhar Zam bridge then climbs to **Surey** village, with its mandarin orchards, cardamom fields and lhakhang just above the village. The Gurung Hotel here offers a decent tea spot. Surey's official Dzongkha name is Jigme Choling but most locals use the Nepali name.

The road climbs past a landslide area with some sphincter-tightening 1000m drops to the right, before reaching a white chorten marking the turn-off to **Shershong tsachhu** (hot spring). The short but steep downhill detour leads to a sheltered complex of five tubular, cement hot tubs. Like elsewhere in Bhutan, the emphasis at the hot springs is on convalescence rather than pampering.

The main road hits the floodplain with a bump at the immigration check-post beside Pasang Zam bridge. A side road here leads to the hilltop Shershong Lhakhang and its important cremation ground. From here it's a short and mercifully flat drive into Gelephu.

Gelephu

☑ 06 / POP 6457 / ELEV 280M

The large, but hardly bustling, border town of Gelephu is the gateway to south-central Bhutan. It's a pleasant enough town but is really just a place to overnight before leaving or entering Bhutan.

If you find yourself with time to kill, visit the weekend market, spin the prayer wheels at the large Buddha statue beside the football ground or visit the large distillery operated by the army welfare division. The Nyimalung Tratsang, 1km north of town, is the winter residence for monks from Nyimalung Goemba in the Chhume valley.

🛏 Sleeping

Hotel Lhaa Zeey   HOTEL $
(📞16925241, 06-251536; phurbalhamo269@gmail.com; s Nu 918-1500, d Nu 1440-2220; ❄🛜) This welcoming place is one of the best choices in town, with a cosy balcony and dining room. The mostly spacious rooms come with hot-water bathrooms. Management can help organise onward travel to India with Indian taxis.

Hotel Kingacholing   HOTEL $
(📞17423177; www.hotelkingacholing.bt; s Nu 1000, d Nu 1400-2800; ❄🛜) Just north of the town centre and the football field is this latest addition to Gelephu's hotel options. All rooms have air-con and many are spacious, with king-size beds, TVs and bathrooms with hot water and tubs. Some rooms sport balconies with views over town or towards the hills. The restaurant has a limited menu of Bhutanese and Indian dishes.

Hotel Kuku   HOTEL $$
(📞17611121, 06-251435; s/d Nu 3000/3960; ❄) A central hotel that offers spacious deluxe rooms with reliable hot water, air-con, comfy mattresses and a cosy restaurant.

ⓘ Information

Bank of Bhutan (🕙9am-1pm & 2-3.30pm Mon-Fri, 9am-noon Sat) Opposite the football field; exchanges cash but not travellers cheques. Has another ATM at Hotel Kuku.

Bhutan National Bank (🕙9am-1pm & 2-3.30pm Mon-Fri, 9-11am Sat) Has an ATM and exchanges cash.

ⓘ Getting There & Away

Druk Air (p141) flies from Paro (direct or via Jakar) to Gelephu airport, west of town.

Sealed roads run north to Trongsa, either bypassing or via Zhemgang, and northwest to Wangdue Phodrang via Sarpang and Damphu.

Royal Manas National Park

Royal Manas National Park is home to a wide variety of animals, including elephants, water buffaloes, leopards, between 30 and 50 tigers, clouded leopards, civets, rhinoceroses and more than 360 species of birds. The park abuts the Manas National Park in Indian Assam, forming an important transnational conservation area.

After many years of being off-limits due to security concerns, this remote and enticing national park is open to visitors, and facilities are expanding. Accommodation options are very limited though, and the practicalities of visiting the park and organising activities are still little-known among many of the agents in Thimphu. But it is worth persevering and adding the park to your itinerary.

November to March are the best months to visit. Summer is extremely hot and some of the accommodation closes from June to August. There are several tsechu festivals in the region in the 10th Bhutanese month (November).

⊙ Sights

The drive from Tingtibi to Panbang is a real delight, as the road meanders beside the swift-flowing Mangde Chhu. About 3km before the village of Bobsar there are peculiar 'hanging gardens' of bamboo and Himalayan screw pine clinging to the riverside cliffs. Around 10km before reaching Panbang the road passes the beautiful twin waterfalls of **Lehleygang**. Beside the falls is a picnic ground and a chorten with an incongruous teapot spout, and across the road are some public toilets. Keep an eye out for capped langurs, darker-coated cousins of golden langurs.

🏃 Activities

Tourism is still in its infancy here. Your Bhutanese agent can arrange rafting, trekking and wildlife guides through the River Guides of Panbang (p284). This local outfit can also arrange cultural shows and village visits to witness the local Khenpa culture, including Bon festivals.

In addition to the rafting day trips and boat trips down the Manas between Panbang and **Manas Camp**, the national-park headquarters, three-day river expeditions can be arranged. Longer walks within the national park require hiring a park guide and often require elephants for transport. Visitors should be aware that animal-welfare groups advocate against riding elephants due to health concerns for the animals.

🛏 Sleeping

Panbang Eco-lodge   HOTEL $
(📞77373787, 17584221; kinlaydorji@gmail.com; Panbang; r Nu 1000, breakfast Nu 150, lunch & dinner Nu 350) On a sweeping bend of the Mangde Chhu, this lodge has just four rooms in

ⓘ CROSSING THE BORDER INTO INDIA: GELEPHU TO GUWAHATI & RANGIYA

Border Hours

Bhutan Immigration, at the border, is open 7am to 8pm daily. Here you will be finger-printed and photographed as you enter Bhutan, or you'll just get a passport stamp if leaving Bhutan.

Whether leaving or entering India, don't forget to get an Indian immigration stamp at the easily missed Foreigners' Registration Post at Deosiri, 10km from the Bhutan border. It's open 24 hours.

Foreign Exchange

Both Bank of Bhutan (p153) and Bhutan National Bank (p153) will change Bhutanese ngultrum into Indian rupees. In theory you are required to have your original exchange receipt, a passport copy and an application form, available at the banks.

Bhutanese banks will not exchange Indian rupees for US dollars. For small amounts you are better off changing money with your guide.

Onward to India

Unless you have organised to take your Bhutanese vehicle to Guwahati in India (five hours), the only reliable onward transport option is to hire an Indian taxi, either to Guwahati and its Lokpriya Gopinath Bordoloi International Airport (₹6000 to ₹7000), or to Rangiya (₹3000, three hours), which gives access to trains running east and west across India. Your guide can help arrange a taxi.

Unannounced transport strikes (bandhs) in Assam can cause potential havoc with travel schedules, although in recent years bandhs have become less frequent. The border officials receive very short notice of bandhs, so you may only be made aware of one when you reach the gate and find it closed. The only thing to do is to return to Gelephu. Most bandhs last 12 hours, but some may last up to 48 hours.

stone-and-wood cottages. Each room has a private hot-water bathroom and a sit-down toilet. More rooms are planned. There's also a two-storey restaurant building with river views.

Manas Hotel LOCAL HOTEL $
(Sonamthang; r Nu 2000-2500; 🛜) This impressive local hotel is along the road to Nanglam, about 1km from Panbang. Rooms in the older wing are cosy, with wooden furniture, double beds and air-con. Rooms in the new wing are cool, modern and tiled. The restaurant serves local food and alcohol and the highlight is the games room with two full-sized billiard tables!

★ Marang Forest Lodge TENTED CAMP $$
(📞17497923, 17150141; www.paddlebhutan.com; Bjoka Forest Rd; full board s/d Nu 4000/5250; ⊘closed Jun-Aug) This 'lodge' run by the River Guides of Panbang comprises nine tents mounted on platforms beside the Marangang Chhu. Tents are simple but comfortable, with twin beds and portable electric lights. Hot showers are available in two separate blocks, and a large open-sided pavilion functions as the communal dining area.

✖ Eating

The drive from Tingtibi to Panbang passes several villages with simple roadside restaurants serving packaged cake, tea and instant coffee. Accommodation options in Panbang provide meals and snacks. Look for local options such as *ngala metho tsoem* (jungle banana soup), *pacha* (cane shoots) and *jachu* (river weed or local spinach, whichever 'green' is available).

ⓘ Getting There & Away

There are a few roads into the park. The best way to access Panbang is to drive 55km from Nganglam on the Assam border. However, while this border is open to Indian nationals it is not yet open for other foreigners. Therefore, other visitors need to head to Tingtibi (via Gelephu or Zhemgang) and take the turn-off to Gomphu, followed by Pangtang and down to Panbang. Along this sealed road you can see a beautiful waterfall and a wealth of birdlife and mammals.

Alternative road access (not open to foreigners yet) to Panbang is from Mathanguri in India, just a short boat ride across the Manas Chhu from Manas Camp. A little-used 25km road leads from Gelephu to Kanamakra at the southwestern corner of the park.

Eastern Bhutan

Best Buddhist Architecture

➡ Lhuentse Dzong (p162)

➡ Gom Kora (p170)

➡ Chorten Kora (p171)

➡ Trashigang Dzong (p166)

➡ Trashi Yangtse Dzong (p169)

Best off the Beaten Track

➡ Hiking around Mongar (p160)

➡ Dungkhar (p162)

➡ Bomdeling Wildlife Sanctuary (p173)

➡ Birdwatching around Yong Khola (p157)

Why Go?

Intrepid travellers venturing to the wild and rugged east of Bhutan will be rewarded with fascinating villages and towns little influenced by tourism, group-free dzongs and temples, beautiful silks and amazing embroidery. Most of the population lives in tiny settlements secreted high above roads or in isolated valleys. The remote east is home to minority ethnic groups, some comprising fewer than 1000 people, and is unrivalled in traditional arts and crafts.

Many travellers to the east are lured by the magnificent bird-filled forests – wilderness havens for rare and unique wildlife. While birdwatching is extremely popular here, the east is opening up to other forms of tourism with new hotels and trekking routes being developed. The east of Bhutan sees fewer tourists than the western regions and remains a frontier for travel in Bhutan – reason enough to go!

When to Go

➡ The lower altitudes mean that late spring and summer here are hot, humid and sweaty, with insects aplenty. This is the best time for birdwatching in the lush broadleaf forests.

➡ Monsoon rains between May and August regularly cause havoc on the fragile roads carved into the steep mountains, so expect delays after heavy downpours.

➡ Late February to mid-March is a good time to visit for comfortable temperatures, low-season crowds, interesting festivals and spring blooms.

➡ Snowfalls in winter can also result in temporary road blockages on the high passes.

Eastern Bhutan Highlights

1 Trashigang (p165) Wandering the narrow streets of one of Bhutan's most attractive and lively towns.

2 Yong Khola (p157) Watching and listening for the rare and colourful birdlife for which Bhutan is famous.

3 Taki La (p161) Detouring to the 45m-high statue of Guru Rinpoche on the way to Lhuentse.

4 Khoma (p163) Watching some of Bhutan's finest cloth being woven at this remote weaving village.

5 Gom Kora (p170) Checking your sin levels at this picturesque pilgrimage destination.

6 Trashi Yangtse (p171) Walking around the serene Chorten Kora, and witnessing traditional crafts.

7 Bomdeling Wildlife Sanctuary (p173) Exploring this remote sanctuary, one of the best places to see black-necked cranes.

History

In ancient times eastern Bhutan was ruled by a collection of separate petty kingdoms and was an important trade route between India and Tibet. Goods flowed via Bhutan through what is now Singye Dzong in the Lhuentse district to the Tibetan town of Lhodrak.

The most important figure in this region's history was Chhogyel Mingyur Tenpa. When he was *penlop* (governor) of Trongsa, he led his armies to eastern Bhutan to quell revolts in Bumthang, Lhuentse, Trashigang, Mongar and Zhemgang. His efforts brought eastern Bhutan under the rule of the *desi* (secular ruler of Bhutan) and went a long way towards the ultimate unification of the country. Mingyur Tenpa built the dzong at Trongsa and was responsible for the construction of most of the dzongs in eastern and central Bhutan. In 1668 he was enthroned as the third *desi* and ruled until 1680.

MONGAR DZONGKHAG

The Mongar district is the northern portion of the ancient region of Khyeng. Shongar Dzong, Mongar's original dzong, is in ruins, and the new dzong in Mongar town is not as architecturally spectacular or historically significant as others in the region. Drametse Gocmba (p164), in the eastern part of the district, is an important Nyingma monastery, perched high above the valley.

Jakar to Mongar
193KM / 7 HOURS

It takes about seven hours to travel between Jakar and Mongar. Most travellers passing through will admire forest scenery and spectacular waterfalls; a small number of binocular-armed visitors will be hoping to catch a glimpse of a rufous-necked hornbill or a nuthatch bird. The trip crosses two passes and takes in numerous sheer drops on what is one of the most spectacular drives in the country, descending 3200m over a distance of 84km. During winter the Thrumshing La is occasionally closed for a day or two during heavy snowfall.

Ura to the Thrumshing La
36KM / 1¼ HOURS

Beyond the office of the Phrumsengla National Park, past the turn-off to the Nangar–Ura bypass, the main road crosses the small Lirgang Chhu on a bridge called Liri Zam to enter the territory of the national park. It climbs past overhanging cliffs and cedar trees, more often than not framed in mist, and crosses a ridge that is labelled Wangthang La on some maps. It then drops into the Geyzam Chhu valley and starts climbing again past a road workers' camp. The ground is unstable and the road has left a large scar on the hillside.

Three kilometres before Thrumshingla pass there is a small park that features over 20 species of rhododendron. It's possible to follow the trail inside the **In Situ Rhododendron Garden** and hike up through the forest for 40 minutes to the pass. If you have a keen interest in rhododendrons and are here between late March and May, it's often possible to get the park ranger to accompany you and point out the different species; mention this to your guide in advance and ask at the national park office in Ura.

If you are lucky enough to travel on a clear day, watch for a view of Gangkhar Puensum (at 7570m it is often cited as the world's highest unclimbed mountain) as you approach the pass. A *mani* wall (Buddhist dry-stone wall with sacred inscriptions), chorten and prayer flags adorn the pass. This is **Thrumshing La** (3750m), 85km from Jakar, and the border of Mongar Dzongkhag; you are now officially in eastern Bhutan.

Thrumshing La to Sengor
22KM / 1 HOUR

Once you've crossed into eastern Bhutan, you'll find this side of the pass much rockier. The road switches back down through a fir forest. At about 3000m, 20km from the pass, the route emerges from the trees and enters the pastures of the Sengor valley. The settlement at **Sengor** has a few houses near the road, although the main part of the village, about 20 houses, is in the centre of the valley below. The roadside **Kuenzang Hotel & Bar** (☑17866423; Sengor; set meals Nu 500; ⊘6am–10pm) and Hotel Tshewangmo can whip up set lunches for tourists, or a local-style *ema datse* (chillies with cheese).

Sengor to Kuri Zampa
62KM / 1¾ HOURS

The next stretch of road is the wildest in Bhutan. Five kilometres beyond the Sengor valley the road begins a steep descent into

WORTH A TRIP

HIKING & BIRDING IN PHRUMSENGLA NATIONAL PARK

The wild landscapes between Thrumshing La and Shongar Dzong offer lots of opportunities for some adventurous forest hikes. Hardy birdwatchers in particular will love the three-hour hike from Thrumshing La down to Sengor through beautiful old-growth forest. The two-day walk from Sengor to Yong Khola also takes you through one of the best birdwatching spots in Bhutan (360 species live here) and many birding groups base themselves at Yong Khola or the Norbugang campsite around 5km ahead of Yong Khola. The best months for birdwatching are April, October and November.

Another good hiking and birding option is to follow the steep day-long hiking trail from Latong La down to Menchugang, via Saling and Shongar. In general, September to November and February to March are the best times to hike in this region.

For more details on these and other adventures and to pick up a local guide (essential) visit the Ecotourism department at the Phrumsengla National Park Visitor Centre (p151) in Ura.

the Kuri Chhu valley, clinging to the side of a rock cliff, with numerous streams and waterfalls leaping out onto the road. The frequent fog and cloud on this side of the pass make it difficult to see what's below – for which you should be profoundly grateful, since more often than not, there's nothing.

Ten kilometres past Sengor the road swings past a chorten and telecommunications tower at Latong La. Three kilometres further a turnout offers views down onto the **Namling Waterfall**, which plunges from beneath the road and is spectacular after monsoonal rainfalls. There are several chortens on this stretch – erected as memorials to the almost 300 Indian and Nepali contract labourers who were killed during the construction of this portion of the road. As you drive along the narrow track that was hacked into the side of a vertical cliff, it's hard not to be concerned that you might well join them soon. Prayer plaques and Shiva tridents offer some limited spiritual protection. There are no settlements here except for a camp at **Namling**, 20km from Sengor, a base for road crews who maintain the road and stop it from tumbling down the mountainside.

About 17km from Namling, after a long descent that traverses the side of a cliff, the road reaches safer ground and leaves the territory of the Thrumshing La National Park. At **Yong Khola** it emerges into the upper part of a large side valley of the Kuri Chhu, a lush, semitropical land of bamboo, ferns and leeches (and good birdwatching). The roadside **Trogon Villa** (📱 77110133; www.bhutan heritage.com; Yong Khola; s/d Nu 2880/3360; 🛜) here is a tourist-grade hotel specifically built to attract birders from around the world. Each of the 12 spacious rooms here sport

avian names and a superb bird photograph. The best times for the birds are April, October and November. You pass cornfields and descend past the new Tidangbi Lhakhang to the valley floor on a road that winds around like a pretzel. Rice terraces appear and tropical fruits such as mango and pineapple flourish.

Atop a hill on the opposite side of the river, near Menchugang village at Km 123, is a view of the ruined **Shongar Dzong**. There's not much to see – just some stone walls almost hidden by trees on the top of a hillock – but this is believed to have been one of the earliest and largest dzongs, perhaps built as early as 1100. Like Trongsa, Shongar was powerful because the dzong was ideally situated to control movements between eastern and western Bhutan. The new dzong was built in Mongar town when the old one was destroyed by fire in 1899. You can hike to the dzong in around 20 minutes on a sweaty trail that's rich with birdlife.

A couple of kilometres further along the road, **Lingmethang** (650m), 57km from Sengor, boasts adjacent roadside hotels, all offering hot drinks, cold beer and early-season fruit.

The road swings north at a chorten that marks the junction of the main Kuri Chhu valley. At **Kuri Zampa** (570m) you finally hit the valley floor with a bump – an amazing descent of 3200m from the pass. Step out of your vehicle and breathe in the thick syrupy air before frantically stripping off three layers of clothing. On the east side of a prayer-flag-strewn bridge is a large concrete **chorten** that is patterned after Bodhnath in Nepal; it is said to contain relics from the original Shongar Dzong. Beside the bridge is a deserted factory that used to extract oil from the wild lemongrass that is so abundant here.

A secondary road leads downstream to the new town of Gyalpozhing and the Kuri Chhu power project, beyond which a new road leads further downstream to Nganglam on the Indian border.

Kuri Zampa to Mongar

25KM / 45 MINUTES

The road to Mongar climbs through chir-pine forests up the eastern side of the Kuri Chhu valley. To the north you can see the road to Lhuentse traversing the side of the valley. This road leaves the Mongar road at Gangola, 12km before Mongar, and travels 65km to Lhuentse.

The Mongar road climbs up and up through cornfields towards a cluster of houses on top of the hill. A final switchback leads into Mongar.

Mongar

📱 04 / POP 4452 / ELEV 1600M

Many people spend a night in Mongar before continuing to Trashigang. There is, however, little of interest to see here. In eastern Bhutan most towns, including Mongar, are on

the tops of hills or ridges, notably different to many towns in the west that are situated in valleys. It takes about 11 hours to drive from Jakar to Trashigang, which often means driving at night; this is a waste in such interesting and spectacular countryside.

◉ Sights

The pleasant main street is worth a stroll. It is lined with traditionally painted stone buildings decorated with wooden facades and colourful potted plants and prayer wheels on the verandas. More modern buildings, each one housing similar general-produce stores, flank the bizzare, sunken children's park. North of the park is a vegetable market and dairy outlet. Archers sharpen their aim on the football ground on most afternoons.

A large **prayer wheel** near the clock tower attracts reverential old-timers who come to catch up on local news.

Mongar Dzong   BUDDHIST MONASTERY
The Mongar Dzong was established in 1930 to replace the original Shongar Dzong, although the original *utse* (central tower) dates from an earlier age. It's unusual because it has two entrances. There are four lhakhangs in the *utse,* including a

Mongar

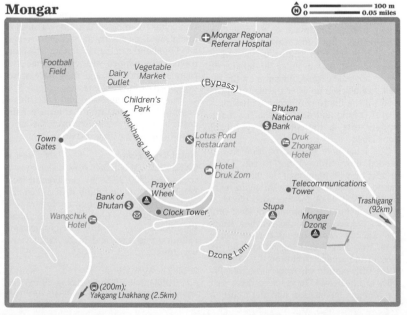

HIKES AROUND MONGAR

If you have a half- or full day spare in your itinerary, there is some fine off-the-beaten-track hiking in the hills south of Mongar. The following route offers ridge walks, valley views and some remote retreats and lhakhangs in a three-quarter-day hike. For an easier 2½-hour walk, do it in the opposite direction, starting at Phurji Laptsa and getting picked up at Phongchu La.

From **Yakgang Lhakhang** drive or hike uphill for 45 minutes (take the shortcuts past the chortens to avoid the dirt road) to the ridgetop monastery at **Phongchu La**. There are expansive views down to the Kuri Chhu and the lushly forested Kheng region to the south, while the monastery itself has some interesting puppets of local protector deity Dorji Gyeltsen.

From Phongchu La it's 25 minutes downhill to tiny **Senlung Goemba**. The main chapel is often locked but there's an unusual personal meditation tent at the entrance.

A steep climb of 40 minutes through forest leads you past two chortens to the ruins surrounding **Jaiphu Lhakhang** on top of the hill. Ten minutes' detour downhill is the charming Jaiphu meditation retreat. From here trails continue steeply down to the lhakhang and village of Kadam and on to Mongar.

The main route continues along the ridgetop from Jaiphu Lhakhang to Shami (Sainu) Goemba, then continues 20 minutes further to the road pass at **Phurji Laptsa**. You can get picked up here, or hike 40 minutes downhill to the impressive Zangto Pelri Lhakhang at Kilikhar (Kyilhor) Shedra, on the main Mongar–Trashigang highway. After tea and a chat with the monks, it's a short 4km drive back to Mongar.

goenkhang (chapel dedicated to protective deities) and the Sangay Lhakhang.

The week-long Mongar tsechu is held here in November or December (from the seventh to the 10th days of the 10th lunar month).

Yakgang Lhakhang   BUDDHIST TEMPLE

A short drive southwest of town is this little-visited but interesting lhakhang, founded in the 16th century by the son of Pema Lingpa. As you enter the main hall, notice how the original entrance on the far wall was blocked up after the arrival of the road (in the interests of security), leaving a mixture of old and new murals. The handwritten texts in the corner were brought from Tibet.

The lama here holds a position that is handed down from father to son. Upon request he will often open the lhakhang in the house next door, where the main relics are displayed. Look for the wood blocks, a *drangyen* (lute), and puppets of local protectors Gelong Daksen and Penchen Tsam. The ancient *cham* (ritual dance) masks were crafted by Pema Lingpa's son and are used in the annual tsechu on the 10th day of the fifth month, when the most valuable relics are displayed. To get here, drive past the Mongar bus station and the Court of Justice with its traditional architecture to the Sherub Reldri private secondary school.

🛏 Sleeping

★**Wangchuk Hotel**   HOTEL $$

(☑ 04-641522; www.wangchukhotel.com; r Nu 5400, deluxe r Nu 6600; 🌐) The impressive Wangchuk dominates the Mongar accommodation scene with 32 spacious rooms, good food and a delightful setting. The large rooms, all equipped with comfy beds, TVs, room safes, heaters and fans, have views over town or forested hills.

You can get a massage and an espresso here, while the restaurant/bar terrace is the perfect place to reminisce over the drive from Bumthang with a stiff drink.

Hotel Druk Zom   LOCAL HOTEL $$

(☑ 17251819, 04-641206; hoteldrukzom@yahoo. com; s/d Nu 2500/3500; 🌐) A welcoming local hotel with 10 rooms whose sizes and configurations vary in a seemingly haphazard way. All rooms have a ceiling fan, TV and phone. Bathrooms vary in size. The multicuisine restaurant is light and bright, with views over town.

Druk Zhongar Hotel   HOTEL $$

(☑ 17111684, 04-641587; drukzhongar@gmail.com; s/d from Nu 3600/4180; ste Nu 5040; 🌐) This well-run, friendly hotel has average rooms equipped with TVs and fans, and some have a balcony. The restaurant is also decent, if a little gloomy, serving surprisingly good food. Avoid the basement rooms, and be aware that while the suites are big they are not luxurious.

🍴 Eating

Lotus Pond Restaurant INTERNATIONAL $
(☏17611588, 04-641387; mains Nu 50-200; ⊗8am-9pm) For a change of scene seek out this cheerful local restaurant with an ambitious veg and nonveg menu that includes Bhutanese, Chinese, Indian, Tibetan and continental dishes. We recommend the chicken chilli and *momos* (dumplings). You can also pick up a bottle of the owners' homemade fragrant lemongrass oil here.

ℹ Information

Bank of Bhutan (⊗9am-1pm Mon-Fri, 9-11am Sat) Has an ATM.
Bhutan National Bank (⊗9am-4pm Mon-Fri, 9-11am Sat) Also has an ATM.
Mongar Regional Referral Hospital (☏04-641112) Located just below the vegetable market.
Post Office (⊗8.30am-5pm Mon-Fri, 8.30am-1pm Sat)

LHUENTSE DZONGKHAG

Formerly known as Kurtoe, the isolated district of Lhuentse is the ancestral home of Bhutan's royal family. Although geographically in the east, it was culturally identified with central Bhutan, and the high route over Rodang La was a major trade route until the road to Mongar was completed. Many Lhuentse women have looms at home and the village of Khoma is especially famous for its *kushutara* (brocade) weaving.

Mongar to Lhuentse

77KM / 2¾ HOURS
Lhuentse is 63km from the junction at Gangola and around three hours' drive from Mongar. It's a dramatic trip, frequently taking you alongside cliffs high above the river valley, but since you follow the main valley it's a comfortable ride, as long as there haven't been any recent landslides.

Mongar to Autsho

38KM / 1¼ HOURS
It is 12km down the hill from Mongar to the junction of the Lhuentse road at Gangola (1110m), where local women sell packets of cornflakes, oranges and peanuts. The Lhuentse road winds around the hill to Chali and Palangphu and then passes the suspension bridge to Banjor village (a previous bridge further upstream was washed away when a glacial lake burst, sending floodwaters surging down the valley). The road crosses the unstable Dorji Lung slide area (and its protective chortens) to descend to the banks of the Kuri Chhu and the two shops that make up the village of Rewan.

Passing a large, white Tibetan-style brick chorten surrounded by 108 smaller chortens, the road reaches the extensive cornfields and languid riverside location of **Autsho** (920m). Near the river you may be able to spot Assamese macaques playing on stones, capped langurs in the trees and black cormorants diving for fish. The riverside Phayul Resort (p162) here has a relaxed vibe, with a delightful garden. It's a fine lunch spot or rural overnight stop, with 12 clean and comfortable rooms with attached bathrooms and hot water.

Autsho to Tangmachu

26KM / 1 HOUR
The road passes towering cliffs, often half hidden in the mist, en route to Fawan. It then switchbacks 100m above the river to the small and neat roadside settlement of Gorgan, opposite the large valley of the Noyurgang Chhu, which enters from the west. Near this part of the road, in Umling, are said to be the remains of an ancient underground stone castle built by Bangtsho Gyalpo in about 1500 BC.

After a while the Kuri Chhu valley begins to widen. Just beyond a large white chorten (in the middle of the road), the road crosses to the west bank of the river on a Japanese-built arch-suspension bridge at Thinleypang. Across the bridge there is an intersection; go straight ahead for Khoma and Lhuentse, or turn left to climb 14km to **Taki La** (1762m), the site for a colossal 45m-high **Guru Rinpoche statue** (Guru Nangsi Zilnon; www.drukodiyana.org; Taki La) in the form of Guru Nangsi Zilnon, via the village of **Tangmachu**. The statue claims to be the tallest Guru statue in the world, beating a similarly Herculean rival in nearby Sikkim, at a cost of over US$2 million. Visit the website for more information. It's certainly an impressive if incongruous sight way up here in the mountains.

Tangmachu to Lhuentse

13KM / 30 MINUTES

The road traverses the foot of the Tangmachu valley for about 6km, passing a road construction camp and a hydrology station at Sumpa. Rounding a corner there's a view of **Lhuentse Dzong**, which dominates the head of the valley. An intersecting road leads to a bridge across the river, providing access past a large chorten and cremation ground at a river confluence up a side valley to Khoma village.

A short distance along the main road, the valley narrows and the road begins climbing towards **Lhuentse**. Just before the road passes the hospital, there is an excellent view of the dzong perched dramatically atop a bluff. The road to Dungkhar branches off by the hospital.

Lhuentse

📱 04 / POP 1500 / ELEV 1440M

The dzong in Lhuentse town is one of the most picturesque in Bhutan. There is otherwise little to see here, however. Just above the dzong is a *dratshang* (college), built to house the monastic community, while the hillsides are dotted with quarters for government officials who have been posted to this remote area where housing is scarce.

It's worth driving up to the Royal Guest House for views of the dzong and the snow peaks at the head of the Kuri Chhu valley. The peak at the head of the valley to the northwest of the guesthouse is Sheri Nyung.

As you leave Lhuentse for Mongar, look out for the ancient ruined bridge in the valley a couple of kilometres below, just before the bend in the river.

👁 Sights

Lhuentse Dzong   BUDDHIST MONASTERY

Lhuentse Rinchentse Phodrang Dzong, as it is correctly known, sits high on a rocky outcrop overlooking the Kuri Chhu valley, with near-vertical drops on all sides. It has been renovated several times, most recently to repair damage caused by an earthquake in 2009. A three-day tsechu fills the dzong to capacity in December/January.

Although Pema Lingpa's son Kuenga Wangpo established a small goemba on this site early in the 16th century, the dzong itself was built by the Trongsa *penlop* Mingyur Tenpa in 1654.

Visitors can visit seven lhakhangs, assuming you can find someone with the keys to gain access. The 100 or so resident monks see few tourists and are very friendly, which perhaps explains why visitors here have more freedom to explore than they do in any other dzong in Bhutan.

🛏 Sleeping

You can visit Lhuentse as a day trip while remaining based in a hotel in Mongar. Alternatively, overnight in one of the professionally run homestays in the village of Khoma. Another option is the delightful **Phayul Resort** (📱 17624046; Autsho; r Nu 1565-3000) at Autsho. The **Royal Guest House** (📱 17700935; r Nu 500) in Lhuentse town is another, if less reliable, option.

🍴 Eating

It's best to arrive in Lhuentse with a packed lunch (organised in Mongar); otherwise, your tour guide can organise lunch at a homestay in Khoma, or you could try your luck at the local **Shangrila Hotel** (📱 17741915; mains Nu 90-140; ⊙ 8am-9pm) for *ema datse* (chillies with cheese) and perhaps *momos* (dumplings).

Around Lhuentse

A highly recommended excursion from Lhuentse is to the weaving village of Khoma (p163). Bhutanese travel companies can offer three-day tours of surrounding weaving villages with homestay accommodation, including Gonpokarpo, Chenling, Shyam, Minje and Nyilamdun (Ngangladung), all of which are linked by farm roads.

Dungkhar

An unpaved but good-quality road runs from Lhuentse for 40km to the small village of Dungkhar, named because the ridge upon which it sits is shaped like a conch (*dungkhar*). Pema Lingpa's son Kuenga Wangpo settled here, and it is through him that Bhutan's royal family, the Wangchucks, trace their ancestry to the Kurtoe region. Jigme Namgyal, father of the first king, was born here in 1825 and left home when he was 15

KHOMA

If you're interested in weaving, and even if you're not, it's worth making the drive up to this traditional weaving village. The village produces some of Bhutan's most sought-after and expensive *kushutara* weavings; almost all of the 30 or so houses in the village have traditional back-strap looms set up on their porches. The weavings are so elaborate that they resemble embroidery and are generally used as *kiras* (women's traditional dress), though bags and other smaller pieces are produced. The village is comparatively wealthy and most households boast a TV and carbon-fibre archery bows.

The **Zangto Pelri Lhakhang** sits on a spur overlooking the river junction. If you have time to kill, get directions to the **Sangay Lhodrup Lhakhang**, a 20-minute hike on the hillside above Khoma.

On the drive up to the village look also for the white hermitage of **Drak Kharpo**, visible on the far cliffs across the valley.

Most travel agencies can arrange a homestay in the village. There are nine homestays: four recognised by the Bhutan Tourism Council and five recognised by the national parks authority. The simple, traditional and welcoming **Homestay of Chhimi Yuden** (☑17708618, 17576688; r Nu 1200, breakfast Nu 350, lunch/dinner Nu 500) is right in the heart of the weaving community.

to eventually become Trongsa *penlop* and the 51st *desi*.

The road from Lhuentse climbs high above the river to Zhamling before dropping down again to Dungkhar. A return trip here from Lhuentse will take at least five hours.

The renovated 16th-century **Dungkhar Naktshang** sits above the village beside the school and houses the government *gewog* (lowest administrative level) offices. They hold a tsechu here on the same dates as the one held at Lhuentse dzong, on the eighth to 11th days of the 10th lunar month. Just below in the village is the unassuming birthplace of Jigme Namgyal. Much more impressive is the **house of the Choeje Naktshang**, a fine century-old country estate whose family are happy to show visitors their charming rooftop lhakhang.

Guru Rinpoche meditated in a cave at Rinchen Bumpa peak, a hard day's hike high above Dungkhar, and locals still make an overnight trek there once a year to circumambulate the peak and visit the small lhakhang. Pema Lingpa visited the Dungkhar area many times and built the **Goeshog Pang Lhakhang**, a two-hour walk up the valley.

At **Thimyul** – en route to Dungkhar, around 9km from Lhuentse, on the far side of the river – there is a photogenic country house and large white chorten. A suspension bridge offers foot access if you fancy some exploring.

TRASHIGANG DZONGKHAG

Trashigang is the heart of eastern Bhutan and was once the centre of important trade with Tibet. There are several goembas and villages that make a visit worthwhile, but a lot of driving is required to reach this remote region. To avoid the drive back consider exiting at Samdrup Jongkhar or flying back to Paro from Yongphula.

Mongar to Trashigang

91KM / 3½ HOURS

The journey from Mongar to Trashigang is easier and shorter than the trip from Jakar to Mongar, but you'll still need about 3½ hours to cover the 91km between the two towns, plus an extra two hours if you detour to Drametse Goemba. The road crosses one low pass, spirals down into the valley, then follows a river before making a final climb to Trashigang.

Mongar to the Kori La

17KM / 30 MINUTES

Leaving Mongar, the road climbs past fields of corn to the *shedra* (Buddhist college) and Zangto Pelri Lhakhang at Kilikhar. Soon the road swings into a side valley, passing through a deep and dark forest of rhododendrons and orchids.

About 3km past Kilikhar a paved side road leads down 2km to **Wengkhar**

DETOUR TO DRAMETSE

The biggest and most important monastery in eastern Bhutan, **Drametse Goemba** (Drametse) is an 18km, hour-long drive on a dirt track off the main road at Thungari. The rough road gains 1350m, and you'll need a 4WD vehicle if it's been raining.

The monastery was founded in 1511 by the granddaughter (some say daughter) of Pema Lingpa, Ani Chhoeten Zangmo, in a place she named Drametse, which means 'the peak where there is no enemy'.

The monastery has about 100 monks and *gomchen* (lay or married Nyingma monks), and is famous as the home of the Nga Cham drum dance that features in many tsechus; it was proclaimed a Masterpiece of the Oral and Intangible Heritage of Humanity by Unesco in 2005.

This is potato-growing country, and in autumn there are huge piles of potatoes waiting for trucks to carry them down to eventual sale in India and Bangladesh.

In the main chapel, to the right of a central Guru Rinpoche, is the gold funeral chorten of Chhoeten Zangmo beside a statue of Pema Lingpa that was fashioned by himself in a dream (and thus is a mirror image). The long box here holds a *thondrol* depicting Pema Lingpa, which is unveiled at dawn on the 15th day of the 10th lunar month (November) during an annual three-day festival. A *thondrol* – a huge *thangka* (painted or embroidered religious picture) – guarantees liberation (*drol*) through the sight of it (*thon*).

The middle floor has chapels dedicated to the protectors Palden Lhamo (Sri Devi) and the 'horse-necked' Tamdrin (Hayagriva). The upstairs **Goenkhang Chenmo** (Great Protector Chapel) is jam-packed with weapons, a stuffed lynx, a dead flying fox (that looks like it's been blown up with a foot pump), an assault rifle, and the three local protector deities of Pekar, Drametse and Tsong Tsoma. Make an offering to receive a sacred thread, be blessed by the *phurba* (ritual dagger) and then roll the dice to get a reading from an ancient book of divination.

The next-door **Tseringma Lhakhang** houses images of the long-life deity, as well as five versions of the Himalayan protector Tseringma, all riding different mythological beasts.

Finally, the **Kanjur Lhakhang** houses a box of sacred relics, including the cymbals used in all previous tsechus.

Visit Drametse on your way to Trashigang or Mongar and find accommodation and meals in these two regional centres.

Lhakhang, founded by the third Zhabdrung near the site of his birthplace. Clothes and relics of the Zhabdrung are displayed here on the 10th day of the third lunar month.

The road passes a nunnery at Kitar and starts switchbacking at Chompa. A footpath here leads up for 90 minutes or so to the photogenic and little-visited cliffside retreat of **Larjung (Larjab Drakar Choeling) Lhakhang**. Rather than return the same way, it's possible to continue on foot to the Kori La. The path isn't obvious, so it's a good idea to arrange a guide in advance; this can be done at the Coffee Café.

About 1km further is the **Kori La** (2400m), where there is an array of prayer flags, a small *mani* wall, and a building containing hundreds of butter lamps. If these are lit, step inside for instant warmth but note the lack of oxygen. The adjacent **Coffee Café** (☑17284451; Kori La; ⊙7am-8pm)

can produce a hot instant coffee or tea with biscuits. The forest surrounding the pass is a good place for birdwatching; keep an eye out for great Indian hornbills.

Nearby is the start of the **Kori La–Golishing Nature Trail**, a former trade route which traverses 2.75km (45 minutes) of pleasant downhill forest trail before ending at a side road, 3km from the main road, where your driver can pick you up.

Kori La to Yadi

21KM / 1 HOUR

The road drops from the pass into the upper reaches of the extensive Manas Chhu drainage, switchbacking down through broadleaf forests to the charming private lhakhang near the village of **Naktshang**.

The road continues its descent past fence-like prayer flags (the Bhutanese equivalent of road-safety barriers) to the substantial village of **Yadi** (1480m). The **Choden Hotel General Shop Cum Bar & Lodge** (☏04-539113, 77737617; Yadi; ☺6am-9pm) next to the giant prayer wheel is a decent place to break for a cup of masala tea. Passengers pile out of buses coming from Trashigang heading to Mongar, Bumthang and Thimphu to get breakfast here.

Below Yadi, a dirt road branches off 17km to **Shershong** (Serzhong) and the two- or three-day pilgrimage trek to **Aja Ney**. The 'A' of Aja is a sacred letter and 'ja' means 'one hundred'. Guru Rinpoche placed 100 letter-As on rocks here, and for devotees it's like a spiritual treasure hunt: the more you see the more merit you gain. Those without sin usually find the most.

Yadi to Thungdari

33KM / 1 HOUR

Beyond Yadi a long stretch of prayer flags lines the road; below are numerous switchbacks, nicknamed the **Yadi Loops**, that lead down through a forest of sparse chir pine with an understorey of fragrant lemongrass, dropping 350m in 10km. There is a good viewpoint where you can see the road weaving down the hill; photos taken from here often appear in books and brochures to illustrate just how circuitous Bhutan's roads are.

The **Monkey Shoulder Cafe** (Tshoki Restaurant; ☏1/596475; Zalaphangma; set meals Nu 600, coffee Nu 120; ☺9am-9pm) at Zalaphangma has pleasant indoor and outdoor seating and serves set meals by arrangement. It's also a good place to stop for a coffee. Zalaphangma translates to 'Monkey Shoulder', hence the commonly used name of the restaurant. Officially it changes names with every new leasehold but guides and drivers still know it as the Monkey Shoulder Cafe. The unpaved road that heads west from here leads 11km to the village and to two lhakhangs of Chaskhar.

After more switchbacks, the road crosses a bridge painted with the eight Tashi Tagye symbols and continues for 10km to **Sherichhu** (600m). Climb out of the Sherichhu valley to a chorten and cross a ridge to meet the large Drangme Chhu, which flows from the eastern border of Bhutan. The road winds in and out of side valleys for 12km to **Thungdari**, 71km from Mongar, where a side road leads to Drametse Goemba.

Thungdari to Trashigang

20KM / 45 MINUTES

Back down on the main road you'll catch glimpses of Trashigang Dzong high above the south bank of the Drangme Chhu.

After passing a Public Works Department (PWD) camp at Rolong, the road reaches a 90m-long bridge at **Chazam** (710m). This place was named after the original chain-link bridge here, said to have been built by the Tibetan bridge builder Thangtong Gyalpo in the 15th century (*cha* means 'iron', *zam* means 'bridge'). The large building that formed the abutment of the old bridge has been partially restored and turned into a lhakhang just a short distance upstream of the new bridge. Look for the ruins of watchtowers on the ridge above the old bridge.

On the south side of the bridge is an immigration checkpoint where police inspect your travel permit. The road north from here follows the Kulong Chhu valley and then climbs to Trashi Yangtse.

The road switchbacks up towards Trashigang, passing the turn-off to Samdrup Jongkhar before continuing 3km to Trashigang, well hidden in a wooded valley.

Trashigang

☏04 / POP 3037 / ELEV 1070M

Trashigang (Auspicious Mountain) is one of Bhutan's more interesting towns and is a good base for excursions to Trashi Yangtse, Khaling, Rangjung and the Merak-Sakteng trek. The picturesque town is at the foot of a steep wooded valley with the tiny Mithidang Chhu channelled through it. Trashigang's focal point is a tiny plaza that becomes crammed with parked cars.

Accommodation here is fairly limited, but there is a variety of restaurants and you're bound to find at least one amusing place to drink at among the town's numerous bars. Not many tourists make it to Trashigang, but many Canadian teachers worked here in the past and the people of Trashigang are used to Westerners.

Villagers come to town on holy days, which occur on the first, 10th and 15th days of the Bhutanese month, to trade and partake in the local *arra* (spirit distilled from rice).

Trashigang

◉ Sights

Trashigang Dzong   BUDDHIST MONASTERY
The dzong is on a thin promontory overlooking the confluence of the Drangme Chhu and the Gamri Chhu. It was built in 1667 by Mingyur Tenpa, Bhutan's third *desi*. The entire eastern region was governed from this dzong from the late 17th century until the beginning of the 20th century. Several tame *jaru* (goral *or* mountain goat) roam the exterior courtyards. Extensive renovations to the dzong were completed in 2019.

This dzong is unusual in that both the administrative and monastic bodies face onto a single *dochey* (courtyard). By the entry gate look left for the fine *mani lhakhang* and its slate carving of Seng Doma, a local protector who is half-male, half-female.

Inside are a half-dozen lhakhangs, though what you get to see will depend on which monks are around. The 1st-floor *goenkhang* features paintings of a yeti, while another chapel is dedicated to the deity Choegi (Yama) Gyelpo, the wrathful aspect of Chenresig. He is a protector of the faith, the god of death and the king of law, who weighs up the good and evil at the end of a person's life.

Many lama dances are performed in Trashigang to appease Yama, especially during the three-day **tsechu** in November/December, which also includes the unveiling of a large *thangka* and the displaying of a statue of Guru Rinpoche on the last day.

Prayer Wheel   BUDDHIST SITE
This large prayer wheel and the pedestal on which it spins sits in the centre of Trashigang's tiny town square, and doubles as a meeting point and taxi shelter.

🛏 Sleeping

Trashigang's best accommodation options are found a few kilometres outside town: Druk Deothjung Resort at Phomshing and Lingkhar Lodge at Lengkhar, on the road to Samdrup Jongkhar.

Druk Deothjung Hotel   LOCAL HOTEL $
(☑04-521214; drukdeothjung@gmail.com; r Nu 600) This 12-room hotel near the central prayer wheel is the best of the local places in the centre of town. It is owned by the same family that runs the Druk Deothjung Resort, where most foreign guests will be directed. Some groups choose to lunch here, though, for a change of scenery.

★ Lingkhar Lodge   HOTEL $$
(☑77116767,   17111722;   www.lingkharlodge.com; Lengkhar; s/d Nu 4200/4560, deluxe s/d 4320/5040, ste Nu 6480) The Lingkhar comprises a charming collection of spacious, well-appointed   boutique   cottages   surrounded by bird-filled gardens and fruit trees. There is a community lounge with TV and a restaurant with an outside terrace and lovely views. It's well run, peaceful and thoroughly recommended.

Druk Deothjung Resort
Phomshing   HOTEL **$$**
(☑04-521440, 17119909; drukdeothjung@gmail.com; Phomshing; s/d Nu 3540/4260, ste from Nu 5760; ☎) Located a couple of kilometres southwest of Trashigang up a steep rough access road, this huge hotel comprises two separate buildings. The upper building is the main hotel for travellers. Rooms are large and comfortable, all with views of the valley. It is the most popular place to stay in the area.

Rangshikhar Homestay   HOMESTAY **$$**
(per person incl breakfast Nu 2000) Run by the same family that operates the Lingkhar Lodge, this delightful homestay is in a noble family's ancestral house. The traditional building is perched on a ridge sharing sweeping views with a neighbouring lhakhang, and is surrounded by rolling fertile farmland. Rooms are authentically simple, yet comfortable, and the traditional meals are generous.

✖ Eating

Druk Deothjung Bakery   BAKERY **$**
(cakes Nu 35-50, bread loaf Nu 80; ⊗8am-9pm) Inside the Druk Deothjung Hotel; just follow your nose. Ask what has been baked that day – it could be doughnuts, chocolate cake or cream horns, and usually arrives from the oven around noon. Bread is also available.

🛍 Shopping

Thinley Choden Handicraft   ARTS & CRAFTS
(⊗8.30am-8.30pm) This small shop beside the Druk Deothjung Hotel is the place to load up on crafts such as traditional boots, painted masks and woven and embroidered textiles.

Pema Bakery &
General Tsongkhang   FOOD
(☑04-521196; ⊗8am-8.30pm) On the road to the Trashigang Dzong, this fascinating general store stocks a decent range of imported goodies. The odd smell comes from the sacks of dried fish.

ℹ Information

Bank of Bhutan (⊗9am-1pm & 2-4pm Mon-Fri, 9am-noon Sat) Changes cash and has an ATM.
Bhutan National Bank (⊗9am-4pm Mon-Fri, 9-11am Sat) Changes cash and, oddly, has a Bank of Bhutan ATM attached.
Post Office (⊗9am-5pm Mon-Fri, 9am-1pm Sat) Above the town centre, near the hospital.

ℹ Getting There & Away

From Trashigang it's 280km by road to Bumthang (two days), 350km to Trongsa and 550km to Thimphu (three days).

The domestic **Yongphula Airport** (☑17170022) is about an hour's drive from Trashigang and hosts thrice-weekly flights to Paro (Tuesday, Thursday and Sunday).

From the **bus stand** there are daily local buses to Thimphu (Nu 805, two days, 6.30am), Samdrup Jongkhar (Nu 270, nine hours, 7.30am and 8am) and Mongar (Nu 100, four hours, 1pm).

Trashigang to Merak
114KM / 6½ HOURS

Most people heading out this way are trekking to and between the twin villages of Merak and Sakteng (p205), each the centre of its own secluded valley within the 741-sq-km **Sakteng Wildlife Sanctuary**. The two villages are home to the Brokpas, a semi-nomadic ethnic group, traditionally yak herders by trade. Katie Hickman gives a good description of her visit to the region on horseback in her travelogue *Dreams of the Peaceful Dragon*. The Merak-Sakteng trek and the villages and their homestays are best reached on foot, but ongoing road construction has shortened the trek to just a few days.

Merak and Sakteng were closed to foreigners from 1995 to 2010 in an effort to protect the traditional culture of the area from undue global influence. The ban was lifted and several roads have since been carved into this region, so it is not as secluded as it once was. You can now drive to Merak from Trashigang, though the road is very rough from Phongme. Soon you will be able to drive to Sakteng also. Nevertheless, while the roads have potentially shortened the trekking routes, this is by no means the end of trekking in the region, or a reason not to visit. The Merak-Sakteng trek (p205) was always primarily a cultural trek: it's a chance to visit the Brokpas in their homelands and experience village life up close, and this is still the prime reason to visit. Day hikes and side trips to several lhakhangs and goembas can be arranged and the Brokpas have their own unique festivals in honour of their protective deity, Aum Jomo.

Apart from the Brokpa, the sanctuary's most famous resident is the *migoi* (yeti), for whom the sanctuary was allegedly established in 2002.

EASTERN BHUTAN TRASHIGANG TO MERAK

MIGOI: THE BHUTANESE YETI
· ·

The Bhutanese name for the yeti is *migoi* ('strong man') and they are believed to exist throughout northern and northeastern Bhutan, particularly in the Sakteng Wildlife Sanctuary.

The *migoi* is said to be covered in hair that may be anything from reddish-brown to black, but its face is hairless, almost human. It is similar to the yetis of Nepal and Tibet in that the breasts of the female are large and sagging, and both sexes have an extremely unpleasant smell. But Bhutanese *migoi* are special because they have the power to become invisible, which accounts for the fact that so few people have seen them. Another feature that helps them escape detection is that their feet may face backwards, confusing people who try to follow them.

The book *Bhutanese Tales of the Yeti* by Kunzang Choden is a wonderful collection of tales told by village people in Bhutan who claim to have seen, or have met people who have seen, a *migoi*.

Trashigang to Rangjung

16KM / 45 MINUTES

The road descends from Trashigang, weaving in and out of side valleys to the banks of the Gamri Chhu at 820m. A sealed side road crosses the river here and leads uphill for 19km in great zigzagging gashes to the Chador Lhakhang and *shedra* at **Bartsam**, where the most famous relic is a thumb-sized image of Chana Dorji.

The main Rangjung road stays on the south side of the river, passing through a flat area affected by flooding (the chorten in the middle of the floodplain provides divine protection against floods). Shortly afterwards is the village of **Lungtenzampa**.

After traversing fields for 6km, past the large Vocational Training Institute at Buna, the road crosses the small Kharti Chhu and makes a short climb to **Rangjung** at 1120m. Beyond the secondary school, an elaborate chorten dominates the charming centre of town, which is worth a brief stroll.

Just above the town is the **Rangjung Yoesel Chholing Monastery**, a large Nyingma goemba founded in 1990 by Garub Rinpoche. The main statues are of the Gelog Choksum, the trio of Guru Rinpoche, Indian abbot Shantarakshita and Tibetan king Trisong Detsen. The *torma* (sculptures of barley and butter) depict the five senses, with eyeballs, earlobes, nostrils, a tongue and skin. *Cham* dancing ends a 10-day **drupchen** (festival) in the 12th month (January).

The monastery has a good **guesthouse** (☑ bookings 17246076; Rangjung; r Nu 3000, breakfast/lunch/dinner Nu 350/480/490) up the hill that is occasionally booked by tourists, particularly Buddhist groups. The 24 rooms have private bathrooms and offer great views over the goemba, but must be booked in advance. Alternatively, try the local **TT Hotel** (☑ 17610238, 04-561232; Rangjung; r Nu 3000; 🛜) below the monastery.

Rangjung to Khardung

13KM / 40 MINUTES

The road continues east, climbing through large rice terraces and fields of corn for 8km to Radi.

Just 1.5km past Rangjung is **Pema Lhundup Handicrafts** (☑ 16461124; ⊘ by appointment), a private house turned weaving centre that sells beautiful embroidered cloth, shawls and scarfs made from *bura* (raw silk – literally 'insect fibre') or *sechu* (spun silk) by women from the surrounding villages, including Tzangkhar. *Kiras* (women's traditional dresses) vary in price from Nu 10,000 to 60,000, while silk scarves are around Nu 1500 to 16,000. The knowledgeable owner Peden offers displays on spinning and weaving.

Weaving enthusiasts can also visit **Tzangkhar** from a turn-off by a hairpin loop just before Radi (Km 23). Many of the women here are weavers and you might be able to buy silks directly from them.

Beyond Radi (1570m) the road climbs past terraced hillsides for 3km, passing above the large modern **Thekchok Kunzang Choeden Nunnery**. At **Khardung** village a very rough road heads southeast towards the Mon La (3278m), entering the wildlife sanctuary after 30km, and on to **Merak** (55km).

Four kilometres beyond this intersection, on the main road, is the collection of shops that is **Phongme** (1840m). From here a rough road plunges down to cross the

Gamri Chhu to join the the road to Thakthri. Another rough road continues eastwards on this side of the river to Jyonglhar.

On the hill just before and above the village is the 150-plus-year-old **Phongme Lhakhang**. The central statue is of Chenresig with 1000 arms and 11 heads. A rolled-up *thondrol* (a building-sized *thangka*) hangs from the rafters and *cham* costumes are stored in boxes at the foot of the statues, ready for the annual festival on the 15th day of the eighth lunar month (September).

Khardung to Merak

85KM / 5 HOURS

From Khardung, a rough farm road (4WD only) and foot trails lead south and east to the remote village of Merak. At the time of research the road reached **Merak** while another road north of the Gamri Chhu reached Thakthri, a few hours' walk from Sakteng. The road through Phongme continues to near Jongkhar, south of the Gamri Chhu, located a six- to seven-hour walk to/from Sakteng. The office of the **Sakteng Wildlife Sanctuary** is 1km east of Phongme. If you are staying overnight, your Bhutan agent will organise a full camping set-up (kitchen, tents etc) to use at the official campgrounds, or you might stay in unofficial homestays in Brokpa villages.

TRASHI YANGTSE DZONGKHAG

Previously a *drungkhag* (subdistrict) of Trashigang, Trashi Yangtse became a fully fledged *dzongkhag* (district) in 1993. It borders the Indian state of Arunachal Pradesh, and there is some cross-border trade and significant cross-border foot traffic. The old trade route between east and west Bhutan from Trashi Yangtse, over the mountains to Lhuentse and then over Rodang La (4160m) to Bumthang, is now a popular trek route. The district lies at the headwaters of the Kulong Chhu, and was earlier known as Kulong.

Trashigang to Trashi Yangtse

53KM / 2 HOURS

The drive from Trashigang to Trashi Yangtse takes about 1¾ hours of driving time, but you should budget extra time to visit Gom Kora on the way. There's lots to see en route and it's a great day trip from Trashigang. Even if you don't have time to drive all the way to Chorten Kora and Trashi Yangtse, do make the effort to take the short trip to Gom Kora.

Trashigang to Chazam

9KM / 15 MINUTES

To get from Trashigang to **Chazam**, follow the switchbacks down to the bridge at Chazam. Just past Chazam, an unpaved side road leads steeply uphill to Gangthung village and goemba, and Yangnyer, where a replica of the Bodhgaya chorten was constructed in 2009. The complex that's visible a short distance up this road is a jail.

Chazam to Gom Kora

13KM / 30 MINUTES

From Chazam, the road is level as it winds its way through sparse clumps of chir pine above the west bank of the Drangme Chhu

---

MEET THE BROKPAS

The 6000 or so Brokpas of Merak and Sakteng trace their origins from Tshona in southern Tibet, but have lived in Bhutan for centuries now. They are culturally distinct from neighbouring ethnic groups and are recognisable by their unique dress; most notable is their *shamo*, a beret-like black hat made from the chest hair of a yak, with spider-like tentacles descending from its edges to deflect rainwater. Women wear a red-and-white-striped silk dress called a *shingkha*, while men wear a red wool jacket known as a *tshokhan chuba*. Most practise transhumance, moving with their yaks between the highlands in summer and lower pastures in winter.

The Brokpas still engage in the barter system, and travel down to Phongme, Radi and Trashigang in winter to trade their stocks of *chora* (fermented cheese), butter and dried meat in exchange for salt, tea and grains. Most families own livestock, barring a few who stay back in their village dwellings through the cold season. With the introduction of tourism the entrepreneurial Brokpas have started to open homestays and offer equipment rental.

DON'T MISS

GOM KORA

An extraordinarily picturesque temple, **Gom Kora** is located 13km north of Chazam. The lush green fields, the monks' red robes and the temple's yellow roof combine with colourful Buddhist carvings and the rushing river to create an idyllic scene.

The correct name for the site is Gomphu Kora. Gomphu denotes a sacred meditation site of Guru Rinpoche and *kora* means 'circumambulation'. The Guru meditated here and left a body impression on a rock, similar to that in Kurjey Lhakhang in Bumthang.

The central figure in the temple is Guru Rinpoche. To the right is Chenresig, in his 1000-armed aspect. To the far right is an image of the snake demon Gangan Yonga Choephel, who holds a golden mirror in his right hand. The wall murals to the far right are believed to date from the 15th century.

There are numerous sacred objects locked in a glass cabinet that either miraculously appeared here or were brought by the Guru. The largest item is a *garuda* egg, which is a very heavy, perfectly shaped, egg-like stone. Other relics include the traditional boot print of the Guru, the footprint of his consort Yeshe Tsogyal (aged eight), the hoof print of Guru Rinpoche's horse and a phallus-shaped rock belonging to Pema Lingpa.

Gom Kora's celebrated old *thondrol,* unique because it is painted, not appliquéd, is either kept in the box here or in Chorten Kora, depending on which source you believe. Gom Kora has a 'new' *thondrol,* which is displayed at the **tsechu** on the 10th day of the second lunar month (March/April). This festival is different from most other tsechus in that pilgrims circumambulate the goemba and sacred rock throughout the night.

Behind the goemba is a fantastical large black rock. It is said that Guru Rinpoche was meditating in a small cave near the bottom of the rock when a demon in the shape of a cobra suddenly appeared. The Guru, alarmed, stood up quickly, leaving the impression of his pointed hat at the top of the cave, and then transformed himself into a *garuda,* leaving the imprint of his wings nearby. The Guru then made an agreement with the demon to stay away until the end of his meditation. The contract was sealed with thumbprints, which are still visible on the rock. The serpent also left a light-coloured print, with his hood at the top of the rock.

A small sin-testing passageway leads from the cave to an exit to the side of the rock – one successful participant reported that you must indeed move like a snake to get through the cave. Visitors also test their sin levels and rock-climbing skills by trying to climb up the side of the rock (the 'stairway of the *dakinis*'; female celestial beings) – only the virtuous can make it. On certain auspicious days, holy water, believed to be the Guru's nectar of immortality, flows down from a crevice in the rock and pilgrims line up to spoon it into bottles. You may also see childless women carrying a hefty holy stone around the *kora* path to boost their chances of conceiving.

Gom Kora has no accommodation, but is only a 45-minute (22km) drive from Trashigang, the best place to eat and sleep in the area. To get here from Trashigang, drive the 9km (15 minutes) to Chazam and take the turn-off towards Trashi Yangtse; after 13km you will see the yellow roof of Gom Kora below the road. There is a parking area but this is woefully inadequate during festival time.

to Gom Kora. A couple of kilometres before Gom Kora, by the side of the road, is a *ney* (holy place), where a rock shrine is covered in cone-shaped *tsha-tshas* (small offerings moulded in clay) and brass images of the Rigsum Goenpo – the Buddhist trinity of Chenresig, Jampelyang (Manjushri) and Chana Dorji. Also here is a natural chorten, wisely painted white since it stands in the middle of the main road!

Gom Kora to Trashi Yangtse

28KM / 1¼ HOURS

The drive from Gom Kora to Trashi Yangtse is very pleasant and for the most part follows the Kulong Chhu, affording great views of the river and the diverse vegetation on the opposite bank. In spring the spectacular Bauhinia trees splash the mountainsides with purple and white blossoms. Keep an eye out for troops of capped langurs right beside the road.

Two kilometres from Gom Kora is the sleepy village of **Duksum** (860m), the roadhead for many large villages higher in the valley. A couple of shops (try the Dondup Tsongkhag) sell colourful patterned cloth and belts woven by local women using back-strap looms. Duksum's iron chain-link bridge, believed to have been the last surviving example of those built by Thangtong Gyalpo, was destroyed in 2004. Some links were used in the reconstructed bridge at Tamchhog Lhakhang and others lie on display at Gom Kora.

The road turns northwest and follows the Kulong Chhu valley towards Trashi Yangtse. The eastern fork of the river flows from Arunachal Pradesh in India and is known as the Dawung Chhu. A hydro power project is under construction along the upper section of the Kulong Chhu.

Climbing high above the Kulong Chhu, the road passes the junction of a paved road at Zangpozor. Die-hards can drive 9km up this road to the ruined walls of **Tshenkarla dzong**, which was built in the first half of the 9th century by Prince Tsangma, the eldest son of Tibetan king Trisong Detsen. The prince established himself in eastern Bhutan after he was banished from Tibet. The old name of this town is Rangthang Woong. The ruins sit in a field of wild lemongrass just above the school. A little further is the charming new Zangto Pelri Lhakhang, which offers a fine place for a picnic with views stretching as far as Arunachal Pradesh.

Back on the main road, the habitation gets more sparse as the valley becomes steeper and less suitable for cultivation. Snowy peaks at the head of the valley come in and out of focus. After you traverse along a rocky cliff, an impressive building appears on a promontory where a side stream, the Dongdi Chhu, joins the valley. This is the original **Trashi Yangtse Dzong**, built by Pema Lingpa alongside the former trade route; it now houses the town's community of 300 monks. The *dratshang* (monastic college) has a dramatic main assembly hall and an *utse*, which holds the dzong's most precious relic, a statue of Chenresig that flew here from Ralung in Tibet. The dzong is 1.5km up a side road, past a wonderful traditional cantilevered bridge. The old trade route from Bumthang ended here, as does its modern equivalent: the six- to eight-day Rodang La trek.

Trashi Yangtse

🏠 04 / POP 3187 / ELEV 1700M

The orderly and sleepy settlement of Trashi Yangtse occupies a large bowl-shaped valley in one of the furthest corners of the kingdom, 550km from Thimphu. The town and its new dzong sit just above the ancient and serene Chorten Kora, 3km from the old dzong. The road from Trashigang enters from the south, passing the large Chorten Kora and then entering the subdued bazaar area marked with an elaborately decorated Bhutanese-style chorten. From here, one road leads straight to the headquarters and visitor centre of the Bomdeling Wildlife Sanctuary; another branches right to the new dzong and administrative offices, on a ridge 130m above the town. The dzong was inaugurated in 1997 and has little historical or architectural significance, though the archery ground below the dzong is worth a visit if a tournament is under way.

Trashi Yangtse is known for the excellent wooden cups and bowls *(dapa)* made here from rhododendron, avocado wood and maple wood. A small number of craftspeople still use water-driven and treadle lathes; the majority use electric lathes. Trashi Yangtse is also a centre of daphne-papermaking, using the *tsasho* technique with a bamboo frame to produce a distinctive pattern on the paper.

◉ Sights

Chorten Kora   BUDDHIST MONUMENT
Chorten Kora is large, but not nearly as large as the stupa of Bodhnath in Nepal, after which it was patterned. It was constructed in 1740 by Lama Ngawang Loday in memory of his uncle, Jungshu Phesan, and to subdue local spirits.

In front of the chorten is a natural stone stupa, the *sertho*, which used to sit atop the chorten and is considered sacred. There is also a small goemba here. The popular Bhutanese film *Chorten Kora* was shot here.

The story behind the chorten is that Lama Ngawang Loday went to Nepal and brought back a model of Bodhnath carved in a radish. He had it copied here so that people could visit this place instead of making the arduous trip to Nepal. The reason that Chorten Kora is not an exact copy of Bodhnath is because the radish shrank and was distorted during the return trip.

During the first month of the lunar calendar (February or March) there is an auspicious *kora* held here, where people gain merit by walking around the main chorten and its inner *kora*. It is celebrated on two separate dates (the 15th and 30th days of the lunar month). The first date (Dakpa Kora) is for the people from the Dakpa community in Arunachal Pradesh, India, who make the three-day pilgrimage here to celebrate the sacrifice of an eight-year-old girl from Arunachal Pradesh, who was enshrined in the chorten to appease a troublesome demon. The second *kora* (Drukpa Kora) is for the Bhutanese, who come from all over eastern Bhutan, including from the Merak and Sakteng regions, to attend the local fair and gain some good karma by witnessing the unfurling of a giant *thondrol*. Dozens of stalls and gambling stands give pilgrims a chance to catch up on some shopping and local gossip. A month before the festival the chorten is whitewashed anew. This is paid for with funds earned from rice grown in the fields surrounding the chorten.

National Institute for Zorig Chusum
ARTS CENTRE

(☑ 04-781141; ☺ 9am-noon & 1-3.45pm Mon-Fri, 9am-noon Sat) `FREE` This arts and crafts institute south of town was opened in 1997 to provide vocational training opportunities for those who aren't continuing in the higher education system. Ten of the Zorig Chusum (Thirteen Arts) are studied here, including *thangka* painting, embroidery, sculpture, metalwork and woodturning. You can visit the school, watch the students at work and take photographs. The showroom has a decent variety of paintings, carvings, sculptures, bowls and masks for sale.

The students are on holiday from December to February and for all of July.

🛌 Sleeping

Bomdeling Wildlife Sanctuary Guest House
GUESTHOUSE $

(☑ 04-781155; bwstrashiyangtse@gmail.com; r Nu 600-1000) The sanctuary visitor centre complex just to the northwest of Trashi Yangtse has four simple rooms with private bathrooms and balconies; the upper-floor rooms are the best. The location is a bit isolated and you will need to bring your own food supplies. You and your guide can use the kitchen for a token fee.

Karmaling Hotel
HOTEL $$

(☑ 04-781113, 17731140; s Nu 3000, d Nu 4200-6000) This is the sole tourist hotel in town, with a restaurant, bar and conference centre. Modern rooms sport comfy beds, rugs, electric heaters and tiled bathrooms with hot water. There are 12 upstairs rooms reserved for foreign tourists; the six boasting the town views are best.

The owner served the second and third kings of Bhutan as a personal clerk.

🛍 Shopping

Wood Turning & Laquering Cluster
ARTS & CRAFTS

(☺ 9am-5pm Wed-Mon) This cooperative of local woodturners sells polished products in a small outlet near the dzong. The *dapas* turned from rhododendron wood (and other trees) are priced from Nu 800 to over Nu 20,000. There is a treadle lathe in a back room to display traditional woodturning methods.

Thinley Dendup General Shop & Handicraft
ARTS & CRAFTS

(☺ 7am-7pm) This local store by the central-town junction stocks textiles, *dapa* (wooden bowls), oboes, brass butter lamps and other religious paraphernalia.

Around Trashi Yangtse

The little-visited environs of Trashi Yangtse are ideal for off-the-beaten-track exploration. In an effort to promote tourism in the area, hiking trails, mountain-bike routes, campsites and homestays have been developed, but remain seldom used. You will need to make travel enquiries through your Bhutanese agent, who should have no trouble organising an itinerary.

One recommendation is to combine a visit to Dechen Phodrang and Dongzom village, in the Bomdeling Wildlife Sanctuary, via the sacred **Rigsum Goenpo Lhakhang**, overnighting at a homestay or campsite. Depending on the time of year you could catch glimpses of rare birds, such as black-necked cranes, and spectacular endemic butterflies.

There are numerous other day hikes and extended treks available in the east; Bhutanese agents will have their favourites. Wherever you go you can be sure you will find yourself very far from the madding crowd out here.

Dechen Phodrang

Hidden in a side valley high above Trashi Yangtse town is this delightful and little-known pilgrimage site. The current chapel dates from the 18th century and is built around the *kurjey* (body print) of Guru Rinpoche. Pilgrims lift one of two stones in front of the print to increase their chances of getting a boy or girl. With its towering cypress trees, many sacred stones and carved mantras, the site has a dreamy, timeless feel.

The easiest way to get here is along the bumpy, rutted 12km feeder road to the school at Womenang (also called Do Nakpo), from where it's an easy 45-minute hike via Solamang village. Hiking trails continue via Bumdir and Birting villages to either Dongzom village (3½ hours) or the Rigsum Goenpo Lhakhang via Pelri Goemba (four hours).

Bomdeling Wildlife Sanctuary

Bomdeling Wildlife Sanctuary is a 40-minute drive north of Trashi Yangtse, across the traditional bridge at the north end of town. It is the roosting place in winter (November to early March) of around 100 black-necked cranes. Other overwintering birds include bar-headed geese and ibisbills. The sanctuary is also home to capped langurs, red pandas, tigers and snow leopards. In 2012 Bomdeling was ratified as a Ramsar wetland of international significance due to its ecological importance.

The **Bomdeling Wildlife Sanctuary Visitor Centre** (☑04-781155; bws@druknet. bt; ⊙9am-5pm Mon-Fri), just a few minutes' drive northwest of Trashi Yangtse town, has a small museum with some vaguely interesting displays on the geology and natural history of the 1520-sq-km sanctuary. While the moth-balled, amateurishly stuffed wildlife adds little value, the friendly staff can advise on hiking and homestay options in the sanctuary.

At **Dongzom** (Dungzam) village, 9km from Trashi Yangtse, rangers can lead you to spot roosting cranes at dawn and dusk. Around 3km before Dongzom is the **Phenday Paper Factory**, where you can watch traditional paper being made from local daphne bushes.

There are good hikes from Dongzom up to the Buddhist sites of Dechen Phodrang and Rigsum Goenpo Lhakhang; the latter is a long day hike or easy overnighter. You can combine all three in a leisurely two- or three-day walk around the valley rim, a hike many agents refer to as the Orchid trek.

SAMDRUP JONGKHAR DZONGKHAG

Entering the country at the border crossing with India at Samdrup Jongkhar offers quick access to the east from India's Assam state. In the other direction, the only reason to make the tortuous drive into southeastern Bhutan is to leave it via this border crossing. Political tensions and strikes *(bandhs)* in Assam can make transport options uncertain, though these have become infrequent in recent years. Your Bhutanese agent will be able to make enquiries as to the current situation, but you should be prepared for last-minute delays.

Trashigang to Samdrup Jongkhar

174KM / 6 HOURS

The winding drive from Trashigang down to Samdrup Jongkhar takes at least six hours.

Trashigang to Kanglung

22KM / 45 MINUTES

Three kilometres from Trashigang bazaar, the southern road turns off the Mongar road and climbs past the town's petrol station.

Climbing around a ridge and heading south the road passes the settlement of **Pam**, whose main village and lhakhang are on the hillside above. The narrow unpaved road running uphill from here leads to Rangshikhar Goemba and an unusual but rather gaudy two-storey statue of Sakyamuni as a starving ascetic. Locals say it's possible to hike from here over the ridge to Trashigang in three hours. Rangshikhar boasts a homestay (p167) aligned with Trashigang's Lingkhar Lodge.

The main road soon passes the excellent Lingkhar Lodge (p166), a charming collection of boutique cottages surrounded by gardens and fruit trees. It's well run, peaceful and thoroughly recommended.

Descend into a side valley, cross a stream and climb through rice terraces to the prosperous farming community of **Rongthung**,

17km from Trashigang. The road then climbs to a ridge and enters **Kanglung** (1870m), where you can see the Zangto Pelri Lhakhang near the entrance to the clock tower and extensive campus of **Sherubtse College**.

The late Father William Mackey, a Jesuit priest, was instrumental in setting up Sherubtse (Peak of Knowledge), Bhutan's first college, in the late 1970s. Foreigners may know of the college through reading Jamie Zeppa's *Beyond the Sky and the Earth,* which chronicles her time teaching here as a Canadian volunteer. The clock tower and green lawns give the town the air of a Himalayan hill station.

Kanglung to Khaling
32KM / 1 HOUR

The road climbs through fields of corn and potatoes, then switchbacks around a line of eight chortens. There are fine views down over the college and as far as Drametse Goemba, far across the valley. Hidden on a ridge above the road in a highly improbable hilltop location is Yongphula Airport (p167), with flights to Paro.

The road crosses the **Yongphu La** (2190m), offering you a last glimpse of the Himalaya, and swoops past Barshong Lhakhang, along the top of the Barshong valley, and past the impressive **Karma Thegsum Dechenling Goemba**, a huge new Kagyud-school institution headed by the eighth Zuri Rinpoche.

Rounding several corners in the convoluted landscape, the road enters **Khaling**, spread out in a large valley high above the Drangme Chhu. Above the valley is a small lhakhang. In the centre of the valley below Khaling is the **National Institute for the Visually Impaired**. This well-organised institution tries to assimilate students from all over Bhutan who are blind or otherwise disabled into the local educational system by providing special resources and training. One of its accomplishments is the development of a Dzongkha version of Braille.

Three kilometres beyond Khaling is the **National Handloom Development Project** (04-581140; 8am-noon & 1-5pm Mon-Fri, 8am-noon Sat Apr-Dec), operated by the National Women's Association of Bhutan (NWAB). It contracts out weaving and provides cotton yarn on credit to about 200 villagers, who then return the finished product to be sold here, in Trashigang or at Handicraft Emporiums in Thimphu, Paro and Bumthang.

Particularly interesting are samples of the plants that are used to produce the natural dyes, including rhododendrons (pale yellow), an insect secretion called *lac* (purple) and the stem of the madder creeping plant (pale pink). Photography of the workshops and the design samples is strictly prohibited. Prices for a length of woven cloth vary from Nu 1000 up to 30,000, and there are also shawls for sale. Most of the basic cotton is imported from Kolkata (Calcutta).

Khaling to Wamrong
27KM / 45 MINUTES

Beyond Khaling, the road traverses above scattered houses and cornfields before climbing to the head of a rhododendron-filled valley and crossing the **Kharung La** at 2350m. There's a short descent through crumbling hills, then another climb to another pass at 2430m.

Curling around the valley, the route descends past a side road to Thrimshing, then curves round the **Zangto Pelri Lhakhang**. This may well be the last Bhutanese goemba you'll see, so consider stopping to check out the wonderfully detailed murals and ceiling mandalas. Two kilometres below the lhakhang is the pleasant town of **Wamrong** (2130m), where you can get a good lunch at one of the local-style restaurants. The recommended **Dechen Wangdi Restaurant** (Wamrong; lunch set meals Nu 550; lunch & dinner) also runs a pleasant rural homestay a few kilometres from town. Wamrong is a *drungkhag* and so has a small dzong.

Wamrong to Pemagatshel Junction
20KM / 45 MINUTES

The road here descends for 6km to Riserboo and its Norwegian-funded hospital. There is a good view down the huge valley as the road traverses in and out of side valleys past the hamlet of **Moshi**, halfway between Trashigang and Samdrup Jongkhar. At a bend in the road at Km 77 you get your first glimpse of the Assam plain below.

Before long you meet the junction to **Pemagatshel**, whose name means 'Blissful Land of the Lotus'. This rural *dzongkhag* is Bhutan's smallest district. There are plans to create a multiday trekking route around the village rim, staying in homestays en route.

On the way to Pemagatshel village is **Yongla Goemba**, one of the holiest shrines in eastern Bhutan. It was founded in the 18th century by Kheydup Jigme Kuenduel, who was advised by the great *terton* (discoverer of *terma*) Rigzin Jigme Lingpa to establish a monastery on a mountain that looked like a *phurba* (ritual dagger) and overlooked the vast plains of India. Later the goemba was used as a base for religious ceremonies by Trongsa *penlop* Jigme Namgyal during the great Duar War with the British in 1865.

Pemagatshel Junction to Deothang

55KM / 1¾ HOURS

Below the junction comes the day's most dangerous section of road, the **Menlong Brak** (*brak*, or *brag*, means cliff in Sharchop), high above the upper Bada valley. The fragile road passes prayer flags, prayer plaques and chortens to reach the Dantak-sponsored Hindu shrine at **Krishnagiri**, where your car (and occupants) can get a *tika* (blessing in the form of a mark on the forehead) from the resident Nepali *babu* (holy man or sadhu). It's an amazing descent, with sheer drops putting the fear of Shiva into you.

From the two-road village of **Narphung** (with its one-way system!), the road passes the Narphung La at 1698m. It crosses a ridge and climbs to 1920m before beginning the final descent to the plains.

The road weaves down, reaching the PWD camp at Morong (1600m), whose workers are responsible for the Indian-style homilies that line the roads here: 'Speed thrills but kills', 'After whisky driving is risky' and our favourite: 'It is not a rally, enjoy the valley'.

The Choekyi Gyatso Institute for Advanced Buddhist Philosophy marks the outskirts of **Deothang** at 850m. Founded by important Rinpoche (and film director and author) Jamyang Khyentse Norbu, the institute recycles all of its refuse in an attempt to become a zero-waste community. The town's old name was Dewangiri, and it was the site of a major battle between the Bhutanese and the British in 1865. Fittingly, the town is dominated by a large Royal Bhutan Army (RBA) camp and to the south is a chorten with the names of all those who died building Bhutan's roads.

Deothang to Samdrup Jongkhar

18KM / 30 MINUTES

The road eventually hits the valley floor with a thud, as a farewell rock painting of Guru Rinpoche marks the end of the Himalayan foothills. The road curves through the final ripples of the continental collision zone, passing the Dickensian Bhutan Chemical Industries to the fairly cursory checkpoint at **Pinchinang**, 4km or so before Samdrup Jongkhar.

Samdrup Jongkhar

07 / POP 1713 / ELEV 170M

It's fascinating to see the morning tide of Indian workers crossing the border to work in the town of Samdrup Jongkhar. There's little reason to linger in this often sweltering border town, however. The highway enters Samdrup Jongkhar from the north, passing the small modern dzong with its goemba and traditional-style courthouse. The main road passes the Bank of Bhutan and crosses a bridge, then turns left into the surprisingly neat and compact bazaar area. (If you are coming from India the clean, level sidewalks and streets will be a pleasant shock.) In the bazaar you'll find hotels, shops and restaurants. If you continue south instead of turning left, you will hit the border. A Bhutanese-style gate decorated with a dragon and *garuda* bids you farewell as you collect your passport exit stamp and cross into the heat and chaos of India.

If you have time to kill, you can visit the modern **Rabdey Dratshang** behind the dzong or the **Zangto Pelri Lhakhang** down the road near the football ground.

🛏 Sleeping

Druk Mountain HOTEL $

(07-251178, 77750100; drukmountainhotel@gmail.com; r Nu 2400; ❋ ➘) Take the stairs up one floor to this modern hotel with welcoming staff, spacious rooms with TVs and private bathrooms, and a capacious, bright and airy multicuisine restaurant and bar. Upgrades were coming soon according to management when we visited.

❶ CROSSING THE BORDER: SAMDRUP JONGKHAR TO DARRANGA & GUWAHATI

Border Hours

Bhutan **Immigration** (Dungsam Lam; ⊘ 7am-8pm) is next to the police booth at the border gate. Here you will be fingerprinted and photographed as you enter Bhutan, or just get a passport stamp if leaving Bhutan.

Don't forget to stop at the Indian Foreigners' Registration Post (theoretically open 24 hours), by the bridge 5km south of the border at Darranga, to get an Indian entry stamp (or exit stamp if headed to Bhutan). It is essential to bring a photocopy of your Indian visa and passport information pages.

Foreign Exchange

Both Bank of Bhutan and Bhutan National Bank in Samdrup Jongkhar will change ngultrum into Indian rupees. In theory you are required to have your original exchange receipt, passport copy and an application form, available in the banks.

Bhutanese banks will not give Indian rupees for US dollars. For small amounts you are better off changing money with your guide.

Onwards to India

It is possible for your Bhutanese driver to take you to Guwahati, and this can be the easiest option if there are no political problems in Assam affecting the movement of Bhutanese vehicles.

A cheaper way to get to Guwahati is to arrange an Indian taxi with your hotel; figure on at least ₹4000 for the 100km (three-hour) drive to the city or airport. Check to see if your Bhutanese agent will pay for this.

Buses from the Indian town of Darranga, a 10-minute walk or rickshaw ride over the border, depart for Guwahati at 6.30am and 2pm. Alternatively, take a taxi to Rangiya (₹800 to ₹1000) where there are numerous train options east or west.

Bear in mind that strikes (*bandhs*) in Assam can close the border and cripple transport options in Assam without warning and for days at a time. However, these have been less frequent in recent years.

★**Tashi Gasel Lodge**　　　　HOTEL $$
(☑ 07-251553; tashigasel@gmail.com; s/d Nu 2400/3000; ❋ 🛜) Probably the best option in Samdrup Jongkhar, this hotel is 3.5km north of town by the Pinchigang check-post. The eight spacious rooms are colourful and surrounded by breezy balconies, and there's a verdant garden attracting birds. The best feature is the terrace restaurant overlooking the town below, a fine place to toast the end of your tour with a beer and some tasty Indian food.

TD Guest House　　　　HOTEL $$
(☑ 1/596607, 07-251764; tdguesthouse2017@gmail.com; Pelri Lam; s/d Nu 2450/3600; ❋ 🛜) This place, the newest of Samdrup Jongkhar's accommodation options, is about 500m north of the centre of town. TD has just eight spacious rooms, each with two double beds, TV and modern attached bathrooms. There's also a cosy but rather impersonal multicuisine restaurant.

❶ Information

Bank of Bhutan (☑ 07-251149; ⊘ 9am-1pm & 2-4pm Mon-Fri, 9-11am Sat)
Bank of Bhutan ATM In the TLT Hotel building.
Bhutan National Bank (⊘ 9am-4pm Mon-Fri, 9-11am Sat) Also changes cash.

Treks

Best Views

➡ Jangothang (p190)

➡ Thanza (p200)

➡ Pangalabtsa pass (p184)

➡ Chebisa valley (p195)

➡ Soi Yaksa valley (p193)

Best Cultural Sights

➡ Jili Dzong (p181)

➡ Lingzhi Dzong (p191)

➡ Laya village (p197)

➡ Nabji village (p205)

➡ Bumdrak hermitage (p185)

Why Go?

Almost two-thirds of Bhutan still lies beyond the reach of any road. Composed of rugged Himalayan summits, high passes, pristine forests, turquoise lakes, rolling yak pastures, traditional villages and a healthy sprinkling of exotic wildlife from hornbills to snow leopards, this is perhaps one of the world's best-preserved (and least-explored) landscapes.

Bhutan offers a wide range of treks, from tough high-altitude expeditions to the base camps of snowcapped Himalayan giants to relaxing community-based village trails linked by subtropical forest. And with walks ranging from two days to one month, there's a trek for everyone.

Perhaps the best part of all is that you can trust your Bhutanese tour agent, guide and cook to take charge of every conceivable camping chore, leaving you to simply relax, enjoy the trail and soak up the extraordinary scenery. Shangri-La indeed.

Top Tips

➡ You'll enjoy your trek much more if you are in decent physical shape, so spend a month or more beforehand doing some training hikes and breaking in your trekking shoes.

➡ During the day you won't have access to your main bag on a trek, so always carry the following items in your daypack: sun hat, rain shell, spare T-shirt, camera, MP3 player, fleece, water bottle and purification, and trail bars.

➡ For the same reason always have the following emergency items on your person: toilet paper, blister kit, sunscreen, first-aid kit, headache tablets, acetazolamide (Diamox), whistle and torch.

➡ You won't find much electricity on longer treks so consider a solar charger. During particularly cold nights keep your batteries in your sleeping bag to stop them from draining.

TREK ROUTES

The Tourism Council of Bhutan (TCB) sanctions around two dozen official trekking routes across the country. Moreover, new routes and variations are popping up all the time. Many routes can be trekked in the reverse direction, logistics permitting.

In recent years road construction has taken a real toll on trekking routes. Several former routes such as the Gangte trek and Samtengang winter trek are no longer recommended and days have been cut off the Jhomolhari trek and Laya trek. You'll have to check with your agent to see how road construction is affecting your proposed route and which new routes are fully functioning.

Route Descriptions

Some treks that follow old trade routes are seldom used by people today. Since there is usually no one around to ask for directions, you need to stay reasonably close to your guide or horsemen to ensure you are on the correct path.

Daily Stages

Route descriptions are divided into daily stages, and give an estimate of the number of days required for each trek. The stages are marked by campsites designated by the TCB, and the rules state that you must camp at these places, although alternative campsites are sometimes identified.

Before you start out, make sure you have a detailed itinerary, including rest days, worked out in advance. While discussing the trek with your staff, be careful to ensure that everyone agrees on the places where you will camp. In the past, horsemen have sometimes set off for a campsite beyond the expected stage, leaving trekkers stranded in the wilderness. Besides, some Bhutanese trekking staff have a rather relaxed approach to schedules, and late morning starts are common – often resulting in arrivals at camp after dark.

Times & Distances

The route descriptions list approximate daily walking times, based on personal experience and information produced by the TCB. The estimates are 'tourist times', factoring in a leisurely pace with plenty of breaks and sightseeing. Bhutanese horsemen and over-enthusiastic trekkers can reduce walking times considerably. The distances given are those published by the TCB. They are estimates and have not been determined by any more empirical method of measurement.

Rest Days

The route descriptions are based on a reasonable number of days needed to complete the trek. You will enjoy the trek more if you add the occasional day for rest, acclimatisation or exploration – even at the cost of an extra US$250.

Altitude Measurements

The elevations given are composites, based on measurements with an altimeter or GPS and checked against maps. There is no definitive list of elevations or names of peaks and passes in Bhutan, and various maps and publications differ significantly. In most cases, peak elevations are those defined in the mountain database produced by the Alpine Club in Britain. All other elevations are rounded to the nearest 10m.

Directions & Place Names

Bhutan is a complex maze of valleys and rivers that wind around in unexpected twists and turns. It is, therefore, difficult to define the exact compass direction of a river at a particular spot. So instead of referring to north or south banks, the slightly technical 'river right' or 'river left' have been used. This refers to the right or left side of the river as you face downstream, which is not necessarily the direction you are walking. In the route descriptions, right and left in reference to a river always refers to river right or river left.

Several mountains and places in the descriptions do not match names in other descriptions or maps of the same route. The variance occurs because most maps were made before the Dzongkha Development Commission produced its guidelines for Romanised Dzongkha. Lonely Planet uses the Romanised Dzongkha standards for all place names in Bhutan.

HEALTH & SAFETY

Once you are on a trek in Bhutan you can't rely on getting any medical attention, so be sure to minimise your risks beforehand. Make sure you and your gear are ready for

Treks

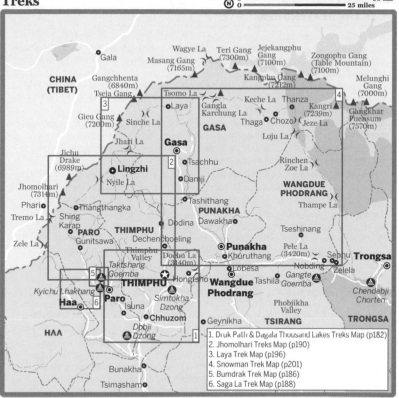

N 0 — 50 km
0 — 25 miles

1. Druk Path & Dagala Thousand Lakes Treks Map (p182)
2. Jhomolhari Treks Map (p190)
3. Laya Trek Map (p196)
4. Snowman Trek Map (p201)
5. Bumdrak Trek Map (p186)
6. Saga La Trek Map (p188)

the trek. Walk up and down hills or inclines as much as possible, breaking in your boots in the process. Try carrying a backpack to increase the strength training associated with walking or jogging.

➡ One thing to watch out for is sore or inflamed knees caused by the mild trauma repeated thousands of times on a trekking descent. Anti-inflammatory pills are helpful, as are walking poles and specialised knee supports.

➡ Bring a good pair of polarising sunglasses to prevent snow blindness over snowy passes and bring two water bottles to help ensure you stay hydrated.

➡ People aged over 45 often worry about altitude and potential heart problems. Relax. There's no evidence that altitude is likely to bring on previously undiagnosed heart disease. If you can exercise to your maximum at home, you should not have an increased risk while trekking. However, if

you have a known heart disease and your exercise is already limited by symptoms at low altitude, consult an experienced doctor before committing yourself to a trek.

➡ It's a good idea to have a dental check-up well before arriving in Bhutan. Bring antibiotics and painkillers in case you have a tooth infection while on a trek.

➡ When on the trail remember to always give way to yaks and mules and always stand on the upper or hill side of a trail when livestock are passing. It's not unknown for trekkers to get shoved off a ledge by a pushy mule.

Rescue

Trekking entails a certain amount of risk, and there's always a possibility of courting illness or injury. However, do not panic, as it only makes things worse. Assess the incident with a clear mind before making a decision,

OFF THE BEATEN TREK

As road construction eats away at existing treks and tourist numbers continue to grow in popular trekking areas in peak seasons, the tourism authorities are trying to introduce new trek routes to avoid bottlenecks and spread tourism development into hitherto unvisited corners of the country.

Ask your Bhutanese agent about the following trek routes, currently in the planning stages but due to come online soon. Figure on some exploring if you tackle these routes, as you'll be among the first to trek them.

Nub Tshona Pata trek Five- to seven-day wilderness loop onto the high alpine plateau to the northwest of Haa. The trail crosses half a dozen passes, the highest of which is 4255m, with the third night at Tshona Pata Tsho. The region is connected to Sherab Mebar, the *terton* (treasure finder) who revealed Buddhist texts here.

Naro Six Passes trek This route connects the first five days of the Jhomolhari trek (as far as Lingzhi) with the last couple of days of the Druk Path trek, via the remote Ledi La and Yusa La passes, for a nine-day trek in total. There are a couple of route variations.

Shabjithang trek A seven-day itinerary from Nangsiphel in the upper Chamkhar valley (Bumthang) through Wangchuck Centennial Park. The route leads to Chamba and Waithang villages, then east to Gomthang for fine views of Gangkhar Puensum.

Gangkhar Puensum Base Camp trek A five-day trek from Jakar to the base of the world's highest unclimbed mountain (7570m), with a day there and three days' walk back. Visited by Levison Wood in the British TV series *Walking the Himalayas*.

Duer Hot Springs trek An eight-day trek along the old expedition route to Gangkhar Puensum, taking you over the 4700m Juli La and rewarding with a full day at a *tsachhu* (hot spring), before returning the way you came. The route offers an alternative ending to the Snowman trek (p198).

Bridung La trek This week-long trek through the upper Kheng region starts from Chungphel in the lower Chhume valley, 20km from Ura, and climbs through forest for four days until reaching the plateau lakes of the Bridung La pass and then dropping down to the ancient lhakhang at Buli. April to June and September to November are the best times to trek. The starting point is accessed by farm road from the Pogo junction on the Jakar bypass. Buli is a bumpy 55km (three hours) drive from Zhemgang.

Salt trek This remote five-day route from Samdrup Jungkhar to Cheya (south of Trashigang, near Khentongmani) via Pemagatshel and Yongla Goemba follows a former salt- and silk-trading route through subtropical and temperate broadleaf and pine forest, overnighting in Nelang, Radhingphu, Mongling, Demrizam and Denchung. Because of the low elevations this is a good winter-season trek, walkable between October and March. Come in November to time your trek with the three-day Pemagatshel tsechu.

Juniper trek A short two- or three-day trek from Doga Kha or Chuzomtoe in the lower Paro Valley up to the ridge line separating the Paro and Haa valleys, offering fine views and yak pastures to end at the Chele La.

Rodang La trek A tough, logistically complicated trek along an old trade route and a section of the Great Himalayan Trail. Roads have affected parts of the route in recent years and a road is even planned over the Rodung La itself. The eight-day trek runs from the Tang Valley to Trashi Yangtse across eastern Bhutan, via ancient Khaine Lhakhang.

without jumping to conclusions. Suspected broken bones may only be bruises, a fever may subside overnight, and a dazed person may wake up and be all right in a few hours. In most areas, horses or yaks will be available to help ferry a sick or injured trekker.

Sometimes, however, the seriousness of the situation may call for immediate evacuation. In this case, the only option is to request a helicopter, since land evacuation may be near impossible. Fortunately, this is a reasonably simple process, but once you ask for a helicopter, you will be charged over US$3000 for a helivac, and up to US$10,000 per hour, depending on weather conditions, your exact location and the number of rescue attempts made by the chopper. Your guide and agent will make arrangements. The Royal Bhutan Helicopter Service (p296) based at Paro airport now offers emergency evacuations, as well as sightseeing flights, so helicopters no longer need to come from India.

These days it's normally possible to get local mobile-phone coverage in the major valleys of Jangothang, Lingzhi and Laya, and even on many passes. Simple local phones seem to get a better signal than expensive smartphones.

Foreigners are allowed to bring their own satellite phones into Bhutan, but not India, so you will have problems if routing via India. Some tour operators rent satellite phones to trekkers, though the charges are steep.

DRUK PATH TREK

Linking the dry Paro valley to the forests above Thimphu, the Druk Path is the most popular trek in Bhutan, with around 1200 trekkers tackling it every year. The main draws are mountain monasteries, alpine scenery and the convenience of being able to start trekking from your port of arrival in Bhutan, without losing days of your trip driving to trailheads.

The trek is possible from late February to May and from September to December, but snow sometimes blocks higher stages of the route in late autumn and early spring, and afternoon showers are common in April and May. Pack for warm days and cold nights, and be prepared for snow on the higher stages. Most people walk the route in six days, but fit walkers can do it in five days by combining the last two days. If you are borderline superhuman, you can even race through the trek in a single day: an old punishment for Bhutanese soldiers was a forced one-day march along this route.

Some agencies offer a shortened version of this trail called the Tsaluna trek, which descends to Tsaluna village and trailhead from either Jangchu Lakha (four days) or Jimilang Tsho (five days).

Day 1: National Museum to Jili Dzong

10KM / 3½–5 HOURS / 1115M ASCENT, 40M DESCENT

Traditionally groups have started the trek from Paro's National Museum at 2470m (our

trek stats refer to this full route), climbing past the small Kuenga Choeling Lhakhang (2650m) after 40 minutes. However, the spread of dirt roads in the region means you can now drive as far as **Damchena** (2880m) and the nearby clearing known as **Damche Gom** (2985m), from where it's less than two hours' climb through forests to the **Jili La** (3540m). This means that most groups now start their trek at Damchena after lunch. Well-acclimatised groups could even combine days one and two, walking as far as Rabana in one day. It's even possible to visit Jili Dzong as a day hike from Paro.

Cross the Jili La (marked by a cairn and chorten) and drop to an excellent camping place in a meadow surrounded by rhododendron forests just below the hut-like **Jili Dzong**. This small, solid-looking building sits on an important site. It was the residence of Ngawang Chhogyel (1465–1540), the cousin of Lama Drukpa Kunley, and the Zhabdrung is said to have meditated here before heading down to Paro to defeat an invading Tibetan army. The impressive main lhakhang contains a large statue of Sakyamuni almost 4m high.

Day 2: Jili Dzong to Rabana

10KM / 3–4 HOURS / 425M ASCENT, 50M DESCENT

The second day is short and follows a ridge with relatively small ascents and descents, so there's plenty of time for a morning visit

---

DRUK PATH TREK AT A GLANCE
....

Duration 6 days

Max elevation 4235m

Difficulty Medium

Season February to May, September to December

Start Paro Ta Dzong

Finish Motithang

Access towns Paro, Thimphu

Summary This popular trek climbs past remote lakes and mountain monasteries, before dropping into the Thimphu city limits. Trekking days are short, but the relatively high altitudes make it moderately strenuous.

Druk Path & Dagala Thousand Lakes Treks

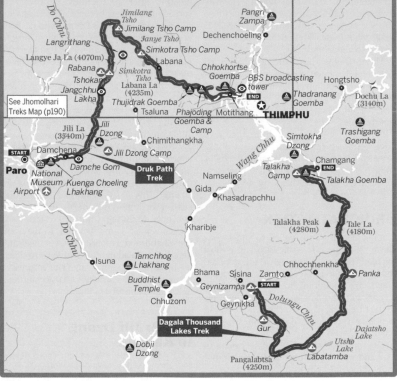

to Jili Dzong. You might see or hear colourful monal pheasants during the day.

From the dzong the route follows prayer flags and descends through rhododendron forest to a saddle at 3550m, before climbing for 40 minutes to great views of Paro and the Bemang Rong valley. If the weather is clear, look for Jhomolhari and other snow-capped peaks in the distance.

The trail crosses to the east side of the ridge offering views down to Gimena village (look for its large goemba). Climb again and circle around the west side of a cone-shaped hill to a saddle (3750m) and, just beyond, the yak pasture of **Jangchhu Lakha** at 3760m. There are two camping options nearby: follow the lower trail to quickly reach an often-boggy camping spot at **Tshokam** (3770m), or take the higher trail for 25 minutes to the yak herders' camp of **Rabana** (3890m), surrounded by rhododendrons.

Day 3: Rabana to Jimilang Tsho

11KM / 4 HOURS / 375M DESCENT, 370M ASCENT

There are two trails to Jimilang Tsho. Most groups take the high trail (described here) because it offers better views, including (in good weather) Jhomolhari and 6989m Jichu Drakye, the peak representing the protective deity of Paro. The lower trail descends from Tshokham into the upper Bemang Rong valley and then climbs via the yak pasture of Langrithang, but it involves some soggy stream crossings.

Following the main trail from Rabana, a horse track ascends the ridge diagonally to a **viewpoint** at 3960m. Traverse for 30 minutes to a meadow, then descend through rhododendrons, heading just left of a small peak topped with prayer flags. An hour from camp you crest the minor **Langye Ja La** (Ox Hump Pass) at 4070m. At the pass, climb 50m to the hilltop for impressive 360-degree views.

From the pass, the rocky descent is hard on the feet, passing a small herders' shelter and then climbing 80m to another pass with, weather permitting, fine views of Jhomolhari. Far below in the Do Chhu valley you may spot the yellow roof of Chumpu Ney, a pilgrimage centre famous for its statue of Dorje Phagmo. You'll soon see the isolated pool of Jimilang Tsho far below you.

After a lunch stop on the next saddle, climb and angle around the ridge to a chorten at 4180m for a final view of Jhomolhari. A steep 30-minute descent leads to the shore of **Jimilang Tsho**, with pleasant camping at the far end of the lake (3885m).

Set in a silent valley, Jimilang Tsho ('Sand Ox Lake') takes its name from a legend about a bull that emerged from the lake and joined the cattle of a family using the area as a summer grazing ground. The lake is also known for its giant trout, which were introduced in the 1970s.

Day 4: Jimilang Tsho to Simkotra Tsho

11KM / 4 HOURS / 820M ASCENT, 400M DESCENT

From the lower end of the lake, the trail climbs through rhododendron forest to a ridge at 4010m, then descends to a stone shelter. Following the ridge, you'll crest at some prayer flags at 4050m overlooking small, still **Janye Tsho**. Descend to a yak herders' camp near the lake at 3880m before climbing again to a ridge at 4150m, with views of **Simkotra Tsho**. Descend to some stone ruins and a camp at 4100m.

Be sure everyone is clear on where to camp on this day. Horse drivers may push to continue over the next ridge to a better camp and grazing land at Labana.

Day 5: Simkotra Tsho to Phajoding

10KM / 3–4 HOURS / 130M ASCENT, 680M DESCENT

Day 5 is a long climb past three false summits, before the trail descends to the herders' camp at **Labana** at 4110m, beside a shallow lake. There's a final longish climb to a group of cairns atop **Labana La** at 4235m. The trail descends gently to crest another minor pass at 4210m, and there are views of Dochu La and Jhomolhari along this stretch.

From here the trail descends to a final 4090m pass marked by a chorten, and the entire Thimphu valley comes into view.

Weather permitting, you might catch sight of Gangkhar Puensum and other Himalayan peaks in the far distance. The main trail descends to the northeast, but after 10 minutes it's worth taking a side trail for 20 minutes southeast down to **Thujidrak Goemba**, a remote meditation centre that clings to the side of a precipitous rock face at 3950m.

Continuing past Thujidrak, you'll soon reach the meditation cells and lhakhangs of **Phajoding Goemba**, scattered across an open, grassy hillside. A descent on a maze of eroded trails leads to a campsite beside the main Jampa Lhakhang at 3640m. Darkness brings the bright city lights far below you and the feeling that you have arrived back at the edge of the world.

Day 6: Phajoding to Motithang

4–5KM / 2½ HOURS / 1130M DESCENT

The final day is all downhill through forest so tie your laces tight and keep your trekking poles handy. A wide trail passes a chorten at 3440m, 40 minutes after which there is a trail junction. The left branch descends via the small, historic **Chhokhortse Goemba** and drops down a prayer-flag-choked spur to reach the **BBS broadcasting tower** at Sangaygang, offering an interesting alternative end to the trek. If you walk this way, your driver will meet you at the tower.

The main route branches right and descends more steeply towards the Thimphu suburb of **Motithang**. There are numerous shortcuts, but they all eventually lead to the same place. Pass another chorten at 3070m and descend steeply to a stream, crossing it at 2820m before following a rough road down to your waiting vehicle.

DAGALA THOUSAND LAKES TREK

If you like the idea of walking for five days and encountering few other trekkers along the way, look no further than this lake circuit south of Thimphu. It's not particularly demanding (despite a few steep climbs), and most trekking days are short. The route is best walked in April and late September through October. However, snow in the high country can often block out the route, and it's not unknown for trekkers to be forced back by the weather.

DAGALA THOUSAND LAKES TREK AT A GLANCE

Duration 5 days

Max elevation 4520/4720m

Difficulty Medium

Season April, September to October

Start Geynizampa

Finish Chamgang

Access town Thimphu

Summary A peaceful trek near Thimphu to a number of lovely, high-altitude lakes (though not quite as many as the name suggests).

Your driver will take you to Geynikha village, a 29km drive south from Thimphu, from where it's a short hike down to the Geynitsang Chhu to reach the suspension bridge at Geynizampa. Some companies use this as the first overnight stop, exploring local villages in the afternoon.

Day 1: Geynizampa to Gur

5KM / 4 HOURS / 550M ASCENT, 60M DESCENT

Crossing the suspension bridge at Geynizampa, the trail turns south along the east side of the Geynitsang Chhu to a side stream, the Dolungu Chhu. Cross the stream and start uphill on an eroded trail through an oak forest. Currently used mainly by yak herders and woodcutters, this trail was once a major trading route between Thimphu and Dagana, headquarters of Dagana Dzongkhag. This accounts for the walls, well-crafted stone staircases and other signs of human intervention along portions of the route.

A long climb leads to an outstanding lookout point at 3220m. The ascent is now gentler, and the trail climbs to the top of the ridge where it makes a tight turn at 3350m. The way to the campsite is along an inconspicuous path that leads off the trail here, going southward through the forest to Gur, amid yak pastures at 3290m.

Day 2: Gur to Labatamba

12KM / 5 HOURS / 1040M ASCENT, 110M DESCENT

Returning to the main trail, continue gently up the ridge on a wide track. A long, stiff climb through blue pines leads to a rocky outcrop where the vegetation changes to

spruces, firs and larches. The trail traverses into a side valley, crosses a stream at 3870m and begins a long, gentle climb through scattered birches and rhododendrons, weaving in and out of side valleys and crossing several tiny streams.

At **Pangalabtsa**, a pass marked by cairns at 4250m, there is a spectacular view of the whole Dagala range. This is prime yak country, with numerous herders' camps scattered across the broad Labatamba valley. Descend from the pass to a herders' hut at 4170m and traverse around the head of a small valley to reach the main valley floor. Climb beside a stream to **Labatamba**, a camp at 4300m near Utsho, a beautiful high-altitude lake with a thriving population of golden trout. The area near the lakes bursts with alpine wildflowers in September. There are numerous other pretty lakes in the vicinity, and you could easily add on an extra day here to explore them and hike up to **Jomo** peak (5050m).

Day 3: Labatamba to Panka

8KM / 6–7 HOURS / 260M ASCENT, 520M DESCENT

There are two possible routes ahead, and pack animals take the lower one. Trekkers can follow the less obvious higher trail that climbs along the western side of the **Dajatsho** to a saddle at 4520m, with good mountain views. From the pass, the trail descends past several herders' camps before dropping to the Dochha Chhu, rejoining the lower trail at about 4200m. Subsequently, it climbs over three ridges and descends to the campsite at **Panka** at 4000m. Water is scarce here in spring, and it may be necessary to descend to an alternative camp 20 minutes' walk below.

Day 4: Panka to Talakha

8KM / 6–7 HOURS / 180M ASCENT, 1100M DESCENT

The route on from Panka leads north to a crest at 4100m, where several trails lead off in different directions. The trail to Talakha climbs steeply to a ruined house and makes a long traverse to **Tale La** at 4180m, which offers a view of the Dagala range and Thimphu, far away to the north. Finally, it's a long descent – first through a mixed forest of spruce, birch, juniper and rhododendron, and then through bamboo – to reach an open hillside and campsite near the **goemba** (Map p74) at **Talakha** (3080m). The views from here along the Thimphu valley are stupendous, and you should be able to see the Buddha Dordenma (p55) dwarfed by its surroundings on the west side of the valley.

Day 5: Talakha to Chamgang

6KM / 3 HOURS / 440M DESCENT

If your driver has a 4WD, you can end the trek at Talakha. A rough and rutted dirt road drops from the goemba to the village of **Chamgang** at 2640m, Despite being the site of Bhutan's main prison, the village is actually very pretty, studded with white village homes adorned with phallus murals. Alternatively, you can walk down to meet your driver at Chamgang in about three hours, following the road and various shortcuts. On your way back to Thimphu, schedule a stop at stately Simtokha Dzong (p75), one of the most impressive sights in the southern part of the valley.

BUMDRAK TREK

This short overnight trek has much to recommend it: great views of the Paro valley, gorgeous sunsets over the mountains of Haa, an interesting cliff-face pilgrimage site, little-visited chapels above Taktshang Goemba and the spectacular Tiger's Nest itself.

The camping accommodation at Bumdrak is the most luxurious in Bhutan, but don't be fooled into thinking that this is an easy stroll. It's all uphill for the first day and all downhill on the second day, and it takes you up to almost 4000m, so you have to be in decent shape to enjoy this trek.

The first day is only a four-hour walk, so you could do some sightseeing in the morning and have a hot packed lunch at a scenic picnic viewpoint below the entrance to Sangchen Choekor Shedra before heading off on the trek. It's worth popping into the *shedra*, a Buddhist college home to about 150 monks, who study for six years before they move on to Tango Monastery upon graduation. Look for the stuffed bear to the side of the main entryway.

To get here you'll have to drive 12km up the Paro Valley north bank road and then 7km up the switchbacking mountainside road, passing excellent views of the Paro Valley.

Depending on how your agent has arranged the trek, you will likely just carry a daypack with what you need for an overnight. Bring warm clothes and a torch (flashlight).

Day 1: Sangchen Choekor Shedra to Bumdrak

7KM / 4 HOURS / 960M ASCENT

The trek starts from Sangchen Choekor Shedra, at 2900m, after a winding drive that drops you 600m above the valley floor. After visiting the chapels here, follow the trail from the car park, branching left as you enter an area of burnt forest. After 15 minutes or so you branch left again, just below the Rinpung Goemba meditation centre (visitors are not allowed).

Continue climbing through blue pine onto the ridge, swinging north through a level section of oak and rhododendron forest that offers a convenient bench on which to rest, one hour into the trek. From here you can see **Choechotse Lhakhang** (3640m), a steep hour-long climb above you. The wooden seats near the lhakhang are a possible lunch spot, offering fine views down the Paro valley. The statue of Denpa here is said to have once saved the valley from a measles epidemic. The caretaker claims the murals are 700 years old.

The trail climbs briefly up to two sets of prayer flags (3780m) before levelling out through a charming forest of larch, silver fir and juniper (known locally as *tsendhen*). Just beyond here is a large pasture and the first views of **Bumdrak Lhakhang** (3900m) from a collection of prayer flags atop a small knoll. Figure on 1¼ hours here from Choechotse.

The semipermanent **campsite** (3860m) lies just below Bumdrak and is the most

TREKS BUMDRAK TREK

BUMDRAK TREK AT A GLANCE

Duration 2 days

Max elevation 3900m

Difficulty Medium

Season Mid-February to May, September to November

Start Sangchen Choekor Shedra

Finish Ramthangkha

Access town Paro

Summary A short but steep hike that gives a top-down perspective on the famous Tiger's Nest.

Bumdrak Trek

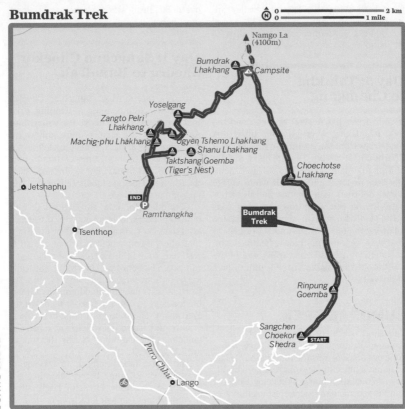

luxurious in Bhutan, complete with sun-loungers, gas heaters and wooden beds. There are fine sunset views over the Haa region and Sikkim beyond. For dawn views climb the low ridge just behind the camp.

The cliff-hugging 17th-century hermitage has a dramatic location, said to have been built on a spot frequented by 100,000 *dakinis* (*bum* means '100,000'). The main deity here is Dorje Phagmo, an emanation of Guru Rinpoche's consort Yeshe Tsogyel. The hillside behind is covered in prayer flags and has a cave connected to Guru Rinpoche.

If you have the time and energy, make the optional 45-minute ascent of **Namgo La** (the 'pass as high as the sky') just behind Bumdrak; the trail starts just behind the campsite. The 4100m peak is crowned by a collection of prayer flags marking a *durtoe* (sky-burial site), where dead babies are brought for sky burial. It's a superbly peaceful place at sunset.

Day 2: Bumdrak to Ramthangkha

7KM / 3 HOURS / 1260M DESCENT

Day 2 is all downhill and can be tough on the knees. After 30 minutes or so of descent, make use of a conveniently located seat to pause and take a final look back at Bumdrak.

From Bumdrak it's a relentlessly downhill 60-minute walk beneath lichen-draped larch and silver pines to Yoselgang (p98), the 'Shining Summit', at 3300m, where you can visit the assembly hall with its beautiful woodblock print depicting Guru Rinpoche's eight manifestations. Yoselgang can also be visited on a hiking tour from Taktshang Goemba (p98).

It's a further 10 minutes to the nearby **Ugyen Tshemo Lhakhang**, at 3300m, then a further 15 minutes to the **Zangto Pelri Lhakhang** (3280m), with its fantastic views down to Taktshang Goemba (p95), a further

20 minutes away at around 3000m. Between Ugyen Tshemo Lhakhang and Zangto Pelri Lhakhang is a steep shortcut path to Takt-shang via the Machig-phu Lhakhang (p96).

After visiting Taktshang it's 90 downhill minutes to the car park at Ramthangkha. You can grab lunch at the cafeteria or at res-taurants near Ramthangkha.

SAGA LA TREK

The overnight Saga La trek follows the tra-ditional route taken by Haa farmers on their annual trips to plant rice in the Paro valley. In return for their labour the Haa farmers would get part of the red rice crop, as rice doesn't grow in Haa.

Some agents take three days for this trek but it's easily done in two, or even one long day hike if you are fit. Each day is really a half-day's walk so you can easily fit in some sightseeing at either end, preferably Yang-thong or Jangtey monasteries in Haa, and the Drukgyel Dzong in Paro. The important thing is to get to the pass early enough in the day to give yourself time to make an excur-sion along the ridgeline for the best moun-tain views.

There are several variants on this trek, including the Cheli La trek, which involves walking for two days along the ridgeline from the Cheli La on the Paro–Haa road to meet the Saga La and then descending into the Paro valley from there. That trek can also be done in the reverse order, starting in the Talung valley.

Day 1: Talung to Khadey Gom

5KM / 2–3 HOURS / 425M ASCENT

Your camping crew will likely overnight at the Chhundu Pang meadow, at the mouth of the Talung valley. You can either start walk-ing at the Makha Zampa bridge at the base of the dirt road to Yangthong Goemba, or you can drive to **Talung** village (3020m) and start there. The first day is only a couple of hours' walking, so you can easily do a half-day's sightseeing at the nearby Yangthong, Tsenkha (just above Talung) or Jangtey monasteries.

If you are starting from the Makha Zampa bridge (2900m), ascend the valley on the true left side of the river, past horse pastures. After less than an hour you meet the trail from Talung village by a water prayer wheel

and a white chorten. As the trail ascends it veers right into the valley as pasture gives way to forest. The trail becomes rockier as it traverses lovely forests of silver fir.

It's a total of two hours to the main camp-ground at **Khadey Gom** (3450m), with another campsite just a few minutes' fur-ther at a junction in the trail where a side trail branches left to the Tibet border. There is a third possible campground 30 minutes higher up the right branch, just below the Saga La pass, but this is only possible from late spring when there is no snow.

Day 2: Khadey Gom to Balakha via Saga La

8KM / 3–4 HOURS / 250M ASCENT, 1140M DESCENT

It's a 45-minute ascent to the 3700m Saga La up a series of eroded horse trails. The earlier you get to the pass the better chance for clear views, so try to arrange an early breakfast or have one on the pass. There are some views of Jhomolhari (7314m) and Jichu Drake (6989) peaks, as well as views west towards the border with Tibet, but you'll get better views further along the ridge.

If the weather is clear, it's well worth mak-ing the excursion south along the ridge to the right of the pass. An hour's walk up the ridgeline to around 4000m brings you to a hilltop series of **stone walls** and buildings and a great **viewpoint**, which is also a good place to turn around. Trails continue along the ridge for two days to the Cheli La on what is known as the Cheli La trek.

From the Saga La it's a steep 45-minute descent to a cramped pasture called **Dongney Tsho** that makes for a possible

---

SAGA LA TREK AT A GLANCE

Duration 2 days

Max elevation 4000m

Difficulty Easy

Season Mid-February to May, September to November

Start Talung village/Makha Zampa bridge

Finish Balakha

Access towns Haa, Paro

Summary Monasteries, villages and superb views of Jhomolhari are the highlights of this easy trek.

Saga La Trek

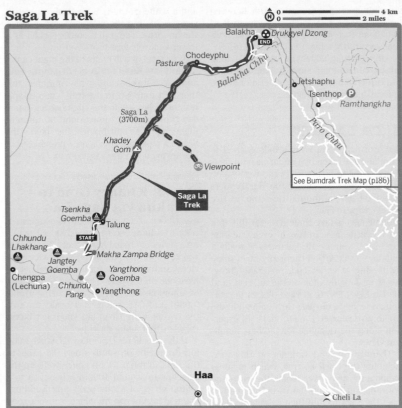

emergency camp. Look for views of Drukgyel Dzong and Taktshang Goemba down the valley along this section of trail. The forest here is lovely but the trail can be very muddy. After a two-hour descent from the summit you finally reach a large pasture that has views of **Chodeyphu** village (2900m) and offers a fine place to camp if you want to turn this into a two-night trek. You can detour to explore the village or descend directly on a dirt logging road, following electricity lines for 45 minutes to reach the main Paro valley road at **Balakha**, not far from Drukgyel Dzong.

JHOMOLHARI TREK

The Jhomolhari trek is to Bhutan what the Everest Base Camp route is to Nepal: a trekking pilgrimage. With two different versions, it's one of the most trodden routes in the country, and almost 40% of all trekkers who come to Bhutan end up following one of the Jhomolhari routes.

The first two days of the trek follow the Paro Chhu valley to Jangothang, climbing gently but continually, with a few short, steep climbs over side ridges. It crosses a high pass and visits the remote village of Lingzhi, then crosses another pass before making its way towards Thimphu. The last three days of the trek cover a lot of distance. The trek also affords an excellent opportunity to see yaks.

Partly because of its popularity, the trek is not exactly in pristine condition. Power pylons now run the entire distance from Sharna to Lingzhi, following the exact route of the trek, including over the Nyile La. There's quite a lot of plastic waste along the trail.

The trek is possible from April to early June and September to November; April and October are most favourable. It's normally warm during daylight hours, but nights can be very cold, especially above Jangothang. There is a lot of mud on this trail and it can be miserable in the rain. Snow usually closes the high passes from mid-November onwards, and they don't reopen until April.

The trek traditionally started from the ruins of Drukgyel Dzong at 2580m, but the road now reaches Sharna Zampa, near the army post of Gunitsawa (2810m), close to the border with Tibet. This trek will soon be further shortened when the road, currently under construction, reaches Barshong.

Day 1: Sharna Zampa to Thangthangka

15KM / 6 HOURS / 770M ASCENT, 10M DESCENT

Brace yourself for a long, hard day with lots of ups and downs, made worse by all the rock-hopping required to avoid mud holes.

Begin the day by climbing through conifers and rhododendrons flanking the Paro Chhu. If the water is high, you might have to scramble over a few small hills to get around the river in places. About 15 minutes beyond Sharna Zampa are the remnants of an old bridge with a house and a chorten on the other side. Welcome to Jigme Dorji National Park.

After about two hours of trekking through oaks, rhododendrons and ferns, and crossing several streams, you will reach **Shing Karap**, a stone house and a clearing at 3110m. Consider stopping here for lunch. Further ahead is the stone-paved trail leading left to Tremo La. This is the old invasion and trade route from Phari Dzong in Tibet, and still looks well-beaten since it's used by army caravans to ferry rations to the border post. Beware: many trekkers have casually ambled down this trail in the past and made a long, exhausting side trip to nowhere (you'll be turned back at an army camp).

Immediately after the trail junction is a wooden bridge over a side stream. Climb a short set of switchbacks over a little ridge, then descend and cross the Paro Chhu to river left on a wooden cantilever bridge at 3230m. The route now goes up and down a rocky trail through forests of birch and fir, followed by blue pine, maple and larch, and crossing an old landslide.

About three hours ahead there's a bridge back to river right at 3560m. The trail climbs to a place where you can see a white chorten on the opposite side of the river. There is a bridge here that leads back across the river. Don't cross it, or it'll take you up the Ronse Ghon Chhu towards Soi Yaksa, the campsite on Day 4 of the Jhomolhari Loop trek.

JHOMOLHARI TREK AT A GLANCE

Duration 7 days

Max elevation 4930m

Difficulty Medium–hard

Season April to June, September to November

Start Sharna Zampa

Finish Dom Shisa/Dolam Kencho

Access towns Paro, Thimphu

Summary Bhutan's popular showcase trek offers a spectacular view of the 7314m Jhomolhari from a high camp at Jangothang.

Follow the trail on river right and climb over a small ridge as the Paro Chhu makes a noticeable bend. Fifteen minutes' walk from the bridge is a lovely meadow with Jhomolhari looming majestically at the head of the valley. This is **Thangthangka** (3610m), with permanent toilets, a small stone kitchen shelter for your crew and a Bhutanese-style house in a cedar grove at the edge of the meadow. Camp fires are not allowed.

Day 2: Thangthangka to Jangothang

13KM / 5 HOURS / 450M ASCENT

This is not a long day, but you'll be left breathless due to the significant elevation gain at high altitude.

Wake up early for good views of Jhomolhari, which will disappear behind a ridge as you climb beyond camp. Less than an hour ahead, at 3730m, there's an army camp with rough stone barracks housing personnel from both the Bhutan army and the Indian Military Training Team (IMTRAT).

The trail crosses a wooden bridge over a fast-flowing stream a short distance beyond the army camp. The hillside on the opposite side of the Paro Chhu is a near-vertical rock face with a few trees clinging to it. Along this stretch the trail can be extremely muddy; there are lots of big stones you can use to rock-hop around mud holes. At 3770m, about one hour from camp, the trail turns sharply right at a whitewashed *mani* wall.

A short climb leads to a small chorten on a ridge. You are now entering yak country and will see these huge beasts lumbering

Jhomolhari Treks

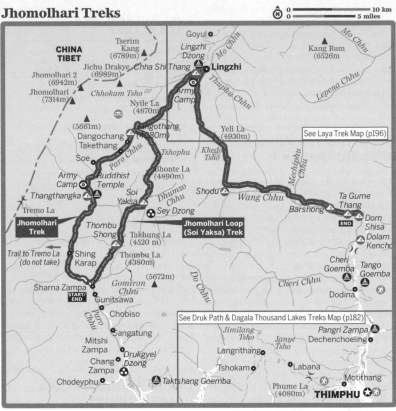

across hillsides and lazing in meadows. There are two trails from here, both contouring up the valley and ending near the river bank, hugging the valley floor as the river bends sharply to the right. Parts of the hillside are covered with larches, which turn a light yellow in autumn. Above the trail is the village of **Soe**. You cannot see it until you are beyond and above it, but you may meet people herding yaks near the river.

One hour beyond Soe is **Takethang**, a cluster of stone houses on a plateau at 3940m. The villagers grow barley and a large succulent plant called *kashaykoni* that is fed to yaks during winter.

The trail follows straight across the plateau, high above the river, crossing a little stream on a bridge made of big stones laid on logs. On the opposite side is a white chorten, an outreach clinic and the few houses of **Dangochang**. The people of this village raise yaks and a few sheep, and some households grow potatoes, turnips and radishes.

This area is snowbound from mid-November until the end of March. From here, it's slow going uphill beside a side stream to the camp at **Jangothang** (4080m), offering a spectacular view of Jhomolhari. As with yesterday's camp there is a stone toilet block and a small kitchen shelter; campfires are not allowed.

Depending on your itinerary, your horse may be exchanged for yaks from Soe or fresh horses from Dangochang.

Day 3: Acclimatisation Day & Exploration of Jangothang

If you're pressing on to Lingzhi, you should spend a day lazing in Jangothang for acclimatisation. If you are returning to Sharna Zampa via the Jhomolhari Loop and Soi Yaksa valley (p193), a day in Jangothang is the highlight of the trek; the views don't get any better than here. The horsemen also take the day off, and can be seen lazing around and playing *dego*, a traditional discus game.

There are four major possibilities for day hikes from Jangothang (also called Jhomolhari Camp). The first, and best, is a four-hour excursion up the **ridge** to the north of the camp. There's no trail, but it's a broad open slope and you can just scramble up. The ridge seems endless, but after an hour or so you get an excellent view of Jichu Drakye. Jhomolhari is hidden behind the ridge here, but becomes visible if you continue to the highest point at 4750m. You are likely to encounter grazing yaks, and, occasionally, blue sheep, on the upper slopes.

An alternative, which can be combined with the walk up the ridge, is to trek up the **main valley** towards the last house, then continue up the valley towards Jichu Drakye. This is the same country you'll be walking through tomorrow, so only consider this if you are doing the Jhomolhari Loop.

A third hike goes up towards the head of the valley in the direction of **Jhomolhari**. There is a very rough overgrown trail that cuts across moraines and brush, leading to the foot of the mountain. You can't get very far, but there are good views in the upper part of the valley.

The last option (if you are not following the Jhomolhari Loop itinerary) is an expedition to **Tshophu**, a pair of lakes that sit high on the opposite side of the river to the east, with a good supply of brown trout. To get to the lakes, follow the trail north to the last settlement in the valley. It takes about one hour to get to the top of the ridge and then another 30 minutes following a stream to the lake.

Day 4: Jangothang to Lingzhi

18KM / 6–7 HOURS / 840M ASCENT, 870M DESCENT

If you are having problems with the altitude at Jangothang, consider returning. Otherwise, push ahead past three stone houses inhabited by park rangers. This is the last settlement in the valley and it's extremely isolated. Around a corner, there's a spectacular view of Jichu Drakye.

Descend and cross a log bridge at 4160m to the left bank of the Paro Chhu, then start up a steep traverse heading back downstream. The trail crests at the foot of a side valley and goes eastwards. Jichu Drakye towers above the Paro Chhu valley and soon the top of Jhomolhari appears over the ridge above the camp at Jangothang. The snow peak in the middle is a secondary summit of Jhomolhari.

At 4470m, the trail traverses under the big rocks that were visible from the camp, leads left and enters a large east–west glacial valley with numerous moraines. Apart from a few small gentians, it's just grass, tundra and small juniper bushes that grow here. You may spot blue sheep on the hillside above and see marmots darting into their burrows.

Past a false summit with a cairn at 4680m, the trail approaches the ridge and you can see Jichu Drakye to the northwest. The trail dips and then climbs back up a moraine, offering spectacular views of the sharp ridge jutting out from Jichu Drakye. The final pull is up a scree slope to **Nyile La** (4870m), three to four hours from camp. You can climb higher to the northwest, where you'll see Jhomolhari 2 and Jichu Drakye on one side, and Tserim Kang (6789m) on the other. Nyile La is frequently very windy, so descend quickly

CAMPING AT JANGOTHANG

Jangothang is clearly among the most popular campsites in the entire Himalaya. In October, it's packed to the gills with trekkers, and the joke among guides is that if you're yearning to catch up with a long-lost mountain-loving pal, simply land up in Jangothang in autumn! The two-day **Jomolhari Festival** at Dangochang in mid-October brings more crowds, despite the fact that there's not a great deal to the festival. You are unlikely to have the camp to yourself even in the lean season.

The campsite derives its name (meaning 'land of ruins') from the remains of a small fortress that sits atop a rock in a side valley leading northwest to Jhomolhari. There's a community hall with a kitchen here for the benefit of trekkers, and several large flat spots for camping. A chain of snow peaks lines the eastern side of the Paro Chhu valley, and it's possible to spot blue sheep on the lower slopes. Despite being located at the foot of Jhomolhari, Jangothang has, interestingly, never been used as base camp by any expedition scaling the summit.

MOUNTAINEERING IN BHUTAN

While they may not physically measure up to the iconic 8000m-high peaks in Nepal and Tibet, the mountains of Bhutan are ruggedly beautiful. Jhomolhari was a famous landmark for early Everest expeditions. On the approach march for the 1921 British Everest Expedition, George Leigh Mallory thought it to be an astounding mountain, but one which filled him with a cold horror. It was climbed from Tibet in 1937 by F Spencer Chapman and Passang Lama, and again in 1970 by a joint Indo-Bhutanese team.

Michael Ward and Dr Frederic Jackson made an extensive and pioneering survey of Bhutan's mountains from 1964 to 1965. Climbing several peaks of around 5500m, they categorised the Bhutan Himalaya as a defined group of mountains. Climbers were allowed in for a short period from 1983 to 1994. A Bhutanese team scaled Thurigang (4900m), north of Thimphu, in 1983. Jichu Drakye was attempted thrice before being climbed in 1988 by an expedition led by Doug Scott. In 1985 Japanese expeditions climbed Gangri (7239m), Kari Jang, Kang Bum (6526m) and Masang Gang (7165m).

Gangkhar Puensum still remains the highest unclimbed peak in the world after unsuccessful attempts by Japanese and British teams in the 1980s. Even its height remains uncertain, with a Chinese team recently measuring it at 7570m, while the Bhutanese stick with the more traditional 7541m.

Climbing peaks above 6000m was subsequently prohibited in Bhutan, owing to religious beliefs and reservations of villagers residing near them.

through scree along the hillside, down to a stream on the valley floor at 4450m. There is some vegetation here, mostly grass, juniper and cotoneaster. It's an excellent lunch spot.

The trail now goes north, contouring along the hillside high above the valley. It's a good trail with a few small ups, but is mostly down and level. Eventually you can see an army camp near the river below; the white tower of Lingzhi Dzong is visible in the distance. Following a long walk to a lookout at 4360m, the trail now descends into the large Jaje Chhu valley, making many switchbacks through rhododendrons and birches to a yak pasture on the valley floor. Jichu Drakye and Tserim Kang tower over the head of the valley and you can see some remarkable examples of moraines on their lower slopes. The camp is at **Chha Shi Thang** near a large stone community hall (4010m) used by both Bhutanese travellers and trekking groups. **Lingzhi** is up the obvious trail on the opposite side of the Jaje Chhu.

If you take a spare day here, you can make an excursion to **Chhokam Tsho** at 4340m near the base camp of Jichu Drakye. During the hike you may encounter blue sheep and musk deer. If you are continuing to the Thimphu valley, schedule a rest day here. The village and dzong at Lingzhi (also spelt Lingshi) are worth visiting, and it's useful to rest up for the following strenuous trek day. Lingzhi is also a stop on the Laya trek (p195).

Day 5: Lingzhi to Shodu

22KM / 8–9 HOURS / 940M ASCENT, 920M DESCENT
Start early today: you have a long and tiring trek ahead of you. Climb towards a white chorten on a ridge above the camp, then turn south up the deep Mo Chhu valley. The trail stays on the west side of the valley, crossing numerous side streams, most without bridges. About three hours from camp it crosses the Mo Chhu. There is no bridge and the river has broken into many small channels, presenting a tedious route-finding exercise through hummocks of grass and slippery rocks.

The trail climbs steeply up the side of the main valley and crosses into a large side valley, climbing above a stream. It then makes an impressive climb up the headwall, zigzagging through rocks to a large cairn atop **Yeli La** at 4930m. Avoid walking with the pack animals because the trail here is carved into a rock cliff and is quite narrow. From the pass, on a clear day, you can see Jhomolhari, Gangchhenta and Tserim Kang.

Descending to a hanging valley after passing a small lake at 4830m, the trail tracks the outflow from the lake, and goes down to another huge valley with a larger lake, **Khedo Tsho**, at 4720m. Watch for grazing blue sheep. The trail then crosses the upper reaches of the Jaradinthang Chhu and descends along the valley, following the river southwards, crossing several side streams.

After crossing back to the east bank on a log bridge at 4340m, the trail reaches a chorten at 4150m, where it turns eastwards into the upper Wang Chhu valley. Descending and crossing to the south bank (river right) on a log bridge, the trail traverses a narrow, sandy slope to a camping spot at **Shodu** (4080m), just at the treeline.

Day 6: Shodu to Barshong

16KM / 5–6 HOURS / 250M ASCENT, 670M DESCENT

Upon leaving Shodu, you cross to river left and pass an abandoned army camp and a small alternative campsite. The trail traverses under steep yellow cliffs with a few meditation caves carved into them, where the Zhabdrung supposedly spent some time. Down a steep stone staircase, the trail reaches the river, crossing it on a log bridge at 3870m. For the next three hours, the trail crosses the river five more times, slopping through muddy cypress forests on the south slope and hugging the steep canyon walls and crossing large side streams on the north slope, eventually ending up on the north bank (river left) at 3580m.

The route climbs gradually for one hour to **Barshong**, where there is a dilapidated community hall and the ruins of a small dzong. The designated camp is below the ruins at 3710m, but it is in a swampy meadow, and most groups elect to continue to a better camp by the river, about 1½ hours further.

It won't be long before roads reach Barshong from Thimphu, making Barshong the end of the trek. As it is, many groups already extend this day's walk to Dom Shisa and meet their vehicle there. Check with your agency on the state of play.

Day 7: Barshong to Dolam Kencho

7KM / 1¾ HOURS / 350M DESCENT

The trail descends gently through a dense forest of rhododendrons, birches and conifers, and then drops steeply on a rocky trail to meet the Wang Chhu. Thirty minutes of walking through a larch forest leads to a clearing known as **Ta Gume Thang** (Waiting for Horses) at 3370m. Most groups camp here or 15 minutes further on at **Dom Shisa** (Where the Bear Died) instead of Barshong.

Dirt roads currently reach Dom Shisa, so most people meet their vehicle here.

Otherwise you'll continue down to **Dolam Kencho**, a pleasant camp in a large meadow at 3320m.

JHOMOLHARI LOOP (SOI YAKSA) TREK

If you fancy sighting Jhomolhari and Jichu Drakye from up close, but want to avoid the tiring slog all the way to Lingzhi, this trek is for you. While it's possible to return from Jangothang to Sharna Zampa by the same route taken on the way up, most trekkers choose to take this alternative route, which is less strenuous than the classic Jhomolhari trek and can be completed in less time. Despite its relative ease, however, be warned that this route still reaches elevations that could cause problems.

This trek is sometimes called the Jhomolhari 2 or Soi Yaksa trek after the valley it traverses.

Days 1–3: Sharna Zampa to Jangothang

Follow Days 1 to 3 of the main Jhomolhari trek (p189).

Day 4: Jangothang to Soi Yaksa

16KM / 6–7 HOURS / 810M ASCENT, 1090M DESCENT

From Jangothang, the return trail initially leads north to the last settlement in the valley, before dropping to the Paro Chhu, crossing it on a wooden bridge. After crossing the

> ### JHOMOLHARI LOOP (SOI YAKSA) TREK AT A GLANCE
>
> **Duration** 6 days
>
> **Max elevation** 4890m
>
> **Difficulty** Medium
>
> **Season** April to June, September to November
>
> **Start/finish** Sharna Zampa
>
> **Access town** Paro
>
> **Summary** The shorter version of the main Jhomolhari trek goes to the Jhomolhari base camp at Jangothang, returning via several high lakes and three passes.

YAK & JYI
....

Westerners tend to oversimplify the yak's many manifestations into a single name, yet it is only the full-blooded, long-haired bull of the species *Bos grunniens* that truly bears the name yak. In Bhutan, the name is pronounced 'yuck'. Females of the species are called *jyi* (or *jim*), and are prized for their butterfat-rich milk, used to make butter and cheese.

Large, ponderous and clumsy looking, yaks can move very quickly when startled. If you are trekking with yaks, give them a wide berth, stay upslope of them on a path, and don't put anything fragile in your luggage.

Though some yaks are crossbred with local cows, there are many purebred yaks in Bhutan – massive animals with thick furry coats and impressive sharp horns.

river, you begin a gradual climb, following a set of sharp switchbacks for about 300m up the side of the hill. Along the way, you can get fabulous views of Jhomolhari, Jhomolhari 2, Jichu Drakye and Tserim Kang if the weather is good. From here, it's a relatively even and smooth hike all the way to a large cirque nestling the lakes of **Tshophu** (4380m), a pair of splendid high-altitude water bodies inhabited by a flock of ruddy shelducks and known to feature a healthy population of brown trout deep in their placid waters. While it's possible to set up camp in between the two lakes, most trekkers continue on along the trail, which now climbs high above the eastern side of the first lake, passes the second lake along the way and finally climbs across a scree slope to the crest of a ridge. From here, it descends into a hidden valley, before climbing steeply to **Bhonte La** (4890m), the highest point on this route.

Descending from Bhonte La, the route now runs past a scree slope, and then winds down a ridge with a lot of criss-crossing yak trails. Finally, it switchbacks down to the **Soi Yaksa** valley (also known as the Dhumzo Chhu valley), a beautiful setting for a camp at 3800m with rocky cliffs, wildflower meadows, a few nomadic settlements and a waterfall at the end of the valley. All through this day, keep your eyes trained on the wilderness for a host of regional wildlife, such as blue sheep, golden marmots and the elusive snow leopard.

Day 5: Soi Yaksa to Thombu Shong

11KM / 4–5 HOURS / 720M ASCENT, 340M DESCENT

Starting out from camp, today's walk initially takes you past hillsides lush with a crop of azaleas and rhododendrons, before gradually climbing above the treeline. You will also cross forests of birch and oak on the way. The trail ascends about 100m over a ridge, before dropping to a meadow with a chorten and a *mani* wall, and a babbling stream. If you have enough time on your hands, you can make a quick detour to the ruins of the **Sey Dzong**, in a side valley nearby. Otherwise, you can simply continue ahead from the *mani* wall, cross the stream on a wooden bridge, and follow the trail heading up the hillside.

Not long after, it drops into a small side valley, before emerging onto a ridge. Here the trail bifurcates, and it can be quite confusing since both the tracks look very similar. Don't go left – this route will eventually take you to Lalung La, a pass that leads on to an extremely roundabout way back to Drukgyel Dzong. Go right instead.

The track will first take you through a wooded area, and then climb steeply for about an hour, ascending past a few huts and chortens to **Takhung La** (4520m). Spectacular views of Jhomolhari, Jichu Drakye and Tserim Kang can be seen from the pass, and on a clear day, the formidable Kanchenjunga (8586m) can be sighted far away on the western horizon.

From Takhung La, the trail holds out for a while, before gradually meandering down to **Thombu Shong** (4180m). It's a grassy pasture dotted with three yak herders' huts, and has traditionally been used by animal herders as a campsite at various times of year.

Day 6: Thombu Shong to Sharna Zampa

13KM / 4–5 HOURS / 200M ASCENT, 1650M DESCENT

After breaking camp, follow the trail leading out of the valley through a marshy patch. From here, the well-defined track suddenly begins to gain elevation, and climbs steeply for a good 200m. This hike can prove tiring, especially since you now have several days of vigorous trekking behind you, although you will have adjusted well to the altitude by now, if that's any consolation. All along, you will be traversing through a gloriously beautiful garden of wildflowers, also rich with a crop of rhododendrons, which is especially breathtaking through late spring and summer. At the end of the climb, you will finally cross over **Thombu La** at 4380m, where the trail eventually exits the valley. Stop here for a last good look at Kanchenjunga and Drakye Gang (5200m), among other peaks.

On the other side of Thombu La, the trail begins to amble down steeply through upland forest, and the long descent ahead can prove to be rather brutal on your knees. Leading down from the pass, the total loss in elevation all the way to the end of the trek is a whopping 1800m, all within a span of about three hours. The first part of the descent is gradual, winding down to about 4000m, after which the trail makes a steep descent, zigzagging down the ridge through wildflower bushes, mostly edelweiss, before finally reaching the helipad at **Gunitsawa** (2730m). Cross the river and go upstream to reach your Day 1 starting point at **Sharna Zampa** (2580m), hopefully in time to enjoy a hot packed lunch before driving back to Paro.

LAYA TREK

This trek takes you into remote and isolated high country, introducing you to the unusual culture of the Layap community and allowing you to cross paths with takins (Bhutan's national animal). If you're lucky, you might also spot the exotic blue poppy, Bhutan's national flower.

The trek begins in the Paro valley and follows the same route as the Jhomolhari trek as far as Lingzhi, before heading north into the highlands. Snow can sometimes close the high passes, but they are generally open from April to June and mid-September to mid-November. The best trekking month in the Laya region is April.

Some groups time their trip with the new **Royal Highlander Festival** in the third week of October. Activities include wrestling, horse races and yak competitions, as well as a 26km marathon (the Snowman Run) the day before.

Days 1–4: Sharna Zampa to Lingzhi

Follow Days 1 to 4 of the Jhomolhari trek (p188).

Day 5: Lingzhi to Chebisa

10KM / 5–6 HOURS / 280M ASCENT, 410M DESCENT

Cross the stream below the Chha Shi Thang camp on a wooden bridge and climb up the opposite side to a chorten below Lingzhi Dzong, sitting at 4220m atop a ridge and accessible via a diversion from the trail. Also known as Yugyel Dzong, it was built to control travel over the Lingzhi La, a trade route between Punakha and the Tibetan town of Gyantse. Home to a few monks, the dzong is quite small, with a few offices along the outside wall and a two-storey *utse* (central tower) in the centre.

Walk down from the dzong and rejoin the lower trail leading into Lingzhi village, hidden in a valley formed by the ridge. Wheat and barley fields carpet the upper part of the side valley. The trail crosses the lower part, dotted by a few houses, a school and a post office (with a telephone) at 4080m. The Lingzhi region has a wide variety of herbs, many of medicinal value. The National Institute of Traditional Medicine in Thimphu has a herb-collecting and drying project here.

About one hour from Lingzhi, the trail turns into a side valley past a cairn and prayer flags on a ridge at 4140m. It then makes a long gradual descent to **Goyul** (3870m), a cluster of unusual stone houses by a stream, with dramatic rock walls towering above. Leaving Goyul, the trail climbs for an hour to a chorten. A short descent leads into the spectacular Chebisa valley, with a frozen waterfall at its head. The campsite is on a meadow opposite **Chebisa** (3880m). Upstream of the camp is the village of **Chobiso**.

LAYA TREK AT A GLANCE

Duration 10 days

Max elevation 5005m

Difficulty Medium–hard

Season April to June, September to November

Start Sharna Zampa

Finish Koina

Access towns Paro, Punakha

Summary This trek is an extension of the Jhomolhari trek, with a pit stop at the far-flung village of Laya. It offers diverse flora and fauna and a good opportunity to spot blue sheep.

Laya Trek

CHINA
TIBET

Tseja Gang (6833m)

Limithang

Laya

Army Camp

Zamdo Nangi Chhu

Gieu Gang (7200m)

Sinche La (5005m)

Bahitung Chhu

Jholethang Chhu

Kohi La (3300m)

END Koina

Isheri Jathang

Robluthang

Koina Chhu

See Snowman Trek Map (p201)

Jhari La (4750m)

Shomuthang

Bari La (3900m)

Chachim

Shakshepasa

Gasa Dzong

Gogu La (4440m)

Mo Chhu

Gasa

Chobiso

Chebisa

See Jhomolhari Treks Map (p190)

Mo Chhu

Goyul

Gayza

Gasa Tsachhu

Lingzhi Dzong

Kang Bum (6526m)

Lepena Chhu

Gun

Lingzhi

Damji

Chha Shi Thang

Thuphu Chhu

Sharna Zampa

Dodina

Punakha (20km)

Day 6: Chebisa to Shomuthang

17KM / 6–7 HOURS / 890M ASCENT, 540M DESCENT

Start out by climbing the ridge behind Chebisa, and then tackle a long, steep ascent up a featureless slope. There are large herds of blue sheep living in the rocks above. Watch for bearded vultures and Himalayan griffons flying overhead. At about 4410m the trail levels out and traverses to **Gogu La** (4440m), before crossing a ridge and descending into a side valley through rhododendrons.

Descend to a stream at 4170m, and then climb over a small ridge through a cedar forest. The trail crests the ridge at 4210m and descends on a muddy path into the main Jholethang Chhu valley, in a deep forest of fir and birch. There's a little climb over the side of the valley and down to **Shakshepasa** (3980m), the site of a helipad, marked by a big 'H'. Below, there's a marsh and a messy

stream crossing, with a good lunch spot on the other side.

The trail now goes steeply up the northern side of the valley, levelling out at about 4200m, passing a couple of herders' huts and traversing high above the valley floor on river right to **Chachim**, a yak pasture at 4260m. The camp is in a cluster of brush beside a stream at the base of the valley, at **Shomuthang** (4220m).

Day 7: Shomuthang to Robluthang

18KM / 6–7 HOURS / 700M ASCENT, 760M DESCENT

The trail climbs up the valley, starting on river right, crossing to river left and then crossing back again at 4360m. Edelweiss abounds along the trail; the snow peak visible to the southeast is Kang Bum (6526m).

Climb out of the valley through desolate country to **Jhari La** (4750m), about two hours from camp. North of the pass, the trail switchbacks down to a little stream at 4490m, then becomes a rough, rocky route through rhododendrons on the stream's left. Follow the stream gently downhill through bushes on river left as it makes its way to the main valley. It's a gradual descent to a meadow by the Jholethang Chhu at 3990m, which you cross on a log bridge about 1km upstream.

There is a camp called **Tsheri Jathang** by the river. Herds of takin migrate to this valley in summer and remain here for about four months. Takins are easily disturbed by the presence of other animals, including humans. Sometimes it might be necessary to take a one-hour diversion in order to leave the beasts undisturbed. The valley has been declared a special takin sanctuary and yak herders have agreed not to graze their animals in the valley while the takins are here.

The trail climbs steeply on the northern side to a crest at about 4150m. It then traverses into a side valley past a tiny lake. There are good camping places in a rocky meadow named **Robluthang** at 4160m.

Day 8: Robluthang to Limithang

19KM / 6–7 HOURS / 850M ASCENT, 870M DESCENT

Climb past the remnants of a burnt forest and up the hillside through some boggy patches. Switchback to a shelf at 4390m, before turning into another large glacial side valley. Follow a stream for a while, crossing to river right on an icy log bridge at 4470m, then climb onto a moraine and traverse past lots of marmot holes. You may be able to spot blue sheep high on the slopes to the north before the trail crosses back to stream left.

It's a tough climb from here to the pass at **Sinche La** (5005m), passing a false summit with a cairn. The trail levels out a little before reaching the cairns and prayer flags on the pass, with the snow-covered peak of Gangchhenta filling the northern horizon.

The descent is on a rough, rocky trail that follows a moraine into another glacial valley. Eventually you arrive at the Kango Chhu, a stream below a terminal moraine that forms the end of another valley to the west.

Cross the Kango Chhu to river left on a log bridge at 4470m. A short distance beyond is a yak pasture and camping spot next to a huge rock. However, it's best to continue on to Limithang to camp. Follow the valley northwards, staying high as the stream falls away below you. Beyond an uninhabited

stone house, the trail descends steeply to the valley floor. It switchbacks down with the terminal moraine looming above, crossing the Kango Chhu on a bridge at 4260m. After a short climb through rhododendrons, the trail levels out on a plateau above the Zamdo Nangi Chhu. It's then a short walk through a cedar forest interspersed with small meadows to **Limithang** (4140m), a lovely campsite in a big meadow by the river. Gangchhenta towers over the campsite in the distance.

Day 9: Limithang to Laya

10KM / 4–5 HOURS / 60M ASCENT, 340M DESCENT

After you've walked for 20 minutes, the trail crosses to river left and enters a deep cedar forest, crossing several muddy side streams. Ahead, there's a herders' hut of stone where the vegetation changes to fir trees draped with lichen.

Cross a large stream that flows in from the north and make a steep rocky descent down the side of the valley to the river at 3800m, then cross to river right on a wooden cantilever bridge. A short distance later, cross back and make a stiff climb.

It's a long walk through the heavily wooded, uninhabited valley. Descend to cross a waterfall flowing across the trail, then traverse several ups and downs. Near a point where you can see a single house on a ridge to the east, there is an inconspicuous trail junction. The lower trail leads to the lower part of the village. If you take the upper trail, you will cross a ridge and see the stone houses and wheat fields of **Laya** laid out below you, with some abandoned houses and a goemba above.

Gangchhenta dominates the skyline to the west of the village, and from some places you can get a glimpse of Masang Gang (7165m). In the village centre is a community school, a hospital, an archery field and the first shop since the Paro valley. You can camp in the fields below the school at 3840m. Many groups include a rest day in Laya.

Day 10: Laya to Koina

19KM / 6–7 HOURS / 260M ASCENT, 1070M DESCENT

Layaps are not noted for their punctuality, so horses may arrive late. Below the village, the trail drops back to the river. The trail exits the village through a *khonying* (arch chorten), then passes another chorten at Taje-kha as it descends on a muddy trail to a stream.

LAYA

Spread out over a hillside near the Tibetan border, Laya is one of the highest and remotest villages in Bhutan, at 3700m. The terrain forms the country's primary yak-breeding area. Villagers raise turnips and mustard and produce a crop of wheat or barley each year before winter. During summer people move to high pastures and live in black tents woven from yak hair.

The Layaps have their own language, customs and distinct dress. The women keep their hair long and wear conical bamboo hats with a bamboo spike at the top, held on by a beaded band. They dress in black woollen jackets with silver trims and long woollen skirts with a few stripes in orange or brown. They wear lots of silver jewellery on their backs; on many women, this display includes an array of silver teaspoons.

Laya is starting to change. High prices for the cordyceps (p275) collected in the surrounding valleys have brought considerable wealth to the region, which is now just a day's walk from the road trailhead.

The womenfolk often offer to sell their bamboo hats for about Nu 200. Be wary of the ones offering to sell beads, as they are often family heirlooms. Laya women also frequent trekking camps selling jewellery; most of this is made in Nepal.

Zhabdrung Ngawang Namgyal passed through Laya, and in a small meadow below the village is a chorten with the footprints of the Zhabdrung and his horse. The region is believed to be a *bey-yul* (hidden land) protected by an ancient gate that leads to Laya village. The Layaps perform an annual ceremony in honour of the protective forces that were said to have turned all the stones and trees around the gate into soldiers to repel Tibetan invaders.

There is an alternative camping place on a plateau at 3590m, next to the large Togtsherkhagi Chhu. Cross the river on a wooden bridge and climb to the stone buildings of the **army camp**. There's a radio station here, and a checkpoint where your names will be registered. The road from Gasa will eventually reach this army camp, but only after two substantial bridges are completed, so it may take a few years.

The route now follows the Mo Chhu downstream to Tashithang. About 30 minutes from the army post is an inconspicuous trail junction at 3340m, where the route for the Snowman trek leads uphill on a tiny path. The route to Gasa keeps going downstream on a muddy trail. Soon, it turns a corner into a side valley before crossing the **Bahitung Chhu** at 3290m, the lunch spot for the day.

The trail then trudges along the Mo Chhu to an overhanging rock that forms a cave, then crosses to river right at 3240m on a cantilever bridge. The canyon closes in, and the trail makes several climbs over side ridges while making its way downstream. Beyond, another cave formed by a large overhanging rock is a long steep climb, cresting on a ridge at 3390m. It's a 150m descent to a clear side stream, and the trail then wanders up and down near the river, before climbing once again to **Kohi La** at 3300m.

The muddy trail stays high for about 30 minutes until it reaches a stone staircase, where it turns into a side valley, before dropping to the Koina Chhu. Welcome to **Koina** (3050m), a muddy bog in the forest filled with ankle-deep sludge. This was for many years the worst camp on the trek, but recent road construction means it's now the trailhead, so you'll most likely meet your vehicle here and make the drive down to Gasa. As road construction inches up the valley you can expect the actual pick-up point to change.

SNOWMAN TREK

The combination of distance, altitude, remoteness and weather makes this trek a tough and expensive journey. Even though there are reduced rates for long treks, many people baulk at the cost of a 24-day trek. Western trek companies charge over US$6000 for the trip. It is said that more people have summitted Everest than have completed the Snowman trek.

If you plan to trek this route, check your emergency evacuation insurance. If you get into Lunana and snow blocks the passes, the only way out is by helicopter, a costly way to finish an already expensive trek. Other obstacles that often hamper this trek are bridges, in remote regions, that get washed away by deluges.

The Snowman trek is frequently closed because of snow, and is impossible to undertake during winter. The window is generally considered to be late September to mid-October, after the main monsoon rains, but before snow closes the high passes. Start too late and you run the risk of being stuck. Don't plan a summer trek; this is a miserable place to be during the monsoon.

This classic trek follows the Jhomolhari and Laya treks to Laya. Many walking days can be saved by starting in Gasa (via Punakha) and trekking north over the Bari La.

There are several alternative endings to the Snowman trek. One of the most popular is to continue southeast from Danji via the Gophu La and Duer Hot Springs, past fine views of Gangkhar Puensum, to end at Duer in the Bumthang valley (seven to eight days from Danji); a total of 25 or 26 days.

Days 1–4: Sharna Zampa to Lingzhi

Follow Days 1 to 4 of the Jhomolhari trek (p188).

Days 5–9: Lingzhi to Laya

Follow Days 5 to 9 of the Laya trek (p195).

Day 10: Rest & Acclimatisation Day in Laya

If you have trekked from Sharna Zampa, you should spend a day recuperating in Laya and preparing for the rigours ahead. If you've trekked from Gasa, you should also walk up to Laya to acclimatise. You may well get mobile-phone service in Laya. In an emergency, the army camp below Laya has a radio.

Day 11: Laya to Rodophu

19KM / 6–8 HOURS / 1030M ASCENT, 70M DESCENT
The trek leads down to the Lunana trail junction, then climbs for 40 minutes to a hilltop with good views over the Mo Chhu and the Rhodo Chhu. It continues up the Rhodo Chhu valley, first through mixed conifers, then through rhododendrons, above the treeline. Atop a large rock slide there is a view of the glacial valley and a massive glacier on Tsenda Kang (7100m). The **Rodophu** camp is just beyond a wooden bridge across the Rhodo Chhu at 4160m.

If you're acclimatising here for a day, consider a short 2km hike up the valley to a knoll with excellent views of the valley and mountains, continuing to the base of the glacier. Another option is to follow a small trail starting about 500m upstream from camp and up the hill to the north, ending in a small yak pasture with a hut at 4500m.

Day 12: Rodophu to Narethang

17KM / 5–6 HOURS / 720M ASCENT
The path crosses the wooden bridge and follows the river for 20 minutes through rhododendron shrubs before turning right up the hill. Climb to a high open valley at 4600m and then through meadows to **Tsomo La** (4900m), which offers good views towards the Tibet border and Jhomolhari. Next up is a flat, barren plateau at around 5000m with yak trails criss-crossing everywhere – your guide will know the way. The camp is at **Narethang** (4900m), below the 6395m peak of Gangla Karchung.

Day 13: Narethang to Tarina

18KM / 7–8 HOURS / 270M ASCENT, 1200M DESCENT
It's a one-hour climb to the 5120m **Gangla Karchung La**, with Kang Bum (6526m) to the west and Tsenda Kang, Teri Gang (7300m) and Jejekangphu Gang (7100m) due north. The path descends along a large moraine to the edge of a near-vertical wall

SNOWMAN TREK AT A GLANCE

Duration 24 days

Max elevation 5320m

Difficulty Hard

Season September to October

Start Sharna Zampa

Finish Upper Sephu

Access town Paro

Summary The Snowman trek travels to the remote Lunana district and is said to be one of the most difficult treks in the world. Fewer than half the people who attempt this trek eventually finish it, either because of problems with altitude or heavy snowfall on the high passes.

TREKS SNOWMAN TREK

with breathtaking views. A massive glacier descends from Teri Gang to two deep turquoise lakes at its foot, 1km below you. The glacial lake to the left burst through its dam in the early 1960s, causing widespread damage downstream, and partially destroying Punakha Dzong.

The path now becomes very steep as it descends into the valley. When wet, this stretch can be rather nasty, with lots of roots and slippery mud. At the base of the U-shaped valley, the trail turns right, following the Tang Chhu downstream. There are several good campsites along the river, both before and after the trail crosses the river at **Tarina**.

Day 14: Tarina to Woche

17KM / 6–7 HOURS / 275M ASCENT, 330M DESCENT

The walk leads through conifers down the Tang Chhu on river left, passing some impressive waterfalls. The trail climbs gently out of the valley past several huge landslides, and eventually climbs steeply to the northeast into the high side valley of **Woche**. The first village in the Lunana region, Woche is a small settlement of five houses at 3940m.

Looking up the valley you can see the following day's route to Lhedi. There have been reports of theft here; keep all your gear safely inside your tent.

Day 15: Woche to Lhedi

17KM / 6–7 HOURS / 980M ASCENT, 950M DESCENT

The trail climbs the Woche valley, crossing a stream and going over a moraine before descending to a wooden bridge across the Woche Chhu. It then climbs on a wide trail past a clear lake to **Keche La** (4650m), with excellent views of the surrounding mountains, including Jejekangphu Gang's triple peak, the source of the Woche Chhu.

The route now descends into the Pho Chhu valley and reaches **Thaga** village (4050m). Dropping towards the Pho Chhu, the path then turns northeast towards Lhedi. Passing a few scattered settlements and crossing below a waterfall on a wooden bridge, the trail descends to the banks of the Pho Chhu, continuing along the riverbed to **Lhedi** at 3700m.

Lhedi is a district headquarters with a school, a Basic Health Unit (BHU) and a wireless station, but there is no shop here (or anywhere else in the Lunana district). Everything is carried in by yak trains across

5000m passes. There are strong winds up the valley in the late afternoon, making it bitterly cold in autumn and winter.

Day 16: Lhedi to Thanza

17KM / 4–5 HOURS / 400M ASCENT

The trail follows the north bank of the Pho Chhu past several small farms. Floods have destroyed parts of the trail so an alternative path winds its way among boulders in the riverbed. Around lunchtime the trail passes **Chozo** village at 4090m, which has a functioning dzong.

If you are pressed for time, you can take a direct trail to Tshochena from here, but most trekkers continue to Thanza (4100m), a couple of hours up the valley. The first part of the trail leads through yak pastures on river flats, giving way to a large expanse of fine glacial sand. Eventually, the trail leaves the riverbed and climbs a bluff overlooking the villages of **Thanza**, straight ahead, and **Toencha**, on the other bank of the river. The 7100m Zongophu Gang (Table Mountain) forms an immense, 3000m-high wall of snow and ice behind Thanza. Most groups camp in Toencha (4150m), but there are places to camp in Thanza as well.

Day 17: Rest Day in Thanza

Schedule a rest day here. This is often as far as yak drivers from Laya go, and it takes time to round up yaks for the rest of the trek. Capitalise on the day by exploring the villages and glacial lakes up the valley. The closest lake, **Raphstreng Tsho,** is 100m deep and caused a flood in 1994 when a moraine holding back its waters burst. A large crew of Indian workers dug a channel through the moraine to prevent a recurrence, but there are other lakes in the area posing a similar risk.

Day 18: Thanza to Danji

8KM / 3–4 HOURS / 80M ASCENT

If you're feeling fit, you can hike to Tshochena in one day, but it's a long, hard walk at high altitude and is best split in two parts.

Climbing to a large boulder on the hill south of the village, the trail then turns east up a side valley. After a couple of hours of easy walking, the trail enters **Danji**, a yak

Snowman Trek

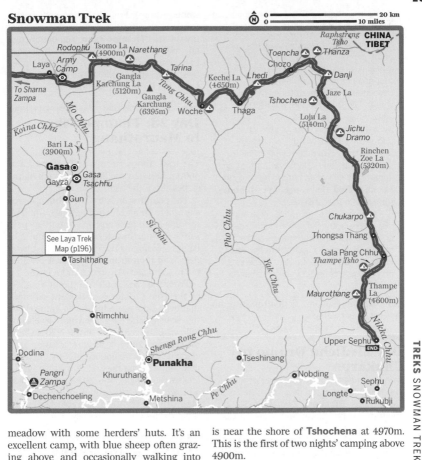

meadow with some herders' huts. It's an excellent camp, with blue sheep often grazing above and occasionally walking into camp.

A few hundred metres up the valley, a small trail climbs the ridge to the left, leading to a higher valley. The top of the ridge offers excellent views of surrounding mountains.

Day 19: Danji to Tshochena

12KM / 5–6 HOURS / 490M ASCENT, 240M DESCENT

From the junction near camp, the trail up the valley leads to Gangkhar Puensum base camp and Bumthang. The path to the end of the trek crosses the creek and leads up a rocky side valley – a long climb across several false summits to **Jaze La** at 5150m, with views of mountains in all directions. From the pass, the path descends between snow-covered peaks past a string of small lakes. The camp

is near the shore of **Tshochena** at 4970m. This is the first of two nights' camping above 4900m.

Day 20: Tshochena to Jichu Dramo

14KM / 4–5 HOURS / 230M ASCENT, 140M DESCENT

The trail follows the shore of the blue-green lake before climbing to a ridge at 5100m, with a 360-degree panorama of snowy peaks. Far below, the Pho Chhu descends towards Punakha. The road and microwave tower at Dochu La are visible in the distance.

The path makes several ups and downs over small rounded hills, but the altitude can slow you down. Past a glacial lake before **Loju La** at 5140m, many trails wander around high-altitude yak pastures, and it's easy to wander astray. The correct path is across a small saddle at 5100m into a wide glacial valley, and then down to the camp at

THE SHY PREDATOR

Locally referred to as *chen*, the critically endangered snow leopard is a solitary and elusive creature that lives in rocky mountain folds above the treeline, descending to lower altitudes during winter. The snow leopard is extremely agile in high terrain, and can effortlessly move through nearly 1m of snow. Its dappled fur offers wonderful camouflage in its icy habitat. Preying on blue sheep and the occasional yak calf, it can sometimes stray into human territory in search of food. However, direct confrontations with humans are rare.

The holy grail of an entire generation of wildlife photographers and film-makers, the snow leopard remains one of the most pursued creatures in the wild. If you manage to spot one of these cats on your trek, consider yourself blessed.

Jichu Dramo (5050m), a small pasture on the east of the valley.

Day 21: Jichu Dramo to Chukarpo

18KM / 5–6 HOURS / 320M ASCENT, 730M DESCENT

The trail climbs through a moraine to the picturesque **Rinchen Zoe La** (5320m), dividing the Pho Chhu and Mangde Chhu drainages. Rinchen Zoe peak (5650m) towers above, Gangkhar Puensum is visible in the east, while the Thampe Chhu valley stretches below to the south.

Descending into a broad, marshy valley with a string of lakes, the trail follows the left (east) side of the valley. Eventually, it descends steeply down the face of a moraine to a yak pasture in the upper reaches of the Thampe Chhu. Cross to the west bank (river right) here, as there is no bridge further down. The vegetation begins to thicken, and consists of rhododendrons and junipers. The camp is a couple of hours away at **Chukarpo** (4600m); a better site sits an hour further on at **Thongsa Thang** (4400m).

Day 22: Chukarpo to Thampe Tsho

18KM / 5–6 HOURS / 400M ASCENT, 640M DESCENT

Descend along the right bank of the river until you reach a yak pasture at **Gala Pang Chhu** (4010m). From here, the path begins to climb steeply through junipers and silver firs towards **Thampe Tsho**. The path generally follows a stream to the beautiful, clear, turquoise lake, set in a bowl and surrounded by steep mountain walls. The camp is at the far end of the lake at 4300m.

Day 23: Thampe Tsho to Maurothang

14KM / 5 HOURS / 280M ASCENT, 1020M DESCENT

The trail climbs steeply to **Thampe La** at 4600m. You may see blue sheep high on the slopes above the trail.

The path descends to **Om Tsho**, a sacred site where Pema Lingpa found a number of *terma* (sacred texts and artefacts). The path skirts the northwestern shore of the lake before crossing its outlet, marked by prayer flags, and then drops steeply past a waterfall to a smaller lake, about 100m lower.

From the second lake to the headwaters of the Nikka Chhu is a descent so steep that even yaks are reluctant to come down this stretch. The path eventually levels out, following the left bank of the Nikka Chhu. After about 2km, it reaches a large open glade near the confluence of a major tributary coming from the east. A wooden bridge crosses the Nikka Chhu to river right, where a broad path leads through mixed forest to **Maurothang** (3610m), a large clearing by the river beside a few herders' huts.

Day 24: Maurothang to Upper Sephu

11KM / 3 HOURS / 730M DESCENT

If horses are not available at Maurothang, your guide will probably send someone ahead to arrange for them further down. Yaks cannot walk all the way to the road because of the low altitude and the many cows in the area.

A well-used trail continues down the west side of the Nikka Chhu for about 30 minutes before crossing to the east bank into a mixed deciduous and bamboo forest. It descends gradually through forests and pastures, emerging onto a large grassy area overlooking upper Sephu village. Your vehicle should meet you here. If not, it's around 7km down a farm road to the main paved highway at **Sephu**, next to the new Nikka Chhu bridge (2600m), marked by shops and a small restaurant.

OWL TREK

Keen to sample some 'nightlife' out in the mountains? Well, you could always consider walking the Owl trek, a route exploring the Bumthang region that owes its name to the apparently frequent hooting of owls that can be heard at campsites through the night. A two- or three-day itinerary, the Owl trek starts at either Chutigang or Menchugang village (5km north of Toktu Zampa) and ends at either Tharpaling Goemba or Jakar Dzong. March to May and October to December are the best times for trekking, though spring can be muddy.

Day 1: Chutigang to Shona Campsite

7KM / 3 HOURS / 555M ASCENT

The original trail goes from Menchugang, just north of Jakar, and includes a 90-minute climb to Chutigang. Some itineraries also visit Duer village at the start of the trek. There is, however, a road leading to the timber depot, suspension bridge, and water-driven flour mill at **Chutigang** (2685m) and this is where most itineraries now start. The trail leaves the forestry road just before the timber depot, following the true right bank of the babbling Drangngela Chhu, in a southerly direction.

The gentle climb leaves behind the ubiquitous blue pine to enter a forest of giant fir trees with an understorey of daphne. The stream is crossed on a makeshift bridge of planks before the trail zigzags up a steep, mossy and slippery slope. At the top, the trail follows a spur to a small clearing full of thorny Japanese silverberries – a favourite autumnal food for Himalayan black bears that seasonally frequent this and other similar glades.

OWL TREK AT A GLANCE

Duration 3 days

Max elevation 3870m

Difficulty Medium

Season March to May, October to December

Start Chutigang

Finish Tharpaling Goemba

Access town Jakar

Summary Dense rhododendron and fir forests make way for exposed, elevated winter yak pastures, with a panoramic view of Himalayan peaks from Kitephu. A short but moderately challenging and moderately high trek along old yak herders' trails.

Above the glade, the trail meets a forestry road; turn left and follow the road as it contours along an east-facing slope that has been cleared for pasture, offering valley views. Again the trail leaves the road and the track becomes steep and heavily eroded. Towering fir trees, blooming rhododendrons and drifts of snow announce increasing elevation. Upon exiting the dark forest, the **Shona campsite** (3240m) is heralded by a stream and views north to snowy ridges, and, unfortunately, a rather large amount of litter.

Day 2: Shona Campsite to Kitephu

6KM / 5 HOURS / 630M ASCENT

The climb out of Shona meanders through giant fir trees festooned with old man's beard. The ascent is gentle as you negotiate

TREKS OWL TREK

MULTIDAY HIKES IN BUMTHANG

There are so many great hiking trails in the Bumthang valley that it's possible to link together a string of day hikes to make a multiday walk that avoids the inconvenience, discomfort and expense of a full camping trek.

From Menchugang you could start with a full day hike to Luege Rowe (or even Shugdrak), before hiking up the south bank of the Chamkhar Chhu to Ngang Lhakhang. Overnight at Ngang Lhakhang or a homestay in nearby Tsangling or Tashiling, before making the long day hike over the Phephe La to Ogyen Chholing (the Bumthang Cultural trek).

On the third day, make the rewarding return day hike to Thowadrak Hermitage. Then on the fourth day, return to Jakar by car or drive to Kunzangdrak Goemba and hike over the ridge to Pelseling Goemba and then down to the Swiss Guest House or Tamshing Goemba.

For a full week's walking with some camping, add on the three-day Owl trek in the reverse direction, starting at Tharpaling Goemba and picking up this itinerary at Menchugang.

a tangle of moss-carpeted roots. The trail follows a rocky stream bed past cairns of boulders and twists up a gully that can be quite deep with snow drifts even into late spring.

After about two hours' walk from the campsite a string of prayer flags and a stiff breeze welcomes you to **Rang La pass** (Drangela; 3595m). Views to the southeast encompass Gaytsa and Chhumey valley below the snowy peaks of the Black Range. Here the trail turns east to follow the ridge as it ascends through winter yak pastures. Yaks and horses and interesting makeshift huts populate the exposed pastures.

Beyond the pastures there is a series of short climbs through stunted forests of willow, birch and juniper before reaching the exposed campsite at **Kitephu** (3870m). The campsite sits below the ridge beside a small stream that may not be flowing. If there is insufficient water your crew will want to press on to make camp at Tharpaling Goemba. There's plenty of time in the afternoon to savour the views by hiking up to the top of the ridge.

Day 3: Kitephu to Tharpaling Goemba

3KM / 1½ HOURS / 330M DESCENT

If you do overnight at Kitephu, get up early on the third morning for magnificent views towards Gangkhar Phuensum and the main Himalaya range. The trail from Kitephu takes you for 90 minutes to a campsite just above the impressive **Tharpaling Goemba** and Choedrak Hermitage (where Guru Rinpoche is said to have meditated). Keep an eye out for colourful Himalayan monal near the monastery. From here you have the choice of meeting your vehicle, descending on foot via Samtenling Lhakhang to Domkhar in the Chhume valley, or climbing back over the ridge behind Tharpaling to descend through forest to Jakar.

NABJI TREK

If you are looking for a low altitude winter trek, or if village life, birdwatching and family interactions are more important than mountain views, the Nabji trek could well be your cup of tea.

This trail pioneered community-based tourism in Bhutan, whereby local villagers

NABJI TREK AT A GLANCE

Duration 3–4 days

Max elevation 1635m

Difficulty Easy

Season October to March

Start Tongtongphey

Finish Nimshong

Access town Trongsa

Summary A low-altitude trek passing through the land of the isolated Monpa people.

are employed on a rotating basis to offer services and amenities such as porterage, village tours, cultural shows and food at semideveloped campsites along the route. Campsite fees go into a community fund to support education, conservation and tourism development.

The trailheads of this winter trek are on the road between Trongsa and Zhemgang, and the trek itself offers a chance to spot some exotic local creatures such as the golden langur, the rufous-necked hornbill and the serpent eagle, among others.

As with so many treks in Bhutan, road-building is nibbling away at both ends of the trek, and you will probably find yourself walking on farm roads at some stages. Depending on how much walking on roads is desirable, you may end the trek at Nabji or Nimshong. This trek can easily be done in the opposite direction.

Day 1: Tongtongphey to Jangbi

9KM / 3–4 HOURS / 950M ASCENT, 640M DESCENT

From Tongtongphey (1060m) you walk on a farm road for about one hour before meeting the old trail to Jangbi. Descend steeply to the bridge crossing the Mangde Chhu, before ascending to Jangbi (1370m), a village in the homeland of the Monpa people. The campsite at Jangbi overlooks the Mangdue Chhu valley.

Day 2: Jangbi to Kudra

14KM / 6–7 HOURS / 265M ASCENT

From Jangbi it's an easy hike to **Phrumzur** village (1400m), a good spot for lunch.

Phrumzur, another Monpa village, has a temple from where you can take in good views of the valley. Today's trail to Kudra is littered with fabulous evidence of Guru Rinpoche's visit to the region – footprint, dagger, hat, you name it.

The campsite at **Kudra** village (1635m) is smack in the middle of the forest. There are three Monpa households nearby and filtered views all the way down to Nyimshong.

Day 3: Kudra to Nabji

13KM / 6–7 HOURS / 335M DESCENT

Today's trek is on the ancient trail through magnificent forest, supposedly a habitat for tigers and leopards, although sightings are rare. Emerging from the orchid-festooned forest and bamboo thickets, the trail finally arrives at **Nabji** (1300m) at a spot marked by a holy tree. The camp is located amid rice fields near the village.

Take some time to explore the village and visit the temple and the historically important stone pillar commemorating an 8th-century peace treaty negotiated by Guru Rinpoche and signed between King Sindhu of Bumthang and King Nauchhe (Big Nose) from Assam. In the village you'll also see the rocky remains of a blacksmith, believed to be connected to Pema Lingpa.

It is possible to cut the trek short here, meet your car at Nabji, and return to Trongsa.

Day 4: Nabji to Nimshong

23KM / 9 HOURS / 200M ASCENT, 200M DESCENT

It is two to three hours' trekking to **Korphu** (1500m), a village of about 600 people, to visit the village temple, which houses the sacred relics of Pema Lingpa. It's possible to stay at the community-run campsite, which offers fine views over the valley, especially if you are doing the trek in the reverse direction or require a shorter final day.

Hike along the road through a lush broadleaf forest teeming with regional fauna, such as golden langurs and rufous-necked hornbills, to the village of **Nimshong** (1320m). This section is well regarded for birdwatching. Nimshong is a village of about 60 households where you will be welcomed with much song and dance. At Nimshong you can tour the village and possibly take in a cultural show, before picking up your transport back to Trongsa.

MERAK–SAKTENG TREK

Closed to foreigners from 1995 to 2010, this trek in the far-eastern corner of the country promises an unparalleled cultural and natural experience, for the moment at least.

The trek passes through the Sakteng Wildlife Sanctuary, an unspoilt and delicate ecosystem that's home to the endangered snow leopard and red panda, the Himalayan black bear, the Himalayan red fox and perhaps even the legendary *migoi* (yeti). The region is also home to the isolated Brokpa people, one of the Himalaya's most interesting ethnic groups.

As with so many trekking routes in Bhutan, roads are encroaching upon these routes. A road reaches Merak and another, north of the Gamri Chhu, will probably soon reach Sakteng. Homestays are available in both villages. Alternative paths have been developed to avoid the bulk of the new roads. April and May are the best months to visit for lovely spring blooms.

It's possible to start the trek from Merak, or from several villages closer to Trashigang. One option to avoid the bulk of the new roads is to start trekking from Merak to Namchena: the next day involves camping near Tangling-Tsho, and Day 3 takes you over Preng-La pass (4267m) to reach Khaling by lunch, following the old migration route of Merak villagers. The most popular option is to begin at Damnongchu, but you could conceivably start at Jaling, Khardung or Phongme. If you want a shorter trek or to spend a full day in and around Sakteng village, skip Day 1 of this itinerary and start walking from Merak.

MERAK–SAKTENG TREK AT A GLANCE

Duration 3–4 days

Max elevation 3480m

Difficulty Medium

Season Mid-March to May, September to November

Start Damnongchu or Merak

Finish Thakthri or Jyongkhar

Access town Trashigang

Summary A star attraction offering a sneak peek into one of the most secluded regions in Bhutan.

'PEOPLE OF DARKNESS'

Numbering around 3000 individuals, the Monpas inhabit a cluster of ancient villages dotting the mountain slope overlooking the Mangde Chhu near Jangbi. The word 'Monpa' loosely translates to 'people of darkness', and refers to their isolated existence in Bhutan. The tribe is believed to be the earliest settlers in the country, with ethnic roots that can be traced back to Arunachal Pradesh in India, where their population exceeds 50,000.

The Monpas practise a mix of Buddhism and animistic shamanism. While they were originally hunters and gatherers, the Monpas have, over time, developed artisanal skills such as cane weaving, bamboo crafting and basket making.

Day 1: Damnongchu to Merak

5 HOURS

The trail leading out of Damnongchu involves a series of gentle ups and downs along a stream. About 45 minutes before Merak you pass the village and lhakhang at Gengu, which is said to house the mummified body of Buchang Gyalwa Zangpo, the son of Thangtong Gyalpo.

The final stretch is an easy and gradual ascent through yak meadows into the village of **Merak** (3480m), home to around 140 families. Camp is usually made just before the village, in a spot offering fantastic views of the mountains and the village. Alternatively, you can choose to stay at the village guesthouse or in a local homestay. The Samtenling Lhakhang boasts the saddle and phallus of local mountain deity Jomo Kuenkhar's horse.

Day 2: Merak to Miksa Teng

7–8 HOURS

Today's trek scales the 4140m Nagchung La for fine Himalayan views, after which the route descends steadily to a river. After following the river for an hour, it's another steep one-hour climb and then descent to **Miksa Teng** (2850m; a *teng* is a ledge or terrace). The campsite is surrounded by rhododendrons, which are in riotous bloom in April.

Day 3: Miksa Teng to Sakteng

4 HOURS

From Miksa Teng, climb 300m to a small pass, then descend through beautiful woods to **Sakteng** (2985m). If you're lucky, you might see a red panda amid the forest along the way. There's a campsite on the outskirts of the village, but you can also sleep at the village guesthouse. Some groups include a rest day in Sakteng, which is a good idea.

Day 4: Sakteng to Jyongkhar via Thakthri

6–7 HOURS

After a small pass, today's walk is mostly downhill, to the village of **Thakthri** (2200m), which is connected by a new road to Rangjung and is where you can end the trek. Alternatively, you can cross the Gamri Chhu and continue to the village of **Jyongkhar** (1850m), which is linked by another road to Phongme, Radi and then Rangjung.

Understand
Bhutan

Bhutan Today

Bhutan remains a unique and very special country, but for better or worse it's opened its doors to the outside world and joined the global community. There's now almost one mobile phone for every Bhutanese and more than 75,000 registered vehicles (but still no traffic lights). The challenge for the government is to use the benefits of globalisation and capitalism to meet the growing expectations of its people without undermining the very things that Bhutanese cherish about their culture.

Best in Print

The Raven Crown (Michael Aris; 1995) Definitive history of Bhutan's monarchy, lavishly illustrated with rare photographs.

The History of Bhutan (Karma Phuntsho; 2014) Comprehensive and detailed history of the nation.

The Hero with a Thousand Eyes (Karma Ura; 1995) Historical novel based on the life of Shingkhar Lam, a retainer who served in the court of the second, third and fourth kings of Bhutan.

Treasures of the Thunder Dragon (Ashi Dorji Wangmo; 2006) An engaging portrait of Bhutan from the wife of the fourth king.

Best on Film

Travellers & Magicians (2003) Whimsical tale from the Bhutanese rinpoche-director.

The Other Final (2003) When the world's bottom football (soccer) team, Montserrat, meets second from the bottom, Bhutan.

Crossing Bhutan (2016) Chronicles a 42-day trek across Bhutan, investigating notions of Gross National Happiness.

Politics & Parliament

Bhutan's fledgling (and initially somewhat reluctant) democratic system continues to mature. The 2018 elections saw victory for the new Druk Nyamrup Tshogpa party, meaning that three separate parties have won the three national elections since democracy was introduced in 2007.

Challenges remain for the new government. Border disputes with China continue to flare up, most recently in 2017 on the Doklam plateau at the junction of Bhutan's Haa region, Tibet's Chumbi Valley and the Indian Sikkim state. China's attempt to build a road in Bhutanese territory resulted in a tense three-month military standoff between India and China.

Despite its image abroad as a modern Shangri-La, Bhutan does not live outside the demands of the modern world. Even remote mountain communities like Laya are changing quickly, thanks to the booming trade with China in the valuable medicinal parasite cordyceps. The modern world is slowly gaining ground in Bhutan.

Challenges & Changes

Bhutan is a tiny nation with a small, sustainable population squeezed between two giant countries with massive populations and economies. This situation has presented opportunities but also threats in recent decades.

A rapidly growing economy and increased consumerism have led to soaring imports, primarily from India. The flow of Indian rupees (to which the Bhutanese ngultrum is pegged) out of the country resulted in a cash crisis in 2012. Many Bhutanese say they have simply caught the global bug of overspending and overborrowing. The irony of this happening in the country that introduced Gross National Happiness is not lost on the Bhutanese and is openly discussed. Increased mobility and aspiration have also led to unprecedented migration from rural villages to urban centres where youth unemployment is rising.

As tourism grows so does the number of hotels, and this, combined with the 600% growth in roads over the last decade, risks taking the shine off Bhutan's exclusive image. It remains to be seen how long it can continue to charge foreign tourists US$250 per day, while much larger numbers of Indian tourists pay no tariffs and often drive their own vehicles, creating a much larger environmental and cultural impact.

Modernisation & Gross National Happiness

Despite the rapid uptake of technology, democracy and global trends, Bhutan's government continues to assume a protective role in Bhutanese society. Bhutan was the first country to ban not only smoking in public places but also the sale of tobacco. Also banned are Western-style advertising billboards and plastic bags.

Issues of sustainable development, education and healthcare, and environmental and cultural preservation are therefore at the forefront of policy making, as are the tenets of Buddhism, which form the base of Bhutan's legal code. Every development project is scrutinised for its impact on the local population, religious faith and the environment. Bhutan's strict adherence to high-value, low-impact tourism is just one example of this.

Bhutan is one of the few places on earth where compassion is valued as much as capitalism, and well-being is measured alongside productivity. This unique approach is summed up in the much-celebrated prioritising of Gross National Happiness over Gross Domestic Product. And yet things are not as simple as they seem. According to the 2018 UN World Happiness Report, Bhutan ranks 97th, just above Somalia.

The Environment

At the 2015 Climate Summit in Paris, Bhutan pledged not only to be carbon neutral, but also to remain carbon negative, the world's only such country. The tiny, well-forested nation absorbs three times the carbon its economy produces.

Hydro power is seen as the holy grail of Bhutan's sustainable development. Currently Bhutan has five operating schemes, six schemes under construction and five proposed projects. Bhutan gets 27% of its government income from hydroelectricity exports to India, but these projects have created 50% of its rising foreign debt. The future earnings from the hydro-power projects under construction are already earmarked for Bhutan's burgeoning foreign debt.

To further its green credentials, Bhutan is aiming to cut its fossil fuel dependency on India by moving to electric cars, banning export logging and achieving 100% organic food production. Despite its challenges, in terms of spiritual and environmental issues Bhutan remains a model for the world.

POPULATION: **766,397**

LIFE EXPECTANCY: **70 YEARS**

GDP: **US$3438 PER CAPITA**

INFLATION: **3.1%**

UNEMPLOYMENT: **2.4%**

if Bhutan were 100 people

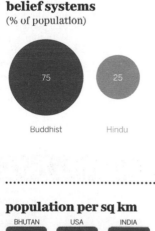

50 would be Ngalop
35 would be Nepali
15 would be tribal

belief systems
(% of population)

75 Buddhist

25 Hindu

population per sq km

BHUTAN   USA   INDIA

≈ 20 people

History

Bhutan's history is steeped in Buddhist folklore and mythology – even museum captions and school textbooks describe shape-shifting demons and the miracle-working saints who bested them. On a prosaic level the uneasy balance of secular, royal and religious power dominates Bhutan's history, as does the country's relationship with its northern neighbour Tibet, but to truly get to the heart of Bhutan's past, you'll have to suspend your disbelief and embrace its magical blend of fact and fiction.

The Spread of History

Researchers have attached dates to many events and protagonists in Bhutan's vibrant history, though these often do not seem to fit together into a credible and accurate chronology. Sources of historical fact include folk songs, local lore, religious biographies and storytellers. Try visualising the spirit of the happenings rather than rationalising events as historical truth. This will, in part, help prepare you for a visit to a land where spirits, ghosts, *migoi* (yetis), snake spirits and lamas reincarnated in three different bodies are accepted as a part of daily life.

Bhutan's medieval and modern history is better documented than its ancient history, but is no less exotic. This is a time of warlords, feuds, giant fortresses and castles, with intrigue, treachery, fierce battles and extraordinary pageantry all playing feature roles. The country's recent history begins with a hereditary monarchy that was founded in the 20th century and continued the country's policy of isolationism. It was not until the leadership of the third king that Bhutan emerged from its medieval heritage of serfdom and seclusion.

Until the 1960s, the country had no national currency, no telephones, no schools, no hospitals, no postal service and no tourists. Development efforts have now produced all these – plus airports, roads and a national system of free healthcare and education. Despite the speed of modernisation, Bhutan has been famously cautious in opening its doors to tourism, TV and the internet in an effort to preserve its national identity and the environment.

TIMELINE	1500–2000 BC	6th century AD	7th century
	Present-day Bhutan is inhabited by nomadic herders who seasonally migrated between low-lying valleys and alpine pastures.	The animist Bon religion is established across the Himalayan region, including several valleys of what is now Bhutan.	Buddhism becomes established in Bhutan with the first Buddhist temples built in AD 659, including Kyichu Lhakhang near Paro, and Jampey Lhakhang in Bumthang.

Compare Bhutan's recent political history with that of its neighbours Sikkim (absorbed by India), Tibet (controlled by China) and Nepal (its royal family overthrown) and its cultural and national strength seem even more remarkable.

Early History & the Arrival of Buddhism

Archaeological evidence suggests the low-lying valleys of present-day Bhutan were inhabited as early as 1500 to 2000 BC by nomadic herders who moved their grazing animals to high pastures in summer. Many Bhutanese still live this way today. The valleys of Bhutan provided relatively easy access across the Himalaya, and several valleys were used as migration and trade routes from India to Tibet.

Some of the early inhabitants of Bhutan were followers of Bon, the animistic tradition that was the main religion throughout the Himalayan region before the advent of Buddhism. It is believed that the Bon religion was introduced in Bhutan in the 6th century AD.

Buddhism was possibly first introduced to parts of Bhutan as early as the 2nd century AD, although most historians agree that the first Buddhist temples were built in the 7th century under the instruction of the Tibetan king Songtsen Gampo.

Many of the important events in the emerging country's early history involved saints and religious leaders and were therefore chronicled only in scriptures. Unfortunately, most of these original documents were destroyed in fires in the printing works of Sonagatsel in 1828 and in Punakha Dzong in 1832. Much of what was left in the old capital of Punakha was lost in an earthquake in 1897 and more records were lost when Paro Dzong burned in 1907. Therefore, much of the early history of Bhutan relies either on reports from British explorers, on legend and folklore, or the few manuscripts that escaped these disasters.

Guru Rinpoche

Guru Rinpoche (Precious Master) is one of the most important of Bhutan's historical and religious figures, and his visit to Bumthang in AD 746 is recognised as the true introduction of Buddhism to Bhutan. He is a notable historical figure of the 8th century and his statue appears in almost all Bhutanese temples.

He is also regarded as the second Buddha possessing miraculous powers, including the ability to subdue demons and evil spirits, and his birth was predicted by Sakyamuni, the historical Buddha. His birthplace was Uddiyana in the Swat valley of what is now Pakistan. Uddiyana is known in Dzongkha as Ugyen, and some texts refer to him as Ugyen Rinpoche. He is also known as Padmasambhava. *Padma* is Sanskrit for

Travel in Bhutan is generally easiest following the main north–south river valleys, so many Bhutanese travelled to Tibet for trade, education, pastures or pilgrimage, rather than to east–west valleys in Bhutan.

746	841	9th century	10th century
Guru Rinpoche (Padmasambhava) is invited by the king of Bumthang to visit his land and subdue evil spirits. He is credited with converting the king and others to Buddhism.	The Tibetan king Langdharma bans Buddhism in Tibet and banishes his brother prince Tsangma to eastern Bhutan.	Many Tibetan Buddhists take refuge in Bhutan as the Bonpo gain power in Tibet and Buddhists are persecuted.	Further turmoil and the decline of Buddhism in Tibet sees various schools of Tibetan Buddhism established in Bhutan.

ORIGIN OF THE NAME BHUTAN

Few agree on the origin of the name Bhutan. It may have evolved from the Sanskrit 'Bhotant', meaning the end of Tibet, or from 'Bhu-uttan' meaning 'high land'. Early British explorers called it Bootan or Bhotan, and they believed the name derived from 'Bhotsthan', meaning 'Land of the Bhotias' (Bhotia is Sanskrit for people from Tibet).

The Tibetans originally called the region Mon, Tibetan for 'darkness', and referred to its people as Monpa, meaning 'those living in darkness' (ie without the light of Buddhism). Tibetans also called Bhutan Menjong (The Land of Medicinal Herbs) for its immense botanical richness, particularly compared to the high-altitude desert of Tibet.

Although now known as Bhutan to the outside world, the country has been known as Druk Yul, 'Land of the Thunder Dragon', to its inhabitants since the 13th century. The people call themselves the Drukpa.

'lotus flower' and is the origin of the Tibetan and Bhutanese name Pema; *sambhava* means 'born from'.

He travelled in various manifestations throughout Tibet, Nepal and Bhutan, meditating in numerous caves, which are now regarded as important 'power places'. He preserved his teachings and wisdom by concealing them in the form of *terma* (hidden treasures) to be found by enlightened treasure discoverers called *tertons*. His consort and biographer, Yeshe Chhogyel, urges us not to regard Guru Rinpoche as a normal human being, because by doing so we will fail to perceive even a fraction of his enlightened qualities.

Bhutanese and Tibetans differ over a few aspects of his life; we refer here to the Bhutanese tradition.

> Guru Rinpoche is credited with the founding of the Nyingma lineage – also known as the 'old' or 'Red Hat' sect – of Mahayana Buddhism, which became for a time the dominant religion of Bhutan. Its followers are known as Nyingmapa.

The Story of Kurjey Lhakhang

In AD 746 Guru Rinpoche made his first visit to Bhutan. At this time, the Indian Sendha Gyab had established himself as the king of Bumthang, with the title Sindhu Raja. He was feuding with Naochhe (Big Nose), a rival Indian king in the south of Bhutan, when Naochhe killed the Sindhu Raja's son and 16 of his attendants. The raja was so distraught that he desecrated the abode of the chief Bumthang deity, Shelging Kharpo, who then angrily took revenge by turning the skies black and stealing the king's life force, bringing him near to death.

One of the king's secretaries thus invited Guru Rinpoche to Bumthang to use his supernatural powers to save the Sindhu Raja. The Guru came to Bumthang and meditated, leaving a *jey* (imprint) of his *kur* (body) in the rock, now surrounded by Kurjey Lhakhang.

Guru Rinpoche was to be married to the king's daughter, Tashi Khuedon. He sent her to fetch water in a golden ewer. While she was away, the

12th century	1180	12th century	1184–1251
Gyalwa Lhanangpa, founder of the Lhapa Kagyu lineage, establishes Tango Goemba in the Thimphu valley and a system of forts based on Tibetan dzongs.	The founding of Druk Monastery in Ralung (Tibet) by Lama Tsangpa Gyarey Yeshe Dorji signals the beginning of Drukpa Kagyu lineage.	Many Drukpa lamas leave Tibet for Bhutan because of persecution at the hands of the rival Gelugpa. Most settle in western Bhutan and establish Drukpa monastic orders.	Lifespan of Lama Phajo Drukgom Shigpo, who cements the Drukpa Kagyu as the dominant school of Buddhism in Bhutan, giving the region its distinctive form of Buddhism.

Guru transformed into all eight of his manifestations and, together, they started to dance in the field by the temple. Every local deity appeared to watch this spectacle, except the stony-faced Shelging Kharpo who stayed hidden away in his rocky hideout.

Guru Rinpoche was not to be set back by this rejection, and when the princess returned he changed her into five separate princesses, each clutching a golden ewer. The sunlight flashing off these ewers finally attracted Shelging Kharpo, but before he ventured out to see what was going on, he first transformed himself into a white snow lion. On seeing the creature appear, the Guru changed into a *garuda,* flew up, grabbed the lion and told Shelging Kharpo in no uncertain terms to behave himself. He therefore recovered King Sendha Gyab's life force, and for good measure converted both the rival kings to Buddhism, and by doing so restored the country to peace.

Shelging Kharpo agreed to become a protective deity of Buddhism; to seal the agreement the Guru planted his staff in the ground at the temple – its cypress-tree descendants continue to grow and tower over the Kurjey Lhakhang.

Sampa Lhundrup Lhakhang, part of the Kurjey Lhakhang complex in Bumthang's Chokhor valley, houses an impressive 10m statue of Guru Rinpoche flanked by his eight manifestations.

Further Visits by Guru Rinpoche

The Guru returned to Bhutan via Singye Dzong in Lhuentse and visited the districts of Bumthang and Mongar as well as Lhuentse. He was returning from Tibet where, at the invitation of the Tibetan king Trisong Detsen, he had introduced Nyingma Buddhism and overcome the demons that were obstructing the construction of Tibet's first monastery at Samye.

At Gom Kora, in eastern Bhutan, he left a body print and an impression of his head with a hat. He flew in the form of Dorji Drakpo (one of his eight manifestations) to Taktshang in Paro on a flaming tigress, giving the famous Taktshang Goemba the name 'Tiger's Nest'.

It is believed that Guru Rinpoche also made a third visit to present-day Bhutan during the reign of Muthri Tsenpo (764–817), the son of Trisong Detsen and the 39th king of Tibet.

The Eight Manifestations of Guru Rinpoche

The Guru is depicted in eight forms (Guru Tshengay). These are not really different incarnations but representations of his eight main initiations, in which he assumed a new personality that was symbolised by a new name and appearance. Because initiation is equivalent to entering a new life, it is a form of rebirth. Therefore the eight forms follow the chronology of Guru Rinpoche's life.

He emerged as an eight-year-old from a blue lotus on Lake Danakosha in Uddiyana, and was adopted by King Indrabodhi. Then he was

1433	1450–1521	1455–1529	1616
Thangtong Gyalpo, the Iron Bridge Lama, visits Bhutan from Tibet in search of iron ore; he builds eight bridges.	The much-heralded life of Pema Lingpa, the most important *terton* (discoverer of sacred texts and artefacts) in Bhutan.	Lifespan of Lama Drukpa Kunley, the Divine Madman, who travelled throughout Bhutan preaching an unconventional approach to Buddhism and life.	The first Zhabdrung, Ngawang Namgyal, arrives in Bhutan from Ralung, Tibet, marking the ascendancy of the Druk Kagyu lineage.

called Tshokye Dorji (Diamond Thunderbolt Born from a Lake). He later renounced his kingdom and went to receive teachings and ordination from the master Prabhahasti in the cave of Maratrika (near the village of Harishe in eastern Nepal), becoming Sakya Senge (Lion of the Sakya Clan). In this form he is identified with Sakyamuni, the historical Buddha.

After studying the teachings of the Vajrayana and mastering the sciences of all the Indian *pandits* he became Loden Chogsey (Possessor of Supreme Knowledge). He took as his consort Mandarava, the daughter of the king of Zahor (in the Mandi district of Himachal Pradesh, India). This enraged the king, who condemned them both to be burned, but through his powers the Guru turned the pyre into a lake and converted the kingdom to Buddhism. Then he was called Padmasambhava.

He returned to Uddiyana to convert it to Buddhism, but was recognised as the prince who had renounced his kingdom and was condemned to be burned along with his consort. Again he was not consumed by the fire and appeared sitting upon a lotus in a lake. This lake is Rewalsar – also called Tsho Pema (Lotus Lake) – in Himachal Pradesh, and is an important pilgrimage spot. His father, King Indrabodhi, offered him the kingdom and he became Pema Gyalpo (Lotus King), remaining for 13 years and establishing Buddhism.

When he was preaching to the *khandromas* (female celestial beings) in the eight cremation grounds, he transformed the evil deities into protectors of Buddhism and became known as Nyima Yeozer (Sunbeam of Enlightenment). Later, 500 heretic masters tried to destroy the doctrine of Buddha, but he vanquished them through the power of his words and brought down a thunderbolt destroying the non-Buddhists in a flash of hail and lightning. He was then called Sengye Dradrok (Roaring Lion).

When he came to Bhutan the second time and visited Singye Dzong in Kurtoe and Taktshang in Paro, he was in the form of Dorji Drolo (Fierce Thunderbolt). He subdued all the evil spirits hindering Buddhism and blessed them as guardians of the doctrine. In this form, Guru Rinpoche rides a tigress.

Medieval Period

The grandson of Trisong Detsen, Langdharma, ruled Tibet from AD 836 to 842. As a follower of Bon, he banned Buddhism, destroyed religious institutions and banished his brother, Prince Tsangma, to Bhutan. It is believed that many monks fled from Tibet and took refuge in Bhutan during this period. Despite the assassination of Langdharma and the reintroduction of Buddhism, Tibet remained in political turmoil and many Tibetans migrated to western Bhutan.

1621	1627	1629	1637
The first monk body is established at Cheri Goemba, which was built by Zhabdrung Ngawang Namgyal a year earlier.	Portuguese Jesuits, Fathers Cacella and Cabral, become the first European visitors to Bhutan, meeting the Zhabdrung in Cheri Goemba.	A coalition of five Bhutanese lamas representing opposing lineages attacks Simtokha Dzong, the first dzong in the country, and challenges the Zhabdrung.	Punakha Dzong is constructed as the second dzong in the country. The town remains the capital of Bhutan until the mid-1950s.

Between the 9th and 17th centuries, numerous ruling clans and noble families emerged in different valleys throughout Bhutan. The various local chieftains spent their energy quarrelling among themselves and with Tibet, and no important nationally recognised political figure emerged during this period.

Establishing the Bhutanese Form of Buddhism

Back in Tibet, Lama Tsangpa Gyarey Yeshe Dorji (1161–1211) founded a monastery in the town of Ralung, just east of Gyantse, in 1180. He named the monastery Druk (Dragon), after the nine thunder dragons that he heard in the sky as he searched for an appropriate site upon which to build a monastery. The lineage followed here was named after the monastery and became known as Drukpa Kagyu.

In the 11th and 12th centuries there was a further large influx of Tibetans into Bhutan. Many Drukpa lamas left Tibet because of persecution at the hands of the followers of rival Buddhist lineages. Most of these lamas settled in western Bhutan and established branches of Drukpa monastic orders. Western Bhutan became loosely united through the weight of their teachings. Charismatic lamas emerged as de facto leaders of large portions of the west, while the isolated valleys of eastern and central Bhutan remained separate feudal states.

One of the most important of these lamas was Gyalwa Lhanangpa, who founded the Lhapa Kagyu lineage. He established the Tango Goemba on a hill above the northern end of the Thimphu valley and built a system of forts in Bhutan similar to the dzongs found in Tibet.

Lama Phajo Drukgom Shigpo (1184–1251), a disciple of Lama Tsangpa Gyarey, came to Bhutan from Ralung in 1222 and defeated Lama Lhanangpa. He and his companions developed the small Dho-Ngen Dzong on the west bank of the Wang Chhu and took control of Tango Goemba. Lama Phajo is credited with forging the Bhutanese form of Buddhism by converting many people to the Drukpa Kagyu lineage. Other lamas resented his presence and success, and they tried to kill him through the casting of magic spells. Phajo, though, turned the spells back on these lamas, destroying several of their monasteries. Many of Bhutan's old nobility trace their family heritage back to Phajo Drukgom Shigpo.

Between the 13th and 16th centuries, the Drukpa Kagyu lineage flourished and Bhutan adopted its own religious identity. Several important Druk Kagyu teachers from Ralung were invited to preach and set up monasteries in western Bhutan. Among the visitors to Bhutan during this period was Lama Ngawang Chhogyel (1465–1540). He made several trips and was often accompanied by his sons, who constructed several

The three main lineages spreading Buddhist teachings in Bhutan were the Nyingmapa, the Kagyupa and the Sakyapa. A fourth school, the Gelugpa, emerged in Tibet in the 15th century. This lineage was viewed by the Bhutanese from the 17th century onwards as hostile to Bhutan.

HISTORY MEDIEVAL PERIOD

1639	1644	1668	1705
Tibet finally recognises Zhabdrung Ngawang Namgyal as the supreme authority in Bhutan.	Zhabdrung orders the construction of Paro Dzong.	Mingyur Tenpa is enthroned as the third *desi* (secular ruler). He rules for 12 years, during which time he extends the boundaries of Bhutan westwards to Kalimpong, now part of India.	The much-delayed announcement is made of the demise of the Zhabdrung Ngawang Namgyal.

monasteries. They are credited with building the temple of Druk Choeding in Paro and Pangri Zampa and Hongtsho goemba near Thimphu.

Perhaps the most famous Druk Kagyu teacher was the colourful and unconventional Drukpa Kunley (1455–1529). He is remembered today with immense affection and faith by the Bhutanese and is closely associated with the beautiful temple of Chimi Lhakhang between Lobesa and Punakha.

The Divine Madman by Keith Dowman is a wonderful translation of the poems and works of the extraordinary Lama Drukpa Kunley.

Hidden Treasures & Pema Lingpa

Between the 11th and 16th centuries, numerous *terma* (sacred texts) hidden by Guru Rinpoche in caves, rocks and lakes were discovered, as he had prophesied, by tantric lamas called *tertons* (treasure finders).

Pema Lingpa (1450–1521) was one of the five great *tertons* of Nyingma Buddhism, and the most important *terton* in Bhutan. The texts and artefacts he found, the dances he composed and the art he produced have significantly shaped Bhutan's cultural heritage. He is also considered to be a reincarnation of Guru Rinpoche.

He was born in the hamlet of Drangchel in Bumthang's Tang valley, near Kunzangdrak Goemba. As a boy he learned the craft of blacksmithing from his grandfather; indeed, two of the chain mails he forged are still on display at Tamshing and Thangbi goembas.

At age 25, he discovered his first *terma* after he dreamed a monk handed him a scroll in *dakini* script that gave instructions on how to find a treasure chest deep in a pool in the Tang valley. Pema eventually managed to translate the scroll but this was a huge project, because in *dakini* script each word stands for 1000 human words. Later, assisted by the *khandromas (dakinis)*, he used the text as a basis for teachings. His residence at the time was in Kunzangling, which is on a cliff above the Tang valley and is now the site of the Kunzangdrak Goemba.

During Pema Lingpa's life he found a total of 34 statues, scrolls and sacred relics in Bhutan and as far away as Samye in Tibet. Many of the statues and relics he discovered are preserved in lhakhangs (inner temples) throughout Bhutan, including Bumthang's Tamshing and Kunzangdrak goembas, which he founded.

After his death he was reincarnated in three forms, consisting of *ku* (body), *sung* (speech) and *thug* (mind). These lineages continue to this day.

Through his six sons, one daughter and numerous reincarnations, Pema Lingpa's legacy still influences much of Bhutan. One of his grandsons, Gyalse Pema Thinley, who was also a reincarnation of Pema Lingpa, founded Gangte Goemba in the Phobjikha valley. The Gangte Trulku lineage continues there, with Kuenzang Pema Namgyal, born in 1955, as the

1730	1768	1772	1774
Druk Desi Mipham Wangpo assists Gya Chila, the ruler of Cooch Behar, to defeat invaders and to settle a family feud; Bhutan is then allowed to station a force in that southern kingdom.	The *desi* tries to suppress the influence of the religious establishment in Bhutan. To do so he establishes alliances with the Panchen Lama in Tibet and with King Prithvi Narayan Shah of Nepal.	Bhutan invades Cooch Behar and kidnaps its king. The British East India Company agrees to assist Cooch Behar in return for payment.	George Bogle leads a trade mission to Bhutan and Tibet, and plants potatoes in Bhutanese soil.

ninth 'mind' reincarnation. The royal family of Bhutan, the Wangchuck dynasty, is also descended from this line.

The Rise of the Zhabdrung

By the 16th century the political arena was still fragmented between many local chiefs, each controlling their own territory and engaging in petty feuds with the others. There were numerous monasteries competing for superiority, and the lamas of western Bhutan were working to extend their influence to the east of the country.

Everything changed in 1616 when Ngawang Namgyal (1594–1651) came to Bhutan from Ralung, the spiritual home of the Drukpa Kagyu in Tibet. He was a descendent of Tsangpa Gyarey, the founder of Ralung Monastery. At age 12, he was recognised as the reincarnation of Pema Karpo, the prince-abbot of Ralung. This recognition was challenged by the ruler of another principality in Tibet, and Ngawang Namgyal found his position at Ralung very difficult. When he was 23, the protective deity Yeshe Goenpo (Mahakala) appeared to him in the form of a raven and directed him south to Bhutan. He travelled through Laya and Gasa and spent time at Pangri Zampa, Thimphu, which was established by his great-great-grandfather, Ngawang Chhogyel.

As Ngawang Namgyal travelled throughout western Bhutan teaching, his political strength increased. Soon he established himself as the religious ruler of Bhutan with the title Zhabdrung Rinpoche (Precious Jewel at Whose Feet One Prostrates), thereby becoming the first in the line of Zhabdrungs. He built the first of the current system of dzongs at Simtokha, just south of present-day Thimphu. While the primary function of earlier Bhutanese dzongs was to serve as fortresses, the Simtokha Dzong also housed a monastic body and administrative facilities, as well as fulfilling its defensive function. This combination of civil, religious and defensive functions became the model for all of Bhutan's subsequent dzongs.

The Zhabdrung's rule was opposed by the leaders of rival Buddhist lineages within Bhutan. They formed a coalition of five lamas under the leadership of Lama Palden and attacked Simtokha Dzong in 1629. This attack was repelled, but the coalition then aligned itself with a group of Tibetans and continued its opposition. The Zhabdrung's militia thwarted the Tibetans in battle on several occasions, and the influence of the rival lineages diminished. Finally, after forging an alliance with the brother of King Singye Namgyal of Ladakh, the Zhabdrung's forces defeated the Tibetans and their coalition ally. In 1639 an agreement was reached with the king of Tsang in Tibet, recognising Zhabdrung Ngawang Namgyal as the supreme authority throughout Bhutan.

In his visions, Pema Lingpa often visited Zangto Pelri, Guru Rinpoche's celestial paradise, where he observed the dances (pacham) of the khandromas and yidam (tutelary deities). He taught three of these dances to his disciples, and several are still performed as part of Bhutan's tsechus (dance festivals).

HISTORY THE RISE OF THE ZHABDRUNG

1776 & 1777	1783	1826	1828
Dr Alexander Hamilton travels to Punakha and Thimphu to negotiate land disputes between Britain and Bhutan.	Captain Samuel Turner leads a grand British Raj expedition to Bhutan and Tibet.	Bhutan and Britain start bickering over the sovereignty of the duars (the southern Bhutanese hills).	Many original historical documents are destroyed in fires in the printing works of Sonagatsel.

The Zhabdrung further enhanced his power by establishing relations with neighbouring kings, including Rama Shah, the king of Nepal, and Raja Padmanarayan of Cooch Behar (India) to the south of Bhutan. It was at this time that the king of Ladakh granted the Zhabdrung a number of sites in western Tibet for the purpose of meditation and worship. These included Diraphuk, Nyanri and Zuthulphuk on the slopes of the holy Mt Kailash.

The Bhutanese administration of these monasteries continued until the Chinese takeover of Tibet in 1959. Other Tibetan monasteries that came under Bhutanese administration were Rimpung, Doba, Khochag and De Dzong, all near Gartok in western Tibet. A Bhutanese lama was sent as representative to Nepal, and Bhutanese monasteries were established at Bodhnath (Chorten Jaro Khasho) and Swayambhunath in Kathmandu. Bhutan administered Swayambhunath until after the Nepal-Tibet war of 1854–56, when it was retaken by Nepal on the suspicion that Bhutan had helped the Tibetans.

The Zhabdrung established the first *sangha* (community of monks) at Cheri Goemba near Thimphu. When Punakha Dzong was completed in 1635, the *sangha* was moved there and became the *dratshang* (central monk body), headed by a supreme abbot called the Je Khenpo.

> The arrival in 1616 of the Zhabdrung Ngawang Namgyal marks the transformation of Bhutan and the ascendancy of the Druk Kagyu lineage.

Invasions from Tibet

In the meantime, strife continued in Tibet, between the Nyingmapa (known as 'Red Hat') group of Buddhists and the Gelugpa ('Yellow Hat'); the latter are headed by the Dalai Lama. The Mongol chief Gushri Khan, a patron of the Dalai Lama, led his army in an attack on Tibet's Tsang province, where he overthrew the Rinpong dynasty and established the supremacy of the Gelug lineage in the region.

In 1644 the Mongols and Tibetans, who were used to the extremely high plains of Tibet, launched an assault from Lhodrak in southern Tibet into Bumthang, but found themselves overpowered by the forests and heat of Bhutan. Zhabdrung Ngawang Namgyal personally led the successful resistance and several Tibetan officers and a large number of horses were captured. Drukgyel Dzong was built at the head of Paro valley in 1647 to commemorate the victory and to prevent any further Tibetan infiltration.

One of the strongest of Tibet's Dalai Lamas was the 'Great Fifth'. During his administration, he became jealous of the growing influence of the rival Drukpa on his southern border and mounted further invasions into Bhutan in 1648 and 1649. Each attempt was launched via Phari in Tibet, from where the Great Fifth's forces crossed the 5000m-high Tremo La into Paro valley. They were repelled, and again the Bhutanese captured

> During his reign, Zhabdrung Ngawang Namgyal ordered the construction of many monasteries and dzongs throughout Bhutan. Of these, the dzongs at Simtokha, Paro, Punakha and Trongsa are still standing.

1832	1862	1864	1865
Further losses of historical documents occur in the devastating fire in the library of Punakha Dzong.	Ugyen Wangchuck – son of 'the Black Regent' Jigme Namgyal, the battle-hardened Trongsa *penlop* – is born.	The ill-fated Ashley Eden expedition gets a humiliating reception in Punakha and sours relations between Bhutan and Britain.	Bhutan and Britain go to war over the *duars;* the conflict is finally resolved with the Treaty of Sinchula, which sees Bhutan's territory greatly reduced.

large amounts of armour, weapons and other spoils. Some of this booty may still be seen in the National Museum in Paro.

Ngawang Namgyal's success in repelling the Tibetan attacks further consolidated his position as ruler. The large militia that he raised for the purpose also gave him effective control of the country. Mingyur Tenpa, who was appointed by the Zhabdrung as *penlop* (governor) of Trongsa, undertook a campaign to unite all the valleys of the central and eastern parts of the country under the Zhabdrung's rule, which he accomplished by about 1655. At this time the great dzongs of Jakar, Lhuentse, Trashi Yangtse, Shongar – now Mongar – Trashigang and Zhemgang were constructed.

A Bhutanese Identity Emerges

The Zhabdrung realised that Bhutan needed to differentiate itself from Tibet in order to preserve its religion and cultural identity. He devised many of Bhutan's customs, traditions and ceremonies in a deliberate effort to develop a unique cultural identity for the country.

As a revered Buddhist scholar, he had both the astuteness and authority to codify the Kagyu religious teachings into a system that was distinctively Bhutanese. He also defined the national dress and instituted the tsechu (series of dances) celebrations.

The Zhabdrung created a code of laws that defined the relationship between the lay people and the monastic community. A system of taxes was developed; these were paid in kind in the form of wheat, buckwheat, rice, yak meat, butter, paper, timber and clothing. The people were subject to a system of compulsory labour for the construction of trails, dzongs, temples and bridges. These practices lasted almost unchanged until the third king eliminated them in 1956.

In the 1640s, the Zhabdrung created the system of Choesi: the separation of the administration of the country into two offices. The religious and spiritual aspects of the country were handled by the Zhabdrung. The political, administrative and foreign-affairs aspects of the government were to be handled by the *desi* (secular ruler), who was elected to the post. The office of the Zhabdrung theoretically had the greater power. Under the system at that time, the Zhabdrung was the spiritual ruler and the Je Khenpo was the Chief Abbot and official head of the monastic establishment. The Je Khenpo had a status equal to the *desi* and sometimes held that office.

The first *desi* was Tenzin Drugyey (1591–1656), one of the monks who came with Ngawang Namgyal from Ralung Monastery. He established a system of administration throughout the country, formalising the position of *penlop* as that of provincial governor. There were initially three districts: Trongsa in the centre, Paro in the west and Dagana in

Much of the armour and many weapons that were taken during the 1644 battle with the Mongols and Tibetans is on display in Punakha Dzong.

1865	1870	1878	1885
After the *duar* war, the saying goes that Bhutan's border is where a rock rolled down the hill finally stops.	The Penlop of Trongsa, Jigme Namgyal, is enthroned as the 51st *desi*, consolidating his growing power and influence.	At just 16 years of age, Ugyen Wangchuck, the son of Jigme Namgyal, is briefly taken hostage in Paro's Ta Dzong while accompanying his father's campaign to recapture Paro Dzong.	After decades of civil unrest and the Battle of Changlimithang, Ugyen Wangchuck emerges as the most powerful figure in the country.

the south. The *penlops* became the representatives of the central government, which was then in Punakha. There were three officers called *dzongpens* (lords of the dzong) who looked after the affairs of the subdistricts of Punakha, Thimphu and Wangdue Phodrang.

Zhabdrung Ngawang Namgyal went into retreat in Punakha Dzong in 1651. He didn't emerge again, and although it is likely that he passed away very early in the period of retreat, his death remained concealed until 1705. It is believed that the four successive *desis* who ruled during this period felt that the continued presence of the Zhabdrung was necessary to keep the country unified and Tibet at bay. Nonetheless, Tibet mounted seven attacks on Bhutan between 1656 and 1730.

Civil Wars

When the Je Khenpo finally announced the death of the Zhabdrung in 1705, he said that three rays of light emanated from the Zhabdrung's body, representing the *ku sung thug* (body, speech and mind) of Ngawang Namgyal. This indicated that the Zhabdrung would be reincarnated in these three forms, though only the reincarnation of the Zhabdrung's mind was considered to be the head of state. Because the position of *zhabdrung* was a continuing one, it was necessary for the mind incarnation to be reborn after the death of the previous incarnation.

This structure resulted in long periods when the *zhabdrung* was too young to rule and the *desi* often became the de facto ruler. Because the *desi* was an elected position, there was considerable rivalry among various factions for the office. These factions also took advantage of uncertainty over which of the three incarnations of the Zhabdrung was the 'true' incarnation. None of the successive incarnations had the personal charisma or political astuteness of Ngawang Namgyal.

The next 200 years were a time of civil war, internal conflicts and political infighting. While there were only six mind incarnations of the Zhabdrung during this period, there were 55 *desis*. The longest-serving *desi* was the 13th incumbent, Sherab Wangchuk, who ruled for 20 years; and the most important was the fourth, Gyalse Tenzin Rabgye, who ruled from 1680 to 1694. Few of the rulers finished their term; 22 *desis* were assassinated or deposed by rivals.

The political situation became so unstable that some of the rival factions appealed to the Tibetans for assistance. In 1729 and 1730 Tibet took advantage of Bhutan's instability and invaded the country three times. The lamas in Tibet initiated a truce that eventually ended the hostilities. The rival Bhutanese factions submitted their case to the Chinese emperor in Beijing for mediation. The issue was only finally resolved when several of the Bhutanese protagonists died, leaving the currently recognised mind incarnation of the Zhabdrung as the ruler. At the same

A Political and Religious History of Bhutan by CT Dorji chronicles the major personalities in the religious and political spheres of Bhutan's history.

1897	1904	1906	1907
On 12 June the great Assam earthquake destroys the dzongs and many original documents in Punakha and Lingzhi, and severely damages many other buildings.	Ugyen Wangchuck assists Francis Younghusband in his invasion of Tibet and assists with the negotiations for a treaty between Britain and Tibet.	Sir Ugyen Wangchuck is invited to Calcutta to attend the reception for the Prince of Wales.	Ugyen Wangchuck is unanimously elected as the hereditary ruler of Bhutan, the Druk Gyalpo, in Punakha.

time, formal diplomatic relations were established between Bhutan and Tibet, which helped solidify Bhutanese independence.

Involvement of the British

In his book, *Lands of the Thunderbolt,* the Earl of Ronaldshay wrote, 'it was not until 1772 that the East India Company became conscious of the existence, across its northern frontier, of a meddlesome neighbour'. The first contact the British had with Bhutan was when the claimants to the throne of neighbouring Cooch Behar (in present-day West Bengal) appealed to the East India Company to help drive the Bhutanese out of their kingdom.

Because the East India Company was a strictly commercial enterprise, its officers agreed to help when the deposed ruler of Cooch Behar offered to pay half of the revenues of the state in return for assistance. In December 1772, the British governor of Bengal, Warren Hastings, sent Indian troops and guns to Cooch Behar and, despite suffering heavy losses, routed the Bhutanese and restored the king to the throne. However, Cooch Behar paid a very high price for this assistance. Not only did its rulers pay Rs50,000, but in 1773 they also signed a treaty ceding substantial powers and future revenue to the East India Company.

The British pushed the Bhutanese back into the hills and followed them into Bhutan. The British won another major battle in January 1773 at the garrison of Chichacotta (now Khithokha) in the hills east of what is now Phuentsholing. A second battle was fought near Kalimpong in April 1773. The Bhutanese troops were led by the 16th *desi* but, after the second defeat, he was deposed by a coup d'état.

First Treaty with the British

The new *desi* wanted to make an agreement with the British and appealed to the Panchen Lama in Tibet for assistance. The Panchen Lama then wrote what the British described as 'a very friendly and intelligent letter' that was carried to Calcutta (now called Kolkata) by an Indian pilgrim. The British, although more eager to establish relations with Tibet than to solve the issue of Bhutan, agreed to comply with the Tibetan request. The result was a peace treaty between Bhutan and the British signed in Calcutta on 25 April 1774. In this treaty the *desi* agreed to respect the territory of the East India Company and to allow the company to cut timber in the forests of Bhutan. The British returned all the territory they had captured.

The British in India attached their own names, derived from Sanskrit, to the titles used by the Bhutanese. They called the Zhabdrung the '*dharma raja*', and the *desi* '*deb raja*'.

> Although spoken as a native language from Haa to Wangdue Phodrang, Dzongkha only became a written language in the 1960s, using the Tibetan alphabet and its Uchen script for formal writing.

> **HISTORY** INVOLVEMENT OF THE BRITISH

> *Bhutan and the British* by Peter Collister is a comprehensive account of the interaction between Britain and Bhutan from 1771 to 1987.

1907	1910	1926	1927
Numerous collections of historical documents and treasures are lost when Paro valley's Rinpung Dzong is engulfed in a devastating fire.	The Treaty of Punakha is signed, guaranteeing Bhutan's sovereignty and giving Britain a hand in its external relations.	His Majesty Ugyen Wangchuck dies and is succeeded by his son Jigme Wangchuck, the second Druk Gyalpo.	British officer Lt Col FM Bailey attends the official coronation of the second king of Bhutan, Jigme Wangchuck.

Exploration by Western Travellers

Some of the most interesting stories of Bhutan, and much of Bhutan's recorded history, came from the descriptions provided by early European explorers. These records provide an insight into what they observed and also reveal the extraordinary attitudes of some of the envoys Britain sent to negotiate with Bhutan.

Several records of the early European exploration and missions to Bhutan have been reprinted by Indian publishers and are readily available in bookshops in Thimphu, Delhi and Kathmandu, or on Google Books.

George Bogle

The first British expedition arrived in Bhutan in 1774, just after the first British treaties with Bhutan and Tibet were signed. The Court of Directors of the East India Company sent a mission to Tibet via Bhutan to find out about goods, 'especially such as are of great value and easy transportation'. The expedition team, led by George Bogle, planted potatoes wherever they went, providing a new food crop for Bhutan and a lasting legacy of this mission. They spent five months in Thimphu and then travelled on to Tibet. The written account of this mission provides the first Western view into the isolated kingdom of 'Boutan'. Bogle found the Bhutanese 'good-humoured, downright, and so far as I can judge, thoroughly trustworthy'. He did, however, note that the practice of celibacy by many monks led to 'many irregularities' and the cold resulted in 'an excessive use of spirituous liquors'.

Alexander Hamilton & Samuel Turner

In the next few years two small expeditions travelled to Bhutan. Dr Alexander Hamilton led a group to Punakha and Thimphu in 1776, and another in 1777, to discuss Bhutanese claims to Ambari Falakati (a town northwest of Cooch Behar) and to consolidate transit rights through Bhutan to Tibet that had been negotiated by Bogle's mission.

Lands of the Thunderbolt, Sikhim, Chumbi & Bhutan by the Earl of Ronaldshay is a very readable, very British account of regional history and an expedition to Bhutan in the early 20th century.

The next major venture into Bhutan was in 1783, when Samuel Turner led a grand expedition with all the accoutrements of the British Raj. They travelled through the *duars* (southern Bhutanese hills) in palanquins (sedan chairs) and followed Bogle's route to Thimphu. They also visited Punakha and Wangdue Phodrang before crossing to Tibet. Among the members of the 1783 expedition was Samuel Davis, who was a draftsman and surveyor. His journal and outstanding paintings provide one of the earliest views of Bhutan. Much of Davis' material is presented in *Views of Mediaeval Bhutan* by Michael Aris.

The Humiliation of Ashley Eden

Minor British expeditions to Bhutan were made in 1810, 1812, 1815 and 1837, for the most part in order to settle border disputes and conflict over the *duars*. The Ashley Eden expedition attempted to settle these issues.

1928	1931	1949	1952
The future third king, Jigme Dorji Wangchuck, is born at Thruepang Palace in Trongsa on 2 May.	Lt Col JLR Weir travels to Bumthang to present King Jigme Wangchuck with the insignia of Knight Commander of the Indian Empire.	Bhutan signs a treaty with newly independent India in Darjeeling and gains a small concession of land bordering the region known as the *duars*.	King Jigme Wangchuck, the second king, dies and is succeeded to the throne by his 24-year-old son Jigme Dorje Wangchuck.

The British had managed to extend their influence into Sikkim, making it a British protectorate, and subsequently decided to send a mission to Bhutan to establish a resident British representative and encourage better communication. Among the members of Eden's expedition was Captain HH Godwin-Austin of the Indian topographical Survey. Godwin-Austin had explored (present-day) Pakistan's Baltoro Glacier in 1861, and on some maps K2, the second-highest peak in the world, is named after him.

Despite reports of political chaos in Bhutan, Ashley Eden, the secretary of the government of Bengal, set out from Darjeeling in November 1864 to meet the *desi* (or *'deb raja'*). Ignoring numerous messages from the Bhutanese that the British mission was not welcome, Eden pushed on past Kalimpong, through Daling, Haa and Paro, reaching Punakha on 15 March.

It's not clear whether it was more by accident or by design, but Eden's party was jeered, pelted with rocks, made to wait long hours in the sun and subjected to other humiliations. Both Bhutanese and British pride suffered badly. As Eden describes it in *Political Missions to Bootan:* 'The Penlow *[penlop]* took up a large piece of wet dough and began rubbing my face with it; he pulled my hair, and slapped me on the back, and generally conducted himself with great insolence.'

Eden exacerbated the situation by sending the Lhengyal Shungtshog a copy of a draft treaty with terms that he had been instructed to negotiate. His actions implied that this was the final version of the treaty that the Bhutanese were to sign without any discussion. The Bhutanese took immediate exception to Eden's high-handedness and soon presented him with an alternative treaty that returned all the *duars* to Bhutan. One clause in the treaty stated: 'We have written about that the settlement is permanent; but who knows, perhaps this settlement is made with one word in the mouth and two in the heart. If, therefore, this settlement is false, the Dharma Raja's demons will, after deciding who is true or false, take his life, and take out his liver and scatter it to the winds like ashes.'

Reading this, it's little wonder that Eden feared for the safety of his party. He signed the treaty, but under his signature added the English words 'under compulsion', which, naturally, the Bhutanese could not read.

Eden's party crossed the Cheli La from Haa into the Paro valley in February and had an extremely difficult time in the deep snow. Some years later, John Claude White suggested that Eden might have been given incorrect directions, perhaps on purpose. It is astounding that, even having admitted failure, Eden still viewed his as a 'friendly mission'. His report certainly was a major factor in British annexation of the *duars*. He advocated a punitive policy to teach the Bhutanese that they would not

Political Missions to Bootan by Ashley Eden is a pompous Victorian account of the history of Bhutan. After reading a few pages, you'll have some idea as to why Eden was treated so badly when he arrived in Punakha.

1953	1956	1958	1959
The 130-member National Assembly (Tshogdu), the country's first legislature, is established by the king to promote democratic governance.	The age-old system of serfdom is abolished by King Jigme Dorji Wangchuck, who also decrees that all derogatory terms associated with serfs be abolished.	The Indian Prime Minister, Jawaharlal Nehru, and his daughter, Indira Gandhi, visit Bhutan to symbolise improving communications with India.	Bhutan loses administrative control of several monasteries on the slopes of Mt Kailash and near Gatok after the Chinese annexation of Tibet.

be allowed to 'treat our power with contempt'. He later went on to build the toy train in Darjeeling.

John Claude White

Sikhim and Bhutan, Twenty-one Years on the North-east Frontier by J Claude White describes the 1905 expedition to present the first king, Ugyen Wangchuck, with the insignia of Knight Commander of the Indian Empire.

There were no formal expeditions to Bhutan for more than 40 years after Eden's, but the Survey of India sent several agents disguised as lamas and pilgrims to explore Bhutan and Tibet in 1883 and 1886.

By 1905 the Bhutanese and British were friends due to the assistance that the *penlop* of Trongsa, Ugyen Wangchuck, had provided the 1904 Younghusband expedition to Lhasa. John Claude White, a British political officer, came to present the insignia of Knight Commander of the Indian Empire to the *penlop*. White had been a member of the 1904 expedition and was an old friend of Ugyen Wangchuck.

White and his large party travelled from Gangtok, in Sikkim, into Haa and Paro, en route to the investiture ceremony in Punakha. Later, White and his party were guests of Ugyen Wangchuck at his new palace of Wangdichholing in Bumthang. The expedition later returned with the first photographs of dzongs and the court of Bhutan.

In 1906 White made a reconnaissance through eastern Bhutan to southern Tibet. He made a third trip in 1907 when he was invited as the British representative to the coronation of Ugyen Wangchuck as the first king of Bhutan. A summary of White's account appeared in the April 1914 issue of the *National Geographic,* and made Bhutan known to the world for the first time.

Other British Political Officers

Between 1909 and 1947 the British government dealt with Bhutan in the same way as it did with other Indian princely states, but it never specifically defined its relationship with Bhutan. Starting with CA Bell in 1909, several British political officers visited Bhutan and presented the king with decorations. In 1921 the Earl of Ronaldshay, who was described as a 'closet Buddhist', travelled to Bhutan as a guest of the first king. He travelled from Gangtok to Paro, where he was met with great fanfare. The party visited Taktshang Goemba and witnessed the Paro tsechu, but never met the king, who was in Punakha, ill with influenza.

The Duar Wars & the Rise of Ugyen Wangchuck

The area of plains between the Brahmaputra River up to and including the lowest of the hills of Bhutan was known as the *duars* (literally, 'doors' or 'gates'). The western part of this area, known as the Bengal Duars, had been annexed by the third *desi*, Mingyur Tenpa, in the late 17th century and the Bhutanese considered it their territory. The eastern part, the

1961	1961	1962	1964
Bhutan warily emerges from self-imposed isolation and begins a process of controlled development, undertaking modernisation.	The capital moves from Punakha to Thimphu (some sources say 1955 or 1966).	The ninth Zhabdrung flees Bhutan aged six, spending the rest of his life in Manali and then Kalimpong in India.	Prime Minister Jigme Palden Dorji, a leading proponent of change, is assassinated on 5 April in Phuentsholing.

Assam Duars, had long been administered in a complex rental agreement between Bhutan and Assam.

After the Burmese war (1825–26), the British took over the peculiar land rental arrangement for the Assam Duars, along with what were described as 'very unsatisfactory relations of the Assamese with the Bhutanese'. Disagreements over payments and administration between Britain and Bhutan escalated into military skirmishes. Other than the area's strategic importance, the British were attracted to the *duars* because they were excellent tea-growing country.

The British annexed the two easternmost *duars* in 1840 and the rest of the Assam Duars in September 1841, agreeing to pay Bhutan an annual compensation of Rs10,000. Lord Auckland wrote to the *deb* and *dharma rajas* that the British were 'compelled by an imperative sense of duty to occupy the whole of the duars without any reference to your Highnesses' wishes, as I feel assured that it is the only course which is likely to hold out a prospect of restoring peace and prosperity to that tract of country'.

Perhaps more revealing is a letter from Colonel Jenkins, the agent of the governor-general, outlining the need for taking over the Assam Duars. He wrote: 'Had we possession of the Dooars, the Bhootan Government would necessarily in a short time become entirely dependent upon us, as holding in our hands the source of all their subsistence.'

The Trongsa Penlop Gains Control

During this period the Trongsa *penlop,* Jigme Namgyal (1825–82), established effective control of the country through a series of shrewd alliances. This was the first time peace had prevailed since the time of the first Zhabdrung. Jigme Namgyal was working to strengthen his power and that of the central government when he had an inconvenient visit from the British government representative Ashley Eden.

Although the British considered Eden's mission a failure, and reprimanded him for his conduct, they continued the dispute with Bhutan over payment for the Bengal Duars. The Bhutanese, in turn, were furious the British had renounced the treaty Eden had signed. In November 1864 the British summarily annexed the Bengal Duars, gaining effective control of the entire south of Bhutan. The Trongsa *penlop* mounted a carefully planned counterattack. His troops, protected by shields of rhinoceros hide, captured two British guns and drove the British forces out of Bhutan in January 1865.

The British regrouped and recaptured various towns, including Samtse (then called Chamurchi). A fierce battle at Dewangiri on 2 April essentially ended the war, with the British destroying all the buildings and slaughtering their captives. Negotiations continued through the summer. Eventually the Bhutanese returned the captured guns and

Although the *duars* were excellent for growing tea, they were also a malarial jungle, and the British had a very difficult time keeping their troops healthy.

1968	1971	1972	1974
King Jigme Dorji Wangchuck continues to reform the government by surrendering his veto power on the decisions of the National Assembly.	Bhutan finally joins the UN as a full member after spending three years holding observer status.	King Jigme Dorji Wangchuck is succeeded to the throne by his son, 16-year-old Jigme Singye Wangchuck.	The official coronation of King Jigme Singye Wangchuck, the fourth Druk Gyalpo.

NEPALI REFUGEES

In the late 19th and early 20th centuries immigrants from Nepal began settling along the southern border of Bhutan, partly in an attempt to break free from the rigid caste system of their homelands. They are called Lhotshampa (literally, 'the people of the southern border'), are a mixture of mostly Hindu Rai, Limbu, Tamang, Bahun and Chhetri ethnic groups, and form approximately 25% of Bhutan's population.

Major tensions between the Drukpa and the Lhotshampa emerged in the late 1980s, as the government began to focus on preserving what it saw as Bhutan's threatened national identity. Mindful of Bhutan's porous border and attractiveness because of its fertile land, low population and free health and education facilities, the government conducted a nationwide census to identify what it saw as illegal immigrants.

Thousands of ethnic Nepalis lacked proper documentation and a sense of fear and insecurity led to an exodus of Nepali speakers from Bhutan. How much of the migration was voluntary remains a matter of tense debate, but between 1988 and 1993 tens of thousands of Nepali speakers left Bhutan for camps in southeastern Nepal. By 2019 there were only about 6500 people left in two United Nations High Commissioner for Refugees (UNHCR) protected camps. Over 113,000 of the refugees have been resettled in the West, with 92,000 settling in the USA alone.

accepted a treaty. The treaty of Sinchula was signed, under duress, by the Bhutanese on 11 November 1865. In it the Bhutanese ceded the *duars* to Britain forever and agreed to allow free trade between the two countries.

Through this treaty, Bhutan lost a major tract of valuable farmland and a large portion of its wealth. Its borders became the foot of the hills bordering the plain of India. It is often said that Bhutan's border is where a rock rolled down the hill finally stops. Among the important landmarks the Bhutanese lost were the town of Ambari Falakati, northwest of Cooch Behar, the town of Dewangiri (now called Deothang) in the east and the territory on the east bank of the Teesta River, including what is now the town of Kalimpong.

Back in Bhutan's heartland there were continuing civil wars, but Jigme Namgyal retained his power and in 1870 was enthroned as the 51st *desi*. The next 10 years were again a time of intrigue, treachery, power broking and continual strife. The *penlop* of Paro and the *dzongpens* of Punakha and Wangdue Phodrang conspired to challenge the position of Desi Jigme Namgyal and his successor, who was his half-brother. After he retired as *desi*, Jigme Namgyal remained in firm control of the country and in 1879 appointed his 17-year-old son, Ugyen Wangchuck, as Paro *penlop*.

After Jigme Namgyal died, his son consolidated his own position following a feud over the post of *penlop* of Trongsa. At the age of 20,

1974	1980s	1988	1991
The first 'tourist group' explores the country's sights, paving the way for international visitors.	Government policies aimed at preserving national identity begin to polarise the Nepali-speaking southerners.	The government conducts a nationwide census aimed at identifying illegal immigrants, defined as those who cannot prove family residence before 1958.	An eventual mass movement begins of Nepali speakers from Bhutan to refugee camps just over the border in Nepal.

Ugyen Wangchuck marched on Bumthang and Trongsa and in 1882 was appointed *penlop* of Trongsa, while still retaining the post of *penlop* of Paro. Because his father had enhanced the powers of the office of the Trongsa *penlop,* this gave him much more influence than the *desi.* When a battle broke out between the *dzongpens* of Punakha and Thimphu, Ugyen Wangchuck tried to mediate the dispute.

He sent in his troops after unsuccessful negotiations and his forces defeated the troops loyal to both *dzongpens* and seized control of Simtokha Dzong. The monk body and the *penlop* of Paro tried to settle the conflict and in 1885 arranged a meeting at the Changlimithang parade ground in Thimphu. During the meeting a fight broke out, the representative of the Thimphu *dzongpen* was killed and the *dzongpen* fled to Tibet. Following the battle, Ugyen Wangchuck emerged as the most powerful person in the country, assumed full authority, installed his own nominee as *desi,* and reduced the post to a ceremonial one.

Trongsa was important to the early kings. The father of the first king rose to power here, the first two kings ruled from here in winter and the third king was born in the town's Thruepang Palace.

The First Dragon King

In order to re-establish Bhutan's sovereignty and help consolidate his position, Ugyen Wangchuck developed closer relations with the British. He accompanied Francis Younghusband during his invasion of Tibet in 1904 and assisted with the negotiations that resulted in a treaty between Tibet and Britain. The British rewarded the *penlop* by granting him the title of Knight Commander of the Indian Empire. In 1906 the then Sir Ugyen Wangchuck was invited to Calcutta to attend the reception for the Prince of Wales and returned to Bhutan with a better appreciation of the world that lay beyond his country's borders.

In 1907 the *desi* died and Ugyen Wangchuck was elected as the hereditary ruler of Bhutan by a unanimous vote of Bhutan's chiefs and principal lamas. He was crowned on 17 December 1907 and installed as head of state with the title Druk Gyalpo (Dragon King). This coronation signalled the end of the *desi* system and the beginning of a hereditary monarchy – among the youngest in existence today. King Ugyen Wangchuck

HISTORY THE FIRST DRAGON KING

THE 1897 EARTHQUAKE

One of the most devastating natural disasters in Bhutan was the great Assam earthquake that occurred at 5.06pm on 12 June 1897. The epicentre was about 80km south of Bhutan in Assam and had an estimated magnitude of 8.7 on the Richter scale, which seismologists categorise as 'catastrophic'. The earthquake destroyed the dzongs in Punakha and Lingzhi and severely damaged the dzongs of Wangdue Phodrang, Trongsa, Jakar and the *utse* (central tower) of Trashi Chho Dzong. Paro Dzong escaped largely unharmed.

1992	1993	1998	1998
Up to 80,000 Nepali speakers who claim they are from Bhutan are housed in seven camps in the Jhapa district of southeastern Nepal.	The exodus of Nepali speakers stops and the UN High Commissioner for Refugees establishes a screening centre at Kakarbhitta on the Nepal–India border.	King Jigme Singye Wangchuck transfers full executive authority to an elected Council of Ministers.	Taktshang Goemba, the most famous monastery in Bhutan, is all but destroyed in a fire.

THE BEGINNING OF TOURISM

••

Until the beginning of King Jigme Dorji Wangchuck's modernisation efforts in 1960, most of the non-Indian foreigners who entered Bhutan were British explorers. A few foreigners were permitted into the country during the 1960s, but only the royal family had the authority to issue invitations, so almost all visitors were royal guests.

Early trekkers included Desmond Doig, a friend of the royal family who trekked in 1961 on assignment for *National Geographic*. In 1963 Professor Augusto Gansser travelled throughout the country studying geology, and in 1964 a group of British physicians, Michael Ward, Frederic Jackson and R Turner, mounted an expedition to the remote Lunana region.

The coronation of the fourth king in 1974 was the first time that a large number of foreign visitors had entered the kingdom. After the coronation, small groups of tourists were allowed into the country and given permission to visit the dzongs and goembas in Thimphu and Paro. From these beginnings, the pattern for Bhutan's tourism industry evolved.

The first group of paying tourists arrived in 1974, organised and led by Lars Eric Lindblad, founder of Lindblad Travel in Connecticut, USA, a pioneer of modern-day group tours. Lindblad encouraged the government to limit tourism and to charge high fees.

Paro airport was opened in 1983 and the newly formed national airline, Druk Air, started operating flights from Kolkata. The airport runway was extended in 1990 and Druk Air began operating jet aircraft, with direct international connections. Until 1991 tourists were handled by the Bhutan Tourism Corporation, a government agency. Tourism was privatised that year and soon numerous agencies were established, most run by ex-employees of the now-disbanded government agency.

---

continued to maintain excellent relations with the British, partly in an effort to gain some security from the increasing Chinese influence in Tibet.

In wider terms the establishment of the royal lineage also signalled a wrenching of power away from the Zhabdrung and the monk body. The seventh Zhabdrung, Jigme Dorji, was removed to Talo Goemba and was the last Zhabdrung to be formally recognised by the Bhutanese government. Both the seventh and eighth Zhabdrungs died young, the latter just 14 years old, and the ninth fled to India as a boy, dying there in 2003.

The Treaty of Punakha

British-Bhutanese relations were enhanced by the treaty of Punakha, which was signed in 1910. This treaty stated that the British government would 'exercise no interference in the internal administration of Bhutan'. It was agreed, though, that Bhutan would 'be guided by the advice of the British Government in regard to its external relations'. The compensation

1999	2001	2001	2003
TV and the internet are officially introduced to Bhutan in a managed continuation of the modernisation process.	The drafting of the first Constitution of the Kingdom of Bhutan begins.	A verification process of refugees in the Nepal camps is initiated under a bilateral process between Nepal and Bhutan.	The Royal Bhutan Army, led by the fourth king, removes Bodo militant camps from Bhutanese territory.

for the *duars* was increased to Rs100,000 per year and Bhutan agreed to refer disputes with Cooch Behar and Sikkim to the British for settlement.

Bhutan still refused to allow the appointment of a British resident, and continued to maintain a policy of isolation aimed at preserving its own sovereignty in an era of colonisation. In 1911 King Ugyen Wangchuck attended the great *durbar* (royal court) held by King George V at Delhi and was given the additional decoration of Knight Commander of the Order of the Star of India.

The Second King

Ugyen Wangchuck died in 1926 and was succeeded by his 24-year-old son, Jigme Wangchuck. He ruled during the time of the Great Depression and WWII, but these catastrophic world events did not affect Bhutan because of its barter economy and isolation.

Jigme Wangchuck refined the administrative and taxation systems and brought the entire country under his direct control. He made Wangdichholing Palace in Bumthang his summer palace, and moved the entire court to Kuenga Rabten, south of Trongsa, in the winter.

After India gained independence from Britain on 15 August 1947, the new Indian government recognised Bhutan as an independent country. In 1949 Bhutan signed a treaty with independent India that was very similar to its earlier treaty with the British. The treaty reinforced Bhutan's position as a sovereign state. India agreed not to interfere in the internal affairs of Bhutan, while Bhutan agreed to be guided by the government of India in its external relations. The treaty also returned to Bhutan about 82 sq km of the *duars* in the southeast of the country, including Dewangiri, that had been annexed by the British.

The Third King & the Modernisation of Bhutan

King Jigme Wangchuck died in 1952. He was succeeded by his son, Jigme Dorji Wangchuck, who had been educated in India and England and spoke fluent Tibetan, English and Hindi. To improve relations with India he invited the Indian prime minister, Jawaharlal Nehru, and his daughter, Indira Gandhi, to visit Bhutan in 1958.

When the Chinese took control of Tibet in 1959, it became obvious that a policy of isolationism was not appropriate in the modern world. The king knew that in order to preserve Bhutan's independence, the country had to become a member of the larger world community. In 1961 Bhutan emerged from centuries of self-imposed isolation and embarked on a process of planned development.

Michael Aris' book *The Raven Crown* gives a detailed description of Bhutan in the early 20th century; it is lavishly illustrated with rare photographs and provides a perspective based on Bhutanese accounts.

In 1931 Lt Col JLR Weir travelled to Bumthang to denominate the king Knight Commander of the Indian Empire – the basis for the book and TV documentary *Joanna Lumley in the Kingdom of the Thunder Dragon*.

HISTORY THE SECOND KING

2005 & 2006	2007	2008	2008
The fourth king abdicates and the draft Constitution of the Kingdom of Bhutan is released.	The first-ever election is held to vote for the 20 members each representing a *dzongkhag* (district) of the 25-member National Council (upper house).	The Bhutanese vote again, this time for the 47-member National Assembly (lower house). Druk Phuensum Tshogpa (DPT; Bhutan Peace & Prosperity) wins 45 seats.	The fifth Druk Gyalpo (Dragon King) Jigme Khesar Namgyel Wangchuck is crowned on 6 November.

Karma Ura's book *The Hero with a Thousand Eyes* gives a wonderful insight into the protocol and workings of the Bhutanese court in the days of the second king, Jigme Wangchuck, and is available in Thimphu.

Bhutan joined the Colombo Plan in 1962. This gave it access to technical assistance and training from member countries in Southeast Asia. The first 'five-year plan' for development was implemented in 1961 and India agreed to help finance and construct the large Chhukha hydroelectric project in western Bhutan. Not all Bhutanese approved of the pace of change. There were clashes between rival power groups and the prime minister, Jigme Palden Dorji, who was a leading proponent of change, was assassinated on 5 April 1964.

Bhutan joined the Universal Postal Union in 1969 and became a member of the UN in 1971. In the same year, Bhutan and India established formal diplomatic relations and exchanged ambassadors.

The king's domestic accomplishments were also impressive. In 1953 he established the Tshogdu (National Assembly) and drew up a 12-volume code of law. He abolished serfdom, reorganised land holdings, created the Royal Bhutan Army (RBA) and police force, and established the High Court. However, as he led Bhutan into the modern world, he emphasised the need to preserve Bhutanese culture and tradition.

The Fourth King & the Introduction of Democracy

King Jigme Dorji Wangchuck died in 1972 at age 44. He was succeeded by his 16-year-old son, Jigme Singye Wangchuck. Like his father, he was educated in India and England, but he also received a Bhutanese education at the Ugyen Wangchuck Academy in Paro. He pledged to continue his father's program of modernisation and announced a plan for the country to achieve economic self-reliance. This plan took advantage of Bhutan's special circumstances – a small population, abundant land and rich natural resources. Among the development goals set by the king was the ideal of economic self-reliance and what he nicknamed 'Gross National Happiness' (GNH). GNH is not a simple appraisal of the smiles on the faces of the populace; rather it encompasses explicit criteria to measure development projects and progress in terms of society's greater good. A more sustainable happiness for the individual is believed to derive from such an approach.

Only from the middle of the 20th century did Bhutan's different valleys and regions start to form a national consciousness. Regional identities such as Kheng (Zhemgang), Mangde (Trongsa) and Kurtoe (Lhuentse) continue to be important.

The coronation of King Jigme Singye Wangchuck as the fourth Druk Gyalpo on 2 June 1974 was a major turning point in the opening of Bhutan, and was the first time that the international press was allowed to enter the country. A total of 287 invited guests travelled to Thimphu for the event, and several new hotels were built to accommodate them. These hotels later provided the basis for the development of tourism in Bhutan.

2008	2009	2009	2010
The Constitution of the Kingdom of Bhutan is officially adopted.	Bhutan and India agree on the construction of 10 new hydropower projects in Bhutan to provide 10,000MW of electricity.	A 6.1 magnitude earthquake centred in eastern Bhutan leaves several dead.	Bhutan hosts the 16th summit of the South Asian Association for Regional Cooperation (SAARC) in Thimphu.

The fourth king emphasised modernisation of education, health services, rural development and communications. He continued the reforms begun by his father in the areas of administration, labour and justice, including the abolition of compulsory labour. He was the architect of Bhutan's policy of environmental conservation, which gives precedence to ecological considerations over commercial interests. He promoted national identity, traditional values and the concept of 'One Nation, One People'.

In 1988 the royal wedding solemnised the king's marriage to the sisters Ashi Dorji Wangmo, Ashi Tshering Pem, Ashi Tshering Yangdon and Ashi Sangay Choedon. In 1998 he gave up absolute power, sharing authority with the National Assembly and Council of Ministers.

In December 2005, the 50-year-old king announced a plan to abdicate the throne in favour of his eldest son, Crown Prince Jigme Khesar Namgyal Wangchuck, and help move the country from an absolute monarchy to a democratic constitutional monarchy in 2008.

Of Rainbows and Clouds: The Life of Yab Ugyen Dorji as Told to His Daughter by Yab Ugyen Dorji and Ashi Dorje Wangmo Wangchuck is a fascinating and intimate account of life in changing Bhutan.

The Fifth King & the First Elected Parliament

King Jigme Singye Wangchuck did not wait until 2008. He formally abdicated in December 2006, bestowing all his authority to his eldest son, who was already travelling to every corner of the country to explain the new constitution, the upcoming election, and their beloved fourth king's

BODO GROUPS & THE UNITED LIBERATION FRONT OF ASSAM

The northeastern region of India has suffered years of separatist violence carried out by militants, some of whom have established bases in the jungles of southern Bhutan from which they mount assaults. The actions of these groups have claimed the lives of more than 20,000 people in the Indian state of Assam.

The Bodos are Mechey tribal people that have two militant groups, the Bodo Liberation Tiger Force and the Bodo Security Force, both of which are fighting for a Bodo homeland. The United Liberation Front of Assam, more commonly known as ULFA, is a separatist group formed in 1979 with the goal of an independent Assamese nation. It has staged numerous attacks on trains, buses and vehicles carrying both Bhutanese and Indian citizens.

In December 2003, after the government felt it had exhausted all peaceful means, the Royal Bhutan Army, led from the front by the king, flushed out the militants from Bhutanese territory. The same groups continue to be active periodically across the border in Assam, so check the situation before exiting or entering Bhutan via the crossing points at Gelephu and Samdrup Jongkhar in southeastern Bhutan.

2011	2011	2012	2013
King Jigme Khesar Namgyel Wangchuck marries commoner Jetsun Pema at Punakha Dzong on 13 October.	A 6.9 magnitude earthquake hits Sikkim and western Bhutan.	Bhutan is rocked by the complete destruction by fire of Wangdue Phodrang Dzong, one of the country's oldest dzongs. Plans for its reconstruction start immediately.	Bhutan goes to the polls for the second time. The tables are turned and the People's Democratic Party (PDP) is swept to power in the National Assembly.

dramatic decision. This peaceful ceding of power in favour of a parliamentary democracy stood in stark contrast to that other Himalayan former monarchy, Nepal.

In December 2007 the first elections for the new parliament were held for the 25-member upper house, called the National Council. Twenty members each represent one of the *dzongkhags* (political districts) and there are five additional members nominated by the king.

This was followed in March 2008 by the first election for the 47-member National Assembly (lower house). With royal encouragement, the sparse population spread over a rugged country managed a remarkable 80% turnout. This election became a landslide victory for the Druk Phuensum Tshogpa (DPT; Bhutan Peace & Prosperity) party, which won 45 of the 47 seats. The People's Democratic Party (PDP) won the other two seats.

The unprecedented sight of the former king crowning the new king with the raven crown was witnessed on 6 November 2008 at the official coronation of 27-year-old Jigme Khesar Namgyel Wangchuck. The momentous occasion took place in the Golden Throne room of Thimphu's Trashi Chho Dzong in front of national and international dignitaries. The following day, the fifth king gave his coronation speech to a packed Changlimithang Stadium, in which he pledged: 'As the king of a Buddhist nation, my duty is not only to ensure your happiness today, but to create the fertile ground from which you may gain the fruits of spiritual pursuit and attain good karma.'

King Jigme Dorji Wangchuck, the third king, became known as the father of modern Bhutan, owing to his reforms to society and economics.

A New Parliament & A New Prince

In 2013 it was time for the second election and, in a climate of economic uncertainty, the PDP was swept into power, winning 32 seats to the DPT's 15. The new government wasted little time in coming to grips with the country's social and economic situation. The prime minister openly and pragmatically admitted that the mantra of Gross National Happiness sometimes overshadowed problems of low living standards, unemployment and corruption, which needed addressing.

In February 2016 the country went into royal overdrive with the birth of the new heir to the throne, Gyalsey (Prince) Jigme Namgyel Wangchuck. A few months later, the proud parents, King Jigme Khesar Namgyel Wangchuck and Gyaltsuen (Queen) Jetsun Pema, hosted British royalty in the form of the Duke and Duchess of Cambridge.

The UN refugee agency (www.unhcr.org) provides the latest facts and figures on the refugee camps in Jhapa, Nepal.

2015	2016	2017	2018
Prime Minister Tshering Tobgay meets with US Secretary of State John Kerry in India in an unprecedented bilateral meeting.	The prince (Gyalsey) Jigme Namgyel Wangchuck is born to King Jigme Khesar Namgyel Wangchuck and Queen (Gyaltsuen) Jetsun Pema.	Military tensions between India and China spike during a three-month stand-off at the Doklam plateau, claimed by Bhutan.	The Bhutan United Party (DNT) wins the national elections, meaning that three different parties have been elected in Bhutan's three elections.

The Bhutanese Way of Life

Bhutan was relatively isolated until the early 1950s; this tiny country has witnessed more change in the last 70 years than in the previous 400 years. To date, Bhutan has retained many of its traditional social structures and has actively sought to preserve its cultural identity in the face of modernisation and increasing external influences.

Everyday Buddhism

Maybe it's your first sight of the monumental Buddha that watches over the Thimphu valley, or the way your driver swerves clockwise around a chorten stuck in the middle of the road, but as a new visitor you quickly realise how Buddhism permeates life in Bhutan. Prayer flags flutter throughout the land, prayer wheels powered by mountain streams clunk gently by the roadside, and images of the Buddha and other religious figures are carved into cliffs, reminding the visitor that every aspect of daily life is shaped by Buddhist beliefs and aspirations. This can be daunting, even alien, for many Western visitors, and a basic knowledge of Buddhism will go a long way towards understanding the Bhutanese. The idea of accumulating merit, having a deep respect of the natural and often sacred environment, and respecting religious practitioners: all are central elements of the unique fusion of Buddhism and older non-Buddhist beliefs.

Buddhism is practised throughout the country; however, in the south, most Bhutanese people of Nepali and Indian descent are Hindu. Relations between Buddhists and Hindus are very good, with major Hindu festivals marked by national holidays. Minority groups practise various forms of ancient animistic religions, including Bon, which predates Himalayan Buddhism.

Urban Bhutan

Until the 1960s, there were no major urban settlements. Since then Thimphu, Paro and Phuentsholing have grown significantly, leading to pressure on land availability in these areas. Elsewhere there has been an increase in land acquisition and settlement, most notably in Gelephu.

As a result of the opportunities created by education and the development of service-industry jobs (such as civil servants, teachers, travel guides, army personnel and police), Bhutan has experienced unprecedented social mobility in recent decades. The rate of rural–urban migration continues to increase, and there has been growing concern over the increasing unemployment rate among educated school leavers, the abandonment of farms, and rapidly rising property values and rents in Thimphu.

The Living Standard Survey 2017 revealed that 36% of Bhutanese now live in urban areas, and 39% of the country's households get the majority of their income from wages. Averaged across the country, agriculture accounts for only 10% of income. For many living in urban areas, average

Until the mid-20th century there were no large urban settlements in Bhutan. By 2017 the population of Thimphu was over 114,000.

DZOE – SPIRIT CATCHER

Sometimes you will come across a strange construction of twigs, straw and rainbow-coloured thread woven into a spider-web shape. You may see one near a building or by a roadside, with flower and food offerings. This is a *dzoe* (also known as a *tendo*), a sort of spirit catcher used to exorcise something evil that has been pestering a household. The malevolent spirits are drawn to the *dzoe*. After prayers the *dzoe* is cast away, often on a trail or road, to send away the evil spirits it has trapped.

household expenditure can represent all or most of their salary, which is why many Bhutanese households supplement traditional income through some form of small business enterprise.

Rural Life

Despite rapid urbanisation, the majority of people still live in rural Bhutan and most are dependent on the cultivation of crops and livestock breeding.

The main crops grown in central Bhutan are rice, buckwheat, barley and potatoes. Chillies are also grown, then dried on the roofs of houses before being stored.

Life for most rural households starts around dawn and ends with sunset; daily life revolves around the care of crops and livestock. Each morning the family will make offerings, typically of water, before the household shrine and a simple breakfast of rice is prepared. Men and women share equally in the day-to-day care of the children, and although women are usually in charge of the household, men are equally able, and expected, to assist with the cooking. Meals consist of rice and a selection of simple shared dishes – *ema datse* (chillies with cheese), perhaps a meat dish or some buckwheat noodles. Children are expected to help with the household and farm chores, like cleaning, collecting water or firewood, or herding the livestock.

In the evening, the water from the offering bowls will be poured away and a butter lamp may be lit and left to burn before the household shrine.

Traditionally Bhutanese were very self-sufficient, often making their own clothing, bedding, floor and seat covers, tablecloths, and decorative items for daily and religious use. There remains a degree of self-sufficiency among the rural Bhutanese, though many everyday items are now imported from Bangladesh, China, India and Thailand.

Rural Migration

The migration from rural zones to the bright lights of urban areas is not unique to Bhutan. The Bhutanese do, however, have their own word for it: *goongtong* (*goong* referring to households and *tong* meaning empty). The number of empty households and fallow fields, especially in the east, is a hot topic. To help stem the flow and revitalise rural enterprises by improving access to markets, the Bhutanese government is duplicating the National Highway from Thimphu to Trashigang and improving road connections to remote *gewogs* (groups of villages). Visitors to Bhutan cannot fail to notice the extensive road building and widening. The government is also investigating solar energy to provide power to small remote communities and helping farmers buy farm vehicles. However, the flow of young people to the urban centres seems to continue unabated.

Literacy in Bhutan is 69% for males and 51% for females (2017). For more information on education in the Himalaya, and on supporting young students, see www.loden.org.

Women in Bhutan

Compared to other areas of South Asia, Bhutanese women enjoy greater equality and freedom with men. The right to inherit often passes property to the woman of the household rather than the man.

Traditionally, women look after the household, preparing food and weaving textiles for family use and for sale. However, they also work in the fields, notably at harvest times when all available labour is required.

Usually women brew the homemade alcohol such as *arra, bang chhang* or *sinchhang*. Decisions affecting the household are jointly made.

While travelling in Bhutan you will notice that Bhutanese women are independently minded and possess a strong entrepreneurial spirit. In Thimphu and the emerging urban centres such as Trongsa, Gelephu and Phuentsholing, women may seek to boost family income by engaging in trade, selling goods from home or renting a small shop.

The introduction of education in the 1960s enabled Bhutanese women to become literate and to seek employment outside of their homes and their local villages. Teaching, the civil service and other office positions provided important opportunities for young, educated Bhutanese women.

However, there are areas in which Bhutanese women are still not equal with their male counterparts. Levels of literacy remain higher among men than women, though this is being tackled by the government through adult learning classes. Although some women have been appointed to higher positions in the government and NGOs, including the first female district court judge appointed in 2003, there remains a gender imbalance at all levels of government. In the first, second and third elections for the parliament's National Council, women accounted for four, none and two, respectively, of the successful 20 candidates. For the 47-member National Assembly elections in September 2018, seven of the 10 women standing (representing two parties) were successful.

The major women's organisation in the country is the National Women's Association of Bhutan. It was established in 1981 and headed by Dasho Dawa Dem, one of the few women to have received the honorific title of Dasho. In 2004, Respect, Educate, Nurture & Empower Women (Renew; www.renew.org.bt), an NGO for women, was established by HM Queen Mother Sangay Choeden Wangchuck. Renew is highly respected and tackles major issues facing contemporary Bhutanese women. It

> Rural women are often presented as the custodians of traditional values. Urbanisation and increasing rural–urban migration have brought new challenges for women separated from their families and social networks.

THE BHUTANESE WAY OF LIFE WOMEN IN BHUTAN

Women in front of a traditional house, Mongar (p159)

ANGELA MEIER / SHUTTERSTOCK ©

DOMA

Doma is an integral part of Bhutanese culture. A popular gift throughout Bhutanese society, it is made up of three main ingredients: *doma* or areca nut *(Areca catechu)*, *pani* or betel leaf *(Piper betel)* and *tsune* or lime (calcium carbonate).

Eating *doma* was an aristocratic practice, with the plant ingredients kept in ornate rectangular silver boxes called *chaka*, while lime had a separate circular box with conical lid called *trimi*. JC White, the British political officer who attended Gongsar Ugyen Wangchuck's enthronement in 1907, reports that *doma* was served to those attending the enthronement. Today people may keep their *doma* in bamboo *bangchung* (ornate covered bowls used to carry food) or a cloth pouch called a *kaychung*. While the red sprays of *doma* spit still stain many walls and floors, young people appear to be slowly turning away from the habit as health warnings begin to make inroads.

is at the forefront of initiatives to combat domestic and gender-based violence.

Marriage

In the past, marriages were arranged. However, since the 1970s the majority of marriages have been love matches. The minimum age is 18 for both women and men. In rural areas, it is quite common for the husband to move into his wife's household and if they divorce he will return to live with his own family.

The women of Laya are particularly noted for their distinctive conical bamboo hats and long black wool dresses.

Polyandry, the practice of taking more than one husband, still exists in certain parts of Bhutan and polygamy is restricted. There remains a large number of Bhutanese couples who, although living together as a couple, are not formally married. The divorce rate is increasing and there is legal provision for alimony to be paid to take care of children.

Personal Names

The system for personal names in Bhutan differs between the north and south of the country. In the north, with the exception of the royal family, there are no family names. Two names are given to children by monks a few weeks after birth. These are traditional names of Tibetan origin and are chosen because of their auspicious influence or religious meaning. Two names are always given, although a few people have three names.

It is often impossible to tell the sex of a Bhutanese person based on their name. A few names are given only to boys, and others apply only to girls – eg Choekyi, Drolma and Wangmo – but most names may apply to either.

Yeewong magazine (www.yeewongmagazine.com) is Bhutan's women's glossy, launched in 2009 and published twice a year. While the poses and the prettiness are globally glamorous, the food and fashions are decidedly Bhutanese.

In the south, with an evident Hindu influence, a system resembling family names exists. Brahmans and Newars retain their caste name, such as Sharma or Pradhan, and others retain the name of their ethnic group, such as Rai or Gurung.

Death Rituals & the Wheel of Life

The Wheel of Life, often evident at the entrances to goembas (monasteries), reminds Bhutanese that death is part of the cycle of samsara separating loved ones and leading to rebirth. Accordingly, death is treated as a major life event. Family and friends are informed and monks, *gomchen* (lay or married monks) or nuns begin to recite from the *Bardo Thodrel* to guide the deceased through the intermediate phase.

Until the cremation, the deceased is placed in a wooden box and covered in a white cloth and kept separate from the family. At the cremation, the corpse is placed on the pyre facing the officiating lama. The first funeral service is held on the seventh day after death, with other rituals performed on the 14th, 21st and 49th days. The lama reminds the deceased that they are dead and during the ritual seeks to help them move on to their next (it is hoped fortunate) rebirth, either as a human being or preferably in a Buddha realm.

At the end of the 49 days, the ashes of the deceased may be scattered; some are placed in a sacred image and donated to a monastery or temple. The anniversary of the death will be marked for the following three years.

Titles & Forms of Address

Titles are extremely important in Bhutan. All persons of rank should be addressed by the appropriate title followed by their first or full name. Members of the royal family are addressed as 'Dasho' if they are male and 'Ashi' if female. A minister has the title 'Lyonpo' (pronounced 'lonpo').

The title Dasho is given to those who have been honoured by the king and have received the accompanying red scarf. In common practice, many senior government officials are addressed as Dasho even if they have not received the title, but officially this is incorrect.

You would address a senior monk or teacher with the title 'Lopon' (pronounced 'loeboen') or, if he has been given the title, as Lam. A *trulku* (reincarnate lama) is addressed as 'Rinpoche' and a nun as 'Anim'.

A man is addressed as 'Aap' and a boy as 'Busu'; a woman is addressed as 'Am' and a girl as 'Bum'. If you are calling someone whose name you do not know, you may use 'Ama' for women and 'Aapa' for men. In the same situation, girls are 'Bumo' and boys 'Alou'. When Bhutanese talk about a foreigner whose name they don't know, they use the word 'Chilip', or in eastern Bhutan 'Pilingpa'.

White silk scarves called *kata* are exchanged as customary greetings among ranking officials and are offered to high lamas as a sign of respect, but they are not exchanged as frequently as they are in Tibet and Nepal.

Dress: Gho & Kira

Bhutan's traditional dress is one of the most distinctive and visible aspects of the country. It is compulsory for all Bhutanese to wear national dress in schools and government offices, and on formal occasions. Men,

Of approximately 7000 formal monks in Bhutan, half are under the patronage of the Je Khenpo; the other half are subsidised privately.

Bhutanese do not shout a person's name at night, as it's believed this may attract a ghost.

BHUTAN'S SILVER SCREEN

The first feature film produced by a Bhutanese film-maker for a non-Bhutanese audience was *The Cup* by Khyentse Norbu, which was nominated as best foreign-language film for the 2000 Academy Awards. *Travellers and Magicians* (2003), also produced by Khyentse Norbu, is the first Dzongkha-language film to be made for an international audience. The film contains two parallel tales and its main theme remains pertinent to contemporary Bhutan. The story focuses on a young frustrated civil servant, Dhundup, who dreams of leaving Bhutan for the USA. He likes rock and roll and Western clothes. Yet on the road to the capital, he encounters a series of people who suggest that contentment can be found among his own people.

Bhutanese of all ages enjoy these films, and part of the enjoyment for many is identifying friends and relatives, as well as the locations. Bhutanese films such as *Khorwa*, made for a Bhutanese audience, often tackle contemporary social problems such as domestic violence, alcoholism and unemployment. The production values and acting are of varying quality, yet a stronger sense of Bhutanese film-making is gradually appearing, with annual awards recognising local film-makers. At the 18th National Film Awards held in February 2019, a total of 16 films were entered. *Tsip Choelo – The Vested Astrologer* won the best film award.

Archery competition near Thimphu (p50)

women and children wear traditional clothing made from Bhutanese textiles in a variety of colourful patterns.

Men wear a *gho,* a long robe similar to the Tibetan *chuba.* The Bhutanese hoist the *gho* to knee length and hold it in place with a woven cloth belt called a *kera.* The *kera* is wound tightly around the waist, and the large pouch formed above it is traditionally used to carry a bowl, money and the makings of *doma.* One man suggested that the best part of the day was when he was able to loosen his uncomfortably tight belt.

According to tradition, men should carry a small knife called a *dozum* at the waist. Traditional footwear is knee-high, embroidered leather boots, but these are now worn only at festivals. Most Bhutanese men wear leather shoes, trainers or trekking boots.

Ghos come in a wide variety of patterns, though often they have plaid or striped designs. Flowered patterns are taboo, and solid reds and yellows are avoided because these are colours worn by monks; otherwise patterns have no special significance. Historically, Bhutanese men wore the same thing under their *gho* that a true Scotsman wears under his kilt, but today it's usually a pair of shorts. In winter it's correct to wear thermal underwear, but it's more often a pair of jeans or a tracksuit. Formality in Thimphu dictates that legs may not be covered until winter has arrived, which is defined as the time that the monks move to Punakha.

Formal occasions, including a visit to the dzong (fort-monastery), require a scarf called a *kabney* that identifies a person's rank. The *kabney* has to be put on so it hangs in exactly the right way. In dzongs, and on formal occasions, a *dasho* or someone in authority carries a long sword called a *patang.*

Ordinary male citizens wear a *kabney* of unbleached white silk and each level of official (male or female) wears a different coloured *kabney*: saffron for the king and Je Khenpo; orange for *lyonpos*; blue for National Council and National Assembly members; red for those with the title

Bhutanese footballers came to the world's attention in 2002 when Bhutan played against the small island of Montserrat. *The Other Final* documentary narrates the lead-up to the football match between the world's two lowest-ranked teams and the crowd's enthusiastic participation.

Dasho and for senior officials whom the king has recognised; green for judges; white with a central red stripe for *dzongdags* (district governors); and white with red stripes on the outside for a *gup* (elected leader of a village).

Women wear a long floor-length dress called a *kira*. This is a rectangular piece of brightly coloured cloth that wraps around the body over a Tibetan-style silk blouse called a *wonju*. The *kira* is fastened at the shoulders with elaborate silver hooks called *koma* and at the waist with a belt that may be of either silver or cloth. Over the top is worn a short, open, jacket-like garment called a *toego*. Women often wear large amounts of jewellery. The whole ensemble is beautiful and Bhutanese women are very elegant in their finery.

The *kira* may be made from cotton or silk (usually synthetic these days) and may have a pattern on one or both sides. For everyday wear, women wear a *kira* made from striped cloth with a double-sided design, and on more formal occasions they wear a *kira* with an embellished pattern woven into it. The most expensive *kira*s are *kushutara*s (brocade dresses), which are made of hand-spun, handwoven Bhutanese cotton and embroidered with various colours and designs in raw silk or cotton thread. Lhuentse is celebrated for its *kushutara* designs.

When visiting dzongs, women wear a cloth sash called a *rachu* over their shoulders or simply over their left shoulder in the same manner as men wear a *kabney*.

Bhutanese at Play

Bhutan's national sport is archery *(datse)*. It is played wherever there is enough space and remains the favourite sport for all ages. There are archery tournaments held throughout the country.

TRADITIONAL MEDICINE IN BHUTAN

Historically, Bhutan was referred to as the 'Land of Medicinal Herbs' and exported herbs to Tibet. Bhutanese were trained in medicine, known as So-ba Rig pa. It represents a blending of Ayurveda from India with Chinese medicine, in the reading of pulses. The earliest medical works date from the 7th and 8th centuries and the main medical teachings are believed to have been transmitted from the Medicine Buddha, Sangye Menlha. They are contained in four volumes, called the *Gyuzhi*.

When the Zhabdrung Ngawang Namgyal came to Bhutan, he brought with him a highly esteemed physician, Tenzin Drukey, who spread the teachings on So-ba Rig pa in Bhutan. Although the basic texts are the same, the Bhutanese tradition of So-ba Rig pa developed independently from its Tibetan origins. Since 1967 the Bhutanese tradition has been formally incorporated into the national health system.

The decision about the kind of treatment necessary for a particular condition is made mainly through reading of the pulses. Unlike Western medicine, which only uses reading of pulses to detect anomalies of the circulatory system, the So-ba Rig pa method claims that it is possible to detect diseases of organs. The eyes, tongue and urine are also examined for signs that will help with the diagnosis.

Several forms of treatment are applied in Bhutanese traditional medicine. Hundreds of medicinal plants, minerals and animal parts form the basic medicines that are used by the practitioner. These basic ingredients are processed and mixed in different combinations to make 300 medicines in the form of pills, tablets, syrups, powders and lotions. The practitioner may also offer advice on, or treatment for, diet and lifestyle.

There are also procedures that include *gtar* (bloodletting), *bsregs* (cauterisation by herbal compounds), *gser bcos* (acupuncture with a golden needle), *tshug* (cauterisation with instruments of different materials), *dugs* (applying heat or cold to parts of the body), *byugs pa* (medicated oil massage), *sman chu* (taking stone-heated baths), *tshachhu* (baths at a hot spring, such as the springs in Gasa) and *lum* (vapour treatments).

SOCIAL ETIQUETTE

The Zhabdrung Ngawang Namgyal established a code of etiquette for monastic and government officials. Over the centuries this system of etiquette spread to lay people. Called *driglam namzha*, the code of conduct specifies how to dress when visiting a dzong (fort-monastery), the polite way to greet one's boss and officials, and the correct way to sit, eat and so forth. Many of the ceremonies performed at the start of an official event (*chipdrel, marchang*) or an archery match are part of *driglam namzha*.

The government has actively promoted *driglam namzha* since 1989 in an attempt to preserve Bhutanese traditions, notably enforcing the requirement to wear *gho* and *kira* when visiting government offices, dzongs and temples.

Closely linked to *driglam namzha, thadamthsi* refers to the Bhutanese belief in respect towards one's parents, elders and other members of the community. Based on the Buddhist teachings on devotion, *thadamtshi* is an important concept in Bhutanese society. It is often illustrated by the story of the Four Friends (p255).

Linked to *thadamtshi* and less formal than *driglam namzha* is the concept of *bey cha*, which emphasises the aesthetics of performing everyday tasks gracefully and with care and consideration for others.

Archery contests act as an affirmation of Bhutanese cultural identity as well as popular entertainment. The tournaments begin with a short ceremony and breakfast. The targets are placed 140m apart. Players often stand close to the targets and call how good or bad the aim of their opponent is – if the contestant hits the target, his teammates will perform a slow dance and sing his praises, while he slips a coloured scarf into his belt. If he misses, the opposition mock his ability.

Women, usually wearing their finest clothes and jewellery, often stand to one side of the archery field and act as cheerleaders. They dance and sing during breaks from the shooting. Their songs and shouts can be quite ribald! While it remains a male-dominated sport, there is a growing interest in women's archery.

Khuru is a darts game played on a field about 20m long with small targets similar to those used by archers. The darts are usually homemade from a block of wood and a nail, with some chicken feathers for flights. If a chicken can't be found, bits of plastic make a good substitute. Teams compete with a lot of shouting and arm waving, designed to put the thrower off his aim. The game is a favourite of monks and young boys but women's teams and competitions are on the rise; beware of dangerous flying objects if you are near a *khuru* target or an archery field.

Other sports, notably football (soccer), basketball, cricket, cycling, golf, tae kwon do and tennis, continue to grow in popularity with both men and women. There are national men's and women's teams for both football and basketball.

Bhutan's first foray into the Olympic Games happened when an archery team of three men and three women participated in the 1984 games. Since then Bhutan has participated in all the Olympics.

Buddhism in Bhutan

Buddhism is inscribed into the very landscape of Bhutan – fluttering prayer flags, gleaming white chortens and portraits of Buddhist saints carved into the rock dot the countryside. Whether you are visiting a dzong or chatting to your guide, if you want to understand Bhutan, it is essential to have a basic understanding of Buddhism. In essence, everything from festival dances and monastery art to government policy serves the same purpose in Bhutan: to encapsulate and promulgate basic Buddhist teachings.

The Buddha

Buddhism originated in northern central India around the 6th or 5th century BC, from the teachings of Siddhartha Gautama – better known as Sakyamuni Buddha. Little is known for certain about the young Siddhartha. According to legend his parents, King Suddhodana and Queen Maya, lived in a small kingdom, Sakya, which lay on the border between the present-day states of Nepal and India. Shortly after his birth, a wandering ascetic prophesied to King Suddhodana that the young prince would either be a world-conquering king or a liberator of living beings from suffering. The king took various precautions to ensure that his son would never have cause to follow a spiritual path. However, the young prince grew restless and during various excursions from his palace Siddhartha Gautama saw a number of examples of suffering that inspired him to escape from his sheltered palace life.

After fleeing the palace (and leaving his wife and child behind), Siddhartha became a wandering ascetic, fasting and meditating. Finally at Bodhgaya in Bihar, India, Siddhartha began meditating beneath a bo *(pipal)* tree, declaring that he would not stop until he had achieved enlightenment. He had realised there must be a middle path between the extremes of his luxurious palace life and the severe ascetic practices that brought him only exhaustion. As dawn broke on the morning of his third night of meditation Siddhartha became a Buddha (an awakened one).

Bhutan's oldest Buddhist temples are the Kyichu Lhakhang in the Paro valley and Jampey Lhakhang in the Bumthang valley. Both were built by the Tibetan king Songtsen Gampo in the 7th century.

Schools of Buddhism

Buddhism is perhaps the most accommodating of the world's religions. As Buddhism has spread, it has adapted to local conditions and absorbed local beliefs and aesthetics, creating new schools of thought. Over the centuries two principal schools of Buddhism emerged: Theravada and Mahayana.

Theravada, sometimes referred to as Hinayana, focused on pursuing liberation for the individual. Mahayana took Buddhism in a different direction, emphasising compassion and the liberation of all living beings. The Theravada teachings retreated to southern India before becoming established in Sri Lanka, Thailand, Myanmar (Burma) and Cambodia. The Mahayana teachings were developed in the new Buddhist universities in northern India before being transmitted northwards in a huge arc along the Silk Road to China, Tibet, Bhutan, Japan and Korea. It is the Mahayana teachings on compassion that permeate the religious beliefs and practices of the Bhutanese.

To learn more about Tibetan Buddhism try the book *What Makes You Not a Buddhist*, by Dzongsar Jamyang Khyentse, the celebrated Bhutanese *rinpoche* (reincarnated lama) and director.

Despite these differences, the basic tenets of Buddhism have remained the same and all schools of Buddhism are united by their faith in the value of the original teachings of Buddha.

Tantrism (Vajrayana)

A new school called Vajrayana (Diamond Vehicle) emerged from the Mahayana in about AD 600. Both the Theravada and Mahayana schools studied the Sutras that recorded the teachings of Sakyamuni; however, the followers of Tantrism believed that he had left a collection of hidden esoteric teachings to a select few of his early disciples. These were known as Tantra *(gyu)*.

Over the centuries Tantric Buddhism in Tibet gradually divided into various schools, each with their own philosophical, spiritual and political emphasis. In central and eastern Bhutan, the oldest school of Himalayan Buddhism, Nyingmapa, is most popular. The Nyingmapa school was introduced during the earliest phase of Buddhist propagation and experienced a revival through the discovery of *terma* (hidden texts believed to have been buried by Guru Rinpoche at various sites across Bhutan). In other parts of Bhutan, particularly the west, the Drukpa Kagyupa school is pre-eminent. The Drukpa school was founded in Ralung in Tibet by Tsanpa Gyare (1161–1211) and spread to Bhutan in the 13th century.

Tantra (Sanskrit meaning 'continuum') most often refers to the literature dealing with tantric teachings. Tantrism relies heavily on oral transmission between teacher and student, as well as the practice of identifying with a tutelary deity through meditation and the recitation of mantras. The two most well-known mantras are *om mani padme hum* of Chenresig (Avalokiteshvara) and *om vajra guru padme siddhi hum* of Guru Rinpoche (Padmasambhava).

In Bhutan ritual objects such as the *dorji* (thunderbolt), *drilbu* (bell), skull cup and hand drum are all derived from tantric teachings, as is much of the imagery on the walls of monasteries and temples. They display the many different aspects of enlightenment – at times gentle but at other times wrathful.

Buddhist Concepts

Buddha's first sermon at Sarnath's Deer Park is commemorated by the bronze statues of two deer flanking the Wheel of Law that adorns each monastery roof.

Shortly after gaining enlightenment, the Buddha gave his first public teaching in the Deer Park at Sarnath (present-day Uttar Pradesh, India). The Buddha started his teachings by explaining that there was a middle way that steered a course between sensual indulgence and ascetic self-torment. The Middle Way can be followed by taking the Eight-Fold Noble Path, underpinned by the Four Noble Truths. The Four Noble Truths set out the laws of cause and effect. Buddhism is thus not based on a revealed prophecy or divine revelation but rather is firmly rooted in human experience. In a modern sense, Buddhist thought stresses nonviolence, compassion, equanimity (evenness of mind) and mindfulness (awareness of the present moment).

Four Noble Truths

The Four Noble Truths underpin Buddhist philosophy and are the basic tenets linking ignorance and enlightenment, suffering and freedom set forth by the Buddha in his first formal discourse in Sarnath.

The first Noble Truth is that life is suffering, the Truth of Suffering. This suffering is the result of an unenlightened life and is maintained by the constant process of rebirth in the different realms of existence. Inherent in the suffering of life is the pain of ageing, sickness and death, the loss of things we are attached to and the failure to achieve the things we desire.

The reason for this dissatisfaction and suffering is contained in the second Noble Truth, which refers to our desire for things to be other than they actually are. This dissatisfaction leads to actions and karmic consequences that merely prolong the cycle of rebirths.

The third Noble Truth was described by the Buddha as True Cessation – the stopping of all delusions, desires and attachment to samsara (the cycle of birth, death and reincarnation). With the cessation of desire and attachment, we are able to break the cycle of rebirth and suffering and reach a state of nirvana, the ultimate goal of Buddhism.

The fourth Noble Truth, True Paths, refers to the correct means through which an individual is able to overcome attachment and desires in the pursuit of liberation from samsara. These are often described as the Eight-Fold Path: with dedication and practice it may lead to accumulation of merit, then enlightenment and liberation. The eight components of the path to enlightenment: right understanding, right thought, right speech, right action, right livelihood, right effort, right mindfulness and right concentration.

The doctrine of the Four Noble Truths is the foundation on which the whole path to liberation and enlightenment is built. Therefore a deep understanding of these truths, cultivated through reflection and meditation, is an indispensable basis for following the Buddhist path.

Rebirth & the Wheel of Life

In Buddhism, life is seen as a countless cycle of rebirths as living beings 'wander' in samsara. There is not just one world but myriad worlds in which beings may be reborn – according to Buddhist doctrine, there are six different realms of existence. It is important during one's lifetime to accumulate enough merit to avoid being reborn in one of the three lower realms. Rebirth, or cyclic existence, emerges from fundamental ignorance through a process known as the 12 links of dependent origination. When this fundamental ignorance is reversed, cyclic existence itself can be reversed and nirvana attained, freeing the individual from suffering and the processes of rebirth. The six realms of existence and the 12 links of dependent origination are what is depicted in the popular Wheel of Life illustration at monastery entrances.

LUSO (FOLK RELIGION)

Vestiges of Bon, the pre-Buddhist belief system prevalent across the Himalaya, can still be found in Bhutan and are closely tied to the rich folk religion known as *luso*. Customs such as hanging prayer flags from a mountain pass have their roots in Bon practice. Every locality, mountain, lake, river or grove of trees in Bhutan has its own sacred geography and the invocation of these local and protective deities is an essential part of daily ritual in Bhutan. In the morning, most Bhutanese burn aromatic herbs (juniper) or incense as an offering to the mountain deities. On certain days, a single flag is raised on every house and particular deities are invoked.

Bhutanese folk beliefs are also concerned with a range of spirits or *nep* (local deities) who act as the custodian of particular valleys, such as Chungdu in Haa, or Radak in Wangdue Phodrang. There are also *tshomen*, mermaid-like goddesses who inhabit the lakes, and *lu* or *naga*, snake-bodied spirits who dwell in lakes, rivers and wells. *Sadak* are lords of the earth and *tsen* are air spirits who can bring illness and death.

Many of the local deities are believed to have originally been Bon deities converted to Buddhism by Guru Rinpoche. Bon traditions and rituals are still practised in parts of Bhutan, especially during the celebration of local festivals. Many Bon traditions have subsequently merged into mainstream Buddhism.

An interesting, if rare, category of female religious figures is the *delog*. A *delog* is a woman, though occasionally a man, who has died and travelled to the other side, where they have watched the judgement of the dead and encountered various important figures in Buddhism (eg Chenresig or Guru Rinpoche), before returning to life. The *delogs* stress the importance of leading virtuous lives and refraining from causing harm to living beings.

Karma

As beings are reborn in samsara, their rebirths in the different realms of existence are determined by their karma, a kind of psychic baggage that follows each being from rebirth to rebirth. In Buddhist doctrine, karma refers to three important components: actions, their effects and their consequences. Buddhist teachings liken karma to a seed (action) that ripens into a fruit (effect).

Mahayana teachings say it is important to dedicate the merit of one's wholesome actions to the benefit of all living beings, ensuring that others also experience the results of one's positive actions. The giving of alms to the needy and to monks, the relinquishing of a son into the monkhood and acts of compassion are all meritorious and have a positive karmic outcome.

Pilgrims earn merit from the donation of food, money and oil for butter lamps, from sponsoring religious ceremonies or prayer flags, or from simply attending a festival or religious ritual on a particularly auspicious date.

Buddhism in Modern Bhutan

The modern state of Bhutan reflects an age-old system constructed by the first Zhabdrung. At the pinnacle of the new structure was the Zhabdrung. Below him he created the Je Khenpo (Chief Abbot), who was responsible for all religious matters. His secular counterpart was the *desi,* who was responsible for all political matters.

Organisation of the Religious Community

The *dratshang* (central monk body) refers to the government-supported monks who are under the authority of the Je Khenpo. He is assisted by four *lonpons* (masters), each in charge of religious tradition, liturgy, lexicography or logic. The Je Khenpo moves between Punakha Dzong in winter and Thimpu's Trashi Chho Dzong in summer. During this two-day journey, the roads are lined with Bhutanese seeking his blessings.

Each dzong has a *lam neten,* who is responsible for the monk body in each *dzongkhag.* Each dzong will have a master of grammar, master of liturgy, master of philosophy, an *umdze* (choirmaster) and a *kundun* (disciple master), who carries a rosary of large beads and a whip.

Traditionally, Bhutanese families would, if they were able, send one son to join a monastery. This was viewed as creating merit for the family and household and a blessing for the child. The fourth *desi,* Tenzin Rabgye, introduced a monk tax in the late 16th century. The reason for this tax, which required one child to be sent to become a monk, was to promote the Drukpa Kagyu sect.

Although there is no longer a monk tax, young boys continue to enter the monkhood. Visitors to Bhutan will see long snaking lines of maroon-robed boy monks walking near the dzongs in Paro and Punakha. Often they come from poor rural families and may or may not have expressed an interest in becoming a monk. Once in the monastery, their daily lives revolve around learning to read and write.

Monks are required to be celibate and must abstain from smoking and drinking alcohol, but they are not required to be vegetarian and may eat in the evening, unlike their counterparts in Southeast Asia.

Typically, the young monks will sit in class with a monk-teacher in the mornings and in the afternoon sit with friends in small groups, reciting their texts. Monastic schools for younger monks are known as *lobras,* as opposed to more advanced *shedra*s. Throughout a monk's education there is an emphasis on memorisation. So each day the monk will memorise a set amount of text and prayers, and will be tested by his teacher. When they are still young, the monks do not understand the meaning of the texts. Once they are in their mid-teens, they will be examined individually and they will either proceed to the *shedra* (Buddhist college) or perhaps join the ritual school. The *shedra* develops the young monk's knowledge and understanding of a range of Buddhist texts and teachings, while the school trains the monk in the correct procedures for a wide range of rituals.

While the government currently provides basic needs (accommodation, food and clothing), the monks are permitted to keep money received from lay people for performing rituals. They may be requested to attend the blessing of a new house or the consecration of a new chorten, or to conduct prayers for the well-being of the household. These events take a great deal of preparation for the sponsor, who will need to ensure that all the necessary ritual items are available. The sponsor will provide food for the monks and often the household will be filled with neighbours attending the ceremony. These events renew and strengthen the bonds between the lay and religious community.

Monks continually take vows as they progress from novice to fully ordained monk. A few monks join monastic orders after adolescence, but they are not the norm. Monks may renounce or return their vows at any time in order to return to lay life, often to start a family, and have to pay a token fine. These former monks are called *getres* or 'retired' monks and there is no social stigma attached to this choice. Some may even act as lay religious figures, called *gomchens*, and perform prayers and ceremonies for a range of daily activities, especially if there is no monastery nearby.

Domestic Rituals

Every house has a *choesum* (altar or shrine room). Each altar usually features statues of Sakyamuni, Guru Rinpoche and the Zhabdrung. In most homes and temples, devotees place seven bowls filled with water on altars. This simple offering is important because it can be given without greed or attachment. If offerings are made to the protective deities, such as Mahakala, then there are only five offering bowls. As all Himalayan Buddhists do, Bhutanese devotees prostrate themselves in front of altars and lamas, first clasping hands above the head, again at throat level and then at the chest. This represents the ultimate desire to attain the body *(ku)*, speech *(sung)* and mind *(thug)* of a Buddha.

Rites are performed for events and crises in life such as birth, marriage, promotion, illness and death. The rituals take place in front of the household shrine, or outside with an altar erected with an image of Buddha (representing the Buddha's body), a religious text (representing the Buddha's speech) and a small stupa or chorten (representing the Buddha's mind). The basic rituals of initiation, purification, consecration and the offering of a *torma* are included. For example, a water or incense purification ceremony is performed after a birth, while more elaborate rituals involving the offering of the eight auspicious symbols (ie Tashi Tagye) may be offered at a promotion or marriage. Astrology may be used to decide the timing of the rituals. Bhutanese often consult *tsips* (astrologers) before embarking on a journey or a new undertaking. Astrology plays an important role in overcoming misfortune and deciding the most appropriate time to perform rituals to avert misfortune.

Ordinary men and women do not typically engage in meditation or Buddhist philosophical studies, though many will attempt to complete the preliminary practices and will seek the blessings of lamas before embarking on new ventures, for their children and prosperity.

On special occasions monks prepare *torma* (ritual cakes), multicoloured sculptures made from *tsampa* (barley flour) and butter, as symbolic offerings to deities. Each deity is associated with a particular form of *torma*.

Some monks may be trained as painters or sculptors, or as tailors and embroiderers for the various items required for the monastery.

OTHER RELIGIONS

Not all Bhutanese are Buddhist. Many of the Lhotshampas, the descendants of Nepali migrants, are Hindu – as are the majority of the casual labourers from Assam and Bengal. There are still traces of animistic pre-Buddhist beliefs in the countryside and there's a small number of Christian converts. Bhutan is tolerant of all religions, but does not permit proselytisation. The Constitution upholds freedom of belief and does not make any religion the official religion of Bhutan. It does, however, recognise the importance of Bhutan's Buddhist heritage to the country's cultural identity.

Important Figures of Buddhism in Bhutan

This is a brief guide to the iconography of some of the main figures of Buddhism in Bhutan. This guide is neither exhaustive nor scholarly; rather it seeks to enable you to identify the main figures on altars and in the temple murals encountered during your trip. The Bhutanese names are generally given first with the Sanskrit (where applicable) in parentheses.

Buddhas

Sakyamuni

Sakyamuni

Sakyamuni is the historical Buddha (of the present age), whose teachings are the foundation of Bhutanese Buddhism. Typically in Bhutan, as in Tibet, Sakyamuni is represented as seated with his legs crossed on a lotus-flower throne. His tightly curled hair is bluish-black and there is a halo of enlightenment around his head. His right hand touches the ground in the 'witness' *mudra* (hand gesture) and his left rests on his lap, usually with an alms bowl in the left palm. His body is marked with 32 signs of enlightenment, including a top knot, three folds of skin on his neck and elongated ear lobes. He is often seen in the Dusum Sangye: the trinity of past, present and future Buddhas. A bowl of *drilbu* sits in front of all Sakyamuni statues in Bhutan, a gift from the fifth king to his people.

Opagme (Amitabha)

The Buddha of Infinite Light is one of the five *dhyani* (meditational or cosmic) Buddhas and resides in the Blissful Pure Land of the West (Sukhavati in Sanskrit or Dewachen in Dzongkha – also the name of several hotels in Bhutan). He is closely associated with Tsepame and Chenresig and represents the transformation of lust into wisdom. He is depicted seated cross-legged on a lotus throne, with his hands resting on his lap in meditative pose and holding an alms bowl. His body is red in colour.

Tsepame

The Buddha of Longevity, like Opagme, is red and holds his hands in meditation gesture, but he holds a vase containing the nectar of immortality. He is often seen in groups of nine.

DOS & DON'TS WHEN VISITING TEMPLES

Himalayan Buddhism has a generally relaxed approach to religious sites, but you should observe a few important rules if you are invited to enter a lhakhang (chapel) or goemba (monastery).

➜ It is customary to remove one's shoes upon entering the important rooms of a temple. You will most likely be escorted by a caretaker monk, and you can follow his example in removing your shoes at the appropriate doorway. Leave umbrellas and hats outside.

➜ Always move in a clockwise direction and do not speak loudly. If there is a ceremony being performed inside, always check first that it's OK to enter.

➜ It is customary to leave a small offering of money (Nu 10) on the altar. When you make this offering, the monk accompanying you will pour a small amount of holy water, from a sacred vessel called a *bumpa*, into your hand. You should make the gesture of drinking a sip of this water and then spread the rest on the top of your head.

➜ While male visitors may be permitted to enter the *goenkhang* (protector chapel), always ask before entering and remember that these are off-limits to all women. Do not walk behind an altar set before the *goenkhang*.

Jampa (Maitreya)

The future Buddha is said to be residing as a bodhisattva in Ganden (Tushita) – a heavenly realm where bodhisattvas reside awaiting full enlightenment and rebirth – until his time to incarnate on earth as a Buddha. Statues of Jampa, often giant, are the focal point in most older lhakhangs built before the visit of Guru Rinpoche. He is shown seated with his feet on the ground and hands in front of his chest, in the 'turning the wheel' *mudra*.

Jampa

Sangye Menlha (Medicine Buddha)

Sangye Menlha is a deep-blue Buddha who emanates healing rays of light and teaches the science of medicine *(men)*. Buddhism values medicine as a means to alleviate suffering and prolong human life, thereby improving the opportunity to attain enlightenment. The Medicine Buddha sits cross-legged on a lotus throne, with a bowl containing three medicinal fruits. He may be surrounded by a group of eight other medicine Buddhas.

Bodhisattvas

A bodhisattva (hero of enlightenment) seeks enlightenment for the sake of all living beings, out of heartfelt compassion and self-sacrifice, rather than seeking liberation from samsara for her or himself. This altruistic attitude is referred to as *bodhicitta* (mind of enlightenment).

Unlike Buddhas, bodhisattvas are often shown decorated with crowns and princely jewels. Keep a look out in goembas and lhakhangs for the Rigsum Goenpo – a trinity of Chenresig, Jampelyang and Chana Dorje.

BUDDHISM IN BHUTAN IMPORTANT FIGURES OF BUDDHISM IN BHUTAN

Chenresig (Avalokiteshvara)

The white Bodhisattva of Compassion is probably the best-known deity in Bhutanese Buddhism. Chenresig appears in a variety of forms. He is the 'glorious gentle one' – one of the four great bodhisattvas and the special guardian of Bhutanese religion – pictured sitting in a lotus position, with the lower two (of four) arms in a gesture of prayer.

There is also a powerful 11-headed, 1000-armed version known in Bhutan as Chaktong Chentong or Chuchizey. The head of this version is said to have exploded when confronted with myriad problems to solve. One of his heads is that of wrathful Chana Dorje (Vajrapani), and another (the top one) is that of Opagme (Amitabha), who is said to have reassembled Chenresig's body after it exploded. Each of the 1000 arms has an eye in the palm.

Chenresig

Jampelyang (Manjushri)

The 'princely lord of wisdom' – the embodiment of wisdom and knowledge – carries a flaming sword in his right hand to cut through delusion. As the patron of learning and the arts he cradles a scripture in his left arm. He is generally yellow.

Jampelyang

Chana Dorje (Vajrapani)

'Thunderbolt in hand' – this is the god of power and victory. His thunderbolt, representing power, is a fundamental symbol of Tantric faith; it is called a *dorji* in Tibetan and *vajra* in Sanskrit. He is pictured in a wrathful blue form with an angry face and one leg outstretched. You'll often see him flanking the entryway to chapels alongside the red deity Tamdrin.

Drolma (Tara)

There are 21 emanations of Drolma. The two most common representations are as Drolma, a green, female bodhisattva seated on a lotus flower with her right leg extended and said to have been born from a tear of compassion falling from Chenresig's face. The other form, known as

Chana Dorje

Drolma
(Green Tara)

Drolkhar
(White Tara)

Drolkhar (White Tara), is seated in the full lotus posture and has seven eyes, including one in her forehead, and one on each of her palms and the soles of her feet. Drolma is often seen as part of the Tsela Nam Sum longevity trinity, alongside Tsepame (Amitayus) and Namgyelma (Vijaya).

Protective Deities

Even the smallest lhakhang has a *goenkhang* (protector chapel) chockfull of terrifying wrathful deities, often engulfed in flames, dripping blood and holding an array of fearsome weapons. These can be specific local guardian deities, more general *yidam* (tutelary deities) or *dharmapala* (protectors of Buddhism), or symbols of malevolent beings that were subdued and converted by tantric forces. On an entirely other level they can also represent powerful attributes of the mind or ego, human beings' inner psychological demons if you will, with their many arms and weapons symbolising different powers. Often you'll see a protector deity in the *yab-yum* pose of sexual union with a female consort, in a symbolic representation of compassion and wisdom.

Most of Bhutan's valleys have their own local protective deity. Statues of Thimphu's protector, Gyenyen Jagpa Melen, appear in Dechenphu Lhakhang near Dechenchoeling and in Neykhang Lhakhang next to the dzong. He is also seen as a national protective deity, with Bhutanese visiting his temple to seek his blessings before a new venture or if leaving the country for any length of time. Among the other regional protective deities are Jichu Drakye in Paro, Chhundu in Haa, Talo Gyalpo Pehar in Punakha, Kaytshugpa in Wangdue Phodrang and, in Bumthang, Keybu Lungtsan and Jowo Ludud Drakpa Gyeltshen. These deities are gods who have not left the world and therefore have not gained enlightenment.

Nagpo Chenpo (Mahakala)

Mahakala (Great Black One) appears in a variety of forms in Bhutan and is one of the fiercest protective deities, aptly recognised as the guardian deity of Bhutan. He is also known as Yeshe Goenpo, often described as the overlord of all the mountain gods, and is a tantric Buddhist form of the Hindu god Shiva. Most Bhutanese monasteries and temples have a shrine dedicated to him and he is invoked to help remove obstacles to a new undertaking, or in times of danger. His worship in Bhutan was popularised by the Zhabdrung Ngawang Namgyal, who adopted the protector as his personal deity. According to legend, Mahakala appeared to the Zhabdrung in his raven form (Gompo Jarodanden) and advised him to go to Bhutan. The raven-headed Mahakala is the inspiration for the Raven Crown worn by the Bhutanese monarchs.

Mahakala is black with reddish hair that rises upwards. He has three eyes, wears a cloak of elephant skin, and is surrounded by fire and smoke. He wears various bone ornaments and a skull garland. He carries a curved knife in his right hand and a skull cup in his left. Depending on the form depicted, he may have two, four, six or more arms.

Palden Lhamo (Mahakali)

The Glorious Goddess is a fierce protective deity and is closely associated with Yeshe Gompo (Mahakala). Palden Lhamo is invoked in times of difficulty and special pujas are performed to avert misfortune, like natural disasters and wars. She has a ferocious appearance and is quite distinctive. Her body is dark blue, while the palms of her hands and the soles of her feet are red. She holds the moon in her hair, the sun in her belly and a corpse in her mouth, and wears a crown of five skulls and earrings made of snakes. She carries a skull cup in her left hand and brandishes a club in her right. She rides on a wild ass and her saddle cloth is a flayed human skin.

The Eight Auspicious Symbols (Tashi Tagye) are associated with gifts made to Sakyamuni and appear as protective motifs across Bhutan. They are the knot of eternity, wheel of law, lotus flower, fair of golden fishes, victory banner, previous umbrella, white conch and vase of treasure.

Top: Buddha Dordenma
(p55), Thimphu

Bottom: Prayer flags
(p250)

Historical Figures

Guru Rinpoche (Padmasambhava)

Seeds of Faith: A Comprehensive Guide to the Sacred Places of Bhutan (Volume 1, West Bhutan), by the KMT Research Group, is an expensive but excellent locally produced guide to Bhutan's spiritual places.

'The Lotus Born' was an Indian Buddhist adept, saint and tantric magician who, according to local tradition, helped found Buddhism in Bhutan in the 8th century. Popularly known as Guru Rinpoche (Precious Teacher), but also known as Pema Jungne or Padmasambhava (Lotus Born) in Sanskrit, he was born in Oddiyana (Ugyen in Dzongkha) in the modern-day Swat valley. He is viewed as nothing less than the Second Buddha by the Nyingma lineage. Dozens of caves and rock markings across Bhutan claim a sacred connection with the guru.

He is depicted seated in a half-lotus position on a lotus throne. He wears a blue inner robe with a golden robe and an outer red cloak. His hat is known as the 'lotus cap' and is adorned with a crescent moon, the sun and a small flame-like protuberance that signifies the union of lunar and solar forces. The hat is surmounted by a *dorji* (thunderbolt) and also an eagle's feather, which represents the Guru's soaring mind, penetrating the highest realms of reality. He has long flowing hair, bug eyes and a curly moustache. In his extended right hand he holds a *dorji* and in his left hand, resting on his lap, is a skull cup filled with nectar. A

PRAYER FLAGS

Prayer flags are ubiquitous in Bhutan, found fluttering on mountain passes and rooftops, and in dzong and temple courtyards.

Prayer flags come in five colours – blue, green, red, yellow and white – symbolising the elements of water, wood, fire, earth and iron, respectively. They also stand for the five *dhyani* (meditation Buddhas); the five wisdoms; the five directions; and the five mental attributes or emotions. The prayer for the flag is carved into wooden blocks and then printed on the cloth in repeating patterns.

Goendhar

The smallest prayer flags, *goendhars*, are those mounted on the rooftops of homes. These white banners have small blue, green, red and yellow ribbons attached to their edges. They invoke the blessings and patronage of Mahakala, the main protective deity of Bhutan. The flags are replaced annually during a ceremony that honours the family's personal local deities.

Lungdhar

The *lungdhar* (wind flag) is erected on hillsides or ridges and can be for good luck, protection from an illness, the achievement of a personal goal or the acquisition of wisdom. These flags are printed with the Wind Horse (Lungta), which carries a wish-fulfilling jewel on its back.

Manidhar

The *manidhar* is erected on behalf of a deceased person, and features prayers to the Bodhisattva of Compassion, Chenresig. These white prayer flags are generally erected in batches of 108 and are placed at strategic high points from which a river can be seen. In this way, the belief is that the prayers will waft with the wind to the river, and be carried by the river on its long and winding journey.

Lhadhar

The largest flag in the country is the *lhadhar* (god flag). These huge flags can be seen outside dzongs and other important places and represent victory over the forces of evil. There is normally no text on these flags; they are like a giant version of the *goendhar*. The only difference, apart from size, is at the top, where the *lhadhar* is capped by a colourful silk parasol. You must be formally dressed in traditional Bhutanese attire for Bhutanese and in appropriate dress for foreigners to enter any place where a *lhadhar* stands.

staff, known as a *katvanga,* topped with a freshly severed head, a decaying head and a skull, rests in the crook of his left arm. A *phurba* (ritual dagger for subduing demons) is tucked into his belt.

Guru Rinpoche commonly appears in eight manifestations known as the Guru Tshengye, of which the most eye-catching is the tiger-borne Dorji Drolo. He is often flanked by his two consorts Yeshe Tsogyel and Mandarava and is joined by his 25 main disciples. He is often depicted in his Copper Mountain paradise known as Zangto Pelri.

Guru Rinpoche

Milarepa

A great Tibetan magician (1040–1123) and poet of the Kagyu lineage, the 'Cotton Clad' magician-poet is believed to have attained the supreme enlightenment of Buddhahood in the course of one life. He travelled extensively throughout the Himalayan borderlands and is said to have meditated at Taktshang in Bhutan, where he composed a song. Most images of Milarepa picture him smiling and holding his hand to his ear as he sings. He is normally depicted in green due to his extended diet of nettle soup.

Milarepa

Drukpa Kunley

The wandering ascetic, Drukpa Kunley (1455–1529), is one of the main figures of the Druk Kagyu. His ribald songs and poems were unconventional and have earned him the affection of the Bhutanese. In Bhutan he is often depicted with a bow-and-arrow case and accompanied by a small hunting dog. In Chimi Lhakhang, Drukpa Kunley is depicted dressed similarly to the great Indian sages known as the Mahasiddhis, with a bare torso and a loincloth. Elsewhere he is shown wearing normal lay dress with boots.

Pema Lingpa

The blacksmith and *terton* (treasure finder) Pema Lingpa (1450–1521) was born in Tang valley, Bumthang. The best-known statue of Pema Lingpa was made by Pema Lingpa himself and is kept at Kunzangdrak Goemba, Bumthang. Pema Lingpa holds a *bumpa* (vase symbolising long life) in his hands and wears a hat similar to that worn by Guru Rinpoche, with the notable addition of two *dorjis* crossed at the front of it.

Zhabdrung Ngawang Namgyal

Zhabdrung Ngawang Namgyal (1594–1651) is regarded as the founder of Bhutan, where he arrived from Tibet in 1616. The Zhabdrung has a distinctive white, pointed beard and wears monastic robes, and is seated in the lotus posture. In his left hand he holds a *bumpa* and his right hand is in the 'witness' *mudra.* Over his right shoulder is a meditation belt. The Zhabdrung wears a distinctive ceremonial hat of the Druk Kagyu order.

Zhabdrung
Ngawang
Namgyal

BUDDHISM IN BHUTAN IMPORTANT FIGURES OF BUDDHISM IN BHUTAN

Arts & Architecture

Bhutan's vibrant art, dance, drama, music and even the characteristic architecture all have their roots in Buddhism. Almost all representation in art, music and dance is a dramatisation of the Buddha's teachings. Bhutanese architecture is one of the most striking features of the country. Massive dzongs (fort-monasteries), remote goembas (monasteries) and lhakhangs (temples), as well as the traditional houses, all subscribe to a characteristic Bhutanese style.

The Artistic Tradition in Bhutan

The development of Buddhist arts and crafts in Bhutan can be traced to the 15th-century *terton* (discoverer of sacred texts) Pema Lingpa, who was an accomplished painter, metalworker, sculptor and architect. The country's artistic tradition received a further boost when, in 1680, the fourth *desi* (secular ruler), Gyalse Tenzin Rabgye (r 1680–94), opened the School of Bhutanese Arts & Crafts, which has evolved into the National Institute for Zorig Chusum.

Traditional Bhutanese artistry is maintained through the support of all levels of society. The royal family, nobility and clergy continue to provide important patronage. Meanwhile, the common people support the arts because they depend on artisans to provide the wide variety of wooden and metal objects indispensable to typical Bhutanese households and painting, both inside and outside homes.

Traditional art has two important characteristics: it is religious and anonymous. The Bhutanese consider commissioning paintings and statues as pious acts, which gain merit for the *jinda* (patron). The name of the *jinda* is sometimes written on the work so that their pious act may be remembered. However, the artist's name is rarely ever mentioned, although there are some artists whose names do become well known due to the exceptional quality of their work.

There are strict iconographical conventions in Bhutanese art and the Bhutanese artists observe them scrupulously. However, artists do express their own personality in minor details (eg the shading of clouds or background scenes).

> Paintings and sculptures are usually executed by monks or laymen working in specialist workshops. The disciples of a master, as part of their training, will do all the preliminary work, while the fine work is executed by the master.

The Thirteen Arts

The Thirteen Arts are the traditional arts and crafts (Zorig Chusum) believed to have been categorised during the reign of the fourth *desi*, Tenzin Rabgye. Zorig Chusum refers to those physical activities that assist, teach or uplift others.

Shingzo (Carpentry)

Skilled carpenters are involved in a range of activities ranging from building dzongs (fort-monasteries) temples, houses and palaces; to making tools and other practical instruments used in the everyday life of the Bhutanese people.

Dozo (Masonry)

This covers the building of chortens, dzongs and temples as well as making the heavy millstones and stone pestles.

Parzo (Carving)

The Bhutanese are highly skilled at wood, stone and slate carving. Examples of their work are evident throughout Bhutan, from the slate carvings depicting the Buddha and other religious figures inserted in stupas to the wooden printing blocks used for printing sacred texts.

Lhazo (Painting)

Lhazo encompasses drawing and painting in Bhutan. It includes the painting of *thangkas* (religious pictures), murals and frescoes in temples and dzongs, as well as the colourful images on the exterior walls of Bhutanese homes. Drawing and painting are governed by strict geometric rules of proportion and iconography.

Jinzo (Sculpture)

One of the arts in which the Bhutanese excel is the creation of delicate clay sculptures, occasionally set in amazing landscapes. These sculptures, ranging from small- to large-scale statues, are generally created around a hollow frame with the mud or clay built up to form the image.

As well as statues, *jinzo* includes the production of a range of ritual items, notably the moulded offerings *(torma)* and masks worn during tsechus (dance festivals), and the more prosaic activity of preparing mud walls on new buildings.

Lugzo (Casting)

Casting, usually in bronze, refers to the production of musical instruments, statues, tools and kitchen utensils, as well as slip casting for pottery and jewellery.

Bhutan's Agency for Promotion of Indigenous Arts has introduced the Bhutan SEAL to establish a quality and authenticity benchmark for handicraft products.

ARTS & ARCHITECTURE THE THIRTEEN ARTS

TEXTILE TRAVELS

Watching the mesmerising weaving and appreciating the fine skills and sheer hard work is just part of the fun of chasing traditional textiles. With your guide you can start conversing with the weavers, perhaps picking up a few century-old tricks of the trade. Some friendly bartering is sure to follow. Handwoven fabric is the most traditional and useful item you can buy in Bhutan. The quality is almost always good, but the price will vary depending on the intricacy of the design and whether any expensive imported silk was used in the weaving. Handwoven fabric is sold in 'loom lengths' that are 30cm to 45cm wide and 2.5m to 3m long. Bhutanese sew three of these lengths together to make the traditional dress of *gho* and *kira*.

Some of the most striking fabrics feature intricate designs called *trima*, created via an embroidery-like technique where extra weft threads are coiled around the warp yarns to create distinctive geometric patterns. A *kira* with *trima* designs can take months to complete, and these fine pieces command huge price tags; prices of over US$1000 are not uncommon. Some of the most sought-after styles are *ngosham* on a blue ground and *kushuthara* pieces on a white silk ground.

The traditional centres of sophisticated weaving are in eastern Bhutan, especially Dungkhar and Khoma in Lhuentse, Khaling and Radi in Trashigang, and Duksum in Trashi Yangtse. Zungney village in Bumthang is the centre for the weaving of wool into strips called *yathra*. For those interested in textiles, visits to these places, in addition to Thimphu's National Textile Museum (p53), will provide an invaluable insight into Bhutan's cultural identity.

Garzo (Blacksmithing)

Generally, these craftspeople produce axes, plough blades, chains, knives and swords and other practical items.

Troko (Smithing)

This includes all ornaments made from gold, silver or copper. They are often cut out, beaten, drawn or engraved.

Tshazo (Bamboo Work)

There is a wide variety of these products, as seen in the markets across the country. They include *bangchung* (covered bowls with intricate designs, used to carry food), long *palang* (used to store beer or other liquor), the *tshesip* (box), *belo* (small hat worn for sun protection), *redi* (mat), *luchu* (used for storing grain), *balep* (bamboo thatch) and, of course, the bow and arrow.

Thagzo (Weaving)

Thagzo covers the whole process: the preparation of the yarn, the dyeing and the numerous designs. This is the largest craft industry in terms of the variety and number of craftspeople involved throughout Bhutan.

Tshemzo (Embroidery)

There are two special categories within this craft. The first is those items that are sewn and embroidered (ranging from clothing to intricate and rare embroidered *thangkas*). The second refers to appliqué and patchwork items made from stitching cloth together. This includes the large *thondrols* displayed during tsechu festivals, as well as hats and the elaborate boots worn with the *gho* on official occasions.

Shagzo (Woodturning)

Skilled woodturners produce a range of delicate wooden bowls, turned with expertise from special parts of a tree or roots. The large wooden *dapa* (serving dishes), wooden plates, buckets, ladles and *phop* (small cups), as well as the various small hand drums beaten during religious ceremonies, are among the products of this craft.

Dezo (Papermaking)

The art of making paper from the bark of the daphne plant, and more recently bamboo and rice stalks, is under threat from the loss of skilled craftsmen. The word *de* refers to the daphne plant.

Painting

Aside from spectacular architecture, the most visible manifestation of Bhutanese art is painting. There are three forms of traditional painting: *thangkas,* wall paintings and statues. A painting is invariably religious in nature depicting a deity, a religious story, a meditational object or an

Bhutan's wonderful wooden bowls are turned from lumpy 'burls' that usually grow around an infection or insect attack on a tree. Only the most intricately patterned burlwood goes into making the magnificent and highly valued *woogzo* bowls, so named for their owl-feather patterns.

PRAYER WHEELS

Spinning prayer wheels are an ubiquitous sight in Bhutan. The revolving cylinders are filled with printed prayers that are 'activated' each time the wheel is turned. Prayer wheels can be intricately decorated hand-held affairs *(mani lhakhor)* or building-sized *(mani dungkhor)* and every size in between. Some are effortlessly turned by diverted streams of water *(mani chhukhor)* or even hot air above a flame, whereas monks and devotees turn human-powered wheels to gain merit and to concentrate the mind on the mantras and prayers they are reciting. Remember to always turn a prayer wheel clockwise.

THE FOUR FRIENDS

One of Bhutan's favourite paintings is based on the popular fable of the Four Friends. In Dzongkha the name of the story is *Thuenpa Puen Shi* (Cooperation, Relation, Four) and it illustrates the concept of teamwork. You will see paintings illustrating this story on temples, homes and shops throughout the country.

The story tells how the elephant, monkey, peacock and rabbit combined forces to obtain a continual supply of fruit. The peacock found a seed and planted it, the rabbit watered it, the monkey fertilised it and the elephant guarded it. When the fruit was ripe, the tree was so high that they could not reach the top. The four animals made a tower by climbing on one another's back, and plucked the fruit from the high branches.

array of auspicious symbols (such as the Tashi Tagye – Eight Auspicious Symbols – or Four Friends). Paintings were traditionally done not for sale but for specific purposes – though this is slowly changing.

Paintings, in particular the portrayal of human figures, are subject to strict rules of iconography. The proportions and features must be precise, and there is no latitude for artistic licence in these works. The initial layout is constructed with a series of geometrical patterns, using straight lines to lay out the proportions of the figure, which are defined in religious documents called *zuri pata*. In other cases the initial sketch is made with a stencil of the basic outline, which is transferred to the canvas by patting the stencil with a bag filled with chalk dust. Traditionally, paints were made from earth, minerals and vegetables, though now chemical colours are also used. The material is first reduced into powder and then mixed with water, glue and chalk. The brushes are handmade from twigs and animal hair.

Thangkas are painted on canvas that is stretched and lashed to a wooden frame. When the painting is completed it is removed from the frame and given a border of colourful brocade, with wooden sticks at the top and bottom used for hanging. Although some *thangkas* are hung permanently, most are rolled up and stored until they are exhibited at special occasions. This applies particularly to the huge appliqué *thondrols* that are displayed briefly in the early morning during a tsechu. The same iconographical rules apply to the images on a massive *thondrol,* which demonstrates the skills of the Bhutanese artisans.

The interior walls of dzongs and lhakhangs are usually covered with paintings. In Bhutan most wall murals are painted on a thin layer of cloth applied to the wall using a special paste. Nowadays old paintings are treasured because of their historic and artistic value; however, until quite recently old wall paintings were often repainted or even painted over during restoration work.

Most statues are painted with sharply defined facial features typical to each individual figure. Many statues in lhakhangs are made from unfired clay. In addition to the face, the entire surface of these large figures is painted, often in a gold colour. On bronze statues only the face is painted.

Statues only gain their sanctity when sacred texts and juniper incense are secreted inside the statue; they are blessed and their eyes are painted open. You'll sometimes see unfinished statues with bandages around their unpainted eyes.

If you are interested in creating your own Bhutanese art, look out for *Tibetan Thangka Painting: Methods and Materials* by David P Jackson and Janice A Jackson.

Textiles

Weaving, more than the other Zorig Chusum, is the most distinctive and sophisticated of Bhutanese arts and crafts. The richness of this art form can be seen at the permanent exhibition in the National Textile Museum (p53) in Thimphu. Everyday articles such as clothing, wrappers for goods and cushion covers are stitched from cloth woven at home. Until the mid-20th century, certain taxes were paid in cloth and collected at the regional dzong. The authorities distributed the cloth as 'payment' to monastic and civil officials and to monasteries. Until quite recently, it was common to present cloth as a gift to mark special occasions or promotions. Bhutanese women still have trunks filled with fine fabrics that may be sold when money is required.

Unlike *thangka* painting, which has very precise religious rules, weaving provides the weaver with an opportunity to express herself. Designs, colours, sizes and even the finish have always reflected the materials available and the changes in technology and fashion. Bhutan's weavers specialise in working additional decorative warps and wefts into the 'ground' fabric. The most elaborate weavings are usually for the traditional *kira* and *gho* and these garments may take up to a year to weave in silk.

Legend states that weaving was introduced to Bhutan by the wife of Songtsen Gampo. Each region has its own weaving traditions and designs; that of Lhuentse, the ancestral home of the royal family, is the most renowned. The weavers in Lhuentse specialise in decorating *kira* and other textiles with intricate patterns that resemble embroidery. Other parts of eastern Bhutan are famous for their distinctive striped garments woven from raw silk. Bumthang weavers produce another popular fabric – *yathra,* hand-woven strips of woollen cloth, stitched into blankets, jackets, cushion covers and even car seats.

Though *yathra* was traditionally produced on back-strap looms, pedal looms were introduced from Tibet in the mid-20th century, while Indian spinning wheels are faster than the drop spindle. Today, all these technologies can be seen being used by weavers in their homes.

More recently, with assistance from the government, items such as bags, decorations and even bed and table linen have been developed both for the local and international markets.

> The royal Wangchuck dynasty's ancestral home is in the pre-eminent weaving district of Lhuentse, and perhaps this is why royal patronage has been so influential in the development of textile art, with dozens of weavers employed by all the royal households.

> The simple back-strap loom sometime used for weaving in Bhutan is similar to looms found throughout Southeast Asia and Tibet. The loom is easily transported and is ideal for setting up in a warm kitchen, on the porch of a house or beside a tent.

Literature

The development of *jo yig,* the cursive Bhutanese script, as distinct from a Tibetan script, is credited to a monk by the name of Lotsawa Denma Tsemang. However, the Bhutanese script is based on the Tibetan script introduced by Tonmi Sambhota during the reign of the Tibetan king, Songtsen Gampo. For the most part, the literary culture of Bhutan has been dominated by Buddhism; first as a means of translating Buddhist scriptures from Sanskrit, and later by local scholars as a means of developing Himalayan Buddhist thought.

Wood-block printing has been used for centuries and is still the most common form of printing in the monasteries. Blocks are carved in mirror image, then the printers working in pairs place strips of handmade paper over the inked blocks and a roller passes over the paper. The printed strip is then set aside to dry. The printed books are placed between two boards and wrapped in cloth. There is an excellent exhibition in the National Library (p56) in Thimphu, showing the printing process as well as examples of rare texts.

> Mountain Echoes (www.mountain echoes.org) is an annual literary festival that attracts writers, poets, artists and film-makers. It's held in Thimphu in August

Music

There are four main traditional instruments in Bhutan, beyond the ritual instruments used in religious ceremonies: the ornate *drangyen* or Bhutanese lute; the *pchewang,* with only two strings; *lyem* (bamboo flute); and the *yangchen* (zither) made from hollow wood, with 72 strings that are struck lightly with two thin bamboo sticks.

There are various performers who specialise in folk or religious songs, like Aum Thinlay Om. Jigme Drukpa *(Folk Songs from Bhutan)* performs a wide selection of the two main styles of folk singing: *zhungdra,* which developed in Bhutan in the 17th century, and *boedra,* influenced by Tibetan folk music.

There is a series of four CDs from the Monasteries of Bhutan, with the misleading title *Tibetan Buddhist Rites* (John Levy, Lyrichord). This collection includes a wide range of sacred and folk music, including a hauntingly beautiful recording of a *manip* (an itinerant ascetic) reciting a song recollecting the Zhabdrung Ngawang Namgyal's arrival in Bhutan.

Theatre & Dance

The main forms of dance are the spectacular and theatrical masked dances called *cham,* performed at the tsechus and other religious festivals held throughout Bhutan.

The main dances performed at tsechus are described here.

Durdag (Dance of the Lords of the Cremation Grounds)

Four dancers mostly clad in white and wearing white skull masks and long white gloves stamp out this dance with white boots on the first day of the tsechu. The dancers bend backwards, touching the earth to liberate the spirits of the deceased. The dance was composed by the Zhabdrung Ngawang Namgyal and the dancers represent the protectors of the religion who live in the eight cremation grounds on the edges of the symbolic Mt Meru.

Pacham (Dance of the Heroes)

This energetic dance based on a vision by Pema Linga is thought to lead believers directly to the presence of Guru Rinpoche. The dancers wear yellow skirts and golden crowns but do not wear masks. They carry a *dri-lbu* (small bell) and a *damaru* (small drum).

Shawa Shachi (Dance of the Stag & Hunter)

Based on the story of Milarepa's conversion of the hunter Gonpo Dorji to Buddhism, this dance is split into two parts. The first part is comic, with the hunter preparing to set out on a hunting expedition and his servants joking very irreverently with him. The second part is more serious. The hunter and his dog are in pursuit of a deer when the deer seeks shelter with the yogi Milarepa, identifiable by his white cotton robe, who sings a song that converts all three to Buddhism. The conversion is symbolised by a rope that both the dog and hunter must jump over.

Dranyeo Cham (Dance with the Dranyen)

This dance celebrates the diffusion of the Drukpa lineage in Bhutan by the Zhabdrung Ngawang Namgyal. The dancers carry swords and wear a circular headdress, felt boots and heavy woollen clothes. One dancer carries a *drangyen,* a stringed instrument similar to a lute.

Music of Bhutan Research Centre (www.musicofbhutan.org) promotes traditional music and has recorded many of Bhutan's living repositories of rare and regional music. It sells CDs and books online.

ARTS & ARCHITECTURE THEATRE & DANCE

In Thimphu, the Royal Academy for the Performing Arts trains young Bhutanese dancers and musicians in religious and folk dances. The quality of the dancing is exceptional and the program they offer is breathtaking in its colour and vitality.

BHUTAN BEAT

The music scene in Bhutan is small and the most popular local music, *rigsar,* is constantly evolving. *Rigsar* is typically performed on modern instruments, notably electric piano and synthesiser. *Rigsar* blends elements of traditional Bhutanese and Tibetan tunes, and is influenced by Hindi film music. Popular male and female *rigsar* performers often appear in locally produced films.

While contemporary and traditional Bhutanese music is widely available from little booths throughout Bhutan, groups struggle in a small market where massively popular karaoke has all but plundered every centimetre of available stage space. Check out Mojo Park (p69) in Thimphu for the latest in live music.

Sha Na Cham (Black Hat Dance)

This dance, on one level, commemorates the killing of the anti-Buddhist Tibetan king Langdarma in 842 by the Buddhist monk Pelkyi Dorji. It also represents the transformation of the dancers into powerful tantric yogis, who take possession of the dancing area and drive out all evil spirits as they stamp the ground. The dancers wear brocade dresses, wide-brimmed black hats, and black aprons with an image representing protective deities.

For a blend of traditional and modern music, look out for the beautiful recording of chants by Lama Gyurme and Jean-Philippe Rykiel: *The Lama's Chants – Songs of Awakening* (Sony, 1994) and *Rain of Blessings* (Real World Records, 2000 and 2017).

Pholay Molay (Dance of the Noblemen & Ladies)

This is less a dance than a crude play about the two princesses left with an old couple by two princes who leave for war. The two princesses and an old woman are corrupted by some *atsaras* (clowns). On their return, the princes are furious and punish the women by cutting off their noses. Eventually, everybody is reconciled and the princes marry the princesses.

Drametsi Nga Cham (Dance of the Drametsi Drummers)

Based on a vision by Kunga Gyeltshen, the son of Pema Lingpa, this dance depicts 100 peaceful and wrathful deities. The dancers wear animal masks and knee-length yellow skirts, and carry a large hand drum in their left hand and a drumstick in their right.

Dungtam (Dance of the Wrathful Deities)

In this dance, the deities are the entourage of one of the eight manifestations of Guru Rinpoche, Dorji Drolo. Dorji Drolo and his entourage are armed with *phurba* (special daggers) that execute and thereby redeem an evil spirit (represented by a small mannequin). This represents Buddhist teachings on the liberation of consciousness from the body. The dancers' costumes are beautiful brocade dresses, boots and terrifying masks.

Raksha Mangcham (Dance of the Rakshas & the Judgement of the Dead)

This is one of the highlights of the tsechu. It represents a spiritual drama as two newly deceased men are brought before the Lord of the Underworld, represented by a large mannequin surrounded by an entourage of *raksha*s (figures or spirits of the underworld). The first to be judged is a sinner, dressed in black. After hearing from Black Demon and White God, the prosecution and defence, his sins outweigh his good actions and he is dragged to the hell realms. The second figure is dressed in white; again the Lord of the Underworld hears about his good and bad actions, and he is found to be virtuous. After a brief attempt by Black Demon to grab the virtuous man, he is led to the pure lands.

Folk dances are often performed during breaks in the main tsechu performances. The dancers form a circle or a line and move in a series of steps with graceful arm movements. One person may lead the singing, with the other dancers picking up the song or answering with a refrain.

Guru Tshengay (The Eight Manifestations of Guru Rinpoche)

The eight manifestations are different forms of Guru Rinpoche, who is accompanied by his two consorts, Yeshe Tshogyel (on his right) and Mandarava (on his left). This is both a dance and a drama and starts with Dorji Drolo, wearing a terrifying red mask, entering the dance area, followed by a long procession with the eight manifestations.

Chhoeshey (Religious Song)

This commemorates the opening of the eastern gate to the pilgrimage site at Tsari in Tibet by Tsangpa Gyarey, the founder of the Drukpa Kagyu.

Architecture

One of the first things you notice about Bhutan is its distinctive architecture. The solid, rammed-earth farmhouses, the cliff-hugging goembas (monasteries) and lhakhangs (temples), and the impressive dzongs (fort-monasteries) follow a traditional pattern. Yet the absence of written plans means that there are many variations on the theme dictated by the local topography and available materials.

Dzongs

Bhutan's dzongs are perhaps the most visibly striking architectural aspect of the kingdom. They are outstanding examples of grand design and construction. These huge, white citadels dominate the major towns and serve as the administrative headquarters of all 20 *dzongkhags* (districts) and the focus of secular and religious authority in each.

As well as the large, active district dzongs, there are a few dzongs that have been destroyed or abandoned, or are now used for other purposes, such as Dobji Dzong, south of Chhuzom. And not all dzongs are ancient monuments; eg, a new dzong was inaugurated in Chhukha (near Phuentsholing) in 2012.

Many dzongs had a *ta dzong* (watchtower), which was either part of the building, as in Jakar Dzong (p136), or a separate structure, as in Paro (p79) and Trongsa (p129) dzongs. This structure was also used as an ammunition store and dungeon. Many dzongs were accessed by cantilever bridges as an additional protective measure. Most dzongs have inward-sloping walls, an architectural feature known as battered walls, which can fool the eye and make the building look imposing and larger than its actual dimensions.

Because dzongs were usually placed on ridges, a tunnel was often constructed to the nearest water supply so that those in the dzong could survive a long siege.

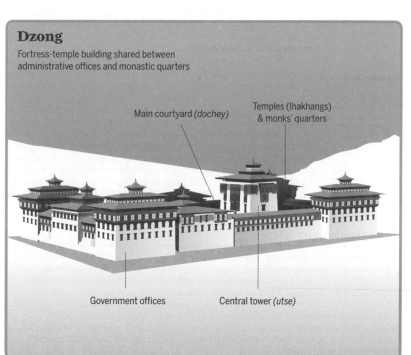

Dzong

Fortress-temple building shared between administrative offices and monastic quarters

Main courtyard (*dochey*)

Temples (lhakhangs) & monks' quarters

Government offices

Central tower (*utse*)

Bhutan's dzongs were built of stone or pounded mud, and a considerable amount of timber, including massive beams and wooden shingle roofs. This, combined with the large number of butter lamps used in temples, has caused fires in almost all dzongs. All important dzongs have been (or are being) rebuilt using traditional construction methods, though in many places corrugated-iron roofs have replaced wooden shingles.

Bhutanese proclaim proudly that no nails are used to construct dzongs. Furthermore, dzong architects don't prepare any plans or drawings. They rely only on a mental concept of what is to be built, and this was how Thimphu's Trashi Chho Dzong (p51) was reconstructed in 1966.

Each dzong has unique details, but most follow the same general design principles. Most dzongs are divided into two wings: one containing temples and monks' quarters and the other for government offices. The monastic wing of many dzongs actually serves as a monastery, with the resident monk body called a *rabdey*. In early days, most dzongs had a *rabdey,* but today only the dzongs of Thimphu, Chhukha, Punakha, Paro, Mongar, Trongsa, Jakar, Gasa and Trashigang serve as monasteries. The *dratshang* (central monk body) maintains monastic schools in the dzongs of Punakha, Trongsa and Paro. Punakha Dzong (p109) is the seat of the Chief Abbot, His Holiness the Je Khenpo.

The main courtyard of the dzong is the *dochey,* which is paved with large flagstones. Along the outer walls of the dzong are several storeys of rooms and galleries overlooking the paved courtyard; these rooms are the monks' quarters and classrooms. Because the monastic wing of the dzong is physically separate from the secular wing, many dzongs have two *docheys,* the second being surrounded by administrative offices.

The central structure of the dzong is a tower-like building called the *utse.* In most dzongs, the *utse* has a series of lhakhangs, one on each floor. On the ground floor of the *utse* is the primary lhakhang.

Goembas & Lhakhangs

In Dzongkha, a monastery is called a goemba, and the word is pronounced quite differently from the corresponding Tibetan word, *gompa.* A primary reason for selecting the location of a monastery is to have a remote location where the monks can find peace and solitude. This is particularly evident in Bhutan where goembas are built atop rocky crags or on remote hillsides.

All Bhutanese goembas are different, but they all possess certain common features. They are self-contained communities, with a central lhakhang (temple) and separate quarters for sleeping. The lhakhang is usually at the centre of a *dochey* (courtyard), similar to that of the dzongs, which is used as a dance arena during festivals. The term lhakhang can be a bit confusing because it can refer to both the building itself and

Don't-Miss Dzongs

....

Punakha Dzong (Punakha)

....

Paro Dzong (Paro)

....

Trongsa Dzong (Trongsa)

....

Trashi Chho Dzong (Thimphu)

DEFENDING THE DZONG

During the time of Zhabdrung Ngawang Namgyal (1594–1651), the dzongs served their primary function as fortresses well. Each was the stronghold of a *penlop* (governor). Many of the feuds and battles for control during the 17th to 20th centuries were waged by *penlops* whose troops attacked neighbouring dzongs. The key to success in these battles was to capture the dzong of the opposing *penlop,* thereby gaining control of that district. Dzongs often feature defensive windows with firing positions and usually have only one massive door, which leads into a small passage that makes two right-angle turns before it enters the main courtyard. This is a design feature to obstruct invaders from storming the dzong.

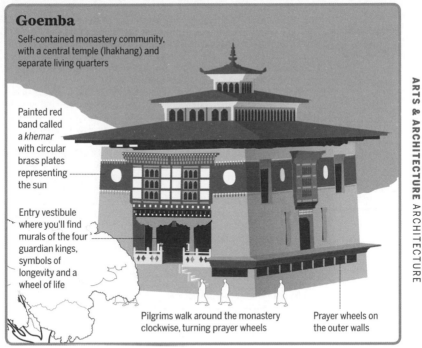

Goemba

Self-contained monastery community, with a central temple (lhakhang) and separate living quarters

Painted red band called a *khemar* with circular brass plates representing the sun

Entry vestibule where you'll find murals of the four guardian kings, symbols of longevity and a wheel of life

Pilgrims walk around the monastery clockwise, turning prayer wheels

Prayer wheels on the outer walls

to the primary chapel inside the building. Some goembas have several lhakhangs within the central building.

On all religious buildings in Bhutan, and on dzongs too, a painted red band called a *khemar* runs just below the roof. One or more circular brass plates or mirrors representing the *nima* (sun) are often placed on the *khemar*.

The following are often depicted at the entrance to goembas:

➡ The Wheel of Life, which is held and turned by Yama, Lord of Death; it is a representation of the cycle of samsara, separating loved ones and leading to rebirth. The inner circle depicts a cockerel (representing desire or attachment) biting a pig (ignorance or delusion) biting a snake (hatred or anger). Surrounding this is a band of figures ascending and descending according to their karma. Outside this are six segments, each depicting the six realms of samsara or rebirth. And outside this are the 12 segments that depict the 12 links of dependent origination representing the processes by which we all live, die and are reborn.

➡ The Six Symbols of Longevity (Tshering Samdrup) are of Chinese origin and include an old man, peach tree, conch-shaped rock, river, cranes (usually a pair) and a deer.

➡ The geometric poem set in a grid of squares (looking somewhat like a quilt) that is dedicated to the Zhabdrung.

A typical lhakhang has a cupola and a gilded bell-shaped ornament, called a *serto,* on top of the yellow-painted roof. Most have a paved *kora* path around the circumference of the building. On the outside wall are racks of prayer wheels, which monks and devotees spin as they circumambulate the building.

The entrance to the lhakhang is through the *gorikha* (porch), which is covered with murals, usually depicting the Guardians of the Four

One way that lhakhangs in Bhutan differ from those in Tibet is that they feature a pair of elephant tusks alongside the altar to symbolise good. Buddhists revere the elephant because when the Buddha was born, his mother had a vision of a white elephant.

Directions (p265) or the Wheel of Life. Entry is via a large painted wooden door that is often protected by a heavy cloth or yak-hair curtain. The door opens to a *tshokhang* (assembly hall), also called a *dukhang* or *kunre*. The hall is usually so large that it has rows of pillars to hold up the roof, and the walls are storyboards of Buddhist paintings.

At the far end of the *tshokhang* is an elaborately decorated altar *(choesum)* that can be part of the main room or else be housed in a separate room or lhakhang. The two-tiered *choesum*, with its large gilded statue, is a focal point of the lhakhang, and depending on when and why the lhakhang was built, the statue may be of Sakyamuni, Guru Rinpoche or another figure. Jampa is the central figure in many lhakhangs built before Guru Rinpoche's visits to Bhutan.

On a monastery or chapel altar, you'd see sacred rocks with self-arisen *(rangjung)* hand or footprints; a ewer of holy water with a peacock feather in it; a mandala-shaped offering of seeds; a pair of dice used to divine the future; dried seeds; plus elephant tusks and seven bowls of water, referring to the first seven footsteps of Buddha or the first seven ordained monks at Samye in Tibet. On the altar you will also see delicately carved and usually garishly coloured *torma* (ritual ornamental cake), made from sugar, butter and flour.

The halls often have cymbals, conch shell *(dungkhar)*, oboes *(jaling)* and long telescopic trumpets known as *dungchen*. The altar often has the bell *(drilbu)* and thunderbolt *(dorji)*, tantric implements that symbolise wisdom and compassion, respectively. Also in the halls are libraries of traditional texts and prayer books, usually wrapped in cloth.

In most lhakhangs, often on the upper floor, is a chapel called a *goenkhang*, which is devoted to the protective deities. The statues in these rooms are usually covered except when rituals are performed.

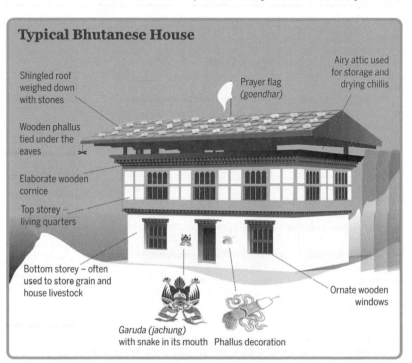

Typical Bhutanese House

Shingled roof weighed down with stones

Wooden phallus tied under the eaves

Elaborate wooden cornice

Top storey – living quarters

Bottom storey – often used to store grain and house livestock

Prayer flag (goendhar)

Airy attic used for storage and drying chillis

Ornate wooden windows

Garuda (jachung) with snake in its mouth   Phallus decoration

GUARDIANS OF THE FOUR DIRECTIONS

Paintings or statues of the Guardians (or Kings) of the Four Directions appear on the *gorikha* (porch) to guard the entrance to most lhakhangs. The guardians have an origin in ancient Mongolian tradition, and each one holds a different object. They are warriors who guard the world against demons and earthly threats.

Chenmizang The red king of the west; holds a chorten and a snake, and is the lord of the *nagas* (serpents).

Yulkhorsung The white king of the east; plays the lute and is the lord of celestial musicians.

Namthose The gold king of the north; holds a mongoose and a banner of victory. He is a god of wealth and prosperity.

Phagchepo The blue king of the south; holds a sword in his right hand.

Weapons are stored in this room and may include old muskets, armour and round shields made from rhinoceros hide. Teams of archers sometimes sleep in a *goenkhang* before a major match, but women are never allowed to enter and the monks are often reluctant to allow entry to visitors.

Houses

If, for the moment, we ignore the concrete blocks that are steadily taking over the major towns, the Bhutanese build distinctive housing depending on the region, particularly the elevation. Thatched bamboo houses predominate in the lower altitudes in the south of the country, whereas at very high altitudes most homes are simple stone structures or even yak-hair tents. In central and eastern Bhutan, at midrange altitudes, houses are often made of stone, whereas in the west the walls are usually made of compacted earth, an extremely strong and durable structure.

A typical western Bhutanese house is two storeys high with a large, airy attic used for storage. In rural areas, the ground floor is always used as a barn and the upper floor as the living quarters. In most houses, one elaborately decorated room called a *choesum* serves as a chapel.

On the lower floor, an opening for a door, and perhaps some windows, is left in the earth wall that forms the front of the house, which traditionally faces south. The upper floor is supported by wooden beams that fit into holes in the wall. Central columns support the beams, because it is difficult to find a single piece of timber to span the entire width of the house. The earthen walls for the upper floor form only the rear wall and back half of the two exterior side walls. The front portion of the living area is always built of timber, which is sometimes elaborately decorated, with large divided windows facing south. The wooden portion of the house extends out over the front and side earthen walls, giving a top-heavy appearance.

In older houses the windows are sliding wooden panels, not glass. Above all, windows in Bhutan comprise a cut-out of a curved trefoil motif, called a *horzhing*. In Bhutan there are often several explanations for everything, and this motif is said to be either of Persian influence or simply a practical design that allows a person to look out of the window while the smoke blows out through the opening above. An elaborate wooden cornice is usually built along the top of the wall, directly under the roof of the house. Traditional roofs are pitched and covered with wooden shingles (often weighed down by large stones as safeguards from the wind), but shingles need to be replaced frequently and most people now choose corrugated iron for their roofs. The internal walls,

Many houses are decorated with carved wooden phalluses, often crossed by a sword, which are hung at the four corners of the roof or over the door to ward off evil.

and often parts of the external walls, are built with a timber frame that is filled in with woven bamboo and plastered with mud. This construction is called *shaddam* (weave-mud).

Stairways to the upper floors and attic are often crude ladders made by carving steps into a whole tree trunk. If you find yourself climbing one of these ladders, reach around behind the right edge and you may find a groove cut there to serve as a handrail. Traditional Bhutanese long-drop toilets hang precariously off the side of the upper storey of old houses.

After a house is built, the all-important decoration begins. Wooden surfaces are painted with various designs, each with a special significance. Swastikas, floral patterns representing the lotus, cloud whirls and the Tashi Tagye (Eight Auspicious Symbols) are the most common. Beside the front door are larger paintings, often of mythical animals such as the *garuda*, or large red phalluses. The phallus is not a fertility symbol; it is associated with the Lama Drukpa Kunley and is believed to ward off evil. A prayer flag called a *goendhar* is erected on the centre of the roof of all Buddhist homes.

Chortens

A chorten is literally a receptacle for offerings, and in Bhutan all chortens contain religious relics. Chortens are often situated in locations considered inauspicious – river junctions, crossroads, mountain passes and bridges – to ward off evil. The classical chorten shape is based on the ancient Indian form of a stupa. Each of the chorten's five architectural elements has a symbolic meaning. The square or rectangular base symbolises earth. The hemispherical dome symbolises water. The conical or pyramidal spire symbolises fire (the spire has 13 steplike segments that symbolise the 13 steps leading to Buddhahood). On top is a crescent

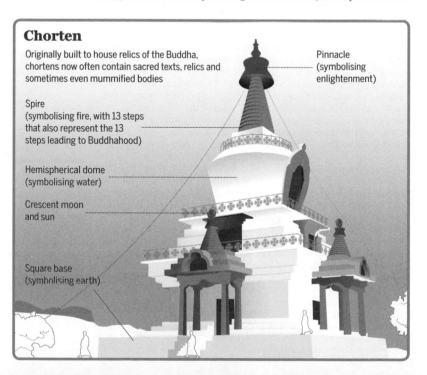

Chorten

Originally built to house relics of the Buddha, chortens now often contain sacred texts, relics and sometimes even mummified bodies

Pinnacle (symbolising enlightenment)

Spire
(symbolising fire, with 13 steps that also represent the 13 steps leading to Buddhahood)

Hemispherical dome
(symbolising water)

Crescent moon
and sun

Square base
(symbolising earth)

POUNDING THE WALLS

The massive compacted earth walls of typical western Bhutanese houses are 80cm to 100cm thick. To build these walls, a wooden frame is constructed then filled with mud. The mud is compacted by being pounded with wooden poles to which a flat ram is attached. When the wall reaches the top of the frame, the frame is shifted upwards and the process begins again.

The pounders are usually teams of women, who sing and dance as they beat the walls. Although Bhutanese women are usually shy and modest with outsiders, they traditionally loosen their inhibitions and exchange ribald comments with men as they perform the pounding, which can take several weeks for a large house. Once the mud wall is finished, it is either left in its natural colour or is whitewashed.

moon and a sun, symbolising air, and a vertical spike symbolising ether or the sacred light of the Buddha. Inside is placed a carved wooden pole called a *sokshing,* which is the life-spirit of the chorten.

Some chortens, such as the National Memorial Chorten (p53) in Thimphu, are built in memory of an individual. Others commemorate the visit of a saint or contain sacred books or the bodies of saints or great lamas. Bhutan has three basic styles of chorten, usually characterised as Nepali, Tibetan and Bhutanese.

The Nepali-style chorten is based on the classical stupa. On Nepali chortens the four sides of the tower are painted with a pair of eyes, the all-seeing eyes of Buddha. The prototypes for the Nepali chortens in Bhutan are Swayambhunath and Bodhnath in Kathmandu. The large Chorten Kora (p171) in Trashi Yangtse and Chendebji Chorten (p128) near Trongsa are two examples of the Nepali style of chorten.

The Tibetan-style chorten has a shape similar to the stupa, but the rounded part flares outward instead of being a dome shape. Thimphu's National Memorial Chorten (p53) is an excellent example of this style.

The Bhutanese design comprises a square stone pillar with a *khemar* near the top. The exact origin of this style is not known, but is believed to be a reduced form of the classical stupa, with only the pinnacle and square base. Some Bhutanese chortens have a ball and crescent representing the moon and sun on top.

Several other types of chorten are also found in Bhutan. The *khonying* (two legs) is an archway that forms a gate over a trail. Travellers earn merit by passing through the structure, which is decorated with interior wall paintings and a mandala on the roof. The *mani chukor* is shaped like a Bhutanese chorten, but is hollow and contains a large prayer wheel. It is built over or near a stream so that the water turns a wooden turbine below the structure, which then turns the prayer wheel.

When approaching a chorten, large prayer flag or a *mani* wall, always walk to the left, just as you would keep a lhakhang on your right side as you circumambulate it.

The Natural World

Bhutan boasts a tremendous diversity of plants and animals flourishing in a range of ecosystems, from subtropical jungle barely above sea level to snowbound mountains. Scientists have long considered the eastern Himalaya to be globally important in terms of biological diversity. Add to this the relatively recent history of isolation, the inaccessibility of much of the country and a low human population with a reverence for all life forms, and you have the ingredients for an outstanding showcase of nature.

The Lie of the Land

Bhutan is a landlocked country about 300km long and 150km wide, encompassing 46,500 sq km. It is bounded on the northwest and north by Tibet, and the remainder by India: on the east by the state of Arunachal Pradesh; on the south by Assam and West Bengal; and on the west by Sikkim. Tibet's Chumbi valley, the old trade and expedition route from India to Lhasa, lies between the northern parts of Bhutan and Sikkim.

Almost the entire country is mountainous and with elevations ranging from 100m to the 7541m Gangkhar Puensum peak on the Tibetan border. It can be divided into three major geographic regions: the high or Greater Himalaya of the north; the hills and valleys of the Inner Himalaya; and the foothills and plains of the south.

Millions of years ago the space now occupied by Bhutan was an open expanse of water, part of the shallow Tethys Sea. The Tibetan plateau ('Roof of the World') was beachfront property.

Greater Himalaya

A range of high Himalayan peaks forms much of the northern and western borders of Bhutan. These are the thrones of the gods; almost none has been climbed, many are virtually unexplored and some are not even named. There are several high mountain passes that cross the Himalaya, but for the most part it remains an impenetrable snow-clad barrier (20% of the country is under perpetual snow). The Himalayan range extends from Jhomolhari (7314m) in the west to Kulha Gangri (7554m), near the centre point of the northern border. A chain of lower peaks extends eastwards to the Indian state of Arunachal Pradesh.

The Lunana region, just south of the midpoint of Bhutan's border with Tibet, is an area of glacial peaks and high valleys that are snowbound during winter. A range of high peaks forms the southern boundary of Lunana, isolating it from the rest of the country.

Inner Himalaya

Trees and Shrubs of Nepal and the Himalayas, by Adrian and Jimmie Storrs, is the best field guide to the forests of Bhutan.

South of the high peaks is an area of broad, deep valleys and steep forested hills ranging from 1100m to 3500m in elevation. This is the largest region of Bhutan and all the major towns, including Thimphu, are here. This region is a labyrinth of deep ravines formed by fast-flowing rivers. The hillsides are generally too steep for farming, and so most have remained covered in forest.

The greater part of Bhutan's western border is formed by the Himalayan range, including the peaks of Jhomolhari and Jichu Drakye (6989m). Several forested ridges extend eastwards from this range, and these define the large valleys of Thimphu, Paro, Haa and Samtse. Between

Punakha and Thimphu lies a well-defined ridge that forms the water-shed between Thimphu's Wang Chhu and Punakha's Puna Tsang Chhu. The east–west road crosses this ridge over a 3050m pass, Dochu La.

A range called the Black Mountains lies to the east of the Puna Tsang Chhu watershed, forming the major barrier between eastern and western Bhutan. Pele La (3420m) is the most important pass across the Black Mountains.

A north–south range of hills separates the Trongsa and Bumthang valley systems. The road crosses this ridge via Yotong La (3425m). Further east, the Donga range of hills follows the border separating the Bumthang and Lhuentse districts, with Thrumshing La (3780m) as the crossing point for the road. Eastern Bhutan, which encompasses most of the Manas Chhu watershed, lies to the east of this range.

The Duars

The southern foothills rapidly drop down to the great plain of India, and with the large and powerful rivers flowing from the north they comprise a region of lush fertile valleys known as the *duars*. *Duar* is a Sanskrit word meaning 'passes' or 'gates', and is the origin of the English word 'door'. Before the British annexed Bhutan's southern regions, each *duar* was under the control of a Bhutanese *dzongpen* (lord of the dzong), but as they were malaria-infested they were largely unoccupied by the Bhutanese, who stayed in the northern hills.

Each *duar* is named after a river valley that leads out of Bhutan, though the *duar* itself is actually the land between two rivers. The land ranges from an elevation of about 100m to almost sea level at the Brahmaputra River, and the slope is barely perceptible.

Seven of the *duars* abut the border of Assam between the Dhansiri (Durlah) and Manas Rivers. The remaining 11, from the Manas River to the Teesta River in the east, border on the state of West Bengal.

Mighty Rivers

Rivers (*chhus*) play an important role in Bhutan's geography, and their enormous potential for hydroelectric power has helped shape the economy. Most of the rivers have their headwaters in the high mountains of Bhutan, but there are three that flow across borders into the country. The Amo Chhu flows from Tibet's Chumbi valley across the southwestern corner of Bhutan, where it becomes the Torsa Chhu, and exits at Phuentsholing. Two tributaries of the Manas, in eastern Bhutan, originate outside the country. The Kuri Chhu has its headwaters in Tibet (where it is known as the Lhobrak Chhu) and crosses into Bhutan at an elevation of only 1200m; the other tributary, the Gamri Chhu, rises in India's Arunachal Pradesh.

All of Bhutan's rivers eventually flow through the fertile *duars* to become part of the Brahmaputra, which is known in Tibet as the Yarlung Tsampo, with a source near Mt Kailash in the far west.

BHUTAN ON A PLATE

The Himalaya continue to buckle and rise under the influence of plate tectonics; and the consequences are regularly felt in Bhutan. In 2009 a 6.1 magnitude quake, centred in Mongar, shook the entire country, causing fatalities and destruction. In 2011 the 6.9 magnitude Sikkim earthquake also caused damage and one death in Bhutan. The devastating Nepal earthquake of 2015 was felt in Bhutan, but there was no significant damage. While Bhutan does not yet have a permanent seismometer network, a temporary network was set up in 2013–14, which indicated numerous small earthquakes occur on a daily basis, most of which are undetectable by humans.

Bhutan's Green Vault

An astonishing array of plants grows in Bhutan: over 5000 species, including more than 600 species of orchid, 300 species of medicinal plants and about 46 species of spectacular rhododendrons. Few countries could boast the variety of habitats from subtropical jungle to alpine tundra in such a compact area. Because glaciation had no impact on the lower reaches of the Himalaya, these foothills remain repositories of plants whose origins can be traced back before the ice age. This area is home to some of the most ancient species of vegetation on earth.

Forests are found up to 4500m and serve not only as a source of fuel, timber and herbs, but also as a cultural resource, as they form the basis of many folk songs and ritual offerings. Though the government policy is to maintain at least 60% of the land as forest, the present ratio is higher, and that is indeed good news. However, it's hard to separate myth from fact. Estimates as high as 71% forest cover include shrubland, abandoned farmland and conifer and broadleaf forests. Furthermore, in recent years there has been significant development in Bhutan's forests with increased efforts in forestry, mining, road building and hydro projects, plus an increase in forest fires, all impacting forest cover negatively. On the plus side there have been large-scale reafforestation initiatives. In 2015 Bhutan claimed a Guinness world record for planting 49,672 trees in one hour, and in 2016, in celebration of Prince Jigme Namgyel Wangchuck's birth, 108,000 saplings were planted across the nation.

> Wild Rhododendrons of Bhutan, by Rebecca Pradhan, is a beautiful guide to Bhutan's rhododendrons, with photographs of all 46 species.

Warm & Wet Subtropics

Subtropical evergreen forests growing below 800m are unique repositories of biodiversity, but much of the rich vegetation at these lower elevations has been cleared for pasture and terraced farmland. In the next vegetation zone (900m to 1800m) are the subtropical grasslands, including groves of fragrant lemon grass and bamboo. Forests here comprise chir pine, oak, walnut and sal. Numerous varieties of orchid and fern grace the branches of the forest giants.

> You can easily distinguish the chir pine from the blue pine, because the needles of the chir pine are in groups of three and those of the blue pine are shorter and in groups of five.

Deep & Dark Forests

The subtropical vegetation of the lower altitudes gives way to the diverse, dense and dark forests of oak, birch, maple, magnolia and laurel of the temperate zone (1800m to 3500m). On most hills, the sunny south side takes on countless shades of green with a variety of broadleaf species. The damp, shady north side displays a more dour appearance with blue pine and soaring deodars and firs festooned with old man's beard. Spring is the time to see the magnificent red-, pink- or cream-flowering rhododendrons of Bhutan that feature on the mountain passes of Dochu La, Pele La and Yotung La.

Alpine Flower Meadows

Between the treeline and the snow line at about 5500m are found low shrubs, dwarf rhododendrons and flowering herbs. Junipers can also be seen in a dwarf form at altitudes over 4000m.

> Between March and May the hillsides are ablaze with the deep red flowers of the *etho metho*, the country's most famous rhododendron. Ranging from small shrubs to 20m trees, 46 species of rhododendron occur throughout the country.

As the snows begin to melt at the end of winter, the high-altitude grazing lands are carpeted with wildflowers, which remain in bloom until early summer. After the onset of the monsoon in July, a second and even more vibrant flowering occurs, which extends until late August. Some of the magnificent blooms found at these higher elevations include anemones, forget-me-nots, dwarf irises, primulas, delphiniums and ranunculus.

Wildlife

Mammals

Large mammals abound in the wilds of Bhutan, but unless you are trekking or exploring Royal Manas National Park (p153) you will be very lucky to see more than a few examples. The neighbourhood of Royal Manas is home to a large variety of well-known south Asian species: water buffalo, gaur, serow, wild pig, smooth-coated otter and several species of deer (sambar, muntjac, chital and hog). It is also the best place to see Asian elephants and the very rare greater one-horned rhinoceros.

While trekking on the high trails you may well be lucky enough to spot herds of blue sheep (bharal). Blue sheep are goat-antelopes, taxonomically somewhere between goats and sheep, that turn a bluish grey in winter and are found at between 1800m and 4300m. Other mammals that prefer the high life include wolves, yaks and the diminutive, unusual musk deer. The male's musk gland is a highly valued perfume ingredient and this secretive deer is a target for indiscriminate poaching. Fat marmots whistle as you pass their burrows in the high alpine pastures and the curious takins can be seen in northwestern and far northeastern Bhutan. However, the most likely place to spot a takin is in the Motithang Takin Preserve (p56) in Thimphu.

Monkeys

Several species of monkey are found in Bhutan and some of these are active throughout the day and may be seen not far from villages or a main road – so keep an eye on the roadside trees on those long drives. Most common are the Assamese macaques: reddish-brown, stumpy-tailed monkeys travelling on the ground in troops of 10 to 50 individuals. They are found throughout Bhutan up to 2900m. Rhesus macaques are similar and are the dominant monkey of the Indian plains. In Bhutan the bold rhesus is confined to the southern foothills.

Langurs are elegant, arboreal monkeys with graceful limbs, extraordinarily long tails and a charismatic presence. Three species of langur make a home in Bhutan's forests – up to 3600m in altitude, and usually high up in the forest canopy. The common grey or Hanuman langur is found west of Pele La; the capped langur is found east of the Manas Chhu in eastern Bhutan; while the famous golden langur is only found from the Puna Tsang Chhu in the west to the Manas Chhu in the east. Keep an eye out for troops of them on the drive from Trongsa to Zhemgang. This beautiful primate's existence was not even known to the scientific

---

Best Places for Wildlife-spotting

Bomdeling (p173) – capped langurs

Jhomolhari trek (p188) – blue sheep

Kori La (p164) – hornbills, barbets and more

Phobjikha valley (p116) – black-necked cranes

Zhemgang (p151) – golden langurs

The most authoritative guide to Bhutan's mammals, their identification, behaviour and distribution is *A Field Guide to the Mammals of Bhutan*, by Tashi Wangchuk, available in most Thimphu bookshops.

THE BLUE POPPY

The blue poppy, Bhutan's national flower, is a delicate blue- or purple-tinged bloom with a white filament. In Dzongkha it is known by the name *euitgel metog hoem*. It grows to nearly 1m tall on the rocky mountain terrain found above the treeline (3500m to 4500m). The flowering season occurs during the early monsoon, from late May to July, and the seeds yield oil. Adding to its mystery, fascination and appeal with plant lovers is its strange flowering behaviour. It takes several years to grow, then it eventually flowers for the first and last time, produces seeds, and dies. Poppies can be found atop some high passes from the far eastern parts of the country all the way across to the west.

At one time the blue poppy was considered to be a Himalayan myth, along with the *migoi* (yeti). In 1933 a British botanist, George Sherriff, who was in Bhutan studying Himalayan flora, found the plant in the remote mountain region of Sakteng in eastern Bhutan. Despite this proof, few people have seen one; a mystique surrounds the species in the same way it does the snow leopard.

community until the 20th century. Not surprisingly, its distinctive feature is its lustrous blonde-to-golden coat. Also around Zhemgang are troops of mixed capped and golden lineage.

The grey, golden and capped langurs have a specially adapted stomach for digesting forest leaves and are not an agricultural pest.

Big Cats

Several species of cat, ranging from the moggy-sized jungle cat to the powerful tiger, prowl the forests, valleys and mountains of Bhutan. The other cats are the Asiatic golden cat, marbled cat, Pallas's cat, leopard cat, fishing cat, lynx, clouded leopard, common leopard and the enigmatic snow leopard.

The essentially solitary tiger is a symbol of great reverence in Bhutan. There are only around 100, mostly in and around Royal Manas National Park (p153), though tigers roam throughout Bhutan, even to high altitudes (4100m), and as far north as Jigme Dorji National Park. In 2012 a tiger was photographed on a camera trap near Dochu La.

Several tiger-conservation measures have been implemented in Bhutan and, coupled with the strong protected-areas system, have provided a favourable environment for the animal. It is believed the protected

THE TAKIN – BHUTAN'S NATIONAL ANIMAL

The reason for selecting the takin as the national animal is based both on its uniqueness and its strong association with the country's religious history and mythology. When the great saint Lama Drukpa Kunley, the Divine Madman, visited Bhutan in the 15th century, a large congregation of devotees gathered from around the country to witness his magical powers. The people urged the lama to perform a miracle.

However, the saint, in his usual unorthodox and outrageous way, demanded that he first be served a whole cow and a goat for lunch. He devoured these with relish and left only the bones. After letting out a large and satisfied burp, he took the goat's head and stuck it onto the bones of the cow. And then with a snap of his fingers he commanded the strange beast to rise up and graze on the mountainside. To the astonishment of the people, the animal arose and ran up to the meadows to graze. This animal came to be known as the *dong gyem tsey* (takin) and to this day these clumsy-looking animals can be seen grazing on the mountainsides of Bhutan.

The takin continues to befuddle taxonomists. The famous biologist George Schaller called it a 'beestung moose'. In summer, takins migrate to subalpine forests and alpine meadows above 3700m to graze on luxuriant grasses, herbs and shrubs. By migrating they escape the leeches, mosquitoes, horseflies and other parasites of the monsoon-swept lower valleys. This is also the time when the alpine vegetation is richest in nutrition and takins gain weight easily: some males become massive, weighing a tonne or more. Summer is also the time when takins mate. The gestation period is between seven and eight months, and their young – usually a single calf – are born between December and February. Sometimes the Himalayan black bear will follow a pregnant takin and immediately after she has given birth, chase her away and eat the calf.

In late August takins start their slow descent to the lower valleys where the herds begin to break up. They arrive at the winter grazing grounds in temperate broadleaf forests between 2000m and 3000m by late October.

Hunting is banned by law and poaching is limited since there is no high economic value placed on the body parts of the takin. In traditional medicine, however, the horn of the takin, consumed in minute amounts, is supposed to help women during a difficult childbirth.

The major threats that the takin faces are competition with domestic yaks for grazing in the alpine meadows and the loss of habitat in the temperate forests.

regions of Bhutan and India provide sufficient habitat to sustain viable breeding populations, although this has to be put in context: the world's tiger population has been reduced by over 95% in the last century owing to human expansion and intervention.

With its extraordinarily beautiful dappled silver coat, the snow leopard has been hunted relentlessly throughout its range and is in danger of extinction. This elusive cat is almost entirely solitary, largely because a single animal's hunting territory is so vast and its prey is so scarce throughout its high-altitude habitat. However, when its favourite prey, the blue sheep, migrates to lower valleys in winter, the snow leopard follows them. It is then that the sexes meet.

Bears & Red Pandas

There are two species of bear found in Bhutan. The omnivorous Himalayan black bear is a bane to farmers growing corn and fruit near the temperate forests (1200m to 3500m) it frequents, whereas the sloth bear is principally a termite eater and honey pirate found at lower altitudes. Bears do occasionally attack humans, probably because their poor eyesight leads them to interpret that a standing person is making a threatening gesture.

The red panda is known in Bhutan as *aamchu donkha* and is most commonly found near Pele La, Thrumshing La and parts of the Gasa district. It is bright-chestnut coloured, about 50cm long, including its bushy, banded tail, and has a white face. The red panda is nocturnal, sleeping in trees during the day and coming to the ground to forage on bamboo and raid birds' nests at night.

Birds

Each year Bhutan's extensive bird list grows longer, a consequence of Bhutan's rich biodiversity and relatively small amount of systematic birding that has been done in the kingdom. Over 600 species have been recorded and birdwatching tours are extremely popular.

Bhutan is rightly famous for its wintering populations of the vulnerable black-necked crane (p272). Less well known are the winter populations, mainly as solitary individuals, of the critically endangered white-bellied heron, listed as one of the 50 rarest birds in the world with no more than 250 individuals worldwide. This graceful bird may – with luck – be seen from the road in the vicinity of Punakha, Wangdue Phodrang and Zhemgang, especially along the Mangde Chhu valley.

Some bird species are even more transient, migrating through Bhutan between Tibet and northern India in autumn and spring. Pallas's fish eagle, which is considered rare, is regularly seen migrating up the Punak Chhu near Wangdue Phodrang in spring. It is often in the company of ospreys, a wide range of ducks, waders such as the pied avocet, and other birds that breed in Tibet.

The raven is the national bird of Bhutan. A raven guided the Zhabdrung to Bhutan in 1616, and it gives its name to the raven-shaped crown worn by the kings of Bhutan.

Winter brings numerous species down to lower altitudes, including accentors, rosefinches, grosbeaks, snow pigeons and pheasants, such as the satyr tragopan, the Himalayan monal and the blood pheasant. Observant early morning walkers can often find these on the mountains and passes around Thimphu. In summer many lowland species move to higher altitudes to breed; these species include the comic-looking hoopoe, various species of minivets, cuckoos (one can commonly hear at least five different species calling), barbets, warblers, sunbirds, fulvettas and yuhinas.

Bhutanese Tales of the Yeti, by Kunzang Choden, describes Bhutanese beliefs about where and how this mysterious creature may live.

The musk deer is a primitive deer that has no antlers; both sexes have oversized protruding canine teeth that are up to 7cm long in males and used in territorial battles.

THE NATURAL WORLD WILDLIFE

THE BLACK-NECKED CRANE

The rare and vulnerable black-necked crane occupies a special place in Bhutanese hearts and folklore. Its arrival every autumn from Tibet inspires songs and dances; it usually heralds the end of the harvesting season and also the time when farming families start migrating to warmer climates.

Many legends and myths exist about the bird, which the Bhutanese call *thrung thrung karmo*. Wetlands of the high mountain valleys of Phobjikha, Bomdeling and Gaytsa serve as the winter habitat for about 600 birds. Like other cranes, these have an elaborate mating ritual, a dance in which pairs bow, leap into the air and toss vegetation about while uttering loud bugling calls. It can be difficult to distinguish the sexes because the colouration is so similar, but the females are slightly smaller. The crane's preferred delicacies include fallen grain, tubers and insects.

The world's entire population of 9000 to 11,000 black-necked cranes breeds in Tibet and Ladakh. As well as in Bhutan, they winter in south-central Tibet and northeastern Yunan province in China.

The Royal Society for Protection of Nature (www.rspnbhutan.org), which is involved in conservation, education and inspiring the Bhutanese populace, annually monitors the black-necked cranes in the Phobjikha and Bomdeling valleys and has produced videos of them. For more on cranes generally, including a downloadable field guide, visit the International Crane Foundation (www.savingcranes.org).

Given the density of forest cover and the steep vertical descents, the road is often the best place from which to spot birds. Recommended stretches include the road down from Dochu La to Wangdue Phodrang (the adventurous can take the old trail, which is even better), from Wangdue Phodrang to Nobding (on the way to Pele La), and from Tingtibi to Panbang. For those who go east, the 2000m descent between Sengor and Lingmethang is spectacular: the rufous-necked hornbill and Ward's trogon have been recorded in this area. But stay on the lookout on all the roads – we spotted a pair of rufus-necked hornbills near Gedu, on the road between Thimphu and Phuentsholing.

Trekking will provide you with a greater chance of seeing high-altitude birds, including the lammergeier, the Himalayan griffon, the raven, the unique high-altitude wader, the ibisbill and several colourful pheasants.

National Parks & Protected Areas

There are five national parks, four wildlife sanctuaries and one nature reserve, which together constitute about 43% of the country, or 16,396 sq km. An additional 3307 sq km is designated as a network of biological corridors linking all nine protected areas, putting 52% of the country under some form of protection.

Birds of Bhutan, by Carol Inskipp, Tim Inskipp and Richard Grimmett, is a comprehensive, illustrated guide to Bhutan's avian treasures.

All but three of the protected areas encompass regions in which there is a resident human population. Preserving the culture and fostering local tradition is part of the mandate of Bhutan's national-park system. The government has developed an integrated conservation and development program to allow people living within a protected area to continue to farm, graze animals, collect plants and cut firewood.

Bhutan established its national-park system to protect important ecosystems, and for the most part they have not been developed as tourist attractions. Apart from one or two exceptions, you won't find the kind of facilities you may normally associate with national parks, such as entrance stations, campgrounds and visitor centres. In many cases you won't even be aware that you are entering or leaving a national park.

Top: View from Khamsum Yuelley Namgyal Chorten (p113)

Bottom: Takin, Bhutan's national animal (p270)

MATHIAS BERLIN / SHUTTERSTOCK ©

WWLOECK / GETTY IMAGES ©

Environmental Challenges

Bhutan entered the 20th century with much of its forests and ecosystems intact. But now, with an increasing population, improved and expanding roads and limited farming land, a major effort is required to protect the country's natural heritage.

Growing awareness of environmental issues has prompted appropriate conservation measures. Among these are nationwide bans on the commercial export of raw timber and the use of plastic bags. While Bhutan has consciously decided to forego immediate economic gain from exploitation of its natural resources in order to preserve its environment for long-term sustainable benefits, the pressure to develop and keep up with neighbours China and India is a hot topic across the nation.

Global Warming & Glacial Timebombs

It's no small tragedy that the tiny villages of rural Bhutan, which insignificantly contribute to greenhouse gases, are on the front line of global warming's consequences. Bhutan is the only country that can boast being carbon negative on a planet rapidly warming as more and more greenhouse gases are pumped into the atmosphere. Across the Himalaya, glacier lakes are filling up with many millions of cubic metres of meltwater as glaciers recede at 30m to 60m per decade. In recent decades there has been a tenfold increase in glacier-lake outbursts. In Bhutan there are 25 lakes considered to be in danger of bursting.

In 1994 a glacier-lake outburst swept 10 million cubic metres of water down the Po Chhu. It flooded a number of villages and killed 23 people in Punakha, 80km downstream. In 2015 Lemthang Tsho suddenly emptied its entire volume into the Mo Chhu system, thankfully without much damage. In addition to increased monitoring of glacial lakes, current mitigation efforts include reducing lake levels by digging outflow channels. However, the threat of a sudden outburst remains significant.

Poaching in Shangri-La

While the Bhutanese generally observe their own conservation policies, the open southern and northern borders offer opportunities for poaching of both plant and animal life. Many species are sought for their alleged medicinal or other valuable properties. Killing and poaching are unacceptable in Buddhist tradition, but the high prices that wildlife products such as rhino horn, tiger bone, musk and caterpillar fungus command outside Bhutan present major challenges to conservationists.

The Department of Forests & Park Services operates effective antipoaching programs designed to protect endangered plants and animals, enforce forestry rules, and control trade in wildlife parts and products. A national network of foresters regulates timber harvesting, and there are road checkpoints throughout the country to monitor the transportation of forest products.

Firewood

Managing firewood harvesting is a major problem in remote regions of Bhutan. Wood is still used as the primary heating and cooking fuel in rural areas and Bhutan's per-capita consumption of firewood is one of the highest in the world. In urban areas cooking gas or kerosene is commonly used, but there are high hopes that both rural and urban Bhutan will receive electricity supplies from the large and small hydro projects currently in development, although the bulk of that energy

THE CATERPILLAR & THE FUNGUS

According to one study, upwards of US$10 billion is spent each year by Asian markets on a fungus with purported powers matched only by rhino horns, elephant tusks and tiger penises. Most of the purchasers hope it will increase potency in males. Some Chinese swimming coaches and practitioners of traditional medicine have so talked up the value of *yartsa goenbub* (winter-worm summer-plant) that it is now one of the most valuable commodities by weight (if not the most valuable). Also known as caterpillar fungus or cordyceps, *Ophioordyceps sinensis* is a peculiar fungus that parasitises then kills its moth caterpillar host. It is only found in the high-altitude meadows of the Himalaya and Tibet.

Tibetan yak herders wandering in and out of Bhutan traditionally scooped up the fungus to augment their meagre living, but the increased demand for cordyceps in China has brought dramatic changes, with gatherers swarming the meadows of Nepal, Tibet and Bhutan, which is not surprising – prices, usually around US$20,000 to $50,000 per kilogram, can peak as high as US$100,000 per kilogram!

Bhutan legalised the harvesting of cordyceps in 2004, and since then there has been a massive increase in harvesting effort, raising concerns for its sustainability. Although the trade in cordyceps is officially regulated, the high stakes mean unlawful collection and black-market trading is rife.

A tragic knock-on effect linked to this sudden Himalayan wealth bonanza was a swath of poaching of big cats across Asia as increasingly wealthy Tibetans demanded cat skins for new *chuba* (cloaks) and for decorating their homes. This prompted a proclamation by the Dalai Lama for Tibetans to respect nature and discard their cat skins, which was popularly supported with thousands of Tibetans burning their cat skins. Nevertheless, China remains the main destination for products from poached big cats.

is earmarked for sale to India. Nevertheless, rural electrification has made inroads in per-capita consumption of firewood and small electric cookers are being introduced throughout the country.

Grazing & Farming

Conservation issues centre on conflicts between humans and wildlife, such as crop and livestock depredation by wild predators, and the deterioration of high-altitude wildlife habitat from grazing pressure. There are government and NGO programs under way to balance the needs of traditional herders and farmers with wildlife protection.

A significant amount of shifting cultivation ('slash and burn'; called *tseri* in Dzongkha) is practised in Bhutan, particularly in the east. The practice is officially banned and several methods, including education and fertiliser supply, are being implemented to change this practice.

THE NATURAL WORLD

WANGCHUCK CENTENNIAL PARK

Size 4914 sq km

Bhutan's newest and largest national park was inaugurated in 2008. This high-altitude park links Jigme Dorji National Park with Bomdeling Wildlife Sanctuary and protects the headwaters of four major rivers as well as snow-leopard and takin habitat.

JIGME DORJI NATIONAL PARK

Size 4319 sq km

The second-largest protected area in Bhutan with habitats ranging from subtropical (1400m) to alpine (7000m), it protects several endangered species, including takins, snow leopards and tigers. Villagers farm and harvest indigenous plants in the park. (p73)

JIGME KHESAR STRICT NATURE RESERVE

Size 610 sq km

This reserve is located where the Torsa Chhu enters from Tibet. The reserve was set aside to protect the temperate forests and alpine meadows and is the only protected area with no resident human population.

Thanza

Gasa

THIMPHU

Punakha

Trongsa

Wangdue Phodrang

Paro

Haa

Chhukha

Dagana

Sibsu

Chengmari

Samtse

Phuentsholing

Damphu

Lamidranga

Sarpang

Gelephu

Kalikhola

INDIA
(ASSAM)

JIGME SINGYE WANGCHUCK NATIONAL PARK

Size 1730 sq km

Protecting the Black Mountains that separate eastern and western Bhutan, it harbours tigers, Himalayan black bears, red pandas and golden langurs. An amazing 450 species of bird have been catalogued. The Phobjikha valley, wintering place of black-necked cranes, is included in the park. (p128)

PHIBSOO WILDLIFE SANCTUARY

Size 269 sq km

On the southern border of Bhutan, it was established to protect the only remaining natural sal forest in Bhutan. Several protected species thrive here, including chital deer, elephants, gaurs, tigers, golden langurs and hornbills.

Protected Areas

Biological Corridors

0   50 km
0   30 miles

PHRUMSENGLA NATIONAL PARK

Size 905 sq km
This national park was set aside to protect old-growth temperate forests of fir and chir pine. It is also home to red pandas and several endangered bird species, including the rufous-necked hornbill and satyr tragopan pheasant. (p151)

BOMDELING WILDLIFE SANCTUARY

Size 1521 sq km
The sanctuary protects the habitat of blue sheep, snow leopards, red pandas, tigers, capped langurs, Himalayan black bears and musk deer. It also protects a large area of alpine tundra and is a wintering ground of the black-necked crane. (p173)

SAKTENG WILDLIFE SANCTUARY

Size 741 sq km
The sanctuary protects several endemic species, particularly rhododendrons, within its temperate forests of blue pine and mixed conifers. It is also renowned as the only reserve in the world that protects the habitat of the *migoi* (yeti). (p167)

CHINA
(TIBET)

Lhuentse

Jakar

Trashi
Yangtse   Sakteng

Trashigang

Zhemgang   Mongar

Wamrong

Pemagatshel

INDIA
(ARUNACHAL
PRADESH)

Pangbang   Nganglam   Bhangtar   Daifam

Samdrup
Jongkhar

JHOMOTSHANGKHAR WILDLIFE SANCTUARY

Size 335 sq km
In far southeastern Bhutan, the this wildlife sanctuary protects wild elephants, gaurs, leopards, pygmy hogs, hispid hares and other tropical wildlife.
This sanctuary adjoins a comparable reserve in India.

ROYAL MANAS NATIONAL PARK

Size 1057 sq km
Adjoining India's Manas National Park, it forms a protected area running from the plains to the peaks. It is the home of rhino, buffalo, tigers, leopards, bears and elephants. It is also home to rare species, including the golden langur, capped langur and hispid hare. (p153)

The Bhutanese Table

The Bhutanese love chillies, so much in fact that some dishes consist entirely of chillies, and are accompanied by chilli-infused condiments! However, the buffets put on by tourist hotels are typically not packed with the same firepower. Since most travel in Bhutan is via an all-inclusive package, most of your meals will be in the form of a hotel buffet comprising continental, Indian, Chinese and one or two toned-down Bhutanese dishes.

Staples & Specialities

The mouth-scorching local meals will bring tears of joy to the eyes of chilli lovers, though don't expect the aromatically spiced dishes typical of the subcontinent. These can only be found in the Nepali-influenced south of Bhutan or at an Indian restaurant.

Hotel (and trekking) buffets usually include at least one meat dish and several vegetarian options and always rice. The vegetable ingredients are nearly always fresh and locally grown, and the food is fine. But it is specifically created to not offend anyone, so it can be bland. Small groups and individuals can often order from the menu, though the buffet meals usually offer a wider selection. If you find the tourist food bland, request some of what your guide is eating. It will be much tastier, if you can take the heat.

Beef and fish come from India or Thailand, usually flown in frozen and safe. During the summer you may be limited to chicken, or a vegetarian diet in more remote parts of the country. Yak meat is available, but only in winter.

Although there is plenty of white rice, the Bhutanese prefer a locally produced red variety, which has a slightly nutty flavour. At high altitudes wheat and buckwheat are the staples. In Bumthang, *khule* (buckwheat pancakes) and *puta* (buckwheat noodles) replace rice as the foundation of many meals.

Dessert is most often a modest presentation of fruit. For a proper sweet treat, you probably will need to head to one of the luxury hotels or the bakeries in Thimphu and Paro.

Pork fat is a popular dish throughout Bhutan because of its high energy content. To the uninitiated it can be a challenge to swallow a lump of fat with no meat and sometimes with remnants of hairy skin attached.

Bhutanese Dishes

Bhutan's national dish is *ema datse*: large green (sometimes red, but always very hot) chillies *(ema),* prepared as a vegetable, not as a seasoning, in a cheese sauce *(datse).* The second most popular dish is *phak sha laphu* (stewed pork with radish).

Other typically Bhutanese dishes, always served with chillies, include *no sha huentsu* (stewed beef with spinach), *phak sha phin tshoem* (pork with rice noodles) and *bja sha maroo* (chicken in garlic and butter sauce).

Hotel and trekking cooks make some excellent nonspicy dishes, such as *kewa datse* (potatoes with cheese sauce) and *shamu datse* (mushrooms with cheese sauce). These dishes also come with chillies, eg *shamu ema datse,* so be careful. More seasonal are the delicious wild asparagus and unusual *nakey* (fiddlehead fern fronds); the latter is typically smothered in the ever-present *datse.*

Foremost among several Tibetan-influenced snacks are *momos*: small steamed dumplings that may be filled with meat, vegetables or cheese – delicious when dipped in a chilli sauce. Fried cheese *momos* are a speciality of several Thimphu restaurants.

Drinks in Bhutan

Tea (sweet, Indian-style chai or a teabag) and coffee (predominantly of the instant variety) are drunk throughout Bhutan and are readily available. For espresso and quality tea you'll need to head to the cafes of Thimphu or, away from Thimphu, an upmarket hotel. Bottled beer and wine are readily available throughout the country, while many places like to make a point of introducing visitors to the local brew, *bang chhang*, and sinus-clearing firewater, *arra*.

Nonalcoholic Drinks

Indian-style sweet milky tea *(ngad-ja)* is widely available and often referred to as either masala tea, chai or 'ready-made' tea. Less satisfying is the tourist equivalent, a tea bag that you only get some flavour from after endless prodding. Bhutanese frequently drink *sud-ja*, Tibetan-style tea with salt and butter, which is more like soup than tea, and surprisingly tasty and warming on a cold day. Filter coffee and espresso is available in top-end hotels and a few cafes in Thimphu and Paro, but elsewhere 'coffee' is invariably of the instant variety.

Excellent Bhutanese apple juice is served in most hotels and is preferable to the imported 'juices' in small cartons that are typically sugary concoctions rather than natural juice.

Alcoholic Drinks

Microbreweries have recently arrived in Bhutan, offering several craft beers to challenge the old-school favourite, Red Panda, a tangy unfiltered *weissbier* (wheat beer) brewed and bottled in Bumthang. On a larger scale, Bhutan Brewery produces Druk Lager and the high-alcohol (8%) Druk 11000. Imported beers, such as Singha and Tiger, are sometimes available.

Wine is available but it's expensive for the quality. There are imported bottled wines and locally bottled imported wine. The latter includes Raven and Vintria, both Shiraz. The locally bottled white wine, Zumzin, is very sweet and confusingly labelled as 'Peach Wine'. In fact it is a blend of Colombard and Muscat, and certainly boasts a certain 'peachiness'. If you prefer dry whites this wine is not for you.

There are several brands of Bhutanese whisky, but the most common local brew is *bang chhang,* a warm beer-like drink made from wheat. The favourite hard drinks are *arra*, a spirit distilled from rice, and *sinchhang*, which is made from millet, wheat or rice.

Drinks, including bottled water, are usually charged as extras, and payment is collected at the end of the meal or when you check out of the hotel.

While travelling through Bhutan and visiting local shops, look for the strings of rock-hard, dried yak cheese *(chugo)* hanging from shop rafters. Soften it in your mouth and be careful of your teeth.

Avoid drinking untreated tap water anywhere in Bhutan. Bottled water is widely available and filtered spring water is a feature of several rural hotels. Most hotel rooms have kettles for boiling water.

THE BHUTANESE TABLE DRINKS IN BHUTAN

CHEWING THE NUT

One of the great Bhutanese vices is chewing *doma* nut, also known by its Indian name, *paan*. The nut (from an Areca palm) is mixed with lime powder (the ash, not the fruit), and the whole collection is rolled up in a heart-shaped betel leaf and chewed slowly. It's a bittersweet, mildly intoxicating concoction and it stains the mouth bright red. The blood-like stains you see on Bhutanese pavements are the result of spat out *doma* effluent. Or they're just bloodstains...

HIMALAYAN CRAFT BEER

The global rise of craft beer has spread as far as the foothills of the Bhutan Himalaya, making it perhaps the remotest beer destination in Asia.

The oldest brewery in Bhutan is the Bumthang Brewery (p137), started by early Swiss development expert Fritz Mauer before the word 'microbrewery' was even invented. Their fruity, tangy Panda Beer is still many expats' brew of choice but, thanks to its short shelf life, it can be hard to find. Grab one whenever you find it.

The Namgyal Artisanal Brewery (p90) in the Paro valley is currently Bhutan's biggest craft brewery. The founder got the beer bug while studying in Switzerland and set up the operation in 2017, using Canadian know-how, Indian technology and American Cascade hops. The most popular beer is the Red Rice lager, made with local Paro valley red rice, but they also make a hoppy IPA, a dark ale, wheat beer, Pilsner, and an oddly refreshing pineapple gose (sour beer) made with pink salt and local yogurt. Naturally, a red chilli ale is in the pipeline. Bottles of the lager and dark ale are available in many supermarkets in Paro, but for the IPA you'll have to head to the brewery or the Namgyal hotels in Paro or Thimpu.

Bhutan's other main microbrewery is Ser Bhum Brewery (p104), named after one of the eight auspicious symbols of Tibetan Buddhism, and based in the countryside near Hongtsho, 12km from Thimphu, on the way to the Dochu La. The brewery produces an excellent amber ale and a Dragon Stout, and also stocks bottles of its Kati Patang amber ale (www.katipatang.in), brewed here for exclusive export to the Indian market. The oddly rural location is all due to the purity of the local spring water.

All three breweries offer tours; if you have an interest, ask your agent to ring in advance.

If you just want to drink, Park 76 (p91) in Paro and Mojo Park (p69) in Thimpu have the best selection of craft beers in the country, while the Namgyal hotels in Paro and Thimphu offer their beers on tap and stock bottles in the room minibars.

Packed Lunches & Local Restaurants

On long day drives or hikes you may not return to your hotel for lunch, and most tour operators will arrange a packed lunch (often called a picnic lunch). This is usually delicious and can even be a hot lunch packed inside a series of metal containers packed inside a wide insulated flask.

The food in hotels is often the best in town, but if you want to sample local restaurants, especially in Thimphu or Paro, your guide can arrange it. Your tour operator should pay for your restaurant meals, with the exception of a few upper-end restaurants in Thimphu and casual visits to cafes for snacks. In almost all restaurants it's a good idea to order an hour or more in advance, or expect to wait forever. If you are ordering from a menu, don't be surprised if many of the offerings are not available.

Due to the unique nature of travel in Bhutan, restaurant opening hours have little meaning. Almost all tourists will have breakfast in their hotel and guides will prearrange lunch and dinner in restaurants or hotels, which will normally offer a buffet or set meal at whatever time your guide determines.

Survival Guide

Directory A–Z

Accessible Travel

Touring Bhutan is a challenge for a traveller with physical disabilities, but you'll have a guide, driver and vehicle at your disposal, so this is possible with some planning. The Bhutanese are eager to help, and agencies should be able to arrange a strong companion to assist with moving about and getting in and out of vehicles.

Mobility impaired travellers will find that roads are rough and pavements, where they exist, often have holes and sometimes steps. Hotels and public buildings rarely have wheelchair access or lifts, and only a few hotels at the top end have bathrooms designed to accommodate wheelchairs.

Download Lonely Planet's free Accessible Travel guides from http://lptravel.to/AccessibleTravel.

Accommodation

Tour operators will book you into hotels or homestays approved by the Tourism Council of Bhutan (TCB). Since most visitors effectively pay the same rate across the category, it makes sense to ask for information about the various options when you make your travel arrangements.

Homestays The only accommodation in some parts of the east; provide unparalleled immersion into local culture.

Hotels Tourist-quality hotels range from simple but comfortable rooms included in the daily fee to luxurious five-star resorts attracting a premium tariff.

Local hotels Tend to be noisier and have firm mattresses; a last resort only.

Hotels

Hotel accommodation in Bhutan ranges from simple pine-clad cabins to five-star luxury resorts, though most tourists will stay in comfortable midrange tourist hotels equipped with electricity, telephone, TV, private bathroom and hot water. Every hotel has a restaurant that serves buffet meals when a group is in residence and offers à la carte dining at other times. Most hotels in Bhutan have wi-fi, but internet connectivity can be slow as you head away from the cities.

Larger hotels offer standard, deluxe and suite accommodation, although the difference between standard and deluxe in many hotels is minimal. When you book a trip, you may specify which hotel you wish, but your agent may have a list of hotels with whom they have contracts or relationships. Changes and cancellations will be much simpler and upgrades more likely in these hotels. You'll find that smaller agencies often have a hard time getting guaranteed rooms at hotels owned by larger tour companies. During the low season (December to February and June to August), hotels often discount their rooms by as much as 30%, so you may be able to negotiate an upgrade during these months.

During tsechu (dance festival) time, tourist hotels add a hefty surcharge, but they still get booked up and you may well find yourself 'bumped' into budget digs, such as the local hotels used by domestic and Indian travellers and traders. Also out east, where there is not an oversupply of hotels, your only choice may be a local hotel. These can still be comfortable, though the mattresses (thin) and toilet facilities (squat or with makeshift plumbing) may not be quite what you're used to.

A confirmed hotel reservation does not always guarantee a booking in hotels as small as those in Bhutan. A large tour group can exert a powerful influence and you may discover that there is an extended negotiation taking place between your guide and the desk clerk when you check in. Don't worry: *something* will be arranged.

Bhutan has a growing number of luxury options, including the Uma, Aman-kora, Zhiwa Ling and Terma-linca resorts. For these you will have to pay a substantial supplement on top of the standard tourist tariff. These hotels are marked as 'luxury'. For these luxury hotels you should get at least a 30% discount off the full rate during the low season.

Winter is cold in Bhutan and central heating is rare. In Thimphu and Paro there are small electric heaters, and in Bumthang many hotel rooms are heated by a wood stove called a *bukhari,* which often has a pile of rocks on the top to retain the heat. These stoves are flued to the outside and should not be at risk of causing carbon monoxide poisoning. Nevertheless, not all flues are 100% sealed and fires do consume oxygen, so some venting, such as opening a window, is recommended. Unless you are trekking,

---

HOT-STONE BATHS

Many hotels offer a *dotsho* (traditional hot-stone bath), a simple coffin-like wooden box containing water warmed with fire-heated rocks. The red-hot rocks tumble and sizzle into the water behind a grill that protects the bather's skin. More traditional places add natural herbs such as artemisia. You'll need to book a couple of hours in advance for the rocks to be heated; expect to pay around Nu 2000 for the experience, double this in top-end places. Bring a towel and soap in cheaper places.

---

you won't need to carry bedding or a sleeping bag.

If there is an electric water heater (called a geyser) in the room, check that it's turned on when you check in. The better hotels supply bottled drinking water in the rooms, but if you come across an open water flask in your room, don't drink from it.

Indian travellers and resident foreigners often get an automatic 20% or 30% discount on hotel room rates, while Bhutanese may get 50%.

For those paying their own way, most hotels charge 10% Bhutan Sales Tax (BST) and a 10% service charge (or less commonly 5%). These taxes are included in the prices listed for hotels.

Activities

There are numerous opportunities to leave the vehicle for a day and stretch your legs. You won't regret organising a day hike to take in the views and mountain air, particularly if you are moving quickly between regions. There are also more serious treks, ranging from three to 24 days.

Birdwatching

Bhutan is rightly celebrated for its wintering populations of the vulnerable black-necked crane, but with over 600 recorded bird species and a spectacular range of habitats, this tiny country is a birdwatcher's paradise.

Although the following companies specialise in

---

birdwatching tours, Bhutan's plentiful mature forests and lack of hunting make any travel in the countryside a bird-spotting opportunity.

Bhutan Birding & Heritage Travels (☑02-332302; www.bhutanheritage.com)

Sunbird Tours (www.sunbird tours.co.uk)

Wings (www.wingsbirds.com)

Cycling

Mountain biking is popular with Bhutanese and expats alike. Companies that specialise in cycling tours, have repair shops and bikes for hire, and can advise on routes include **Wheels for Hills** (Map p74; ☑02-340185; www.bhutanmountain bike.com; near Shearee Sq Mall, Olakha; ⊙9am-6.30pm) and **Yu-Druk Bike Shop** (Map p54; ☑02-323461; www.yudruk.com; Thori Lam; ⊙10am-6pm Mon-Fri, 10am-2pm Sat); the latter also stocks e-bikes. Internationally, check out Bhutan By Bike (www.bhutanbybike.com). Some adventure-travel companies organise trips that allow bikers to bring their own bikes and travel throughout Bhutan accompanied by a support vehicle; otherwise local mountain bike hire costs an extra US$35 per day.

Long journeys are challenging because there's a lot of uphill pedalling and approaching vehicles roar around corners, not expecting cyclists. Local cycling excursions in the Paro, Thimphu and Bumthang valleys offer a safer and less-strenuous mountain

TOUR OF THE DRAGON & DRAGON'S FURY

Bhutan's premier mountain-bike event is the tortuous Tour of the Dragon (www.touroftthedragon.com), a race of 268km from Bumthang to Thimphu in just one day. The course gains 3790m and descends 3950m and crosses four mountain passes on Bhutan's famously winding roads. The tour takes place on the first Saturday in September and international registration costs US$250. If all that sounds a little too extreme, there is the gentler Dragon's Fury, a mere 60km doddle ascending 1740m from Metshina to Dochu La before the roll down to Thimphu. It's run on the same day as the Tour of the Dragon and international registration costs US$100.

biking experience. Suggested places include the following:

Cheli La For a wild ride, get dropped off at the top of this pass and ride 35km nonstop, downhill, either on the main road or on logging roads via Gorina.

Paro valley The paved road to Drukgyel Dzong and the return trip along the unpaved western farm road from Satsam make this a 30km day trip.

Phobjikha Bike trails here are part of the local ecotourism initiative, and there are also new opportunities for using graded logging roads to Tsele La and overnight to Tikke Zampa.

Punakha Offers several dedicated mountain bike trails (p110).

Tango and Cheri A fine day trip north of Thimphu, combining biking and hiking.

Thimphu to Paro An interesting ride, though traffic can be heavy as far as Chhuzom (the turn-off to Phuentsholing).

Fishing

Fishing with lure or fly for brown trout is possible in many rivers, though it is frowned upon by many Bhutanese for religious reasons. A licence (Nu 500 per day) is required (ask your tour agency) and fishing is prohibited within 1km of a monastery, temple, dzong or *shedra* (Buddhist college). A closed season applies from October to December and fishing is banned on many religious days throughout the year.

A legendary game fish of subcontinent rivers, the golden mahseer is considered threatened in Himalayan rivers because of habitat destruction, dam building for hydroelectric power projects, and pollution; several Bhutanese tour operators, including **Yangphel Adventure Travel** (☑02-323293; www.yangphel. com; Thimphu), offer 'catch and release' fishing trips where you can fly-fish for these magnificent fish without harming the wild population.

Golf

The international-standard golf course, **Royal Thimphu Golf Club** (Map p54; ☑02-335521; www.golfbhutan. com; Chhophel Lam; green fees SAARC national/adult Nu 2500/US$60, club hire per day US$30; ☺8am-5pm), in Thimphu, and the Indian Army **golf course** (green fees weekday/weekend Nu 500/1000; ☺9am-5pm Thu-Tue) in Haa are open to nonmembers.

Rafting & Kayaking

The rafting scene in Bhutan is still developing and those who have scouted the rivers feel that it has great potential even with the threat of more dams being developed. Paddlers have been exploring 14 rivers and over 22 different runs that vary from Class II (beginner with moderate rapids) to Class V (expert only). However, unless you are a seasoned river rat, and can organise the special permission required,

there are essentially only three day trips on offer: the Pho Chhu and Mo Chhu, both in the Punakha valley (p112), and the Manas Chhu.

Most companies can book you on these trips. The per-person fees depend on the group size: as an example, in a group of six or less you'll pay the minimum US$250 per raft. The following companies run rafting and kayaking trips:

Druk Rafting Service (☑02-584545, 17612586; www. raftingbhutan.com; Punakha)

Northwest Rafting Company (www.nwrafting.com/bhutan) US-based operator with a four-day trip on the Drangme Chhu in Eastern Bhutan.

River Guides of Panbang (☑17150141, 17497923; www. paddlebhutan.com; rafting packages for up to 8 passengers from Nu 9000)

Xplore Bhutan (☑17139999, 02-335671; www.xplorebhutan. com)

Children

Children aged under five are exempt from the minimum daily tariff and five-to-12-year-olds get a 50% discount, so travelling with children in Bhutan doesn't have to be financially crippling. However, kids may become bored with long, monotonous drives, steep walks to monasteries, hotel buffet food and the general lack of entertainment. On the other hand, they will be immediately accepted by local kids and their families. Lonely Planet's *Travel with Children* has lots of useful advice and suggestions.

Practicalities

Despite the welcome exemptions from the daily tariff, Bhutan is not well set up for travel with children. Child car seats are hard to find, and the minivans used for transporting tourists may not have seat belts to anchor a seat to if you bring your own. Some parents have reported being able to secure child car seats

Climate

Thimphu

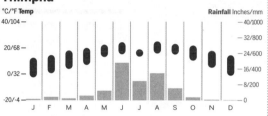

Phuentsholing

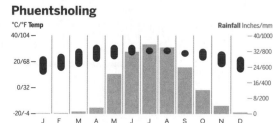

Type C
220V/50Hz

Type D
220V/50Hz

with straps brought from home. Most tourist-class hotels can arrange an extra bed, but cots are harder to find; bring a travel cot from home for younger children.

Upmarket restaurants in larger cities may have high chairs; they are non-existent elsewhere. Imported disposable nappies (diapers) are sold in larger cities, but nappy-changing facilities are very rare. Bhutan has one of the highest rates of breastfeeding in the world, but breastfeeding is done discreetly; local people would be surprised to see a tourist breastfeeding in public.

Customs Regulations

You will receive a baggage declaration form to complete when you arrive in Bhutan. For tourists, the main purpose of this form is to ensure that you re-export anything you bring into the country. List any expensive equipment that you are carrying, such as cameras and laptops. Don't lose the form as you must return it when you leave the country.

Duty-free allowances include 1L of liquor. You can bring in just one carton of 200 cigarettes and these attract a 200% duty upon arrival. A packet or two is normally allowed in gratis. There are no restrictions on other personal effects, including trekking gear, brought into the country.

Departure formalities are straightforward, but you'll need to produce the form that you completed on arrival and may need to show all of the items listed on it. A lost form means complications and delays. If you lose the form, let your guide know as soon as possible so that special arrangements can be made to avoid any inconvenience.

The export of antiques and wildlife products is prohibited. If you wish to purchase a souvenir that looks old, have your guide clear it as a non-antique item with the Division of Cultural Properties, part of the Department of Culture inside the Ministry of Home and Cultural Affairs. Customs authorities pay special attention to religious statues. It would be prudent to have any such statue cleared, whether old or not.

Embassies & Consulates

Visas are not available from Bhutanese embassies abroad. All tourist visa applications must be channelled through a tour company and the **Tourism Council of Bhutan** (TCB; Map p54; ☎02-323251; www.tourism.gov.bt; Tarayana Centre, Yardren Lam,

Chubachhu; ⊗9am-5pm Mon-Fri) in Thimphu, and from there through the Ministry of Foreign Affairs.

Only a handful of foreign countries have an official presence in Bhutan. Bhutan's relations with other countries are handled through its embassies in Delhi and Dhaka.

Bangladeshi Embassy, Thimphu (Map p54; ☑02-322539; Thori Lam, Thimphu; ⊗9am-5pm Mon-Fri, to 4pm in winter)

Indian Embassy, Thimphu (Map p54; ☑02-322162; www.indembthimphu.gov.in; India House, Zhung Lam, Jungshina; ⊗9.30am-1pm & 2-5.30pm Mon-Fri, closed Indian holidays)

Indian Consulate, Phuentsholing (Map p123; ☑05-252101; www.consulatephuentsholing.nic.in; Gaki Lam; ⊗9am-1.30pm & 2-5.30pm Mon-Fri)

Thai Honorary Consulate-General, Thimphu (Map p54; ☑02-323978; www.royalthaiconsulate.bt; 2nd fl, National Textile Museum complex, Norzin Lam; ⊗9am-4pm Mon-Fri)

Food & Drink

Your guide will arrange all your meals (p278), whether that's at a roadside restaurant or your accommodation. They should also be able to suggest a new venue if you are staying in the same hotel for several days.

Cafes Espresso and cream cakes are slowly making inroads into Bhutan.

Hotel restaurants Most of your meals, especially breakfast and

---

EATING PRICE RANGES

The following price ranges refer to a standard set meal.

$ less than Nu 250

$$ Nu 250–500

$$$ more than Nu 500

---

dinner, will be a buffet at your accommodation.

Local hotels and restaurants Not always as hygienic as they should be; will test your chilli tolerance.

Roadside restaurants Well organised with prearranged buffets, but if you turn up unannounced the pickings may be slim.

Insurance

Although few people have problems in Bhutan, a travel insurance policy to cover theft, loss and medical problems is always recommended. Most policies will cover costs if you are forced to cancel your tour because of flight cancellation, illness, injury or the death of a close relative. This can protect you from major losses, given Bhutan's prepayment conditions and hefty cancellation charges.

Some insurance policies specifically exclude 'dangerous activities', and these can include motorcycling, rafting and even trekking. Read your policy carefully to be sure it covers ambulance rides or an emergency helicopter airlift out of a remote region, or an emergency flight home. Keep in mind that if you can't afford travel insurance, you certainly won't be able to afford to deal with a medical emergency overseas.

You may prefer a policy that pays doctors or hospitals directly rather than you having to pay on the spot and claim later. If you have to claim later, make sure you keep all documentation. Some insurance companies ask you to call them (they suggest reversing the charges, an impossibility from Bhutan) at a centre in your home country, where an immediate assessment of your problem is made.

Worldwide travel insurance is available at www.lonelyplanet.com/travel-insurance. You can buy,

extend and claim online anytime – even if you're already on the road.

Internet Access

There are very few internet cafes in towns, but free wi-fi is offered in most tourist hotels and many cafes and restaurants in larger cities. Bhutan Telecom and Tashi Cell offer 3G and 4G networks that are constantly expanding, and buying a local SIM is an inexpensive way to use data on your mobile phone.

Language Courses

The **Dzongkha Language Institute** (Map p74; ☑02-333869; dzongkhalanguageinstitute@yahoo.com; Babesa) can arrange language courses in Dzongkha lasting one to six months at its campus south of Thimphu.

Laundry

Most hotels offer a laundry service, normally with quite high charges, and larger towns have a laundry or dry-cleaners. During wet weather, smaller hotels may return your laundry damp, or not until the following day. If you are on a tight schedule, ask about the drying facilities before you hand over your laundry.

Legal Matters

Although you will probably notice cannabis growing in any bit of spare dirt, even in the towns, there is not a tradition of use and possession is illegal. Littering is prohibited, as is urinating in public; both incur a fine of Nu 1000.

Smoking in public places is prohibited, except in the dedicated smoking rooms found in some bars and restaurants; the fine for violating the ban is Nu 500. You can bring in up to 200 cigarettes for your own use but be prepared to be taxed 200% at customs. Don't sell any cigarettes brought into the country as this is illegal.

If you are arrested in Bhutan, contact the nearest embassy for your home country (this may be in Nepal or India). Note that embassy officials may not be able to do much more than put you in contact with a local lawyer.

LGBTIQ+ Travellers

In June 2019 Bhutan's National Assembly approved a bill to decriminalise homosexuality, repealing two sections of Bhutan's penal code. There are growing calls for gender recognition for transgender people. Like most Asians, the Bhutanese believe that what one does in private is strictly a personal matter, and public displays of affection are not appreciated. Everyone, regardless of orientation, should exercise discretion.

Maps

A good map can be hard to source outside the country. Bookshops in Kathmandu are the best bet for finding a map. International Travel Maps produces a 1:345,000 *Bhutan & Northern India*, and Nepa Maps produces a 1:380,000 *Bhutan*, and *Bhutan Himalaya Trekking Routes*.

In Bhutan, bookshops sell Thimphu and Paro city maps as well as country maps produced by the **Survey of Bhutan** (Map p54; ☑02-321217; Rm 35, National Land Commission, Serzhong Lam, Motithang; ☺9am-5pm Mon-Fri). The Survey publishes a large 1:250,000 satellite country map overlaid with roads and major towns and district boundaries, as well as several specialised maps showing historical places

LOCAL ETIQUETTE

Bhutan is a deeply traditional society and certain codes of conduct apply.

Visiting temples & monasteries Shoes should be removed before entering any dzong, goemba or religious building. Photography is banned inside chapels, but is usually permitted in temple courtyards. Walk around chortens and shrines in a clockwise direction. Avoid revealing clothing – locals dress modestly so follow their lead.

Physical contact It is considered rude to touch anyone on the head, or point your feet towards someone. Shaking hands is becoming common in urban areas, but the traditional Bhutanese greeting is a bow with the arms low and outstretched.

Social etiquette When dining with a group of people, wait till everyone has been served before you start. If you offer something to a local person – for example a tip for your guide or driver – it is customary for them to initially decline the offer before they accept.

and points of interest. However, many Survey of Bhutan maps are restricted and cannot be sold to visitors.

Money

The unit of currency is the ngultrum (Nu), which is pegged to the Indian rupee. The ngultrum is further divided into 100 chetrum. There are coins to the value of 25 and 50 chetrum and Nu 1, and notes of Nu 1, 5, 10, 20, 50, 100, 500 and 1000. The Nu 1 coin depicts the eight auspicious symbols called Tashi Tagye, while each note depicts a different dzong.

Indian rupees may be used freely anywhere in Bhutan (don't be surprised if you get change in rupees). Officially 500 and 1000 Indian rupee notes are not accepted due to large amounts of counterfeit notes; however, in practice 500s are usually accepted. Ngultrums cannot be used in India.

It is OK with the Bhutanese if you bring a reasonable amount of Indian currency into Bhutan, though Indian regulations officially prohibit currency export.

Unspent ngultrums can be changed into US dollars on departure from Paro airport.

ATMs

Bank of Bhutan (BoB), Bhutan National Bank and Druk PNB Bank ATMs accept some foreign credit cards, but ATMs in Bhutan use the magnetic strip rather than digital chips, and some foreign banks do not permit withdrawals via this method. The government also periodically blocks international ATM transactions for short periods to combat fraud. It always pays to carry cash in case you have problems. ATM transactions are limited to Nu 10,000 or Nu 15,000.

Bargaining

Bargaining is not a Bhutanese tradition, and you won't get very far with your haggling skills here, except with trail-side vendors on the hike to Taktshang and in the local handicrafts section of the Thimphu Weekend Market. Almost all shops have fixed prices, and these are typically high compared to other countries in the region.

Changing Money

Tours are fully prepaid, so you could in theory manage in Bhutan without any local money at all, though you'll probably want to change at least US$50 to US$100 to pay for laundry and drinks, plus whatever you need for souvenirs and tips.

The exchange counters at the airport, larger hotels and the banks in Thimphu and Phuentsholing can change major currencies, and some smaller currencies from Asia and Scandinavia. Indian rupees are used interchangeably with ngultrums and are not officially exchanged at banks.

If you are heading to central and eastern Bhutan, you will do better sticking to US dollars. The exchange rate for US-dollar bills in denominations less than US$100 is around 10% lower than for large bills. US-dollar bills that are pre-1993 are generally not accepted.

You may change your unused ngultrums back into US dollars on departure at Paro airport (including in the airport bookshop). Travellers departing overland didn't have this facility at the time of research. You may need to produce your original exchange receipts. Ngultrums are useless outside of Bhutan (except as a curiosity).

Bhutan has two major banks, the Bank of Bhutan (www.bob.bt) and the Bhutan National Bank (www.bnb.bt), each with branches throughout the country. Smaller banks with forex include T-Bank and Druk PNB, with branches in larger cities. In addition, you can change money at many hotels and some shops.

Credit Cards

Cards are accepted at major handicraft stores and some of the larger hotels in Thimphu and other towns, but a surcharge of up to 5% often applies to cover the fees levied by the credit-card companies. PINs have to be four digits.

Tipping

Hotels At your discretion, but hotel staff will appreciate a small tip for carrying your bags.

Restaurants Restaurant bills include service tax, and tipping is not common.

Taxis It is not customary to tip taxi drivers.

Tour guides It is customary to tip your guide and driver at the end of an organised trip. Allow US$10 to US$15 per day for guides, and US$8 to US$10 per day for drivers.

Opening Hours

Banks 9am to 5pm (4pm winter) Monday to Friday, 9am to 11am or 1pm Saturday

Bars Close at 11pm on weekdays and midnight on Friday and Saturday. Closed Tuesday – the national 'dry' day.

Clubs Generally close at midnight most weekdays, and at around 2am or 3am on Wednesday, Friday and Saturday

Government Offices 9am to 1pm and 2pm to 5pm summer, until 4pm winter, Monday to Friday

Shops 8am to 8pm or 9pm

Photography

Bhutan is generally liberal about photography by tourists. There are a few places, though, with signs prohibiting photography, such as the telecommunication tower above Thimphu. It would also be prudent to refrain from taking pictures of military installations and around border crossings.

There are no restrictions on photographing the outside of dzongs (fort-monasteries) and goembas (monasteries), but photography is *strictly* prohibited inside goembas and lhakhangs (temples). There are several reasons for this. One is that in the past tourists have completely disrupted holy places with their picture taking. Another is the fear that photos of treasured statues will become a catalogue of items for art thieves to steal. And thirdly, some early tourists made photographs of religious statues into postcards that were then sold, offending local religious sensibilities.

During festivals you can photograph from the dzong courtyard where the dances take place. Remember, however, that this is a religious observance and that you should behave respectfully. Don't photograph a member of the royal family, even if you happen to be at a festival or gathering where they are present.

There is an extensive set of rules and restrictions for filming in Bhutan, including payment of additional royalties for commercial movie making. See the website of the Bhutan InfoComm & Media Authority (www.bicma.gov.bt/bicmanew) for details.

Post

The mail service from Bhutan is reliable, and no special procedures are necessary.

Bhutan Post (www.bhutanpost.bt) offers both outgoing and incoming Expedited Mail Service (EMS), a reliable and fast international mail delivery facility that is cheaper than using a courier. There is also a Local Urgent Mail (LUM) service for delivery within Thimphu.

If you have made a purchase and want to send it home, it's easiest to have the shop make arrangements for you. Keep the receipt and let your guide know what you are doing so they can follow up in case the package does not arrive. Send all parcels by air. Sea mail, via Kolkata (Calcutta), takes months and items can go missing. Alternatively, **DHL** (Map p54; ☎02-324730; 19-13 Thori Lam;

PRACTICALITIES

Magazines Glossy magazines come and go, but the most successful magazine in Bhutan is *Yeewong* (www.yeewongmagazine.com) aimed at Bhutanese women. The free in-flight magazine *Tashi Delek,* provided on Druk Air flights, has some interesting articles on local culture.

Newspapers *Kuensel* (www.kuenselonline.com) is the daily (except Sunday) national newspaper of Bhutan. Private newspapers include *Bhutan Today* (www.bhutantoday. net, biweekly), *Bhutan Times* (www.bhutantimes.com, Sunday), *The Bhutanese* (www. thebhutanese.bt, Saturday) and *Business Bhutan* (www.businessbhutan.bt, Saturday).

Radio Bhutan Broadcasting Service (www.bbs.com.bt) broadcasts English news at 11am and 2pm on 96FM. Kuzoo FM 105 is a private English- and Dzongkha-language station with a mix of music and chat, or try Radio Valley at 99.9FM.

Smoking Officially prohibited in public places, except designated smoking rooms at some bars, restaurants and hotels. The sale of tobacco is banned in Bhutan, but travellers can import a single carton of 200 cigarettes subject to a 200% tax at customs. Selling cigarettes brought into the country is illegal.

TV BBS TV broadcasts evening news in English. Most tourist hotels have Indian satellite TV packages including international channels such as the BBC and CNN.

Weights & measures The metric system is used throughout the country. In villages, rice is sometimes measured in a round measure called a gasekhorlo. There is a scale called a sang that is used for butter and meat.

⊙9am-5pm Mon-Fri, 9am-1pm Sat) has an office in Thimphu.

Public Holidays

Public holidays follow both the Gregorian and lunar calendars and are decided by the Royal Civil Service Commission (www.rcsc.gov. bt) – dates are posted on its website.

Birthday of the Gyaltse (crown prince) 5 February

Birthday of Fifth King 21–23 February

Birthday of Third King 2 May

Coronation of Fourth King 2 June; also marked as 'Social Forestry Day'

Coronation of Druk Gyalpo 1 November

Constitution Day/Fourth King's Birthday 11 November

National Day 17 December; the date of the establishment of the monarchy in 1907

The following holidays are set by the traditional lunar calendar and Gregorian dates vary:

Losar January/February, New Year

Zhabdrung Kuchoe April/May; death of the Zhabdrung

Buddha Parinirvana/Saga Dawa May/June; enlightenment and death of Buddha

Birthday of Guru Rinpoche June/July

First sermon of Buddha July/August

Dashain September/October; Hindu celebration

Several major festivals are considered local public holidays, including Thimphu's *dromchoe* and tsechu (dance festival) celebrations in September or October. Note that dates for festivals can vary by several weeks each year, especially if they are adjusted to conform to auspicious dates. Before you schedule a trip around a specific festival, check with a tour operator or the **Tourism Council of Bhutan** (TCB; Map p54; ☏02-323251; www.tourism.gov.bt; Tarayana Centre, Yardren Lam, Chubachhu; ⊙9am-5pm Mon-Fri) for the correct dates.

In the Bhutanese lunar system, months have 30 days, with the full moon on the 15th. The eighth, 15th and 30th days of the month are auspicious and you'll notice increased activity and prayers in monasteries across the country.

Safe Travel

Bhutan is a remarkably safe destination, but note the following:

➡ Some treks climb to elevations where Acute Mountain Sickness can be a risk; take time to acclimatise.

➡ Street dogs make a lot of noise at night and rabies is a risk; always be cautious around guard dogs in the hills.

➡ Rain, cloud, snow and rockfalls can affect travel by road and by air; double-check departure times the day before you fly.

➡ Roads are rough and winding; anti-motion medication such as Dramamine can help with carsickness symptoms.

➡ Theft is rare but keep an eye on your belongings as a precaution.

➡ Indian separatist groups are active across the border from southeastern Bhutan, so check the latest news before visiting the far southeast.

Telephone

Public call offices (PCOs) are becoming rare throughout the country, as the mobile service is generally excellent. Most hotels can arrange local and international calls for a premium, though few have in-room direct-dial facilities.

Local calls cost Nu 1 per minute, or Nu 2 per minute long distance. International calls cost Nu 15 to 35 per minute to most destinations, or Nu 4 to India. Call ☎1600 for domestic and international directory enquiries.

Mobile Phones

You can easily buy and top-up a B-Mobile or Tashi Cell SIM card as long as your phone is unlocked.

B-Mobile (www.bt.bt/tourist-sim) has the best coverage; its numbers start with 17. A B-Mobile SIM card for tourists is available from telecom shops in Thimphu for Nu 150. This includes talk time worth Nu 100 and is valid for one month. Further top-ups are available from phone shops across Bhutan. Show your passport at the time of purchase.

Tashi Cell (www.tashicell.com) has similar rates but

more limited coverage; its numbers start with 77. A tourist SIM costs Nu 250, including Nu 200 worth of calls. Package deals with larger call and data bundles are available at Paro Airport.

Local mobile call charges vary from Nu 0.40 to 0.70 per 15 seconds, depending on the time of day and network called. Some tour operators have satellite phones or they can rent them but the charges are significantly higher than for normal mobile calls.

Time

Bhutan time is GMT/UTC plus six hours; there is only one time zone throughout the country. The time in Bhutan is 30 minutes later than in India, 15 minutes later than Nepal, and the same as the time in Bangladesh. When it is noon in Bhutan, standard time is 6am in London, 4pm in Sydney, 1am in New York and 10pm the previous day in San Francisco.

Toilets

Most hotels provide Western toilets and toilet paper, though there are some exceptions, particularly in local hotels in eastern Bhutan. There are very few public toilets, so take full advantage of hotel and restaurant facilities before that long drive. Most public toilets are of the Asian squat variety and toilet paper isn't provided, though

a container of water should be present.

Tourist Information

The **Tourism Council of Bhutan** (TCB; Map p54; ☎02-323251; www.tourism.gov.bt; Tarayana Centre, Yardren Lam, Chubachhu; ⊙9am-5pm Mon-Fri) has a comprehensive website and it can refer you to tour operators who can assist with arrangements to visit Bhutan. The TCB office in Thimphu is not really set up to answer tourist questions – you are better off speaking to your guide. There is no official government tourist office outside Bhutan.

Visas

Unlike in most countries, visas for Bhutan are issued only when you arrive in the country, either at Paro airport or (if entering by road) at Phuentsholing, Gelephu or Samdrup Jongkhar. You must apply in advance through a tour operator, as part of a prepaid all-inclusive tour, and receive visa approval before you travel to Bhutan.

Applications for tourist visas must be submitted by a Bhutanese tour operator for approval by the Ministry of Foreign Affairs in Thimphu. The agency will submit an online visa application with a copy of the photo page of your passport to the **Tourism Council of Bhutan** (TCB; Map p54; ☎02-323251; www.tourism.gov.bt; Tarayana Centre, Yardren Lam, Chubachhu; ⊙9am-5pm Mon-Fri) in Thimphu. They in turn will check that you have completely paid for your trip (including the US$40 visa fee) and then issue an approval letter to the tour operator. With this approval in hand, the tour operator then makes a final application to the Ministry of Foreign Affairs, which takes up to three days to process the visa.

You may be asked to fill out the visa form yourself, but many agencies will do this stage for you. What you will need to do is send a scan of your passport photo and your passport information pages to the agency. You may also need to provide your permanent address and occupation.

Once the visa clearance is issued by the Ministry of Foreign Affairs, it sends a visa confirmation number to the tour operator and to Druk Air/Bhutan Airlines. The airline will not issue your tickets to Paro until it receives this confirmation number, and check-in staff will recheck the visa information before allowing you to board your flight.

The actual visa endorsement is stamped in your passport when you arrive at one of the permitted ports of entry for tourists. You will receive a visa for the exact period you have arranged to be in Bhutan; if some unusual event requires that you obtain a visa extension, your tour operator will arrange it.

The system is surprisingly efficient considering all the time, distance and various levels of bureaucracy involved. While your details will all be on the computers of immigration officials, it's very helpful to have a printout of the scanned visa authority to aid the immigration officials and airline to find your information quickly.

Visas for Neighbouring Countries

INDIA

Nationals of most countries need a visa to visit India. If you are travelling overland to or from Bhutan via Phuentsholing, Gelephu or Samdrup Jongkhar, you will need an Indian visa.

The government of India strongly prefers that you obtain your Indian visa in the country that issued your passport. Citizens of most countries can apply for an e-visa online at www.indianvisaonline.gov.in. These visas allow two entries and are valid for 60 days, but you must enter India via one of 26 approved airports (you can leave via any immigration checkpoint, including at land border crossings).

If you need a 'regular' six-month tourist visa, you can file an application on the same website and then take the paperwork to your local Indian embassy (or its approved visa application centre) along with your passport, passport photos and supporting documents.

Tourist visas are generally issued for six months, are multiple entry, and are valid from the date of issue of the visa, not the date you enter India. This means that if you first enter India five months after the visa was issued, it will be valid for one month.

NEPAL

Visas for Nepal are available on arrival at Kathmandu airport and at all of Nepal's land border crossings, including Kakarbhitta, the crossing nearest to Bhutan. The fee for a 15-/30-/90-day visa is US$25/40/100. If you fly into Kathmandu's Tribhuvan airport, you can scan your machine-readable passport into a visa registration machine, which will take your photo, and fill out the form digitally. At other crossings, you'll need to fill out the form manually and provide a passport photo.

If you are making a side trip to Bhutan from Kathmandu, you can get a multiple-entry visa the first time you arrive in Nepal. However, you can also simply get another visa on arrival when you return to Nepal. You can also obtain a visa for Nepal in advance from embassies abroad.

If you are simply transiting through Kathmandu, you can get a 24-hour transit visa for US$5.

Travel Permits
RESTRICTED-AREA PERMITS

All of Bhutan outside of the Paro and Thimphu valleys is classified as a restricted area. Tour operators obtain a 'road permit' for the places on your itinerary, and this permit is checked and endorsed by the police at immigration checkpoints strategically located at important road junctions. The tour operator must return the permit to the government at the completion of the tour, and it is scrutinised for major deviations from the authorised program. In general you won't be aware that any of this is going on in the background.

There are immigration checkpoints in Hongtsho (east of Thimphu), Chhukha (between Thimphu and Phuentsholing), Rinchending (above Phuentsholing), Wangdue Phodrang, Chazam (near Trashigang), Wamrong (between Trashigang and Samdrup Jongkhar) and in Samdrup Jongkhar. All are open from 5am to 9pm daily.

PERMITS TO ENTER TEMPLES

Outside of festivals, tourists are allowed to visit the courtyards of dzongs and usually the *tshokhang* (assembly hall) and one designated lhakhang in each dzong, but only when accompanied by a licensed Bhutanese guide. This provision is subject to certain restrictions, including visiting hours, dress standards and other rules that vary by district.

The TCB has a small list of places tourists *cannot* visit, with the assumption that all other places can be visited. You can generally visit any lhakhang that is private or village run. Dzongs are open to all during the time of a tsechu, when you may visit the courtyard, but not the lhakhangs. Your tour company will deal with all the necessary paperwork, so let them

INDIAN TRAVELLERS IN BHUTAN

Indian nationals (and citizens of Bangladesh and Maldives) are allowed to travel independently in Bhutan without a visa, either with or without the services of a Bhutanese tour operator. On arrival at Paro or Bhutan's land border crossing at Phuentsholing, Indian travellers can obtain a seven-day entry-cum-stay permit from the immigration office upon presentation of a passport or government-issued ID such as a voter's registration card.

This permit allows travel only to Phuentsholing, Thimphu and Paro, but it can be extended at the **Immigration Office** (Map p54; ☎02-323127; 79 Norzin Lam; ◎9am-5pm Mon-Fri) in Thimphu up to a maximum of 30 days. Indian tourists can also request a route permit here to travel beyond the three aforementioned towns. If you are driving yourself, you will need a route permit from the Royal Safety Transport Authority (RSTA; www.rsta.gov. bt), based at the bus station at Phuentsholing.

Indians without stay permits can wander freely in Phuentsholing and go 5km into Bhutan during the day, but must return to India before 10pm.

know in advance if there are specific goembas or chapels you wish to visit.

If you are a practising Buddhist, you may apply for a permit to visit certain dzongs and religious institutions that are usually off-limits. The credibility of your application will be enhanced if you include a letter of reference from a recognised Buddhist organisation in your home country.

Volunteering

Bhutan is highly selective about the type of projects it wants in the country, and opportunities for volunteer work are limited. The UN has numerous programs in Bhutan, all coordinated through the UN Development Programme (UNDP), and many different agencies feed into the program.

Smaller agencies that operate programs in Bhutan include ACB (Austria), Danida (Denmark), GTZ (Germany), Helvetas (Switzerland), JOCV & JICA (Japan), Save the Children, SNV (Netherlands) and VSA (New Zealand). Lonely Planet does not endorse any organisations we do not work with directly, so research any project throughly before signing up to make sure that it takes appropriate steps to protect and benefit local people.

Volunteers are not subject to the normal rules for tourists and the agency employing you will arrange your visa. Volunteers are allowed two visitors a year; the visitors must be close relatives and are not subject to the tourist tariff.

Women Travellers

While Bhutan has some patriarchal traditions, women are rarely subject to harassment and do not need to take any special precautions over and above the general behaviour you might follow at home. Men have a reasonably liberated attitude towards their relations with women and female travellers rarely report any problems in Bhutan.

However, female travellers should be aware that romantic liaisons between tourists and Bhutanese guides are not uncommon, so be cautious about being over-familiar in case this is misinterpreted. Visiting the home of a guide by yourself, without the rest of your group, might be interpreted as a sign of romantic interest. Women are generally not allowed to enter the goenkhang (protector chapel) of a monastery or lhakhang, but these chapels are often closed to male visitors as well.

Work

The popular Teach in Bhutan (www.teachinbhutan. org) program is run by the Bhutan-Canada Foundation (www.bhutancanada.org) and it places qualified teachers at schools in Bhutan. The program is not limited to Canadian citizens, and English-speaking, qualified teachers from other countries can apply. Salaries are paid by the Bhutanese government.

Transport

GETTING THERE & AWAY

The vast majority of travellers to Bhutan arrive by air at Bhutan's only international airport in Paro. Some travellers enter Bhutan by road at Phuentsholing, Gelephu or Samdrup Jongkhar on the southern border with India.

Flights, cars and tours can be booked online at lonelyplanet.com/bookings.

Entering the Country

Entry procedures are generally simple because your tour guide will meet you on arrival. You'll need your visa authorisation form from the Ministry of Foreign Affairs to board your flight into Bhutan and you should present it again to get your visa stamped into your passport on arrival.

Passports

Ensure that your passport has more than six months of validity remaining as many countries in the region will not issue visas to anyone whose passport is about to expire.

Keep your passport safe. No country other than India has the facility for issuing a replacement passport in Bhutan. If you lose your passport, you must travel 'stateless' to another country to get it replaced. You should carry some additional form of identification and a photocopy of your passport to help in such an event.

Indian, Bangladeshi and Maldivian travellers do not need a passport to visit Bhutan, but will need some form of (photographic) identification, such as a voter's registration card.

Air

Airports & Airlines

Bhutan has one international airport, **Paro** (Map p86; ☑08-271423), and two airlines: government-owned **Druk Air** (Map p54; ☑02-332154, toll free 1300; drukairthimphu@ druknet.bt; Thori Lam; ☺9am-10pm Mon-Fri, 10am-noon Sat & Sun), and private airline **Bhutan Airlines** (Map p62; ☑02-334052, toll free 1234; www.bhutanairlines.bt; lower fl, Tashi Mall, Norzin Lam; ☺9am-5pm Mon-Fri, 9am-1pm Sat, 10am-1pm Sun), a division of the Tashi Group. Both have offices in Thimphu, and in the countries they fly to – see the websites for details.

The Druk Air and Bhutan Airlines schedules change by season, but there are usually daily flights from Kathmandu, New Delhi and Bangkok, and less frequent flights to Bagdogra and Kolkata (Calcutta) in India, Dhaka in Bangladesh, and Singapore. Periodically, flights also connect Paro to Gaya in India (for Bodhgaya). Longer flights often involve a stop at another airport en route. Extra flights are put on during the Thimphu tsechu (dance festival) in October and the Paro tsechu in April.

There are only a few aircraft that can operate on a runway as short and high as at Paro and only a handful of Bhutanese pilots are licensed to fly on this challenging manual landing route. All landings and take-offs in Paro are by visual flight rules (VFR), which means that the pilot must be able to see the runway before landing, and see the surrounding hills before take-off.

This means that no flights can be operated at night or in poor visibility, so when the Paro valley is clouded in, flights are delayed, sometimes for days. When this happens your tour program will have to be changed and everything rebooked. The upside of such a delay is that you can probably add some spontaneity into your schedule in Bhutan and make a few modifications as you go.

A few tips for travelling by air from Paro:

➡ Reconfirm your flight before departure and also once in Paro, to ensure that the schedule has not changed.

➡ Check in early for flights as they occasionally depart before the scheduled time, especially if the weather starts to change for the worse.

IN-FLIGHT ENTERTAINMENT

The flight from Kathmandu to Paro provides the most dramatic view of Himalayan scenery of any scheduled flight, so check in early and ask for a window seat on the left of the aircraft. As you take off from Kathmandu's Tribhuvan airport, look for the impressive Bodhnath stupa to the north. Soon a continuous chain of peaks appears just off the left wing.

The captain will point out key peaks such as Everest (8848m), Makalu (8462m) and the huge massif of Kanchenjunga (8598m), but if you have trekked in Nepal and are familiar with the mountains you can pick out many more. The elusive Shishapangma (8013m) is sometimes visible inside Tibet, and it's often possible to spot Gauri Shankar (7185m), with its notched shape, Cho Oyu (8153m), Nuptse (7906m), with its long ridge, Lhotse (8501m), Chamlang (7319m) and dome-shaped Kumbhakarna (Jannu; 7710m).

Once past Kanchenjunga, the peaks are more distant. This is the Sikkim Himalaya; the major peaks, from west to east, are Chomoyummo (6829m), Pauhunri (7125m) and Shudu Tsenpa (7032m). As the plane approaches Paro you may be able to spot the beautiful snow peak of Jhomolhari (7314m) and the grey ridge-shaped peak of Jichu Drakye (6989m).

The plane then descends, often through clouds, banking steeply into the wooded valleys of Bhutan. Depending on the approach pattern that day, you may see Taktshang Goemba and Paro Dzong as you descend. The bombing-run-style final approach to Paro airport is often described as the scariest landing in the world, but Bhutanese pilots are highly experienced and the views are amazing, as the plane banks and turns almost within touching distance of the mountainous terrain.

➜ Flights are often delayed because of weather and local airlines recommend that you travel on nonrestricted tickets for any onward connections, allowing at least 24 hours' transit time before your connecting flight.

Tickets

Druk Air and Bhutan Airlines tickets can be purchased online using a credit card on the airlines' websites. There are no discounts or student fares, except for citizens of Bhutan and SAARC nationals. Be sure to select the correct status when you book – if you try to board with a Bhutanese or SAARC ticket and you are not from the relevant country, your ticket will be cancelled.

It's also possible to have your agent book your tickets and email you the e-ticket. In the event of a cancellation you are likely to get a refund quicker this way and your agent should get direct notifications if there are changes to the flight times. Your agent will also email you a scan of your visa clearance from the Department of Immigration and you may need to show

a printout of this when you check in.

You may need to also buy a ticket to and from the place where you will connect to Druk Air. For most travellers this essentially means Delhi, Bangkok, Singapore or Kathmandu, depending on where you are travelling from and which city you'd rather transit through. Delhi, Singapore and Bangkok offer the most international connections, but Kathmandu will give you an extra taste of the Himalaya. Other connections via Kolkata or Dhaka are possible, but fewer discounted international airfares are available to these places.

Transit Baggage

Although Bhutan's airlines say they have transit agreements with other carriers, your ticket to Paro will be separate from your other international tickets. This means you cannot check your baggage all the way through to Paro via a connecting flight. You will need to reclaim your baggage and recheck it at the Druk Air or Bhutan Airlines counter.

As a result, you may need to go through immigration at

your transfer airport to pick up your luggage in order to check in again. You may need a visa, even if you're only entering the country to check in your bags. Transiting through Singapore, Bangkok or Kathmandu is usually easiest as you can get either a free visa on arrival or an inexpensive transit visa.

When you depart from Bhutan, Druk Air claims it can check bags through to your final destination if you give staff the flight details during check-in, but be aware that this information is handwritten on the baggage tags, so it's not the foolproof computer system that usually ensures bags reach their final destination.

Land

Crossing between Bhutan and India (and then to Nepal) is relatively straightforward at the following three points found along Bhutan's southern border. On an organised tour, your driver and guide will arrange to meet you at the border (or sometimes across the border in India) and transport you on to your

INTERNATIONAL FLIGHTS TO & FROM PARO

DEPART	ARRIVE	FREQUENCY	COST (US$)
Paro	Bagdogra (India)	2 weekly	142
Paro	Bangkok (Thailand)	daily	485
Paro	Dhaka (Bangladesh)	3 weekly	213
Paro	Guhawati (India)	4 weekly	153
Paro	Kathmandu (Nepal)	daily	234
Paro	Kolkata (Calcutta; India)	4 weekly	238
Paro	New Delhi (India)	daily	364
Paro	Singapore	2 weekly	539

first destination. For non-SAARC visitors, visas (p290) must be applied for in advance through the agency arranging your tour and will be stamped into your passport on arrival in Bhutan. Possible crossing points are:

Phuentsholing The primary border crossing from India into Bhutan, on the border with the Indian state of West Bengal.

Samdrup Jongkhar Much less used but still possible for exit or entry, in the far east on the border with the Indian state of Assam.

Gelephu Another little-used crossing for exit or entry, on the border with Assam.

To/From Phuentsholing (India)

The gate between Phuentsholing and Jaigaon (just across the border) opens at 6am and closes at 9pm for vehicles, but people can cross on foot until 10pm. If you are travelling to or from Bhutan via Phuentsholing, all roads lead through Siliguri in West Bengal. From Siliguri, it's easy to travel by bus or jeep to the Indian hill stations of Darjeeling (77km), Gangtok (Sikkim; 114km) or Kalimpong (66km), and also to the Nepali border crossing at Kakarbhitta (35km).

If you are headed into Bhutan from Siliguri, Bhutan Transport Services operates direct buses daily to Phuentsholing (₹120 to ₹150, five hours) at 7am, 12.30pm and 2pm from the Howrah Petrol

Pump stop on Burdwan Rd. Indian bus companies operate frequent buses from Siliguri's Central Bus Terminus to Jaigaon (₹170) on the Indian side of the border crossing.

Heading into India from Bhutan, there are easy bus connections from Phuentsholing or Jaigaon to Siliguri (169km, six hours). On arrival in Siliguri, you can charter a taxi or autorickshaw to reach the busy train station at New Jalpaiguri (NJP) on the main line between Kolkata (Calcutta) and Northeast India. Bagdogra airport, served by flights from across India, is just 12km west of Siliguri.

Alternatively, you can arrange transport from Jaigaon to the small train stations at Hasimara or Alipurduar, on the rail line between Siliguri and Guwahati in Assam.

Bhutanese vehicles may travel freely in India and a Bhutanese tour operator can easily arrange a vehicle to any of these destinations. There are also taxis and shared jeeps available in both Phuentsholing and Siliguri.

Since Phuentsholing offers decent lodging options, few choose to halt at Jaigaon. If you absolutely must stay on the Indian side of the border, there are some reasonable hotels near the immigration checkpoint and on MG Rd.

FOREIGNERS

Travelling into Bhutan, your guide will meet you at the

gate and help you obtain your Bhutanese visa from the local immigration checkpoint.

Don't forget to get your passport stamped when leaving India. If your transport has already deposited you in Bhutan, you can simply walk back across the border to complete the paperwork. If you fail to get your passport stamped, you may have problems trying to re-enter India at a later date.

INDIAN NATIONALS

To go through immigration at Phuentsholing, Indian nationals are required to submit a passport-size photograph, a copy of their identification document (this can be a passport or voters' identity card) and a filled-in application form at the **Main Immigration Office** (Map p123; Zhung Lam; ⊙9am-5pm Mon-Fri), located in front of Hotel Druk. A permit is then handed out by the immigration authorities, which must be stamped at the checkpost in Rinchending, en route to Thimphu.

Note that these rules can change at short notice, especially during politically sensitive periods on either side of the border.

To/From Samdrup Jongkhar & Gelephu (India)

Tourists are also allowed to enter or exit Bhutan at Samdrup Jongkhar (eastern Bhutan) and Gelephu (cen-

CLIMATE CHANGE & TRAVEL

Every form of transport that relies on carbon-based fuel generates CO_2, the main cause of human-induced climate change. Modern travel is dependent on aeroplanes, which might use less fuel per kilometre per person than most cars but travel much greater distances. The altitude at which aircraft emit gases (including CO_2) and particles also contributes to their climate change impact. Many websites offer 'carbon calculators' that allow people to estimate the carbon emissions generated by their journey and, for those who wish to do so, to offset the impact of the greenhouse gases emitted with contributions to portfolios of climate-friendly initiatives throughout the world. Lonely Planet offsets the carbon footprint of all staff and author travel.

tral Bhutan). Be aware that strikes (bandhs) can occur at short notice in Assam, and can result in road and border closures. Assamese newspaper The Sentinel (www. sentinelassam.com) has up-to-date news on the region.

The main reason to exit into Assam is to avoid the long drive back over the mountains to Thimphu or Paro after visiting central and eastern Bhutan. From either Samdrup Jongkhar or Gelephu, buses and taxis provide transport to the Assamese capital, Guwahati, which has train connections to destinations across India (including Kolkata) and a busy airport served by flights from major Indian hubs. Coming from Gelephu, you can also take local transport to the town of Bongaigaon, on the main train line between Siliguri and Guwahati.

It is important to get your entry/exit stamp on your way into or out of India. For Gelephu, the Foreigners' Registration Post is 10km south at Deosiri. For Samdrup Jongkhar, the post is 6km south at Darranga. Both are open 24 hours.

To/From Nepal Via India

If you are travelling overland from Nepal, Bhutanese agencies can send a driver to pick you up at Panitanki (aka Raniganj) in West Bengal, across from the Nepal border post at Kakarbhitta. It's also easy to travel on from Panitanki by bus or shared jeep

to Siliguri (₹100, one hour) and pick up transport there to Phuentsholing and other entry points for Bhutan.

Travelling overland into Nepal, the Kakarbhitta/Panitanki border crossing is open from 6am to 6pm. From the bus stand in Kakarbhitta, local buses run to towns in eastern Nepal, and overnight buses make the 17-hour dash to Kathmandu (NRs 1400 to NRs 1685). Bhadrapur Airport, 23km southwest of Kakarbhitta, has daily flights to Kathmandu.

GETTING AROUND

The only way to explore Bhutan is on foot or by road, or via the rather limited domestic air service. If you are travelling on a tourist visa, the cost of all transport is included in the price of your trip and you'll have a vehicle available for both short- and long-distance travel.

There is one main road: the National Hwy, a stretch of well-maintained tarmac that winds its way up and down mountains, across clattering bridges, along the side of cliffs and over high mountain passes. Sections of the road are being widened to double lanes. Until you experience the mountain roads of Bhutan you may not be able to fully appreciate the logistics involved in forging a path through this rugged terrain.

Nevertheless, flooding, mudflows and rockfalls

present continual hazards, especially when it rains. Roads can also become blocked due to snow in winter. Where there is a blockage, the army is quickly mobilised to clear the highway, but this can take anywhere from an hour to several days.

Air

Bhutan has just a handful of domestic air services. There are small airstrips at Gelephu (in southern Bhutan, near the border with India), at Bumthang (Bathpalathang/Jakar, central Bhutan) and Yongphula (south of Trashigang in the far east). **Druk Air** (Map p54; ☑02-332154, toll free 1300; drukairthimphu@druknet.bt; Thori Lam; ☺9am-10pm Mon-Fri, 10am-noon Sat & Sun) flies several times a week from Paro to Bumthang and from Paro to Yongphula via Gelephu. Check with your tour company or the airline for the latest schedules.

The **Royal Bhutan Helicopter Service** (Map p86; ☑17170964, 08-271396; www.rbhsl.bt; Paro) operates charter and sightseeing flights, along with medical evacuations from its base in Paro.

Bicycle

Some travellers bring their mountain bikes to Bhutan, and several agencies in Thimphu and elsewhere rent bicycles and arrange dedicated mountain biking tours (p283).

Bus

Only locals, residents and Indian tourists are likely to travel on buses in Bhutan. Public buses are crowded bone-shakers, and Bhutan's winding roads make them doubly uncomfortable. The minibuses run by the Bhutanese government have earned the nickname 'vomit comets' as so many passengers suffer from motion sickness when travelling in them. Private operators such as Dhug, Metho and Sernya use more comfortable Toyota Coasters that cost about 50% more than the minibus fare.

From Thimphu, buses run throughout the day to Phuentsholing, and several buses run daily from Thimphu to Paro, Haa and Punakha. Long-distance buses run daily from Phobjikha, Trongsa, Bumthang and Gelephu. Multiday trips to Mongar, Lhuentse and Trashigang leave less frequently.

A public bus service operates throughout Thimphu, running as far as Dechenchoeling Palace in the north and Simtokha and Babesa to the south, but few travellers use it.

Car & Motorcycle

For most travellers, all transport is provided by the tour agency. If you are outside of the daily fee system, you can charter a car or jeep and driver in most towns. This is preferable to driving yourself: although Bhutanese drivers tend not to speed, roads are narrow and trucks roar around hairpin bends, appearing suddenly and forcing oncoming vehicles to the side.

A number of agencies arrange specialist motorcycle tours of Bhutan, including Nepal-based Himalayan Roadrunners (www. ridehigh.com) and local company **Knight Adventure**

Tours (☑02-339138; www. bhutanknight.com; Thimphu). Contact the Black Dragons Motorcycle Club (www. facebook.com/pages/ Bhutan-Dragons-Motorcycle/516531518397044) in Thimphu for advice on tackling Bhutan's roads.

Bringing Your Own Vehicle

If you are travelling into Bhutan with your own vehicle, you can get a 14-day permit at the Phuentsholing border. You will need the help of a tour operator to handle the paperwork. If you are driving a vehicle that is registered overseas, you'll need a carnet in order to get through India.

Indian visitors may travel throughout most of Bhutan in their own vehicle, upon getting all relevant documents such as registration papers, insurance policies, emission and fitness certificates, and individual driving licences endorsed by the Road Safety & Transport Authority (www.rsta.gov.bt) at the border. Traffic regulations are the same as in India and are strictly enforced.

Driving Licences

NGO staff and volunteers who need to drive in Bhutan must obtain a driving licence issued by the Road Safety & Transport Authority (www.rsta.gov.bt). Bhutanese licences are also valid throughout India.

An International Driving Permit is not valid in Bhutan. An Indian driving licence is valid in Bhutan, and it's possible for Indian nationals to drive in Bhutan, but unless you are an accomplished mountain driver, it's safer to hire a car and driver.

Road Rules

Traffic keeps to the left and is much more orderly than in most other south Asian countries. Speeds are low in towns and on rural roads; you will be lucky to average more than 30km/h on roads

in the hills. Nevertheless, trucks can pose a serious hazard, appearing suddenly around corners and blocking the road. Watch for dogs and livestock on the road too.

As is the case throughout Asia, it is important that the police establish who was at fault in any traffic accident. This means that the police must arrive and make the decision before any of the vehicles can be moved, even if the vehicles are blocking a narrow road. A relatively minor accident can stop traffic for hours while everyone waits patiently for the police to arrive from the nearest town.

Taxi

There are local taxi services in Thimphu, Paro, Phuentsholing and Jakar. Taxis usually have meters, but drivers rarely use them. For long-distance trips they operate on a flat rate that is rarely open to negotiation. Taxi drivers have a habit of charging foreigners, including Indians, as much as they can – one of Bhutan's few rip-offs.

You should expect to pay Nu 100 for a local trip within Thimphu, or Nu 2000 for a full day of sightseeing. If you are travelling between Thimphu and a nearby town, look for a taxi that is from the place you are travelling to, as you may be able to negotiate a lower price.

The MyDrukRide taxi-booking app (www. drukride.com) allows users to book taxis from mobile phones.

Supplementing the bus services, Bhutan has an army of shared taxis, which buzz back and forth between the major towns. These small cars charge per passenger and leave when full, or you can charter the whole vehicle by paying for all the seats.

Health

The main health concerns in Bhutan are similar to those in other south Asian destinations: there is a relatively high risk of acquiring traveller's diarrhoea, a respiratory infection or a minor skin infection, and it pays to obtain immunisations and take other precautions to avoid more serious illnesses.

Infectious diseases can interrupt your trip and make you feel miserable, but they are rarely fatal. If you go trekking, there are also risks from avalanches, rockfalls and altitude sickness. Falling off trails as you trek is rare but can happen.

The following advice is a general guide only and does not replace the advice of a doctor trained in travel medicine.

BEFORE YOU GO

Pack medications in their original, clearly labelled containers. A signed and dated letter from your physician describing your medical conditions and medications, including generic names, is also a good idea. If carrying syringes or needles, be sure to have a physician's letter documenting their medical necessity. If you have a heart condition, bring a copy of your ECG taken just prior to travelling.

If you take any regular medication, bring double your needs in case of loss or theft. You can't rely on a full range of medications being available from pharmacies in Bhutan.

Insurance

Even if you are fit and healthy, don't travel without health insurance – accidents do happen and illness isn't always avoidable. Declare any existing medical conditions you have – the insurance company *will* check if your problem is pre-existing and will not cover you if it is undeclared.

You may also require extra cover for adventure activities such as rock climbing and trekking at altitude. If your health insurance doesn't cover you for medical expenses abroad, consider getting specialist insurance – for more information, check Lonely Planet (www.lonelyplanet.com). If you're uninsured, emergency evacuation is expensive; bills of over US$100,000 are not uncommon.

Find out in advance if your insurance plan will make payments directly to providers or reimburse you later for overseas health expenditures. (In many countries, doctors expect payment in cash.) You may prefer a policy that pays doctors or hospitals directly rather than you having to pay on the spot and claim later. If you have to claim later, make sure you keep all documentation. Some insurance companies ask you to call them at a centre in your home country, where an immediate assessment of your problem is made.

Vaccinations

Specialised travel-medicine clinics can give specific recommendations for you and your trip, or visit your usual doctor before you travel. Most vaccines don't produce immunity until at least two weeks after they're given, so get your jabs four to eight weeks before departure. Ask your doctor for an International Certificate of Vaccination, which will list all the vaccinations you've received.

Recommended Vaccinations

The only vaccine required by international regulations is for yellow fever. Proof of vaccination will only be required if you have visited a country in the yellow-fever zone within the six days prior to entering Bhutan. If you are travelling to Bhutan from Africa or South America, you should check to see if you require proof of vaccination.

Malaria is present in southern Bhutan, but cases are rare and many travellers only take prophylaxis if they are spending long periods in rural areas.

MEDICAL CHECKLIST

Recommended items for a personal medical kit:

➡ Antifungal cream, eg Clotrimazole

➡ Antibacterial cream, eg Muciprocin

➡ Antibiotic for skin infections, eg Amoxicillin/Clavulanate or Cephalexin

➡ Antibiotics for diarrhoea, eg Norfloxacin or Ciprofloxacin for bacterial diarrhoea; Tinidazole for giardiasis or amoebic dysentery

➡ Antihistamine, eg Cetirizine for daytime and Promethazine for night

➡ Antiseptic, eg Betadine

➡ Antispasmodic for stomach cramps, eg Buscopan

➡ Contraceptives

➡ Decongestant, eg Pseudoephedrine

➡ DEET-based insect repellent

➡ Diarrhoea treatment – an oral rehydration solution (eg Gastrolyte), diarrhoea 'stopper' (eg Loperamide) and antinausea medication (eg Prochlorperazine)

➡ First-aid items such as scissors, bandages, gauze, thermometer, sterile needles and syringes, safety pins and tweezers

➡ Ibuprofen or other anti-inflammatory

➡ Iodine tablets (unless you are pregnant or have a thyroid problem) to purify water

➡ Laxative, eg Coloxyl

➡ Paracetamol

➡ Permethrin to impregnate clothing and mosquito nets

➡ Steroid cream for allergic/itchy rashes, eg 1% to 2% hydrocortisone

➡ Sunscreen

➡ Throat lozenges

➡ Thrush (vaginal yeast infection) treatment, eg Clotrimazole pessaries

➡ Ural or equivalent if you're prone to urine infections

The World Health Organization recommends the following vaccinations for travellers to Bhutan (as well as being up to date with measles, mumps and rubella vaccinations):

Diphtheria and tetanus (for adults) Single booster recommended if none taken in the previous 10 years. Side effects include sore arm and fever.

Hepatitis A Provides almost 100% protection for up to a year; a booster after 12 months provides at least another 20 years' protection. Mild side effects such as headache and sore arm occur in 5% to 10% of people.

Hepatitis B Now considered routine for most travellers, it is given as three shots over six months. A rapid schedule is also available, as is a combined vaccination with Hepatitis A. Side effects are mild and uncommon: usually headache and sore arm. Lifetime protection occurs in 95% of people.

Polio Bhutan's last case of polio was reported in 1986, but it has been reported more recently in nearby Nepal and India. Only one booster is required for an adult for lifetime protection. Inactivated polio vaccine is safe during pregnancy.

Typhoid The vaccine offers around 70% protection, lasts for two to three years and comes as a single shot. Tablets are also available; however, the injection is usually recommended as it

has fewer side effects. Sore arm and fever may occur.

Varicella If you haven't had chickenpox, discuss this vaccination with your doctor.

The following immunisations may be recommended for long-term travellers (more than one month) or those at special risk:

Japanese B encephalitis Three injections in all. Booster recommended after two years. Sore arm and headache are the most common side effects. Rarely, an allergic reaction comprising hives and swelling can occur up to 10 days after any of the three doses.

Meningitis Single injection. There are two types of

vaccination: the quadrivalent vaccine gives two to three years' protection; meningitis group C vaccine gives around 10 years' protection. Recommended for long-term backpackers aged under 25.

Rabies Three injections in all. A booster after one year will then provide 10 years' protection. Side effects are rare – occasionally headache and sore arm.

Tuberculosis A complex issue. Adult long-term travellers are usually recommended to have a TB skin test before and after travel, rather than vaccination. Only one vaccine given in a lifetime.

Websites

There is a wealth of travel health advice on the internet. Useful resources include:

Centers for Disease Control & Prevention (www.cdc.gov) Good general information on travel health issues.

MD Travel Health (www.redplanet.travel/mdtravelhealth) Provides complete travel health recommendations for every country.

World Health Organization (WHO; www.who.int) The global body overseeing public health.

Further Reading

Recommended references include *Traveller's Health: How to Stay Healthy Abroad* by Dr Richard Dawood and *Travelling Well* by Dr Deborah Mills – check out the website www.travellingwell.com.au.

IN BHUTAN

Availability & Cost of Healthcare

There is one private health clinic in Thimphu, but most healthcare in the country is provided by the government.

All district headquarters towns have a hospital, and will accept travellers in need of medical attention. The best facility is the **Jigme Dorji Wangchuck National Referral Hospital** (☏02-322496; www.jdwnrh.gov.bt; Gongphel Lam) in Thimphu. It has general physicians and several specialists, labs and operating rooms. Treatment is free, even for tourists.

If you are seriously ill or injured, you should consider evacuation to the excellent medical facilities in Bangkok. It is difficult to find reliable medical care in rural areas. Your closest embassy and insurance company are good contacts.

Self-treatment may be appropriate if your problem is minor (eg traveller's diarrhoea), you are carrying the appropriate medication and you cannot attend a recommended clinic. If you think you may have a serious disease, especially malaria, do not waste time – travel to the nearest quality facility to receive attention. It is always better to be assessed by a doctor than to rely on self-treatment.

Most towns have fairly well-stocked pharmacies. Most of the medical supplies mentioned in this section are available without a prescription.

Infectious Diseases

Coughs, Colds & Chest Infections

Respiratory infections usually start as a virus and are exacerbated by urban pollution, or cold and altitude in the mountains. Commonly, a secondary bacterial infection will intervene – marked by fever, chest pain and coughing up discoloured or blood-tinged sputum. If you have the symptoms of an infection, seek medical advice.

Dengue Fever

This mosquito-borne disease is becomingly increasingly problematic in lowland areas of Bhutan. As there is no vaccine available it can only be prevented by avoiding mosquito bites. The mosquito that carries dengue bites day and night, so use insect avoidance measures at all times. Symptoms include high fever, severe headache and body ache. Some people develop a rash and experience diarrhoea. There is no specific treatment, just rest and paracetamol – do not take aspirin though, as it increases the likelihood of haemorrhaging. See a doctor to be diagnosed and monitored.

Hepatitis A

A problem throughout the region, this food- and water-borne virus infects the liver, causing jaundice (yellow skin and eyes), nausea and lethargy. There is no specific treatment for hepatitis A – you just need to allow time for the liver to heal. All travellers to Bhutan should be vaccinated against hepatitis A.

Hepatitis B

The only sexually transmitted disease that can be prevented by vaccination, hepatitis B is spread by body fluids, including in sexual contact. The long-term consequences can include liver cancer and cirrhosis.

Hepatitis E

Hepatitis E is transmitted through contaminated food and water and has similar symptoms to hepatitis A, but is far less common. It is a severe problem for pregnant women. There is currently no readily available vaccine, and prevention is following safe eating and drinking guidelines.

Influenza

Present year-round in the tropics, influenza (flu)

TRAVELLER'S DIARRHOEA

Traveller's diarrhoea is by far the most common problem affecting travellers – between 30% and 50% of people will suffer from it within two weeks of starting their trip. In over 80% of cases, traveller's diarrhoea is caused by a bacteria, and therefore responds promptly to treatment with antibiotics, such as Norfloxacin. Keep in mind, though, that a couple of loose stools are little cause for concern.

Loperamide is just a 'stopper' and doesn't get to the cause of the problem. It can be helpful, for example, if you have to go on a long car trip. Don't take Loperamide if you have a fever, or blood in your stools, and seek medical attention quickly if you do not respond to an appropriate antibiotic.

Amoebic dysentery is very rare in travellers but is often misdiagnosed. Symptoms are similar to bacterial diarrhoea: fever, bloody diarrhoea and generally feeling unwell. You should always seek reliable medical care if you have blood in your diarrhoea. Treatment involves two drugs: Tinidazole or Metronidazole to kill the parasite in your gut, followed by a second drug to kill the cysts.

Giardia lamblia is a parasite that is relatively common in travellers. Symptoms include nausea, bloating, excess gas, fatigue and intermittent diarrhoea. The parasite will eventually go away if left untreated, but this can take months. The treatment of choice is Tinidazole.

symptoms include high fever, muscle aches, runny nose, cough and sore throat. It can be very severe in people over the age of 65 or in those with underlying medical conditions such as heart disease or diabetes; vaccination is recommended for these individuals. There is no specific treatment, just rest and paracetamol.

Japanese B Encephalitis

This viral disease is transmitted by mosquitoes and is rare in travellers. Like most mosquito-borne diseases it is becoming a more common problem in affected countries. Most cases occur in rural areas and vaccination is recommended for travellers spending more than one month outside cities. There is no treatment, and a third of infected people will die, while another third will suffer permanent brain damage.

Malaria

Malaria is present in Bhutan but the risk to travellers is small, unless you will be spending time in rural areas in southern Bhutan. Seek expert advice as to whether your trip actually puts you

at risk, and the most appropriate course of prophylaxis. Even if you take a course of antimalarial tablets, it always pays to take steps to avoid being bitten by mosquitoes, which can also carry dengue fever and other infections.

Malaria is caused by a parasite transmitted by the bite of an infected mosquito. The most important symptom of malaria is fever, but general symptoms such as headache, diarrhoea, cough or chills may also occur. Diagnosis can only be made by taking a blood sample.

Travellers are advised to prevent mosquito bites by taking these steps:

➡ Use a DEET-containing insect repellent on exposed skin. Natural repellents such as citronella can be effective, but must be applied more frequently than products containing DEET.

➡ Sleep under a mosquito net impregnated with pyrethrin.

➡ Choose accommodation with screens and fans (if not air-conditioned).

➡ Impregnate clothing with pyrethrin in high-risk areas.

➡ Wear long sleeves and trousers in light colours.

➡ Use mosquito coils.

➡ Spray your room with insect repellent before going out for your evening meal.

If you are advised to take antimalarial medication, there is a variety of options. The effectiveness of the Chloroquine and Paludrine combination is now limited in many parts of south Asia. Common side effects include nausea (40% of people) and mouth ulcers.

The daily tablet Doxycycline is a broad-spectrum antimalarial that has the added benefit of helping to prevent a variety of tropical diseases, including leptospirosis, tick-borne diseases and typhus. The potential side effects include photosensitivity, thrush, indigestion, heartburn, nausea and interference with the contraceptive pill. More serious side effects include ulceration of the oesophagus – you can help prevent this by taking your tablet with a meal, and never lying down within 30 minutes of taking it. It must continue to be taken for four weeks after leaving the risk area.

Lariam (Mefloquine) is a weekly tablet. Serious side effects are rare but include

TAP WATER

→ Never drink tap water in Bhutan.

→ Bottled water is generally safe – check the seal is intact at purchase. Most hotels provide purified water for guests.

→ Avoid ice.

→ Avoid fresh juices – they may have been watered down.

There are several options for purifying your own water while trekking.

→ Boiling – this is the most efficient method; bring water to a rolling boil for at least one minute (or five minutes above 2000m).

→ Chemical purification – the best chemical purifier is iodine but its use is now discouraged because of potential health risks and chlorine is used instead.

→ Water filtration – travel water filters should also filter out viruses; ensure your filter has a chemical barrier and a small pore size, eg less than four microns.

depression, anxiety, psychosis and having fits. Anyone with a history of depression, anxiety, another psychological disorder, or epilepsy should not take Lariam. It is considered safe in the second and third trimesters of pregnancy. Tablets must be taken for four weeks after leaving the risk area.

Malarone is a combination of Atovaquone and Proguanil. Side effects are uncommon and mild: most commonly nausea and headache. It is the best tablet for those on short trips to high-risk areas. It must be taken for one week after leaving the risk area.

Rabies

Rabies is considered to be endemic in Bhutan. This fatal disease is spread by the bite or lick of an infected animal – most commonly a dog or monkey. You should seek medical advice immediately after any animal bite and commence post-exposure treatment as a precaution; it could save your life. Having a pre-travel vaccination means the post-bite treatment is greatly simplified. If

an animal bites you, gently wash the wound with soap and water, and apply iodine-based antiseptic. If you are not pre-vaccinated you will need to receive rabies immunoglobulin as soon as possible.

Tuberculosis

While rare in travellers, medical and aid workers and long-term travellers who have significant contact with the local population should take precautions. Vaccination is usually given only to children under the age of five, but adults at risk are recommended to have pre- and post-travel tuberculosis testing. The main symptoms are fever, cough, weight loss, night sweats and tiredness.

Typhoid

This serious bacterial infection is spread via food and water. It gives a high and slowly progressive fever, headache and may be accompanied by a dry cough and stomach pain. It is diagnosed by blood tests and treated with antibiotics. Vaccination is recommended for all travellers spending

more than a week in Bhutan. Be aware that vaccination is not 100% effective so you must still be careful with what you eat and drink.

Environmental Hazards

Even on a cloudy day sunburn can occur, especially at altitude where the atmosphere is thinner. Minimise the risk by applying sunscreen and wearing sunglasses and a hat outdoors.

Food

Eating in restaurants is the biggest risk factor for contracting traveller's diarrhoea. Ways to avoid it include eating only freshly cooked food, and avoiding shellfish and food that has been sitting around in buffets. Wash and/or peel fruit and vegetables before eating.

High Altitude

If you are going to altitudes above 3000m you should get information on preventing, recognising and treating Acute Mountain Sickness (AMS). AMS is a notoriously unpredictable condition and can even affect people who are accustomed to walking at high altitudes. AMS has been fatal at 3000m, although most fatalities occur above 3500m.

SYMPTOMS

Mild symptoms of AMS are very common in travellers visiting high altitudes, and usually develop during the first 24 hours at altitude. These will generally disappear through acclimatisation in several hours to several days.

Symptoms tend to be worse at night and include headache, dizziness, lethargy, loss of appetite, nausea, breathlessness and irritability. Difficulty sleeping is another common symptom.

AMS may become more serious without warning

and can be fatal. Symptoms are caused by the accumulation of fluid in the lungs and brain, and include breathlessness at rest, a dry irritative cough (which may progress to the production of pink, frothy sputum), severe headache, lack of coordination (typically leading to a 'drunken walk'), confusion, irrational behaviour, vomiting and eventually unconsciousness.

The symptoms of AMS, however mild, are a warning – be sure to take them seriously! Trekkers should keep an eye on each other as those experiencing symptoms, especially severe symptoms, may not be in a position to recognise them. One thing to note is that while the symptoms of mild AMS often precede those of severe AMS, this is not always the case. Severe AMS can strike with little or no warning.

ACCLIMATISATION

With an increase in altitude, the human body needs time to develop physiological mechanisms to cope with the decreased oxygen. This process of acclimatisation is still not fully understood, but is known to involve modifications in breathing patterns and heart rate, and an increase in the blood's oxygen-carrying capabilities.

These compensatory mechanisms usually take about one to three days to develop at a particular altitude. Once you are acclimatised to a given height you are unlikely to get AMS at that elevation, but you can still get ill when you travel higher. If the ascent is too high and too fast, these compensatory reactions may not kick into gear fast enough.

PREVENTION

To prevent Acute Mountain Sickness:

➡ Ascend slowly and allow for frequent rest days, spending two to three nights at each rise of 1000m.

➡ Climb high, but sleep low. Always try to sleep at a lower altitude than the greatest height reached during the day.

➡ Once above 3000m, care should be taken not to increase the sleeping altitude by more than 400m per day. If the terrain won't allow for less than 400m of elevation gain, take an extra acclimatisation day before tackling the climb.

➡ Drink extra fluids. Mountain air is dry and cold, and moisture is lost as you breathe and sweat, which may result in dehydration.

➡ Eat light, high-carbohydrate meals for more energy.

➡ Avoid alcohol as it may increase the risk of dehydration, and don't smoke.

➡ Avoid sedatives.

➡ When trekking, take a day off to rest and acclimatise if you feel overtired.

➡ Don't push yourself when climbing up to passes; rather, take plenty of breaks.

TREATMENT

Treat mild symptoms by resting at the same or lower altitude until recovery, usually in a day or two. Take paracetamol or aspirin for headaches. If symptoms persist or become worse, however, *immediate descent* is necessary – even 500m can help.

The most effective treatment for severe AMS is to get down to a lower altitude as quickly as possible. In less severe cases the victim will be able to stagger down with some support; in other cases they may need to be carried down. Whatever the case, do not delay, as any delay could be fatal.

AMS victims may need to be flown out of Bhutan as quickly as possible – make sure you have adequate travel insurance.

The drugs acetazolamide (Diamox) and dexamethasone are recommended by some doctors for the prevention of AMS. However, while these drugs can reduce the symptoms, they may also mask warning signs; severe and fatal AMS has occurred in people taking these drugs. Drug treatments should never be used to avoid descent or to enable further ascent.

Insect Bites & Stings

Bedbugs and fleas don't carry disease but their bites are very itchy. You can treat the itch with an antihistamine.

Ticks are contracted after walking in rural areas. Ticks are commonly found behind the ears, on the belly and in armpits. If you have had a tick bite and experience symptoms such as a rash at the site of the bite or elsewhere, fever or muscle aches, you should see a doctor. Doxycycline prevents tick-borne diseases.

Leeches are found in humid rainforest areas. They do not transmit diseases but their bites are often intensely itchy for weeks afterwards and can easily become infected. Apply an iodine-based antiseptic to any leech bite to help prevent infection.

Bee and wasp stings mainly cause problems for people who are allergic to them. Anyone with a serious bee or wasp allergy should carry an injection of adrenaline (eg an EpiPen) for emergency treatment. For others, pain is the main problem – apply ice to the sting and take painkillers.

Skin Problems

Fungal rashes are common in humid climates. There are two common fungal rashes that affect travellers. The first occurs in moist areas that get less air such as the groin, armpits and between the toes. It starts as a red patch that slowly spreads and is usually itchy. Treatment involves keeping the skin dry, avoiding chafing and using an antifungal cream such as Clotrimazole or Lamisil. *Tinea versicolor* is also common – this fungus causes small, light-coloured patches, most commonly on the back, chest and shoulders. Consult a doctor.

Cuts and scratches become easily infected in humid climates. Take meticulous care of any cuts and scratches to prevent complications such as abscesses. Immediately wash all wounds in clean water and apply antiseptic. If you develop signs of infection (increasing pain and redness), see a doctor.

Women's Health

In urban areas of Bhutan, sanitary products are readily available. Birth-control options may be limited, so bring adequate supplies of your chosen form of contraception.

Heat, humidity and antibiotics can all contribute to thrush. Treatment is with antifungal creams and pessaries such as Clotrimazole. A practical alternative is a single tablet of Fluconazole (Diflucan). Urinary tract infections can be precipitated by dehydration or long road journeys without toilet stops; bring suitable antibiotics.

Pregnant women should receive specialised advice before travelling. The ideal time to travel is in the second trimester (between 16 and 28 weeks), when the risk of pregnancy-related problems are at their lowest. During the first trimester there is a risk of miscarriage and in the third trimester complications such as premature labour and high blood pressure are possible. It's also wise to travel with a companion.

Always carry a list of quality medical facilities available at your destination and ensure you continue your standard antenatal care at these facilities. Avoid rural travel in areas with poor transport and medical

facilities. Most of all, ensure travel insurance covers all pregnancy-related possibilities, including premature labour.

Malaria is a high-risk disease during pregnancy. WHO recommends that pregnant women do *not* travel to areas that have Chloroquine-resistant malaria. Lariam (Mefloquine) is considered safe for use in the second and third trimesters, but Doxycycline and Atovaquone/Proguanil are not recommended at any time during pregnancy.

Traveller's diarrhoea can quickly lead to dehydration and result in inadequate blood flow to the placenta. Many of the drugs used to treat various diarrhoea bugs are not recommended in pregnancy. Azithromycin is considered safe.

Although not much is known about the possible adverse effects of altitude on a developing foetus, many authorities recommend not travelling above 4000m while pregnant.

Language

The official language of Bhutan is Dzongkha. While Dzongkha uses the same script as Tibetan – and the two languages are closely related – Dzongkha is sufficiently different that Tibetans can't understand it. English is the medium of instruction in schools, so most educated people can speak it fluently. There are English signboards, books and menus throughout the country. Road signs and government documents are all written in both English and Dzongkha. The national newspaper, Kuensel, is published in three languages: English, Dzongkha and Nepali. In the monastic schools Choekey, the classical Tibetan language, is taught.

As a result of the isolation of many parts of the country, a number of other languages survive, and it's common for regional minorities to have their own language. Some are so different that people from different parts of the country can't understand each other. In eastern Bhutan most people speak Sharchop (meaning 'language of the east'), which is totally different from Dzongkha. In the south, most people speak Nepali. Bumthangkha is a language of the Bumthang region. Also spoken are Khengkha from Zhamgang, Kurtoep from Lhuentshe, Mangdep from Trongsa and Dzala from Trashi Yangtse.

PRONUNCIATION

The simplified pronunciation system used in this chapter is based on the official Romanisation system (used for writing Dzongkha in Roman script), so if you read our coloured pronunciation guides as if they were English, you'll be understood. There are three accent marks: the apostrophe represents a high tone (eg 'ne) or a 'soft' consonant (eg g'), the circumflex accent (eg ê) represents long vowels, and the diaeresis (eg ö) alters the pronunciation of some vowels, namely ä (as the 'a' in 'hat'), ö as the 'ir' in 'dirt' (without the 'r' sound), and ü (like saying 'i' with the lips stretched back).

An h after the consonants c, d, g, l, p and t indicates that they are 'aspirated' (released with a slight puff of air) – listen to the 'p' sounds in 'pip'; the first is aspirated, the second is not.

Practise pronouncing the ng sound (as in 'sing') at the beginning of a word, eg ngawang (a name). The 'dental' consonants, t and th, are pronounced with the tongue tip against the teeth. Note also that c is pronounced as the 'ch' in 'church', and zh as the 's' in 'measure'.

BASICS

Hello.	kuzuzangbo la
Goodbye.	
(by person leaving)	läzhimbe jön
(by person staying)	läzhimbe zhû
Thank you.	kadinchey la
Good luck.	trashi dele
Yes.	ing/yö
No.	mê
Maybe.	im ong
How are you?	chö gadebe yö?
I'm fine.	nga läzhimbe ra yö
What's your name?	chö meng gaci mo?
My name is ...	ngê meng ... ing
Where are you from?	chö gâti lä mo?
I'm from ...	nga ... lä ing
Where are you going?	chö gâti jou mo?
I'm staying at ...	nga ... döp ing
I know.	nga shê
I don't know.	nga mi shê
Can I take a photo?	på tabney chokar la?
Can I take your photo?	chögi på ci tapge mä?
That's OK.	di tupbä
It's cold today.	dari jâm-mä
It's raining.	châp cap dowä

TREKKING & COUNTRY LIFE

alpine hut	bjobi gâ
alpine pasture	la nogi tsamjo
bridge	zam
cold (weather)	sîtraktra
hills	ri
house	chim
lake	tsho
mountain	gangri
mountain pass	la
mule track	ta lam
plain or meadow	thang
prayer flag	dâshi
river	chhu/tsangchhu
steep downhill	lam khamâ zâdra
steep uphill	khagen gâdra
stone carved with prayers	dogi mani
tired	udû/thangche
trail	lam/kanglam
village	ü
warm (weather)	drotokto/tshatokto

Which trail goes to ...?	... josi lam gâti mo?
Is the trail steep?	lam zâdra yö-ga?
Where is my tent?	ngê gû di gâti in-na?
What's the name of this village?	ani ügi meng gaci zeu mo?
Let's go.	jogey-la

bird/chicken	bja
cow	ba
dog	rochi/chi
horse	ta
pig	phap
water buffalo	mahe
yak (male/female)	yâ/jim

barley	nâ
buckwheat	bjô
corn (maize)	gäza/gesasip
husked rice	chum
millet	membja
standing rice	bjâ
wheat	kâ

daughter	bum
elder brother	phôgem
elder sister	azhim
father	apa
friend	totsha/châro
mother	ama
son	bu
younger brother	nucu
younger sister	num/sîm
hers	mogi
his	khogi
mine	ngêgi
yours	chögi

big	bôm
cheap	khetokto
clean	tsangtokto
dirty	khamlôsisi
enough	tupbä/lâmmä
expensive	gong bôm
good	läzhim
happy	gatokto
heavy	jice

not good	läzhim mindu
small	chungku
that	aphidi
this	di

DIRECTIONS & TRANSPORT

What time does the bus leave?	drülkhor chutshö gademci kha jou inna?
I want to get off here.	nga nâ dögobe
How far is the ...?	... gadeci tha ringsa mo?
Is it near?	bolokha in-na?
Is it far?	tha ringsa in-na?
Go straight ahead.	thrangdi song

behind	japkha
here	nâ/nâlu
left	öm
in front of	dongkha
next to	bolokha
opposite	dongko/dongte
right	yäp

there	phâ/phâlu
where	gâti
north	bjang
south	lho
east	shâ
west	nup

EATING & DRINKING

Where is a ...?	... gâti mo?
local bar	changkha
restaurant	zakha
Do you have food now?	chö dato to za-wigang in-na?
I don't eat meat.	nga sha miza
I don't like food with chillies.	nga zhêgo êma dacikha miga
This is too spicy.	di khatshi dû
This is delicious.	di zhim-mä
Please give me a cup of tea.	ngalu ja phôp gang nang
It's enough.	digi lâm-mä

Key Words

food	zhêgo/to
hot (spicy)	khatshi yömi
hot (warm)	tshatom
slices	pa
tasty	zhimtoto

Meat & Vegetables

cabbage	banda kopi
cauliflower	meto kopi
chicken	bja sha
cooked vegetable	tshöse tsotsou
fish	ngasha
meat	ha
potatoes	kewa
radish	laphu
turnips	öndo
vegetable	tshöse

Other Foods

cheese	datse
chilli	êma

NUMBERS

1	ci
2	nyî
3	sum
4	zhi
5	nga
6	drû
7	dün
8	gä
9	gu
10	cuthâm
11	cûci
12	cunyî
13	cûsu
14	cüzhi
15	cänga
16	cûdru
17	cupdü
18	côpgä
19	cügu
20	nyishu/khächi
30	sumcu/khä pcheda nyî
40	zhipcu/khänyî
50	ngapcu/khä pcheda sum
60	drukcu/khäsum
70	düncu/khä pcheda zhi
80	gepcu/khäzhi
90	gupcu/khä pcheda nga
100	cikja/khänga
1000	ciktong/tongthra ci
10,000	cikthri
100,000	cikbum/bum
1,000,000	saya ci

corn	(maize) gäza/gesasip
egg	gongdo
mushroom	shamu
mustard	päga
noodles	bathu/thukpa
rice (cooked)	to
salad	ezay

Drinks

beer (local)	bang chhang
boiled water	chhu kököu
cold/hot water	chhu khöm/tshatom

tea	ja
water	chhu
whisky (local)	ârra

HEALTH & EMERGENCIES

I'm ill.	nga nau mä
I feel nauseous.	nga cûni zum beu mä
I feel weak.	nga thangchep mä
I keep vomiting.	nga cûp cûsara döp mä
I feel dizzy.	nga guyu khôu mä
I'm having trouble breathing.	nga bung tang mit shubä

doctor	drungtsho
fever	jangshu
pain	nazu

SHOPPING & SERVICES

The word khang means building; in many cases it's only necessary to add the word for the type of building.

Where is a ...?	... gâti mo?
bank	ngükhang
bookshop	pekhang
cinema	loknyen
hospital	menkhang
market	thromkhang
monastery	goemba
police station	thrimsung gakpi mâkhang
post office	dremkhang
public telephone	manggi jüthrin tangsi
shop	tshongkhang
temple	lhakhang
toilet	chapsa

I want to see ...	nga ... tagobe
I'm looking for ...	nga ... tau ing
What time does it open?	chutshö gademci lu go pchiu mo?

POLITENESS

To be polite, you can add -la to the end of almost anything you say in Dzongkha, and even to English words you might use in Bhutan. So when talking to a government minister, a lama or someone older than you, you can say eg 'yes-la' or 'okay-la', and you'll be showing respect.

What time does it close?	chutshö gademci lu go dam mo?
Is it still open?	datoya pchidi ong ga?
What is this?	di gaci mo?
I want to change money.	nga tiru sôgobä
How much is it?	dilu gadeci mo?
That's too much.	gong bôm mä
I'll give you no more than.	ngâgi ... anemci lä trö mitshube
What's your best price?	gong gademcibe bjinni?

TRANSPORT

What is the time?	chutshö gademci mo?
(Five) o'clock.	chutshö (nga)
afternoon	pchiru
day	nyim/za
day after tomorrow	nâtshe
morning	drôba
night	numu
sometime	retshe kap
today	dari
tomorrow	nâba
yesterday	khatsha
Sunday	za dau
Monday	za mîma
Tuesday	za lhap
Wednesday	za phup
Thursday	za pâsa
Friday	za pêm
Saturday	za nyim

GLOSSARY

ABTO – Association of Bhutanese Tour Operators

anim – Buddhist nun

anim goemba – nunnery

atsara – masked clown that badgers the crowd at a *tsechu*

bangchung – round bamboo basket with a tight-fitting cover

BHU – Basic Health Unit

bodhisattva – a being who has the capacity of gaining Buddhahood in this life, but who refuses it in order to be reincarnated in the world to help other beings

Bon – ancient, pre-Buddhist, animistic religion of Tibet; its practitioners are called Bon-po

Brokpa – minority group in eastern Bhutan

bukhari – wood-burning stove

bumpa – vase, usually used to contain holy water in *goembas*

cham – ritual religious dance

chang – north

chhang – beer made from rice, corn or millet, pronounced 'chung'

chhu – river, also water

chilip – foreigner

choesum – chapel

chorten – stone Buddhist monument, often containing relics

Dantak – Indian Border Roads Task Force

datse – traditional archery; also cheese

desi – secular ruler of Bhutan

dharma – Buddhist teachings

dharma raja – British name for the Zhabdrung, the religious ruler, during period 1652–1907

dochey – inner courtyard of a *dzong*

doma – betel nut, also known by its Indian name, *paan*

dorji – a stylised thunderbolt used in rituals; *vajra* in Sanskrit

drak – cave or hermitage

dratshang – central monk body

driglam chhoesum – code of etiquette

driglam namzha – traditional values and etiquette

Druk Gyalpo – the king of Bhutan

Drukpa Kagyu – the official religion of Bhutan, a school of tantric *Mahayana* Buddhism

drungkhag – subdistrict

dukhang – assembly hall in a *goemba;* also called a *tshokhang*

dzong – fort-monastery shared between government office and monks' quarters

dzongdag – district administrator

Dzongkha – national language of Bhutan

dzongkhag – district

dzongpen – old term for lord of the *dzong*

gangri – snow mountain

gho – traditional dress for men

goemba – a *Mahayana* Buddhist monastery

goenkhang – chapel devoted to protective and terrifying deities, usually *Mahakala*

gomchen – lay or married monk

gorikha – porch of a *lhakhang*, literally 'mouth of the door'

Guru Rinpoche the common name of Padmasambhava, the founder of *Mahayana* Buddhism

gyalpo – ruler or king

himal – Sanskrit word for mountain

IMTRAT – Indian Military Training Team

Je Khenpo – Chief Abbot of Bhutan

kabney – scarf worn over the shoulder on formal occasions

khandroma – a female celestial being; *dakini* in Sanskrit

khenpo – abbot

khonying – archway chorten

kira – traditional dress for women

kora – circumambulation

la – mountain pass

lam – path or road

lama – *Mahayana* Buddhist teacher or priest

lha – god or deity

lhakhang – temple, literally 'god house'

lho – south

Lhotshampa – southern Bhutanese people, mainly Nepali-speaking

Losar – Bhutanese and Tibetan New Year

lu – serpent deities, called *naga* in Sanskrit

Mahakala – Yeshe Goenpo, the guardian god of Bhutan, who manifests himself as a raven

Mahayana – school of Buddhism, literally 'great vehicle'

mandala – cosmic diagram; *kyilkhor* in *Dzongkha*

mani stone – stone carved with the Buddhist mantra *om mani peme hum*

mantra – prayer formula or chant

migoi – the abominable snowman; also known as yeti

naktshang – temple dedicated to warlord or protective deity, literally 'place of vows'

NCCA – National Commission for Cultural Affairs

ney – sacred site

Ngalop – people of Tibetan origin

ngultrum – unit of Bhutanese currency

nup – west

Nyingma – lineage of Himalayan Buddhism; its practitioners are Nyingmapa

om mani peme hum – sacred Buddhist mantra, roughly translates as 'hail to the jewel in the lotus'

outreach clinic – health posts in remote villages

PCO – Public Call Office

penlop – regional governor, literally 'lord-teacher'

phajo – priest

prayer flag – long strips of cloth printed with prayers that are 'said' whenever the flag flaps in the wind

prayer wheel – cylindrical wheel inscribed with, and containing, prayers

rabdey – district monk body
RBA – Royal Bhutan Army
rinpoche – reincarnate lama, usually the abbot of a *goemba*
river left – the left bank of a river when facing downstream
river right – the right bank of a river when facing downstream
RSPN – Royal Society for Protection of Nature

SAARC – South Asia Association for Regional Cooperation; this includes the seven countries of Bangladesh, Bhutan, India, Maldives, Nepal, Pakistan and Sri Lanka

Sakyamuni – one name for Gautama Buddha, the Historical Buddha
shar – east
shedra – Buddhist college
shing – wood
sonam – good luck
stupa – hemispherical Buddhist structure from which the *chorten* evolved

terma – texts and artefacts hidden by *Guru Rinpoche*
terton – discoverer of *terma*
thang – plain
thangka – painted or embroidered religious picture
thondrol – huge *thangka* that is unfurled on special occasions, literally 'liberation on sight'
torma – ritual cake made of *tsampa*, butter and sugar
trulku – a reincarnation; the spiritual head of a *goemba*

tsachhu – hot spring
tsampa – roasted-barley flour
tsechu – religious dance festival
tshamkhang – small meditation quarters
tsho – lake
Tshogdu – National Assembly
tshokhang – assembly hall in a *lhakhang*

utse – the central tower that houses the *lhakhang* in a *dzong*

yathra – strips of woven woollen cloth
yeti – see *migoi*

Zangto Pelri – the celestial abode or paradise of *Guru Rinpoche*
Zhabdrung, the – title of the reincarnations of the Zhabdrung Ngawang Namgyal

FOOD GLOSSARY

arra – homemade spirit distilled from barley, wheat or rice

barthu – noodles
bja sha maroo – chicken in garlic and butter sauce

chhang – beer made from rice, corn or millet, pronounced *chung*
chugo – dried yak cheese

dal – lentil soup

ema datse – chilli with cheese sauce

hogey – salad of cucumber, Asian pepper, red chilli, spring onion and tomato

kewa datse – potatoes with cheese sauce
khule – buckwheat pancakes

momo – steamed dumpling filled with meat or cheese

nakey – fiddlehead fern fronds
no sha huentseu – stewed beef with spinach

olo choto – literally 'crow beak', a hooked-shaped broad bean

phak sha laphu – stewed pork with radish
phak sha phin tshoem – pork with rice noodles
puta – buckwheat noodles

shamu datse – mushrooms with cheese sauce
sip – fried, beaten corn
sud-ja – Tibetan-style tea with salt and butter

thukpa – noodles, often served in a soup
tsampa – roasted-barley flour

zao – fried rice

Behind the Scenes

SEND US YOUR FEEDBACK

We love to hear from travellers – your comments keep us on our toes and help make our books better. Our well-travelled team reads every word on what you loved or loathed about this book. Although we cannot reply individually to your submissions, we always guarantee that your feedback goes straight to the appropriate authors, in time for the next edition. Each person who sends us information is thanked in the next edition – the most useful submissions are rewarded with a selection of digital PDF chapters.

Visit **lonelyplanet.com/contact** to submit your updates and suggestions or to ask for help. Our award-winning website also features inspirational travel stories, news and discussions.

Note: We may edit, reproduce and incorporate your comments in Lonely Planet products such as guidebooks, websites and digital products, so let us know if you don't want your comments reproduced or your name acknowledged. For a copy of our privacy policy visit lonelyplanet.com/privacy.

WRITER THANKS

Bradley Mayhew

Thanks to Karma Gyeltsen at Bhutan Mountain Holiday for organising my travel and to my excellent guide Sangay and driver Rinchen, who made the trip. Thanks to Joe Bindloss for many years of commissioning and co-authoring; I hope to work with you again soon. Thanks to Gar Powell-Evans for his useful updates from the road. And to Carolyn for offering her desk with a view of a volcano.

Joe Bindloss

I'd like to dedicate my work on this project to my sons Tyler and Benjamin and my partner Linda. In Bhutan, thanks to Karma Tshering and Ugyen Tshering for excellent guide services, impressive off-road driving and the heavy lifting of hauling camera gear up mountain trails. Also for going without lunch to keep to my exacting schedule. Thanks also to Pema Nidup, Abhi Shrestha and Niraj Shrestha at Rural Heritage for support with logistics and general helpfulness during my trip.

Lindsay Brown

Thanks to Rinzin Wangchuck, Thinley Wangchuk and Sonam Wangmo at Yu Druk Tours & Treks. Special thanks to Chador Wangdi and Tandin Gyeltshin for the expert guidance, and to Harka Bahadur Rai for the patient driving skills. Thanks to all those in Bhutan who assisted me with information, advice and suggestions, and to co-writers Joe Bindloss and Bradley Mayhew.

ACKNOWLEDGMENTS

Climate map data adapted from Peel MC, Finlayson BL & McMahon TA (2007), 'Updated World Map of the Köppen-Geiger Climate Classification', *Hydrology and Earth System Sciences*, 11, 1633–44.

Cover photograph: Dance of the Lord of Death and his Consort (Shinje Yab Yum) at Paro Tsechu, Blaine Harrington III/Alamy Stock Photo ©

THIS BOOK

This 7th edition of Lonely Planet's *Bhutan* guidebook was researched and written by Bradley Mayhew, Joe Bindloss and Lindsay Brown. Bradley and Lindsay also wrote the previous three editions. This guidebook was produced by the following:

Destination Editor
Joe Bindloss

Senior Product Editors
Kate Chapman, Anne Mason

Regional Senior Cartographer
Valentina Kremenchutskaya

Product Editors
Hannah Cartmel, Bruce Evans, Saralinda Turner

Book Designer Wibowo Rusli

Assisting Editors
Michelle Bennett, Nigel Chin, Peter Cruttenden, Anne Mulvaney

Cover Researcher
Naomi Parker

Thanks to Joel Cotterell, Robert DeLoach, Karen Henderson, Catherine Naghten, Charlotte Orr, Gabrielle Stefanos, Angela Tinson, Sam Wheeler, LeAnne Woon

Index

Map Legend

Sights
- Beach
- Bird Sanctuary
- Buddhist
- Castle/Palace
- Christian
- Confucian
- Hindu
- Islamic
- Jain
- Jewish
- Monument
- Museum/Gallery/Historic Building
- Ruin
- Shinto
- Sikh
- Taoist
- Winery/Vineyard
- Zoo/Wildlife Sanctuary
- Other Sight

Activities, Courses & Tours
- Bodysurfing
- Diving
- Canoeing/Kayaking
- Course/Tour
- Sento Hot Baths/Onsen
- Skiing
- Snorkelling
- Surfing
- Swimming/Pool
- Walking
- Windsurfing
- Other Activity

Sleeping
- Sleeping
- Camping
- Hut/Shelter

Eating
- Eating

Drinking & Nightlife
- Drinking & Nightlife
- Cafe

Entertainment
- Entertainment

Shopping
- Shopping

Information
- Bank
- Embassy/Consulate
- Hospital/Medical
- Internet
- Police
- Post Office
- Telephone
- Toilet
- Tourist Information
- Other Information

Geographic
- Beach
- Gate
- Hut/Shelter
- Lighthouse
- Lookout
- Mountain/Volcano
- Oasis
- Park
- Pass
- Picnic Area
- Waterfall

Population
- Capital (National)
- Capital (State/Province)
- City/Large Town
- Town/Village

Transport
- Airport
- Border crossing
- Bus
- Cable car/Funicular
- Cycling
- Ferry
- Metro station
- Monorail
- Parking
- Petrol station
- Subway station
- Taxi
- Train station/Railway
- Tram
- Underground station
- Other Transport

Routes
- Tollway
- Freeway
- Primary
- Secondary
- Tertiary
- Lane
- Unsealed road
- Road under construction
- Plaza/Mall
- Steps
- Tunnel
- Pedestrian overpass
- Walking Tour
- Walking Tour detour
- Path/Walking Trail

Boundaries
- International
- State/Province
- Disputed
- Regional/Suburb
- Marine Park
- Cliff
- Wall

Hydrography
- River, Creek
- Intermittent River
- Canal
- Water
- Dry/Salt/Intermittent Lake
- Reef

Areas
- Airport/Runway
- Beach/Desert
- Cemetery (Christian)
- Cemetery (Other)
- Glacier
- Mudflat
- Park/Forest
- Sight (Building)
- Sportsground
- Swamp/Mangrove

Note: Not all symbols displayed above appear on the maps in this book

OUR STORY

A beat-up old car, a few dollars in the pocket and a sense of adventure. In 1972 that's all Tony and Maureen Wheeler needed for the trip of a lifetime – across Europe and Asia overland to Australia. It took several months, and at the end – broke but inspired – they sat at their kitchen table writing and stapling together their first travel guide, *Across Asia on the Cheap*. Within a week they'd sold 1500 copies. Lonely Planet was born.

Today, Lonely Planet has offices in Franklin, London, Melbourne, Oakland, Dublin, Beijing and Delhi, with more than 600 staff and writers. We share Tony's belief that 'a great guidebook should do three things: inform, educate and amuse'.

OUR WRITERS

Bradley Mayhew

Curator, Western Bhutan Bradley has been writing guidebooks for 20 years. He started travelling while studying Chinese at Oxford University, and has since focused his expertise on China, Tibet, the Himalaya and Central Asia. He is the co-writer of Lonely Planet guides *Tibet, Nepal, Trekking in the Nepal Himalaya, Bhutan, Central Asia* and many others. Bradley has also fronted two TV series for Arte and SWR, one retracing the route of Marco Polo via Turkey, Iran, Afghanistan, Central Asia and China, and the other trekking Europe's 10 most scenic long-distance trails. Bradley has also written for Rough Guides, has contributed chapters to *Silk Road: Monks, Warriors & Merchants* and is a co-writer of Insight Guide's *Silk Road*. Bradley also worked on the History chapter, Plan section and a number of treks.

Joe Bindloss

Thimphu Joe first got the travel bug on a grand tour of Asia in the early 1990s, and he's been roaming around its temples and paddy fields ever since on dozens of assignments for Lonely Planet and other publishers, covering everywhere from Myanmar and Thailand to India and Nepal. Joe was Lonely Planet's destination editor for the Indian subcontinent until 2019. See more of his work at www.bindloss.co.uk. Joe also worked on the Directory, Transport and Health chapters and a number of treks.

Lindsay Brown

Central Bhutan, Eastern Bhutan Lindsay started travelling as a young bushwalker exploring the Blue Mountains west of Sydney. Then as a marine biologist he dived the coastal and island waters of southeastern Australia. He continued travelling whenever he could while employed at Lonely Planet as an editor and publishing manager. Since becoming a freelance writer and photographer he has co-authored more than 45 Lonely Planet guides to Australia, Bhutan, India, Malaysia, Nepal, Pakistan and Papua New Guinea. Lindsay also worked on the Bhutanese Way of Life, Buddhism in Bhutan, Arts & Architecture, Natural World and Bhutanese Table chapters and a number of treks.

Published by Lonely Planet Global Limited
CRN 554153
7th edition – Jun 2020
ISBN 978 1 78701 348 3
© Lonely Planet 2020   Photographs © as indicated 2020
10 9 8 7 6 5 4 3 2 1
Printed in Singapore